THE FAMILY

From Traditional to Companionship

FOURTH EDITION

the late ERNEST W. BURGESS
Formerly University of Chicago

HARVEY J. LOCKE
Emeritus Professor at the University of Southern California

MARY MARGARET THOMES
California Lutheran College

VAN NOSTRAND REINHOLD COMPANY
New York / Cincinnati / Toronto / London / Melbourne

Van Nostrand Reinhold Company Regional Offices:
Cincinnati   New York   Chicago   Millbrae   Dallas
Van Nostrand Reinhold Company International Offices:
London   Toronto   Melbourne
Copyright © 1971 by Litton Educational Publishing, Inc.
Library of Congress Catalog Card Number: 76-146603
All rights reserved. Certain portions of this work copyright
© 1963, 1960, 1953, 1950, 1945 by Litton Educational Publishing, Inc. No part
of this work covered by the copyrights hereon may be reproduced or
used in any form or by any means—graphic, electronic, or
mechanical, including photocopying, recording, taping, or
information storage and retrieval systems—without written
permission of the publisher. Manufactured in the United States
of America.
Published by Van Nostrand Reinhold Company
450 West 33rd Street, New York, N.Y. 10001
Published simultaneously in Canada by
D. Van Nostrand Reinhold Ltd.

Preface

The central theme of this book is that in the last few decades the family has been in transition from a traditional to a companionship form. This transition is in part the result of major social changes which have placed families in a radically different environment from that of the past. Important changes are the shift from a rural to an urban society, from stability of residence to mobility, from familism to individualism, and from a relatively short family life cycle to one which continues for years after the children have established homes of their own. All of these changes have occurred in the United States, and most of them have taken place in other countries. Most of these changes led to situations in which impersonal, secondary associations predominate, and the kinship group and the nuclear family units become the major areas of intimate, affectional association. This has facilitated the growth of the companionship family, characterized by the mutual affection, sympathetic understanding, and comradeship of its members.

Throughout the book we present knowledge derived, as far as possible, from research investigations. There is no direct concern with the application of this knowledge to the preparation of persons for marriage or to the solving of family problems. On the other hand, it is our conviction that reliable knowledge is the most adequate basis for preparation for marriage and for solving family problems.

The book is divided into four parts. Part I analyzes family relationships under different social conditions and different periods of time. After a consideration of the various forms of the family in several countries and the United States, the ways in which the family has adapted itself to major social changes are discussed. Part II examines interaction and socialization within the family and the way these influence personality development. Specifically, consideration is given to social, emotional, and cultural factors in personality development. Part III considers ways in which families are organized and the possibility of predicting success or failure in marriage. It traces the process of family formation from courtship and mate selection to the development of family unity and to relationships in the middle and later years of marriage. Part IV describes the family in transition. It includes an analysis of the effect of certain social processes on family crises and disruptions and suggests conditions for meeting the needs of the American family.

Several distinctive features have been included in the new edition. Personal documents were used systematically to illustrate the problems discussed in each chapter and to clarify the concepts employed for analysis. Life histories and other personal documents reveal the attitudes, desires, and values of family members that are difficult to perceive in external behavior or from reports of outsiders.[1]

A second feature of the book is its research emphasis. The findings of pertinent and recent studies are found throughout the book. Moreover, research projects are presented at the end of each chapter, indicating that although the family has been studied more intensively than most other groups, there are still wide gaps in our knowledge of it.

A third feature is a carefully selected annotated bibliography for each chapter. A list of books and articles at the end of a chapter is not particularly useful. It is our hope that a brief description of a book or article will stimulate a student to read beyond the required course assignments.

The first question one is likely to ask about a new edition is to what extent it has been revised. While all chapters have been extensively revised, a few are completely new. This is particularly true for the first seven chapters. Chapter 1 includes the analysis of the family as a valued object; our conceptual framework with an emphasis on symbolic interaction; and a comparison of the traditional and companionship family systems. About half of Chapter 2 is new; this is a description of family patterns and behavior in five non-American communities studied by anthropologists. Chapter 4, on the urban family, is completely new. It includes a discussion of the importance of the kinship group in urban areas of the United States and other countries; a comparison of suburban and central-city families; and types of families found in central cities, largely different social classes: nonfamily men of Skid Row, poverty families of the slums, and middle- and working-class families. Much of Chapter 5 on the Negro family is new. Since

---

[1] The case studies in the text, unless otherwise indicated, are documents in the files of the authors. Names of persons and other identifying information have been changed. These personal documents, as well as quotations from articles and books, have sometimes been slightly adapted by the omission of words, phrases, and sentences, but with care not to alter the meaning.

1960 major changes have taken place in Negro families, and there has been a great increase in studies on the Negro family. These new studies have been taken into account in this chapter. The three chapters in Part II are largely new and have a changed emphasis—interaction and socialization. Chapter 17, on the family in transition, includes a new section on the historical change from the patriarchal to the democratic family and an analysis of birth control in terms of family values.

Another way of judging the degree to which an edition is revised is the number of new references. Of the total footnotes to the text, one-half were not in the third edition; of the annotated bibliographies, one-third are new. And, of course, statistical data have been brought up-to-date.

We want to thank the various authors and publishers who have generously given us permission to quote from their books and articles. A formal statement of acknowledgments will be found in Appendix B. Footnote references cannot fully express our appreciation for the research and work of persons whose ideas and materials we used.

Locke and Thomes, along with many others, had the privilege of working with Ernest W. Burgess (1886–1966) over a period of many years. Many of the ideas of the book were formulated as we thought, talked, and worked together. We are sure that he would favor the changes made in this fourth edition, for he always insisted that old knowledge must be modified if new knowledge made it necessary. We are indebted to him not only for research and scholarship but for the privilege of associating with a kind, generous, objective, and tough-minded person.

Harvey J. Locke
Mary Margaret Thomes

Contents

1 Definitions and Conceptual Viewpoint   *1*

PART ONE
Variations in the Family

2 Variations in Marital and Family Behavior   *13*
3 The Rural Family   *34*
4 The Urban Family   *59*
5 The Negro Family   *99*
6 The Family in the Soviet Union   *130*
7 The Family of Japan, China, and India   *156*

PART TWO
The Family and Personality

8 Culture and Socialization   *179*
9 Interaction and Socialization   *205*
10 Expectations and Roles   *233*

PART THREE
Family Organization

11 Courtship   *265*
12 Mate Selection   *292*
13 Measuring Success in Marriage   *315*
14 Predicting Adjustment in Marriage   *336*
15 Family Unity   *364*
16 Family Relations in the Middle and Later Years   *387*

PART FOUR

Changing Patterns of Family Behavior

17 The Changing American Family   415
18 Mobility and the Family   448
19 Family Conflicts and Accommodations   472
20 Family Crises   501
21 Family Disruption   526
22 War and the Family   559
23 The Family in Process of Change   581

APPENDIX A Premarital and Marital Items Associated with Marital Adjustment   599

APPENDIX B Acknowledgments   631
Index   633

FIGURES

1. Labor-saving machines on farms, 1940 and 1968, in thousands	36
2. Employment status of farm men and women, by percents, 1966	42
3. Farm population, farms, and farm size, 1940–1968	46
4. Number of men per 100 women, by states, 1960	49
5. The farm family's food dollar, 1955 and 1965	51
6. Percent of rural-farm, rural-nonfarm, and urban homes having television sets, 1950, 1955, and 1961	52
7. Median money income for males, by occupation, 1967	54
8. Number of families having given family income from 1947 to 1966, in constant 1966 dollars	77
9. Percent of ever-married women 14 years old or older who were separated or divorced, by age and color, 1968	106
10. Characteristics of Negro and white families, 1968	107
11. Percent of those 25 to 29 years of age who completed four or more years of high school or four or more years of college, by race, 1950, 1964, and 1968	111
12. Percent of whites and Negroes residing in central cities, metropolitan rings, and nonmetropolitan areas, 1969	118
13. Correlations between selected child behaviors and similar adult behaviors	197

14. Marital-success profiles of husband and wife — 328
15. Percent distribution of new permanent dwelling units constructed in nonfarm areas (urban plus rural-nonfarm) by type of dwelling, 1920–1968 — 421
16. Number of births per 1,000 population, 1870–1969 — 426
17. Size of the family household, by states, 1940 and 1960 — 429
18. Percent of babies born in hospitals and not in hospitals, 1935–1967 — 430
19. Percent of nonfarm and farm wives in the labor force, 1950, 1960, and 1967 — 433
20. Percent of mothers in the labor force, by age of children, 1967 — 434
21. Years of school completed by persons 20 years of age or older, 1947 and 1968 — 437
22. Percent of population one year old or older moving to a given area in a one-year period, 1947–1969
23. Percent of all dwellings having at least one television set, 1950–1969 — 459
24. Development of social distance between a husband and wife — 478
25. Total persons receiving relief through public assistance and federal works programs in the United States, 1933–1939 — 516
26. Annual marriages and divorces per 1,000 population, 1925–1941 — 517
27. Divorces per 1,000 population, 1870–1969 — 534
28. Divorces per 1,000 population by states, 1940 and 1966 — 536

TABLES

1. Legal age for marriage in 78 countries, 1968 — 23
2. Percent of rural and urban boys and girls answering given MMPI items as true — 44
3. Average size of the family, urban and rural areas, 1910–1960, and rural-farm, and rural-nonfarm areas, 1930–1960 — 48
4. Men per 100 women in rural-farm, rural-nonfarm, and urban areas, 1920–1960, and farm and nonfarm, 1968 — 49
5. Percent married persons are of all persons 14 years old or older, by sex, urban and rural, 1910–1960 — 50
6. Percent of all rural-farm, rural-nonfarm, and urban dwellings having certain facilities, 1940 and 1960 — 55
7. Social characteristics of central cities and suburbs of the 10

largest standard statistical metropolitan areas, by percent, 1960	70
8. Percent with given marital status of men and women in central cities, suburbs, and rural areas, 1960	73
9. Percent of Negroes and whites completing 4 or more years of high school and 4 or more years of college, 1960–1966, by sex	110
10. Percent distribution of Negroes and whites by metropolitan and nonmetropolitan areas, 1950, 1960, and 1969	117
11. Percent Negro of the total population and population of urban, rural-nonfarm, and rural-farm, 1920–1960	119
12. Marital status by race and sex of those 14 years of age and older, by percent, 1968	120
13. Social class of conjugal role relationships	247
14. Place of meeting of happily married and divorced couples, by percent	300
15. An instrument to measure adjustment in marriage	329
16. An index to predict adjustment in marriage	341
17. Percent of first marriages, married in 1950–1944 and 1945–1949, dissolved by divorce or death by 1960, by age at marriage, sex, and color	351
18. Percent of adjusted and unadjusted men and women reporting parental approval of mate before marriage, four studies	352
19. Marital problems of couples married 3 years or less and those married 18 years or more, by percent	394
20. Median family income by age of head	395
21. Average number of persons per family household, 1790–1968	427
22. Percent of private families having specified number of persons, 1790, 1900, 1930, and 1968	428
23. Percent of homes with given appliances, 1953, 1960, 1967, 1968 and 1969	432
24. Gainfully employed married women, their number, and the percent they are of all married women, 1890–1968	432
25. Percent of Terman's subjects born before 1890 and in 1910 or later reporting premarital intercourse	439
26. Percent of Locke's subjects born before 1890 and in 1910 or later reporting premarital and extramarital intercourse	440
27. Percent of happily married and divorced persons checking items as serious marital difficulties	479
28. Divorce rate in 1910-1914 and 1966 per 1,000 population for specified countries, with ratios of 1966 to 1910–1914	531

29. High divorce rates in nine states, 1940, 1950, 1960, and 1966 — 537
30. Marriages per 1,000 population in certain countries, 1911–1924, and 1935–1950 — 563
31. Birth rates for selected countries, 1937–1949 — 565
32. Total employed workers and percent women were of total employed, 1940–1952 — 576
33. Percent distribution of families receiving given money income, 1967 and 1947, in 1967 dollars — 587
34. Premarital items associated with adjustment in marriage — 599
35. Marital items associated with adjustment in marriage — 618

Chapter 1
Definitions and Conceptual Viewpoint

Marriage is a socially sanctioned union of one or more men with one or more women in the roles of husband and wife. The family is a group united by marriage, blood, or adoption, residing in a single household, communicating with each other in their respective roles, and maintaining a common culture. In this book our objective is to apply sociological methods of analysis to the family. This involves analysis and description of the family in terms of social groups and structures, roles and statuses, social processes, culture, demography, and symbolic interaction. The family is in transition from a traditional family system controlled by mores, public opinion, and law to a companionship family system based on mutual affection, intimate communication, and mutual acceptance of division of labor and procedures of decision-making.

THE FAMILY AS A VALUED OBJECT

The family is one of man's most valued possessions. One way to test the value of anything is to ask yourself what you would be willing to give up in order to retain it. Most persons, if presented with the choice of giving up their family or material possessions would not hesitate to give up their material possessions. If presented with a choice between all their friends or their family, most persons would choose their family with little hesitation. Likewise, faced with a choice between giving up all enjoyable recreational activities or their family, there is little doubt that most persons would choose to retain their family. Fortunately, for the most part one can have his family and also other valuable things as well.

The value placed on the family is especially high when its members consist of husband, wife, and minor children. In America, young adults are expected to leave their parental homes to establish homes of their own. Consequently, over the years there is a decrease in their attachment to the parental home and an increase in their attachment to their new nuclear family.

There are, of course, families which are not cherished as prized possessions by some members. But even those people who experience divorce seem to prize the family situation sufficiently so that almost all remarry. The divorced who get married again are about as successful as those being married for the first time. In the United States, a little under 70 percent of all persons 14 years of age and older are married. Apparently most people like the married state and enter into it with the expectation that it will be satisfying and successful.

Let us consider some of the characteristics of family life which make it so valuable to family members. First, family members secure emotional support through mutual expression of love and affection. American society places a high value on love in the marriage relationship. It is not surprising, therefore, that young people entering marriage expect to find love and affection in this relationship and place a high value on families in which love and affection are present. Second, the family provides a long-term environment in which members engage in interdependent activities, share experiences, and enjoy companionship. Third, the family has as one of its primary functions the care and rearing of children. Fourth, from the standpoint of society as a whole, the family is one of the primary agencies in the transmission of folkways and mores from generation to generation.

CONCEPTUAL FRAMEWORK

Sociology is concerned especially with six interrelated conceptual areas which are also areas of interest in the study of the family: (1) social groups and structures; (2) roles and statuses; (3) social processes; (4) culture; (5) demography; and (6) symbolic interaction. The sociological frame of reference offers distinct advantages in analyzing marriage and family behavior and in securing knowledge about the family. We shall, therefore, refer to these six conceptual areas in our analysis and description of the family:

1. The family is a small group with a discernible structure. It is a social system or network of interpersonal relationships; its structure includes designated positions, the allocation of authority, and division of labor. It has been characterized as a primary group, with emphasis on intimate, informal, and unrestricted communication.

2. Role behavior is an integral part of any family. Each society prescribes appropriate roles for the wife and mother, husband and father, son, daughter, older and younger children, and relatives. Each family member has a status in the family and the family as a whole has a status in the community.

3. Social processes impinge on the family and bring about changes within it. Major social processes such as urbanization, industrialization, and mobility are long-term influences that create changed social situations to which families must adjust. In adjusting, new relationships within the family emerge.

4. Culture prescribes expected forms of behavior in marriage and the family. These include folkways, such as marriage rites and ceremonies, types of living arrangements, and particular ways of rearing and training children. Culture also includes mores, such as monogamy, support of children, and presentation of an outward appearance of harmony between the husband and wife.

5. Demographic statements, generally given in statistical form, provide summary statements of human behavior. Analysis of several demographic characteristics can provide a profile of changes in family behavior. These might include the effect on families of the shifting distribution of the population in urban, rural-nonfarm, and rural-farm areas; the changing distribution of Negroes, Mexican Americans, and foreign-born; the differential density of different sections of metropolitan areas; sex ratio in different areas; trends in the birth rate and size of families; trends and distribution of divorces; and differential life expectancy of husbands and wives.

6. Symbolic interaction may be described as emotional and intellectual communication through verbal or nonverbal means. It is directly related to three of the above main interests of sociology: groups, roles, and culture. Symbolic interaction or communication is necessary to maintain a group; to know the roles expected by a society or group; and to transmit folkways and mores. Mead emphasized the importance in personality development of symbolic interaction in the form of language:

> There is the language of speech and the language of hands, and there may be the language of expression of the countenance. One can register grief or joy and call out certain responses. There are primitive people who carry on elaborate conversations just by expressions of the countenance.[1]

Symbolic interaction is a major conceptual framework of this book. Burgess, the first family sociologist to use symbolic interaction, defined the family as a unity of interacting personalities:

---

[1] George H. Mead, *Mind, Self, and Society* (Chicago: University of Chicago Press, 1934), p. 147. See also pp. 135–222.

By a unity of interacting personalities is meant a living, changing, growing thing. . . . The actual unity of family life has its existence not in any legal conception, nor in any formal contract, but in the interaction of its members. For the family does not depend for its survival on the harmonious relations of its members, nor does it necessarily disintegrate as a result of conflicts between its members. The family lives as long as interaction is taking place and only dies when it ceases.[2]

Burgess' explanation of family unity was influenced by earlier scholars' use of interaction. Analyzing the family in terms of symbolic interaction was particularly congenial with the views of such men as James, Cooley, and Mead. In 1890 James presented two ideas: (1) the conception or image one secures of himself is from the definitions given him by others; and (2) a person plays several roles which are expected of him in different groups.[3] The looking-glass self and the primary group are two ideas for which Cooley is particularly noted. A person's self-concept is formed from his perceptions of what others think of him. Primary groups are those characterized by certain types of symbolic interaction—that which is intimate, informal, and unrestricted. Cooley cites the family as an example of a primary group.[4]

Mead accepted the view that man is not born with a self, but is born into groups in which symbolic interaction is going on and becomes a self, or an object to himself, in the process of communicating with others and with himself. The ability to communicate and the internalization of meaningful gestures are the two fundamental prerequisites to the development of the self. Through the conversation of significant gestures, the attitudes of other individuals and the more generalized community attitudes are internalized within the individual. These internalized attitudes or beginnings of acts form the raw material out of which the self emerges.[5]

There are other conceptual approaches to the study of the family than that of symbolic interaction. Hill and Hansen have outlined some of these.[6] The institutional approach compares marriage and family behavior in different societies and traces historical developments. The structural-functional approach sees the family as a social system with component parts bound together through interaction and interdepend-

---

[2] Ernest W. Burgess, "The Family as a Unity of Interacting Personalities," *Family*, 7 (1926): pp. 3–9.

[3] William James, "The Consciousness of Self," *The Principles of Psychology* (New York: Henry Holt, 1890), Chapter 10.

[4] Charles H. Cooley, *Human Nature and the Social Order* (New York: Charles Scribner's Sons, 1902), pp. 183–184.

[5] Mead, pp. 164–178.

[6] Reuben Hill and D. A. Hansen, "The Identification of Conceptual Frameworks Utilized in Family Study," *Marriage and Family Living*, 22 (1960): pp. 299–311.

ence. The developmental approach views the family as having a life cycle through which members travel from infancy to old age. These approaches are not exclusive but rather closely interrelated. When appropriate, aspects of these other approaches will be used in addition to symbolic interaction.

MARRIAGE AND THE FAMILY DEFINED

Marriage Marriage may be defined as a socially sanctioned union of one or more men with one or more women with the expectation that they will play the roles of husband and wife. Marriage implies a ceremony, a union with social sanctions, a recognition of obligations to the community assumed by those entering this relationship. Every human society in the past and throughout the world has regarded marriage as important for the welfare of society and has been concerned, therefore, with its regulation and control.

There are wide variations among different societies in the ceremonies performed to give social sanction to the union of a man and woman in engagement and marriage. In some societies livestock and other goods are given to the parents of the bride,[7] while in other societies money and goods are given to the groom and his parents by the parents of the bride.[8] Parties and feasts almost always accompany engagement and marriage ceremonies. In one society, at the conclusion of negotiating the settlement the groom's father will give to the new family, wine is poured over the clasped hands of the prospective fathers-in-law.[9] The following is a description of ceremonies associated with marriage in a village in the Philippines:

> By far the greatest number of marriages are performed in the Problacion church. This is a simple early morning ceremony, which is looked on as a formality. Far more important is the subsequent day of feasting to which everyone related to or friendly with either the bride's or groom's family is invited. Most of the guests are assembled in the decorated *sala* by the time the couple, accompanied by a small party of friends, returns from the church. Upon entering, both bride and groom slowly circle the room, greeting each guest. The bride also embraces and tearfully says good-bye to her family and the "companions of her youth." Both then sit on either side of the family shrine where offerings to the ancestor spirits (plates of coconut-milk, rice, and bowls of wine) and two candles have been placed. On the floor in front of the shrine is laid a mat on which are placed two

---

[7] Beatrice B. Whiting, (ed.), *Six Cultures: Studies in Child Rearing* (New York: John Wiley and Sons, 1963), pp. 64–65.
[8] *Ibid.*, p. 264.
[9] *Ibid.*, p. 743.

new white baskets heaped with well-polished white rice for the new household.

There is feasting and dancing in the yard, led by the bridal couple until midafternoon. At that time guests are reassembled in the *sala,* and the couple again take chairs next to the shrine. One of the groom's sponsors now reads aloud the settlement contract, and at the mention of each item the audience shouts, "Is this correct?" The bride's father answers, "Yes, it is correct" and property transfer papers are signed if necessary. The sponsors then group relatives and friends of the groom on one side of a mat, those of the bride at the other, and a spirited contest begins in which each group tosses money onto the mat. The sponsors urge each side to equal the other's donations with cries, "Who will buy the rice pot?", "Who will buy a basket?" When as much money as possible has been donated, it is then totaled, the amount announced (generally about 100 pesos) and presented to the couple.[10]

The Family A definition of the family must include what is common to the great variety of human groups to which the term *family* has been applied. The following characteristics are common to the human family in all times and all places and differentiate the family from other social groups:

1. The family is composed of persons united by ties of marriage, blood, or adoption. The bond between husband and wife is that of marriage; and the relationship between parents and children is generally that of blood, though sometimes of adoption.

2. The members of a family typically live together under one roof and constitute a single household; or, if they live apart, they consider the household their home. The term household refers to a group of persons residing at the same place and constituting a single housekeeping unit. Sometimes the household is large, consisting of as many as three, four, or even five generations. In the United States today the household is small, generally limited to husband and wife without a child, or with only one, two, or three children.

3. The family is composed of persons who interact and communicate with each other in their social roles, such as husband and wife, mother and father, son and daughter, brother and sister. The roles are defined by social expectation, but in each family they are powerfully reinforced by feelings arising out of experiences within the family itself and from one's parental family.

4. The family maintains a common culture. It is derived mainly from the general culture, but each family has some distinctive features. The distinctive culture of a family arises through the communication of

[10] *Ibid.,* pp. 743-744.

family members in which they merge their individual patterns of behavior. These differential patterns may be brought to the marriage by the husband and wife, or may be acquired after marriage through the different experiences of husband, wife, and their children. The merging of cultural patterns transmitted from the two sides of the family, in interaction with outside cultural influences, creates the distinctive cultural patterns of every new family.

The family may now be defined as a group of persons united by ties of marriage, blood, or adoption; constituting a single household; interacting and communicating with each other in their respective social roles of husband and wife, mother and father, son and daughter, brother and sister; and creating and maintaining a common culture.

Families have different configurations such as conjugal, nuclear, and extended. The conjugal family denotes the husband-wife unit. The nuclear family is defined as the husband and wife with or without children. The extended family includes relatives beyond the nuclear family, such as grandparents and brothers and sisters of the husband and wife and their children. The term *family* also applies to the family of orientation and the family of procreation. These designate the relationship of an individual to his family. If one is or has been a child in a family, that family is his family of orientation; and, if a person is or has been a parent in a family, that family is his family of procreation.

THE COMPANIONSHIP FAMILY SYSTEM

From the Traditional to the Companionship Family System A basic thesis of this book is that the family has been in transition from a traditional family system, based on family members playing traditional roles, to a companionship family system, based on mutual affection, intimate communication, and mutual acceptance of division of labor and procedures of decision-making. The companionship form of the family is not to be conceived as having been realized but as emerging.

Spencer, writing in 1876, made an interesting prediction on the relative roles of law and affection in family relationships:

> While permanent monogamy was being evolved, the union by law (originally the act of purchase) was regarded as the essential part of marriage and the union by affection as nonessential; and whereas at present the union by law is thought the more important and the union by affection the less important, there will come a time when the union by affection will be held of primary moment.[11]

---

[11] Herbert Spencer, *Principles of Sociology* (New York: Appleton-Century, 1897 —first edition, London, 1876), 1, p. 765.

Spencer's prophecy appears to be on the way to realization. Mutual affection is becoming the essential basis of marriage and the family.

The family as a traditional system and as a companionship represent two polar conceptions. The most extreme conceptual formulation of the traditional family system would be one in which its unity would be determined entirely by the traditional rules and regulations, specified duties and obligations, and other social pressures impinging on family members. The family as a companionship system focuses on the unity which develops out of mutual affection, intimate communication, and mutual acceptance of a given division of labor and given procedures of decision-making by a husband, wife, and children.

Of the historical and existing types of families, the extended patriarchal illustrates a traditional family system, with its combination of powerful sanctions of the mores, religion, and law, and the subordination of the family to the authority of the patriarch. In the companionship family the members enjoy a high degree of self-expression and at the same time are united by bonds of love, congeniality, and common interests. The companionship family is democratic but the democratic family is not necessarily a companionship family.

A comparison of the historical approximations of the small democratic family and the patriarchal family will indicate the outstanding differences between them. (1) The patriarchal family is authoritarian and autocratic, with power vested in the head of the family and with the subordination of his wife, sons and their wives and children, and his unmarried daughters to his authority. The democratic family is based on equality of the husband and wife, with consensus in making decisions and with increasing participation by children as they grow older. (2) Marriage is arranged by the parents in the patriarchal family, with emphasis on prudence, on economic and social status, and on adjustment of the son-in-law or daughter-in-law to the family group. In the democratic family, selection of a marriage partner is in the hands of young people and choice is on the basis of affection and personality adjustment to each other. (3) Compliance with duty and the following of tradition are major expectations of the patriarchal family, while the objectives of the small democratic family are the achievement of happiness and personal growth of the individuals. (4) The primary historic functions of the family—economic, educational, recreational, health, protective, and religious—are found in their highest development in the patriarchal family. These historic functions have been greatly modified in the small democratic family.

The Emerging Companionship Family For decades the American family has been evolving from a small-patriarchal type revolving around the father and husband as head and main authority to the democratic type. Accompanying this evolution has been the decreasing size of the family, the diminishing control of the kinship group and of the community over the family unit, and a growing sense of equality of family members. The external factors making for family stability, such as control by custom and community opinion, have been weakened. The permanence of marriage and the family more and more depends on bonds of love and affection, intimate communication, congeniality, and mutual interests.

The American family is moving toward the companionship family system, which may be described as follows: (1) affection is the basis for its existence; (2) husband and wife have mutual acceptance of procedures in decision-making; (3) major decisions are by consensus; and (4) common interests and activities coexist with mutual acceptance of division of labor within the family and individuality of interests. In most families the control is still moderately patriarchal; in some it is more or less matriarchal; and in only a small proportion is it by consensus of husbands, wives, and children. The proportion that includes participation of children is extremely small.

SUMMARY

In this chapter we have dealt with four points. (1) For almost all persons the family is one of the most important values of life. We seldom ask ourselves or others to list those things which we value most. But, if we did, the family would be at or near the top of the list. (2) In this book we use the sociological conceptual framework for analysis and description of the family. It includes six interrelated conceptual areas: social groups and structures, roles and statuses, social processes, culture, demography, and symbolic interaction. (3) Marriage is defined as a socially sanctioned union of one or more men with one or more women with the expectation that they will play the roles of husband and wife. The family is defined as a group of persons united by marriage, blood, or adoption, constituting a single household, interacting with each other in their respective roles, and creating and maintaining a common culture. (4) The family has been and is in transition from a traditional family system to a companionship family system.

QUESTIONS AND EXERCISES

1. Why do persons value the family so highly? Do you place a high value on your parental family?

2. The term *family* is applied to different kinds of groups. Select three of these and define each.
3. Outline the essential characteristics of each of the six sociological conceptual areas.
4. What is the essential difference between marriage and the family?
5. What is the essential difference between the democratic and the companionship family?
6. Outline the primary characteristics of the companionship family.

BIBLIOGRAPHY

Hill, Reuben; and Hansen, D. A. "The Identification of Conceptual Frameworks Utilized in Family Study," *Marriage and Family Living*, 22 (1960): pp. 299–311.

> This is an attempt to identify conceptual frameworks used in the study of the family. The authors describe five conceptual approaches used by sociologists: institutional, the structural-functional, interactional, situational, and developmental.

Nye, F. Ivan; and Berardo, Felix M. (eds.) *Emerging Conceptual Frameworks in Family Analysis*. New York: Macmillan, 1966.

> Presents eleven conceptual frameworks for the study of the family, each described by a different author. The most useful frameworks are the anthropological, structure-functional, institutional, interactional, situational, social psychological, and developmental.

Rodman, Hyman. *Marriage, Family, and Society*. New York: Random House, 1965, Part 8.

> Deals with the discussion of the companionship family as given by Burgess, Locke, and Thomes and the characteristics of the American family as developed by Parsons.

Stryker, Sheldon. "The Interactional and Situational Approaches," in *Handbook of Marriage and the Family*, ed. Harold T. Christensen. Chicago: Rand McNally, 1964, Ch. 4.

> Gives the historical development of symbolic interaction in the writings of James, Cooley, Thomas, and Mead. Distinguishes between theory and a conceptual framework. Indicates that symbolic interaction is particularly applicable to socialization and personality.

Part I
Variations in the Family

Variations and changes in family behavior are central themes of this book. Part I, in particular, is concerned with family relationships in widely different societies and within the United States. Chapter 2, a general discussion of variations in marital and family behavior, is followed by five chapters describing changing patterns of family life in diverse situations: the rural-farm, the urban, the Negro, the Russian, and the family in Japan, China, and India. The many different family forms and practices demonstrate the high adaptability of the family to social change and to divergent situations.

Many of the changes in the American rural-farm family can be traced to modern methods of agriculture and to the relative decline of farming in the national economy. The urban family has been profoundly changed by alterations in economic and other functions under conditions of industrialization, the influx of rural people into cities, and the growth of cities. The Negro family exemplifies the great adaptability of the family to such conditions as being transplanted to a new region, living in slavery, and facing the growing opportunity to participate freely in the economic and political life of the country. The Russian family was in a slow process of change long before the Revolution of 1917. It has been greatly modified by the pressures, propaganda, and programs of Soviet authorities. Finally, the family of Japan, China, and India is undergoing great changes.

Chapter 2
Variations in Marital and Family Behavior

One way to understand the American family is to compare it with families in other societies. Different societies sanction different forms of marriage, such as monogamy, polygyny, or polyandry, and also have different customary forms of the family, such as the extended-patriarchal, the small-patriarchal, or the modern democratic. A description of variations in non-American societies will help us understand the influence of mores and folkways on marriage and family forms. Finally, an analysis of variations within the United States will demonstrate the adjustability of the family to different situations and conditions within a society.

SEX AND MARRIAGE IN NYANSONGO

Courtship, mate selection, and family behavior vary greatly within the United States. There are, however, even greater variations among different parts of the world. Let us compare, for example, American conceptions of the proper age for marriage, desirable physical features in the person one selects for a mate, the giving of presents at the time of marriage, and living arrangements immediately after the marriage ceremony with those attitudes discovered by the LeVines during their anthropological study of Nyansongo, an east African community. The LeVines' work was one of six field studies in a program designed and implemented by senior anthropologists at Harvard, Yale, and Cornell. The following selection from their report on Nyansongo describes premarital activities preliminary to marriage:

> Three traditional rules provide the setting for Nyansongon sexual and marital behavior: (1) No one may marry into his own clan, for all of its

members are classified as relatives. Intermarrying clans are traditional enemies and in the past carried on blood feuds, as expressed in the Gusii proverb "Those whom we marry are those whom we fight." (2) At marriage the wife must go to live at the homestead of her husband and his parents. There she is granted economic rights and a legitimate social position neither of which would be obtainable had she remained at the home of her parents. Eventually a woman becomes incorporated into her husband's kin group, but as a newlywed she is conscious of being a stranger in the enemy camp. (3) A respectable marriage requires the payment of cattle and goats to the bride's father, in number and quality satisfactory to him, before she takes up residence at her husband's home. The bridewealth cattle give the husband exclusive sexual rights over the wife and the custody of all children to whom she gives birth. If he dies, these rights are inherited by a real or classificatory brother of the husband. The rights may only be relinquished by the husband's clan on return of the entire bridewealth. Thus the marriage system of Nyansongo is characterized by clan exogamy, patrilocal residence, bridewealth, and the levirate.

Girls are 15 years old on the average when they marry, while males average 18 to 20 years old at their first marriage. There is more variability in age on the male side, since the possession of the bridewealth cattle is required and proves a temporary barrier for many of the less fortunate young men. . . .

For most individuals, sexual activity begins long before marriage, although premarital liaisons are not approved by older people and must be carried on privately. Young people are particularly afraid of having their sexual activity come to the attention of their parents or other persons of the parental generation. A circumcised boy has his own hut within the homestead and is not subject to intense supervision by parents so long as he is discreet enough not to bring his sexual behavior forcibly to their notice. From the age of 14 or 15 onward, boys are active in seeking heterosexual affairs. . . .

When a youth reaches the maturity of 17 or 18 years, he turns to girls outside his own community and clan for sexual relationships. One reason for this is his fear that continued intercourse with girls of his own community will result in pregnancy and an incest scandal. (The incest taboo includes sexual intercourse with any member of the clan.) . . .

Nyansongo girls are not frank about their sexual feelings; they feign extreme reluctance, even when they will yield quite easily to sexual advances. Young men woo them with gifts, flattery, and serenading. . . . Even when a girl goes willingly to a youth's hut or into the woods with him, she puts up some resistance to his sexual advances. He expects this and enjoys overcoming it, taking pleasure from her protestations and cries of pain. Aside from this patterned pose, most girls have sincere misgivings about premarital sexuality. . . .

The appearance of a girl is an important criterion of her desirability as a mate. Girls who are considered beautiful are much sought after for marriage, while ugly girls have a slightly more difficult time getting married. Characteristics considered attractive in a girl are brown skin (as opposed to black), firm and erect breasts (as opposed to those which are too small or too pendulous), smooth, soft skin, shapely hips and buttocks (as opposed to those which are too straight or too fat), full calves and thighs (as opposed to thin ones). . . . Facial characteristics are also important although more difficult to formulate. Small eyes, a narrow mouth, and a space between the upper incisors are considered attractive in girls. . . .

Once a young man has decided on a girl whom he is not prohibited from marrying and whom he considers attractive, he finds an intermediary. . . . There are two questions the intermediary must answer: What is the girl's sexual reputation? and, Is there witchcraft in her family? . . .

The witchcraft issue is an important one in mate selection. If there is known to be witchcraft in a girl's family, then it is deemed likely that she herself practices witchcraft and will cause trouble in any family she marries into. . . .

A month after the transfer of (bridewealth) cattle the bride must be taken from her father's homestead to the home of the groom. . . . Five young clansmen of the groom come to take the bride and two immediately find the girl and post themselves at her side to prevent her escape, while the others receive the final permission of her parents. When it has been granted, the bride holds onto the house post and must be dragged outside by the young men. Finally she goes along with them, crying and with her hands on her head. This traditional resistance is usually token and not really intended to break off the marriage.

When the reluctant bride arrives at the groom's house, the matter of first importance is the wedding night sexual performance. This is a trial for both parties in that the impotence of the groom may cause the bride to break off the marriage and the discovery of scars or deformities on the bride's body (including vaginal obstruction) may induce the groom to send her home and request the return of the bridewealth. The bride is determined to put her new husband's sexual competence to the most severe test possible. She may take magical measures which are believed to result in his failure in intercourse. The groom for his part is determined to be successful in the face of her expected resistance; he fortifies himself by being well fed, which is believed to favor potency, by eating bitter herbs, and nowadays by eating large quantities of coffee beans. . . .

Numerous young clansmen of the groom gather at the homestead in a festive mood; chickens are killed for them to eat, and they entertain themselves by singing and dancing while waiting for the major events of the wedding night.

The bride usually refuses to get onto the bed; if she did not resist the groom's advances, she would be thought sexually promiscuous. At this point some of the young men may forcibly disrobe her and put her on the bed. The groom examines the bride's mouth for pods or other magical devices designed to render him impotent. As he proceeds toward sexual intercourse, she continues to resist, and he must force her into position. . . . Brides are said to take pride in the length of time they can hold off their mates. . . .

Once penetration has been achieved, the young men sing in jubilation and retire from the house to allow the groom to complete the nuptial sexual relations. They are keenly interested in how many times he will be able to perform coitus on the first night, as this is a matter of prestige and invidious comparison. He will be asked it by all male relatives of his generation, and the bride will also be questioned on this score when she returns to visit her own family. It is said that the groom's clansmen also question the bride in order to check on the groom's account of his attainment. Six is considered a minimally respectable number of times and twelve is the maximum of which informants had heard. They claimed that it was traditional to achieve orgasm twelve times, but that performances in recent years were lower. . . .

After the wedding night, the bride remains at the home of the groom for a period ranging from two weeks to three months, following which she is allowed to return to her father's homestead (or "to her mother" as Nyansongans say) for as much as two months. When she comes home to her parents, the bride may plead for a termination of the marriage. . . . The father of the bride may yield to her plea if her feelings seem so strong that she may desert her husband if forced to go back. Many fathers attempt to persuade or coerce their daughters into going back, however, particularly if the bridewealth cattle have already been used to bring another wife into the extended family. While she is at her parents' home, the bride, even if she intends to return to her husband, may accompany her unmarried friends to the marketplace, pretending to be unmarried in order to encourage would be seducers to give her gifts. She does not have intercourse with them, however, for fears of supernatural sanctions against adultery.[1]

There are similarities in the general conditions of marital and family behavior with which we are familiar and those of Nyansongo. We, too, have rules and prerequisites of marriage; a preferred age for marriage; values attached to physical features; a degree of premarital sexual relations, the expectation that sexual intercourse will occur the first night of the marriage; and attitudes regarding where the newlyweds will live. The differences lie in the customary activities associated with these events.

This chapter describes (1) various forms of marriage, (2) variations in family types, (3) variations in five non-American communities, and (4) variations in the American family.

FORMS OF MARRIAGE

There are four possible forms of marriage, determined by the number of husbands and wives: one husband and one wife, or monogamy; one

[1] Robert A. LeVine and Barbara B. LeVine, "Nyansongo: A Gusii Community in Kenya," in *Six Cultures: Studies of Child Rearing*, Beatrice B. Whiting (ed.) (New York: John Wiley and Sons, 1963), pp. 59–67.

husband and two or more wives, or polygyny; two or more husbands and one wife, or polyandry; and two or more husbands united to two or more wives, or group marriage. Since group marriage is very infrequent, we will discuss only monogamy, polygyny, and polyandry.

Monogamy The marriage of one man to one woman in practically all societies—whether preliterate, ancient, medieval, or modern—has unquestionably been the prevailing form of marriage. Except in certain ancient societies having polygyny as the preferred form of marriage and among a few scattered groups which practice polyandry, monogamy generally has been the approved form of marriage. Among many modern peoples it has the sanction of public opinion and law. But even in countries where monogamy is sanctioned by the mores and by religion, there may exist, as in the United States today, what is in effect successive polygyny or polyandry permitted by the device of divorce; or among the Nyansongo with a man inheriting a deceased brother's wife.

Although the monogamous American family of husband, wife, and children arising out of and maintained by affection, companionship, and mutual interests may seem to us the most natural form and way of life in the family, it is something new in human history.

Polygyny Marriage of one husband to two or more wives exists in many preliterate societies. It was present in most ancient societies and, until recently, in most Oriental societies. Even where it is socially approved and has the highest status, polygyny has never been universal. Most marriages are monogamous.

Women in polygynous societies may be willing to have co-wives in the family because of companionship and the sharing of labor. In some Indian tribes in America the women urged their husbands to marry their blood relatives.

From about 1843 until 1890, when it was officially banned by the church, polygyny was practiced by the Mormons. Brigham Young, who officially announced the doctrine of plural marriage which he believed had been divinely revealed to Joseph Smith, was survived by 17 wives and 47 children. Polygyny had the highest approval, since plural marriage was a cardinal religious principle of the early Mormons.

Kimball Young, a student of the Mormon family, has made an extensive study of the reasons Mormon husbands married more than one wife.[2] Men entered into the system of plural marriage as a result of persuasian by church officials, at the suggestion of a wife or wives, by a desire to obtain relief from an unsatisfactory previous marriage, by a

[2] Kimball Young, *Isn't One Wife Enough?* (New York: Holt, Rinehart and Winston, 1954).

wish for children where there were none by a first wife, and because of sexual motives.

Young rated the degree of success or failure of 110 polygynous marriages for which he had sufficient data. Five categories of success or failure were set up: (1) highly successful, (2) reasonably successful, (3) moderately successful, (4) considerable conflict and marital difficulty, and (5) severe conflict, including, in some instances, separation or divorce. The following summarizes his findings:

> On the basis of these ratings, nearly 53 per cent, or more than half of our cases fall into the "highly successful" or "reasonably successful" classification, one-fourth of them fall in the middle or "moderate" position, and slightly less than one-quarter (23 per cent) were rated as "considerable conflict" and "severe conflict." While it must be realized that I have no idea as to how representative my sample of family stories is, and while the judgments are my own, and, like other such ratings, subjective, nonetheless the figures do give some notion as to how these plural families look to a man who has been observing and studying them for practically a lifetime.[3]

Polyandry In the polyandrous form of marriage two or more husbands establish a single conjugal group by sharing one wife. Such a family is generally of the fraternal type like that of Tibet, though it may be nonfraternal.

Polyandrous marriages and practices are much less frequent than polygynous behavior. In a great majority of societies in which polyandrous practices occur, they are the exceptional rather than the approved form of marriage. In almost all cases polyandrous practices in these societies represent the right or the opportunity of younger brothers to have access to the wife of an older brother, rather than freedom of sexual choice by women.

Prince Peter, a Danish anthropologist, on the basis of field work in Tibet, describes one possible explanation for polyandry—to keep property undivided:

> Tibetans were very keen not to divide their property and anxious, also, not to let their family name die out. In order to attain these two objectives they practised polyandry and both patrilineal and matrilineal inheritance, the latter type, however, only when there was no male heir, so that a generation in which there were only girls might be bridged. In such a case, the elder daughter inherited everything and took a husband or husbands as she pleased.
>
> The Tibetan household was like a pivot around which all the interests of the family revolved. Polyandry was practised because in this way a

[3] *Ibid.*, pp. 56–57.

number of brothers living on a family property could keep it undivided by taking one wife in common and sharing her, the land and the children among themselves.[4]

The following account of polyandrous practices among the Todas, a small tribe of five or six hundred in India, describes marital arrangements:

> The Toda female marries one male and at the same time becomes the wife of his brothers. Should other brothers be born subsequently they will also share equally in marital rights. Insofar as only brothers share a wife, the union may more precisely be termed fraternal polyandry. This form has predominated, but on occasion the marriage will include classificatory brothers—those of the same sib and age group—who may reside in the same or in other villages. Family life arrangements differ accordingly. When all live in one household and one of the brothers is with the wife, he places his cloak and staff outside the hut as a warning to the rest not to disturb him. (Peter found that this was not practised in Tibet.) The marital privileges rotate equitably among the brothers, and there is remarkably little friction or jealousy engendered by the arrangement.
>
> When a wife becomes pregnant, there is no call to determine the biological father. Instead a rather remarkable practice is carried out to give the child a "social" or "legal" father. In a ceremony held about the seventh month of pregnancy, one brother, usually the eldest, is chosen to "give the bow." The pregnant woman retires to a wood accompanied by the chosen husband. There he fashions a ceremonial bow and arrow from twigs and grass and, in front of the relatives, presents these objects to the wife. By this gesture he becomes the recognized "legal" father of the unborn child.[5]

FAMILY TYPES

Families may be classified in three ways: according to descent, location of residence, and authority. The recognized form of descent—whether on the male or female side—provides a classification of families as patrilineal or matrilineal. The place of residence of a couple after marriage—either with or near the husband's or the wife's parents—permits the classification of families as patrilocal or matrilocal. A more significant classification is the matriarchal, patriarchal, and democratic family. In the matriarchal family, members of the extended family live together under the authority of the mother and trace descent through the mother.

---

[4] Prince Peter of Greece and Denmark, "The Tibetan Family System," in *Comparative Family Systems*, M. F. Nimkoff (ed.) (Boston: Houghton Mifflin, 1965), pp. 197–198.
[5] Stuart A. Queen and Robert W. Habenstein, *The Family in Various Cultures* (3rd ed. Philadelphia: Lippincott, 1967), pp. 21–22.

In the patriarchal family the members are under the authority of the father and trace descent through him. In the democratic family authority is shared among the members.

The Matriarchal Family Among preliterate peoples the family is usually of the extended form. In some preliterate communities it is composed of the old matron, her sons, her daughters, and the children of her daughters. After marriage her sons continue to live with their mother and are only visitors in the homes of their wives, who also dwell with their own mothers. The control of children is therefore in the hands not of their fathers but of their uncles, the brothers of their mother.

Among the Hopi Indians the husband moves to his wife's dwelling but remains loyal to his clan.[6] Children belong to the mother and her clan. For the most part the husband eats and sleeps at the wife's home, but on ceremonial and feast days he returns to his own clan. The husband is expected to provide food and clothes for his wife and children, but the fields and the produce from them belong to the mother.

The Iroquois man, too, moves into the home of his wife, which is under the control of her mother. Among the Iroquois the individual family does not have a separate dwelling; each adult woman with her children has a compartment in the "long house." The husband continues to spend most of his time with his mother's group and is socially obligated to do all he can for his sisters' sons. His own sons are held to him only by bonds of affection developed through personal contact.

The dominance of the woman in the family organized on the matriarchal principle varies widely among societies. Typically the old matron will rely on a brother or a son to carry out her orders. Some societies which are matrilineal in descent have variations in matrilocal residence and matriarchal authority. This will be illustrated by the Zuni and Navaho, two of the five groups in New Mexico described by Florence Kluckhohn and Fred Strodtbeck. The following is their description of the Zuni family:

> The most important economic and social unit in Zuni is the extended family, which is matrilineal in descent and predominantly matrilocal in its residence pattern. . . . The household consists of several nuclear families, each often assigned to a separate room, which by lineage are usually dominated by the eldest woman of the matrilineage and in day-to-day affairs often governed by her husband.[7]

---

[6] Dorothy Eggan, "Hopi Marriages and Family Relations," *Marriage and Family Living*, 6 (1944): p. 1.

[7] Florence R. Kluckhohn and Fred L. Strodtbeck, *Variations in Value Orientations* (New York: Harper & Row, 1961), p. 56.

Among the Navaho, polygyny is permitted. The traditional form of dwelling is a one-room, six-sided hogan, or house:

> A single nuclear family usually occupies a particular hogan, and sometimes one finds a nuclear family living alone in isolation from its relations. The more common pattern is the clustering of a group of two or more hogans which house the members of related nuclear families that form an extended family. Sometimes these are the families of two women, often sisters married to one man, for this is a society where polygyny . . . is not infrequent. But in other cases, and more typically, the extended family of this group, which like the Zuni reckons its descent matrilineally, is that of "an older woman with her husband and unmarried children, together with her married daughters and their husbands and unmarried children."[8]

In many societies there are some individual families in which the dominant control is in the hands of a woman. Even in pre-1949 China, with its highly developed patriarchal system, a wife, if she were a woman of ability, might succeed her husband as manager of the affairs of an extended family. And in the United States there is an occasional large-family group dominated by a matriarch. More often in our society there is the small-family group controlled by the wife. The ridicule implicit in the phrases "the henpecked husband" and "the wife wears the pants" suggests that this matriarchal role is not socially sanctioned but arises in personal interaction.

The Patriarchal Family In the patriarchal family, authority resides in the father. Various adaptations of this pattern are found. The two chief historical forms are the extended-patriarchal family and the small-patriarchal family.

Even today a large proportion of societies approve the extended-patriarchal type of family organization. In the Philippines, for example, the extended-patriarchal family is the approved form:

> The fundamental social unit in the Philippines is the family. As in other countries with the same family system, its characteristics are: (1) absolute control by the head of the family, the father in this case; (2) it functions as the economic, social, religious, and political unit; and (3) three or more generations constitute a household. Despite the fact that urban families are breaking away from this pattern, it is still strong, though less inclusive than formerly.
>
> Filipino families are characterized by paternal dominance, discipline, romantic love subordinate to parental approval, premarital association is chaperoned, no divorce, high birth rate, large family-group relations, and

[8] *Ibid.*, p. 58.

the goal is not individual happiness as in Western culture but an integrated and prosperous kinship family group.[9]

The Industrial Revolution in the eighteenth century, with the consequent growth of towns and cities, resulted in problems for the social organization of the extended family. There was not only the problem of moving an entire extended family but of housing it in an urban environment. A man working in an industrial city was removed from the control of his rural kinship family. Thus the extended family was superseded by the small-patriarchal family composed of husband, wife, and children, with perhaps the presence of one or two grandparents, one or more unmarried brothers or sisters of the parents, or other relatives. The dominance of the male head of the family, whether father or grandfather, over the other members was unquestioned.

The Modern Democratic Family The Industrial Revolution established conditions not only for the transition from the extended-patriarchal to the small-patriarchal family but also for the breakdown of the patriarchal family. With young men and women in the city getting factory jobs, the authority of parents was greatly weakened. Wives also could work for wages as domestics or in business or industry, a situation which weakened the patriarchal type of family relations. Young people became inclined to arrange their own marriages and set up their own homes. In the United States, pioneer conditions, the rise of the public school, and the extension of democratic principles accelerated the development of the democratic family.

The modern democratic family has the following characteristics: (1) freedom of choice of a mate on the basis of romance, companionship, compatibility, and common interests; (2) independence of the young people from their parents after marriage; (3) the assumption of equality of husband and wife; (4) decisions reached by discussion between husband and wife, with children participating increasingly with advancing age; and (5) maximum freedom for its members consistent with the achieving of family objectives. These characteristics will be described more fully in later chapters of the book.

VARIATIONS IN FIVE NON-AMERICAN COMMUNITIES

Anthropologists at Harvard, Yale, and Cornell in the mid-1950's developed a program to study several communities in different parts of the world using the same general topics, such as daily activities, economic activities, family behavior, social organization, and child training. Some

---

[9] Amparo E. Santos, "Marital Adjustment of Filipino Couples in Los Angeles," M.A. thesis, University of Southern California Library, 1962.

of the results of these studies have been published under the title *Six Cultures: Studies of Child Rearing*.[10] The six communities studied include the following. (1) Nyansongo, an area in east Africa with a very high population density, consists of 18 families with a total population of 208. Its inhabitants are called Gusii. (2) The second community comprises a section of Khalapur, a town of considerable size in India. Its inhabitants, called Rājpūts, are land owners. (3) The third area studied was the village of Taira in Okinawa. (4) Juxtlahuaca, a town in southern Mexico, contains a section called Santo Domingo which is inhabited entirely by Indians. The investigators found aspects of the Mixtec Indian culture and so called the 600 persons studied Mixtecans. (5) Tarong in the Philippines is a small community five miles from the nearest town. The road is almost impassable and so communication with the town is minimal. This strictly rural area is composed of steep mountain ridges and narrow valleys. (6) The sixth study was of a small New England village. The marital and family behavior there is similar to that of most areas of the United States. The description below will be limited to the five non-American areas.

In examining the anthropological reports on these five areas, one is impressed by the great diversity of marriage and family patterns. Variations are apparent regarding age at marriage, methods of mate selection, sexual behavior, forms of marriage, forms of the family, and division of labor. These will be considered in this section.

Age at Marriage Among the Gusii of Nyansongo and the Rājpūts of India, the age of brides is 15 or 16, the age of grooms 18 to 20. In

Table 1. **Legal age for marriage in 78 countries, 1968***

	NUMBER OF COUNTRIES	
Age	Brides	Grooms
12	12	
14	16	13
15	14	4
16	22	21
17	3	1
18	11	30
19		0
20		2
21		7

**Demographic Yearbook*, United Nations, 1968, pp. 748–756.

[10] Whiting. See also Lee Minturn and William Lambert, *Mothers of Six Cultures: Antecedents of Child Rearing* (New York: John Wiley and Sons, 1964).

Okinawa the average age of brides is 22 and in Tarong it is "after 20." The respective age of grooms is 25 and "18 or so."

The variations in the age at marriage in these areas is similar to that of various countries of the world. Most have a much lower legal age for marriage than the United States. A survey of 78 countries for which the legal age for marriage is available reveals that in 71 countries the age for grooms is lower than 21 years, and in 67 the age of brides is lower than 18. Table 1 shows that the legal age for grooms in 38 countries is 16 years of age or younger and the legal age for brides in 42 countries is 15 years or younger.

Mate Selection In four of the five countries studied there are parental arrangements for mate selection, generally using a relative or close friend as a go-between. The degree of control varies greatly. In Nyansongo, for example, there is strict control, for the son is dependent on the father for the bridewealth cattle which is a prerequisite to marriage:

> Before he (a son) can arrange a legitimate marriage for himself a young man must be permitted by his father to use some of the family's cattle for bridewealth. Even if the marriage of his uterine sister has provided the family with bridewealth, the youth must obtain his father's consent to use that bridewealth for his own marriage. A son who does not bother to obtain paternal consent may find himself arrested for theft by tribal policemen on the basis of a complaint registered by his father. The father may withhold consent in order to use the bridewealth for his own secondary marriage or because he wants to punish a particular son; in the latter event the cattle might be granted to a different son for his marriage. . . . When a man has obtained paternal consent for his use of bridewealth in marriage, he can proceed to select a mate. In so doing he must conform to Gusii incest regulations, which forbid not only marriage within the clan but also marriage with cross-cousins and others of his mother's kin group. Furthermore, he may not choose as a mate any girl whom his father had only considered taking as a secondary wife, even if negotiations for the marriage had broken off early.[11]

In Okinawa mate selection is arranged by parents, but if the girl objects violently the parents withdraw their choice. Parental selection of a mate is nominal in Tarong, for a girl can veto the selection. The father of the groom has more control, for the father provides a marriage settlement on the new family:

> If the boy successfully courts a girl, a secret agreement may be reached between the young people. . . . Traditional negotiations may be completed within a minimal three meetings of the prospective in-laws: the father of the boy, a man known as a talented speaker and a variety of other relatives, but not the boy himself, go to see the parents of the girl. The

[11] *Ibid.*, p. 62.

request for the girl's hand is made in a stylized fashion and her parents respond vaguely. Hints of the marriage settlement to be offered may be made by the speakers for the boy, and if the suit is favored by the girl's parents, they will set a date for a second meeting within a week or two, when the girl's answer will be given.

The girl may appear at any time during the meeting and indicate her rejection of the suitor, usually accompanied by "I am too young" or a like excuse. If she does not show herself, it is proof that the boy's suit is at least under consideration. If the boy is a cousin, neighbor, or in some other way a desirable match, her parents will encourage her assent. But no girl is forced to accept a suitor against her will. . . .

At the second meeting the girl's answer is given, and if favorable, either another meeting date is set or discussions are immediately begun concerning the marriage settlement, given by the groom's father and, ideally, sufficient to make the new family self-sustaining. One by one the categories of the marriage settlement are discussed: money, work animals, house and plot, and land.[12]

Sexual Behavior Premarital sexual relations vary among the five communities. In Nyansongo "sexual activity begins long before marriage, although premarital liaisons are not approved by older people and must be carried on privately."[13] Boys are active in seeking sexual relations from the age of 14 or 15. At first they have sexual relations with girls of their own clan but by the age of 17 or 18 they turn to girls outside their community and clan. Among the Rājpūts there are strict mores against sexual relations outside marriage and "sexual immorality, particularly among women, is a great disgrace, and therefore a carefully guarded secret."[14] In the Okinawan village of Taira, men have more sexual freedom than women. They are at liberty to have affairs with other women outside the village.[15] The following is a description of the emphasis on chastity by the people of Tarong:

> The essential quality the girl must have is chasteness. If she is known to be unchaste or has an illegitimate child, her marriage chances considerably diminish unless her family can force the guilty man to marry her. Generally this is impossible for almost all the men so involved are already married. But such lapses among young marriageable girls are exceedingly rare. Beyond the age when she is marriageable except to an older bachelor or widower, that is about 30, there is only mild gossip at any sexual liaison she might have and her social status or that of the children she might have is not affected.[16]

[12] *Ibid.*, pp. 741–743.
[13] *Ibid.*, p. 59.
[14] *Ibid.*, p. 303.
[15] *Ibid.*, p. 423.
[16] *Ibid.*, pp. 741–742.

Among the Mixtecans of Mexico various forms of sexual behavior, including modesty, imitative sex play, and masturbation, are handled in a rather casual way during childhood:

> There are no specific or severe rules concerning any of these activities at the beginning of early childhood. A young child may go around nude without causing any special comment or evoking any punishment or discipline from the caretaker. In contrast, during the latter part of early childhood, children will be lightly ridiculed for going around nude. Thus there is a gradual learning process regarding modesty during early childhood.
>
> Masturbation and imitative sex play between small children are treated with equal casualness. Parents and caretakers tend to be very permissive concerning these activities at the beginning of early childhood and gradually extinguish such activities, mainly through ridicule, toward the end of that stage. The observations of these activities indicate that masturbation and imitative sex play are not particularly common although by no means unusual.[17]

There are great differences in attitudes toward illegitimacy. The birth of a child to an unmarried girl is considered extremely disgraceful in Nyansongo. Most frequently, however, "the unmarried mother is simply taken as a secondary wife by an elderly man wealthy enough to pay a high bridewealth rate for proven fecundity but too old to be able to demand a girl of high moral virtue."[18]

The Rājpūts are extremely strict in their attitudes toward illegitimacy:

> An illegitimate baby, born to an unmarried girl during our stay, was delivered by the girl's father, who then killed and buried it. The village women were highly critical of the parents for having raised their daughter so badly but made no comment about the killing of the baby. Furthermore, the village officials took steps to see that the police would not investigate the incident. Murder of such children is evidently accepted as a necessary step for the preservation of the family honor.[19]

The treatment of illegitimate children in the Okinawan village is in direct contrast to the above:

> An illegitimate child is loved by everybody and treated like any legitimate child. The bastard's name is listed in the registry under his mother's and his illegitimacy noted. Since World War II the distinguishing red ink mark is no longer used in recording these children. Unless the mother marries the child's real father, the offspring has no legal rights of inheritance. If she marries another man, the child may receive affectionate treatment from the stepfather, but he remains legally her son. Socially such a child does not suffer any form of ostracism, but adults make reference

[17] *Ibid.*, p. 659.
[18] *Ibid.*, p. 133.
[19] *Ibid.*, pp. 303–304.

to his status within his earshot. One such girl proudly said that people had told her that she was half-Japanese.[20]

Forms of Marriage In the four reports dealing with forms of marriage, three communities definitely sanction or permit polygyny and the fourth claims that "monogamy is the ideal and only sanctioned form of marriage" but sororal polygyny (marriage to the sister of one's wife) does occur rarely.[21] The investigators of Nyansongo report that polygyny is the sanctioned form of marriage:

> Polygyny is viewed as the ideal form of marriage. In Nyansongo 15 men are monogamists, 11 men have two wives each, and 1 has three wives. Of the married women, 21 are plural wives, 19 are monagamous wives or widows, and 3 are the unattached widows of a polygynist continuing to live as co-wives. Despite the roughly equivalent number of polygynous and monogamous adults, more than two-thirds of the community's children have polygynous parents.[22]

Forms of the Family Four of the five communities have an extended family form. Tarong of the Philippines has the nuclear family with separate houses for each family. The extended family in Nyansongo is a territorial group:

> The extended family homestead is a clearly defined social and territorial entity which includes one or more mother-child households. It has such autonomy as a residential unit that educated Gusii refer to it in English as "village," although it is much smaller than a village in the ordinary sense. The residents of a homestead are: the man who is the homestead head, his wives, his unmarried children, and his married sons and their wives and children. . . . The homestead has its own land and cattle and is separated from other homesteads by boundary hedges, trees, and jointly used pastures.[23]

The extended family is prevalent among the Rājpūts. Of the 36 families in this group, 28 are extended families: 9 with two generations, 16 with three generations, and 3 with four generations.[24]

Division of Labor There is great variation in these communities regarding responsibility for outdoor work. The report on Nyansongo indicates that the wife primarily has this role:

> The married woman (except the newly married, who eats at the house of her mother-in-law) has her own house, fields, and granary and is re-

[20] *Ibid.*, p. 431.
[21] *Ibid.*, p. 72.
[22] *Ibid.*, p. 39.
[23] *Ibid.*, p. 44.
[24] *Ibid.*, p. 231.

sponsible for the cultivation of the fields as well as for preparing food for her unmarried children (most of whom live in her house), her husband, and overnight visitors.[25]

Among the Rājpūts and the Mixtecans responsibility for outdoor work is assumed by the men. In the summer the Rājpūt men must get to the fields early and do the morning work before the blazing sun drives them to the shade for a noonday siesta. The men finish feeding and milking the animals before they come in for breakfast.[26] Among the Mixtecans the wife arises first and when her husband gets up she serves him some coffee and a cold tortilla. He then goes to the fields and works until breakfast time at about 9 o'clock. After breakfast the husband returns to the fields.[27]

Husbands and wives in the Okinawan village share much of the outdoor work. They work in the fields together and they go to the mountains and gather wood together.

There is no record of sharing household chores in any of the five communities. This is invariably done by the wives.

VARIATIONS IN THE AMERICAN FAMILY

The diversity of folkways and mores within the United States is reflected in wide variations in family patterns and relationships. Individual cases of practically every conceivable form of family behavior can be found. Only a few of these variations will be described: those concerning the member vested with authority, family composition, age and years married, cultural background, rural-urban area, and social class.

The Member Vested with Authority   At present families in the United States differ widely in the authority exercised by the various family members. The extended-patriarchal family is occasionally found, and in such families the patriarch dominates his wife, his sons, their wives and children, and his unmarried daughters. The matriarchal family, too, is occasionally observed, particularly in Negro families. Although undergoing rapid change, the small-patriarchal family, where the husband and father exercises control over his wife and children, is still found.

The trend of the family in the United States appears to be in the direction of the companionship family with control by consensus. The current economic behavior of fathers almost always involves their working away from home. Nearly four out of ten of their wives also work

---

[25] *Ibid.*, p. 55.
[26] *Ibid.*, pp. 243–244.
[27] *Ibid.*, p. 657.

outside the home. The family no longer has a single dominant head who controls the behavior of family members. Increasingly, decisions are made through informal discussions between the father and mother, with children free to participate.

Composition of Families In the American family there are great variations in the number and characteristics of family members. There are differences, for example, in families with no children; one child, two, three, four or more children; the presence of an adopted child or stepchild; by sex of the children; or differences in age of children by one, two, or three or more years. The composition—and therefore the behavior—of families varies also according to the presence or absence of others in the family circle, such as grandparents or other relatives, servants, or lodgers. There is considerable variation, too, according to the previous marital status of the spouses.

Age and Years Married A family in which the husband and wife were married in their teens will be different from one in which marriage occurred at a much later age. While the social expectation and usual practice in America is for the husband to be older than the wife, not infrequently the wife is older than the husband. Obviously there are variations, also, by the number of years married.

Cultural Background The American family differs from those in other countries. These differences may be appreciated best by illustrations of family patterns in other nations, such as the harem in Turkey before the revolution, the chaperonage of unmarried women in Italy, the role of the geisha girl in Japan, the *dot*, or dowry, arrangement in France, the great subordination of daughter-in-law to mother-in-law in nineteenth-century China, and the great part played by women in industrial and military activities in the Soviet Union.

Within the United States there are considerable differences in family structure and relationships by national origin. Cultural patterns transplanted from the Old World or from Mexico tend to persist longer in immigrant colonies and to disappear with the Americanization of the second and third generations.

Rural and Urban Families The rural family under the leadership of its head is an economic unit with its members participating in the occupation of farming. Within the rural family there are wide differences—by farm ownership or tenancy, by types of agricultural employment, and by proximity to the town or city.

Urban families, like rural families, vary widely from each other. For example, in progression from the smaller to the larger city there may be an increase in secularization of activities.

Social Class Families differ also by the social class to which they belong. In nearly every community there are differences in status, with the "old" and the "best" families at the top of the social hierarchy. The class position of an adolescent's family is a major determinant of his social contacts, his continuing in or dropping out of school, his occupation, and his choice of a mate.[28]

SUMMARY

There are various socially sanctioned forms of marriage determined by the number of husbands and wives: one husband and one wife, or monogamy; one husband and two or more wives, or polygyny; and two or more husbands sharing one wife, or polyandry. There are also variations in the forms of the family, particularly on the basis of the authority pattern in the family. In the matriarchal family authority resides in an older woman; in the patriarchal it resides in an older man; and in the democratic it is shared by members—husband, wife, and children as they advance in age. An analysis of five non-American communities studied by anthropologists shows great variations in age at marriage, methods of mate selection, patterns of sexual behavior, forms of marriage and of the family, and division of labor. There are also great variations among families within the United States based on, for example, the member vested with authority, composition of the family, age of the husband and wife and years married, cultural background, residence in rural or urban areas, and social class.

PROBLEMS FOR RESEARCH

Changes in the Extended-Family System It will be shown in Chapter 7 that the extended family is still present in several countries. Comparative studies of the likenesses and differences should be undertaken of the extended family in process of social change in Japan, India, China, and other societies. Knowledge of the effect of industrialization, urbanization, mobility, and other social processes on the extended-family system in various societies would contribute to general sociological knowledge.

Polygyny Young in his exhaustive study of Mormon polygyny describes some personal and family problems of persons who were con-

[28] August B. Hollingshead, *Elmtown's Youth: The Impact of Social Classes on Adolescents* (New York: John Wiley and Sons, 1949).

verted to Mormonism.[29] This involved a shift from monogamy, which was strongly entrenched in religious mores, to polygyny, which was highly approved by the Mormon church. Young also describes problems of polygynous families when the Mormon church abandoned this system of marriage under federal political pressure. The change from polygyny to monogamy is occurring in some countries today, particularly a few of the new nations of Africa. What are the problems of persons and families who shift from polygyny to monogamy? Are they different from those faced by Mormons when they changed to polygyny or when they moved from polygyny back to monogamy?

Authority Systems in Families Family behavior is influenced by the social and cultural life of a given time and place, and studies of family life should be made within the context of the larger economic and social organizations of a society. This is particularly true for studies of the authority systems of families. Smith, in his analysis of the role of the lower-class Negro husband and father in British Guiana, suggests that even a moderately patriarchal form of the family is unlikely when the economic position of men is markedly inferior to other classes in the system.[30] Studies should be made to determine under what economic and cultural conditions matriarchal, patriarchal, or democratic forms of the family are found.

The Family in a Changing Society Sociologists have the hypothesis that basic changes in one part of a society result in changes in other parts of the society. Major social and political changes have occurred and are occurring in many societies, particularly those in the Orient and in Africa. If the hypothesis is correct one would expect that in these societies the family is undergoing significant changes. A longitudinal study of the family in one or more of these countries would make a contribution to sociological knowledge by seeing if the hypothesis is supported, is refuted, or has to be modified.

QUESTIONS AND EXERCISES

1. What are the similarities and differences between marital and family relations of Nyansongo and those of the United States?
2. Define polygamy, polygyny, polyandry, and monogamy.
3. To what extent were plural marriages of Mormons in Utah successful?
4. Make an outline of the age at marriage, methods of mate selection,

---

[29] Young, *Isn't One Wife Enough?*
[30] Raymond T. Smith, *The Negro Family in British Guiana* (New York: Humanities Press, 1956).

patterns of sex behavior, forms of marriage, and forms of the family in the five non-American communities discussed in this chapter.
5. Differentiate patriarchal, patrilineal, and patrilocal from matriarchal, matrilineal, and matrilocal.
6. How do you explain the change from the extended family of earlier times to the small-patriarchal family of modern times?
7. What are some of the factors leading to the development of the modern democratic or companionship family?

BIBLIOGRAPHY

Calhoun, Arthur W. *A Social History of the American Family from Colonial Times to the Present.* 3 vols. Cleveland: Arthur H. Clark, 1917–1919.
> Volume 1 deals with the family in colonial times to the War of Independence; volume II from independence to the Civil War; and volume III from the Civil War to 1919.

Coser, Rose Laub (ed.). *The Family: Its Structure and Functions.* New York: St. Martin's Press, 1964.
> This is an excellent sourcebook on variations of the family in the United States and in other countries. This is particularly true of Part Two on limitations on marital selection; Part Three on role distribution; Part Four on socialization; and Part Five on the societal network.

Erlich, Vera St. *Family in Transition: A Study of 300 Yugoslav Villages.* Princeton, New Jersey: Princeton University Press, 1966.
> Material collected from 305 teachers in different villages, who filled out extensive questionnaires on family life in their communities. The objective was to describe the Yugoslav rural family at the beginning of World War II and the changes taking place in it. Includes almost all important aspects of marriage and family relationships. Delightful description in the Preface of various techniques of preserving the research materials in war-torn Europe.

Firth, Raymond. *We the Tikopia.* London: George Allen & Unwin, 1957, particularly Chs. 4, 5, 6, 9, 14, and 15.
> These chapters deal with the social organizations of the Tikopia, with emphasis on the kinship system. Describes daily routine of the family, care of the young, grandparents, and incest.

Kephart, William M. *The Family, Society and the Individual.* Boston: Houghton Mifflin, 1966, Chs. 3 and 4.
> Describes variations in forms of marriage, consanguine as against conjugal, family relations, courtship, premarital sex behavior, marital and sexual variations. Presents historical variations in marriage and the family among the Hebrews, the Greeks, Romans, early Christians, and in the Middle Ages, the Renaissance, and Reformation.

Ogburn, William F. (ed.). "International Issue on the Family," *Marriage and Family Living*, 16 (1954).
> Entire issue devoted to articles on the family in different areas and nations: the Arab world, the Balkans, Brazil, China, England, France, Germany, India, Israel, Italy, Japan, Mexico, Scandinavia, Thailand, and the Soviet Union.

Queen, Stuart A.; Habenstein, Robert W.; and Adams, John B. *The Family in Various Cultures*. Philadelphia: J. B. Lippincott, 1967.
> Describes marriage and the family in selected societies and at various periods of time.

Whiting, Beatrice B. (ed.). *Six Cultures: Studies of Child Rearing*. New York: John Wiley and Sons, 1963.
> A study designed and promoted by senior anthropologists at Harvard, Yale, and Cornell, with field work done by younger anthropologists. Deals with six groups in different parts of the world. Describes basic economic conditions, social organization, daily routine, sex, marriage and the family, religion, social control, ceremonies connected with death and disease, pregnancy and childbirth, and socialization of children.

Young, Kimball. *Isn't One Wife Enough?* New York: Holt, Rinehart and Winston, 1954.
> An objective analysis of Mormon polygyny, based on a lifetime of interest and study of this institution. Considers the origin of Mormon polygyny and reactions of non-Mormons to it, courtship and marriage, success and failure of plural marriages, and children of polygynous marriages.

Chapter 3
The Rural Family

Today about one in twenty families in the United States live on farms; fifty years ago this was true of one third of the population, and 100 years ago it was more than two-thirds. Those moving to urban areas and those remaining on farms both have faced new conditions and situations. The newcomer to industrial urban centers may not have the skills necessary for a job in industry. Power machinery, good roads, and cooperatives have made the independent small farmer almost a thing of the past. Those remaining on farms have been influenced by the impact of the urban way of life on rural areas and those moving to cities have taken their folkways with them.

FROM FARMING AS A WAY OF LIFE TO FARMING AS A BUSINESS

A major emphasis in this chapter is on recent changes in the farm family. It would be a mistake, however, to believe that the beginnings of these changes were in the immediate past. Actually, most of them can be traced to the period around World War I. The following case history was written about a quarter of a century ago by a woman whose childhood was before World War I. It gives a vivid account of changes from the self-sustaining independent farm family of her grandfather's time to the commercial farm family of her time:[1]

> My grandfather was a farmer and operated a general store. His twelve children helped farm. My father became a farmer because he knew no other way of life. He has liked farming, but always regretted his meager education. He resolved to give his children educational opportunities.

[1] As was indicated in the preface, all cases without footnote citations are from the files of the authors.

He married at twenty-four. To this union were born four children. My older brother, Robert, is a teacher in a high school. His high scholastic record led him into teaching. His wife is also a teacher. They have two girls, aged twelve and ten.

My other brother, George, left the farm at the age of seventeen, took a business course, and began his career as a salesman. As a youngster, he always liked to make trades and often auctioneered cakes and pies at the local church picnics. At the age of twenty-five he married a secretary who is still employed. They have one girl, aged nine.

Father would have been pleased if either of the boys had decided to farm, but he was not opposed to their leaving. I believe they would have as much money if they had bought farms in this community and operated them together with modern machinery. But neither had the type of wife that would be an efficient helpmate on a farm.

My sister, Grace, and I are elementary teachers. We attended the local high school, and each of us has three years of college training. We live with our parents, and drive back and forth to work. Neither of us is married.

Grandpa's farm was practically self-sufficient. They packed sauerkraut, green beans, and pickles in barrels; dried peaches and apples; jellied blackberries and huckleberries; buried apples and potatoes; and made butter in a dasher churn. Hogs were butchered and the meat cured in the smokehouse. They cooked the food on a wood stove which also provided heat in the winter, and obtained water from a cistern.

In my childhood our farm was a self-sufficient unit much as in my grandfather's day. The summer months were a constant routine of berry picking and feverish preparation of foods for the winter. My mother canned and preserved every kind of fruit and vegetable, and it was our job to prepare and clean them. Mother made vinegar, butter, and catsup. Mother dried apples, too. She made the bread for the family, and raised hop vines to make her own yeast cakes. She made all our clothing except our shoes, stockings, caps, hats, and overshoes. We bought beef once a week from a meat peddler.

Today we raise and can our own green beans, tomatoes, corn, apples, peaches, and pears, and make jellies and sauerkraut. But we buy all our meat except poultry, and for years the Donaldson bakery has delivered bread and rolls to our door three times a week. My grandmother washed her clothes on a washboard and used flatirons, but our tasks are lightened by the use of an electric washer, iron, and sweeper. The bottled-gas range furnishes instant heat for cooking, and the furnace provides uniform heat for the entire house.

People walked or rode horseback to Grandfather's store to barter butter, eggs, and chickens for dry goods, shoes, sugar, coffee, quinine, nails, and occasionally, coffins. Grandfather rode in a spring wagon over muddy roads to cities as far as 100 miles away, and brought back merchandise for his customers. The advent of the automobile, road-building programs, and telephones changed all this.

Farm machinery and rural electrification have changed farming conditions since Grandfather's day. The farm is no longer an independent unit, but is a part of a complex economic organization. The industrialization of our country with its shifting population from rural to urban areas has provided expanding markets for farm produce, and this has produced a demand for modern farm equipment. The mechanization of farm life has resulted in large-scale production. Grandfather dropped the corn in furrows by hand, cradled his grain, and cut hay with a scythe. Today, the tractor provides the motor power for plows, disks, wagons, binders, threshing machines, corn pickers, combines, buck rakes, and hay scoops.

My father was one of the organizers of the first cooperative market in our community. Now we have a nationally known berry-marketing center, with co-operative markets handling a million-dollar business every year. Another change, undreamed of fifty years ago, has been the introduction of government agencies to regulate farm prices and production to assure economic stabilization.

The automobile, the daily newspaper, the telephone, and the radio not only provide entertainment but give information on local, national, and international events. Farmers are no longer isolated by distance and their manner of living, for industrialization and urbanization have brought them together and nearer their city neighbors.

There are striking contrasts between farming by the grandfather and by the father of this woman. The outstanding changes were (1) the decline of the family as a self-sustaining unit; (2) the shift from the family working together as a unit to the dispersion of the children to the city for education and nonfarm occupations; (3) the decrease in the attachment to the land and in loyalty to the rural way of life; (4) a transition from traditional to scientific methods of farming; (5) the change from farming as a way of life to farming as a business unit of a large-scale commercial enterprise; (6) the growing urbanization of farm life, with the mechanization of agriculture, the utilization of labor-saving devices and conveniences in the household, and (7) the intro-

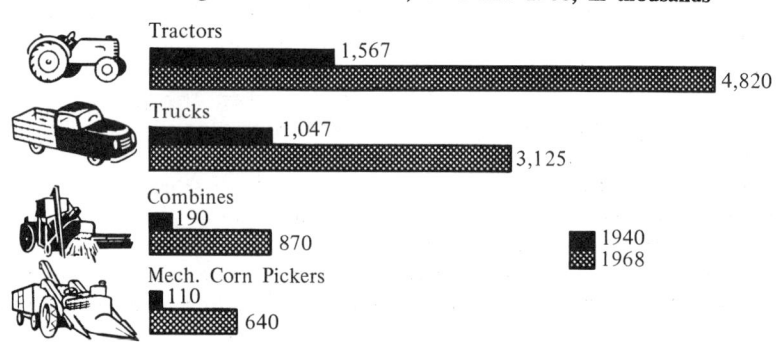

Figure 1. Labor-saving machines on farms, 1940 and 1968, in thousands*

Tractors: 1,567 / 4,820
Trucks: 1,047 / 3,125
Combines: 190 / 870
Mech. Corn Pickers: 110 / 640

1940
1968

Statistical Abstract of the United States, 1969, p. 599.

duction of modern means of transportation and communication, such as automobiles, telephones, radios, and, of course, today television. Figure 1 strikingly reveals the increase in the use of such labor-saving devices as tractors, trucks, combines, and mechanical corn pickers.

The purpose of this chapter is to analyze the changes which have occurred in the farm family and to examine its present characteristics. The chapter will deal with four points: (1) family organizations and systems of land tenure, (2) farming and familism, (3) social characteristics of farm families, and (4) the changing farm family.

FAMILY ORGANIZATIONS AND SYSTEMS OF LAND TENURE

Through the centuries there has been a close relationship between the system of land tenure and the form of family organization. By "system of land tenure" is meant the approved pattern of holding land within the family, including the method of its transmission at the time of marriage and inheritance in the case of death. "Family organization" refers to a form or system of family interrelationships, particularly of roles and statuses.

Certain forms of the family, at least until recently, have been maintained in the interest of ensuring the effective operation of various sanctioned systems of land tenure. The relationship between land tenure and forms of the family will be illustrated by the following cases: (1) the polyandrous family; (2) the stem-family of France described by Le Play; and (3) the Irish rural family.

The Polyandrous Family A number of factors in combination appear to be associated with polyandry (the marriage of two or more husbands to one wife). A basic factor is the scarcity of land coupled with its low productivity. The development of polyandry was related to the desire to leave an estate and family undivided. Under the usual polyandrous pattern of family organization, the wife is formally married to the oldest brother, with recognition of marital rights for the younger brothers. Under custom and law, all the offspring are recognized as children of the oldest brother. On the death of the brothers the estate becomes the property of the sons, who also marry one wife and form a single family. Thus polyandry is associated with a system of land tenure that transmits an estate intact from generation to generation.[2]

The Stem-Family The stem-family is the name given by Frédéric Le Play to a form of the small-patriarchal family operating under a system of land tenure with inheritance which guarantees the transmission of

[2] Y. S. Parmar, *Himalayan Polyandry* (Lucknow, India: Lucknow University Library, 1943).

the estate, family name, and traditions from generation to generation. Le Play applied the term to "the family which maintains a homestead for its immediate members and sends the other members elsewhere to make their own living."[3]

Under the law of primogeniture, on the death of a father the family estate was inherited by his oldest son. In France the latter had the obligation to support his unmarried brothers and sisters on the ancestral farm, and the duty to assist his sisters in making suitable marriages. He might also help his brothers by placing them as apprentices or by contributing toward their professional education. A younger brother would frequently remain at home working for little or no remuneration. If need be, the welfare and happiness of the younger sons were sacrificed. This type of family organization provided a system of land tenure that preserved the integrity of the estate.

The Irish Rural Family The rural districts of County Clare, Ireland, are characterized by an intricate system of family relationships. The transfer of the land of the father to the son is connected with the son's marriage. When the father is ready to retire, he chooses a son who is to work the farm. To settle the son on the land the father and son look around for a farmer who has a marriageable daughter and who is willing to bestow on his daughter a dowry equivalent to the value of the farm of the prospective father-in-law. This amount is paid to the father of the son before the marriage takes place, and the farm is then presented to the son. The money received by the father may be used for the marriage of a daughter or to assist another son to emigrate to the United States or otherwise provide for him.

This matchmaking is not merely a device for keeping the land intact. As Arensberg and Kimball point out, it is also a mechanism for the preservation of family unity through a sequence of generations, the dominant interest of the parents in the new woman being to provide heirs.[4]

A student of one of the authors sent the above description of marriage to her mother, who had migrated to the United States from rural Ireland. The following is from a letter received by the student:

> That's a good definition of matchmaking, as they call it over there in Ireland. My three sisters got married that way. They get along well. There are no divorces, so they choose wisely. They usually marry someone like themselves. I remember that my sister had two others who tried to match-

---

[3] Carle C. Zimmerman and Merle E. Frampton, *Family and Society* (New York: Van Nostrand Reinhold Company, 1935), p. 99.

[4] Conrad M. Arensberg and Solon T. Kimball, *Family and Community in Ireland* (2nd ed. Cambridge: Harvard University Press, 1968).

make with us and they were rejected. They just didn't suit, so they let it go at that and there were no hard feelings. Of course money is a factor. The more money the girl has the better farm she gets and the money goes to her husband's family. For instance, if your brother would marry a girl, the money would be divided between you and Katherine and Milly to get you three girls married to other farmers.

FARMING AND FAMILISM

This section will describe the nature of familism and then analyze farming as a common cooperative enterprise.

The Nature of Familism There are four characteristics of familism.
1. There is a feeling of belonging to the family group.
2. The integration of individual activities for the achievement of family objectives is manifested more clearly in farming than in other occupations. Traditionally farming has been an enterprise which requires the participation of all family members in diversified roles. This cooperation is an expression of family solidarity without conscious consideration of individual self-interest or demand for remuneration. The children have work to do which contributes to the welfare of the whole group.
3. The conception of a common interest in family property, with the obligation of supporting and helping individual members in need is another characteristic of familism. This is shown clearly in the Old Amish, where the family universally recognizes its responsibility to give relief to needy members and to provide for aging parents. Among this group it is considered natural that on retirement the parents will move to a separate part of the house. This is described in a study of the Old Amish by the United States Department of Agriculture:

> When the time comes to retire from active farming—usually when the youngest son or daughter marries—the aging parents move to a separate part of the house known as "Grossdawdy house." Sometimes this is an addition to the main house and sometimes it is a separate unit.
> Grossdawdy does not retire from all work when he retires to his part of the house. He finds as much work outside as he cares to do. Grossmutter sews during the day for the children and grandchildren. This work keeps both of them healthily occupied as long as they are active. If they need attention younger members of the family are near. It is doubtful that old people anywhere are more contented than the occupants of the Grossdawdy house who can associate daily with their children and grandchildren and yet can be separate.[5]

[5] United States Department of Agriculture, Bureau of Agricultural Economics, *Culture of a Contemporary Rural Community, Rural Life Studies: The Old Amish of Lancaster County, Pennsylvania* (by Walter M. Kollmergen, 1940), pp. 62–63.

4. Interest in the perpetuation of the family group through maintaining continuity between the old parental family and new family offshoots is indicated by the parental aid given sons in establishing themselves occupationally and in setting up their family households. The Amish, particularly, have as a fundamental value the obligation to establish their sons and daughters on farms and in households:

> The son may receive various kinds of livestock upon marriage. The daughter may receive full household equipment, and perhaps several dozen chickens. Following the marriage, the son may rent from his parents for a share or for cash, but in either case he is almost certain to have a good bargain. Cash rent payments may be low and if land is rented for a share the chances are that the father will supply somewhat more of the seed or fertilizer than he is required to furnish.[6]

Thus the characteristics of familism are as follows: (1) the feeling on the part of members that they belong preeminently to the family group and that other persons are outsiders; (2) integration of individual activities for the achievement of family objectives; (3) the assumption that land, money, and other material goods are family property, involving the obligation to support individual members and give them assistance when they are in need; and (4) concern for the perpetuation of the family as evidenced by helping an adult offspring in beginning and continuing an economic activity in line with family expectations, and in setting up a new household.

Farming as a Common Cooperative Occupation One characteristic of familism, the integration of individual activities for the achievement of family objectives, is particularly characteristic of the farm family. The farm family is an economic partnership with all members having an interest and a stake in the success of the enterprise. On the farm the father, mother, and children work together in making the living, with the father doing the outside work, the mother taking care of the house, and the children being given and accepting responsibilities.

Wives on farms fulfill their role of taking care of the house to a greater extent than city wives and, more than city wives, they take over certain activities usually considered masculine. These conclusions are derived from interviews with 178 Michigan farm wives and 731 wives from metropolitan Detroit.[7] The two groups were asked to indicate the degree to which the husband and wife performed each of eight

---

[6] *Ibid.*, pp. 30–31.
[7] Robert O. Blood, "The Division of Labor in City and Farm Families," *Marriage and Family Living*, 20 (1958): pp. 170–174. See also Robert O. Blood and Donald M. Wolfe, *Husbands and Wives: The Dynamics of Married Living* (Glencoe, Illinois: The Free Press of Glencoe, 1960).

tasks or roles. There were five possible responses: husband always, husband more than wife, husband and wife exactly the same, wife more than husband, and wife always. A much larger percent of farm than city wives performed by themselves activities associated with taking care of the house: shopping for groceries, getting the husband's breakfast, doing the dishes, and straightening up the house. On usual masculine activities, a larger percent of farm than city wives reported that they always repaired things around the house and mowed the lawn.

Using a representative sample of 500 Wisconsin farm families, Wilkening and Bharadwaj found that (1) wives contribute 20 hours a week to barn chores and 20 days a year to field work; (2) there is a high correlation between the husband's expectation and the wife's actual involvement in tasks; and (3) husband and wife specialize in decision-making as well as in the performance of tasks, with shared involvement in certain areas.[8]

The following excerpt from a personal document illustrates the integration of roles by family members, particularly children, to make the farm enterprise a success:

> My home is in a rural community. My mother and father were both raised in agricultural communities, and both were interested in agriculture as an occupation. They have been farmers in the same community for a number of years.
>
> Farming has been largely a family enterprise. My father is manager. In our community it was considered the husband's place to manage the farm. He hired what help was needed, directed and usually worked with the hired help in the fields or about the livestock, gathered and marketed the crops, did the banking, and assumed the role of "governor" of the home.
>
> On the farm we children had duties to perform. My sister helped Mother prepare meals and do the laundry, cleaning, and other things about the house. My brothers and I had tasks to do when we were five or six years old. At first it was small jobs, later caring for stock and working in the garden, and by the age of ten or twelve, working in the field. We all worked together to make the farm go.

The integration of activities for the achievement of the common objective of making the farm a success probably is not as prevalent as it was a decade or so ago. Figure 2 shows a trend from living and working on the farm to living on the farm but working in nonfarm jobs. It

---

[8] Eugene A. Wilkening and Lakshmi K. Bharadwaj, "Dimensions of Aspiration, Work Roles, and Decision-Making of Farm Husbands and Wives in Wisconsin," *Journal of Marriage and the Family*, 29 (1967): pp. 703–711. See also E. A. Wilkening and Denton E. Morrison, "A Comparison of Husband and Wife Responses Concerning Who Makes Farm and Home Decisions," *Marriage and Family Living*, 25 (1963): pp. 349–351.

shows that 26 percent of farm men and 20 percent of farm women in 1966 were employed in nonagricultural work. Students of the rural family, while pointing out the difficulty of making valid generalizations because of the diversity of types of rural families, are agreed that the one fundamental characteristic of the farm family is that its members work together as a unit to a greater extent than do urban families.

Figure 2. Employment status of farm men and women, by percents, 1966*

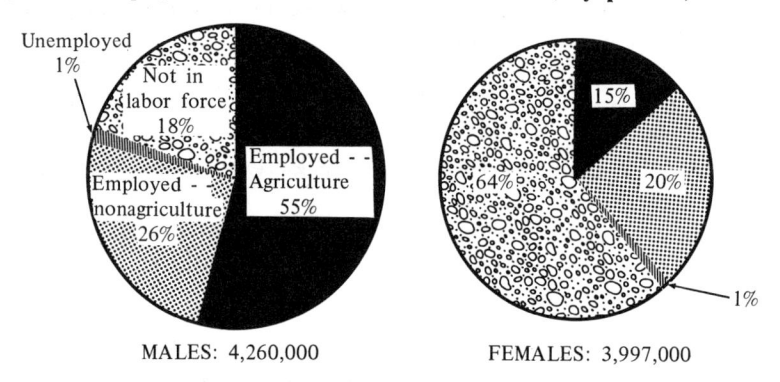

Unemployed 1%
Not in labor force 18%
Employed - nonagriculture 26%
Employed - Agriculture 55%

MALES: 4,260,000

15%
64%
20%
1%

FEMALES: 3,997,000

Relates to farm population 14 years old and over.
Data from Bureau of the Census and Economic Research Service.

*United States Department of Agriculture, *Handbook of Agricultural Charts*, 1967, p. 53.

SOCIAL CHARACTERISTICS OF FARM FAMILIES

Parent-Child Relationships The relationships of parents and children, particularly those of father and son, develop around participation in outdoor farming activities, while those of mother and daughter are centered in the house and garden, with the daughter assisting in "taking care of the house." While both the son and daughter profit from this informal occupational training, their education and recreation may suffer. If parents feel it is impossible to spare them from the farm's labor force some may stop school at an earlier age than urban children.

The question may be raised as to the effect that living in a rural or urban area has on the personality of children. A common belief is that rural children have a better adjustment than children living in cities. Research indicates that rural and urban children differ in personality characteristics, but there is disagreement about which group has better adjustment.

Two studies of the personality characteristics of relatively young rural and urban children have come to almost completely opposite conclusions. Mangus studied the personality adjustment of third- and sixth-grade children in Ohio.[9] His sample included 371 farm, 573 rural-nonfarm, and 285 urban children. He used the California Test of Personality, in addition to the ranking of the children by teachers and classmates. The other study was made by Munson, who studied personality characteristics of children in the fourth through seventh grades.[10] Like Mangus, he used the California Test of Personality. His sample was 150 in a highly urbanized area of New York City, 127 from a suburb of New York City, 170 from a town about twenty miles from New York, and 60 from the hinterland.

Mangus found that "the average level of personality adjustment was significantly higher among farm children than among those living in city homes." Munson reports: "Suburban children exhibited the highest degree of adjustment, urban children were second highest, rural children were third, and town children showed the poorest adjustment." On the following characteristics Mangus found rural children ranked significantly higher than urban, whereas Munson found suburban or urban children to rank the highest: self-reliance, sense of personal worth, sense of belonging, less withdrawal and nervous tendencies, social skills, and school relations.

How can one explain these differences? Do the children in Ohio have different characteristics than those in and around New York City? Is the difference due to the fact that Mangus used third- and sixth-grade children, whereas Munson used all children in grades four through seven? Is it due to Munson's subjects being slightly older? Or is it due to the fact that Mangus added judgments of teachers and classmates to data secured from the California Test of Personality? One or all of these or some other factor may be the explanation for the differences between the two studies on relatively young children. With present evidence, however, the belief that young children have more desirable personality characteristics if reared in a rural area cannot be either supported or disproved.

Two studies of the personality characteristics of adolescents are agreed that city children rank significantly higher in adjustment than rural children. Nye, using an Adolescent-Parent Adjustment Scale, found that adolescent-parent adjustment was lower in rural than in urban areas.[11] A more comprehensive study was made of adolescent behavior in Minnesota in which MMPI[12] data were secured from 11,332 ninth

---

[9] A. R. Mangus, "Personality Adjustment of Rural and Urban Children," *American Sociological Review*, 13 (1948): pp. 566–575.

[10] Byron E. Munson, "Personality Differentials Among Urban, Suburban, Town, and Rural Children," *Rural Sociology*, 24 (1959): pp. 257–264.

[11] F. Ivan Nye, "Adolescent-Parent Adjustment: Rurality as a Variable," *Rural Sociology*, 15 (1950): pp. 334–339.

[12] Minnesota Multiphasic Personality Inventory.

graders residing in 86 communities.[13] Adolescents living on farms as compared with those living in cities, in general, evidenced more shyness, self-depreciation, and suspicion of others. City adolescents were more likely to rebel against authority, and were more sociable, less critical of self, and less suspicious of the motives of others. Table 2 shows MMPI questions which were answered "true" by a significantly larger percent of rural than urban boys and girls.

Table 2. Percent of rural and urban boys and girls answering given MMPI items as true*

ITEMS	PERCENT	
	Rural	Urban
Boys		
I am easily embarrassed	47	32
When in a group of people I have trouble thinking of the right things to talk about	63	38
It makes me uncomfortable to put on a stunt at a party even when others are doing the same sort of things	65	44
I commonly wonder what hidden reason another person may have for doing something nice for me	70	54
I tend to be on my guard with people who are somewhat more friendly than I had expected	60	42
Girls		
I am easily embarrassed	74	55
I wish I were not so shy	64	46
I find it hard to make talk when I meet new people	62	47
I commonly wonder what hidden reasons another person may have for doing something nice for me	70	50
I deserve severe punishment for my sins	49	33

*Starke R. Hathaway, Elio D. Monachesi, and Lawrence A. Young, "Rural-Urban Adolescent Personality," *Rural Sociology*, 24 (1959): pp. 343–344.

Status The city man may be judged a failure by his acquaintances and family if he does not improve himself and his family economically and socially year by year, but not so the farmer. The man who does a good job of looking after his fields and stock and provides for his family gains the approval of the community.

The status of a city woman is determined largely by external signs of

---

[13] Starke R. Hathaway, Elio D. Monachesi, and Lawrence A. Young, "Rural-Urban Adolescent Personality," *Rural Sociology*, 24 (1959): pp. 331–346.

success—living in the best residential neighborhood, engaging in conspicuous consumption, the prestige of her husband's occupational position, and the clubs to which she belongs. The status of a rural woman has changed as the result of modern means of transportation and communication, and the diffusion of urban ways of life to rural areas. A few decades ago a rural woman would attain status if she were a good mother and homemaker, devoted her energies to her family and children, and abided by traditional codes. Today she attains status if the family owns a large farm, lives in a large house, engages in conspicuous consumption, and belongs to the right clubs.

It is easier for rural children to engage in adult activities than it is for city children. At an early age boys and girls do important chores and by their early teens they may do the work of an adult. All members of the family see such work as contributing to the common task of making a living.

Security The rural person finds his greatest security in the family. The youth who goes to the city knows that if he loses his job his family will welcome him back, and he can always work on the farm. Even though they receive no wages such members feel they have a share in the farm enterprise and enjoy security.

Farm families, at a comparable income level, show a greater tendency to build up savings than do city families—that is, they tend to sacrifice immediate needs and save for future security. Financial security is achieved through building up the farm business by ownership of land, by the acquisition of stock, and by the accumulation of farm machinery. The business is increased also by keeping down the standard of living, by making the family as self-sufficient as possible, and by restricting expenditures.

THE CHANGING FARM FAMILY

The primary trends in the farm family will be analyzed, in part, from census data. They will be considered under six topics: (1) decreasing rural population, (2) decline in the size of the farm family, (3) excess of men, (4) rural-urban differences in the proportion married, (5) more things purchased, and (6) increasing communication.

Decreasing Rural Population Since the census of 1790 the number of rural people in the United States has become a smaller and smaller part of the total population. In 1920 only 30.1 percent of the population lived on farms; in 1968 only 5.2 percent of the total population lived on farms. The decline in the farm population in recent decades has been

Figure 3. Farm population, farms, and farm size, 1940-1968

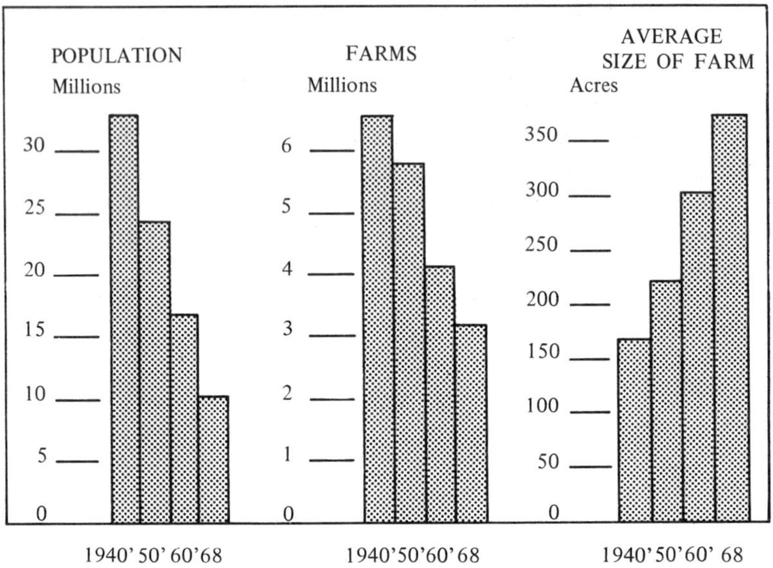

[Bar chart with three panels showing POPULATION (Millions), FARMS (Millions), and AVERAGE SIZE OF FARM (Acres) for the years 1940, '50, '60, '68]

*Statistical Abstract of the United States, 1969, p. 586.

drastic. The farm population as a percent of the total population was in 1930, 24.9; in 1950, 15.3; in 1960, 8.7; and in 1968, 5.2.[14]

Figure 3 gives a dramatic picture of what has been happening to farming during the last quarter of a century. It shows that the farm population and the number of farms have declined decade by decade, while the size of farms has increased each decade. This means that millions of farm families have migrated to urban areas. Also, the capital investment in mechanized equipment requires a large acreage to operate economically. With the exception of a few specialized crops, the day of a farm family operating a small-acreage farm is essentially over.

The shift of rural people into urban areas is shown by an analysis of a broad belt of 18 farm states from Montana to New Mexico on the west and Wisconsin to Mississippi on the east. It reveals that 61 percent of the 1520 counties in these states lost population in the decade between 1950 and 1960.[15] In 13 of the 18 states, 50 percent or more of the counties lost population. In 8 of these states—Kansas, South Dakota, Missouri, Mississippi, Nebraska, North Dakota, Oklahoma, and Arkansas—from 67 to 92 percent of the counties lost population. At the same time the major cities in the 18 states were experiencing explosive population growth. For example, Houston and Wichita each gained 54 per-

[14] *Statistical Abstract of the United States*, 1969, p. 590.
[15] "Cities Crowding—Countryside Losing: Latest on the Way People Are Moving," *U.S. News & World Report* (May 7, 1962): pp. 76–80. Analysis based on census data.

cent; Denver, Fort Worth, and Dallas gained from 46 to 52 percent; and Oklahoma City, Minneapolis-St. Paul, and Kansas City gained from 28 to 30 percent. The migration to cities and the depopulation of rural counties is associated with the increased mechanization of farming and larger size of farms.

What is known about the kind of people who migrate from rural to urban areas? Some of the known facts can be summarized under intelligence, aspirations, and success in competing for jobs. (1) Migration to urban areas by rural youths tends to be selective of those with higher intelligence and superior capabilities. Rural youths who aspire to a college education have higher intelligence than those who do not, and even these definitely rank below the urban students in intelligence. (2) Males who live on farms have lower levels of aspiration than nonfarm males. The levels of aspiration of both rural and urban males depend directly on the socioeconomic status level of their parents. (3) Rural-reared males do not succeed as well as urban males in the urban job market. Those from low socioeconomic backgrounds are limited to manual labor, and the availability of manual labor jobs has declined sharply.[16]

In a follow-up study of 307 rural men in eastern Kentucky 10 years after their enrollment in the eighth grade, Schwarzweller found no relationship between amount of schooling and (1) job status, (2) occupational status, and (3) level of living. Also there was no difference in the level of living of migrant high school graduates and migrant dropouts. Both had a higher level of living than those that did not migrate.[17]

Decline in Size of the Family The rural family, although declining in size, is significantly larger than the urban family. This is shown in Table 3, which gives the average size of the family[18] for urban and rural areas.[19] Between 1910 and 1960 the rural family declined from 4.6 to

[16] Lloyd D. Bender, Daryl Hobbs, and James F. Golden, "Congruence Between Aspirations and Capabilities of Youth in a Low Income Rural Area," *Rural Sociology*, 32 (1967): pp. 278–289. This includes a good summary of research on rural migration.
[17] Harry K. Schwarzweller, "Education, Migration, and Economic Life Chances of Male Entrants to the Labor Force From a Low-Income Rural Area," *Rural Sociology*, 29 (1964): pp. 152–167.
[18] In 1910, 1920, 1940, 1950, and 1960 the average size of the family was the average population per occupied dwelling unit, while that of 1930 was the average size per private family. Thus the different census data are not strictly comparable.
[19] In 1950 the census gave a new definition to urban areas: "(a) places of 2500 inhabitants or more incorporated as cities, boroughs, and villages; (b) the densely settled urban fringe, incorporated or unincorporated, around cities of 50,000 or more; and (c) unincorporated places of 2500 inhabitants or more outside of any urban fringe." All other territory is classified as rural. The rural is divided into rural-farm, those definitely engaged in farming, and rural-nonfarm, or the rest of the rural area.

3.6 or by 22 percent. By contrast, the urban family declined from 4.5 to 3.2, or by 29 percent.

Table 3. Average size of the family, urban and rural areas, 1910-1960, and rural-farm and rural-nonfarm areas, 1930-1960*

Year	Urban	Rural	Rural-Farm	Rural-nonfarm
1960[a]	3.18	3.56	3.77	3.50
1950[a]	3.44	3.93	4.13	3.78
1940	3.61	4.01	4.25	3.78
1930	3.97	4.29	4.57	3.99
1920	4.2	4.5	[b]	[b]
1910	4.5	4.6	[b]	[b]

[a]1950 definition of urban.
[b]Data not available.
*1910 and 1920 from *Fourteenth Census of the United States*, 1920, Population, 2, p. 1273; 1930 and 1940 from *Sixteenth Census of the United States*, 1940, Housing, General Characteristics, 2, Part I, p. 7; 1950 from *United States Census of Population, 1950, Characteristics of the Population*, 2, Part I (U.S. Summary), Table 47, pp. 1–97; and 1960 from *United States Census of Population, 1960, United States Summary*, 1, Table 78.

The census classification of the population, since 1930, into rural-farm, rural-nonfarm, and urban makes it possible to compare the size of families on farms with those in urban areas. Since 1930 the farm family has been 15 to 20 percent larger than the urban family. Farm families in 1967 had an average of 1.40 children, but considering only those with children the number was 2.69, as compared with 2.41 for the United States.[20]

There are relatively large differences in birth rates between rural-farm and urban areas, rural-farm being higher in all age groups. This was the finding of Beegle.[21] He also found differences in birth rates among rural areas, with the lowest rates near metropolitan areas.

Excess of Men Table 4 shows that the sex ratio—the number of men per 100 women—is greatest on farms, next in villages and small towns, and lowest in cities. In 1960 the sex ratio on farms was 107.2, compared with 94.0 in cities. Women, therefore, have a better chance of finding husbands in farming areas, and men have a better chance of finding wives in urban areas.

[20] *Current Population Reports, Population Characteristics*, Series P-20, No. 173, 1968, p. 2.
[21] J. Allan Beegle, "Social Structure and Changing Fertility of the Farm Population," *Rural Sociology*, 31 (1966): pp. 415–427.

Table 4. Men per 100 women in rural-farm, rural-nonfarm, and urban areas, 1920-1960, and farm and nonfarm, 1968*

Year	Rural-farm	Rural-nonfarm	Urban
1968	107.8	93.7	
1960	107.2	103.3	94.0
1950	110.1	102.9	93.5
1940	111.7	103.7	95.5
1930	111.0	105.0	98.1
1920	109.1	106.5	100.4

*Sixteenth Census of the United States, 1940, Population, Characteristics of the Population, 2, Part I, p. 20; United States Census of Population, 1950, Characteristics of the Population, 2, Part I (U.S. Summary), Table 34, pp. 1–87; and United States Census of Population, 1960, United States Summary, I, Table 49; Statistical Abstract of the United States, 1969, p. 26.

Figure 4, which gives the sex ratio by states in 1960, shows that the greatest excess of males is in 11 Western states, with sex ratios of 100 or above; that the 21 states with sex ratios of 97–99 were almost all rural states in the Middle West and in the South Atlantic; and that the three states with the lowest proportion of men to women were New York, Massachusetts, and Pennsylvania, all highly urbanized.

Figure 4. Number of men per 100 women, by states, 1960*

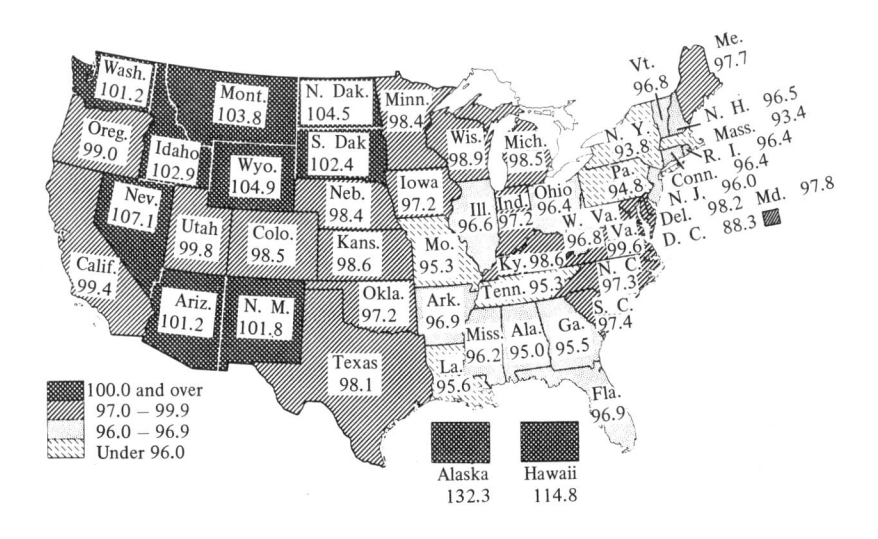

*Statistical Abstract of the United States, 1961, p. 27.

50   The Rural Family

Rural-Urban Differences in Proportion Married   Table 5 shows that the proportion married men and married women are of the total male and female population 14 years of age and older has increased in both rural and urban areas since 1910, the first census in which such tabulations were made. While in 1910 and 1920 the proportion of married men was greater in the country than in the city, since 1930 the proportion has been higher in urban areas. In all census reports the proportion of rural married women exceeded the proportion of urban women. The greater proportion of urban than rural married men in the 1930–1960 period is accentuated when the rural-nonfarm is excluded and the comparison is between urban and farm areas.

Table 5. Percent married persons are of all persons 14 years old or older, by sex, urban and rural, 1910-1960*

	MALE		FEMALE	
Year	Urban	Rural	Urban	Rural
1960	69.9	67.5	64.3	69.8
1950	68.6	65.8	63.8	69.8
1940	61.8	60.4	58.1	65.4
1930	60.5	59.3	58.5	65.0
1920	58.9	59.5	57.6	64.3
1910	54.7	56.8	54.6	63.3

*Computed from data in various United States censuses. Figures for 1910–1940 for persons 15 years old and older.

One explanation of the higher rate of marriage among farm than urban women is the relatively high sex ratio in farm areas. Urban men have the advantage over rural men because of the low sex ratio in urban areas. Where there are fewer available mates, some who otherwise might be rejected as suitable mates are able to marry.

More Things Purchased   The farm family is using home products less and less and using more and more things purchased. Figure 5 shows the great change in the ten-year period, 1955–1965. Home-produced foods declined from 41 to 31 cents of the farm family's food dollar with a corresponding increase in things purchased from stores.

Increasing Communication   In the United States, farmers have less communication with others than urban persons, but the difference is not nearly so much now as even a decade ago. Four indexes will show the increasing communication of farm families: possession of a tele-

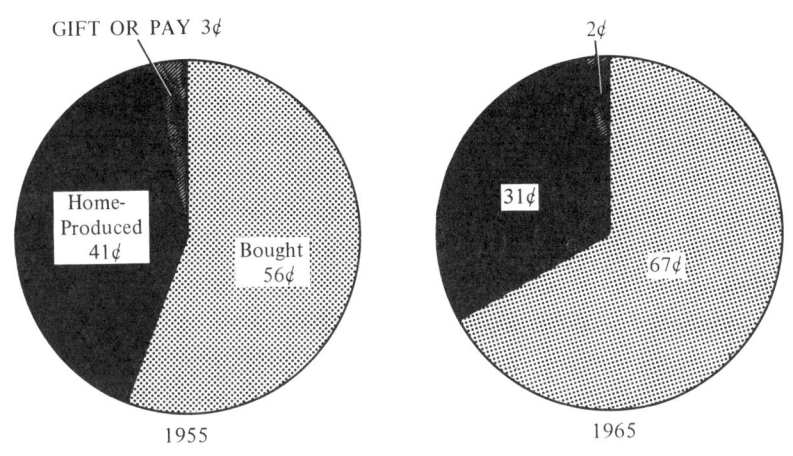

Figure 5. The farm family's food dollar, 1955 and 1965*

GIFT OR PAY 3¢

Home-Produced 41¢

Bought 56¢

2¢

31¢

67¢

1955   1965

Food used at home, 1 week in Spring.

*United States Department of Agriculture, *Handbook of Agricultural Charts*, 1967, p. 59.

phone, possession of a television set, possession of a radio, and amount of education. In the last decade or two there has been a greater increase in having or possessing these things by farm than by nonfarm families.

The Census makes periodic surveys of the prevalence of telephones in urban and rural areas. Recently metropolitan areas were divided into central cities and outside central cities. The results of three surveys were as follows:[22]

	1958	1960	1965
Central Cities	77.7	77.6	81.6
Outside Central Cities	NA	NA	88.1
Farm	45.5	50.3	68.6

The surveys show that farm families have fewer telephones than urban families, but there was an increase of 23 percentage points in less than a decade.

Figure 6 shows that, while in 1950, 1955, and 1961, television sets were less prevalent in rural than in the other two areas, the difference has been rapidly decreasing. In 1969, 95 percent of all households in the United States had at least one television set.[23]

[22] *Current Population Reports, Population Characteristics*, Series P-20, Nos. 96, 1959; 111, 1961; and 146, 1965. (NA means not available.)
[23] *Statistical Abstract of the United States*, 1969, p. 500.

52   The Rural Family

Figure 6. Percent of rural-farm, rural-nonfarm, and urban homes having television sets, 1950, 1955, and 1961*

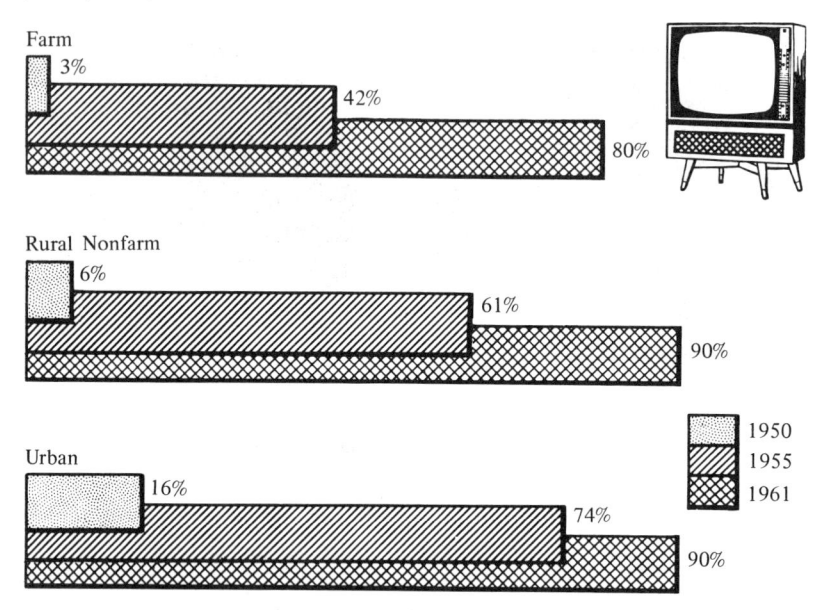

Farm
3%
42%
80%

Rural Nonfarm
6%
61%
90%

1950
1955
1961

Urban
16%
74%
90%

*Statistical Abstract of the United States, 1952, p. 741, and 1961, p. 516; and An Advertising Research Foundation Report based on the Census, National Survey of Television Sets in U.S. Households, May 1961, p. 2.

Using ownership of radios as an index of increasing communication, farm families today have about as much communication as urban families. This is seen in the following comparison of the percent of dwellings having radios in rural-farm, rural-nonfarm, and urban areas in 1940 and 1960:[24]

	1940	1960
Rural-farm	60.2	91.1
Rural-nonfarm	79.0	88.5
Urban	91.9	92.4

Between 1940 and 1960 farm families bought radios to such an extent that today they have about as much communication through radios as do other areas.

The level of educational achievement determines in part the social contacts of persons. Farmers average less education than persons in rural-nonfarm and urban areas. This is indicated by the following com-

[24] Data from censuses of the Bureau of the Census.

parison of the three areas by the percent of those 25 years of age and over who had completed less than 8 years of school in 1940 and in 1960:[25]

	Urban	Rural-nonfarm	Rural-farm
1960	19.7	28.0	29.9
1940	27.2	33.6	46.3

In 1960 the difference between the three areas in the percent with less than 8 years of education was not nearly as great as in 1940. In fact, the percent of rural-farm was only slightly above that of rural-nonfarm.

In 1967 the median years of schooling of persons residing on farms was 8.9 as compared with 12.1 for nonfarm persons. However, the difference is not very great between younger rural-farm and nonfarm persons. The Census has compared younger (under 45 years of age) with older (45 years of age and over) heads of husband-wife families.[26] The younger age groups of rural-farm persons have essentially caught up with nonfarm persons. For the younger farm heads the median grade attained was 12.1 as compared with the younger nonfarm heads of 12.5. The older farm heads of families had a median of 8.7 as compared with 10.8 for the nonfarm.

DISADVANTAGEOUS ECONOMIC POSITION OF AGRICULTURE

One way of ascertaining the economic status of farm families is to compare the median money income of farmers with that of other occupational groups. Figure 7 shows that farm laborers have the lowest income and farmers and farm managers are second. Even nonfarm laborers (unskilled workers) have a higher income than farmers. The median income of the total employed persons in 1967 was nearly twice that of farmers. This great difference cannot be explained entirely by the fact that part of the living expenses of farmers is provided by the farm.

Most data on farm families are for the total rural-farm population. However, certain surveys by the United States Department of Agriculture permit the division of farm families into broad social classes, as

[25] Data for 1960 from *United States Census of Population, 1960, United States Summary*, 1, Table 76; for 1940 from *Sixteenth Census of the United States, 1940, Characteristics by Age, Part 1, United States Summary*, Table 18. See also Lee G. Burchinal and James D. Cowhig, "Rural Youth in an Urban Society," *Children*, 10 (1963): pp. 167–172.

[26] *Current Population Reports, Population Characteristics*, Series P-20, No. 173, 1968.

Figure 7. Median money income for males, by occupation, 1967*

OCCUPATION

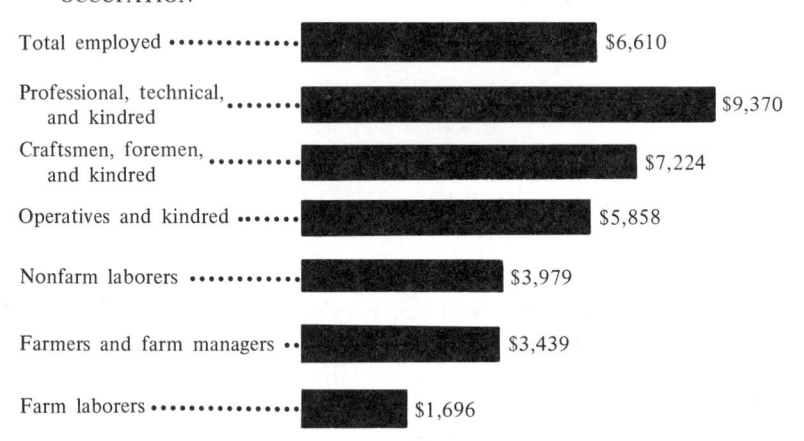

Occupation	Income
Total employed	$6,610
Professional, technical, and kindred	$9,370
Craftsmen, foremen, and kindred	$7,224
Operatives and kindred	$5,858
Nonfarm laborers	$3,979
Farmers and farm managers	$3,439
Farm laborers	$1,696

*Data from *Statistical Abstract of the United States*, 1969, p. 327.

measured by income. Some of these surveys were for low-income farm areas in Texas, Ohio, and Kentucky.[27] A comparison of the general pattern of income for farm families of the United States as a whole and a low-income area in Texas reveals that over a third of all farm families had incomes under $2,000; the income of a third of the low-income farm area was under $1,000. For the United States as a whole there was about the same proportion receiving different sizes of income, while for the low-income area there was a drastic decline in proportions as income increased.

Over half of low-income families secure their income from only off-farm jobs. They spend less for food, shelter, and clothing than farmers as a whole. Young low-income families tend to add to home furnishings and stock, while older-aged families reduce these. Expenditures, incomes, and consumption reach their peak in the age period from 35 to 40 and thereafter decline decidedly. In low-income families the proportion of the budget used for medical care increases as the family head advances in age; the percent of the budget used for medical care in a low-income area in Kentucky for those under 40, 40–59, and 60 and over was, respectively, 8, 11, and 17.

The lower economic status of farm families as compared with rural-nonfarm and with urban is indicated by the relative presence or absence of modern conveniences, such as running water, toilet and bathing facilities, and central heating. Table 6, using data for 1940 and 1960,

[27] Data on low-income families from United States Department of Agriculture, Agriculture Research Service, *Agricultural Outlook Charts*, 1961, pp. 24–28.

shows the increase in these facilities for all areas, and particularly for farms. The table, however, also shows the continued lack of these by many farm families. In 1960, 23 percent of homes had no running water piped to the house; 37.6 percent did not have a flush toilet; 37.5 percent did not have exclusive use of a bathtub or shower; and 71.9 percent did not have central heating.

Table 6. Percent of all rural-farm, rural-nonfarm, and urban dwellings having certain facilities, 1940 and 1960*

Facility	Rural-farm 1940	Rural-farm 1960	Rural-nonfarm 1940	Rural-nonfarm 1960	Urban 1940	Urban 1960
Running water to dwelling	17.8	77.0	55.9	82.3	93.5	99.4
Flush toilet	11.8	62.4	45.0	72.4	90.8	98.1
Exclusive use of bathtub or shower	11.8	62.5	40.8	69.7	77.5	92.6
Central heating system	10.1	28.1	27.0	34.0	58.2	62.0

*Sixteenth Census of the United States, 1940, General Characteristics, 2, Part 1; 1960 in 1960 Census of Housing, 1, States and Small Areas.

The lack of some modern facilities and services for farm families may be explained by various factors. Certain rural areas may have a disproportionate effect on the total farm picture. For example, while the South has caught up to other regions in the electrification of farms, it lags behind in telephones. Other possible explanations are the relatively high cost of installing or securing some of these on the farm, and the fact that some farm families prefer to get along without these conveniences and put the money into machinery and other things necessary for producing crops.

SUMMARY

There is a close relationship between the approved patterns of holding land within the family, including transmission at the time of marriage or inheritance in the case of death, and the form of family relationships, including the polyandrous family, the stem family, and the Irish rural family.

Familism, traditionally found among farm families, is characterized by the following: family members feel that they belong preeminently to the family group; all members participate in the achievement of family objectives and subordinate individual to family interests; family members rally to the assistance of a member if he is in trouble; and the continuity between the parental family and new family units is maintained through helping sons set up their households and establish themselves in an occupation.

In rural-farm areas the family has decreased in size; there is an excess of men; and a higher percent of women are married. Also, there is an increase in the use of telephones, radios, and television; and a higher degree of education.

All available evidence points to the continuing decline of the role of agriculture in the national economy. This is shown by the decreasing proportion of the national population which is rural-farm.

In general the farm family has a standard of living somewhat lower than that of urban families. One reason, of course, is the fact that the farmer has a lower cash income than the urban worker. Another reason is the fact that the farmer tends to put any surplus into the farm business.

Urbanization of rural areas is proceeding at an increasing rate. Improved means of transportation and communication are overcoming both spatial and social isolation, so that the farmer and villager increasingly are participating with other residents of the nation in the social, economic, and intellectual activities of the modern world.

PROBLEMS FOR RESEARCH

Changes in the Farm Family The farm family has changed under the impact of improved means of transportation and communication, the enlargement and mechanization of farms, and the influence of the urban way of life on rural areas. There is little information on what these changes have been. One of the questions which might be examined is the degree to which farm communities have moved toward individualism. Another question is the extent to which large commercial farms have replaced the family farm of a generation ago.

Rural Social Classes There has been increasing interest in the class structure of rural communities. It has long been recognized that there is a great difference, socially as well as economically, between owners, tenants, and farm laborers. With the development of mechanized farming and the increasing size of farms, these differences may be becoming greater. Systematic studies should be made in this field, developing criteria for classifying rural families by social class. Family behavior of the different classes should then be determined, including the degree of familism, the types of authority patterns prevalent, the roles of members, the ways in which the behavior of family members are controlled, and the influences of social class on mate selection. Comparisons should be made between families of similar social class in rural and urban areas. A study of families that have migrated to the city could be made concentrating on their class position in the rural community and the position which they have acquired in the city.

Parent-Child Relations Conflicting findings have been secured on the relative adjustment of farm and urban children. This situation is undoubtedly due to the small unrepresentative samples which have been studied. It is desirable to have more adequate studies made of larger and more representative samples. In these studies improved instruments for measuring adjustment and parent-child relationships should be employed.

QUESTIONS AND EXERCISES

1. Polyandry, the stem-family, and the contemporary Irish rural family were explained as products of different systems of land tenure. Give alternate explanations for each of the three types of families.
2. How do you account for the presence of familism in some families and its absence in other families?
3. How does the status of children and of women on farms compare with their status in cities?
4. What is the relationship between the sex ratio of an area and the proportion of men and women married?
5. Indicate specific ways in which rural areas are becoming urbanized.
6. Analyze the introductory case from the standpoint of (1) the characteristics of familism and (2) the urbanization of rural families.
7. Some question the conclusion of this chapter that familism is relatively absent in cities as compared with farming areas. Interview a sample of city families using questions designed to measure familism.

BIBLIOGRAPHY

Bender, Lloyd D.; and Golden, James F. "Congruence Between Aspirations and Capabilities of Youth in a Low Income Rural Area," *Rural Sociology*, 32 (1967): pp. 278–289.
> This is a longitudinal study of 307 rural men 10 years after their enrollment in the eighth grade. The authors explore the relationships among amount of schooling and job status, occupational status, and level of living.

Blood, Robert O. "The Division of Labor in City and Farm Families," *Marriage and Family Living*, 20 (1958): pp. 170–174.
> Data from interviews with 178 Michigan farm wives and 731 Detroit wives. A comparison of these two groups on eight tasks shows that farm wives had more traditional feminine roles than city wives.

Britton, Joseph H.; Mather, William G.; and Lansing, Alice K. "Expectations for Older Persons in a Rural Community: Community Participation," *Rural Sociology*, 27 (1962): pp. 387–395.
> Interviews with 487 adults in a small Pennsylvania community showed little opposition to participation of older persons in community affairs. The most frequently suggested community services were churches, lodges, and fire company.

Henkel, Ramon E.; and Fuggitt, Glenn V. "Nonfarm Occupational Role Involvement and the Visiting Relationships of Farmers," *Rural Sociology*, 27 (1962): pp. 53–63.
> Sample of 399 male farm operators in 11 Wisconsin townships, showing that nonfarm occupational involvement was associated with visiting friends with nonfarm occupations and those living in cities.

Kolb, John H. "Rural Youth," in *The Nation's Children: Problems and Prospects*, ed. Eli Ginzberg. New York: Columbia University Press, 1960, Part 3, pp. 25–50.
> An analysis of recent changes in farming as a way of life, including consideration of farms organized as businesses and small marginal farms. Discusses social relationships of farm youth and the issues involved in their occupational and educational choices. Brief summary of knowledge about rural youth, but undocumented.

Reiss, Albert J. "Rural-urban and Status Differences in Interpersonal Contacts," *American Journal of Sociology*, 65 (1959): pp. 182–195.
> Based on interviews with males in a metropolitan area, two small villages, and a rural area. Concludes tentatively that residential setting may be less important than occupation in determining the range of social contact. Finds that urban males spend more time in primary contacts than men in villages or farms.

Straus, Murray A. "Family Role Differentiation and Technological Change in Farming," *Rural Sociology*, 25 (1960): pp. 219–228.
> Based on a sample of 903 Wisconsin farm operators classified into high and low technological competence. Found that high technological competence was associated with integrative-supporting marital role of wife.

Wilkening, Eugene A; and Bharadwaj, Lakshmi K. "Dimensions of Aspirations, Work Roles, and Decision-Making of Farm Husbands and Wives in Wisconsin," *Journal of Marriage and the Family*, 29 (1967): pp. 703–711; also, Wilkening, E. A.; and Morrison, Benton E. "A Comparison of Husband and Wife Responses Concerning Who Makes Farm and Home Decisions," *Marriage and Family Living*, 25 (1963): pp. 349–351.
> Study of 500 Wisconsin farm families regarding the amount of time wives work in the fields and the degree to which the husband and wife are involved in decision-making.

Chapter 4
The Urban Family

Industrialization, the growth of cities, and the migration of rural families to cities have been reshaping the urban family. For years social scientists thought that one effect of these factors was the isolation of the urban nuclear family. In reality the vast majority of urban families have relatives living in their area and see them quite frequently. In urban areas, especially in metropolitan areas, there are wide variations in family behavior. One contrast, for example, is between the suburban and the central-city family. There are, however, great differences within each of these. This is particularly true of central cities, for here we find the nonfamily man living on Skid Row, the poverty family, the family of the blue-collar or the working class, and families of the middle class.

WORKING AND MIDDLE-CLASS FAMILIES

The following two cases describe the daily tasks of wives in the urban situation. The first describes the activities of a working-class wife; the second, those of a middle-class wife:

> *Working-Class Wife:* I get up first, make breakfast for my husband and put a load of clothes in my washer while breakfast cooks. Then I wake him up, give him his breakfast and he's off to work. Then I make breakfast for the children. After the children eat I dress them and they go out to play. Then I hang the clothes up and clean lightly through the house. In between times I do the dishes—that's understood, of course. Then I make lunch for the children and myself and I bring them in, clean them up, and they eat. I send them out to play when they're done and I do the dishes, bring the clothes in, and iron them. When I'm done ironing it's

usually time to make supper, or at least start preparing it. Sometimes I have time to watch a TV story for half an hour or so. Then my husband comes home and we have our meals. Then I do the dishes again. Then my husband goes to work again—he has a part-time job—at his uncle's beverage company. Well, he does that two or three nights a week. If he stays home he watches TV and in the meantime I get the kids ready for bed. He and I have a light snack, watch TV awhile and then go to bed.[1]

Middle-Class Wife: I get up at 6:45 A.M. and get every one off—my husband to work, and my daughter to school. Then I get my younger two children dressed for outside so they can play while I do up my dishes and my general housework. In the afternoon I do a lot of sewing—making things for the girls and myself. I have a lot of organizations I belong to and sometimes I attend those if I can find someone to take care of the children. Then my husband comes home—and we have a fairly late dinner, usually, unless he has to run out to attend a couple of his meetings. If he doesn't, he may work around the house, while I read or sew—and then again, we may just watch TV. Right now we're ready to have an open house this weekend—so my husband will probably help me get the place ship-shape.[2]

The working-class wife and the middle-class wife perform similar daily activities in caring for their husbands, children, and homes. Both watch TV when they have the time. Yet they are very different in their attitudes toward marriage and the role of the wife. The working-class wife thinks of her life as dull and monotonous. The middle-class wife experiences more variety in her life. She and her husband are involved in community activities—he attends "his meetings," and she belongs to and participates in some organizations. Also, they entertain friends in their home, and this activity is shared as a common interest.

URBAN-RURAL CONTRASTS

In the preceding chapter some of the characteristics of the rural family were presented by comparing it with the urban family. It will be useful to summarize these facts about the urban family which were explicitly stated or implied in the discussion of the rural family.

1. Individualism is more prevalent in urban than in rural families. This means that family interests are more likely to be subordinated to the desires and interests of the individual members. Individualism tends to separate the person from his family and to weaken family attachments.

---

[1] Lee Rainwater, Richard P. Coleman, and Gerald Handel, *Workingman's Wife: Her Personality, World, and Life Style* (New York: Oceana Publications, 1959), p. 27.

[2] *Ibid.*, p. 34.

2. As will be indicated in the chapter on mobility and the family, more than half of sons whose fathers were skilled or semiskilled engage in skilled or semiskilled work. About a third of sons whose fathers were farmers or unskilled laborers also are farmers or engage in unskilled work. Sons of urban workers, on the whole, do not follow the specific occupation of their fathers. This lack of continuity in the occupations of fathers and sons means that the son lacks an opportunity for apprenticeship in a family business or cannot take advantage of the work experiences of his father.

3. In the city, communication between persons outside the family tends to be impersonal, formal, and secondary, in contrast with the personal, informal, and primary communication between rural neighbors. The fact that no one knows much about anyone else in the city results in less control by the neighborhood and community. But there is a high degree of communication and primary relations in the kinship group and this promotes social control.

4. The city youth has freedom and economic independence, but less family assistance and security than the rural youth.

5. Available statistical data show that the following changes have taken place in the urban family: (a) The increasing proportion of the population living in urban areas has resulted in a greater prevalence of the urban way of life. (b) The decline in the size of the family has been associated with families living in smaller houses and apartments, and with mothers having greater leisure and engaging in more outside-the-home activities. (c) Urban areas have a great excess of women, which means that they have greater competition for available men than rural women. In rural areas men are in greater competition for the available women. (d) The low urban sex ratio results in a higher proportion of men and a lower proportion of women being married in cities than in rural areas. (e) Urban families are less isolated than rural, but the difference has been declining. They have greater residential mobility, more telephones, more television sets, slightly more radios, and a higher educational level. In 1967 urban persons averaged 3.2 more years of school than rural persons. (f) Urban families have higher economic status than rural families. This is seen in their greater cash income and a greater prevalence of modern conveniences. In urban areas there are also more physicians, more babies born in hospitals, and greater per capita expenditures for education.

MAJOR FACTORS RESHAPING THE URBAN FAMILY

To understand the forces affecting the life and behavior of urban families and their problems, it is necessary to have some background knowledge of the modern industrial city, its growth, its differentiated regions, and its effect on the family. Three factors of major importance for the reshaping of the family in the urban environment are (1) industrialization, (2) the transplanting of rural families to cities, and (3) the growth of urban areas.

Industrialization The change from hand crafts to machine work dramatically epitomizes the transition from rural and village to urban life conditions. When all work was done by hand, economic activities were on an intimate, personal basis. Typically, the employer was the friend of his hired men and co-workers. Sentimental as well as economic attitudes entered into their mutual relations. Social life in farm communities, villages, and towns was also intimate and personal. Even with the changes brought about by the motion picture, the automobile, the radio, and television, the village is a social world where personal relations and gossip still hold sway. In an industrial urban society persons work away from home for business corporations, where communication is impersonal, formal, and restricted to prescribed channels.

Transplanting Rural Families to Cities The American family has as its primary characteristics folkways and mores which developed under rural economic and social conditions. Persons living in cities are in large part either migrants from rural areas or descendants of migrants. They brought their folkways and mores with them, particularly those associated with the family and children. Consequently, not only has the urban way of life had an impact on such people, but the rural heritage has also had a significant impact on the urban way of life.

The Growth of Urban Areas A major transformation in the United States has been the increasing concentration of people in urban areas, particularly large cities. In the United States in 1790 only 5.1 percent of the population lived in cities of 2,500 or over, as compared with 69.9 in 1960. Of the three largest metropolitan areas in 1966, New York had a population in 1790 of 49,401 and in 1966, 11,410,000. Even as late as 1850 Chicago had only 29,963 and in 1890 Los Angeles had only 50,395; the respective populations in 1966 were 6,732,000 and 6,789,000. In 1968 there were 235 metropolitan areas with 50,000 population or more in the central city. In the 1960 census more than 43.5 million persons were concentrated in the 10 largest metropolitan statistical areas of the United States. These 10 accounted for about one-fourth of the total population of the 50 states and the District of Columbia.[3]

[3] *Statistical Abstract of the United States*, 1968, pp. 19 and 871; and *United States Census of Population, 1960, United States Summary*, 1, Table 5.

THE KINSHIP GROUP IN URBAN AREAS

The many studies of primary relationships and attachments among relatives in urban areas support the proposition that parents and children generally maintain a close relationship after the children form their own families and that generally siblings and other relatives have a feeling of belonging to the kinship group and assume duties and obligations because of this membership. For example, Sussman and Burchinal, after reviewing research on the kinship family, conclude that in urban areas the kinship family exists, is viable, and performs several functions.[4] In this section we will review some of the kinship studies in the United States, discuss some studies in other countries, and finally consider some functions performed by the large kinship group.

Kinship Studies in the United States A study of 749 persons in Detroit found that about half associated with relatives at least once a week and about one in three visited friends and neighbors at least once a week.[5] Another study found that association with relatives in a large city, Indianapolis, and a smaller city, Terre Haute, was about as frequent as in rural areas and much more frequent than in villages and small cities.[6]

Of the many studies of kinship relationships made by Sussman, one has been selected for presentation here. This is a study of a stratified random sample of 500 families in Cleveland. Sussman found that nuclear family units of the kinship group function along a continuum from isolation from the kinship family to integration with it.[7] About 85 percent had kin living in the metropolitan area of Cleveland and about 75 percent reported a functional relationship with kin at some time during

---

[4] Marvin B. Sussman and Lee Burchinal, "Kin Family Network: Unheralded Structure in Current Conceptualizations of Family Functioning," *Marriage and Family Living*, 24 (1962): pp. 231–240; also, "Parental Aid to Married Children: Implications for Family Functioning," *Marriage and Family Living*, 24 (1962): pp. 320–332; summarized in Marvin B. Sussman, "Relationships of Adult Children with Their Parents in the United States," in *Social Structure and the Family: Generational Relations*, Ethel Shanas and Gordon F. Streib (eds.) (Englewood Cliffs, New Jersey: Prentice-Hall, 1965), Chapter 4.

[5] Morris Axelrod, "Urban Structure and Social Participation," *American Sociological Review*, 21 (1956): pp. 13–18; also, Harry Sharp and Morris Axelrod, "Mutual Aid Among Relatives in an Urban Population," in *Principles of Sociology*, Ronald Freedman and others, (eds.) (New York: Holt, Rinehart and Winston, 1956), pp. 433–439. See also Eugene Litwak and Ivan Szelenyi, "Primary Group Structures and Their Functions: Kin, Neighbors, and Friends," *American Sociological Review*, 34 (1969): pp. 465–481.

[6] William H. Key, *Rural-Urban Differences in Social Participation* (St. Louis: Washington University, 1953), pp. 30, 39, 47, and 60; also, "Rural-Urban Differences and the Family," *Sociological Quarterly*, 2 (1961): pp. 49–56.

[7] Sussman, "Relationships of Adult Children with Their Parents in the United States," pp. 72–73 and 77–78.

marriage on one or more of the indices of functional relationships: visiting, telephone calls, letters, and financial help and services given and received. A second conclusion is that the majority of nuclear family units are members of an integrated kin network both by propinquity and functional relationship and this cuts across lines of class, race, occupation, and education. A third conclusion is that the amount of financial aid is larger in the middle class than in the working class but the willingness to give and receive aid does not differ by class. Fourth, the direction of aid is from parents to their married children during the young families' "launching period."

In a study of 729 married women of a cross-section of married couples in Detroit, Aiken found that 9 out of 10 families had relatives living within the metropolitan area. Almost all contact with kin occurred with closely related persons—parents, grandparents, and siblings. The three factors most highly associated with kinship activities were availability of kin, degree of relationship to kin, and the presence of the wife's mother, who acts as a connecting relative in the kinship family. Aiken also found that the vitality of the kinship unit in urban areas is not on the wane; in fact there is reason to believe that the kinship family is compatible with other features of urban society.[8]

Komarovsky, in her interview study of 58 blue-collar marriages, included questions on kinship relationships.[9] She reports that daily activities center around relatives; that over 9 in 10 of her couples had relatives living nearby; that the wife and mother see each other more frequently than any other pair of relatives; and that relatives play certain functions in the kinship family. Relatives play a part in the socialization of the married couple; they provide emotional support; they serve as confidants; they may be companions in recreation; they provide financial aid in emergencies; they exchange services; and for working-class families relatives tend to be the sole kind of social experiences in a group.

Locke and Thomes have collected interview data from a random sample of 116 white married couples and 61 Negro married couples living in Los Angeles.[10] White and Negro families were approximately matched for socioeconomic level. One part of this study dealt with social participation with relatives and friends. On frequency of association the subjects were asked the extent of visiting in given time periods. The three time periods reported here are the past week, past month, and past six months prior to the interview.

---

[8] Miechel Thomas Aiken, "Kinship in an Urban Community" (Ph.D. Dissertation, University of Michigan Library, 1964).

[9] Mirra Komarovsky, *Blue-Collar Marriage* (New York: Vintage Books, 1967), Chapter 11.

[10] Harvey J. Locke and Mary Margaret Thomes, a study in process.

About a third of the white couples visited both sets of parents at least once during the week prior to the interview;[11] about half at least once in the month prior to the interview;[12] and about two-thirds at least once in the six months prior to the interview.[13] Thus white couples have considerable association with the kinship group of parents and parents-in-law.

Negro couples were found to agree fairly well on the frequency of visiting the husband's parents, but they disagree on frequency of visiting the wife's parents. About 15 percent of the husbands and wives reported that they visited the husband's parents at least once in the week prior to the interview;[14] about a third reported at least once during the month prior to the interview;[15] and about half within the six months prior to the interview.[16] Negro husbands reported visiting the wife's parents much more frequently than did their wives. Visiting the wife's parents at least once in the last week was reported by 42 percent of husbands and 29 percent of wives; at least once in the past month by 51 percent of husbands and 42 percent of wives; and at least once in the last six months by 73 percent of husbands and 61 percent of their wives.

White couples reported about the same frequency of visiting the husband's and wife's parents. Negro couples reported about the same frequency of visiting the husband's parents, but Negro husbands reported more frequent visiting of wife's parents than did their wives.

A significantly larger percent of white than Negro wives reported visiting the husband's parents in the week prior to the interview (t = 2.0). A larger percent of white than Negro husbands reported visiting the husband's parents in the week prior to the interview, though the difference was just below the .05 level of significance (t = 1.8). This suggests that white husbands and wives maintain more frequent contacts with the husband's parents.

Kinship Relations in Other Countries Granted that in urban areas of the United States kinship relations are very prevalent, what is the situation in urban areas of other countries? Information is available for England, Wales, and certain nations of Africa.

---

[11] Respective percents of husbands and wives visiting husband's parents, 34 and 31; visiting wife's parents, 33 and 35.
[12] Respective percents of husbands and wives visiting husband's parents, 46 and 50; visiting wife's parents, 45 and 51.
[13] Respective percents of husbands and wives visiting husband's parents, 66 and 61; visiting wife's parents, 71 and 73.
[14] Respective percents of husbands and wives, 17 and 15.
[15] Respective percents of husbands and wives, 31 and 30.
[16] Respective percents of husbands and wives, 51 and 45.

66   The Urban Family

In a study of Bethnal Green, London, an almost completely working-class area in the center of London, the kinship family was found to be very active.[17] The kinship family provides services for the aged, maintains mother-daughter relationships, and provides a friendly warm kinship atmosphere, as indicated by the reported isolation and loneliness —especially of wives—felt by those who left Bethnal Green to live in a government housing project. The studies of Bethnal Green illustrate the important functions the kinship family plays in the daily lives of nuclear family members:

> Grandmothers look after grandchildren while the mothers are at work, the old and infirm are cared for by their children, social life centers on the family gatherings, and the family circle provides a reliable source of help with all manner of problems.[18]

A study of kinship relationships of two thousand families in the South Wales town of Swansea was made by Rosser and Harris.[19] They described the kinship family as a "variable, amorphous, vague social grouping within which circulate—often over great distances—strong sentiments of belonging, and which is recognizable as a social entity."[20] They found only rare cases of nuclear families completely isolated from kin. The basic kinship family is composed of three nuclear families: the wife and her husband, the wife and her mother, and the husband and his mother. They found that in Swansea industrialization, social mobility, and wide dispersal of family units have not prevented the maintenance of high levels of contact and the interchange of domestic services between members of the kinship family.

Anthropologists and sociologists have made studies of several cities in Africa, among them Timbuctoo,[21] Lagos,[22] Leopoldville,[23] and the cities of Yoruba.[24] One area of interest was the extent and functioning of the kinship group. Researchers concluded that the kinship family is prevalent and fulfills several functions. It meets the recreational, re-

---

[17] Michael Young and Peter Willmott, *Family and Kinship in East London* (New York: Free Press, 1957).

[18] *Ibid.*, p. 99.

[19] Colin Rosser and Christopher Harris, *The Family and Social Change: A Study of Family and Kinship in a South Wales Town* (London: Routledge and Kegan Paul, 1965), particularly Chapter 9.

[20] *Ibid.*, p. 288.

[21] Horace Miner, *The Primitive City of Timbuctoo* (Philadelphia: American Philosophical Society, 1953).

[22] Peter Marris, "Slum Clearance and Family Life in Lagos," *Human Organization*, 19 (1960): pp. 123–128.

[23] Jean L. Comhaire, "Some Aspects of Urbanization in the Belgian Congo," *American Journal of Sociology*, 60 (1956): pp. 8–13.

[24] William Bascom, "Urbanization Among the Yoruba," *American Journal of Sociology*, 60 (1955): pp. 446–454.

ligious, legal, and economic needs of members; serves as a social-security agency; provides for the elderly and the sick; provides for the unemployed; gives shelter and food to new migrants; and forms a friendship network of relatives.

The strength of the kinship family, often called the extended family, may be inferred from four indices: the residing of two or more related nuclear families together; engagement in joint activities; the giving of assistance to individual related persons, based on social expectations of such assistance; and having friendship networks of relatives. Comhaire, after reviewing studies of African cities, reports that social scientists agree that "African societies have an amazing capacity for maintaining kinship ties and other traditional institutions in spite of urbanization."[25] He reports that his study of Leopoldville shows the strength of the kinship family in several ways:

> When newcomers arrive in town and when workers lose their jobs, they usually beg board and lodgings of some relative. The children of prosperous farmers who are sent to town for education customarily stay as paying guests with an uncle, a brother, or a cousin; residents in town often send their children to the village of their birth, since they will be less of a burden if they live on the family estate. Extended family ties are also maintained, thanks to the practice of *matanga*, or urban family rites. The organizations founded on a territorial or professional basis, of which there are many, usually are pseudo-kinship groups, reflecting no disposition to accept the Western urban way of life.[26]

Functions Performed by the Kinship Family Functions performed by the kinship family include mutual aid, social activities in the form of visiting and participation in recreational activities together and in ceremonies, and the performance of services.

Mutual aid takes many forms. It includes the giving of financial assistance, primarily from parents to children in the early years of marriage. Other forms of mutual aid are exchanges of services, gifts, and the giving and receiving of advice. Although the amount of financial aid differs, the giving and receiving of financial assistance is reported about as frequently in the middle class and the working class. Mutual aid in the form of providing information and financial assistance are reported to be two primary functions of the extended kinship system in central Brazil.[27]

[25] Comhaire, p. 12. For another review of these studies, see J. Aldous, "Urbanization, the Extended Family, and Kinship Ties in West Africa," *Social Forces*, 41 (1962): pp. 6–12.
[26] Comhaire, p. 11.
[27] E. A. Wilkening, Joao Bosco Pinto, and Jose Pastore, "Role of the Extended Family in Migration and Adaptation in Brazil," *Journal of Marriage and the Family*, 30 (1968): pp. 689–695.

Visiting kin is the primary form of social activity among urban families and is more frequent than visiting friends and neighbors. Get togethers and recreational activities with kin dominate the social activity of working-class families. Litwak, in his study of 920 married women in Buffalo, found that those who report frequent visiting with kin tend to have more occupational resources and are status oriented.[28]

Services for kinship members include shopping, care of children and ill family members, physical care of the elderly, providing transportation, especially in emergencies, and assistance in occupational mobility.

Let us summarize some of the conclusions about the kinship family in urban areas: (1) A very large proportion of families living in urban areas have kin living in or near the city. (2) Parents and their children generally maintain close relationships after the children form their own families. (3) Contact with kin is predominantly with closely related persons, such as parents, grandparents, and siblings. This is particularly true for mothers and daughters. (4) White couples maintain more frequent contacts with the husband's parents than do Negro couples. (5) Functions performed by the kinship family include mutual aid, social activities in the form of visiting, and the performance of services. (6) There are no substantial differences among various countries regarding social participation with kin in urban areas.

THE SUBURBAN FAMILY

The Attraction of Suburbs Families live in suburbs for the most part because they desire to live close enough to the city to take advantage of its opportunities for employment, shopping, and entertainment, but far enough away to have a yard and garden, a pleasant environment, and enjoyable neighborhood relations. Suburbs, particularly residential ones, in comparison to central cities have a higher sex ratio (the number of men per 100 women), a higher proportion of children, more single than multiple dwellings, a higher percent of home ownership, and more community organizations. Churches, schools, and clubs flourish.

Families move to suburbs for a variety of reasons, the predominant one being the belief that suburbs provide an environment in which their children will be healthy, well adjusted, and well educated. Some parents also believe that it is desirable to have their children grow up in a more homogeneous environment than that found in central cities, associating

---

[28] Eugene Litwak, "Occupational Mobility and Extended Family Cohesion," *American Sociological Review*, 25 (1960): pp. 9–21. See also "The Use of Extended Family Groups in the Achievement of Social Goals," *Social Problems*, 7 (1959–1960): pp. 177–187.

with others whose values are similar to their own. In addition, many whites move to suburbs if the area of the city in which they live has become or is likely to become predominantly Negro.

Social Characteristics The social characteristics of suburbs in comparison to central cities will be analyzed from three sources of data. The United States Census reports some data on central cities, suburbs, and rural areas. The Metropolitan Life Insurance Company has described certain social characteristics of suburbs and central cities within the 10 largest metropolitan areas. It has also described characteristics of 14 metropolitan areas just below the 10 largest areas.[29]

Table 7 gives data on the 10 largest metropolitan areas which permits a comparison of central cities and suburbs on several variables: percent of the population which is white; percent under 18 years of age; average family size; percent which is male; percent which is 65 years of age or older; percent of those 25 years of age or older who are at least high-school graduates; percent engaged in professional or managerial work; percent with family income of $10,000 or more; and percent with family income of under $3,000.

The analysis of the data in Table 7 reveals that whites make up a larger percentage of the population in suburbs than in central cities. The difference in percents of whites in suburbs and central cities in these very large metropolitan areas was 20 percent or more in 5 of the areas; 10-19 percent in 4; and 9 percent in 1. Excluding two extremes —Washington, D.C. with 45 and Boston with 90 percent white—the range of the percent white in central cities was from 71 to 85; in all of the 10 suburban areas of these large metropolitan areas, the percent white was 93 or more, with 6 of them being 95 or more.

Families feel that suburbs are a better place in which to rear their children than central cities. That some have acted on this feeling is shown by the fact that in all of the 10 largest metropolitan areas the percent of the population under 18 years of age was higher in suburbs than in central cities. For central cities the percents ranged from 25 to 31; in suburbs the percents ranged from 34 to 41. For the United States as a whole the respective percents of 18 years of age and younger for central cities, suburbs, and rural areas were 32.3, 37.2, and 39.0.

The average size of families is larger in suburbs than in central cities. In each of the 10 largest metropolitan areas, the average number of persons per household in suburbs was larger than for central cities. For

---

[29] *United States Census of Population, 1960, United States Summary,* 1, pp. 148–157; *Statistical Bulletin, Metropolitan Life Insurance Company,* (February 1962): pp. 5–7; (June 1964): pp. 1–3; and (September 1964): pp. 1–3.

Table 7. Social characteristics of central cities and suburbs[a] of the 10 largest standard statistical metropolitan areas, by percent, 1960[*]

	White	Age under 18	Average family size	Males	Age 65 or over	Age 25 or over, at least high school graduate	Professional or managerial	Income $10,000 or more	Income under $3,000
New York	85	28	2.9	48	11	37	21	19	15
Suburbs	95	37	3.5	49	8	52	31	33	7
Los Angeles[b]	83	31	2.8	48	10	53	26	25	14
Suburbs	93	37	3.3	50	7	54	25	25	11
Chicago	76	31	3.2	49	10	35	17	21	14
Suburbs	99	34	3.4	48	10	52	26	32	7
Philadelphia	73	31	3.0	48	10	31	17	14	17
Suburbs	97	35	3.4	49	9	46	24	23	10
Detroit	71	33	3.2	49	10	34	17	18	19
Suburbs	94	38	3.4	49	8	47	23	25	9
San Francisco[c]	82	25	2.4	49	13	51	23	23	14
Suburbs	94	39	3.5	50	5	58	27	26	10
Boston	90	29	2.9	48	12	45	19	14	17
Suburbs	96	37	3.2	49	8	57	27	24	9
Pittsburgh	83	31	3.1	48	11	35	19	14	18
Suburbs	97	38	3.5	50	7	43	20	16	14
St. Louis	71	31	2.9	47	12	26	15	11	22
Suburbs	94	36	3.5	50	8	41	23	20	11
Washington, D.C.	45	29	2.9	47	9	48	23	22	17
Suburbs	96	41	3.7	50	5	65	35	36	7

[a] The term "suburbs" has been substituted for "outside-central-cities," even though the latter includes areas other than suburbs.
[b] includes Long Beach
[c] includes Oakland
[*] *Statistical Bulletin*, Metropolitan Life Insurance Company, 43 (February 1962): pp. 5–7; and 45 (June 1964): pp. 1–3.

the country as a whole the average size of the private family in central cities, suburbs, and rural areas was 3.50, 3.66, and 3.85.

The sex ratio, or the number of men per 100 women, is higher in suburbs (96.2) than in central cities (92.9), and lower than in rural areas (104.3). The sex ratio of suburbs was higher than that of central cities in 9 of the 10 largest metropolitan areas. Boston, the other metropolitan area, had exactly the same sex ratio in suburbs and central cities.[30]

Persons 65 years of age and older tend to remain in central cities rather than move to suburbs. Generally, their income is drastically reduced at this point and they are able to secure less expensive living accommodations in central cities. It is more difficult for them to commute and, consequently, they may feel more isolated if they live in suburbs.

Parents in suburbs usually have more formal education than parents in central cities. Consequently, they tend to expect and work for better schools more than parents in central cities. Moreover, being in smaller communities, suburban families can be more effective in putting pressure on school boards to improve the schools. In the 10 largest metropolitan areas, the percent of those 25 years of age and older who were at least high school graduates was much higher in suburbs than in central cities for all of the 10 metropolitan areas except Los Angeles.[31] In part, this reflects the fact that the suburban population contains a higher percent of young adults, and, also, suburbs contain a higher proportion of professional persons. Between 1940 and 1960 the proportion of persons with at least high school training increased faster in suburbs than in central cities in all areas except Los Angeles. A larger percent with at least high school education was also found in the 14 smaller metropolitan areas of 1 to 2 million population.

A larger proportion of chief breadwinners in suburbs than in central cities engage in an occupation of high prestige—professional or managerial work. About a fourth of those living in suburbs engage in this kind of work as compared with a fifth or less in central cities. In 10 of the 14 smaller metropolitan areas, suburbs had a significantly higher percent of professional and managerial workers than central cities. Having the chief breadwinner a professional or managerial worker raises the prestige of his family.

Families with high incomes can not only afford to live in suburbs but can afford more spacious living quarters and grounds, more expensive recreational activities, and have more pride in possessions. The percent

[30] Based on percent of males in the given areas.
[31] The city boundaries of Los Angeles extend into what would ordinarily be classified as suburban.

of families with incomes of $10,000 or more was much higher in suburbs than in central cities in 7 of the 10 largest metropolitan areas; this was true for 10 of the 14 next largest metropolitan areas. Families with poverty incomes of under $3,000 were much more prevalent in central cities than in suburbs. In 5 of the 10 largest metropolitan areas they were twice as frequent in central cities as in suburbs. In the 1 to 2 million metropolitan areas, 11 out of the 14 had a larger percent of under $3,000 family incomes in central cities than in suburbs. In 8 of these the proportion was twice as high and in 1 it was three times as high.

The social characteristics described above were typical for large metropolitan areas. These same social characteristics may not hold for smaller metropolitan areas. Schnore and Varley have shown that three of these —education, occupation, and income—are higher in suburbs than in central cities in very large metropolitan areas of 500,000 and over, but they are higher in central cities of smaller metropolitan areas of 100,000 –500,000, and are still higher in central cities of small metropolitan areas of 50,000–100,000. They formulated the following generalization:

> For each socio-economic index the following pattern obtained: the larger the central city, the more likely it is that the socio-economic status of ring residents will be higher than that of city residents. This pattern also appears without exception.[32]

We have found no analysis of differences by size of metropolitan areas for other social characteristics—the proportion of white, the percent under 18 years of age, the average size of the family, the sex ratio, and the percent of persons 65 years of age and over.

Broken Families Table 8 shows the percentage of single and married persons and homes broken by separation, widowhood, and divorce for central cities, suburbs, and rural areas. Suburbs had the lowest percent of single men and women. It will be noted that the percent of men 14 years of age and over who were married was highest in suburbs, with central cities and rural areas being about equal and that for women rural areas and suburbs were equal in percent married and both were much higher than central cities. The percent separated, widowed, and divorced was, for men, lowest in suburbs, next lowest in rural areas, and highest in central cities; for women the percents were about equal

---

[32] Leo F. Schnore and David W. Varley, "Some Concomitants of Metropolitan Size," *American Sociological Review*, 20 (1955): pp. 408–414, particularly pp. 413–414; see also "City-Suburban Income Differentials in Metropolitan Areas," *American Sociological Review*, 27 (1962): pp. 352–355.

for rural areas and suburbs and both were much lower than central cities.

Table 8. Percent with given marital status of men and women in central cities, suburbs, and rural areas, 1960*

Area	Single	Married	Separated	Widowed	Divorced	Total Broken
Men						
Central Cities	25.8	67.3	2.2	4.1	2.8	9.1
Suburbs	21.6	73.9	1.0	2.8	1.7	5.5
Rural Areas	27.2	67.5	1.1	3.6	1.7	6.4
Women						
Central Cities	20.7	61.4	3.1	13.9	4.0	21.0
Suburbs	17.8	69.3	1.4	10.3	2.6	14.3
Rural Areas	18.2	69.8	1.2	10.5	1.5	13.2

*Data from United States Census of Population, 1960, United States Summary, 1, p. 156.

Matricentric Family and Patriarchal Authority Families in suburbs appear to be matricentric in activities and patriarchal in authority. They are matricentric in that the mother is at the center of activity in suburban families. This position is in large part the result of the father's commuting to the central city for work. The centering of many activities around the mother and the flexibility of roles in other activities is described by Mowrer from his studies of suburbs established since World War II:

> The suburban wife finds herself constantly occupied with furnishing transportation for other members of the family; to the railway station to take and meet her husband before and after work, to school and other places of activity to take and bring home the children. In addition there are trips to the neighborhood stores to do the family shopping. Her husband finds himself not only called upon to mow and care for the lawn, but also to become an amateur plumber, house painter, repairer of children's toys and the various gadgets about the household, landscaper, and even construction engineer. . . . When the suburban husband turns indoors he is often joined by his wife and together they become interior craftsmen, painting walls and ceilings, hanging paper, and refinishing furniture.
> Flexibility of role is, in fact, characteristic of suburban family life, the husband often performing characteristically feminine functions and the wife masculine functions. . . . When the children are young, husbands help with the household tasks, sharing in feeding and sometimes diaper-

ing the infants, wives shovel snow from walks and help in caring for the yard and garden. In fact, care of the house, yard, and garden is second only to cooking, sewing and knitting as the most common hobby of suburban wives.[33]

Martin, in his research on the rural-urban fringe, contrasts the roles and social relationships of women living in suburban and rural-urban fringe areas:

> As a result of the daily commuting of males, women play an unusually important role in voluntary association and other interaction situations in the suburbs. As Henderson says, women "are the telephoners, organizers, and arrangers of community organizational life." For many women the suburban situation opens new vistas and provides real avenues for expression and meaningful activity. This is in contrast to the rural-urban fringe situation which frequently leaves a city-reared woman in semi-isolation during the day while the family automobile is parked near her husband's place of work in the city. This restriction on social relationships can be a source of frustration for the woman and a point of contention within the family.[34]

Patriarchal authority seems to be higher in suburbs than in central cities. This is the conclusion of Blood and Wolfe who collected data on families in suburbs and the central city of Detroit. They constructed a power index and found that the mean power score of the father in families living in the suburbs of Detroit was higher than the power score of fathers living in the central city. They indicate that at every status level the suburban husband is more dominant in decision-making than husbands in the central city.[35]

The authors feel this is probably the case. However, there are limitations on the evidence. The data were from a single city, Detroit. The data were exclusively from wives, so the power scores represent the conceptions wives have of the role of husbands in decision-making. Thus the greater patriarchal power of husbands in suburbs as compared with central cities is a hypothesis for additional research.

The discussion above contrasted central cities and suburbs on a number of variables. In central cities there are several different kinds of families. Four have been selected for analysis: nonfamily men of Skid Row, the poverty family of the slums, and the working-class and middle-class family.

---

[33] Ernest R. Mowrer, "The Family in Suburbia," in *The Suburban Community*, William M. Dobriner (ed.) (New York: G. P. Putnam's Sons, 1958), pp. 156–157.
[34] Walter T. Martin, "The Structuring of Social Relationships Engendered by Surban Residence," *American Sociological Review*, 21 (1956): p. 449.
[35] Robert O. Blood and Donald M. Wolfe, *Husbands and Wives* (Glencoe, Illinois: The Free Press of Glencoe, 1960): p. 36.

NONFAMILY MEN OF SKID ROW

Within and adjacent to the central business area is the men's area of Skid Row. In Los Angeles it is along Main and Fifth Streets. In Chicago, nonfamily men are concentrated on three streets running through the central-business area: West Madison, North Clark, and South State. Skid-row areas house a transient population living in cheap hotels and eating at cheap cafeterias. This is an older man's area, with the largest number in the 35–54 age groups. There are essentially no children and no presently married couples.

The objection may be raised that the area of the homeless men is a nonfamily district and so lies outside the field of the urban family. Anyone who has read Anderson's book, *The Hobo*[36] or Sutherland and Locke's *Twenty Thousand Homeless Men*[37] knows how mistaken this is, for the nonfamily skid-row man reflects many of the problems of the family. He is the deserting husband or widower, the man detached from contact with his family and neighborhood, who is seeking escape in restless migration from city to city or in excesses of alcoholism, gambling, or sex.

Sutherland and Locke in their study of homeless men in Chicago during the depression found that those men who had terminated their marriages had done so on the average of 13.5 years before the study. The personal disorganization of the men centered around three closely related factors: occupational instability, family disorganization, and general dissipation. These factors are evident in an interview Mathews had with a resident of Skid Row in Los Angeles:

> Perhaps the bitterest, most obvious and pitiful poverty thrives four blocks south and two blocks east of City Hall—Skid Row, where the alcoholics, the misfits from all strata of society, finally make their way.
>
> For two years, this has been the home of Talmadge Green, a big, soft-spoken Negro of Quixotic moods. He spends his days and his often drunken nights in the missions, the garishly lighted liquor stores and his favorite hotel on 5th St.
>
> Like the others, he drinks "mickeys" of rotgut wine (18 cents for four-fifths of a pint) and often wears the semi-human, glaze-eyed look men get at the end of a long, terrible drunk.
>
> Talmadge, who at 41 says, "I've done nearly every kind of job and I didn't like any of it," has mastered the hard economic facts of the place. He collects $21 worth of chits from the county's Skid Row office every

---

[36] Nels Anderson, *The Hobo* (Chicago: The University of Chicago Press, 1923).
[37] Edwin H. Sutherland and Harvey J. Locke, *Twenty Thousand Homeless Men* (Philadelphia: J. B. Lippincott, 1936).

week, to pay for his room and his meals at a cafe called Tillie's Kitchen. To buy wine, he steals and sells his blood.

"I have to steal," he explains. "I steal whatever I see the best chance to steal. If I'm walking down 5th and I see a guy drunk on the sidewalk, I'll take money out of his pockets. Sure, I know anybody around here would do the same thing to me.

While drunk, Talmadge has been brutally beaten by men he considers his friends and has come to not knowing why he was hurt. Yet, wearing the scars of these battles, he'll share his good fortune if he pawns something he has pilfered from one of the little shops.

Skid Row offers a rough and ready camaraderie and Talmadge talks dreamily of the good times he has had there.

"Sometimes, a couple of us will put our money together, buy chicken necks, potatoes and a little carrot and cook in our rooms. That's real nice."

When he is dried out, Talmadge can rationalize his behavior and explain it in the terms a college psychology major, newly acquainted with Freud, might use.

"My trouble all started when I was 2 years old, when my father killed my mother. I was too young to remember, but my sister told me about it. She used to say, when we get big, we'll kill him, too.

"I was in trouble with the police at 11 or 12, and finally I was sent to reform school. It was bad. In those days they treated kids like they did adults. After being in that environment, there was never any hope of my changing."

Since his first arrest, Talmadge has spent about half his life in prison, with uncounted additional days in jail. He has worked—"when I was forced to," he admits—as a locker room attendant, a fruit picker, a day laborer. . . .

"If I could do anything or be anything I want, "he says, looking out the window of his unspeakably filthy hotel room, "I wouldn't change. I'd just like to be down there on 5th St., drinking wine."[38]

POVERTY FAMILIES IN URBAN AREAS

Extent of Poverty Poverty has been defined in different ways and, of course, the extent of poverty depends on the definition used. The index most commonly used is family income of under $3,000. As will be shown later, in 1967 the Census constructed a poverty index by including other factors besides income.

In 1967, 10.4 percent of all families living in metropolitan areas were below the poverty level: for whites the percent of poor families was 7.8 and for Negroes the percent was 27.8.[39] In recent years the number of poor families has declined; between 1966 and 1967 the number of

[38] Linda Mathews, "What is it Really Like To Be Poor? It's Like This," *Los Angeles Times*, Sept. 9, 1968, Part 1, p. 18.
[39] *Statistical Abstract of the United States*, 1969, p. 328.

poor families declined by 600,000, and there was a significant decline in 1968 and in 1969. Figure 8 shows the decline in families with incomes under $3,000 for the country as a whole in the time period 1947–1966.

Figure 8. Number of families having given family income from 1947 to 1966, in constant 1966 dollars*

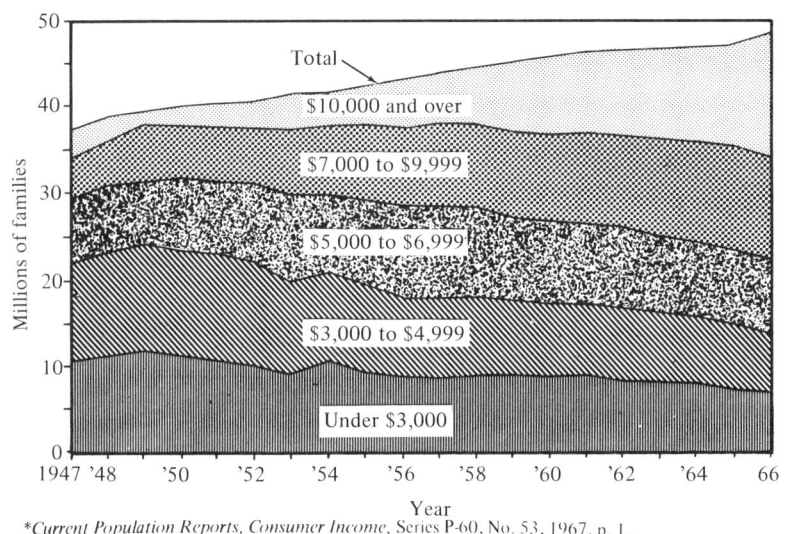

*Current Population Reports, Consumer Income, Series P-60, No. 53, 1967, p. 1.

It also shows the trend in family income for other income categories. In spite of this decline, in 1967 there were 5.4 million families below the poverty line; and there were an estimated 10.5 million children under 18 years of age living in poor families. About 4 million of these poor children were in families with a woman as head; the remaining 6.5 million were in families with a man as head.[40]

Concentration of Poor Families in Poverty Areas The United States Census has constructed an index of poverty areas by using five criteria for census tracts: (1) family income under $3,000, (2) percent of children under 18 not living with both parents, (3) percent of males 25 years of age and over with less than 8 years of schooling, (4) percent of unskilled males, and (5) percent of dilapidated housing units lacking some or all plumbing facilities. Poor families are concentrated in certain sections of metropolitan areas. A comparison of poverty areas with nonpoverty areas revealed that in nonpoverty areas 6.9 percent of all families were poor as against 23.8 percent of all families in poverty areas.

[40] *Current Population Reports, Consumer Income,* Series P-60, No. 55, August 5, 1968.

The percents of poor white families in nonpoverty and poverty areas were respectively 6.3 and 17.0; for Negroes the respective percents were 17.2 and 33.6.[41] Thus both white and Negro poor families are concentrated in poverty areas of cities.

The Culture of the Urban Poor The culture of the urban poor is similar to that of the general culture, but there are discernible differences. In recent years this has been investigated by a large number of scholars. One of the first to describe the culture of the poor was Hollingshead whose study was in a small town of 6,200 plus 3,800 rural persons in a surrounding area. He found his poor families living in a culture with the following characteristics: passivity; a belief in fate; hopelessness; lack of success goals; unskilled work activities; long periods of idleness; limited educational achievement; isolation from organized community activities; frequent contacts with the law; serial marriages; and dilapidated houses.[42]

Many of these same characteristics have been found in more recent studies of poverty families in large cities. These studies describe the culture of the poor as including the following: apathy; hopelessness; nonidentification with middle-class values; low self-esteem; hostility toward others; low level of aspirations; the father as a provider at a minimum level or a nonprovider; a low value placed on education as indicated by dropping out of school early; overcrowded living arrangements; large families; weak marital bonds; precocious sexual interest among children; separate and isolated lives of husbands and wives; limited number of usable roles; and limited styles of communication.[43] The family is the chief agency in transmitting this culture.

Subcultures Among the Poor Students of poverty agree that there are wide differences in subcultures among the poor. A meaningful division of slum families is into stable and unstable. The latter group is characterized by alcoholism, mental illness, disease, addiction, crime and delinquency.[44] The lower-lower-class family lives in more overcrowded

[41] *Statistical Abstract of the United States*, 1968, p. 33. See *Current Population Reports, Consumer Income*, Series P-60, No. 53 for a description of the criteria for the poverty-area index.

[42] August B. Hollingshead, *Elmtown's Youth: The Impact of Social Classes on Adolescents* (New York: John Wiley & Sons, 1949).

[43] See especially Salvador Minuchin, Braulio Montalvo, Bernard G. Guerney, Bernice L. Rosman, and Florence Schumer, *Families of the Slums: An Exploration of Their Structure and Treatment* (New York: Basic Books, 1967), Chapter 2 reviews the literature; H. H. Gans, *The Urban Villagers* (New York: The Free Press of Glencoe, 1962); and Lee Rainwater, *And the Poor Get Children* (Chicago: Quadrangle Books, 1960).

[44] Hyman Lewis, *Culture, Class and Poverty* (Washington, D.C.: CROSS-TELL, 1967).

conditions than the upper-lower-class family. A French study of workers' families found that people with less than 8–10 square meters of space per person had twice as many social and mental disorders as those having 10–14 square meters.[45]

Pavenstedt compares the behavior of upper-lower-class families and lower-lower-class families. She describes as follows the behavior of lower-lower-class families:

> The outstanding characteristic in these homes was that activities were impulse-determined; consistency was totally absent. The mother might stay in bed until noon while the children also were kept in bed or ran around unsupervised. Although families sometimes ate breakfast or dinner together, there was no pattern for anything. The parents often failed to discriminate between the children. A parent, incensed by the behavior of one child, was seen dealing a blow to another child who was closer. Communication by means of words hardly existed. Directions were indefinite or hung unfinished in mid-air. Reprimands were often high-pitched and angry.... As the children outgrew babyhood, the parents differentiated very little between the parent and child role. The parents' needs were as pressing and as often indulged as those of the children. There was a strong competition for the attention of helpful adults.[46]

Courtship There are three distinctive courtship practices of the poor: (1) The poor are more likely to select a marital partner who lives nearby than someone from another area and social class. There is a marked reluctance to engage in primary relations outside the immediate residential area. (2) Courtship is of short duration. (3) There is little emotional involvement between the couple.[47] Rainwater reports that seeking or choosing a marriage partner is done without much enterprise. The poor feel it is a matter of fate, and there is no planning on the time or date of the marriage: "it was just time," "somehow it was settled," or "we just did it." Here is one of the cases Rainwater presents on dating behavior.

> I met him over on Lafflin Street. There's a place I used to go to dance with a gang of us girls. These fellows always came around too. I saw my husband lots of times before I went around with him. A bunch of us decided to go to the beach one night and he asked me. We fooled around

---

[45] From an address before the American Institute of Architects' Convention by Dr. Edward T. Hall. Given in Elizabeth Coit, "Report on Family Living in High Apartment Buildings," Public Housing Administration, May 1965, p. 3.

[46] Eleanor Pavenstedt, "A Comparison of the Child-Rearing Environment of Upper-Lower and Very Low-Lower Class Families," *American Journal of Orthopsychiatry*, 35 (1965): pp. 94–95.

[47] Arthur Besner, "Economic Deprivation and Family Patterns," in *Low-Income Life Styles*, Lola Irelan, (ed.) (Washington, D. C.: U. S. Department of Health, Education, and Welfare, Welfare Administration, Division of Research).

80 The Urban Family

and I liked the way he treated me. I don't know exactly how it happened; we got to going to the beach at night and fooling around some, and then we decided it would be best to get married right away (married 8 years, five children).[48]

Traits of a "Good" Husband and a "Good" Wife The following analysis is based on Rainwater's interviews with 46 men and 50 women of the working class[49] and on Besner's review of the literature on poverty families.[50] Lower-class men and women ranked traits of a good husband and a good wife both for themselves and for their spouses. Lower-class men ranked the parental function of being a good father as first in importance; women for a good husband ranked being a good lover first or second in importance. Men ranked being a good lover as least in importance. The husbands tended to value the home as a place to satisfy their physical needs. The lower-class husband considers a woman a good partner if she prepares the meals, keeps his clothing in order, takes care of the children, and frees him from everyday responsibilities. In essence he values a wife as a housekeeper-mother.

Being a good wife, as viewed by wives, is to be a good lover and friend. They rank being a good parent or a good housekeeper low. Wives value interpersonal relations of love and affection, but men have little or no interest in emotional relationships.

Marital Relations The values attached to marriage by middle-class women as a means of securing love, companionship, and economic support are not realistic values of lower-class women. On the verbal level they rank being a lover and friend high but they do not expect to get these in marriage. Lower-class spouses are relatively isolated from each other emotionally. Besner summarizes research on this as follows:

> Her wish for open expression of affection is not met by the husband who does not see this as important. It is not that she resists the performance of household and motherly duties, rather she resents the husband's limitation of the marital relationship to them. It has been suggested that much of the tension observed in the families of the poor arises from this basic conflict in role expectations.

Hence, the lower class wife must endure emotional deprivation as well as the ever-present fear of physical-economic deprivation. She is handicapped, however, by her subservient position, vis-a-vis her husband and by her view of men, from managing the marital relationship to serve her

[48] Rainwater, p. 62.
[49] *Ibid.*, particularly pp. 66–71. He asked the subjects to rank in order of importance (1) the parental function or being a good father or mother to the children, (2) work activities (a good provider or housekeeper), (3) being a good lover, and (4) being a good friend.
[50] Besner, particularly pp. 18–20.

needs better. What might also be thought of as a handicap is the special significance of marriage to the lower class woman. Women in the lower socioeconomic strata are likely to find it difficult to think of themselves other than in a familial role.[51]

Lower-class men and women cling to old friendships and do not develop common friends. There is a close and dependent relationship with kin. A comparison of two groups, poor and nonpoor, revealed that the poor received substantially more help from relatives than the nonpoor. Moreover they interact with kin more than with others.[52]

There is a sharp separation of roles in the lower-class family. The lower-class wife is assigned many more duties to perform than the middle-class wife. Earning the money is the husband's responsibility, but spending it is in the hands of the wife. The husband's roles are negligible in the lower-class family. While he tends to insist that the man is the head of the house, he expects to have freedom to come and go as he wishes; he expects the wife to take care of all minor and major household tasks.

Mothers and Their Children The mother-child relationship is the strongest and most enduring bond found in lower-class families. A study of lower-class women in Philadelphia showed a greater attachment to the role of the mother than to the role of the wife. The women were asked "If you could only be a wife or mother (but not both) which would you choose?" The majority of both single and married women chose the mother's role.[53]

Lower-class women are more insistent than middle-class women for their children to be obedient, neat, and clean. They emphasize strict discipline more than the middle-class. Lower-class mothers tend to be traditional in the raising of their children, whereas middle-class parents emphasize the personality development of their offspring.

It was reported above that about 4 out of 10 poor children are in a family headed by the mother. We have selected a case secured by Mathews to illustrate the behavior, problems, and deviations from middle-class norms present in this type of family. Mrs. T. is divorced, the mother of seven children, and on welfare:

> Mrs. T., 34, divorced her husband three years ago and receives no alimony. He disappeared after the divorce, maybe back to the Arkansas river town where they were married 16 years ago.

[51] *Ibid.*, pp. 19–20.
[52] *Ibid.*, pp. 16–17.
[53] Reported in Besner, p. 20. Robert R. Bell, "The One-Parent Mother in the Negro Lower Class," a paper read at a meeting of the Eastern Sociological Society, New York, 1965.

Her only regular income is $364 a month from the county and even that is an off-again, on-again matter. Mrs. T. has sometimes failed to report extra income, earned as a short order cook at a local bar, has got into wild disputes with her social worker and been put off the rolls.

She hates welfare anyway—"nigger programs," she calls it.

Her oldest child is 15-year-old Ricky, a barefoot towhead who has had a couple of run-ins with the police and fallen two grades behind at school. She admits she has no control over him and suspects that he sneaks liquor behind her back.

"He just ain't right," complains Mrs. T., spreading her arms over an expansive belly and frowning, thereby showing two visibly rotten incisors. "Sometimes, he'll be so gentle to me and the kids. Other times, he'll knock 'em around and come at me with the butcher knife."

Ricky plans to join the Marine Corps to escape his noisy sisters and brothers and his sometimes harsh mother, who doesn't hesitate to knock any of them across the room.

For the moment, he just avoids the two-bedroom house with the broken front step, the taped-over windows and the dog carcass rotting in what once was a rosebed.

"She's a slut," he says of his mother, "and everybody around here knows it."

Mrs. T.'s babies, 2 and 3, were the result of brief liaisons with men she met at the bar where she once worked. For her, sex is life's greatest pleasure.

"And it's free," she says gamely. "Geeze, I'm still a young woman. Why do I have to go putting men out of my mind?"

Mrs. T. does not believe in postponing pleasures of any other kind either.

"How do I know if I'm going to be alive tomorrow? Sure, I could scrimp and save and stretch the money out, but would we have any more? No, the kids would just feel the pinch all the time."

Instead, Mrs. T. buys roast beef when the welfare check arrives and stocks up on orange pop ("my kids love it") and Hostess cupcakes. On the day before "mother's day"—slang for the day the check comes—the family eats kidney beans, packaged turkey stuffing prepared with saved-up grease or, sometimes, nothing. Mrs. T. doesn't buy many vegetables "because they spoil so easy."

Rarely does the family leave the neighborhood, because of lack of transportation. An old Chevy rusts in the carport, its tires sold long ago for ready cash.

In emergencies, unless she has money for a taxi, Mrs. T. has no way to get to a doctor. Once this summer her 10-year old daughter LuAnn cut her foot on glass in the yard. Strapped for cash, Mrs. T. merely wrapped up the child's foot. When her check arrived two days later, she finally took LuAnn to an emergency hospital where she was told that the foot, with a piece of glass still embedded in it, was badly infected.

Occasionally Mrs. T. goes with two women friends to the bar where she worked.

"They got a song on the juke box there that I like a lot,"she says dreamily, like a young girl. "It's by a colored girl, Aretha Franklin, but it's still a fine song. They call it 'Natural Woman.'

"My girl friends say that's what I am, I'm just a natural woman."[54]

Children of Disorganized Slum Families The child-rearing environment provided by disorganized slum families and the characteristics of their preschool children were studied by a group consisting of psychiatrists, a psychologist, a sociologist, a nursery school teacher, and a social worker. The usual methods of a systematic study with a large or random sample were found to be inappropriate with these disorganized families. Instead, 13 families with 45 preschool children were observed intensively over a period of time and the children were closely observed in a special nursery school set up for the project. The report of this study provides a synthesis of a great deal of meticulous observation, even though it differs from conventional methods of research. Of the families studied, three were Negro and ten were white.[55]

Parallel with the study of the families and children was an intensive program designed to test ways of working with the children so that they would be less likely to follow the disorganized life patterns of their parents.

The project was located in a section of Boston that had long been a slum area, earlier serving as a first-generation immigrant residence and later having a concentration of alcoholics and bums.[56] The families limited their lives almost entirely to this area, rarely if ever making even short excursions to other parts of the city. They did not indicate any consideration of moving from the area.

Observations of the families indicated that most of them depended on welfare payments for income, as had their parents before them, but they rarely if ever made use of other welfare-type services in the community. They lacked the minimum elements of internal organization and motivation to allow them to enter into ordinary relationships in any institutional setting. Routines of life and of housekeeping were extremely haphazard, with tasks being accomplished if at all when the need to do them became so pressing that it could no longer be ignored. This included almost all aspects of child care. The most striking difference

---

[54] Mathews, p. 18.
[55] Eleanor Pavenstedt (ed.), *The Drifters: Children of Disorganized Lower-Class Families* (Boston: Little, Brown, 1967).
[56] *Ibid.*, pp. 45–49.

between these and other families is indicated in the following, written by the sociologist:

> The primary social-psychological characteristic that appeared in the course of our study is the enormous confusion in each family about the differences between adults and children. This can be documented ad infinitum from the record. . . . All of our adults show persisting failure to exercise self-restraint or self-discipline at crucial points when their own anxieties are aroused while dealing with their children. In fact, none of them seem capable of consistently recognizing any specific set of childish capabilities or needs to which they must respond. . . .
>
> My first impression . . . was that we were watching "families of children" in action. You could hardly distinguish the adults from the children except for the fact that the adults were taller. Parents seemed to lack sufficient self-definition and role-playing ability to keep in mind the fact that children are undifferentiated, impulsive beings who have to be nursed and coerced into differentiated growth. This latter capacity is the bare irreducible minimum of child rearing in any culture, regardless of how widely definitions of adult responsibilities and childish faculties might vary. One has the feeling that these parents were never allowed to be children by their own parents, and that they in turn cannot afford to allow or acknowledge, not to mention appreciate, childishness in their children.[57]

Certain prevalent behavior tendencies became apparent as the preschool children of these families were observed in the nursery school or in their homes with their families. From surface appearances the children appeared alert and responsive, with no immediate indications of serious problems. However, with further observations certain characteristic patterns were found. Low self-esteem and frequent devaluation of self were noticeable. There was little confidence in themselves or in their abilities and a lack of pleasure or satisfaction in accomplishment. One striking evidence of the low regard for themselves was unwillingness to look at themselves in a mirror, often declaring that they did not see themselves. When asked who they were, the reply was likely to be "nobody" or "me don't know" or a similar expression indicating lack of self-identification. The children showed very good gross motor coordination for their ages, excellent rhythmic sense and very high rates of motor activity. The motor activity seemed to be used primarily for discharging tension, and frequently served to avoid dealing with a problem or challenge.

In coping with ordinary living situations, their reactions were chiefly submissive and passive, with very little self-initiation of activities or even independent maintenance of activities. This was true even of five-

---

[57] Maurice R. Stein, "Sociocultural Perspectives on the Neighborhood and the Families," in *ibid.*, pp. 312–313.

and six-year olds. If an obstacle was encountered, the usual reaction was to run away from the situation or to collapse in misery on the floor rather than to attempt to solve the problem presented.

The children showed a combination of hyperalertness focused on activities of adults together with conspicuous unresponsiveness to large segments of the external world. They paid great attention to any cues from adults which might help avoid difficulties or discomforts. They were apprehensively alert to cues which might suggest trouble for themselves. Expectation of calamity was a major theme in the ongoing processes in the nursery school. The slightest accident, even a toy rolling off a table, would arouse expectations of disastrous punishment in all the children, usually followed by a frenzy of undirected running about, even out of the room and the building. Loud noises or somewhat startling events, such as the school car stopping abruptly for a red light, were perceived as threatening disaster. At the same time, the urge to investigate, test out, and to master objects and situations was minimal. The children would walk by the most attractive toys, or ignore materials set out for their play. Apparently attentiveness was highly selective in that it was used to look for cues of danger but not for exploring the world.

The observing of language and cognitive development in the nursery school became especially important since the children did not enter into testing situations adequately. The children did have speech, although their vocabularies were well below what would be expected of children in day-care centers. There was an especially marked lack of words for the names and properties of objects. Also, although the children could frequently repeat verbal directions, they frequently could not act upon them until there was a physical demonstration. In cognitive development, the minimal capacity to generalize was most striking, with a newly learned skill not being applied in a context which differed even slightly from the learning situation.

Thus the slum family had a way of life widely deviant from that of the middle class. There was little separation between the roles of parents and children. And the development of personal and social skills in the children was minimal.

WORKING-CLASS AND MIDDLE-CLASS FAMILIES

Information is singularly lacking on a type of family variously called blue-collar, manual, or working-class family; more information is available on the middle-class family, for that is the type of family most studied. The working-class family is composed of skilled, semiskilled, and unskilled workers and their families. Moreover, the blue-collar worker constitutes a very large category: in 1969 about 4 out of 10, 38.6 percent, of all employed workers were classified as blue-collar.[58]

There are significant differences within families classified as working class or middle class. Rainwater shows little concern for these differences. Komarovsky made some comparisons between different educational groups of her blue-collar families. Kohn was aware of the differences and made one small comparison of his subjects on the basis of the five social classes of Hollingshead. However, even between the broad categories of middle- and working-class families significant differences were found.

Rainwater and his associates interviewed 420 working-class married women and 120 middle-class married women.[59] The subjects were residents of four cities: Chicago, Louisville, Tacoma, and Trenton. Several methods of securing information were used, including a projective test of 24 TAT-type pictures. Each subject was asked to tell a story about each picture. Four topics were of special importance: roles of the wife, self-conception, husband-wife relations, and social participation.

Roles of the Wife The working-class wife has five primary activities or tasks: taking care of the house, child-rearing, husband-servicing, watching TV, and visiting with relatives and neighbors. The last two are limited because of the amount of time spent on the first three. Taking care of the house involves fixing meals, washing clothes, dressing the children, doing chores, such as dishes, beds, dusting, and sweeping, mending clothes, washing windows, working out in the yard, shopping for groceries, and sewing. In child-care the working-class wife feeds, clothes, bathes her children, sees that they go to bed on time, and constantly watches out for them, even when they are not in her immediate presence. Taking care of the husband is viewed by some husbands as including taking care of the house and children: "My wife takes good care of my home and my children." More specifically she gets his breakfast, sometimes fixes his lunch, gets his supper, takes care of his clothes, and tries to make the home "peaceful" when he returns from work. Watching TV is a daily activity, generally in the evening. Visiting is almost exclusively with relatives and neighbors.

The middle-class wife views her activities quite differently. She, of course, does many of the same things, but she organizes them more efficiently. Certain days are reserved for certain activities: laundry on Monday, club meetings on Tuesday, shopping on Wednesday, cleaning on Thursday and Friday. The middle-class woman also has a different

---
[58] *Statistical Abstract of the United States*, 1969, p. 222.
[59] Rainwater, et al., *Workingman's Wife*.

attitude toward children. While the working-class mother emphasizes the dull routine of taking care of the children, the middle-class mother reports that the children are always coming up with something new. Also, middle-class mothers are more concerned with the quality of neighborhoods and schools.

Self-Conceptions The self-conception of a working-class wife is that she is a "little person" and that anything that happens to her is determined by the world external to herself and by fate. She tends to think of this external world as fairly chaotic and potentially catastrophic. She has pervasive anxiety over potential deprivations—the death of a family member, the likelihood of violence, and the possibility of economic hardships. Deprivation, loneliness, and fear are characteristic of working-class wives.

Rainwater and his associates describe the reactions of working-class wives and middle-class wives to a picture of a little girl sitting in the doorway of a cabin, with no other details. The tendency was for the working-class wives to identify themselves with the girl, seeing the girl as lonely and watching for somebody's return, or it "looks like the family has gone away and left her." An upper-middle-class wife describes the girl as follows:

> This is a girl at a summer camp. She sees chipmunks and squirrels near the door and she is sitting real still so as not to frighten them away. If she watches long enough, they will come up and take food from her.[60]

Husband-Wife Relationships The husband is the central person in the life of the working-class wife, but at the same time she is not as close to him as is the middle-class wife. Rainwater reports that the working-class wife is concerned with whether she can retain a hold on him and appears afraid to act openly against the husband's wishes. Middle-class women have far less anxiety over whether their husbands are pleased with every little act. On financial decisions middle-class husbands and wives share responsibility whereas working-class wives have control of the money; husbands turn over their pay checks to their wives and assume that they will spend the money wisely.

Social Participation Relatives are viewed quite differently by working-class and middle-class women. Working-class women spend much more time with their relatives and are more emotionally involved with them than are middle-class women. Rainwater and his associates report:

[60] *Ibid.*, p. 47.

For working-class women relatives are the most important other people beyond the immediate family of husband and children. For middle-class women, relatives are very often less important than nonrelatives.[61]

Clubs and voluntary organizations are much less important to working-class women than to middle-class women. If a working-class woman does belong, she joins fewer organizations and she selects those that are child-centered rather than adult-centered. She generally is passive in her attitude toward joining an organization: "Nobody has asked me to join."

Variations Among Blue-Collar Families by Education Komarovsky intensively interviewed 58 stable blue-collar husbands and their wives.[62] For the most part she describes the behavior of the whole group or compares the behavior of husbands with that of wives. In various parts of the study, a comparison is made between high school graduates and those who had not graduated from high school. Twenty-five wives and 18 husbands had graduated from high school; 17 wives and 23 husbands had some high school but had not graduated; and 16 wives and 17 husbands did not go beyond the grades. The comparison between the family behavior of high school graduates and the less-educated is an indirect comparison by social class and shows the wide differences between blue-collar families.

It is not surprising that high school graduates had higher incomes, a higher standard of living, and smaller families than the less educated. It is more surprising that there were wide differences in personal characteristics, economic attitudes, sexual relations, communication, in self-disclosure, and in relationships with in-laws.

In comparison with the less-educated, high school gradutes were more able, more emotionally stable, and more ambitious. For men, the high school graduates had greater understanding of the wife and a higher degree of empathy.

Less-educated husbands and wives lead more separate lives than high-school graduates. For one thing less-educated men have more frequent contact with male friends: 69 percent of less-educated men have more frequent contact with male friends: 69 percent of less-educated husbands compared to 41 percent of high school graduate husbands see friends at least once a week. Less-educated wives report an excess of grievances. For example, they claim that their husbands do not listen to them and often talk about boring things. The high school graduate group places a higher value on psychic compatibility defined as sexual responsiveness,

[61] *Ibid.*, p. 103.
[62] Mirra Komarovsky, *Blue Collar Marriage* (New York: Vintage Books, 1967).

attractiveness, companionship, common interests, emotional support, and love.

Economic attitudes include both the men's activities and the wife's housework. Less-educated women credit the economic failure of their husbands to bad luck. Wives of the high school graduate group say that the economic failure of the husband is due to a lack of drive. The high school graduate wives have a less favorable attitude toward housework than the less-educated wives. Moreover, housework as a source of "bad" moods is reported by a larger percent of high school graduate wives. Less-educated husbands tend to leave housework and child-care entirely to the wife. Husbands of the high school graduate group help more in shopping and in the care of infants.

Less-educated wives believe that woman should give sex to her husband whether she likes it or not. They consider it a woman's moral duty. High school graduate wives resist the husband's sexual advances more frequently than the less-educated. They feel that submission to the husband is necessary, but there is some consideration also for the husband's needs. Good sexual adjustment is somewhat higher for the less-educated wives—one-third for the less-educated and one-fifth for the high school graduate group. The less-educated wives are more likely to have satisfactory sexual adjustment and at the same time be more unhappy in marriage than high-school graduate wives.

High school graduates engage in more communication and self-disclosure between themselves. The following two statements by Kamarovsky show the differences in communication and self-disclosure by educational groups:

> We had expected the level of education to make a difference in the fullness of self-disclosure, but the extent of this difference was surprising. The high-school graduates, both male and female, share their experiences in marriage much more fully than do the less-educated persons.[63]

> Role differentiation in marriage is not so sharp among the better-educated as among the less-educated families. The high-school fathers are somewhat more active in childcare. And there is more discussion of the husband's job.[64]

High school graduates and the less-educated differ in factors associated with parents and in-laws. Fathers of men in the high school graduate group have a higher occupational level than fathers of the less-educated. Over 50 percent of the former are skilled workers, and there are no unskilled workers among them. By contrast, about half of the

[63] Ibid., pp. 144–145.
[64] Ibid., p. 171.

fathers of the less-educated are unskilled. Men in the less-educated group are not involved in child-rearing and neither were their fathers. It can be assumed that the reasons for their estrangement and often hostility toward their fathers were that no close ties to fathers were established in childhood, the continuance in unskilled work like their fathers, and difficulty in communication.

Less-educated men have more conflict with in-laws, for there is an excess of conflict-producing situations. The norms of the less-educated make it difficult to escape the conflicts. For one thing, they are more likely to live with in-laws during marriage. They have a high dependence upon relatives and this makes it necessary to contact and communicate with in-laws even though there is a lack of congeniality.

Social Class and Parental Values Social class and parental values were studied by Kohn who secured data from two representative samples: 200 white working-class mothers and 200 middle-class mothers, all of whom had a fifth-grade child. In addition he secured data from every fourth husband and every fourth fifth-grade child. For the most part his comparisons are between working-class and middle-class families, with most of the analysis being on mothers. The following conclusions can be drawn from his studies:[65]

1. Middle- and working-class mothers share many values for their children. They both value happiness, honesty, consideration, obedience, dependability, and self-control for both boys and girls.

2. The two groups of mothers differ in the emphasis they give to some values. Working-class mothers place more value on obedience, responsiveness of children to parental authority, neatness, and cleanliness. Middle-class mothers place more value on consideration, self-control, curiosity, and behavior based on inner control and sympathetic concern for other people.

3. Middle-class mothers value about the same things for boys and girls. Working-class mothers regard dependability, being a good student, and ambition as desirable for boys and regard happiness, good manners, neatness, and cleanliness as desirable for girls.

4. Fathers hold essentially the same values for children as do their wives.

---

[65] Melvin L. Kohn, "Social Class and Parental Values," *American Journal of Sociology*, 64 (1959): pp. 337–351; "Social Class and the Exercise of Parental Authority," *American Sociological Review*, 24 (1959): pp. 352–366; "Social Class and Parent-Child Relationships: An Interpretation," *American Journal of Sociology*, 68 (1963): pp. 471–480; and with Eleanor E. Carroll, "Allocation of Parental Responsibilities," *Sociometry*, 23 (1960): pp. 372–392.

5. A considerable proportion of mothers whose families were classified as working class hold white-collar jobs. Such mothers are closer to middle-class mothers in their values than are other working-class mothers. Mothers of working-class families who hold manual jobs are further from middle-class values than mothers who do not hold an outside job.

6. Mothers and fathers of each social class agree fairly well on the roles of the mother and the father toward children.

7. Dividing the mothers into the five socioeconomic classes of Hollingshead, it was found that the higher the mother's social class the higher the probability that she values consideration, curiosity, and self-control; the lower the social class, the greater the likelihood that she values obedience, neatness, cleanliness, and honesty.

8. Middle- and working-class parents punish their children physically or refrain from this as a result of different values. Working-class parents want their children to be respectable and if extreme misbehavior is considered a violation of the norm of respectability, physical punishment is likely to ensue. Middle-class parents value internalized standards of conduct by the children; and consideration of how best to produce this determines the choice of techniques of punishment by parents.

Socioeconomic Status and Family Behavior Locke and Thomes have studied family behavior of matched samples of whites and Negroes in the central city area of Los Angeles. The families were selected from census tracts having a median family income in the middle range for the metropolitan area. Husbands and wives of 116 white families and 61 Negro families were interviewed in their homes, using a schedule of questions designed to assess many family variables. One mode of analysis was to examine the relationship between socioeconomic status of the family and several family variables. Socioeconomic status was measured by an index combining the education of the husband, his occupation, and family income.

In the group of white husbands, socioeconomic status was significantly correlated with eight family variables. These variables all dealt with feelings of unity and affection within the family. In each case, favorable feeling about the family increased with an increase in socioeconomic status of the family. The first six of the variables correlated with socioeconomic status dealt with husband-wife relationships, the other two were on parents and children. The significant correlations for husband-wife variables were: (1) feelings of love and affection, (2) satisfaction with the marriage, (3) perceived and actual consensus with the wife on major issues, (4) nonverbal communication, (5) verbal communication, and (6) marital adjustment.[66] The two variables dealing with relationships between parents and children were: (1) feelings of love and affection between the parent and children, and (2) perception of consensus among all family members including children.[67]

Several other variables for white husbands were not related to socioeconomic status. Some of these were on roles and others were concerned with the social milieu. Three were on roles: (1) joint or separate activities of family members in leisure-time pursuits; (2) household or family tasks; and (3) empathy or the ability to take the role of the mate to such an extent that the husband accurately predicts the responses of the wife. Two were related to the social milieu: (1) an indirect measurement of social pressures against separation or divorce; and (2) familism, with questions focused on relationships between parents and children.

Thus, for these men, feelings of affection and closeness within the family were correlated with socioeconomic status while role factors and factors reflecting relationships of the family to the social milieu were not.

For Negro husbands, three variables dealing with unity with the wife were *negatively* correlated with socioeconomic level, indicating less unity as socioeconomic status increased. The three variables were (1) satisfaction with the marriage; (2) perceived consensus with the wife; and (3) marital adjustment.[68] A moderate *negative* relationship was found between socioeconomic level and influences in the immediate social circle tending to promote family stability and unity.[69] This variable consisted of items on the religiousness of the husband and wife and the experience of divorce and separation among their relatives and friends. As the socioeconomic level of these middle-class Negro husbands rose, they experienced fewer such pressures to maintain family stability. This finding suggests that the greatest pressure for maintaining family stability is for Negro men of the lower-middle class who are economically closest to the lower-class Negro family with its higher rates of family instability.

For Negro wives, none of the variables of family unity and affection was related to socioeconomic level, although a negative correlation with satisfaction in the marriage was just below the level of significance. The correlation of socioeconomic level with the influences promoting family stability was similar to that for their husbands.[70]

---

[66] The correlations for these six were respectively .29, .26, .22, .21, .30, and .26.
[67] The respective correlations were .42 and .25.
[68] The respective correlations were −.27, −.20, and −.21.
[69] The correlation was −.37.
[70] The correlation was −.34.

White wives showed fewer variables significantly correlated with socioeconomic status then did their husbands; for wives only four variables were significantly correlated. All of them dealt with feelings of unity with the husband and were among the eight variables correlated with socioeconomic status for the husbands. They were: (1) satisfaction with the marriage, (2) perceived and actual consensus with the husband, (3) verbal communication, and (4) marital adjustment.[71] Again role factors and social milieu factors were not related to socioeconomic status.

The above findings suggest that for lower-middle- and upper-middle-class urban white husbands and wives feelings of affection, closeness and harmony with each other increase with an increase in socioeconomic status. For husbands, feelings of closeness with their children also increase with an increase in socioeconomic status. Family role behavior and relationships to the rest of society are not so related.

For both Negro husbands and wives, the relationships between socioeconomic status and family variables were quite different from those for whites. No family variable was *positively* correlated with socioeconomic level for either Negro husbands or wives. For these middle-class Negro families, higher socioeconomic level did not mean a more satisfactory or unified marriage.

The data from this study of urban families indicate quite different relationships between socioeconomic status and family variables for whites and Negroes, especially on variables measuring family unity and affection. For white families, and especially for husbands, feelings of unity and affection increased with higher socioeconomic status. For Negro families, and especially for husbands, the variables that were correlated with socioeconomic level indicated less unity and affection with higher socioeconomic status. In addition, there was no relationship between socioeconomic level and influences in the environment to maintain family stability for whites, while a negative relationship was found for Negroes. Role behavior factors were not related to socioeconomic level for either whites or Negroes.

Both the white and Negro families in this study were middle class with a wide range of socioeconomic level from lower-middle-class to upper-middle class families. Consequently, the results are applicable within this socioeconomic range. Lower-class families are not included and from studies of slum families somewhat different relationships between family variables and socioeconomic level might be expected for lower-class families.

---

[71] The respective correlations were .20, .21, .21, and .24.

SUMMARY

The urban family, as contrasted with the rural family, is more individualistic, has less occupational continuity, less personal relations, more freedom and economic independence of youth, smaller sized families, lower sex ratio, higher proportion of men married, more education, and a higher economic status.

A large proportion of urban families have kin living in or near the city in which they reside. Parents and their children maintain close relationships after the children have formed homes of their own. White husbands and wives maintain more frequent contacts with the husband's parents than do Negro husbands and wives. The kinship family functions in the giving and receiving of mutual aid, in visiting, and in the giving and receiving of services.

Suburbs as compared with central cities have a higher proportion of whites, a higher proportion of persons 18 years of age or younger, larger family size, a higher sex ratio, smaller proportion of persons 65 years of age and older, more formal education, a larger proportion in prestige occupations, higher incomes, more married, and less broken homes. The central city is composed of several types of families: the nonfamily man of Skid Row detached from his family, the poverty family of the slums, and middle-class and working-class families. Each of these can be subdivided into additional types.

PROBLEMS FOR RESEARCH

Variations Within Social Classes One of the major findings of this chapter is the high degree of variation within given social classes. There are stable and unstable poverty families, residential and industrial suburbs, large and small central cities, and better educated and less educated working-class families. These broad social classes should be studied to determine the subtypes and the family behavior characteristic of each subtype.

Family Behavior and Urban Areas In recent years a great deal of attention has been focused on the effects of the structure of a city on the life of its people. This question has been of particular concern to urban planning commissions in major cities. Investigations should be made of the way of life of families and individuals in different kinds of urban areas. This chapter has stressed differences in family structure in broadly different areas of the city. To what extent are these differences in families related to the physical structure of the area? Is there selective migration of families and individuals to certain kinds of urban areas? Do families as they move through their life cycle move within the urban area to obtain that type of housing and community facilities which most nearly meets their needs at a particular time in their life cycle? Can urban planning influence the kinds of families that will live in certain areas by influencing the physical structure of the area?

Urban Redevelopment Most large cities have undertaken redevelopment projects aimed at the removal of certain deteriorated buildings in a given area and their replacement with either new housing or civic or business buildings. These are some of the questions which might be studied in connection with urban redevelopment: What effect does the forced removal of the occupants of the area have on their personal and family life? It will be recalled that Young and Willmott in their study of kinship in East London found that families that had been moved to a government housing project outside the area of the neighborhood felt isolated and lonesome.[72] If the prior occupants of the area eventually move into new housing in the same area, are there major changes in their way of life because of the changed housing situation, or do these families perpetuate their prior way of life in the new environment? If they move to a new area, what problems do they have in the new area?

Interrelations of the Family with Other Institutions The social organization of the community is now being analyzed by sociologists from the standpoint of its component institutions. The degree of participation of the family in these institutions, such as the school, the church, leisure-time organizations, and voluntary associations is undoubtedly significant for its structure and functions. To what extent do social classes differ in their participation with various institutions and organizations in the city?

QUESTIONS AND EXERCISES

1. What is the extent of kinship contacts in middle-class and working-class families in urban areas? What functions do such contacts perform?
2. Compare suburbs and central cities on as many characteristics as you can. How do you account for these differences?
3. What factors are most important in bringing about personal disorganization of nonfamily men of Skid Row?

---

[72] Michael Young and Peter Willmott, *Family and Kinship in East London.*

4. How do you account for the concentration of poverty families in poverty areas of a city?
5. What are the characteristics of children in extremely disorganized slum families?
6. What are the differences between middle-class and working-class families?
7. Give your reasons for saying that the country or the city is more suitable for (1) the development of stability of family relationships, (2) health of people, and (3) personality development of children.
8. Contrast central cities, suburbs, and rural areas on sex ratio, size of families, marital status, and broken families.

BIBLIOGRAPHY

Adams, Bert N. *Kinship in an Urban Setting.* Chicago: Markham Publishing Company, 1968.
> A study of 799 white young adults in Greensboro, North Carolina. Kin relationships analyzed with reference to occupational class, intergenerational mobility, rural-urban origin, sex, and spatial distance between kin. Has a theoretical emphasis.

Axelrod, Morris. "Urban Structure and Social Participation," *American Sociological Review,* 21 (1965): pp. 13–18.
> Data from interviews with 749 subjects of Detroit. Of the various findings one is of particular interest: visiting with relatives emerged as the most important type of informal group association in the urban area.

Berger, Bennett M. *Working-Class Suburb: A Study of Auto Workers in Suburbia.* Berkeley: University of California Press, 1960.
> Based on interviews with 100 production and maintenance workers who relocated in a suburb when a large plant was moved to the area. Challenges the idea of suburbia as a way of life; workers retained their working-class outlook, aspirations, religion, and leisure-time pursuits.

Besner, Arthur. "Economic Deprivation and Family Patterns," in *Low-Income Life Styles.* United States Department of Health, Education, and Welfare, Welfare Administration, Publication No. 14, pp. 15–29.
> Excellent summary of research findings of marital and family behavior of the poor: courtship, early adjustment to marriage, division of labor, marital values, and single-parent family and child-rearing.

Dobriner, William M. (ed.). *The Suburban Community.* New York: G. P. Putnam's Sons, 1958.
> Consists of 25 articles by recognized authorities on urban-rural areas. Those most related to the family are "The Structuring of Social Relations Engendered by Suburban Residence," by Walter T. Martin; "The Family in Suburbia," by Ernest R. Mowrer; and "Social Choice, Life Styles and Suburban Residence," by Wendell Bell.

Goldstein, Bernard. *Low Income Youth in Urban Areas: A Critical Review of the Literature.* New York: Holt, Rinehart, and Winston, 1967.
: Presents the findings of studies of children and young people in the following areas: family of orientation, education, work, family of procreation, religion, government and law, and leisure-time activities. Over half of the book is an excellent annotated bibliography of urban studies, for the most part dealing with social classes.

Greenfield, Sidney M. "Industrialization and the Family in Sociological Theory," *American Journal of Sociology,* 67 (1961): pp. 316–322.
: Presents ethnographic data to show that in some societies urbanization and industrialization are present without the small nuclear family, and that the small nuclear family is present in some societies without urbanization and industrialization.

Komarovsky, Mirra. *Blue-Collar Marriage.* New York: Vintage Books, 1967.
: Based on extended interviews with 58 working-class families. Discusses the learning of conjugal roles, division of labor, sex and marital happiness, barriers to communication, marriage and power, and kinship relations. Particularly valuable is an analysis of those who were high school graduates as compared with those who had not graduated from high school.

Minuchin, Salvador. *Families of the Slums: An Exploration of Their Structure and Treatment.* New York: Basic Books, 1967.
: A study of 12 highly disorganized lower-class families and 10 lower-class families that were not disorganized. There were many interviews with each of these families. Chapter 2, a review of the literature on poverty families, is particularly valuable.

Rainwater, Lee; Coleman, Richard P.; and Handel, Gerald. *Workingman's Wife: Her Personality, World, and Life Style.* New York: Oceana Publications, 1959.
: Reports a study of 420 working-class housewives in four cities of the United States. Some of the data are compared with material from 120 middle-class housewives. Narrative analysis without statistical documentation. Describes urban working-class housewives' perception of themselves, their lives, and their relationships with their husbands and children.

Starkey, Otis P. *The Anglo-American Realm.* New York: McGraw-Hill, 1969.
: An analysis of the evolution of modern urban economies and the transition from agricultural to urban activities.

Sussman, Marvin B. "Relationships of Adult Children with Their Parents in the United States," in *Social Structure and the Family: Generational Relations,* eds. Ethel Shanas and Gordon F. Streib. Englewood Cliffs, New Jersey: Prentice Hall, 1965, Chapter 4.
: Reviews the findings of studies of kinship relationships in the United States in terms of mutual aid, social participation with kin, and services. Presents

the findings of his and Slater's study of kinship relations in 500 families in Cleveland.

Whyte, William Foote. *Street Corner Society: The Social Structure of an Italian Slum*. Chicago: University of Chicago Press, 1955.
> Data secured through participant observation. Gives vivid description of the activities, code, personalities, and status arrangement of a Cornerville gang, a group of second-generation men in an Eastern city. Of particular interest is the description of the hierarchical structure of social relations binding the men to each other.

Chapter 5
The Negro Family

The American Negro family has experienced great changes in recent years. The gap between Negro and white families has narrowed in some areas, such as income, employment in a high-status, good paying job, and years of schooling completed. At the same time, the gaps in income, type of job, and the quality of education still exist. In recent decades Negroes have been moving to urban areas to such an extent that now seven out of ten Negroes live in metropolitan areas. It is probable that even greater changes and greater mobility will be experienced by the Negro family in the next few years.

The following are excerpts from a life-history document written by an educated Negro woman. The parents of this woman were divorced and she is divorced. She and her sister and brother lived for about five years in foster homes. Finally her father gained custody and gave them a home. He had one ambition for his children. They should be kept from the cycle of poverty, ignorance, and lack of skill which had characterized his life. The document also illustrates the conflict which arises when a husband and wife have radically different values and goals.

Presently, I am 25 years of age, divorced, the mother of two children (a girl four and a boy three) and an honor student completing my last year of college toward a B.A. My background has no doubt had great influence on my present situation. In many respects the goals and values that I have now are a negative reaction to the life that I led. It may be that I am attempting to avoid a repeat of my life situation at all costs. In this respect I owe a great deal to my father. He made many sacrifices and taught us a lot about the world that was out there and available to us, his children, if not for him. The cycle of poverty and ignorance and lack of skill was to be over with his generation and in his own way he worked to see that this was true. I feel that he did an excellent job of instilling the values and goals that he wanted for us. We are still striving for these goals in our own way but the cycle of ignorance, poverty, and lack of skill is broken forever. My father should be complimented on the results as the story of the upbringing of his three children is not one that would have normally or logically led to such positive results.

My mother and father were separated at an early age. My mother was young (16 when my sister was born and we are all one year apart) and my father was not a very responsible person. He worked but he liked to gamble and spend money and paid bills last. My mother also liked to have a good time and really I am sure she realized that when our father left she would not be able to care for us properly. Daddy worked at many jobs but was mostly a waiter. Mother was uneducated and unskilled and worked as a bar maid at night. That is no job for a mother and is certainly not enough money to raise a family. Neither one of them wanted the responsibility at the time. She was the one who actually signed us over for foster care and I don't think my father ever forgave her. But he was also unwilling to care for us himself at that time. Later on he did decide to care for us and did the best he could by us. However, we had by that time lived a pretty rough life and we were all much older than our years.

I have one sister and one brother. My sister and I had always lived together and the first recollection either of us have of our brother was our parents bringing him to visit us at our grandmother's home where we lived at that time. He was three years old. We were four and five. I later learned that he had been in foster placement since he was nine months old. After that visit, my sister and I went to stay with our brother and his foster parents in Chicago for a while.

Mrs. Reeder was our first foster mother. She was a religious woman, as all our foster mothers were. We spent our entire Sundays at church and some evenings during the week. Mrs. Reeder also beat us once a week as some sort of deterrent to evil. One day my sister did something and Mrs. Reeder beat her with an ironing cord. My sister's head had a beautiful knot on it. Coincidentally that day, our mother came to visit and discovered my sister's condition. She took us home with her where we stayed until another placement could be found. We stayed with our mother several times during the various placements that we had. Except for one occasion, each time it was for extreme cruelty to my sister or me. One of our foster mothers died after only a few months placement. She was the only white foster mother that we had. One couple locked my sister and I in the coal bin every evening and delighted in telling us about ghosts and things. Our social worker discovered us there one day. Another foster mother burned the inside of my hand with a hot comb. It just so happened that our social worker was coming down the steps to the beauty shop when the foster mother burned it and she saw her. After this episode, and another stay with our mother, we were placed for the last time, with Mr. and Mrs. John Lake. We remained in this placement for five years.

Except for our last placement and the one foster mother who died, all the rest were mainly interested in the money. Their interest was certainly not in children. They were usually cruel and sadistic. Despite this my sister and I are not too scarred by these experiences. We were only five and six and most of the bad experiences were over quickly. All except the last of our placements were completed in the first year.

The fact that we were finally located with a good family is no doubt due to our social worker, Miss Tubin, who remained with us from the first day of placement until after our father had gained our custody. She was a beautiful person, very young, and good with kids. We delighted in her visits which were infrequent, except to replace us. I think it was about every six months that we saw her. She was white and this experience with a warm white person no doubt was an influence in our liberal attitudes about whites. We grew up with no race hatred, just an awareness that our world was black.

Our childhood with the Lakes was middle-class in orientation and lower-class in discipline. Mr. Lake would punish us by awakening us at four in the morning to do chores before going to school. Mrs. Lake usually did the spanking. In looking back, I would say their discipline was fair. They punished children for being children like everyone else usually does. Other than that, we played baseball in the vacant lot across the street. We played hide-and-seek, hopscotch, marbles, jumped rope.

My father came from Indianapolis to see us about twice a year. He always came around the Fourth of July to take us to Riverview, a huge amusement park in Chicago. My brother would go along with us and we usually rode everything that the park had to offer. It was an all-day affair and, I am sure, an expensive affair. Periodically, daddy would send us clothes, always red in color and always too big or too small. Our mother lived in Chicago but we only saw her infrequently. I think that there were some regulations regarding their visits.

Six years after our first placement, our father gained custody of the three of us and we went to live with him where we remained until we married and left home. Originally, our aunt and uncle came from Los Angeles to stay with us because daddy had to have a legitimate woman in the house to gain custody of the two girls. They had their own marital problems and moved from us and later back to Los Angeles. This left us pretty much on our own.

After our aunt and uncle left and we were mostly on our own we learned a great deal more about the streets. Later in the year, daddy took a job with the railroad running from Chicago to Los Angeles. He was gone for two weeks at a time and we were left alone during these runs. Various families in the building were to keep an eye on us but they did not do too good a job. In one year we grew from very green little kids to very worldly and sophisticated young adults. Our father was not too pleased with the results and he felt he was at fault. He made the decision to come to Los Angeles the next year.

In Los Angeles hard times hit us like a flood. Daddy stopped the railroad and no job could be found to replace it. Sporadic employment was the rule. During this time our clothing was provided by our great aunt from the clothes collected at the church. Again church was an important part of our lives, although transportation to and from church for the four of us (my adult cousin remained with us) from 88th to 23rd was costly. The church youth group, however, was our most important social contact.

We finally had to leave our lovely home and move into the lower income area of the ghetto around 23rd and San Pedro. This was a two-bedroom, roach-infested apartment. We tried to paint it up to make it look better but the building itself always looked as if it would fall down. We remained here one year until we moved in with another family on the westside of Los Angeles. This was a huge furnished apartment on the second floor. It had four bedrooms, two baths, a separate dining room, living room, den, and enclosed porch. The furniture in it was quite good and quite nice. We had five phones. However, this was a facade covering our actual plight. Although we were doing better, we were not doing well. Food was scarce at times and utilities were shut off several times. We remained here one year before moving around the corner to our own separate home. Later that year our father remarried and we had a mother in the home. This brought financial stability to our home that was to remain from that time on. Our new mother worked and daddy found steady employment also. We acquired some new furnishings and we began to acquire new clothes. My sister and I graduated from junior high that year and started attendance at Manual Arts High School. I completed my education there while my sister left high school to get married and had two children by the time of my graduation.

Education in our family was always something that had to be done. We knew we had to be in school each day and there was no discussion otherwise. I had always done well in school having skipped the first, fourth, and seventh grades and graduating high school at 16. I was also an artist. Several of the pictures I painted in school in Chicago were on display at the Museum of Art in that city.

The friends that I cultivated in junior high and high school continue to be my friends today. We were a tight group in high school and even closer in college. We were older then and working part-time in addition to going to school. This gave us more freedom to assert ourselves and do as we pleased. Our group was diverse in many ways. We were interracial, of both sexes, mostly the same age and IQ, were interested in art, music, drama, and just having fun.

I left all this to get married when I was nineteen. I think my marriage failed because I failed to marry one of my group. We were more like brothers and sisters and had never dated each other but only outside the group occasionally. My husband did not and could not share my divergent interests and the goals and values that were a part of my character. I have never been caught up in the success syndrome or captivated by monetary achievements. All that I have ever wanted was enough money to continue to do the things I love best and maybe get a chance to travel. Clothes, furniture, cars have never excited me but having a family did intrigue me. The different goals and values that my husband and I were pursuing were, for him, money for conspicuous consumption. His idea of really making it was to drive a Cadillac, have $200 in his pocket and wear a $300 suit. These are good values and goals for some people but not for me. Especially when he wanted me to work to achieve them for him and leave our children with someone else at a very young age. He was making $800 a month which was more than anyone in his family or my family had ever had. It was more than enough for the four of us and I was not willing to work for these things. As time went by this became one of the sore points of our marriage.

My goals are those of doing things, enjoying life and all that it has to offer. I love theatre, traveling, and conversation. I am willing to work for the ability to travel but not at the expense of my children. Five years from their birth is time enough to go to work. These kinds of differences cannot be overcome and it makes the ordinary, petty things grow out of proportion. Although I was quite willing to be a wife and mother I was never willing to give up my identity. I have wants, needs, likes, dislikes, and the intelligence and common sense to know that to give all these up is not to be myself. If my childhood had taught me one thing it was that we are in charge of a greater part of our destiny than we will admit to.

When I find that I am not happy and discover the reasons why, I change whatever is necessary for my own survival. This is not selfishness or egotism. I suffered a lot when I was a child and I believe that the reason it did not harm me permanently was due to my rationalization that there was nothing I could do about it and I might as well accept it. Whenever I can change any situation, I do immediately. After my husband and I were divorced I worked as a transcriber-typist. However, I missed greatly the academic atmosphere and the logic and rationality of the general student body. I also knew that with a degree I could go into work that challenged the mind with people who could intelligently discuss something. I could change this situation but only at some sacrifice. The sacrifice seemed worth it to me. I applied for admission to the university in May of 1967. That August I applied for a loan and received both the maximum loan and the maximum grant allowable for a total of $1800 for nine months. Out of the $1800 was to come books, tuition, room, board, transportation, clothes, and babysitter's fees. The loan and the grant would be supplemented by child support payments in the amount of $160 per month. The drop in salary would be compensated by my working at change for myself and my family. After all, children cannot be any happier than their parents.

My brother and his family own their own home. My sister and her family are looking for their own home now. Both locations are very middle-class and integrated. They have color televisions and very nice furniture. They also both have new cars, two in each family. They both have three children apiece and no one wants for anything. I feel daddy can be proud of us.

This account illustrates several characteristics of some Negro families. (1) The parents and children of this family are in different social classes: the parents were in the lower class; the children have moved or hope to move into a higher social class. (2) A high value is placed on education as a means of improving a person's or a family's social position. (3) Family disorganization is reported of the parents' family as well as the subject's own family.

Certain questions are pertinent for an understanding of the Negro family. How does it differ in the South and the North, and in the city and rural communities? Many Negroes have risen in the economic and social scale so that now there is a growing number of successful Negro judges, congressmen, artists, writers, scientists, businessmen, and professional people. Does Negro family life in the different social classes correspond to the patterns of behavior in the same social classes among whites?

In this chapter an account will be given of (1) the transition from slavery to the modern Negro family; (2) the changing Negro family; (3) mobility and urbanization, and (4) forms of the family.

FROM SLAVERY TO THE MODERN NEGRO FAMILY

Elimination of the African Heritage Probably never before in history has a group been so completely stripped of its social heritage as were the Negroes who were brought from Africa to America. While students of the Negro social heritage differ as to the exact degree to which Negro African folkways and mores have been eliminated in this country, they agree that in the United States, as contrasted with Latin America, Negroes have more completely substituted Western culture for their African heritage. Elkins, in his thorough and careful study of the historical backgrounds of American Negroes, reports as follows on African survivals:

> Everyone who has looked into the problem of African cultural features surviving among the New World Negroes agrees that the contrast between North America and Latin America is immense. In Brazil, survivals from African religion are not only to be encountered everywhere, but such carryovers are so distinct that they may even be identified with particular tribal groups.[1]

One possible explanation of the almost complete absence of African survivals in the United States in contrast to the West Indies is the fact that "there was less opportunity for a slave to meet one of his own people, because the plantation was considerably smaller, more widely scattered and, especially, because as soon as they were landed in this country, slaves were immediately divided and shipped in small numbers,

---

[1] Stanley M. Elkins, *Slavery: A Problem in American Institutional and Intellectual Life* (Chicago: University of Chicago Press, 1959): pp. 102–103. Copyright 1959 by the University of Chicago.

frequently no more than one or two at a time, to different plantations."[2] A group is necessary for the survival of folkways and mores; if its members are permanently separated, the folkways and mores die out. In the case of the Negroes, new forms of marriage and family relationships emerged as a result of this process of losing their old culture and adopting a new one.

Differential Experience During Slavery The general social and economic forces operating under the system of slavery produced considerable uniformity of attitudes and practices among Negroes. Some different practices, however, did develop. Plantation owners varied widely in the behavior which they permitted or required of their slaves. Some exercised extreme care in safeguarding virginity and controlling marriage; others used Negro women as breeders and the most physically fit Negro men as sires.

House servants, as contrasted with field hands, had much more extensive contacts with whites and assimilated their ideas, sentiments, and beliefs. The house servant took over the attitudes and sentiments of his master toward such things as religion, sexual behavior, and marriage and family patterns. Occasionally, in addition to this informal assimilation, formal instruction and supervision in religion, secular skills, and morals was given all Negroes on the plantation, field hands as well as house servants. House servants, however, adopted white folkways and codes of behavior to a far greater extent than field hands.

Each decade between 1790 and 1860 saw the number of free Negroes steadily augmented; by 1860 there were 488,070, or 11 percent of all Negroes, in this group.[3] To attain his freedom, the Negro had to have habits of thrift and stability. His family and marriage relationships were modeled on those of the whites.

THE CHANGING NEGRO FAMILY[4]

One picture of the contemporary Negro family which could be presented is that in comparison to whites it has more wives as family heads, has more broken families, has more illegitimacy, has a higher

---

[2] Robert E. Park, "The Conflict and Fusion of Cultures," *Journal of Negro History*, 4 (1919): p. 17.

[3] United States Bureau of the Census, *Negro Population in the United States, 1790–1915*, 1918, p. 53.

[4] Some of the census data are for nonwhites. This, of course, is not strictly Negro. Of the 24,137,000 nonwhites in the United States in 1968, 91.4 percent were Negroes. In most States nonwhite is almost exclusively Negro. Consequently, we will use Negro rather than nonwhite.

106   *The Negro Family*

birth rate, has lower incomes and less desirable jobs, has a larger percent with two or more earners, has more unemployment, has more poor families, is more concentrated in large metropolitan areas, has a larger percent on welfare, has less and poorer education, and lives in more dilapidated and overcrowded housing. Figure 9 supports one of these characteristics: the extent of broken families is much higher in Negro

Figure 9. Percent of ever-married women 14 years old and over who were separated or divorced, by age and color, 1968*

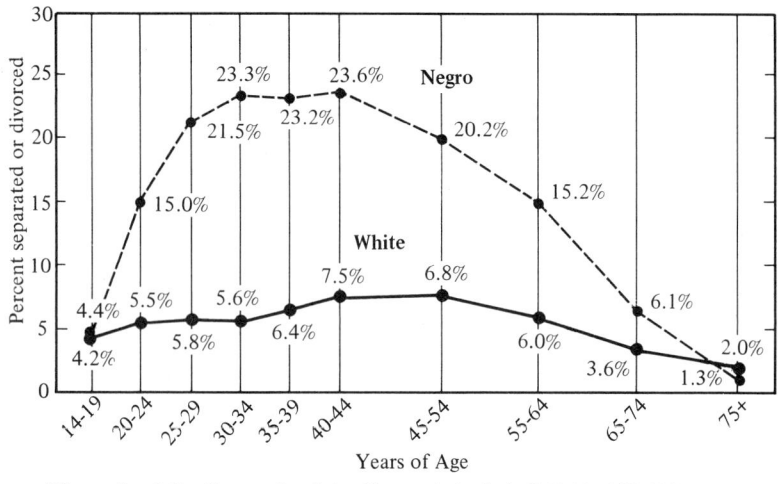

Current Population Reports, Population Characteristics, Series P-20, No. 187, 1969.

than white families. Figure 10 compares Negro and white families on four of these characteristics: female head, average size of the family, broken homes—separated, divorced, and widowed—and income. It shows that Negroes had a female head much more frequently than whites. Families with a female Negro head had the largest number of children, Negro husband-wife families were next, husband-wife white families were next, and those with a white female head were lowest. The percent of those with the marital status of separated, divorced, and widowed was highest for Negro women, next highest for white women, then Negro men, and lowest for white men. Finally, the figure shows that in 1968 the Negro median family income was $3,577 below the white family income.

The above is a correct picture and the one most generally emphasized. The picture, however, is not nearly as bleak as the above indicates. It is true that for some dimensions the problems increased more for Negroes than for whites. For other dimensions the ratio of change for Negroes and whites has been about the same. Finally, there are some

Figure 10. Characteristics of Negro and white families, 1968*

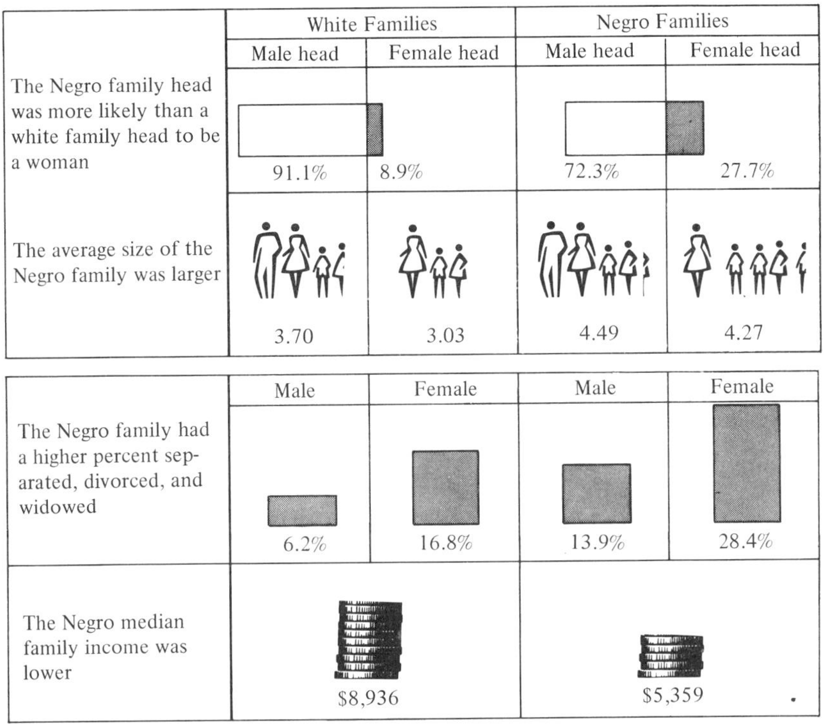

| | White Families || Negro Families ||
	Male head	Female head	Male head	Female head
The Negro family head was more likely than a white family head to be a woman	91.1%	8.9%	72.3%	27.7%
The average size of the Negro family was larger	3.70	3.03	4.49	4.27

	Male	Female	Male	Female
The Negro family had a higher percent separated, divorced, and widowed	6.2%	16.8%	13.9%	28.4%
The Negro median family income was lower	$8,936		$5,359	

*Statistical Abstract of the United States, 1969, p. 26; and Social and Economic Status of Negroes in the United States, Current Population Reports, Series P-23, No. 29, 1970, p. 15.

dimensions for which there is a greater improvement for Negroes than for whites.

Female Heads, Broken Homes, and Illegitimacy Consider problem aspects which have increased more among Negroes than among whites. Female family heads increased from 17.6 percent in 1950 to 27.3 percent in 1969; since 1950 the percent for whites has remained stable at around 9 percent.[5] The incidence of broken homes (separated and divorced) has remained virtually unchanged since 1950. Illegitimacy has been increasing for both Negroes and whites, the largest increase between 1960 and 1965. The percent illegitimate of all live births since 1940 is as follows:[6]

---

[5] Bureau of Labor Statistics and Bureau of the Census, *Social and Economic Status of Negroes in the United States, Current Population Reports*, Series P-23, No. 29, 1970, p. 70.
[6] *Ibid.*, p. 77.

	Negro	White
1940	16.8	2.0
1945	17.9	2.4
1950	18.0	1.8
1955	20.2	1.9
1960	21.6	2.3
1965	26.3	4.0
1967	29.4	4.9

However, the relative increase since 1960 has been much greater for whites than for Negroes.

Poverty Poverty, while still prevalent among Negro and white families, declined for both at about the same ratio between 1959 and 1968. The Census, using certain criteria to establish a poverty level, reports that in 1959 about 54 percent of all Negro families were below the poverty level, while in 1968 the percent was about 29; for whites in 1959 the percent was 16 and in 1968 it was about 8.[7]

A picture of poverty a century ago can be secured from a book written in 1881 by Haygood, President of Emory College. He reports that at that time most of the six million Negroes were very poor, depended for their subsistence on hand labor, and then goes on to say:

> But poor as they all are they are improving their conditions. The tax books show that they are beginning to produce a little more than they consume. They live better, dress better, have better furniture than they had ten years ago.[8]

Decreasing Differences Between Negro and White Families Now let us consider areas and situations in which the differences between Negro and white families have declined. The gap between Negro and white family income has narrowed. The percent of the Negro median family income as a percent of white family income remained stable at around 54 percent between 1950 and 1965; but in 1966 it increased to 58 percent, in 1967 it was 59 percent, and in 1968 it was 60 percent.[9] Negro families are moving in large numbers into the $8,000 or more income group. Thirty-two percent of Negro families in 1968 had incomes of $8,000 or more. Excluding the South, the percent was 43 which was more than three times the amount in 1960. In 1950 the percent of white families having incomes of $8,000 or more was over four times

---

[7] *Ibid.*, p. 22; and *Statistical Abstract of the United States*, 1969, p. 329.
[8] Atticus G. Haywood, *Our Brother in Black: His Freedom and His Future* (New York: Phillips and Hunt, 1881).
[9] *The Social and Economic Status of Negroes*, p. 15.

that of Negro families, but in 1968 it was about two times that of Negro families. In 1968 the median white income was $8,937; the median income of Negroes was $5,590.[10]

In the period 1960 to 1969 the percent of Negro workers in high-skill, high-status, and good-paying jobs, and jobs in manufacturing increased much more sharply than for white workers. In this period the percent increase in occupations for Negro and white workers was respectively as follows: professional and technical, 109 and 41; managers and proprietors, 43 and 12; clerical, 114 and 33; sales, 61 and 9; craftsmen and foremen, 70 and 17; farmers and farm workers declined by 56 percent for Negroes and by 31 percent for whites.[11]

The Negro unemployment rate in 1969 was the lowest since 1953. While the ratio of Negro to white unemployment has remained about 2 to 1, between 1960 and 1969 the Negro unemployment rate dropped by more percentage points than the white: for Negroes 10.2 to 6.5; and for whites 4.9 to 3.2.[12]

The gap between Negro and white adults in the number of school years completed has been almost closed. The major change was after 1960. Table 9 shows that the gap in educational attainment narrowed decidedly since 1960. The percent increase of those completing 4 years of high school or more was greater for Negro men and women than for white men and women. The percent increase of those completing 4 years of college or more was greater for Negro than white men, but it was greater for white than Negro women. The percent increase in the median years of education completed was greater for both Negro men and women than for white men and women. In fact, for those 25–29 years old, Negroes have essentially caught up to whites in the median years of education completed. This is shown, also, by a comparison of all Negroes and the total population (both whites and Negroes) for the age group 25–29. The number of years of school completed in 1960 and 1968 was 10.8 and 12.1 for Negroes; and 12.3 and 12.5 for the total population.[13] The great changes since 1960 makes it safe to predict that the educational gap will be eliminated in the immediate future.

Certain changes have occurred in the type of college or university in which Negroes are enrolled. Negro undergraduate enrollment in 76 predominantly white universities increased significantly between 1969 and 1970—from 1.9 to 2.7 percent of all students enrolled; in 71

---

[10] *Ibid.*, p. 17.
[11] *Ibid.*, p. 41. Of course, the number in each category in 1960 was small and a small increase in numbers might be a large increase in percents.
[12] *Statistical Abstract of the United States*, 1969, p. 213.
[13] *Ibid.*, p. 107.

110 The Negro Family

Table 9. Percent of Negroes and whites completing 4 or more years of high school and 4 or more years of college, 1960-1966, by sex*

	MALES		FEMALES	
	Negro	*White*	*Negro*	*White*
4 years of high school or more (25–29 years old)				
1960	36	63	41	65
1969	60	78	52	77
Percent increase	66.6	23.8	26.9	18.5
4 years of college or more (25–34 years old)				
1960	3.9	15.7	4.6	7.8
1969	7.6	20.2	5.6	12.3
Percent increase	95.0	28.7	21.7	57.7
Median years completed (25–29 years old)				
1960	10.5	12.4	11.1	12.3
1966	12.1	12.6	11.9	12.5
Percent increase	15.2	1.6	7.2	1.6

*Data from *Social and Economic Status of Negroes in the United States*, 1969, Current Population Reports, Series P-23, No. 29, 1970, pp. 51 and 52; and *Social and Economic Conditions of Negroes in the United States*, 1966, Current Population Reports, Series P-23, No. 24, 1967, p. 46.

graduate schools the increase was from 1.9 to 3.3 percent.[14] Moreover, of all Negroes enrolled in college those enrolled in predominantly Negro colleges declined from 51 percent in 1964 to 36 percent in 1968; thus the increase in Negro enrollment in other colleges increased from 49 percent in 1964 to 64 percent in 1968.[15]

Figure 11 shows the percent of Negroes and whites completing four or more years of high school and four or more years of college in 1950, 1964, and 1968. While there has been a great increase in the percent of Negroes completing high school, there has been but a slight increase in the percent completing four or more years of college. However, this is expected to change in the immediate future. Between 1964 and 1968 there was an 85 percent increase of Negroes enrolled in college, while for *all* those enrolled in college the increase was 46 percent.

[14] A report made by the National Association of State Universities and Land-Grant Colleges, published in the *Los Angeles Times*, April 13, 1970, Part 1, p. 3.
[15] *Social and Economic Status of Negroes*, p. 53.

Figure 11. Percent of those 25 to 29 years of age who completed four or more years of high school or four or more years of college, by race, 1950, 1964, and 1968*

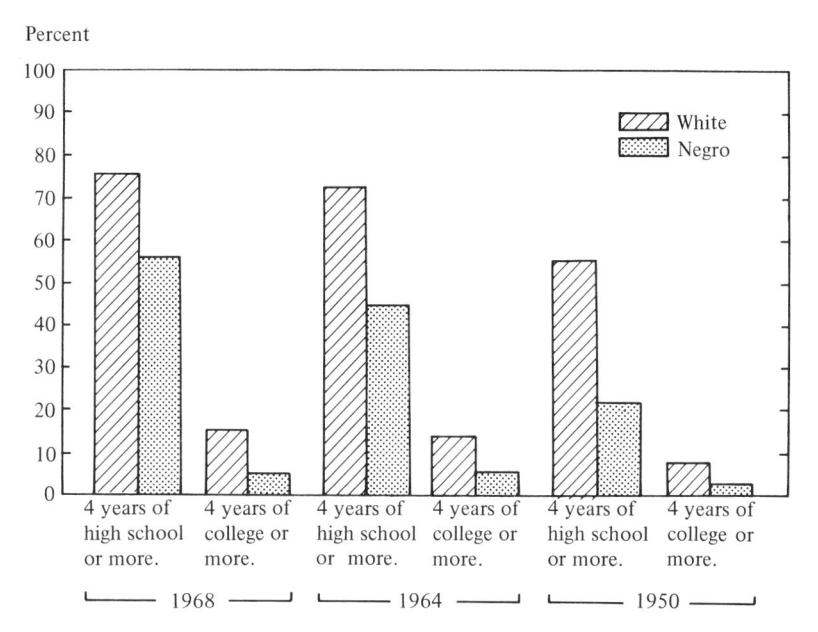

*Current Population Reports, Population Characteristics, Series P-20, No. 182, 1969.

Moreover, in the fall of 1968 Negroes constituted 6 percent of all students in college.

Another way of seeing the great increase among Negroes in years of school completed is to compare younger with older age groups. For Negro husband-wife families with the head under 45 and over 45 the respective medians were 11.5 and 7.9; for whites 12.5 and 10.9.[16]

On educational achievement, however, Negroes fall far below whites. Achievement, measured by national standardized tests on reading, mathematics, and other subjects in 1965 by grade level was as follows:

	TEST GRADE LEVEL	
Grade in school	Negro	White
Sixth	4.4	6.8
Ninth	7.8	9.9
Twelfth	9.2	12.7

[16] *Current Population Reports, Population Characteristics*, P-20, 173, 1968, p. 5.

112   The Negro Family

Thus in the 6th, 9th, and 12th year Negroes were substantially below the given grades in achievement and whites were above the test grade level.[17]

The gap between Negroes and whites on the quality of education is emphasized by a comparison of the two groups on the standardized achievement tests scores on verbal and nonverbal communications, reading, mathematics, and general information. Negroes in the first grade had very much less verbal and nonverbal communication ability than whites, and by the twelfth grade they had fallen even lower. This is seen in the following tabulation:

	GRADE 1		GRADE 12	
	Negroes	*Whites*	*Negroes*	*Whites*
Nonverbal	43.4	54.1	40.9	52.0
Verbal	45.4	53.2	40.9	52.1

The grade 12 gap would have been greater if those who had dropped out of school could have been included.

The following tabulation gives the scores secured by 12th grade children in reading, mathematics, and general information:

Subject	*Negroes*	*Whites*
Reading	42.2	51.9
Mathematics	41.8	51.8
General information	40.6	52.2
Five tests, average	41.1	52.0

It is no surprise that with their lower verbal and nonverbal communication Negroes in the 12th grade would have lower achievement scores than whites in reading, mathematics, and general information.

The very much lower verbal and nonverbal communication scores of Negro than white children in the first grade reflects a difference in the home backgrounds of the two groups. This continues to be a handicap to Negroes as they go through the grades and high school. The low scores of Negro 12th grade children in reading, mathematics, and general information may also reflect, in part, lower educational standards and facilities for Negroes than for whites.

[17] Data for the achievement tests from *Social and Economic Conditions of Negroes in the United States, 1966, Current Population Reports,* Series P-23, No. 24, 1967, p. 49; and from *Statistical Abstract of the United States,* 1969, p. 118.

Deutsch, in discussing the urban Negro child, indicates that one of the factors in the poor performance and deprived psychological state of the Negro child is his sensing that the larger society views him as inferior and expects inferior performance from him:

> It is highly unlikely that any one factor could account for the poor performance and deprived psychological state of the experimental group (Negroes); it is more realistic to see the urban Negro child as subject to many influences which converge on him, all contributing to the effects noted. Among these influences certainly not the least is his sensing that the larger society views him as inferior and expects inferior performance from him, as evidenced by the general denial to him of realistic vertical mobility possibilities. Under these conditions, it is understandable that the Negro child—the experimental group in the present study—would tend strongly to question his own competencies, and in so questioning would be acting largely as others expect him to act. This is an example of what Merton has called the "self-fulfilling prophecy"—the very expectation itself is a cause of its fulfillment. The middle-class orientation of the school helps little in recognizing the realities of the problem, and contributes little toward the development of value systems and activities directed toward breaking this circular dynamic process.[18]

Negro parents have a strong desire to have their children attain a good education. The interest of Negro parents in the education of their children has had a long history. This was observed as early as 1889 and was described as follows:

> The parents show a marked interest in the education of their children; they are anxious that the latter shall attend school, and always require them to do so, unless the children cannot be dispensed with about the house.[19]

Even though there is an intense interest in education, Negro children are in a situation of cultural deprivation, for Negro homes on the whole provide a situation in which their children cannot attain standardized levels of achievement. The educational achievements of the parents provide inadequate models of reading and other academic skills. Also the home situation may not be conducive to doing homework or may not encourage and supervise adequate school work. One important factor is that Negro homes are much more likely to be overcrowded than white homes. In 1960 there were three times as many Negro as white homes

---

[18] Martin Deutsch, "Minority Group and Class Status as Related to Social and Personality Factors in Scholastic Achievement," in M. M. Grossack (ed.), *Mental Health and Segregation* (New York: Springer, 1963), p. 65.
[19] Philip A. Bruce, *The Plantation Negro as a Freeman* (New York: G. P. Putnam's Sons, 1889), p. 7.

which were overcrowded (1.01 or more persons per room); the respective percents were 28 and 10.[20]

Differences Among Negro Families Many whites think of Negro society as homogeneous. Actually, physical, psychological, and social factors have operated to produce great differences. The Negroes brought as slaves from Africa were of different tribal and cultural stocks. Transplantation to the United States destroyed the African forms of social and family organization, and the differential treatment during slavery of the house servants and the plantation workers introduced new family patterns. Variations in mobility after emancipation resulted in further differentiation. More recently the urbanization of a growing number of Negroes and the growth of a middle and upper class has resulted in great differences within Negro society.

These great differences among Negro families should be kept in mind if we are to understand the family behavior of this ethnic group. National data on Negro families tend to submerge these differences.

Families differ by size and the evidence indicates that the larger the family income the larger the size of the family. The size of Negro families (1960–1961) with incomes of under $3,000, from $3,000 to $7,499, and $7,500 and over, was respectively, 2.4, 3.8, and 4.1.[21]

Negro families with men as the head are highest in middle and upper income levels and lowest in lower income levels. Keeping in mind that in 1969, 72.4 percent of all Negro families had men as the head, we find that for middle and upper income levels the percent with men as heads is only slightly lower than for white families—about 9 in 10 for Negroes and 9.6 in 10 for whites. For incomes under $3,000 the percent in 1969 was 44 and for the next income group, $3,000–$4,999, it was 64.[22]

Negro men (25 years and older) vary greatly in education. These differences are reflected in corresponding differences in median income: less than 8 years, $2,376; 8 years, $3,681; 1 to 3 years of high school, $4,278; 4 years of high school, $5,188; and some college, $5,928.[23]

Employment of Negroes differs by marital status. In 1967, 72.6 percent of all Negro families with relatives of the head present were husband-wife families.[24] Married men have much more stability of employment than single, divorced, or widowed men. Of every 100 Negro

---

[20] *Social and Economic Conditions of Negroes*, p. 57.
[21] *Ibid.*, p. 61.
[22] *Social and Economic Status of Negroes*, p. 73.
[23] *Social and Economic Conditions of Negroes*, p. 21.
[24] *Current Population Reports, Population Characteristics*, Series P-20, No. 173, 1968, p. 2.

married men in the labor force in 1967, 96 had a job.[25] Of Negro teenagers in the labor force in 1969, 1 out of 4 were unemployed as compared with 1 out of 10 white teenagers.[26]

Negroes differ by the region of the United States in which they live. In 1969, 52 percent of all Negroes lived in the South, and 19 percent of the total population was Negro.[27] Median family income in 1968 was lowest in the South, $4,278; next lowest in the Northeast, $6,460; and highest in the West and North Central, $7,506 and $6,910, respectively. These differences are also reflected in Negro income as a percent of white income: South, 54; Northeast, 69; West, 80; and North Central, 75.[28]

Jessie Bernard presents a rather convincing argument that the Negro world has two quite different cultures.[29] She calls one the acculturated and the other the externally adapted. She outlines the characteristics of those who are completely acculturated to the standards of the white world and the characteristics of the externally adapted who do not accept these norms but adapt to them. The acultured have internalized and accepted the values of white society. The moral standards of the dominant white group are their moral standards. The externally adapted may know the moral standards of white society but these are not their standards. They look at white culture from the outside and try to get along in it. The acultured strive to be respectable, to maintain stable family life, to conform to high standards of sexual behavior, to monogamous marriage, and to conventional behavior. The externally adapted have illegitimate births, women as head of the family, irregular sexual behavior, and are not interested in being respectable. Bernard indicates that these two cultural forms are found in all social classes and income groups, although the acultured are more prevalent in the upper-middle and upper class and the externally adapted more prevalent in the lower-middle and lower class. She outlines the great chasm between these two worlds as follows:

> The great chasm between the two Negro worlds is so great as to be for all intents and purposes all but unbridgeable, at least until now. Fear and hostility—even hatred and resentment—characterize relations, or lack of relations, between them. The cleavage reaches both ends of the income scale and crosses income-class lines in both cultures; nor is it mitigated by the ambivalence which often characterizes it.[30]

[25] *Social and Economic Conditions of Negroes*, p. 31.
[26] *Social and Economic Status of Negroes*, p. 30
[27] Ibid., pp. 3–4.
[28] *Ibid.*, p. 15.
[29] Jessie Bernard, *Marriage and Family Among Negroes* (Englewood Cliffs, New Jersey: Prentice-Hall, 1966).
[30] *Ibid.*, p. 58.

MOBILITY AND URBANIZATION

Mobility Upon emancipation, families that had attained a fair degree of stability maintained the routine of family living without much disturbance. Where loose attachments had characterized the marriage relationship during slavery, families broke up easily. Freedom often meant freedom of movement, particularly for Negro men. Men with loose familial attachments left their wives and families and wandered into strange communities. Their wives tended to form casual unions.

The migration following emancipation removed many Negroes from their primary-group attachments. By 1910 about one and two-thirds million Negroes had migrated from the state of their birth to other states, most of them going to cities.[31] Many of these migratory Negroes engaged in promiscuous sexual behavior and formed only casual marital and familial attachments.

World War I gave an additional push to migration. The depression also stimulated a considerable movement of individual Negroes and Negro family groups. In World War II large numbers of Negroes under the impact of wartime economic conditions moved to cities and defense-plant areas.

Negroes continued to be mobile in the years after World War II.[32] For example, in 1968, 21.8 percent of Negroes lived in a different house than a year earlier. Another example is that in the ten years between 1950 and 1960 about 1.5 million Negroes left the South. While all Southern states had a net migration loss of Negroes, some had extremely large losses: Mississippi had a net migration loss of 323,000; Alabama, South Carolina, North Carolina, and Georgia had net migration losses of between 204,000 and 224,000; and Arkansas, Louisiana, Virginia, and Tennessee had losses almost as great. California and New York had the largest net migration increase of Negroes: 354,000 and 282,000 respectively; and Illinois, Ohio, Michigan, New Jersey, and Florida had increases of between 101,000 and 189,000. Between 1940 and 1966 there was a net of 3.7 million Negroes who left the South for other regions.

Negroes tend to move to large industrial centers, mostly in the North. The extent to which they move to such industrial centers can be seen by a comparison of the Negro population in certain cities in 1940 and 1960:

[31] United States Bureau of the Census, *Negro Population in the United States, 1790–1915*, 1918, pp. 72–73.

[32] Data for recent Negro migration from *United States Census of Population, 1960, United States Summary*, 1, Tables 56 and 63. See also, *Social and Economic Conditions of Negroes in the United States;* and *Statistical Abstract of the United States*, 1969, p. 33.

	1940	1960
New York	458,444	1,143,952
Chicago	277,731	837,895
Philadelphia	250,880	534,671
Washington	187,266	418,648
Baltimore	165,843	329,597
Detroit	149,119	487,682
Cleveland	84,504	253,179
Los Angeles	63,774	416,475

The tendency of Negroes to move to industrial centers is evident also in the South. Virtually the only Southern cities to experience a growth in the proportion of the population which is Negro are industrial cities like Richmond, Atlanta, Nashville, and Houston.

For those Negroes who had lived in the rural South, migration has meant substituting a new way of urban living for the old rural way of life. It has meant moving into crowded areas, where unskilled jobs are scarce. A partial picture of the degree to which Negroes are crowded into cities is secured by a comparison of Negroes and whites in metropolitan and nonmetropolitan areas in 1950, 1960, and 1969. Table 10 shows that a higher percent of Negroes than whites lived in metropolitan areas in 1969, 70 and 64 respectively.

Table 10. Percent distribution of Negroes and whites by metropolitan and nonmetropolitan areas, 1950, 1960, and 1969*

	NEGRO			WHITE		
	1950	1960	1969	1950	1960	1969
Metropolitan areas	56	65	70	60	63	64
Central cities	43	52	55	34	30	26
Urban fringe	13	13	15	26	33	38
Smaller cities, towns, and rural	44	35	30	40	37	36

*Data from *Social and Economic Status of Negroes in the United States, Current Population Reports*, Series P-23, No. 29, 1970, p. 7.

It also shows that while the percent of Negroes in the urban fringe has remained fairly stable, the percent in central cities has increased dramatically. Whites have been moving out of central cities to suburbs and other nonmetropolitan areas. Small cities, towns, and rural areas lost more Negroes than whites between 1950 and 1969; 44 to 30 percent for Negroes, and 40 to 36 percent for whites. Figure 12 shows that in 1969, 55 percent of Negroes to 26 percent of whites lived in central

118   *The Negro Family*

cities; that 38 percent of whites to only 15 percent of Negroes lived in metropolitan rings, or suburbs; and that a slightly higher percent of whites than Negroes lived in nonmetropolitan areas.

Figure 12. Percent of whites and Negroes residing in central cities, metropolitan rings, and nonmetropolitan areas, 1969*

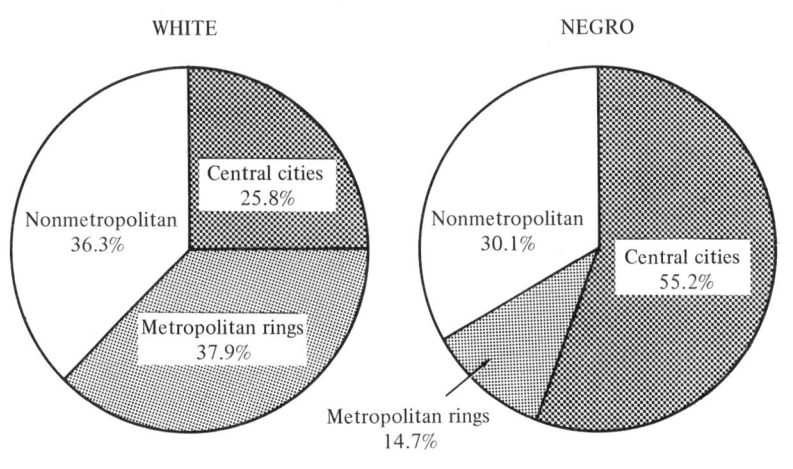

WHITE

- Central cities 25.8%
- Nonmetropolitan 36.3%
- Metropolitan rings 37.9%

NEGRO

- Nonmetropolitan 30.1%
- Central cities 55.2%
- Metropolitan rings 14.7%

*Current Population Reports, Population Characteristics, Series P-20, No. 197, 1970.

The Bureau of the Census collects data on the percent of the population which, on a given date, lives in a different house than the house they lived in a year earlier.[33] Negroes have been found to be much more mobile than whites. Negroes in urban areas and in rural-farm areas have the greatest mobility, with rural-nonfarm being slightly lower.

Three decades ago Frazier pointed out that ideational mobility was beginning to penetrate even the most rural Negro communities:

> Concrete highways are beginning to penetrate the most remote parts of the South. Along these avenues of communication new ideas as well as new means of transportation are finding their way into these twilight zones of civilization. By means of these highways an old automobile brings a modern city as close as a town was before. A trip to the cinema in the city opens up an undreamed world of romance and adventure. Better schools are bringing in better-educated teachers to give new ideas to the younger generation. . . . The effect of these various changes has been to destroy the simple folkways and mores and to create confusion in thought and contradictions in behavior.[34]

[33] *Current Population Reports, Population Characteristics*, Series P-20, No. 113, 1962.

[34] E. Franklin Frazier, *The Negro Family in the United States* (Chicago: University of Chicago Press, 1939), p. 112. Gunnar Myrdal (in *An American Dilemma*) in 1944 and Hylan Lewis (in "The Changing Negro Family," in *The Nation's Children*; Eli Ginzberg, ed.) in 1960 held that E. Franklin Frazier's *The Negro Family in the United States* is an accurate description and analysis.

Ideational mobility among Negroes has increased. The first result of the contact of Negroes with modern means of communication may have been demoralizing and disruptive of family controls. In the long run, however, it prepared the way for reorganization of attitudes and behavior into new forms of family relations.

Urbanization Thousands of Negroes are now city born and reared, but many other thousands are relatively new migrants from rural areas. Table 11 shows that, although the proportion of the population which is Negro has remained fairly constant, the proportion of the urban population which is Negro has increased decade by decade.

Table 11. Percent Negro of the total population and population of urban, rural-nonfarm, and rural-farm, 1920-1960*

Year	Total population	Urban	Rural-nonfarm	Rural-farm
1920	9.9	6.6	9.0	16.3
1930	9.7	7.5	8.5	15.5
1940	9.8	8.4	7.8	14.9
1950[a]	10.0	9.7	8.0	13.7
1960[a]	10.5	11.0	9.4	

[a]1950 definition of urban.
*Sixteenth Census of the United States, 1940, Characteristics of the Population, 2, Part I, pp. 19–20; 1950 from United States Census of Population, 1950, General Characteristics, Series P-B1, United States Summary, Table 36, p. 88; and 1960 from United States Census of Population, 1960, United States Summary, 1, Table 44.

The migration of Negroes to cities is shown by the increased percent of all Negroes living in cities. In 1960 as compared with 1950 the respective percents were 72.4 and 61.7. For whites the respective percents of the population living in cities were 69.5 and 64.3. Another index of the extent to which Negroes reside in urban areas is the fact that between 1950 and 1960 there was an 8.8 percent decline of Negroes in rural areas and a 49.3 percent increase of Negroes in urban areas.[35] Thus there was some migration from farms to urban areas. The natural increase in the Negro population accounts for the rest of the great increase of Negroes in urban areas.

Disorganization of the Negro Family The disorganization of the Negro family as a result of mobility and urbanization is summarized in Table 12. It shows that the Negro family in 1968 had a much higher rate of disorganization than the white family. Separation and divorce are in-

[35] United States Census of Population, 1960, United States Summary, 1, p. 143.

dexes of family disorganization and, together with widowhood, can be used as an index of family disintegration. The table indicates that 14.2 percent of Negro husbands and 28.4 percent of wives were separated, widowed, or divorced; for whites these percents were respectively 6.2 and 16.5.

Table 12. Marital status by race and sex of those 14 years of age and older, by percent, 1968*

	MALES		FEMALES	
Marital Status	White	Negro	White	Negro
Single	26.4	34.9	21.1	26.8
Married (spouse present)	66.8	49.3	60.9	42.5
Separated	0.9	6.3	1.4	9.4
Widowed	3.0	4.8	12.3	14.5
Divorced	2.3	3.1	2.8	4.5

*Statistical Abstract of the United States, 1969, p. 26.

If dissatisfaction with the marriage is used as an index of disorganization, it appears that Negroes are much more disorganized than whites. In a probability sample of 4,452 households in Alameda County, California, Negroes had much higher rates of dissatisfaction than whites. For men, however, dissatisfaction decreased as income increased. For women neither increased income nor increased education reduced dissatisfaction and this was especially true for young Negro women.[36]

The following are excerpts from an account of Negro family behavior in a metropolitan community. This case was secured in a tape-recorded interview with a middle-aged woman engaged in domestic service but with strong aspirations for upward mobility. She placed a high value on education as a means of attaining this higher status and was taking night courses. She had highly negative attitudes toward some forms of Negro behavior.

> My father and mother lived together during the time I was growing up and then they separated. There didn't seem to be much affection between them. My father did not work regularly. He didn't want to work, but wanted to earn a living by doing things that were not in line with the law—peddling moonshine. After he got into trouble with the law, they moved East and then a few years later they separated. I'm from a broken home. I had more affection for my mother than for my father. He has passed on now, but my mother is still living. She is 68 and I'm 48.

[36] Karen S. Renne, "Correlates of Dissatisfaction in Marriage," *Journal of Marriage and the Family*, 23 (1970), pp. 54–67.

I was married 12 years ago and we lived together about 6 years. I liked being married, but I discovered that the man I had didn't make a proper living. He drank too much. An awful lot of Negro men drink up their wages. The majority of Negro women want a nice home, comfortable living, and children, particularly when they are young. I was reaching for a better education by going to night school, but he was content to stay at his own level. He didn't drink so much when we were first married, but then began to drink more and more. He didn't play around with women very much. That wasn't the main reason for our separation; we just didn't agree.

I think a lot of the younger people who do not have an education pick up a lot of ignorance, loose morals, drinking, and being content with where they are from their parents. The ones whose parents are educated do not seem to have these things of the lower class.

My father was educated, but my mother was kind of refined. She did not have very much education, but she believed in education. Maybe I got my strong interest in education from her. I have two brothers and two sisters. One brother has had four years of college education, and has a trade. My other brother drank to excess. One sister works in a restaurant. The other one is just drifting. Her husband drinks and she drinks with him, so they go together. She never rose above that and he didn't either.

I find that in lower-type areas there are quite a few mothers and children without the father being there. They seem to be on the county. The county is supporting them and once in a while they get another child and the county still supports them. I think there is about one out of every five families of this type. That type of behavior I don't understand.

I live in a neighborhood which is not good and is not bad. The reason I live there is that the rent is cheap. Although I don't approve of things that go on in the neighborhood, there are some good families that live there. Right across the street from me is an educated family and the husband is a salesman in an automobile agency in a good business area.

How would my life differ from my mother's life? Well, my mother didn't have an opportunity for education like I have had. I have lived in California since I was 20. I lived in a city in Georgia before that. Here we have beautiful schools. We don't have to pay to go to school. In my mother's day they didn't have schools for Negro children. And I think there is no excuse not to get an education, regardless of race, color, or creed.

The following life-history document, part of which is in the introduction to this chapter, shows the disorganization connected with her mother's second marriage. It shows the reaction of her father, his second wife, and his extended family toward any attempt on the part of this woman, her brother, and her sister to communicate with and help their natural mother:

> She has married and has had eight children since we went to live with

our father. Her husband left her after the last child, who is four, was born. She has been having a most difficult time, before and after her desertion. The three of us have been in intermittent communication with her. My brother saw them when he was traveling through in the Air Force about three years ago. My sister went home to visit two years ago. She told me how bad off my mother is and how she is doing everything for her children, as punishment for having let us go into foster care. The oldest child is 15 and is a boy. She has no control over him or the other ones under him. She does all the cooking, cleaning, ironing, washing, and etc. for those children. She is very sickly and has had two operations in the last year. Whenever we can we send her money and gifts for the children's birthdays and graduation. We are now trying to convince her to come out here with her family. If she came here we would be able to help her more maybe not so much in terms of money as in help with the children. She feels that she could not ask us for this help. She told us that we had responsibilities of our own and we all know that she would feel it was really presumptuous of her to ask our aid after what she did to us.

However, we feel that a parent's only responsibility to their child is to do whatever they consider is best for that child.

Now that we are older we see no reason to hold a grudge against either of them. We also managed to acquire a sense of decency and cannot honestly watch close relatives suffer. Mother's children are our sisters and brothers and the welfare allowance that mother receives for her eight children is barely keeping them from starving. In addition to that, she sacrifices her own needs to try and get things for the children that they want rather than need. We try to get graduation clothes for the kids, but when we cannot or mother does not want to ask she gets such things and skimps on the food or whatever. It is impossible to believe but both my sister and brother report that she has managed to spoil eight children rotten on welfare.

Our attitude disturbs our father somewhat. Our stepmother is very upset about it and my father's family is very, very indignant about it. They scream and fuss and argue with us incessantly. We have never paid them much attention in the past and we don't now. I have tried to explain our attitude but they are in another world. I think that they never liked her from the beginning and feel we betray them by being so concerned. Our stepmother is hurt because she feels we love our natural mother, who did nothing essentially for us, more than her who did so much for so long. It is not a matter of whom we love, it is a matter of who needs us the most. I am sure that if we are able to persuade her to come out there will be increased animosity but we have never been close to our extended family. When daddy needed help with us, all they had were complaints about how we were being raised and how smart lipped we were. The three of us believed only in reality and not good intentions or advice. We did not and do not like phonies and we have never been concerned about pleasing other people at the expense of ourselves or our immediate family. Our father knows this about us and has accepted our decision to try and get our mother out here. I think he is more concerned about how the rest of the family will react to it.

Daddy has always been more concerned about how our extended family feels because he thinks it is a gauge as to how well he raised us. He feels everything we did or do, every mistake we made or make, is his fault for not having gotten us before, or not having done more for us.

FORMS OF FAMILY ORGANIZATION

An analysis of the Negro family shows convincingly that particular forms of marriage and family behavior depend on and arise out of particular social situations. Inasmuch as the Negro has been faced by a variety of social situations, the forms of family organization vary. Such types as the matricentric family, the small-patriarchal family, and the equalitarian family are found in the Negro population.

Matricentric Family Historically the Negro family of the United States has been matricentric. Under slavery the mother remained the important figure in the family. The affectional relations of mother and child developed deep and permanent attachments. If the father was a member of the family group, his relationship was often casual and easily broken. The mother developed the role of mistress of the cabin. The slave mother and her younger children were treated as a group. The wife, relatively free and independent from her husband, developed a keen sense of personal rights. Usually the prospective son-in-law had to get her consent before marriage. This importance of the mother's role in the family during slavery in part accounts for the dominant position of the mother and the presence of the matricentric family form in lower-class and some middle-class families today.

The economic independence of Negro women tends to encourage two family forms: the matricentric in the lower and lower-middle classes and the equalitarian among the upper-middle and the upper classes. Economic independence can be measured by the percent working or seeking work. The 1960 census shows a larger percent of white than Negro men in the labor force (those employed or those seeking work) and a larger percent of Negro than white women. The percent of white and Negro men in the labor force was, respectively, 78.0 and 72.1; for white and Negro women, 33.6 and 41.8.[37]

Small-Patriarchal Family In the small-patriarchal family the husband assumes the role of economic provider and exercises the chief authority.

[37] *United States Census of Population, 1960, United States Summary*, 1, Table 83.

This type of family is found particularly in the middle class. The development of the small-patriarchal family form was directly determined by social and economic conditions. Before emancipation, house servants had assimilated the small-patriarchal form of the white family, along with other white patterns of behavior. Consequently, some Negro fathers had acquired a strong interest in their families. Moreover, some of the nearly half-million Negroes who were free before the Civil War had acquired a proprietary interest in their wives and children by purchase from their owners. The legal status of these wives and children was that of slaves of the husband and father. Some of the Negro owners did not liberate their wives and children immediately, for ownership meant authority over the family; and the penalty of disobedience was the danger of being sold by the husband or father into a more undesirable situation.

The emergence of the small-patriarchal family was also related to the post Civil War economic situation. Plantations were run on Negro contract labor or by tenant farmers. As a rule, contracts were made with Negro men, who insisted that their families be included in the arrangement to work in the fields; the father was held responsible for the behavior of the members of his family and got credit for their work.

Thus the assimilation of the white small-patriarchal family pattern during slavery, the ownership of wife and children by some free Negroes, and the economic arrangements of the Reconstruction period were factors in the development of this family form among Negroes.

The Equalitarian Family The family pattern which stresses equal status of the husband and wife has had two bases among Negroes. One of these, mentioned above, is the economic independence of Negro married women. When the wife contributes her share to the family income, she tends to have an increased voice in family affairs. The second influence making for the rise of the equalitarian family is the tendency for the upper-middle and upper-class families to adopt the new patterns of family relationships of white society. When both husband and wife have a college education or when both are prepared for a business or professional career, husband-wife relations develop on the basis of common interests, congeniality, and mutual respect for the individuality of the other.

Thus different situations are associated with the development of different Negro family forms: the matricentric family, the small-patriarchal family, and the equalitarian family. Despite these variations, the tendency in family organization is toward the type of family predominant among the native-white population of this country.

SUMMARY

Many social changes and different situations were experienced by Negroes during slavery and in the transition to the modern world. In the last few years female family heads and illegitimacy have increased proportionately more in Negro families than in white. The gap has been closing between Negro and white families in income, employment in high-skill, high-status, and good-paying jobs, and in years of schooling. Great differences exist among Negro families in size, men as family heads, education, marital status, age and employment, and regions in which they reside. Millions of Negro families have migrated to cities, particularly in the North and West. Historically the mother has had power and authority, but this is changing, particularly in middle- and upper-income families. Small-patriarchal and equalitarian families have been increasing.

PROBLEMS FOR RESEARCH

Further and continuous research on the Negro family is needed, especially in view of the dramatic changes in the social status of Negroes, their higher educational attainment, their improved economic opportunities, and their increased political power. Little systematic research is being done on the Negro family today, although this group provides a particularly interesting opportunity to study the family under conditions of rapid social changes.

Desegregation and the Negro Family The trend toward desegregation of schools and housing raises many significant questions. What kinds of families are most likely to move into an area of predominantly or completely white housing? To what extent are such moves made by the nuclear families or do such moves involve extended-family members? What are the effects on Negro children when their families make such moves? What kinds of families are likely to be among the first to send their children to schools that have been desegregated under federal order, as in the deep South? What are the effects on white children of attending a school with a substantial proportion of Negro students? Do white students become more or less prejudiced under such conditions? What happens to social life and cross-sex relationships in such schools?

Housing Conditions and Family Life In almost all cities a large proportion of Negro families live in areas of great population density and with relatively poor housing conditions. As the Negro population of an area increases, the population density also increases. This was shown for the Watts area of Los Angeles by census figures computed by the Welfare Planning Council of Los Angeles. The respective percents of Negroes in the total population of the Watts area in 1940, 1950, and 1960 were 30, 71, and 86. The density of population (based on thousands of persons per square mile) in the Watts area in 1940, 1950, and 1960 was respectively 7.3, 12.5, and 13.7, while for Los Angeles city the density was 3.3, 4.3, and 5.5.

Very crowded living conditions may have certain effects on the personalities of children, especially in producing an inability to function satisfactorily in an independent manner and destroying ideals and illusions which may act as important motivating factors. What influence does the crowded housing of Negro areas have on the children? Do these children know about many facets of adult life at an earlier age than children living under less crowded conditions? If there are differences, what effect does this have on the total personality of the children?

Extended Nuclear Families In the past, particularly in the rural South, kinship relationships with the extended family frequently have been very important for the individual Negro both economically and personally. To what extent does this emphasis on extended-family relationships survive in urban areas? The statement has been made that when Negroes migrate to an urban area, certain members of the extended family move first, establish themselves, and then gradually other members of their extended family move to the same area. Research might establish whether this is a typical pattern of the migrant and then compare the interaction with relatives of present-day migrants with that of families which migrated a generation or more ago. Such research would not only give specific information about the Negro family, but also would add to our understanding about the influence of urban conditions on extended-family relationships.

Social Stratification, Marriage, and Family Behavior Studies have already been made indicating the differences by social class in sexual and marital behavior and in parent-child relations. At present Negroes as compared with whites have a large proportion of families of the lower class and a very small upper class. An interesting problem for research would be a comparison of the sex mores, patterns of family behavior, and parent-child interaction between Negroes and whites of corresponding social classes. This would give an answer to the question of whether differences between the classes within both Negro and white society are effective in determining sexual and family behavior. By keeping the class factor constant, it would also be possible to test the hypothesis that changes in codes of behavior in the Negro group lag behind those of whites.

Racial Intermarriage A thorough and systematic study of racial intermarriage should include unions not only between Negroes and whites but between people of other races in order to determine the factors which are general in all racial intermarriage as well as those which are specific between any two races. Especially interesting would be a comparison of racial intermarriage in Brazil and Hawaii, where there is less social discrimination, with racial intermarriage in continental United States, with its racial prejudice. Significant studies of intermarriages should be made to determine the nature and the results of these unions: circumstances of meeting, similarity of social class, marital happiness, parent-child relationships, and problems of adjustment to each other and to the community.

QUESTIONS AND EXERCISES

1. What is the probable explanation of the fact that Negroes in the United States have lost almost all their African heritage?
2. Which differences between Negro and white families have been increasing and which decreasing in recent years?
3. What general conclusions can be made about the movement of Negroes to urban centers?
4. What are the different and similar effects on rural Negro families and on rural white families of moving to the same type of urban area?
5. For each of the forms of the Negro family, indicate (1) where it is most prevalent and (2) how it came to develop.
6. How do you account for the large families among low-income rural Negroes and the small families of upper-class Negroes? How does this difference in number of children affect the individuality of a child?
7. Make a study of the size of the Negro family by states and regions from census data on size of families.

BIBLIOGRAPHY

Bernard, Jessie. *Marriage and Family Among Negroes.* Englewood Cliffs, New Jersey: Prentice-Hall, 1966.
    Emphasizes differences among Negro families in the degree to which they accept and internalize white norms. Discusses illegitimacy and the absence of husbands and fathers. Considers courtship, mate selection, and the socialization of Negro children.

Bureau of Labor Statistics and Bureau of the Census. *Social and Economic Status of Negroes in the United States, Current Population Reports*. Series P-23, No. 29, 1970.
> Excellent summary of statistical information on Negroes and Negro families: their distribution, income, employment, education, housing, living conditions and health, the family, military service, voting, and conditions in low-income areas.

Davis, John P. (ed.). *The American Negro Reference Book*. Englewood Cliffs, New Jersey: Prentice-Hall, 1966.
> This is an excellent collection of articles written for this book by experts on various phases of Negro behavior. "The Urban Negro Family" by Douglass is of special interest to students of the family.

Edwards, G. Franklin. *The Negro Professional Class*. New York: The Free Press of Glencoe, 1959.
> Based on a study of the origins of 300 Negro physicians, dentists, lawyers, and college teachers in Washington, D.C. Data secured on the occupational status of their fathers, grandfathers, and brothers show that about 60 percent of the fathers were in white-collar jobs, and about 33 percent were professional men.

Elkins, Stanley M. *Slavery: A Problem in American Institutional and Intellectual Life*. Chicago: University of Chicago Press, 1959.
> Compares slavery in North America with slavery in Spanish and Portuguese colonies of Latin America. Treats the relation of the Church to the development of slavery; personality development of slaves; the availability of different roles; and the differences between American and British intellectuals in the abolition movement.

Frazier, E. Franklin. *The Negro in the United States*. New York: Macmillan, 1957, particularly Ch. 4, 6, 9, 10, 13, and 24.
> Discusses Negro families at the time of the Civil War, the growth and distribution of the Negro population, a history of the Negro family from slavery to the present, and family disorganization.

Ginzberg, Eli. *The Middle Class Negro in the White Man's World*. New York: Columbia University Press, 1967.
> Reports an intensive interview study of 120 Negro young men, college-bound high school seniors or college students in Northern and Southern urban schools. Students were of middle-class families very much aware of differences between their opportunities and those of their parents. Race did not appear as a crucial factor in determining either their career aspirations and plans or their intentions regarding marriage and family. They anticipated marriages with equal status mates in which companionship would be an important factor.

Jones, Lewis W. "The New World View of Negro Youth," in *Problems of Youth: Transition to Adulthood in a Changing World*, eds. Muzafer Sherif and Carolyn W. Sherif. Chicago: Aldine, 1965, Ch. 4.

Describes the disadvantages of Negro Youth in American society and classifies young Negro orientations to their disadvantaged position: accommodaters, transcenders, social activists, apartheids, and black worlders.

Lewis, Hylan. *Blackways of Kent.* Chapel Hill: University of North Carolina Press, 1955.
A study, under the direction of John Gillin, of Negroes in a small town in the Piedmont area, showing that the Negro subculture was basically similar to the dominant white culture. Describes the inner feelings of Negroes in the community.

Rainwater, Lee. "Crucible of Identity: The Negro Lower-Class Family," *The Psychosocial Interior of the Family,* ed. Gerald Handel. Chicago: Aldine, 1967, Ch. 18.
A description and analysis of slum Negro family patterns including premarital sexual relations, premarital pregnancies, attitudes toward marriage, husband-wife relations, family break-up, and mothers as heads of families.

Rohrer, John H.; and Edmonson, Munro S. (eds.). *The Eighth Generation: Cultures and Personality of New Orleans Negroes.* New York: Harper & Brothers, 1960.
A follow-up of the study by Allison Davis and John Dollard reported in *Children of Bondage* in 1940. Findings based on interviews with 47 of the original cases show no racial stereotypes in the training of Negro children and a great variety of personality patterns. Culturally determined primary role identification seen as significant for personality development.

Chapter 6
The Family in the Soviet Union

The Russian revolution of 1917 eventuated in major changes in the Russian family. At first laws and proposals on marriage and divorce were designed primarily to free persons from restrictions. Then prerequisites to marriage were reinstated and severe legal restrictions on divorce were enacted. This continued up to 1965, at which time some of the restrictions on divorce were withdrawn. Like other Western European countries, the Soviet Union has experienced a decline in family size, a declining birth rate, the emancipation of women, and the enlargement of social services in health and welfare.

THE DISINTEGRATION OF AN EXTENDED FAMILY

The Russian family was in a process of change long before the Revolution of 1917. The peasant family of a hundred years ago was of the extended form, typically patriarchal, with the husband and father as the head and with his wife, unmarried sons and daughters, married sons, and their wives and children living in the same household. On the death of the head the oldest son or sometimes the widow succeeded to his authority. Certain factors making for the disintegration of the extended family are clearly evident in the following description of the breakup of one such family, as given by Kravchīnskii in 1888.

> The Gorshkovs were one of the richest and largest families in Slepoe Litvinovo. Up to the present moment they have always lived under the same roof. There was deep-seated internal discord in the family, which was only held together partly by the skill of the clever and robust old grandmother, whom all were accustomed to obey, and especially by the unwillingness of each one "to be the first to begin the row."

130

This discord was of ancient date. It had been worming itself gradually into the heart of the family almost ever since the time when the necessity for earning something extra first became manifest. One of the brothers went to St. Petersburg during the winter months as a cabman, while another engaged himself as a forester; but the inequality of their earnings had disturbed the economical harmony of the household. In five months the cabman sent one hundred rubles home to the family, while the forester had earned only twenty-five rubles. Now the question was, why should he [the forester] consume with such avidity the tea and sugar dearly purchased with the cabman's money? And in general: Why should this tea be absorbed with such greediness by all the numerous members of the household? True, his [the cabman's] children were fed in the family while he was in town; in the summer he was, however, at home, and worked upon their common land with the rest. His children had a right to their bread. The only thing which made him tolerate his dependency was that the horse and the carriage, which he drove when in town, had been purchased out of the common funds.

The next brother [the forester] also began to ponder and to calculate as to how much of his money was "engrossed" by the eldest brother and his children. A dress for Paranka had been purchased from a peddler with his money. Now, Paranka was the eldest brother's daughter, and able to earn fifty rubles at work which she appropriated to her own private uses. The forester was very vexed and irritated about the dress bought of the peddler. As the grandmother took Paranka's side in the dispute, Alexis, [the forester] took his next month's salary to the public house and spent it all in drink.

The notions as to "mine" and "yours" which disturbed these people's peace of mind were felt in every trifle—in every lump of sugar, cup of tea, or cotton handkerchief. Nicolas [the cabman] looked at Alexis, thinking, "You are eating of that which is mine," conscious, all the while, that at times he too had eaten of something belonging to his younger brothers.

It so happened that the first to rebel was Paranka. She took it into her head that she could not do without a regular woolen townmade dress. All the men resisted this whim for about eighteen months with resolute energy. It was proved to them by the grandmother and the other women, as well as by Paranka herself, that no less than a hundred of Paranka's rubles had been spent upon the family. Finally, the grandmother herself began to wail, and then the men gave way, and it was resolved that a dress should be made.

The next after Paranka to squabble was Nicolas, the cabman. He began to urge that he had long since redeemed the carriage and the horse; but the first to break away from the family was Alexis, the forester, probably because he felt more sincerely and oftener than the others did the burden of being indebted to others. To screw up his courage to break with his family he gave himself up to reckless drinking; he squandered seventy rubles—that is, a whole year's salary—at the public-house, and drank himself mad. . . . In a sober state he would never have had the heart to take his children from the paternal roof-tree, to lead away the cow and the horse.[1]

The chief factor making for the disintegration of the Gorshkov family was the opportunity for its members to earn money by working in the city or in an occupation like forestry outside the village economy. Such openings away from home arose with the urban industrial expansion which followed the emancipation of the serfs in 1861.

THE PREREVOLUTIONARY FAMILY

A description of the family in the Czarist period, both before and after the emancipation of the serfs in 1861, is a necessary background for an understanding of the changes brought about by the Revolution.

Before Emancipation   Before 1861 Russian peasants were serfs bound to the land, which they worked for the lord of the estate. He had complete power over their lives. While marriages were customarily arranged by parents, the lord of an estate, if he wished, could dictate the choice of marriage partners, and, if a man became too difficult, he could always be sent to the army.

The prevalent family system was that of the extended family of three generations living in one household, with authority in the hands of the head of the house and with wife, children, and other relatives subordinate. The son's wives were under the rule of the mother-in-law. The wife's prime duty was "submission to her husband's will," which in no way discharged her from her duty to her parents.[2]

The Domestic Ordinance, which had been drawn up about the middle of the sixteenth century by Pope Sylvester, one of Czar Ivan the Terrible's immediate entourage, defined the proper treatment by the husband of the disobedient and inattentive wife:

> But if a wife refuses to obey, and does not attend to what her husband tells her, it is advisable to beat her with a whip, according to the measure of her guilt; but not in the presence of others, rather alone. Do not strike her straight in the face or on the ear, be careful how you strike her with your fist in the region of the heart, and do not use a rod of wood or iron. . . . Keep to a whip, and choose carefully where to strike: a whip is painful and effective, deterrent and salutary.[3]

---

[1] Adapted from quotation from Uspensky in S. M. Kravchīnskii [Stepniak], *The Russian Peasantry* (New York: Harper & Brothers, 1888), p. 171 ff.
[2] Fannina W. Halle, *Women in the Soviet East* (New York: E. P. Dutton; London: Martin Secker and Warburg, 1938). p. 127.
[3] Quoted in *ibid.*, p. xv.

The bride's father gave the husband a "new whip" before the wedding, symbolizing the authority of the husband. It often was hung over the bridal bed, and was to be used exclusively on the wife.[4] This ancient code persisted into the prerevolutionary period.

In the cities, particularly among the aristocracy and to a lesser degree among the merchant class, family life and the status of women were influenced by contacts with the Western world initiated by Peter the Great at the beginning of the eighteenth century; parents, for example, were forbidden to force a daughter to marry. Many of these changes were superficial, and people easily reverted to traditional practices. Frequently the changes disorganized old family relationships before new customs became firmly established.

Period 1861–1917 After the emancipation of the peasants in 1861, land was sold to them at such high prices that most of them had to continue working on the estates of the landed aristocracy. What land the peasants did own was held in common and allotted for use according to custom by the village *mir*, a communal institution which took charge of the economic and political affairs of the village. After the revolution of 1904–1905, the *mir* received its death-blow by laws which enabled the peasants to own land individually. In 1888 Kravchïnskii gave a picture of the developing spirit of individualism and equality which struck at the domestic despotism of the large family:

> A very important and thorough-going change has taken place in the family relations of the great Russian rural population. The children, as soon as they are grown up and have married, will no longer submit to the bolshak's[5] whimsical rule. They rebel, and, if imposed upon, separate and found new households, where they become masters of their own actions. These separations have grown so frequent that the number of independent households in the period from 1858–1861 [to 1888] increased from thirty-two percent to seventy-one percent of the whole provincial population.[6]

The industrial development of Russia received impetus when many of the landed aristocracy, instead of investing the funds received as compensation for the transfer of land to the liberated serfs in agricultural development as had been expected, placed them in manufacturing enterprises in the cities. Peasants who found it difficult to subsist in the country on the small amount of land which they had bought flocked to cities to work in these new enterprises. The result was the growth

---

[4] *Ibid.*, p. 16.
[5] The bolshak was the head of the extended family.
[6] Kravchïnskii, p. 74.

of an urban group of industrial workers with a slowly rising standard of living. The revolutionary movement, led largely by intellectuals of aristocratic or middle-class origin, made its appeal both to this emerging industrial class and to the peasants. Among the revolutionists, ideas of the equality of the sexes and of new types of family and sex relationships were prevalent. In actuality, however, the wife of the average workingman in the city was under the domination of her husband.

The Russian Revolution The Revolution of 1917 was not merely a political revolution but also an economic and social upheaval. The peasants and laborers who had the lowest status under the Czar were now given a status higher than that of the aristocrat, the merchant, and the priest.

The Communists had long before worked out plans for the family in an economically reconstructed society. They assumed that the bourgeois family, even though communistic within itself, was inseparably linked with the capitalist society through the institutions of private property and inheritance. They determined, therefore, not only to abolish private property as a means of production but to transfer to the community so far as possible the economic functions of the family both in production and in consumption. Some Communists expected that, with the removal of its economic and social functions, the family itself would disappear. After the 1917 Revolution the leaders were ready to put their theoretical program into effect.

The theories of the Communists about the status and form of the family in the new order may be summarized under four points. (1) Marriage and divorce should be private affairs. (2) Communal living quarters should be provided, so that children might be separated from their parents and reared scientifically and with a correct political orientation. (3) Women should be freed from domestic duties by transferring economic activities to the community, and should have equal rights with men in industry, society, and government (4) The community should provide social services for the family against such contingencies as childbirth, sickness, accidents, and unemployment. We will trace the attempt to translate each of these ideas into action, to discover how far and in what ways they were carried out, what concessions had to be made to traditional attitudes, and what practices are features of the Russian family.

MARRIAGE AND DIVORCE

Within a generation the Soviet Union's policies and programs on marriage underwent radical modifications. Immediately following the Revolution the emphasis was on marriage as an individual affair between the two parties and on easy divorce. Today both are under state control.

Early Attitudes Toward Marriage In the early days of the Revolution, isolated instances were reported of proposals for the nationalization of women. These may be regarded as ideological excesses of a few, rather than a serious program sponsored by Communist leaders. The reasoning was that sex was a private matter, like eating and drinking. And if eating was to be communal, why not communism in sex?

A wave of promiscuity among youth followed, but proved to be incidental to the transition from the old to the new order. Lenin denounced casual relations as utterly un-Marxian, unsocial, bourgeois, and a phenomenon of decadence,[7] adding, "Does the normal man drink from the same glass from which a dozen others have drunk?"[8] While no attempt was made to enforce rigid restrictions on young people, recognition was given to the psychological and cutural aspects of sex as well as to its physical significance. The revolution in sex morals was not drastic, for the separation of the sexes was never very strict; this was particularly true of peasants' households, where generally all members of the family slept together in a single room.

Some of the early Communists would have preferred to make marriage and divorce completely an individual matter, with the parties free to enter into and to dissolve a union, but there were psychological considerations to be taken into account. Foremost among these was the fact that marriage under the Czars was a religious matter, with a church ceremony and the blessing of the priest. Transition from this to cohabitation with no community sanction was recognized as being too great for the masses.

The secularization of marriage, or making marriage a civil obligation, was the primary change in the marriage law enacted at the conclusion of the civil war in 1917.[9] The law required persons who entered marriage to sign three statements: on the intention to marry, on an absence of impediments to marry, and on the voluntary or mutual consent to marry.[10] After these statements were signed, the contracting parties were given a certificate of marriage. Moreover, couples who lived together, recognizing each other as husband and wife but not registering their marriages, were also considered to be legally married, as in common-law marriages in some of our states. An overwhelming proportion

[7] Halle, pp. 113–114.
[8] Albert Rhys Williams, *The Soviets* (New York: Harcourt, Brace, 1937), p. 229.
[9] James H. Meisel and Edward S. Kozera, (eds.), *Materials for the Study of the Soviet System* (Ann Arbor: George Wahr, 1950), pp. 39–40.
[10] Free consent was required by law from the beginning of the eighteenth century.

of marriages, however, were registered. Unregistered marriages were confined chiefly to persons in intellectual and artistic groups.

There were practical advantages in having a marriage registered. For one thing, it gave the union an official status, which a house committee would consider if the couple applied for a room or an apartment. There were also obvious advantages in having the date of the marriage officially registered in a divorce case where the fact of marriage needed to be established or in a question of the paternity of a child.

To counteract the surviving interest in religious ceremonies, Communists introduced an announcement dinner to celebrate marriages, and the christening ceremony, where Lenin's picture took the place of the icon. The Communists recognized that the power and control which ceremonies have is hard to break.

Modifications of the Early Marriage Law In 1926, 1936, and 1944 certain clarifications and additions were made in the marriage law.[11] In 1926 it was specifically stated that the registration of marriages was in the interest of the state and society and for the protection of the personal and property rights of husband, wife, and children. The minimum age at marriage of females was raised from 16 to 18. Marriages which had been celebrated according to religious rites before December 20, 1917, were declared to be as legal as civil registered marriages. The coercion of a woman to contract a marriage or to continue cohabitation was made a crime. The payment of a purchase price for brides, or its acceptance, was made a crime. (This was a practice of certain outlying tribes.) Persons in *de facto* marriages—common-law marriages—were given the "right" to register their marriages.

In 1944 the Supreme Soviet passed new laws on marriage, divorce, the family, and motherhood.[12] These laws surrounded the family with more external obligations than it had known since the coming of the Soviets; they lightened the economic burden of parents and used the machinery of the state to strengthen the stability of the family.

Today there are five prerequisites to marriage in the Soviet Union.[13] It will be noted that they are, with minor variations, identical with most states in the United States. (1) The marriage must be registered, with the parties producing evidence of their identity. (2) The parties must have reached the statutory age of 18. (3) They must not be immediate blood relatives. (4) Marriage is based on the free consent of the parties without any form of coercion. (5) There must be no existing undis-

[11] Meisel and Kozera, pp. 172–175.
[12] *Ibid.*, p. 378.
[13] Grigory Sverdlov, *Marriage and the Family in the U.S.S.R.* (Moscow: Foreign Languages Publishing House, 1956), pp. 16–21.

solved marriage. At the time of registering their marriage, the parties must sign a statement that they have informed each other of the state of their health, particularly with regard to venereal disease, tuberculosis, and insanity. And they must indicate the number of times married and the number of their children.

Motherhood Soviet law provides a system of family allowances of three types. A lump sum is paid to married mothers beginning with the third child; small amounts are paid monthly to married mothers beginning with the fourth child; and small monthly payments are given to unmarried mothers. The size of the lump sum is larger for each succeeding child up to the seventh; for the seventh and eighth child the amount is the same and is 6 times that for the third child; and for all children beyond the tenth the amount is 12 times as large as for the third. The monthly payments do not begin until the child attains age 1 and continue for 4 years. Unmarried mothers receive payments until a child reaches 12 years of age.[14]

The laws were devised to stimulate the birth rate. A "Motherhood medal" of first and second class was provided for mothers of 6 and 5 children; an "Order of Glory of Motherhood Medal," first, second, and third class, for 9, 8, and 7 children; and a "Mother Heroine" title for 10 children. Taxes previously imposed on bachelors were extended to childless couples, and small taxes were levied on one-child and two-child families.

The attempt to stimulate the birth rate has not been successful. Strumilin reports that "in recent years the average family in the USSR has no more than 3.7 members."[15] This was the same size of the family in the United States in 1960.[16] However, between 1962 and 1965 there was a substantial decline in first, second, and third births in families:[17]

	1962	*1965*
First births	1,853,200	1,458,100
Second births	1,357,600	1,165,600
Third births	701,300	594,600

[14] United States Department of Health, Education and Welfare, the U.S. Team that visited the U.S.S.R. under the East-West Exchange Program in August–September 1958, *A Report on Social Security Programs in the Soviet Union*, 1960, pp. 66–67.
[15] S. Strumilin, "Family and Community in the Society of the Future," *The Soviet Review: A Journal of Translations*, 2, No. 2, (1961): p. 7.
[16] *United States Census of Population, 1960, United States Summary*, p. 157.
[17] Data from Richard Reston published in the *Los Angeles Times*, January 9, 1967, Part 1, p. 15.

These figures indicate a declining interest of Soviet parents in having a first child, not to mention a second or third.

Moreover, the birth rate in recent years has had a sharp decline. In the six years from 1960 through 1965 the number of births fell by over a million—from 5,341,000 to 4,253,000; and the natural increase of the population fell by a million and a quarter—from 3,812,000 to 2,563,000.

Early Policy Toward Divorce[18]   Divorce, which was almost nonexistent under the Czars, was made relatively easy under the early Soviets. The provisions for securing a divorce in the 1917–1935 period were as follows: (1) In cases of mutual consent, where the husband and wife had agreed on custody of the children and on alimony, a petition for divorce could be filed directly with the bureau of registry of marriages, births, and divorces. This office recorded it and gave the parties certificates of divorce. (2) In contested cases, where only one party desired the divorce or where there was disagreement over custody of the children or over the amount of alimony, the petition was filed with the local court for decision. In such cases the judge decided the custody of the children, to what extent each parent should bear the expenses of maintaining and educating the children, and whether and to what extent the husband must pay alimony to his divorced wife. In actual practice most of the divorces were secured by petition to the bureau of registry.

Changes in Divorce Laws in 1936   In 1936, stock was taken of the Russian experience on divorce. Of primary concern was the development of an irresponsible attitude toward the family and family obligations. Women complained that husbands were becoming prone to discard their middle-aged wives to marry younger women. The 1936 law required the attendance of both parties in divorce preceedings, and raised the fees for divorce from two dollars[19] to ten for the first, thirty for the second, and sixty dollars for the third and following divorces. The courts were authorized to require support of children as follows: one-fourth of the husband's income to the wife to maintain one child, one-third for two children, and one-half for three or more children. The penalty for nonsupport of children was two years' imprisonment. As a result of the new divorce law and an educational campaign which accompanied it, the number of divorces in 1937 was 47 percent lower than in 1936.[20]

---

[18] See Meisel and Kozera, pp. 41–43, and 175–176.
[19] In 1936 one dollar equaled five rubles.
[20] V. Svetlov, *Brak i Sem'ia*, (Moscow, 1939), p. 144.

The Divorce Law—1944–1965 The divorce law passed in 1944 was the law up to 1965. It attempted to discourage divorce by increasing the expense and extending the litigation involved in getting one. Previously a divorce could be secured by both parties' appearing before the registration office and asking for it. The new law required both parties to a divorce to file a petition and to appear in person before a People's Court. It also required that an announcement of application for divorce be published in the local paper. Applications for divorce cost twice as much as did the first divorce under the 1936 law, and this was but the first step in trying to get a divorce.

The People's Court heard the evidence, summoned witnesses, heard the arguments of lawyers, clarified the validity and seriousness of the grounds for the action and, most important of all, endeavored to effect a reconciliation. This court could not grant the divorce. If no reconciliation was reached, the case might be taken to a higher court or to the highest court of the country. The higher court went through the same procedure as the People's Court and might or might not grant the divorce. If the divorce was granted, the cost was from $100 to $400, to be paid by one or both of the parties at the discretion of the court. The law made divorce more difficult in the Soviet Union than in all our states. The financial and legal conditions made divorce almost prohibitive except to persons of the highest income.

Modification of Divorce Law in 1965 In 1965 three changes which made divorce cheaper, easier, and quicker, were made in the divorce law. (1) The cost of divorce was reduced. (2) The requirement for prior newspaper advertisements of divorce plans was abolished. And (3) the requirement that a second court hear the case before a judicial decision was also abolished.[21]

First-hand descriptions of interpersonal conflicts associated with divorce in the Soviet Union are beginning to appear. Husband-wife conflicts over divergent desires and standards of behavior, infidelity, interference of in-laws, differing ways of handling children, and the like can only be inferred from a study of 500 divorce cases from the Leningrad City Court.[22] Two Soviet sociologists analyzing court cases reported that the major causes of divorce were hasty marriages, crowded housing conditions, interference of in-laws, and drunkenness.[23] A more adequate, though incomplete, picture of the family tensions and difficulties in-

---

[21] Data from Vincent J. Burke, published in the *Los Angeles Times*, July 4, 1966, Part 1, p. 5.
[22] A. G. Kharchev, "The Nature of the Soviet Family," *The Soviet Review: Translations in Social Analysis*, 2, No. 5 (1961): p. 12.
[23] Burke, *Los Angeles Times*.

volved in divorce can be secured from documents, such as the following, which review the general background of divorce cases:

> The K's were married in 1946 and had a daughter born in that year. By decision of a court K. had been paying alimony to his wife since 1949. In November 1953 the wife applied for divorce because of the husband's habitual drunkenness and ill-treatment of the family. The plaintiff stated that the father's conduct had a harmful influence on their little daughter. At first the regional court refused to grant divorce on the ground that there was no proof of the defendant's habitual use of intoxicating liquor, that quarrels in the family had been provoked by the plaintiff's relatives and that to preserve the marriage was in the child's interest. But the Supreme Court stated that . . . "Witnesses testified that the defendant was a habitual drunkard, that he systematically ill-treated members of the family and that prior to applying to court the plaintiff had repeatedly complained of her husband's behavior to social Party bodies.
>
> "The plaintiff's allegation of non-support was borne out by the fact that in 1949 a maintenance order was made against the defendant.
>
> "The regional court's statement that the parties could re-establish normal marital relations provided the plaintiff consented to live apart from her parents is wrong on principle. . . .
>
> "The court's statement that the plaintiff's mother is to blame for the defendant's ill-treatment of his family is groundless and contradicts the circumstances of the case." All these considerations guided the Supreme Court of the U.S.S.R. in granting the plaintiff a divorce.[24]

COMMUNAL LIVING

Some Communists in the early years of the Revolution held that the disappearance of the family would come about when children were reared apart from their parents. Large-scale projects were proposed, but were abandoned chiefly because the required outlays were incompatible with expenditures needed for putting the country on a firm industrial basis.

The Ideal of Separate Children's Quarters
Serious consideration was given to the idea of building separate houses or providing separate quarters for children. The following indicates that this ideal has not been abandoned:

> The advantages of public upbringing are so great and evident that they justify any public expenses, on any scale, for *all* the children in the country. Nature has arranged things in such a way that the child is drawn to other children of his own age from the earliest years. . . .

[24] Sverdlov, pp. 39–40.

The Children's collective, particularly if not under pressure and guided by the experienced hand of an educator, can do more to inculcate the best social habits than the most sympathetic and loving mother. . . .

In giving precedence to the public forms of upbringing, it is our task to extend them in the next few years at a tempo that would make them accessible to all—from the cradle to the graduation certification—within fifteen or twenty years. . . .

The question might arise whether such an early separation of the child from the family would not be too difficult for the parents and their children, so sensitive to motherly affection?

This question may be answered as follows: the public organization of upbringing is not aimed at the complete separation of children from their parents. Even now the mothers of infants are able to feed their offspring at the breast during working hours. And it is highly unlikely that anyone will prevent them from visiting their children after working hours, when they will be able to visit the children's premises in their own dwelling house as often as the rules permit.[25]

Rural Communistic Experiments It was chiefly in the country that an extensive attempt was made to try out in the most thorough-going way experiments in communism, including the separation of children from parents. Even before the drive for the collectivization of the farms, enthusiastic Communists had established rural communes at different places throughout the Soviet Union. The following is a picture of the organization of one of these communes visited by Burgess in the summer of 1930:

Originally the members lived together as a big family, working without wages and receiving food, clothing, and shelter from the commune. This was in accordance with the central principle of communism: "from each according to his ability, to each according to his need." This program was abandoned after two years' trial. Two practical reasons were given. First of all, production lagged when there was no relation between the amount of work expended and the reward for it. Second, the women, particularly, got into quarrels because of discriminations, as they thought, in the distribution of dresses and other wearing apparel.

Consequently, wages were introduced and clothing and other personal effects were purchased from the commissary. Other than this, the principle of communism held sway; all land, all dwellings, all machinery of farming, all livestock were held in common. No family or person was allowed to have a house, garden, a cow, a hog, or chickens. Husband and wife had a room in the dormitory; living with them were their small children from two to six years old. All the babies were cared for in the common nursery. Children from six to fourteen had a supervised dormitory in which they slept. The young men over fourteen had a separate dormi-

[25] Strumilin, pp. 10–11.

tory, as did also young women over that age. At fourteen, having completed their elementary education, they became self-supporting workers in the commune. The brighter boys and girls who wished further education were sent to the nearest high school at the expense of the commune.

Meals were not a family but a communal matter. In this particular commune, certain tables were allotted to the men, others to the women, special ones reserved for young people, some for older children, and others for young children.

The family as an institution had almost ceased to exist in this commune. It was still a unit, but an affectional rather than a social group, submerged in the all-embracing unit of the commune.

Now that the agricultural area of the Soviet Union is almost completely collectivized, the dominant unit is not the commune but the collective. The chief difference between the collective and the commune is that in collectives, families generally live in separate houses rather than dormitories. At present, though not at first, families in the collectives are allowed to have their private gardens, chickens, and a cow. The great majority of families in the cities, as well as in rural areas, continue to live in separate family units.

EMANCIPATION OF WOMEN

The Soviet constitution of 1936 stated in unmistakable language the Communist attitude toward the rights of women:

> Women in the USSR are accorded equal rights with men in all spheres of economic, government, cultural, political, and other public activity.
>
> The possibility of exercising these rights is ensured by women being accorded an equal right with men to work, payment for work, rest and leisure, social insurance and education, state aid to mothers of large families and unmarried mothers, maternity leave with full pay, and the provision of a wide network of maternity homes, nurseries, and kindergartens.[26]

Transfer of Activities to the Community The emancipation of women from the domestic duties of the prerevolutionary period was one of the central principles of communism. This was to be accomplished by transferring out of the home all activities that could be established as enterprises in the community, such as baking, canning vegetables and fruits, and making and laundering clothing. This transition was accomplished quite readily in certain cases by merely stopping the sale of a commodity; for example, if flour was not on sale at the stores, everyone had to buy bread from bakeries.

It was highly approved that women should follow activities out of the

[26] Meisel and Kozera, p. 262.

home and become workers in bakeries, laundries, textile factories, and other industries. Dining rooms for workers were opened and day nurseries established in factories.

Equal Economic Rights A cardinal principle of the philosophy of communism was that women should have equal rights with men in industry, society, and government. Women have entered many industries and taken jobs previously regarded as the province of men only. Equal pay is given women and men for the same grade of work.

There has been a steady increase in the number of women in the Soviet Union who are gainfully employed. Before the Revolution women accounted for only 19 percent of the employed; by 1932 they were 27 percent of all industrial workers; by 1939 they were 37 percent of all industrial workers; according to the 1959 census of the Soviet Union women constituted 48 percent of all employed persons.[27] In 1963 women constituted about the same percent of all employed persons (over 48 percent). In 1963 of all women with a higher education, 59 percent were employed.[28]

Equality in Sexual Behavior The Soviets advocate the single standard of sex morals, insisting that men and women should have the same liberties and privileges. They feel that to allow men to enjoy sexual privileges denied to women is no less preposterous than to allow one class privileges withheld from another class. While they are aggressively opposed to promiscuity, some are inclined to accept "the possibility of a second love in one's life" without the disruption of the family.[29]

Equal Political Rights Lenin advocated equal political rights for women. His dictum was "Every cook must learn to run the state." Political education and participation have taken place more rapidly in the city than in the country, where for centuries women have been held in subjection to their husbands. But in both the country and the city, women take part in elections and are themselves elected to office in increasing numbers. In 1922, only five women were elected to the Supreme Soviet,[30]

---

[27] Prerevolutionary and 1959 figures from an article published in *Ekonomicheskaya Gazeta*, December 20, 1960, reproduced in *The Soviet Review: A Journal of Translations*, 2, No. 2 (1961): p. 31; 1932 and 1939 from Leonard E. Hubbard, *Soviet Labour and Industry*. (London: Macmillan and Company, 1942), p. 255; 1951 from *USSR Information Bulletin*, March 8, 1952, p. 134. The figures are not strictly comparable. The 1959 census reports that of all mental workers 54 percent were women.

[28] N. Tatarinova, and E. Korshunova, "Living and Working Conditions of Women in the U.S.S.R.," *International Labour Review*, 82, (1960): p. 346. *See also* "Statistical Data, Women in the USSR," *Soviet Sociology*, 4 (1965–1966): p. 57.

[29] Kharchev, p. 11.

[30] *USSR Information Bulletin*, March 8, 1952, p. 124.

whereas in 1962, 390 or 27.0 percent of the total membership were women; of the total members of the councils of the federated republics, 1,927 or 33.0 percent were women.[31]

HEALTH, EDUCATION, AND DELINQUENCY

Under the Czarist regime individuals depended on assistance from relatives and friends for meeting various problems. Today Soviet leaders feel that the State has the obligation to assist the family in meeting pressing problems, such as those involving health, education, and juvenile delinquency.

Health Attention to public welfare, including health, is one of the most important trends in the Soviet Union.[32] There has been a decided reduction in the death rate, including both infant and maternal mortality rates. An employed pregnant woman is allowed 56 days leave before childbirth and 56 days after, with approximately two-thirds pay during this period.[33] In addition there is a network of centers for maternal and child care and rest homes which provide preventive medical services.

Education The vast majority of persons before the Revolution were illiterate.[34] The last census before the Revolution, 1897, reported that 64 percent of men and 88 percent of women nine years of age and over were not able to read or write. Today illiteracy, except among older persons, has been eliminated by compulsory education for eight years. In addition, there has been a great increase in the number of nurseries and kindergartens. Before the Revolution there were only a few of these. Ten years after the Revolution there were 62,000 nurseries and 120,000 kindergartens. By 1958 the number of nurseries had jumped to 1,135,000 and the number of kindergartens to 2,258,000,[35] and both have had a great increase since then. There is also a widely developed system of secondary and technical schools and a large number of higher educational establishments. Technical instruction is provided in industries, and evening schools are widespread.

Delinquency The civil wars and the famine of 1921 and 1922 created a vast horde of so-called "wild children." These were orphans who lived in basements and dugouts and depended on robbery and burglaries

---

[31] Burke, *Los Angeles Times*.
[32] Strumilin, p. 349.
[33] Tatarinova and Korshunova, p. 349.
[34] *Ibid.*, pp. 343–345.
[35] *Ibid.*, p. 353.

for their subsistence. Finally the authorities rounded up these vagrant children and placed them in institutions.

Juvenile delinquency, however, which had decreased every year since the high peak during the famine until 1929, again became a problem. Between 1930 and 1935 child crime almost doubled. This was alarming, since Communists had held that "child crime, like that of adults, had its origin and development as a direct product of the capitalist class."[36]

An analysis of the cases of juvenile delinquency indicated that the chief causes were parental neglect and undesirable home life.[37] In certain cases the parents of young delinquents were giving all their time to the community to the neglect of their children.

In 1936 the following new measures were enacted to deal with juvenile delinquency: (1) The juvenile commissions, consisting of a justice, a physician, and a pedagogue, were abolished, and juvenile cases were assigned to special branches of the criminal courts. (2) Parental responsibility for the conduct of children was increased. (3) Neigborhood recreation facilities were established. (4) The Young Communist League and the trade unions were given responsibility for dealing with the problem. Especially significant was the recognition of parental responsibility, since in the early years of the Revolution children were encouraged to disregard parental authority.

PARENTS AND CHILDREN

In the Soviet Union there is a vital interest in the well-being of children and parents. Leisure-time activities in the form of clubs and organized groups absorb the attention of children; hobbies and organized groups are available to adults.

Leisure-Time Activities of Children The following is based on a study by Levin (from England) who spent several months traveling in nine republics of Russia, talking with school children, teachers, administrators, and others about the leisure-time activities of children. Because of overcrowding there are many half-day school sessions which, of course, increases the out-of-school time. There are millions of children who participate in one or more clubs or groups outside of lessons, but "there are still plenty who are not involved in anything." There are school clubs in practically every academic subject: chemistry, mathematics, physics, history, geography, literature, biology, languages. In addition, there are technical clubs and groups devoted to drama, music, agricul-

[36] *The Great Soviet Encyclopedia*, 21 (1931): p. 599.
[37] Nathan Berman, "Juvenile Delinquency, the Family, and the Court in the Soviet Union," *American Journal of Sociology*, 42 (1937): pp. 682–692.

ture, sports, science, metal working, and others. The clubs and groups are found in cities, small towns, and rural areas. They are supervised by teachers, older children, young Communists' organizations, retired men (age 60) or retired women (age 55), trade union workers, or persons from institutes. An understanding of the leisure-time activities of Soviet children can be secured, in part, from the following:

> All kinds of parties and celebrations are held during the year; New Year parties around a fir-tree, graduating parties at the end of the school year, May Day celebrations, performances for parents, arts festivals, and all sorts of competitions in sports, chess, mathematics and physics. . . .
> At any time of the day the building is humming, some children are going to lessons, others are hurrying off to a club, in one room there is an arithmetic lesson and in the next there is a film show of cartoons for children of the first and second forms. A rehearsal is going on in the hall and in the garden the trees are being pruned or flower-beds planted. A volley-ball game is on, or, in the winter, the pitch is flooded to make a skating-rink. The reading-room of the library is full, a group is preparing a wall newspaper on Shakespeare, children are reading magazines and periodicals, many of them non-fiction and specialized, others deep in books.[38]

Soviet Ideals for Parents and Children Soviet writers on marriage and the family present certain ideals for husband-wife and parent-child relationships.[39] Husbands and wives "ought" to have mutual love; to recognize equality of husband and wife; to co-operate daily with the partner; to handle together any difficulties that arise; to give mutual aid to family members unable to work, and to children, old people, and invalids; and to enjoy happiness in their relationships.

Ideals for parental care and training of children include seeing that they are healthy and strong; giving them affection; developing in them an urge to work and a love and respect for work; giving them moral training in kindness and justice; and inculcating such cultural values as good personal adjustment, security, happiness, and the pursuit of the rewards of status, security, and income associated with certain occupational and educational activities.[40]

Parental Responsibility A central point in the 1936 and 1944 reforms —the reorganization of education, the control of delinquency, and the changes in marriage and divorce laws—was to stress the importance of

---

[38] Deana Levin, *Leisure and Pleasure of Soviet Children* (London: Macgibbon & Kee, 1966), pp. 25–26.
[39] See Kharchev, pp. 16–19; and Sverdlov, pp. 6–10.
[40] Alex Inkeles and Raymond A. Bauer, *The Soviet Citizen: Daily Life in a Totalitarian Society* (Cambridge: Harvard University Press, 1959), pp. 228–229.

the family and parental responsibility. An educational campaign supported these legislative and administrative measures. Writers in papers and magazines emphasized the duties of fathers as well as of mothers. Three quotations in 1935, 1937 and 1944, respectively, illustrate the emphasis on parental responsibility:

> To be a good family man, this is a matter of duty. A poor family man cannot be a good Soviet citizen or a socially minded person.[41]
>
> The Soviet child has a right to claim his true father as an educator and friend. It is only when the father brings up the new builders of socialism that he can feel himself a worthy citizen of the fatherland.[42]
>
> In human speech there is nothing more pure and exalted, nothing more tender and more holy than the word "Mother."[43]

Reasons for Changes in the Soviet Attitude Toward the Family Three factors appear to have been instrumental in modifying the Soviet attitude toward the family. First is the persistence of attachments of parents to their children in spite of all efforts to change "my" to "our." Second, with the passing of the old and the rising of the new generation indoctrinated in communism and participating in a collectivistic society, the authorities no longer feared the family as a reactionary factor. Third, they perceived in the family a valuable instrument of social control and, above all, an agency for the transmission of communistic ideology and culture to the young. Letters from the newspapers exemplify the nature and spirit of the new socialistic family. One of these illustrates the three points listed above:

> I am a young Communist, married, with a son two years old. My wife is a young Communist; we became acquainted at the Young Communist Club. We are both mechanics; we live very friendly together.
>
> I love my wife, adore my little son, and gladly return home after work. The family does not limit my activity. I study in the Institute. I have little free time, but I take time to devote attention to the family. I wish to rear my son to be a good member of socialist society.[44]

Survivals of Early Practices Geiger reports that "all sources agree that Soviet marital life is tending toward more equality between husband and wife."[45] He also points to certain survivals of early customs and

---

[41] *Pravda*, June 26, 1935, quoted by Berman, p. 691.
[42] *Pravda*, quoted by Williams, p. 296.
[43] *Izvestia*, July 9, 1944, quoted by Maurice Hindus, in a special dispatch to the *St. Louis Post-Dispatch*, July 10, 1944, Part 2, pp. 1 and 4.
[44] Svetlov, p. 110.
[45] H. Kent Geiger, *The Family in Soviet Russia* (Cambridge: Harvard University Press, 1968), p. 225.

traditions, particularly male dominance. Soviet scholars, while emphasizing that the overwhelming majority of Soviet families engage in behavior consistent with Communism, frankly acknowledge some survivals of habits and ideas left over from the past.[46] These include the idea that woman is destined by nature to submit to man, and that she is unworthy of equal standing with him; the "old-world idea" that the family is a stronghold isolated from society; promiscuous sex relations in violation of monogamous marriage; marriages of economic and political interest; parents avoiding responsibility for children and children avoiding responsibility for family members; bringing up children with a spirit of gain, egotism, and laziness; and abduction of brides, buying them, and engaging in polygyny, all of which are still occasionally found in Eastern regions.

SOCIAL-CLASS STRUCTURE

Social-Class Structure and the Family The abolition of the Czarist class system after the Bolshevist Revolution was, according to Communist ideology, to be followed by a classless society. In the new social order people would produce according to their ability and be compensated according to their needs. The ideal of the distribution of income was that of social equality. In the 1920's, differences in income were slight. The pay of the most skilled workers in 1918 was practically the same as that of the least skilled.[47]

During the second and third quarters of the twentieth century Russia was becoming an urbanized, industrialized nation. This is shown by the fact that between 1926 and 1956 the percent of the total population in urban areas more than doubled, from 18 to 39 percent,[48] and between 1956 and 1966 the urban population rose from 39 to 54 percent of the total population.[49] The industrialization of the country under successive five-year plans placed a tremendous emphasis on productivity and led to a re-evaluation of the function of social classes, wage incentives, and the distribution of goods and services. In the 1924–1936 period the following radical modifications of policies were adopted: the acceptance of a class structure as a part of Soviet society; the distribution of goods and services not according to needs, but according to work done; and the use of wage incentives to stimulate production. The first two of these

[46] Sverdlov, pp. 10–11.

[47] Alexander Baykov, *The Development of the Soviet Economic System* (New York: Macmillan, 1947).

[48] The Legislative Reference Service of the Library of Congress, *Soviet Economic Growth: A Comparison with the United States: A Study Prepared for the Subcommittee on Foreign Economic Policy*, 1957, p. 82.

[49] Data from Reston, *Los Angeles Times*.

were outlined before the Eighth Congress of Soviets of the USSR in 1936:

> The capitalist class in the sphere of industry has ceased to exist. And the merchants and profiteers in the sphere of trade have ceased to exist. Thus all the exploiting classes have now been eliminated. There remains the working class. There remains the peasant class. There remains the intelligentsia. . . .
> The fundamental principle of this [first] phase of communism is, as you know, the formula: "From each according to his abilities, to each according to his work." . . . But Soviet society has not yet reached the higher phase of communism, in which the ruling principle will be the formula: "From each according to his abilities, to each according to his needs."[50]

Various incentives are employed to achieve the objective of increased production. Competition between factories and between groups in factories is stressed. Most effective, however, are the measures relating rewards directly to individual output by wage differences, prizes, and social recognition.

Differences in income, as associated with variations in status and power, became the basis for the rise of a new class system. Inkeles offers the following rank order of social classes in Soviet society:[51] (1) *ruling elite*, high party, government, economic and military officials, prominent scientists, artists, and writers; (2) *superior intelligentsia*, intermediate ranks of the above categories, and important technical specialists; (3) *general intelligentsia*, the professions, middle ranks of bureaucracy, managers of small enterprises, junior military officers; (4) *working-class aristocracy*, the most highly skilled and productive workers; including the so-called Stakhanovites; (5.5) *white-collar workers*, petty bureaucrats, accountants, bookkeepers, clerks, and office workers; (5.5) *well-to-do peasants*, both those advantaged because of location, fertility, or crop grown on collective farms and those whose trade, skill, or productivity raises them into a higher income group than that of the average peasant; (7) *rank and file workers* with average incomes; (8.5) *average peasants;* (8.5) *disadvantaged workers* with low income due to lack of skills and/or low productivity; and (10) *forced labor*.

The Soviet family has been greatly affected by the development and open acknowledgement of a new social stratification in the Soviet Union, accompanied as it was by a rise and then a decline in social mobility. Such things as where the family lives, the families with which it intimately associates, the choice of mates by its sons and daughters, and

---

[50] Meisel and Kozera, pp. 231–234.
[51] Alexander Inkeles, "Social Stratification and Mobility in the Soviet Union," *American Sociological Review*, 15 (1950): pp. 466–467.

educational and vocational opportunities are in large part determined by a family's position in the class structure. Moreover, the strengthening of the family, as Inkeles points out, also results in the restriction of social mobility and the reinforcement of social-class lines:

> As the family is strengthened in the Soviet Union, kin relations will play an increasingly important role in determining Soviet youths' opportunities for mobility.... Stories about persons in responsible positions exerting influence to favor their kin have appeared with considerable frequency in recent years, both in the Soviet press and in the reports of first hand observers. There is now a large group of people who have achieved high status by means legitimate within the existing social system, and who wish to pass some of their benefits and privileges on to their children. This creates strong pressures for the establishment of conditions which make it easier for children from this group to improve their position and simultaneously constitute obstacles to effective competition from the children born into families lower in the scale of stratification.[52]

SUMMARY

The capacity of the family to persist under unfavorable conditions has been demonstrated by events in the Soviet Union. The evidence from the Russian experiment seems to prove that the family can survive without the support of law and even in the face of governmental attempts to weaken and undermine it.

The Communists failed to abolish the family—if this was ever the purpose of more than a few extremists. Only a few scattered attempts were made to separate children from parents. The objective of housing all families in communal living quarters has not been achieved. The vast majority of Russian families continue to live in private homes. The making of the registration of marriage permissive rather than required, the providing for divorce at the option of either party, and the disregard of any distinction between legitimate and illegitimate children did not destroy marriage and the family, as many inside and outside the Soviet Union expected. At most these changes in legislation hastened the transition from the old to a new type of family.

The Soviet family today is vastly different from what it was immediately following the Revolution. It is a product of industrialization and urbanization. Women entered the labor force as economic activities were withdrawn from the home. Their increased emancipation is an expansion of an original principle of Soviet society. However, the following five items are quite different from that anticipated by early Soviet writers:

[52] *Ibid.*, pp. 477–478.

1. The prerequisites to marriage in the Soviet Union are as follows: it must be registered, the parties must have reached the statutory age, must not be immediate blood relatives, must be based on free consent, and there must be no prior undissolved marriage.

2. The birth rate has been declining. Family size has likewise declined.

3. Divorce laws in Russia went through a cycle: immediately after the Revolution divorce was very easy, then it was extremely hard, now it is as easy as most states in the United States.

4. A high value is placed on families. There is an emphasis on love as the basis for marriage, parental love for children, cooperation in the solving of problems, and parental responsibility in the training of children.

5. There has developed a social-class structure based on income, education, and the economic and political position of the parental family.

PROBLEMS FOR RESEARCH

There are still many unanswered questions about the Russian family. Research on the Russian family is feasible, for there are translations of many journal articles, pamphlets, and reports, and others which could be translated. In addition there are a few reports based on extended visits to Russia. A glance at the footnotes and the bibliography of this chapter illustrates the wealth and variety of the materials which are available.

Variations in Family Practices Within Russia One sometimes forgets that the Soviet Union is composed of 15 republics stretching from Europe to the Orient. The United States team of social-security experts that visited Russia under an East-West exchange program in 1958 went to several of these republics. This team reported that "in the Oriental republics especially, there appeared to be little or no change in the family as compared with the past or with other countries in this region."[53] This was an impression based on informal interviews with officials and citizens. The statement could be accepted as a hypothesis and might be tested by using reports which have been translated, or UNESCO reports, or articles appearing in Russian journals and periodicals. Here are some questions pertinent to variations in family practices in present-day Russia: What variations in family behavior are there between the 15 republics? Are there variations between rural and urban areas and between

[53] United States Department of Health, Education, and Welfare, The U. S. Team that visited the U.S.S.R. under the East-West Exchange Program in August–September 1958, p. 28.

social classes? If these variations are present, how can one account for them?

Public Scrutiny of the Individual Family   Various reports on the Soviet family indicate that in Russia everyone is expected to be concerned not only with the behavior of his own family and the care of his children but also with the family and care of children of other persons. This, of course, is in direct contrast with the expectation in the United States that one's affairs at home and the care of one's children are essentially private. This public concern is primarily the responsibility of teachers although others also take this obligation seriously. How does public scrutiny of the individual family affect interpersonal interactions and role playing within the Russian family? Does it make for more or less conflict and tension? Is public scrutiny of one's family and care of children accepted without resentment? Is such public concern for the individual family found primarily in European Russia and not in the Oriental republics?

Care of Children by Grandparents and in Public Nurseries   Russian women are encouraged to work and most of them are in the labor force. Some Russian writers imply that most children of working parents are cared for by public nurseries and kindergartens. The report of the team of social-security experts indicates that about a third of the children of working parents are still cared for by grandparents and other relatives.[54] Are there significant differences in personality traits between children cared for by public nurseries and those cared for by grandparents and other relatives? Are there more problem children in one or the other group? Do children in one of these two groups more closely approximate the Soviet ideals for care and training of children described earlier in the chapter?

Marriage and Divorce   Marriage in the Soviet Union, as in the United States, is occurring at an earlier age than formerly. Does this make for happier unions on the hypothesis that younger couples will make adjustments more readily? Or is the outcome greater unhappiness in marriage because of the social immaturity of younger people? What other problems are solved or created by early marriage?

Status of Women   Under the law women in the Soviet Union enjoy equal status. How far is this translated into equality in social status? Women have entered practically every occupational and professional

[54] *Ibid.*

field. While a few have achieved distinction, the outstanding achievements, in general, have been made by men. The question for study is to determine whether there is a survival of the division of labor between men and women; if so, whether this is a growing or diminishing factor.

Social Relations of the Sexes Visitors to the Soviet Union have noted the absence or relatively small degree of sex consciousness in the social relations of young men and women. As compared with young people in other countries, young Russians appear to consider each other primarily as persons and secondarily as of different sex. The problem of research would be, first, to establish this alleged difference and, if it were determined and defined, to seek the explanation: (1) in participation of the sexes together in children's and youth groups, (2) in working together in agriculture and industry, (3) in education in Soviet principles, and (4) in other causes.

QUESTIONS AND EXERCISES

1. Compare marriages and divorce arrangements in prerevolutionary Russia with those in the Soviet Union.
2. Contrast the status of women before and after the Revolution. How do you account for the Soviet interest in equal rights for women and men in economic and political activities?
3. Why were the Soviet leaders interested after the Revolution in reducing the influence of the family?
4. How do you account for the present-day interest in the Soviet Union of increasing the stability of the family?
5. Compare the process of getting a divorce in Russia at present with that of securing one in your state.
6. Some have advocated that communal living quarters be adopted in the United States. Do we have any living arrangements which approximate communal living quarters? What are the advantages and disadvantages of such a program?
7. In size, the family in the Soviet Union and in the United States are almost identical. How do you explain this similarity?
8. Describe the social services in Russia and indicate how they differ from, and in what respects they are similar to, our system.

BIBLIOGRAPHY

Alt, Hershel; and Alt, Edith. *Russia's Children*. New York: Bookman Associates, 1959.

   Describes observations of a summer's visit to Russia by a husband and wife who are professional social workers. Coverage of relevant literature. Part II, "The Child and the State," and particularly Ch. 10, "The Child in the Family" are especially worth reading.

Geiger, H. Kent. *The Family in Soviet Russia.* Cambridge, Massachusetts: Harvard University Press, 1968.

This book is based in part on data collected around 1950: 329 extended life-history interviews and questionnaires from 123 German persons who had been prisoners of war and had lived for years in Soviet families. In addition he reviewed Soviet publications. Describes historical background of the family: Marxist theory and the Revolution. Analyzes variations between classes of Soviet husbands and wives and parents and children.

Inkeles, Alex; and Bauer, Raymond A. *The Soviet Citizen: Daily Life in a Totalitarian Society.* Cambridge: Harvard University Press, 1959, Ch. 8, "Patterns of Family Life: Getting Under Way."

Sketches the historical development of Soviet views on marriage and the family; the stability of endogamy in class and nationality groups; the rise in gainful employment of women; and the declining size of the family. Ch. 9, "Patterns of Family Life: The Inner Family," presents variations in family solidarity, and the substitution of the values of good personal adjustment, security, and happiness for the values of religion, respect for custom, and carrying on the family heritage.

Kharchev, A. G. "The Nature of the Soviet Family," *The Soviet Review: Translations in Social Analysis,* 2, No. 5 (1961): pp. 2–19.

A description of love, duty, and personal happiness as characteristics of the Soviet family. Also describes norms for husband-wife relations.

Levin, Deana. *Leisure and Pleasure of Soviet Children.* London: Macgibbon and Kee, 1966.

An English writer gives a description of leisure-time activities of Russian children. It is primarily a description of clubs and organized groups available to children. Based on several months of traveling and talking to teachers, school children, governmental officials, and others, and on intimate first-hand observation, it gives information, on an area of behavior on which very little is known.

Meisel, James H.; and Kozera, Edward S. (eds.). *Materials for the Study of the Soviet System: State and Party Constitutions, Laws, Decrees, Decisions and Official Statements of the Leaders, in Translation.* Ann Arbor: George Wahr, 1950. See Table of Contents, Nos. 33, 82, 105, 133, 135, 144, and 152.

Consists of constitutional and administrative codes, laws, and ordinances of the Soviet Union.

Petrova, L.; and Gilevskaya, S. (eds.). *Equality of Women in the U.S.S.R.: Materials of International Seminar* (1956). Moscow: Foreign Languages Publishing House, 1957.

Seven reports on women's activities in the Soviet Union, emphasizing equality of women with men. One, "Soviet Women Enjoy Equal Civil Rights with Men," is an excellent description of marriage and family in Soviet Union.

Sverdlov, Gregory. *Marriage and the Family in the U.S.S.R.* Moscow: Foreign Languages Publishing House, 1956.
   A fairly objective description of the Soviet family, marriage and family laws, conditions and manner of contracting marriage, rights and duties of family members, divorce, and excerpts of marriage and divorce laws.

Tatarinova, N.; and Korshunova, E. "Living and Working Conditions of Women in the U.S.S.R.," *International Labour Review*, 82 (1960): pp. 341–357.
   Objective description of the equality of women with men in the Soviet Union, their general education and vocational training, and their employment opportunities and remuneration; protection of the health of mothers and children; social-insurance benefits; the number of nurseries and kindergartens; and women's place in the Soviet economy.

Chapter 7
The Family of Japan, China, and India

Some Western European writers have held that historically the extended-family system was prevalent in Japan, China, and India. It is doubtful, however, if this family form ever predominated in these countries. Loyalty to the lineage or kinship group also has not been universal. In recent decades contacts with new patterns of behavior, movement to industrial cities, and new marriage laws have undermined both the extended-family system and the lineage group, so that now the most universal form is the nuclear-family form familiar to Western European societies. The transformation of family forms has resulted in new roles and statuses.

The following case describes the daily activities of a middle-class, suburban Japanese housewife. Vogel indicates that most wives in the suburb which he studied perform all household tasks daily: washing clothes, shopping for groceries, mopping and sweeping the floors, and meeting and ordering from the errand boys who solicit for various stores.

> She rises at 6 A.M., a full half-hour before anyone else stirs, and opens the wooden storm doors so the house becomes light and airy. She lights the fire for cooking, and since it is winter, she lights the charcoal for the *kotatsu*. After preparing the food, she wakes up the rest of the family. Her husband eats before the children, and she eats part of her breakfast with the others while preparing their lunch. While the husband and older children are dressing, she frantically rushes to find her husband's lost sock and to prepare their shoes and outer garments at the front doorway. She helps them in their coats and sees them off. The older children will have

put their own bedding into the closets, but she puts her husband's and small children's away.

After both older children are off to school, she straps her one-year-old on her back and begins cleaning up the dishes. She then washes out the daily items of laundry and rushes to hang them out on the bamboo poles for fear the clouds might turn to rain. She even takes a few items from the closet to hang outside to prevent them from getting moldy, but she leaves the heavy quilts for a summer day. Although it is cool she opens the sliding glass doors to air out the house and begins her cleaning. By now her baby has fallen to sleep and she is pleased to relieve her back by laying him down for his morning nap. She fluffs the dust off the windows and sliding panels, sweeps the tatami mats and the wooden floor, gets down on hands and knees to pursue every speck of dust with concerted determination, and sweeps the path outside the house leaving fresh broom marks in the dust.

By the time she finishes her cleaning, the errand boys from the canned-goods shop and the fish store, along with the errand girl from the fruit and vegetable store will have taken her orders and delivered their goods, the milk man will have brought the half-pint of milk for the morning, the ice man will have brought ice for the small ice box, and she will have turned away the errand boy from the butcher shop explaining that she didn't need anything. She catches a brief glimpse of the morning paper which the husband read so leisurely at breakfast, and by the time the baby wakes up she has only a few minutes to play with him before going down the street, baby on back, for two or three items at shops which do not send errand boys. While shopping she stops to chat with a few neighbor ladies and hear the morning gossip.

She returns home and prepares a small lunch for herself and the baby and, after cleaning up the dishes, rests and plays with the baby a few minutes while awaiting the return of the older children. She greets the youngest at the door, but as she is busy with the baby, she responds to her older child's announcement of his arrival by yelling her greeting from the kitchen. Both older children join the mother sitting around the *kotatsu* to relate their school exploits for the day, a conversation that is frequently interrupted by the baby who has awakened from his afternoon nap. By the time the older children are through with their snack and a half hour of studying they are off to play, but only after the mother extracts a solemn promise that they will complete their homework immediately after supper. She digs a few weeds from the garden, brings in some flowers and puts them in a vase, sews a few rags into a dish rag, but postpones the other jobs like sewing her daughter's skirt, picking radishes, pasting paper on the torn spots in the sliding panel, and running a few errands.

Her afternoon half-pint of milk is delivered, but she must go out for the rest of the shopping herself. About five o'clock she rushes out, baby on back and basket under arm, to do her evening shopping for bread, crackers, seaweed, bean curd, and spices, but she resists the temptation to talk with her friends in order to get back and prepare supper before the children start nagging. By giving the children a few extra snacks, she manages to keep them from starting to eat before the father's usual arrival time, but when he is late, she allows the children to eat first. While waiting for the father, she fills the bathtub and lights the gas fire to heat the water. Since the food requires no heating, she serves her husband his food as soon as he arrives and sits down to chat with the children. She eats with the father and chats with him as the children resume their studying, occasionally answering some questions which the children bring while the husband catches a few glances at the evening paper.

She interrupts washing the dishes to turn off the gas under the bath and give the bath water a few quick stirs. She announces that the bath water is ready, and the children who by this time have completed their homework and are sitting talking with the father, in turn take their baths. After finishing the dishes, cleaning the table, and sweeping the floor, she gets out the bedding and lies down a few minutes alongside the children to wish them a good night. While the husband is reading the evening paper, playing with the baby, taking his bath, and watching TV, she lays out the children's clothes for the next day, shines the shoes, closes the wooden doors, puts the baby to bed, and takes her own bath. Unlike her country cousin who must stay up a half hour or so after everyone else retires in order to complete her work, the modern wife of a salary man retires with her husband.[1]

The family described above is a close-knit unit with division of labor between the husband and wife. The husband provides financial support for the family. The wife carries on the daily activities of the home, does the shopping, and has a companionable relationship with the children and her husband.

This chapter will discuss the family system and the lineage group, traditional and modern family roles, and those forces tending to break down the extended family and loyalty to the lineage group.

THE FAMILY FORM

The Extended Family   The literature on the Chinese family of a few years ago emphasized that it was an extended-family form, basically associated with an agricultural civilization. Goode, in an extensive analysis of family forms in many countries, including those in Asia, concluded that the change from agricultural to industrial forms of economic activity and from rural to urban population concentrations was accompanied by change from an extended-family system to a nuclear family system.[2]

---

[1] From Ezra F. Vogel, *Japan's New Middle Class: The Salary Man and his Family in a Tokyo Suburb* (Berkeley: University of California Press, 1963), pp. 186–188.

[2] William Goode, *World Revolution and Family Patterns* (New York: Free Press, 1963).

There seems to be ample evidence that much of that which has been written about the extended family of China has overestimated the prevalence of the extended family. Historically the Chinese household has been relatively small. Ho, an expert on Chinese history, gives the average size of the household for four different dates: A.D. 2, 755, 1393, and 1812. The respective sizes were 4.87, 5.95, 5.68, and 5.33. He also reports that most of the pre-1949 sample surveys showed that the Chinese family of that period had an average of about five persons. Ho concludes that "from the standpoint of size, the family has undergone comparatively little change during the past two thousand years."[3]

However, in Japan, China, and India there were areas where the extended or joint family was fairly prevalent. While there are, of course, variations in different societies on the composition of the extended family, the following are probably the most common and general: (1) Three or more generations—the patriarch and his wife, married sons and daughters, grandchildren, and sometimes great-grandchildren—live together or consider themselves a family group. (2) This extended family functions as an economic, social, and religious unit. (3) The chief control of family affairs is in the hands of an elder male member—grandfather, father, or son.

It has been thought that the extended-family system is basically associated with an essentially agricultural civilization. It is tied in with a self-sufficient community economy which has a minimum of commerce and industry. There is some evidence that it also is found in urban areas. Kapadia holds that for India two assumptions about the extended or joint family are invalid: (1) it is essentially rural, and (2) it is dying out. He goes on to say that it is strong in semi-industrial towns and in communities concentrated in industrial cities.[4] This bears out the reports of students of the authors from Japan, free China, and India. The following description is by one of these students:

> I was born in Hong Kong in the home of a midwife who took care of my mother at the time of my birth. Mother never told me why I was not born in a hospital as my elder sister was and I did not trouble to ask, for I fancied that poverty during the second World War was the best explanation.
>
> My memory of childhood is a most delightful one. We lived in a three-story house with our aunts and uncles. My parents, six children, and grandparents, before they died, occupied the ground floor; and my two

[3] Ping-ti Ho, "An Historian's View of the Chinese Family System," in Seymour M. Farber, Piero Mustacchi, and Roger H. L. Wilson (eds.). *Man and Civilization: The Family's Search for Survival* (New York: McGraw-Hill, 1965), pp. 15–30. Specific reference is on p. 18.

[4] K. M. Kapadia, *Marriage and Family in India* (London: Oxford University Press, (1966), p. 331.

aunts' families of my paternal side occupied the next two stories. There was a garden next to our house that faced away from the street.

This arrangement with our relatives living under the same roof gave us many advantages. For one thing we found that we were closely knit together in several respects, such as in recreation and education. My aunt sometimes helped me with my studies while my sister kept her daughter. The one great advantage, as far as I was concerned, was our companionship in games. Nearly all the children in my immediate family had similar age cousins to play with all the time. Our favorite game was "hide-and-go-seek." We were not admitted to school until we reached four years of age, but even then we had a whole afternoon for games. We were expected to know the Arabic alphabet and to identify and copy some fundamental Chinese words. We were exempted from doing any housework because the servants living with us were responsible for the cooking and washing and dusting plus the other jobs in the house. We were encouraged most of all to gain the first place in class and rewards were used as the bait.

Caring for the children was in the hands of the amah or the mother. But because the amah was not educated enough to be a teacher and the mother was too busy, a tutor was usually the teacher in the family. Although she was not very educated, my mother controlled the finances of the house and tried to settle disputes between the servants caused by rivalry. Disputes between the children demanded even greater diplomacy on her part. My cousin and I often quarreled about who was the owner of the garden. I said it belonged to us because we were living on the street level. Actually, the whole house belonged to my uncle upstairs. My mother knew this and tried to bring us to peace. In a way she taught us how to behave in the house, too.

At this stage children are greatly influenced by their parents' attitude toward them. The more love and affection we received from our parents, the more security and respect we felt for ourselves and, hence, we tried to imitate our parents or relatives. My father was a hardworking and honest man and we found that we should study hard and be honest with ourselves, too.

When a child reaches six years of age and his parents are able to afford the expenditure, he is sent to a primary school for six years. At the age of twelve or thirteen he is ready to begin the first year in high school. As high-school students, we were expected to take good care of ourselves. We were urged to form the habit of integration and unity with others. My father often told us the story of the man who could break a piece of stick but was unable to do so with a bundle of them. He pointed out the unity and harmony formed in relationships with his brother and sisters as an example. And he never mentioned how he helped his younger brother finish his education in an American institution. We know from him how we should interact among ourselves. We often felt that conflicts within families, such as sibling rivalry, hardly existed except in other families.

Parental influences on the youngster's selection of a mate still exist in some ways. The most favorable age for a girl to get married is between twenty-two and twenty-five and for a boy, between twenty-six and thirty. My mother often teased us by saying that we should be married at the age of seventeen like my senior aunt. Actually what she meant was that because mate selection was our own concern we should think carefully before we made our decision. An unhappy marriage is usually caused by a hurried decision, especially during the last years of high school.

Divorce was seldom mentioned among my older relatives and friends. Only recently did we hear that a couple of the younger generation had obtained a divorce. The husband was a doctor who received his degree in England, the wife an employee in a camera shop. It was believed that their marriage stemmed solely from romantic love and failed to develop into companionship. Their failure in marriage may have been due to the differences in background, such as the contrasting educational levels of the couple. Furthermore, disharmony with the "in-laws" and temperamental incompatibility of husband and wife may also have been factors in the marital failure. Divorce is not completely condemned nowadays. According to the marriage laws, a final divorce will be granted after seven years of separation, allowing time for possible reconciliation between the couple during the interim years.

Parental consent in marriage is necessary at all ages. The wedding usually takes place in a church during the day and sometimes a reception follows. A feast after a wedding is favored more than a reception, probably because more friends and relatives are able to attend in the evening. Immediately after the wedding ceremony, the bride is expected to change her wedding gown for a Chinese *chan sam* in which she performs her respect and homage to her "in-laws" and relatives of the older generation. The bride performs the task by handing out cups of tea, first to her husband's immediate family and then to more distant relatives. Even my two sisters, who were married during the last five years in the United States, performed these duties, disregarding the influence of Western culture.

After a son gets married he chooses either to live with his parents or with his wife alone. Usually, in the case of economic insecurity or when one of the parents is missing, the new couple live with their parents. Otherwise, they prefer to live separated from their parents but within the same district.

The family members, although scattered because of marriage and work, still perform some of the duties to their parents. Among them is the duty to teach the younger generation to establish unity and harmony within the family. When my uncle was sixty years old last year, all his sons and daughters, thirteen in number, came home from the United States, England, and China to give him a feast for the celebration of his birthday. They all drank to his health, lining up in a row begining with the oldest sons and daughters and going down to the youngest grandchildren. Disregarding the lack of propinquity, family interaction still strongly influences the life of the adults in many ways.

Ancestor worship is a common religious practice in the Chinese family.

It is based on the supremacy of one's own ancestors rather than the supremacy of a particular god. Each day, an adult member of the family is responsible for lighting the candles of a shrine or an altar. In front of the shrine the pictures of the ancestors, usually the grandparents or the great grandparents of the paternal family, are hung with great respect. The members of the family participate in the worship ceremony, either kneeling or standing, and each nods his head three times in front of the pictures to show his homage to his ancestors.

The family described above is a close-knit social unit. It is disintegrating to some extent, however, as a result of contacts with Western culture. The Westerner, in his formal contacts with Japan, China, and India or in reading external descriptions of them has little opportunity to observe the emotional behavior of the people. The narrator of this document takes us behind the scenes of her family and gives us an insight into the privacy of the affectional behavior, and the conflicts which occur.

Maintaining the Family Line At the center of the Japanese family system in the past was the idea of the maintenance of "the single unbroken family line, including both living and dead, and the concept of filial piety."[5] The basic objective of the lineage group was to care properly for the dead ancestors and to maintain the continuity and prosperity of the family line. If a bride entered a new family, she was expected to learn the customs of her new lineage, work hard, be obedient and submissive. The bride was not only the bride of her husband but the bride of the living members of his lineage and referred to as "our bride." Traditionally the lineage group arranged the marriages of sons and daughters.

The son who became the family head had absolute authority theoretically over other family members. The wife was expected to obey her husband, and when her son became family head, she was expected to be obedient to him. Younger brothers had to obey the elder brother. In actual practice there were wide deviations.

The lineage or kinship group in China is a system of relationships dating back to the 11th century. The kinship system was less extensively distributed geographically than is usually thought, being prevalent in South China but "distinctly under-developed and thinly spread in the northern half of China.[6] Even when the kinship group was well endowed and highly organized it did not have the power and authority of the natural family of father, mother, immature children, and occasionally one or both of the aged parents of the husband.

Loyalty of the individual to his group remains today as the most im-

[5] Vogel, p. 165. See also p. 166.
[6] Ho, p. 20.

portant source of respect. In its most extreme form, loyalty comes very close to familism in that the loyal person will place group interests above his own, will maintain an interest in the welfare, comfort, and sense of honor of the others, and believes that members should hold together against outsiders. Loyalty is limited primarily to the nuclear family and the immediate work group. A wife's loyalty to her husband and children takes clear precedence over loyalty to other relatives and friends. The husband's loyalty to his wife and children takes precedence over loyalty to his parents, though usually husbands try to be loyal to both.[7]

ROLES OF FAMILY MEMBERS

The Family Head The head of the family—usually the oldest male—has the highest status. His primary role is that of general manager of activities outside the home. As head he has final authority in all matters. But the authority of the oldest male may be transferred to another male member of the family, usually the oldest son, as the result of such things as the physical disability of the patriarch or a son's personality, ability, and actual achievement.

The subservient role of the wife in India is illustrated by the following incident:

> At one of our Indian seminars we were trying to explain marriage counseling. It seemed very hard to convey the idea.
> "What happens," we asked, "when an Indian husband and wife get involved in a serious quarrel?"
> "It doesn't happen," was the reply.
> "Put it this way then," we tried again. "What happens when an Indian husband and wife disagree about something?"
> "It doesn't happen," was the reply.
> Baffled, we asked why it didn't happen.
> "Because," they explained, "the Indian wife has been trained from childhood to look up to her husband as a god. So in her eyes he can say no wrong and do no wrong.[8]

Many traditional Japanese abhor the idea of a man working in the home. If a husband does help in the home it is considered peculiar and improper by both men and women. While the rigid separation between the role of the husband and the role of the wife remains strong even in contemporary suburban areas, Vogel indicates that a few men are beginning to offer assistance in the home but in almost all families there is a

---

[7] See Vogel, pp. 147, 152, and 154.
[8] From *Marriage: East and West*, pp. 209–210, by David and Vera Mace. Copyright © 1959, 1960 by David and Vera Mace. Reprinted by permission of Doubleday and Company, Inc.

strict division of labor. Some possible explanations of this are tradition, convenience, relative time the husband and wife spend in the home, and the fact that "wives often consider it simpler to do a little more work and avoid the husband's interference."[9]

The Mother Traditionally the mother had two primary functions: to raise sons and to manage the household affairs. If she had many sons and was diligent in looking after the welfare of children and seeing that the work of the house was done efficiently she would have met satisfactorily the expectations of the family and the community. Although the father, theoretically was vested with absolute authority, in actual practice there was division of labor between husbands and wives.

In his exhaustive study of the changing social role of women in Japan, Koyama considered among other things the extent to which women in their housekeeping roles are given the power of operation, management, and decision-making in the household economy. The following is his summary of a study by the Ministry of Labor of nearly 2,000 women above the age of 20:

> Of those married women who answered, 46 percent said "Mainly I work out the plan" and 18 percent answered "I never make the plan" or "My opinion is sometimes asked." From these figures it may be deduced that a considerable number of women who live with their parents-in-law in the extended family after their marriage are not allowed to participate in the operation of the household economy and thus remain in the helpless position of "the bride."
>
> In the operation of the household economy, there exists a wide difference in the wife's role between rural and urban areas, i.e. between farm and nonfarm families. According to the study of the Ministry of Labour, in the homes of medium-scale and small-scale factory workers, 86 percent of the husbands reported that they "hand over all their wages to their wives," but in the farm families 91 percent of the husbands control all household expenditures.[10]

Ho challenges the idea that in the Chinese family women, on the whole, were subservient to the male head of the family. He indicates that historically dynastic codes invariably mentioned the mother along with the father as having authority. Authority was based more on age than on sex. Thus junior family members owed their filial duty to seniors of both sexes.

Moreover, one has to differentiate between high-and low-class families. Only a high-status family could afford to be large and the

---

[9] Vogel, p. 184.
[10] Takashi Koyama, *The Changing Social Position of Women in Japan* (Paris: UNESCO, 1961), pp. 59–60.

mother in such a family had considerable authority. In the low-status family the husband and wife had to toil together to make ends meet and the husband "did not have even the faintest resemblance to the august head of a high-status family.[11]

The suburban Japanese wife has a dual reaction to her role as manager of the home. On the one hand she is pleased that she is able to devote herself to home and family much more than a wife in a poor family. She wants to have a better and fuller life within the home and she wants to manage the activities of the family more efficiently. She would like to lighten the burden of work within the home, but rejects the idea of a maid, or of her mother-in-law doing any work. And she prefers to do the work herself rather than have her husband help her.[12]

The Son Traditionally sons were expected to do two things: be respectful and obedient to parents and to labor for the welfare of the group. The son either worked on the farm or away from home, turning in the wages to the father. In the past in China, the highest official, regardless of his duties and responsibilities and the distance from the parental home, felt obliged on the death of either of his parents to return to his native city to go through the prolonged period of mourning; otherwise he wuld be lacking in filial piety.

The relationship of children with their mother today varies by birth order, sex, and age. The oldest child is called "older brother" or "older sister." The younger children are called by their first name. Vogel reports as follows on suburban children:

> If the father spends little time at home, the mother may share her problems with the older children and treat them like adults, even in their early teens. The mother is particularly dependent on the oldest son, and may have deeper emotional ties toward him, yet she commonly treats him with more respect and less lighthearted affection than she does a younger son. She looks to him for advice and help with younger children and for financial help in her later years.[13]

The Daughter The high valuation of sons in the families of Japan, China, and India meant that a comparatively lower value was placed on daughters. But as they approached the age of marriage their status improved, for they were of some economic value because the families into which they married gave substantial presents for them. While the status of daughters was low, they had a more favored position than their sisters-in-law.

[11] Ho, p. 24.
[12] Vogel, Ch. 9.
[13] *Ibid.*, p. 238.

The Daughter-in-Law A daughter-in-law traditionally was expected to be subservient to her husband, her father-in-law, the unmarried daughters, and particularly her mother-in-law. She was expected to do the work of the house and to engage in many personal services to the mother-in-law. Her role was defined in the Chinese proverb, "A son-in-law must do one half the duty of a son, but a daughter-in-law must do twice as much as a daughter."[14] A hundred years ago a man could secure a divorce on the ground of barrenness, for sons were highly valued.[15]

Koyama points out that when a daughter-in-law enters her husband's family, there already exists a socially sanctioned power structure headed by either her father-in-law or her husband. "As a new member of the group, she is expected to be subservient to the family head, to abide by family ways and to labour for the family."[16] Moreover, since the parents-in-law and the father's brothers and sisters live together, the daughter-in-law is expected to be devoted to them also. Koyama illustrates the power of the extended family in the following case in which the group forced the divorce of the daughter-in-law, even though the son was in love with his wife:

> Family A is a typical extended rural family consisting of six members—husband (age 24), his wife (22), his parents, father (65) and mother (64), his sister (29) and her child (7), all living under the same roof. The husband's sister, once married, has come back with her own child after her divorce. This family is that of an owner-farmer belonging to the middle class. The husband and wife have been married for two and a half years. What has been expected of the new wife by the other members of the family is that she should keep herself constantly busy doing housework and work out in the field, lighten the burden on her parents-in-law and perform innumerable other chores. Having been brought up in a town nearby, this young wife being inexperienced in farming and somewhat delicate in physique, finds herself unable to live up to the role expected of her. She is therefore regarded as lazy by the other members of the family. Understandably, she cannot satisfactorily play the part expected of her. In addition, her sister-in-law being *demodori* (a slightly contemptuous term applied to a divorced woman who has come back to her own parents' home), though somewhat reserved, is always critical of her brother's wife. On the other hand, her father-in-law, who is rather mild and enjoys his life of semi-retirement, does not wield the patriarch's power very effectively. However, her mother-in-law is the harshest in the treatment of her. Her mother-in-law fully expects her son's wife to take

[14] Kang-Hu Kiang, "The Chinese Family System," *The Annals of the American Academy of Political and Social Science*, 152 (1930), p. 41.
[15] P. G. von Mollendorff, "The Family Law of the Chinese and Its Comparative Relations with that of Other Nations," *Journal of the Royal Asiatic Society of Great Britain and Ireland, North-China Branch*, 15 (1879), p. 113.
[16] Koyama, p. 38.

complete charge of all the housework and farm work in order that she, as an aged mother, can lead a carefree life. As her expectations are not fulfilled, she finds herself frustrated, and becomes critical of her son's wife and adopts a hostile attitude towards her. Under these conditions, in spite of A's love for his wife, he is irritated by his mother's endless criticism and her dissatisfaction directed against his wife. And yet, A being the elder son, his sense of responsibility in the matter of family problems overrides his affection for his wife. He decides finally to apply for a divorce so as to appease the dissatisfaction of his mother and sister.[17]

The relationships of daughters-in-law and mothers-in-law in a rural area are quite different from what they are in an urban setting. Vogel reports that conflict is the dominating theme in the relationships between daughters-in-law and mothers-in-law in a suburban community:

> Most homes in Mamachi do not include a mother-in-law and a daughter-in-law, but if they do, the difficulties between them are almost certain to dominate the family scene. In private conversations and in newspaper columns, the relationship between mother-in-law and daughter-in-law is commonly recognized as the most serious problem facing the modern family. Some girls agree to marriage on the condition that the husband make arrangements for his mother to live elsewhere. Some wives have pleaded with their husbands to prevent the mother-in-law from moving in. Some wives and mothers-in-law have tried to adjust to each other, but the arguments have been so vicious that they have been forced to separate. Some wives, who might otherwise be unhappy, console themselves with the thought that at least they do not live with their mothers-in-law. Yet, as much as they both try to avoid living together, the cost of setting up separate households combined with the limited financial resources, the filial feeling toward parents, and the lack of other satisfactory arrangements for elderly people sometimes leaves no acceptable alternative, especially when the young couple is just getting started or after the mother-in-law is widowed.[18]

CHANGES IN THE TRADITIONAL FAMILY

The Chinese saying, "sleeping in the same bed but with different dreams" is applicable to an ever-increasing number of persons living in the traditional family systems of Japan, China, and India. No systematic analysis has been made of the various factors leading to the disintegration of the family-centered social organization, but the factors which seem particularly important are the adoption and diffusion of European

[17] *Ibid.*, pp. 47–48.
[18] Vogel, pp. 203–204.

and American patterns of behavior, industrialization and mobility, new marriage laws, and the disintegration of traditional mores.

New Culture Contacts Contact with groups practicing different ways of behavior has been one of the primary factors in the disorganization of the extended family and of loyalty to the lineage group. As persons came in contact with missionaries and traders, and as students went outside Japan, China, and India for advanced training, they met religious, political, economic, familial, and other practices radically different from their own. When a person became a Christian and gave up ancestor worship, one of the strongest supports of the extended family and the lineage group was withdrawn. The idea of the national state with national solidarity involved a tremendous shift of attitudes from a family-centered to a state-centered way of thinking. The British occupation of India and more recently the presence of American military forces in Japan resulted in the introduction of many Western ideas.

Industrialization and Mobility The establishment of manufacturing plants, which increased the volume of cityward movement, is a second major factor involved in the disorganization of traditional family practices. This development necessitates the movement of persons and marriage-family units away from the large family or kinship group, which is diametrically opposed to the teaching of Confucius: "While one's parents are alive, one should not go abroad." Changes occurred more rapidly in cities than in villages and in seacoast areas more than in the interior.

Koyama indicates that in World Wars I and II and with the industrialization of Japan the number of women working in industry greatly increased.[19] In the ten-year period from 1947 to 1957, the percent of all women 14 years of age and over who were in the labor force increased from 45.1 to 54.5.[20] This has undermined the traditional notion of the Japanese that women should concern themselves solely with domestic affairs and children.

Mobility weakened and often destroyed the power and authority of the lineage group. As families moved away there was a decrease in their willingness to be subservient to a head some distance from them. Arranged marriages by the lineage group are unacceptable to urban young people. They regard arranged marriages as "remnants of antiquated feudalistic society" whereby the lineage group imposes its will on the young people. Japanese young people are much more willing to accept the assistance or suggestions of their parents than those made by

[19] Koyama, p. 98.
[20] *Ibid.*, pp. 101–102.

the lineage group. Despite the undermining of the authority and economic significance of the lineage gruop, there is still sentimental attachment to this idea. Vogel reports that nuclear families "have a strong desire to continue the family line and an overwhelming hope that the family have at least one son to continue the family line."[21]

The decline in the power of the lineage group, in part, is associated with the decline of arranged marriages and the growth of love matches. Blood studied love matches and arranged marriages of 444 married couples in Tokyo. His sample was not representative of Japanese urban families, for he limited his sample to couples in which the wife was under 40. The families were nuclear with no relatives living in the home, and all resided in three government apartment-house projects housing white-collar workers. In this sample he found that 48 percent of his couples had not been introduced formally but had met at work or in various groups, 16 percent had been introduced by a friend, and 37 percent had been introduced as potential marriage partners.[22] The growth of love matches decreases the power of parents-in-law to regulate the affairs of the new family.

Marriage Laws Undermining the Traditional Family System New laws governing marriage in Japan, China, and India have undermined, either directly or indirectly, the traditional family system.[23] All three countries have the following regulations: (1) monogamy is the only approved form of marriage; (2) divorce may be granted equally to men and women; and (3) the civil rights of men and women are equal. In China and Japan the laws state that marriage shall be based on mutual consent. In Japan and India, women have a legal right to inherit property. Governmental and other organizations have made continuous efforts to acquaint people with the new marriage laws and to secure their practice. For the present, though, these new marriage laws may represent objectives to be achieved more than actual practice, particularly in rural areas.

Disintegration of Traditional Mores When Japan, China, and India were isolated from other countries, the practice of parental arrangement of mates was considered natural and proper, and children followed the custom without complaint. According to tradition the bride and groom were not supposed to meet until after the marriage ceremony.

A public opinion study sponsored by the Prime Minister's Office of

---

[21] Vogel, p. 178.
[22] Robert, O. Blood, *Love Match and Arranged Marriage: A Tokyo-Detroit Comparison* (New York: The Free Press, 1967), p. 36.
[23] New Constitution of Japan, 1946; Marriage Law of the Peoples' Republic of China, 1950; and Hindu Code Bill, 1954.

Japan asked the question, "In regard to the choice of a spouse, which of the two is to be preferred—choice made by parents or by oneself?"[24] One finding was that the younger the age, the greater the percent who preferred to choose their own mate: for men and women 20 to 29 years of age, 79 and 77 percent, respectively, favored personal selection of the mate, whereas for those 60 and over the respective percents were 35 and 37. People in large cities favored the personal choice of the mate (77 percent) more than those in middle-sized and small cities (62 percent) and country areas (59 percent). However, what one prefers and what one feels he must do are two different things. In Japan the percent of marriages in 1955 arranged by parents or a matchmaker was 73 in large cities, 86 in farming areas, and 84 in fishing districts.[25]

A Japanese girl in 1962 describes how a young man came to marry her sister:

> This young man met one of my brothers and asked him about his sisters. He decided he would like to marry my sister and so came to see my mother about it. He said he would like to meet my sister. My mother was agreeable and they became engaged. After that he went back to his home some distance from Tokyo, where we live. Then both families began to find out as much as they could about each other. He waited two or three years. The families found nothing against each other and so it was agreed that the marriage should take place. But my sister had a lot of things she had to learn. She had to learn to cook, to do flower arranging, to sew, and to prepare for management of the home. She took formal schooling for most of these. This man is now my brother-in-law.

A Japanese official concerned with technical work for the Japanese government, described to the authors the marriage arrangements for his son and daughter:

> My son has chosen his fiancée entirely by himself. She is a girl he met at school and we knew nothing about her until he said that he was going to marry her and he wanted to bring her to meet us at our home. As it turned out, we were very happy because she is the daughter of a man I have known professionally for many years. My son has chosen for himself and it is a good choice.
>
> As for my daughter, she wants me to arrange a marriage for her in the traditional way.

As the force of traditional mores weakened, the intellectually emancipated began in increasing numbers to demand the control of arranging their own marriages, equality of woman with men, and many other "modern practices." This period of transition led to conflicts within

[24] Koyama, p. 41.
[25] Ibid., p. 43.

families, to new family accommodations, and to problems which were nonexistent when the prevailing system of family relationships was that of the extended family.

Young people imbued with Western ideals of freedom, individualism, and democracy expect that self-arranged marriages will be happier than those dictated by parents. They are finding, however, much the same type of marital maladjustments with which Westerners are familiar. In addition, there are all the complications of a transition period involving the clash of old and new ideas. Even young people who think of themselves as emancipated may find themselves involved in the countercurrents of conflicting trends.

In the following case both husband and wife had been educated in missionary schools and the young people had taken the initiative in their union. When it turned out unhappily, the wife, conforming to the Western idea, wanted a divorce; but the husband wished to take as a concubine another woman with whom he had fallen in love. This the wife would not tolerate. The husband pointed out that the concubine would serve as maid in the home, giving the wife leisure and freedom. Finding herself in this situation of conflict and confusion, the wife wrote as follows to her husband's brother, who had been her confidant:

> If he actually would give up that woman this time, for the sake of you, my beloved brother-in-law, and my only child, I am still willing to go back with him and reconstruct a new and happy family. If he cheats me again, and continues to support that woman, I am resolved by all means to bring about a divorce. I may lack the means which the other woman has to hold his affection, but I am not going to endure this unreasonable oppression any longer.

SUMMARY

Traditionally the extended family and the lineage group have been considered by the people of Japan, China, and India as the best form of family organization. There is no reliable information on the incidence now of these family practices in the different countries. There is evidence, however, that the nuclear family is the form which increasingly is being adopted.

The decreasing number of extended families and the decreasing loyalty to the lineage group should not lead us to ignore the role of these in the village community. Even after the large family has broken up into its component small-family units and the lineage group has lost much of its power, a large measure of control persists. Claims for assistance are made and recognized between brothers and sisters, uncles and nephews, and cousins.

172   *The Family of Japan, China, and India*

The extended family was a self-sufficient unit containing within itself economic, educational, recreational, protective, and political functions. Emphasizing familial solidarity, it stressed the values of stability, continuity, and security.

The extended family system and the lineage group meant precedence of the parent-child over the husband-wife relationship, and of family solidarity over the desires for individual expression of its members. In Japan, China, and India, the breaking up of the extended family system and the lineage group was associated with the migration of young men from the rural village to the city to carry on professional or other work and with the subsequent following by their wives, the potential or actual economic independence of women, and the intellectual emancipation of college-educated people from old traditions.

PROBLEMS FOR RESEARCH

There are numerous opportunities for research in the changing family in Japan, China, and India.

The Effects of Communism on the Family[26]   The Chinese Communists by their land reforms have destroyed the economic basis of the extended family. It will be more difficult to abolish the traditional attitudes and sentiments which will tend to perpetuate ancestor worship, veneration of parents, control by parents of the marriages of their children, and solidarity of the extended family and kinship groups. Research is needed in the order of disappearance of different aspects of the traditional family, relative effectiveness of the educational and corrective programs employed by governments to secure acceptance of the new laws, what provisions of the law are violated or evaded, rural and urban differences in family behavior, conditions under which an increase in the divorce rate takes place, the rapidity with which women take advantage of their new legal status, changes in legislation as a result of experience, and the similarities and differences in the changes in the family as compared with those taking place in the Soviet Union and the United States.

Problems of Modern Marriage   In the United States modern marriage practices are the result of a gradual development over a period of

[26] See, for example, Sripati Chandrasekhar, "Mao's War with the Chinese Family," *New York Times Magazine*, May 17, 1959: pp. 21 and 71–73. Reprinted in Kimball Young and Raymond W. Mack, *Principles of Sociology: A Reader in Theory and Research*, 2nd ed. (New York: Van Nostrand Reinhold Company, 1962), pp. 273–278.

several generations. In Japan, China, and India there is an opportunity to study the problems of modern marriage in the process of change from marriage arranged by parents to marriage controlled by the young people themselves. What are the conflicts and the accommodations which arise when (1) the young people live in the household of the bridegroom's father and (2) when they live in a separate home? Are there indications in these countries that divorce tends to increase when marriage is based on personal choice?

To what extent have the people of these countries adopted the ideals of equality and democracy in familial relationships, with the role of the wife as mother and companion rather than daughter-in-law and servant? What is the process by which new roles are defined and adopted?

Survival of Extended Family Values It may be assumed that traditional values and attitudes persist in persons who have been emancipated from the control of the family. What traditional values are expressed in the nuclear-family unit? What is the explanation for the persistence of some of these traditional attitudes rather than others?

QUESTIONS AND EXERCISES

1. Analyze the introductory case from the viewpoint of (1) the roles played by family members, and (2) its traditional and companionship characteristics.
2. Compare the general characteristics of the extended family with those of the small-family unit.
3. Enumerate some of the customs associated with the extended family and the lineage group. List as many characteristics of the American family as you can which contrast sharply with those of Japan, China, and India. Note especially the differences in courtship, engagement, and marriage practices in these countries as compared with the United States.
4. How does the extended family system and the lineage group handle problems of economic insecurity and divorce?
5. Contrast the roles of mothers, daughters, and daughters-in-law in Japan, China, and India with these roles in the United States.
6. What are the major forces involved in the disintegration of the extended family and the lineage group?

BIBLIOGRAPHY

Blood, Robert O. *Love Match and Arranged Marriage: A Tokyo-Detroit Comparison.* New York: Free Press, 1967,

Deals with various factors related to arranged and love-match marriages. Compares data on husband-wife relationships in Japan and Detroit.

Embree, John F. *Suye Mura: A Japanese Village.* Chicago: University of Chicago Press, 1939.
> A classic study of life in a Japanese village. Describes the form of the family; how, if there are no sons, the family name is perpetuated by adoption; and roles of various family members.

Fried, Morton. "The Family in China: The People's Republic," in *The Family: Its Function and Destiny*, ed. Ruth Nanda Anshen. New York: Harper, 1959, pp. 146–166.
> Documented description of the Chinese marriage law of 1950, how it works in practice; birth control; and the family in communist China.

Goode, William J. *World Revolution and Family Patterns.* New York: Free Press, 1963.
> Describes the family systems of various countries. Makes generalizations that apply to more than one country.

Ho, Ping Ti. "An Historian's View of the Chinese Family System," in *Man and Civilization: The Family's Search for Survival*, eds. Seymour M. Farber; Piero Mustacchi; and Roger H. L. Wilson. New York: McGraw-Hill, 1965, pp. 15–30.
> An excellent summary of the historical evolution of the Chinese family. Challenges some of the Western ideas of the extended family, particularly its large size and the role of women.

Kapadia, K. N. *Marriage and Family in India*, 3rd ed. London: Oxford University Press, 1966.
> Shows the effect on the extended family of the education of women, urbanization, increased industrialization, and marriage laws. Reports on recent studies of the Indian family. Indicates that the extended family is more prevalent in agricultural than in urban areas.

Keyano, Shogo. "Changing Family Behavior in Four Japanese Communities," *Journal of Marriage and the Family*, 26 (1964): pp. 149–159.
> A study of four Japanese communities of different sizes found a fairly direct relationship between population size and the percentage of nuclear families in the communities.

Koyama, Takashi. *The Changing Social Position of Women in Japan.* Paris: United Nations Educational, Scientific and Cultural Organization, 1961.
> Eight Japanese educational and governmental leaders collaborated in collecting data for this excellent description and analysis of the Japanese family. Shows the emergence of the small democratic family along with the continuance of extended family attitudes, particularly in rural areas.

———, *Gendai Kazoku no Kenkyuu* (An Investigation of the Contemporary Family). Tokyo: Koobundoo, 1960.

Compares Japanese family behavior in a modern apartment building, a rural village, and an isolated mountain village. The decline of the traditional family patterns found to be more related to economic organization than to diffusion from an urban center.

Matsumoto, Yoshiharu Scott. *Contemporary Japan: The Individual and the Group, Transactions of the American Philosophical Society*. Philadelphia: The American Philosophical Society, 1960, pp. 16–35.
   Gives results of public opinion polls on such things as marriage, parent-child relationships, planned parenthood, abortion, size of the family, education, prostitution, status of women, and authoritarianism.

Theodorson, George A. "Romanticism and Motivation to Marry in the United States, Singapore, Burma, and India," *Social Forces*, 44 (1965): pp. 17–28.
   Study of college students in four countries comparing an American group with Asian groups. Found significantly higher degrees of romanticism and of desire to marry among Americans. Interpretation suggests that romantic attitudes act as a positive incentive to marriage, especially under conditions of rapid social change.

Vogel, Ezra F. *Japan's New Middle Class: The Salary Man and His Family in a Tokyo Suburb*. Berkeley: The University of California Press, 1963.
   An excellent presentation of the Japanese family in a suburban area. Includes discussion of the decline of the lineage-group ideal, division of labor in the home, decline in patriarchal authority, family solidarity, and child-rearing practices.

Yang, C. K. *The Chinese Family in the Communist Revolution*. Cambridge: Harvard University Press, 1959.
   Excellent description of changes in the Chinese family during the three decades preceding the communist revolution; the contrasts between traditional and communist attitudes and practices in freedom of marriage, remarriage, and divorce; the crumbling of the age hierarchy; the changing status of women; and the changing structure of the family.

Part II
The Family and Personality

Personality has been defined in a variety of ways, but most sociologists and psychologists recognize that it has two aspects, an internal and an external. The internal is the self, which may be formally defined as all those conscious and unconscious characteristics, qualities, traits, drives, habits, attitudes, ideas, values, and expectations which have been acquired from the family, the kinship group, and others, which are internalized and organized in the individual, and which are perceived and identified as one's own. The external aspect of personality is one's behavior in roles, toward goals, and in interpersonal relationships. The external aspect of the self is in action which can be observed by one's self and by others.

The raw material out of which a self develops is derived from the internalization by the child of cultural patterns, language, social expectations, and other ways of behavior. From these ways of behavior, particularly definitions of himself by the family, the child begins to form a conception of himself; he begins to see himself as others see him. He tends to become organized and unified as he acquires group ideas, attitudes, values, and role expectations. The essence of selfhood is the organization of acquired patterns of behavior into a form which is peculiarly one's own.

This part consists of three chapters: culture and socialization, interaction and socialization, and expectations and roles. These three are closely related and are separated only for purposes of analysis **and** *description.*

Chapter 8
Culture and Socialization

Personality develops in a child as he internalizes the cultural patterns of his family and of the subcultures in which his family participates. Communication and interaction are fundamental processes through which this takes place. Personality tends to become organized and unified as the child acquires group ideas, attitudes, values, and expectations. The child forms a conception of himself from the definitions given him by others and estimates his own worth from these definitions.

GROWING UP IN TWO SOCIETIES

A child is born a member of the human race with his own specific genetic and constitutional makeup. He is also born to be reared in a society, a culture, and a group. Regardless of his hereditary and congenital background, the child will learn to speak the language of the group that rears him, to behave in ways that they do, and to adopt many of the attitudes and values of that society and culture. A striking illustration of this fact is shown in two cases described by Scheinfeld. One involved a Chinese who became completely American in culture. The other involved a white American by birth who was reared by a Chinese family in China and, when he first came to the United States, was completely Chinese in culture:

> No experiment could be more convincing than the actual stories of two young men now living in New York and personally known to the author: one, an American-Chinese; the other a Chinese-American. . . . In the first edition of this book, published in 1939, we told about Fung Kwok Keung, born Joseph Rhinehart (of German-American stock), who, at the age of 2, was adopted by a Chinese man on Long Island and three years later taken to China, where he was reared in a small town . . . with the family

of his foster father until he was 20. Returning then to New York (in 1938), he was so completely Chinese in all but appearance that he had to be given "Americanization" as well as English lessons to adapt him to his new life. A few years later, after the outbreak of World War II, he was drafted into the American army and sent to Italy. In many ways he was alien to the other American soldiers and tried continuously to be transferred to service in China, but army red tape held him fast in Italy until the war's end. Back again in New York Rhinehart-Fung at this writing works as a compositor on a Chinese newspaper . . . and still speaks English very imperfectly, with a Chinese accent.

Now for the remarkably opposite case, that of a *racially* Chinese but *culturally* American young man: Paul Fung, Jr., another war veteran and now a comic-strip artist, whom the author has known since his infancy. Of second-generation American-born Chinese stock, Paul, like his parents before him, was educated with and lived among White Americans all of his life. His thinking, behavior, speech, outlook and sense of humor are completely like that of any other American. . . . He has known little of the Chinese language and customs. So it was with the thought of becoming better acquainted with the Chinese people that, after enlistment in the air force at the beginning of World War II and a year of training, he asked for assignment to the American-Chinese unit which had just been organized.

But Paul soon found that he was a stranger among the others of Chinese stock. He couldn't understand them properly; his language and thinking were different; and—no small matter to a G.I.—there was a food problem, for he preferred Ameircan food and couldn't adjust to having Chinese food served him at virtually every meal. Most of the Chinese-American soldiers thought Paul was "putting on an act." Difficulties and conflicts ensued, and he had to seek companionship among White G.I.'s from a nearby camp. His predicament was never fully realized by the military authorities, and it was only the misfortune of his father's death, calling him home just as the Chinese unit was about to go overseas, which led to his transfer to a regular unit of the air force.[1]

These cases dramatically reveal how the personality of each man was shaped by the culture to which he was exposed. They show how the attitudes and values of a person are influenced by the cultural heritage as transmitted through the family and in the behavior of other persons.

The personality of an individual develops through the operation of three related forms of interaction with others: verbal communication, communication through nonverbal signs and gestures, and emotional interaction. This chapter will deal with interaction through the first two of these under the general subject of cultural conditioning. Personality

---

[1] Amram Scheinfeld, *The New You and Heredity* (Philadelphia: Lippincott, 1950), pp. 505–506.

as influenced by emotional interaction will be considered in the next chapter.

The general subjects discussed in this chapter are (1) the nature of cultural conditioning, (2) cultural conditioning within the family, (3) the acquisition of family culture, (4) outside-the-home conditioning, and (5) the development of the self-concept.

THE NATURE OF CULTURAL CONDITIONING

Definition of Cultural Conditioning Human personality is shaped primarily by cultural conditioning. The human infant is potentially capable of learning a great variety of ways of behavior, as evidenced by the wide range of behavior patterns revealed in anthropological studies. From all the possible ways of behavior, a child in a given society develops the specific ways of behavior of his own society and culture, usually of the particular group in that society into which he is born. He comes in contact with models of behavior practiced by the members of the society in his immediate environment, and he incorporates these behaviors in the form of habits, attitudes, and values. He becomes socialized as a member of the society. In his very early years the infant usually interacts primarily with members of his family or persons selected by them and consequently, it is their habits, their attitudes, their values which become the models for initial behavior. This is illustrated by the results of a study of child-rearing practices of culturally deprived, lower-class, urban Negro families. Wortis and associates interviewed 250 mothers of two-and-a-half-year-old children and subsequently 47 of these mothers when the children were five years old.[2] Almost half had no father in the home, and many received care from a number of mother figures. In general, certain child-rearing practices were used because they were easy or convenient for the mother, with no recognized underlying philosophy of child training. Weaning and toilet training were handled permissively because it was easier. There was very little concern with habits of routine living or orderliness, or with reducing aggression toward other children. Physical punishment was used freely, especially for behaviors which were aggressive toward the mother. Some observations were summarized:

> Other elements in the environment were preparing the child to take over a lower class role. The inadequate incomes, crowded homes, lack of consistent familial ties, the mother's depression and helplessness in her own situation, were as important as her child-rearing practices in influencing

[2] H. Wortis, et al., "Child-rearing Practices in a Low Socioeconomic Group," *Pediatrics*, 32 (1963): pp. 298–307.

the child's development and preparing him for an adult role. It was for us a sobering experience to watch a large group of newborn infants, plastic human beings of unknown potential, and observe over a 5-year period their social preparation to enter the class of the least-skilled, least-educated, and most-rejected in our society.[3]

Examples of Cultural Conditioning Among the elements of culture which the family transmits to the child are his habits of eating, dressing, and walking; language; attitudes toward sex, private property, religion, and outgroups; submission to authority; co-operative and competitive behavior; and the history and tradition of the family group. Language and attitudes toward marriage and childbirth have been selected to illustrate the wide variability in cultural behavior to which the child may be conditioned.

The child's random vocalizations, such as gurgling, grunting, sighing, crying, and shrieking, become defined according to the language system of the community in which he is reared, colored by its peculiar tone qualities. The child learns to speak and to think in the specific language of his society; he also learns to use that language with the vocabulary, grammar, and pronunciation of his own family and subculture. For example, there is some research indicating that language may be used differently in families of different social classes. Bernstein reports that in lower-class families, language is used in a restrictive rather than an elaborative fashion.[4] An exclamation or a partial sentence frequently is used instead of a complete sentence or explanation. If a child speaks, the response may frequently be just "yes," "no," "go away," "not now," or simply a gesture. Extensive patterns of verbal interaction may not be established in such a climate. Also, there may be fewer opportunities for verbal family interaction. Family interaction data gathered by Deutsch indicate far fewer family activities in lower-class homes than in middle-class homes.[5] For example, meals were much less likely to be family affairs. In such models of speech and limited opportunities for the use of language in interaction with adults may lie the basis for the relatively poor development of language skills in children from lower-class families.

Initially, a child has relatively undefined sexual impulses which are capable of being satisfied in a variety of ways. If the culture has a pattern of polygyny, the man's attitudes will be conditioned so that he will want more than one wife and the woman's attitudes will be conditioned

[3] *Ibid.*, p. 307.//
[4] B. Bernstein, "Language and Social Class," *British Journal of Sociology*, 11 (1960): pp. 271–276.
[5] Martin Deutsch, *The Disadvantaged Child* (New York: Basic Books, 1967), p. 359.

so that she will expect to have co-wives. Ideas about the enjoyment of sexual relationships vary from society to society, and even within a given society they may vary by social class or by religion. In a number of studies dealing with attitudes about sexual relationships among very poor families there is evidence of attitudes that sexual relationships are an important source of pleasure for men and that pleasure for women is either incidental or actually disapproved.[6] Women may be regarded as abnormal or improper if they show much interest in sexual relationships with their husbands. Moreover, culture determines some patterns associated with even such a biological function as childbearing. For instance, the *couvade* has been practiced among certain groups, especially early inhabitants of the western hemisphere. When a child is born, the mother will resume her work almost immediately, while the father begins to suffer, takes to his bed, and undergoes a period of fasting and dieting. This custom is followed today by the Ainu of the northernmost islands of Japan. The Ainu mother is active within five or six days after childbirth, while the father is confined for 12 days, behaving like an invalid and observing numerous taboos. The Ainu believe that the child's body comes from the mother; the spirit and mind from the father. He needs to recover from the ordeal of passing on his spirit and mind.[7]

The Function of Communication Sociologists assume that the child is born with the potential to develop personality and perhaps with some response tendencies. The newborn infant does not have specific personality characteristics but develops them very rapidly as an infant and young child. He may continue to modify them over a long period of time. His personality is shaped in the processes of interaction and communication with persons in his environment. He learns how to relate to others by the cues and guidelines given as he interacts with them. He learns what he is and how he is regarded through the definitions furnished to him in a wide variety of communications, some verbal, some gestural, and some which are subtle indications of attitudes toward him.

The importance of genetic and congenital factors is not ruled out. In recent years studies dealing with the biological bases for human characteristics and behavior have begun to appear. An excellent example will be found in the work of Alexander Thomas and his associates.[8] They report the first two years of a longitudinal study of 80 children fol-

---

[6] Lee Rainwater, "Marital Sexuality in Four Cultures of Poverty," *Journal of Marriage and the Family*, 26 (1964): pp. 457–466.
[7] Gordon C. Baldwin, *Stone Age Peoples Today* (New York: Norton, 1964), p. 108.
[8] Alexander Thomas, and associates, *Behavioral Individuality in Early Childhood* (New York: New York University Press, 1963).

lowed from the first months of life. The research was designed to study whether children have discernable patterns of reactivity in early infancy and if such patterns persist during the first two years. The results suggest that some ways of behaving, especially intensity of reaction, may be enduring characteristics of a child during this period.

In the viewpoint presented here, however, the emphasis is on the impact of the environment of human interactions within which the person carries out life activities. The fundamental biological equipment of the human provides, among many other things, exceedingly complex mechanisms by which he is able to use symbols for communication.

Communication is the mechanism through which the child learns and incorporates the ways of behavior of his family, his peers, and groups with which he associates. Groups such as the family and the play group which are characterized by intimate, informal, and unrestricted patterns of communication are particularly favorable to the transmission of the culture to the child.

Relative Absence of Communication An understanding of the importance of communication for the development of personality can be secured from a description of cases involving an almost complete absence of communication with others. These cases illustrate the need for a considerable degree of communication with other persons for the formation of a fully functioning personality.

The cases of Anna and Isabelle are instances of extreme isolation from human associations. Anna was an illegitimate child who for more than five years was incarcerated in an upstairs room of a farmhouse in Pennsylvania.[9] The girl's contacts with her mother and others were minimal, the mother feeding her but otherwise leaving her alone. On discovery she was removed to the county home, after nine months to a foster home, and finally to a school for defective children. Between February 4, 1938, when she was discovered, and November 11, 1938, the period in which she was in the county home, she showed considerable improvement. Davis, who made an intensive study of her case, describes the development in this period as follows:

> If we ask why she had learned so little in nine months, the answer probably lies in the long previous isolation and in the conditions of the county home. At the latter institution she was early deprived of her two little roommates and was left alone. In the entire establishment there was only one nurse, who had three hundred and twenty-four other inmates to look after. Most of Anna's care was turned over to adult inmates, many of

[9] Kingsley Davis, "Extreme Social Isolation of a Child," *American Journal of Sociology*, 45 (1939–1940): pp. 554–565.

whom were mentally defective themselves. Part of the time Anna's door was shut. In addition to this continued isolation, Anna was given no stimulus to learning. She was fed, clothed, and cleaned without having to turn a hand in her own behalf. She was never disciplined or rewarded, because nobody had the time for the tedious task.[10]

In the foster home, where she was the sole object of one woman's care, Anna underwent "what was for her a remarkable transformation—she began to learn":

> Anna had been in the foster home less than a month, but the results were plain to see. Her new guardian was using the same common-sense methods by which mothers from time immemorial have socialized their infants—unremitting attention, repetitive correction, and countless small rewards and punishments, mixed always with sympathetic interest and hovering physical presence. These Anna was getting for the first time in her life.[11]

In this, as in similar cases of social isolation of small children, there remains unanswered the tantalizing question: Was Anna feeble-minded because of isolation or was she already defective mentally at the time she was deprived of social contacts? Although no conclusive answer can be given, another case of extreme isolation throws some light on the question.

Isabelle, discovered about the same time as Anna, had lived under similar, yet different, circumstances.[12] There were these similarities: (1) she was an illegitimate child, (2) she had been kept in seclusion, (3) on discovery she appeared to be feeble-minded and had no speech, and (4) she was about six-and-a-half years old when she was found. Two differences were these: (1) her mother, a deaf-mute, was secluded along with the child, and (2) the child was given prolonged systematic, and expert training in speech and other skills by members of the staff of Ohio State University. Davis summarizes Isabelle's rapid development:

> It required one week of intensive effort before she even made her first attempt at vocalization. Gradually she began to respond, however, and, after the first hurdles had at last been overcome, a curious thing happened. She went through the usual stages of learning characteristic of the years one to six not only in proper succession but far more rapidly than normal. In a little over two months after her first vocalization she was putting sentences together. Nine months after that she could identify words and sentences on the printed page, could write well, and could add to ten, and could retell a story after hearing it. Seven months beyond this point she

[10] Ibid., p. 560.
[11] Ibid., p. 561.
[12] Marie K. Mason, "Learning to Speak After Six and One-Half Years of Silence," Journal of Speech Disorders, 7 (1942): pp. 295–304.

had a vocabulary of 1500–2000 words and was asking complicated questions. Starting from an educational level of between one and three years, she had reached a normal level by the time she was eight-and-a-half years old. In short, she covered in two years the stages of learning that ordinarily require six.

Today she is over fourteen years old and has passed the sixth grade in a public school. Her teachers say that she participates in all school activities as normally as other children.[13]

The evidence from this case seems to indicate that even after an extensive period of isolation, a child may become a person through associations and communication with other persons.

Such cases of extreme isolation occur rarely, of course, and in most instances systematic data are not gathered about them. This was the situation with a child discovered in the early 1960's by an Irish social worker who was subsequently a student of one of the authors. In her work in Ireland the social worker was asked to investigate a rumor about an isolated farmhouse. She found a very small boy who spent all of his time naked in a chicken house, crouched on a ledge in a position similar to that of a chicken. He moved his arms only in a flapping-like motion, and ate in a manner that closely copied the chickens. Investigation revealed that he was the son of a widowed farm woman, conceived and born well after the death of her husband. After secluding him in the house during the early months of life, his mother had placed him in the chicken house which was kept somewhat warm and supplied him with food. His only human contact was when food was brought for him and the chickens, and this contact apparently did not involve any significant interaction. He had evidently imitated the behavior of the chickens in his physical motions, and the sounds he produced resembled the noises of the chickens. The child was reported to be about five years of age when he was discovered. He was subsequently taken to a rural hospital where he was confined to a crib and given a routine type of care. He died of an infection shortly thereafter.

Extraordinary cases such as these indicate the dependency of the human infant upon interaction and communication with human models for the formation of human personality.

The Importance of Language The story of Helen Keller, isolated by blindness and deafness at the age of 19 months, is well known. It affords a particularly poignant illustration of the importance of acquiring the symbol system of language for the development of the human

---

[13] Kingsley Davis, "Final Note on a Case of Extreme Isolation," *American Journal of Sociology*, 52 (1947): pp. 432–437.

potential. The letters of Helen Keller's teacher to a friend detail the processes she used:

April 10, 1887

I see an improvement in Helen from day to day, almost from hour to hour. Everything must have a name now. Wherever we go, she asks eagerly for the names of things she has not learned at home. She is anxious for her friends to spell, and eager to teach the letters to everyone she meets. She drops the signs and pantomime she used before, as soon as she has words to supply their place, and the acquirement of a new word affords her the liveliest pleasure. And we notice that her face grows more expressive each day.

I have decided not to try to have regular lessons for the present. I am going to treat Helen exactly like a two-year-old child. It occurred to me the other day that it is absurd to require a child to come to a certain place at a certain time and recite certain lessons, when he has not yet acquired a working vocabulary. I sent Helen away and sat down to think. I asked myself, "How does a normal child learn language?" The answer was simple, "By imitation." . . . He hears others speak, and he tries to speak. *But long before he utters his first word, he understands what is said to him.* . . . *I shall talk into her hand as we talk into the baby's ears.* I shall assume that she has the normal child's capacity of assimilation and imitation. *I shall use complete sentences in talking to her,* and fill out the meaning with gestures and her descriptive signs when necessity requires it.

April 24, 1887

The new scheme works splendidly. Helen knows the meaning of more than a hundred words now, and learns new ones daily without the slightest suspicion that she is performing a most difficult feat.[14]

It is apparent that the application of methods based on the ordinary interaction of older persons with small children resulted in Helen Keller's acquisition of language and with it the opportunity for a greatly increased range of interaction and development.

CULTURAL CONDITIONING WITHIN THE FAMILY

We shall consider the following aspects of cultural conditioning in the family: (1) methods of conditioning behavior; (2) the family as a conditioning agent; and (3) learning deviant behavior in the family.

Methods of Conditioning Behavior What are the methods by which patterns of behavior become habitual in the person? Communication

[14] Helen Keller, *The Story of My Life.* Copyright 1902, 1903 by Helen Keller. Reprinted by permission of Doubleday and Company, New York, pp. 316–318. This book gives a complete account of her teacher's procedure, including the spelling out of words into Helen's hand, which Helen repeated and associated with objects.

with others is the general mechanism through which ways of behavior are incorporated into the person. George Mead developed a theory that the social ways of behavior of a person are formed through the processes of interaction between himself and others.[15] Mead presented concepts useful in an analysis of how an infant becomes a social person and how this process continues later. One concept is the conversation of meaningful gestures and symbols. We shall examine how an infant develops a repertory of acts which he learns to use to enter into interaction with others.

At birth the baby lacks meaningful acts through which to influence the behavior of others or his own behavior. Soon he acquires some signs and symbols associated with desired objects, such as food. His early responses to such symbols are generally excited, relatively unstructured, diffuse gestures. He learns that a particular type of behavior on his part, such as crying, will result in the bringing of food.

Despite widespread acceptance of the importance of early development and theories about the significance of early patterns of interaction, there are very few systematic observational studies of infants in their natural environment. One such study, reported by Moss, observed 30 first-born infants and their mothers, each pair for a total of 28 hours during the first three months of life.[16] Both maternal and child behaviors were systematically rated. Boys slept less, cried more, and experienced more extensive and stimulating interaction with the mother than girls. All babies who were restless and awake had more interaction with their mothers. Significant differences in the responsiveness of the mothers were found. Such differences were partly accounted for by differences in the behavior of the babies. Moss suggests that mutual stimulation and reinforcement of behavior occurs even in these early interactions. The mother responds to the actions of the child by acts of her own and he in turn responds to her actions. Each response acts as a reinforcement for the preceding behavior. In addition, the mother is teaching her child patterns of response. One might speculate that the mother who responds readily and in a gratifying manner to the acts of her child is also teaching the child something about responsiveness.

In time the child acquires more symbols which he can use to communicate his desires to others. His first use of language is simply to name objects, but he very soon learns to use this language to influence the activities of others. Language rapidly becomes more complex and efficient. Over a period of years the person internalizes from his inter-

---

[15] George H. Mead, *Mind, Self, and Society* (Chicago: University of Chicago Press, 1932).

[16] Howard A. Moss, "Sex, Age, and State as Determinants of Mother-Infant Interaction," *Merrill-Palmer Quarterly*, 13 (1967): pp. 19–36.

actions with others a mass of habitual responses, attitudes, values, and expectations which constitute a large part of his personality.

In addition to learning to communicate with gestures and symbols, the child learns to imaginatively put himself in the place of another and to try out the role of the other. When he is very young, he will overtly act out the roles of others. Whether imaginatively or overtly, the child internalizes the roles he tries, at least to some degree.

Also, when he has internalized symbols, a person can introspectively converse with himself or others. This allows him to try out various acts toward others, judge their probable consequences in the form of others' reactions, and modify overt behavior with a greater likelihood of attaining desired responses. The acquisition of language and the ability to take the role of others internally not only increases enormously the extent to which one can regulate his own behavior and the behavior of others for the attainment of given objectives but results in the acquisition of behavior patterns of others.

Copying the models of behavior around him is another method by which a person acquires the patterns of behavior of others. The following excerpts from two recent letters by a mother describing the behavior of her daughter nearly two years of age indicate the rapidity with which a child acquires models of behavior:

October 17

Judy is really changing. Right now she is extremely interested in dolls. Her baby eats, goes night-night, gets rocked in the rocking chair, and about everything else. She sleeps in her big bed and the doll sleeps in her crib. Right now she is sitting in her rocker giving her baby a bottle. She is so cute now. Imitates everything we do. About 4:30 every evening she decides it is time to eat and goes into the kitchen and sets the table. Of course, we end up with twelve forks on the table, but at least she's trying.

November 7

It doesn't seem possible that she will be two in two weeks. She is so much fun and yet I can get so disgusted at her occasionally. She imitates everything. We got her a tea set the other day. She has to have her coffee with mommy. She sweeps the floor, puts groceries away, helps me wash clothes, etc.

Sociologists feel that in unrestricted communication, such as is found in the intimate, personal, informal relationships of the family, there is a certain fusion of personalities in which the behavior of one person is incorporated into the conduct of another. In these intimate, informal relationships, the developing child almost inevitably takes over prevailing ways of speaking, food habits, prejudices, mannerisms, and religious attitudes.

Expectations of desired behavior are also given to children in the intimate, personal, informal interactions within the family. This is illustrated by the behavior of a mother toward her twin sons, three months old. The following shows how even at this early age she was giving definitions of expected behavior to each of the twins:

> MOTHER. "So you would like to see my babies. Come into the bedroom. I have a fourteen-year old daughter and the twins are from my second marriage. We decided to have a child and prayed that it would be a boy. The Lord was good to us and gave us twins."
> INTERVIEWER. "Are they identical?"
> MOTHER. "No! Bobby is more like me and Geney is more like my husband. Geney is the one with the big personality, while Bobby is a pretty boy. Geney already has a butch haircut. When I brush his hair I brush it up on end."
> As she talked to the children Bobby was the more responsive, smiling and cooing in apparent delight. Geney was hardly awake. The mother wanted the "personality baby" to show his smile. With some talking and smiling at him, he finally smiled and the mother was very pleased. "When I come into the room I put on a big smile, regardless of how I feel, for I think that is important for the babies."
> INTERVIEWER. "About what age did you first notice either smiling?"
> MOTHER. "About six weeks, and by two months they were smiling readily."
> Taking Geney by both hands and giving him a very slight pulling movement, the mother said: "I will be glad when you sit up, for you will be even more fun then."
> At the door she said: "I am working to help pay expenses. But I almost resent the time I have to be away from the babies."

Definitions of desired ways of behavior are consciously and unconsciously given to a person by his parents and later by peer and other groups. Many techniques are used to do this. At least three of these can be identified: defining certain ways of behavior as good and desirable and other ways as bad and undesirable; inhibiting undesirable behavior; and rewarding approved or desirable behavior. Smiles and caresses follow approved acts, while frowns and scoldings follow disapproved acts. The child repeats those acts which are the most satisfying and abandons those which fail to bring satisfaction. Of course, if engaging in disapproved ways of behavior secures attention which is not secured in other ways, the disapproved ways of behavior may become habitual.

Let us suppose that a parent wants to create a desire to read in his child. At an early age reading might be defined as desirable behavior and models of this behavior might be presented to him by reading to him.

Other models might be the parents reading in the presence of the child or reading by siblings and other children. The parents may reward the child through praise for his attempts at reading. The point is that children for the most part take over the definitions of behavior of persons with whom they are intimately associated.

Formal training is another way by which the behavior patterns of others become a part of a person. For instance, in training a child to avoid being hit while crossing the street, as the father and daughter walk together, the father repeats over and over to the child, "Look both ways before you cross the street." This becomes so much a habit of the child that she not only looks both ways herself but tells herself, her father and others who may happen to be along to do so too. All day long a child is being given definitions of the way to behave.

The Family as a Conditioning Agent An analysis of life-history documents reveals at least four reasons why the parental family is so influential in the personality development of the child: (1) The child comes in contact with culture as it is embodied in the behavior of particular persons, and for a while the members of his family are the persons with whom he has significant contacts. The family conditions vocal impulses, hunger, various activities, and ways of interaction according to specific patterns; in addition, it defines what the child sees, hears, and smells, and his tastes, wishes, and ambitions—in fact, most of his behavior. (2) Childhood experiences indirectly influence the acquisition of later behavior because they sensitize the person to pay attention to certain things and to neglect others. (3) The person's acceptability or unacceptability to others is, in part, determined by his family, for it gives early direction to his personality traits, such as sociability, adaptability, ability to take the role of the other, and friendliness. (4) Because the family is organized around many common interests over a long period, interdependent relationships and attachments are formed among its members; this results in direct and continuing modification of family members by one another. The strength of these influences is indicated by the fact that interdependent relationships and attachments may only partially disintegrate when children leave and form their own homes or when the husband and wife are separated or divorced. Years of communication between the members tend to perpetuate attachments in spite of later physical separation or divergence of interests.

The definitions given by the family gain added weight because they are acquired during the first months and years of the child's life, they persist over a relatively long time span, and they are given and received in intimate, personal, informal interrelationships, where the transfer of behavior patterns occurs most easily. While some definitions of behavior are consciously instilled in the child, most patterns of behavior are given to him and acquired by him in his day-to-day communication with members of his own family and other persons.

Learning Deviant Behavior in the Family The influence of definitions, family conditioning, and significant models suggests one possible interpretation of a major study of deviant children by Robins—the importance of the father's behavior.[17] Robins followed the life histories of children referred to a psychiatric clinic in the 1920's. About 30 years later, both record and interview data were obtained for 476 patients (89 percent of selected subjects) and 97 normal controls (97 percent of selected subjects). Data were sufficient to allow diagnosis of sociopathic personality of adults, defined as the existence of repeated gross antisocial behavior. The most important finding relating to the family was the relationship between antisocial behavior of the father and a subsequent diagnosis of sociopathic personality in his adult offspring.

> Antisocial behavior in the father of patients seems to be an important predictor of similar behavior in the patients themselves, whether the patients are men or women. The father's behavior appears a better predictor than does behavior of the mother or siblings. . . . When *only* the mother has behavior problems, the risk of sociopathy in the child is no greater than when she does not.
>
> The kinds of behavior in the father which predict behavior problems in the child are desertion, excessive drinking, chronic unemployment, failure to support the family, and arrests.[18]

Lack of adequate supervision and discipline during adolescence was also related to the development of sociopathy in adulthood, while either adequate or too strict discipline was not.[19] Parental discord, including breaking up the home, seemed to be related to sociopathy in the children only when it was a reflection of the father's behavior problem.[20]

ACQUISITION OF THE FAMILY CULTURE

By "family culture" is meant the specific body of customs which is handed down within the home from generation to generation. Each generation has two tasks with reference to culture: acquiring the culture from the past, and transmitting it to the next generation. The acquisition of the family culture occurs in the continuity between the parental family

---

[17] Lee N. Robins, *Deviant Children Grown Up* (Baltimore: Williams and Wilkins, 1966).
[18] *Ibid.*, pp. 178–179.
[19] *Ibid.*, pp. 167–171.
[20] *Ibid.*, pp. 171–174.

and its children, in identification of family members with the family's historical background, in the projection of frustrated parental desires on the child, and in the recreation of the general culture.

Cultural Continuity Families in the past maintained close continuity between one generation and the next. The children almost always adopted the political affiliations, religious preferences, and class identification of their parents. Benjamin Franklin, writing in 1771, reported that from the notes of one of his uncles he learned that his ancestral family had lived in the same English village for at least three hundred years "on a freehold of about thirty acres, aided by the smith's business," which had continued in the family up to that time, "the eldest son being always bred to that business, a custom which he and my father followed as to their eldest sons."[21]

Generally, in our modern society sons are not likely to follow the specific occupations of their fathers. This is not quite so true for broad occupational groupings, but even here occupational continuity is very low. In a later chapter[22] we will show that skilled and semiskilled workers have the highest continuity with the occupations of their fathers, with just over half being in the same occupational level. Unskilled workers and farm laborers rank second in continuity. Clerical and sales workers have the least continuity, with about one in five reporting the same occupations as their fathers. Professional and semiprofessional rank second in vertical mobility—in moving away from the father's occupation. Thus today the family pattern is no longer the sole factor, and not always the chief one, in determining the vocational choices of young people.

Socialization of American children into the political system was investigated by Hess and Torney using a national sample of several thousand school children in grades two through eight.[23] The family seems to play a major role in two aspects of political socialization. One is the development of a strong, positive attachment to the United States as an ideal country. This attitude seems to be firmly established by age seven (grade two, the youngest children studied) and to show relatively little change through the elementary school years. Although the study did not explicitly examine the origin of this attitude, from the young age of the children one may safely assume that attachment to the country developed primarily within the family.[24] Preference for a political party

[21] Percy H. Boynton, (ed.), *The Autobiography of Benjamin Franklin* (New York: Harcourt, Brace, 1926), p. 3.
[22] Chapter 18.
[23] Robert D. Hess and Judith V. Torney, *The Development of Political Attitudes in Children* (Chicago: Aldine, 1967).
[24] *Ibid.*, Chapter 2.

194   *Culture and Socialization*

is also transmitted through the family, with clear-cut similarities of partisanship attitudes among the children in the same family.[25]

Political views of relatively young adolescents closely parallel those of their parents. George Gallup made the following statement in an interview prior to the 1968 election:

> Young persons between the ages of 14 and 18 mirror their parents' views almost 100 per cent—so much so that if you were to poll the high-school students of the United States the week before the election, and if you had a perfect sample, you'd probably have a perfect prediction.[26]

Identification with the Family's Historical Background Many families have some stories and jokes that date back one or two generations. These are told and retold until they become part of the history of the family. They are connected with certain events in the lives of older members of the family, such as weddings, births, economic ventures and opportunities, and locations in which parents and grandparents have lived. This will be illustrated by excerpts from two life-history documents, one on a wedding and the other on an economic possibility:

> My mother likes to tell this story about my father. On the day after their wedding my father and mother were driving to a dance in the community where my father lived and worked. Although he had driven the road many times when he was courting my mother, he got lost three times and had to plod his way through the snow up to farm houses, asking the way to his home community.

> My oldest uncle tells the following story about my great-grandfather. When Grandpa Peterson first came to Minnesota he homesteaded a farm on which downtown Minneapolis later developed. He sold his farm and bought 10 acres on a lake front which is now an exclusive residential district in Minneapolis. Wouldn't it have been great, if my great-grandfather had kept this property and distributed it to his heirs?

As they hear stories such as the above, children acquire a sense of belonging to an ongoing family group with a colorful history. Subsequently they will tell some of these stories to their own children and to those who marry into the family. Young children also delight in stories of their own early history, again building a sense of family identification.

Projection of Parental Aims Often the cultural pattern implanted in the child is the frustrated ambition of a parent. A mother whose un-

---

[25] *Ibid.*, pp. 95–99.
[26] *United States News and World Report*, July 29, 1968, p. 34.

fulfilled girlhood ambition had been to teach school may be determined that her daughter go to college and become a teacher. Or the parent may have aspirations for a great career of noble service for the child:

> Before I was born my mother dedicated me to God in case I should turn out to be a boy, and she interpreted this to mean that I should enter the ministry. My mother feels that her debt to the Lord will not be fully paid unless I enter the ministry. I am firmly convinced that this attitude of hers, linked as it is with my earliest childhood memories and teachings, has had a controlling effect upon my life. On several occasions I have nearly entered business and have always at the last moment given it up, my decision in each case being determined by some unconscious feeling, and not by rational considerations.

In this case it is plausible to infer that influences outside the family came into conflict with the expectation implanted in the boy's thought of himself by his mother.

OUTSIDE-THE-HOME CONDITIONING

Ways of behavior learned in the family, obviously, are added to and modified by such outside-the-home influences as the community, the church, and the school. The following case demonstrates how outside-the-family influences, particularly the church, modify personality:

> Both my parents were church-going Methodists, and my mother was very devout. I grew up in the church, and that was the only place I was ever taken except to visit friends.
> Three weeks before my twelfth birthday, and a few days before Christmas, my father was taken sick with pneumonia. A week later he died.
> My mother, to support us, bought a small rooming house. For two years we struggled along, trying to make both ends meet. When all our rooms were filled, we had an income large enough to make our payments on the house, to pay taxes, and to live.
> Here in the rooming-house I found myself a stranger in a strange land. The street on which we lived was very cosmopolitan, and many nationalities were represented. It was impossible to live in a house with a number of men of all types very long without coming face to face with sex. One roomer taught me masturbation, and I practiced it quite extensively for about a year.
> We continued to go to church every Sunday, and my religious consciousness began to reawaken. I heard preachers preach about "hell fire," and exhort people to get saved. The question of religion was uppermost in my mind. I began to read a chapter in the Bible every day, and to pray more. In recent years a number of my father's folks told me that at about this time I changed from a very bad boy into quite a good boy.

This case brings out clearly the way in which the subjective life of the person, his desires and his attitudes, become culturally conditioned. It also raises the question of what the relation is between the culture of the family and the culture of the environing society. In moving into the rooming-house, the boy was placed in contact with influences in conflict with those of his family and his former surroundings. It was the church that crystallized the trends of his personality development.

Some of the ways in which the family and subsequently the educational, religious, and community systems can socialize the thinking and beliefs of children are illustrated somewhat dramatically by the white communities in South Africa today.[27] Members of both nuclear and extended families are all almost invariably from one of the two white groups, either the Afrikaner (descendants of Dutch settlers) or the English speaking. In the public school which most children attend, a given school will include only teachers and children from one of the white communities. These arrangements are explicit policies designed to maintain a school environment as exclusive as the home situation. For the Afrikaner, the church also reinforces the values of exclusiveness of the white Afrikaner community. Churches of the English-speaking community are generally affiliated with international bodies and do not espouse racial exclusiveness. Almost all contacts of members of both white communities with nonwhites are largely controlled by the governmental policies of *apartheid*, with white children having frequent contacts with nonwhites who are always in subordinate positions and have inferior status. The consistency of family and community socialization practices for the Afrikaner seems to develop persons with a strong sense of moral and intellectual righteousness about conduct and policies which are widely condemned throughout the rest of the world. The English-speaking white South African is in a much more ambivalent position.

The importance of the general culture in developing specified sex-role behaviors is emphasized by results of a major longitudinal investigation. The study was conducted by Fels Institute in Ohio and began in the 1930's.[28] Children and their families were seen at frequent intervals beginning in infancy and continuing through adolescence. The child subjects were subsequently interviewed and tested as young adults in their twenties. A most important finding was that many behaviors assessed in children between six and ten years of age were fairly good predictors of similar behaviors in the young adults. Figure 13 shows the correlations between assessments of certain behaviors at age six to ten

[27] Leonard M. Thompson, *Politics in the Republic of South Africa* (Boston: Little, Brown, 1966), pp. 98–113.
[28] Jerome Kagan and Howard A. Moss, *Birth to Maturity* (New York: John Wiley and Sons, 1962).

with assessments of similar behaviors in young adulthood. These results offer considerable empirical support for the idea that significant aspects of adult personality take shape in relatively early childhood when family influences are important. At the same time, examination of Figure 13 shows that the degree of relationship of childhood to adult

Figure 13. Correlations between selected child behaviors and similar adult behaviors*

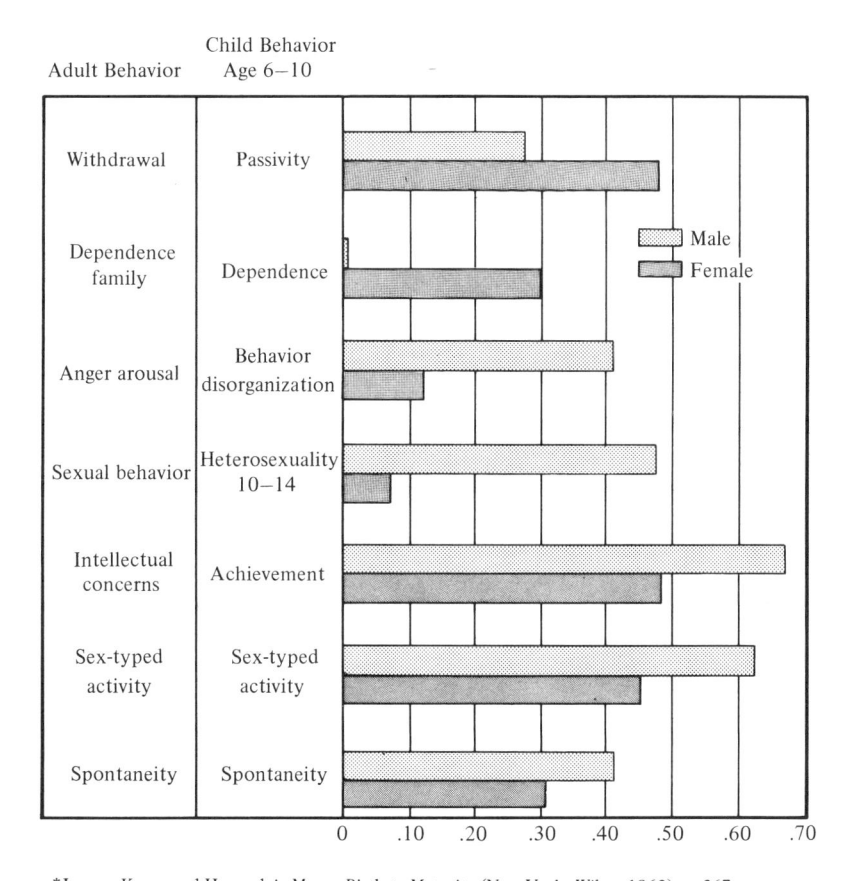

Adult Behavior	Child Behavior Age 6–10	Male	Female
Withdrawal	Passivity	~.28	~.52
Dependence family	Dependence	~.01	~.38
Anger arousal	Behavior disorganization	~.45	~.11
Sexual behavior	Heterosexuality 10–14	~.48	~.05
Intellectual concerns	Achievement	~.68	~.48
Sex-typed activity	Sex-typed activity	~.62	~.44
Spontaneity	Spontaneity	~.40	~.30

*Jerome Kagan and Howard A. Moss. *Birth to Maturity* (New York: Wiley, 1962), p. 267.

behavior is greatly influenced by whether a type of behavior is approved by the traditional standards for sex-appropriate behavior held by the culture outside of the home. Passive or dependent behavior is considered appropriate for women but not for men; indeed, these behaviors show much higher correlations between childhood and adulthood for women than for men. On the other hand, anger and overt aggression as well as frequent and overt sexual interest are much more acceptable in men than women and these behaviors are significantly correlated over time for men but not for women. Intellectual activity and appropriate sex-role activities are approved for both sexes and correlate over time for both sexes. The apparent importance of culturally prescribed behaviors for each sex is striking, with certain behaviors being reinforced and others extinguished or altered between childhood and adulthood. The authors of the Fels study report: "Even the children who were reared by families that did not consciously attempt to mold the children in strict accordance with traditional sex-role standards responded to the pressures of the extrafamilial environment."[29]

Another area in which outside-the-home influences may be important in conditioning behavior is the learning of delinquent behavior. Criminologists hold that both the family and the neighborhood are potent influences in the development of delinquency. Sutherland and Cressey describe five principal processes in the development of delinquency:

> First, a child may assimilate within the home by observation of parents or other relatives the attitudes, codes, and behavior patterns of delinquency. He then becomes delinquent because he has learned delinquency at home. . . . Second, parents determine both the geographic and social class locus of the home in the community, and the locus of the home, in turn, largely determines the kind of behavior pattern the child will encounter. If the home is in a high delinquency area, the probability that the child will encounter many delinquent patterns is higher than it is if the home is located in a low delinquency area. Similarly, being a member of a lower socioeconomic class may greatly affect the child's denial or acceptance of the dominant values of the society. Third, the home may determine the prestige values of various persons and also the types of persons with whom intimacy later develops. . . . He learns, in other words, to pay little attention to the behavior patterns, whether criminal or anticriminal, presented by some persons, and pay close attention to those presented by other persons. Fourth, a child may be driven from the home by unpleasant experiences and situations or withdraw from it because of the absence of pleasant experiences, and thus cease to be a functioning member of an integrated group. . . . Fifth, the home may fail to train the child to deal with community situations in a law-abiding manner.[30]

THE DEVELOPMENT OF SELF-CONCEPT

Definitions of Biological Traits and Self-Conception The relationship between definitions of biological characteristics and the conception one has of oneself is clearly illustrated in the following case:

[29] *Ibid.*, p. 268.
[30] Edwin H. Sutherland and Donald R. Cressey, *Principles of Criminology* (Philadelphia: Lippincott, 1966), pp. 225–226.

The birth of a son, I've been told, was a grand event. I was the first son born to any relative or member of our family.

I was a shy child and guess I still am. I remember being apprehensive about meeting new people or doing new things. I was never the physical type and maybe this had something to do with it. I always seemed to take to heart any criticism I received from my friends. Fear of disapproval or criticism soon became an obsession with me. I often tried to improve in those areas where I lacked. I practiced kicking a football for hours in the vacant lot nearby.

Many things in my past have made me feel insecure and shy. My parents have always set high standards for me. My father always told me that I was going to be a star on a football team and going to a certain university. These were his dreams for me and I felt that I was letting him down whenever I missed the kickball or lost at tether-ball. I had only good grades to show him and this comforted me somewhat.

When I was nine, my family made a big move and came to live in our new house. The environment was completely different. At the new school I continued to get good grades, but my trouble with sports soon reared its ugly head. Soon I would look at the clock and wish it would stop whenever the hour for team games rolled around. I soon learned to hate baseball and getting up to bat because I knew I would miss and strike out and to a young boy this could be the most important thing in his life.

The first time I was ever called a name was when I was about eleven and had a fight with my friend. He was of German descent and in the heat of the fight I called him a Nazi, a term my mother called him, for she didn't like this boy. In turn he called me a dirty Mexican. I guess that was the turning point in my life. From that moment on I vowed that I would become as un-Mexican as possible. I became critical of my father's Mexican accent and his mispronouncing of certain words. If someone asked my nationality I would either mumble the word Mexican or else say Spanish. I began to notice the Mexican children at school. Their skin was darker than mine, though mine was darker than most of the non-Mexicans.

Some of the relationships between social definitions of biological traits and personality characteristics are clear in this boy: the importance of being a male child, his conception of being a failure in those athletic activities so highly valued by his father, and the meaning attached to having the dark skin of a Mexican.

The influence on the self-concept of the social definitions given to physical characteristics, particularly those deviating greatly from the usual, has been emphasized by Macfarlane[31] of the Berkeley Child Guidance Study, and by Sears, Maccoby, and Levin. Both studies found that differences in physical characteristics determine, in part, the con-

---

[31] Jean Walker Macfarlane, "Study of Personality Development," in *Child Behavior Development*, Roger G. Barker, Jacob S. Kounin, and Herbert F. Wright (eds.) (New York: McGraw-Hill, 1943), Chapter 18, particularly pp. 316 and 319.

ception a person has of himself. The following from Sears, Maccoby, and Levin indicates how differences in physical characteristics influence the reactions of persons, particularly the peer group, toward the child and the child's reaction toward himself:

> Take, for example, the consequences of sheer physical size. A boy whose weight is in the lower fourth of the population during his preadolescent and adolescent years is unlikely to play football during his senior year in high school. Whatever may have been his father's hopes for him at birth, he will never have had the opportunity to practice the necessary skills, nor to enjoy the gratifications, of football play. He will never have learned the myriad habits, feelings, attitudes, and interests that characterize the social role of "football player." His peer group choices for friendship and recreation are affected in many ways—negatively in the sense that he cannot be a part of the ball-playing group, positively in the sense that he joins a different kind of group. If his father set great store by athletic success, the boy may have lived with a certain sense of inadequacy; and this in turn will have influenced his reactions to his peers, who in their turn will have responded to his behavior with whatever actions their personalities made possible. These peer group experiences contribute to the boy's own attitudes toward others and toward himself.[32]

Thus the conception a person has of himself seems to depend in part on the meaning his physical characteristics have for him, as defined by his family, his peer group, and by other persons.

The Development of Self-Esteem In developing a self-concept, the child acquires ideas about his own value or worth. He comes to regard himself somewhere on a continuum from high self-esteem to low self-esteem. This estimate of himself is important both for personal satisfaction and effective functioning. Two studies of self-esteem in young persons support the widely held belief that the family is a major influence in the development of self-esteem.

A survey of more than 5,000 high school students was used by Rosenberg to examine the social conditions associated with enhanced and diminished self-esteem.[33] Major social influences, such as social class and ethnic group affiliation, appeared either not related or only slightly related to self-esteem in adolescents but family factors, especially birth order and the relationship with the father, are significantly related. Adolescents who have close relationships with their fathers are likely to have high self-esteem. This type of relationship seems to occur most frequently in families with only one child, especially when the child is a male.

[32] Robert R. Sears, Eleanor E. Maccoby, and Harry Levin, *Patterns of Child Rearing* (New York: Harper & Row, 1957), pp. 452–453.
[33] Morris Rosenberg, *Society and the Adolescent Self-Image* (Princeton, N. J.: Princeton University Press, 1965).

Coopersmith studied a great many aspects of personality and family background of 85 fifth-grade boys selected from a large sample as having specific degrees of self-esteem.[34] He summarizes the antecedents of high self-esteem as total or nearly total acceptance of the children by their parents, the establishment of a structured world in which definite values are espoused and clear limits set, and relatively great freedom within the established structures and limits.[35] In general, parents of boys with high self-esteem are active, poised individuals, on relatively good terms with each other, with many sources of gratification. Coopersmith found that self-esteem is likely to be high among first and only children (who are in a position to receive more parental attention); when the child's rapport with his mother is close; when the child perceives general agreement with his family; when parental control is fairly extensive; and when parental decisions are relatively firm.

SUMMARY

Compared with the young of other animals, the child's original equipment is highly unorganized and plastic. The organization of this random behavior into ingrained habits is the result of cultural conditioning. The child is potentially able to adopt almost any pattern of behavior to which he is consistently exposed. Instances of extreme isolation and cases where communication is difficult because of sensory defects point to the function of association and communication in the formation of personality.

In intimate association within the family the child gets his first attitudes, his first sentiments and values, and the first definitions of expected behavior. The family conditions him to speak a given language, defines eating and sleeping habits, and indicates other ways of acceptable behavior. In modern society the child by the age of two or three may begin to come in contact with outside-the-home patterns of behavior. While these may supplement and reinforce the definitions of behavior given by the family, they frequently are in conflict with those of the home. This becomes increasingly the case as the child grows older. But habits acquired within the family, of which the individual is often unconscious, affect the behavior of the person throughout life.

The handing down within the home of more or less unchanged practices was almost the rule in earlier times. Today family customs frequently undergo considerable change within a single generation. For one thing, as family members become familiar with a wide range of behavior patterns outside the home, their traditional family customs are modified

[34] Stanley Coopersmith, *The Antecedents of Self-esteem* (San Francisco: W. H. Freeman, 1967).
[35] *Ibid.*, p. 236.

and personalities also are modified through cultural conditioning. Cultural conditioning, while it begins in infancy, continues throughout life.

PROBLEMS FOR RESEARCH

Primary Associations What evidence is available or obtainable to prove or disprove the sociological view that behavior patterns are transmitted most easily in intimate, informal, primary associations? It would be significant to study the personality characteristics which differentiate children from homes characterized by formality and relative lack of intimacy and children from homes characterized by a great deal of communication which is intimate, personal, informal, and unrestricted.

Comparative Studies of Personality in Varying Cultures What differences in personality development are associated with varying cultural levels in the United States? The enormous differences in the culture of families in this country have not been fully appreciated. It is not merely the wide variation between urban and rural families. The observable variations in culture seem to be correlated with variations between regions, with differences in occupation and in economic class, and with variations in urbanization.

In what ways does the role of culture in personality development differ in various countries? Among contemporary people it would be feasible to describe and analyze comparatively the cultural conditioning of the person in different family forms, such as the extended family in India and the nuclear family in the United States. There have been a few studies of a community or a group at a given time and then a restudy of it a generation or two later.[36] The primary interest of these studies has been in changes in the culture. These studies could be analyzed to see whether they reveal changes in personality over a period of time. Similar study and restudy of groups should be made with particular emphasis on changes in personality related to social and cultural changes.

QUESTIONS AND EXERCISES

1. Give evidence to support the conclusion that man is not born with a personality but acquires his distinctive personality characteristics in association with others.

[36] Wilson D. Wallis and Ruth Sawtell Wallis, *The Micmac Indians of Eastern Canada* (Minneapolis: University of Minnesota Press, 1955); Robert Redfield, *A Village that Chose Progress: Chan Kom Revisited* (Chicago: University of Chicago Press, 1950); and Margaret Mead, *New Lives for Old: Cultural Transformation— Manus 1928–1953* (New York: Morrow, 1956).

2. What were the methods used by Helen Keller's teacher in her training and socialization of Helen?
2. Anna and Isabelle were about six and Helen Keller almost seven when deliberate attempts were made at training. There were great differences in the personal development of these three girls. What are some general explanations for the differences in the degree of mental and social development attained by persons who are extremely isolated from others for several years?
4. Do you think a family could be conditioned to new material cultural patterns more readily than to new nonmaterial patterns? For instance, would it be easier for a family to become adapted to living in a plastic house and traveling in a helicopter than it would to adjust to having a wage-earning mother and a housekeeping father?
5. Give four reasons why the family is so determinative in the formation of the child's personality.
6. How do you account for the fact that occupational choices are not so much determined by family tradition as they were two or three generations ago?

BIBLIOGRAPHY

Clausen, John A. "Family Structure, Socialization, and Personality," in *Review of Child Development Research*, eds. Lois Wladis Hoffman and Martin L. Hoffman. New York: Russell Sage, 2, 1966.
    Analyzes influences of family structure, family relationships, values, and processes on the socialization and development of children.

Cloward, Richard A.; and Ohlin, Lloyd E. *Delinquency and Opportunity: A Theory of Delinquent Gangs*. New York: Free Press of Glencoe, 1960, Chs. 3 and 4.
    Reviews various theories of delinquent behavior and emphasizes the theory that delinquency is primarily a lower-class way of life and results from unfulfilled aspirations and blocked opportunity. Delinquency is considered a subculture.

Coopersmith, Stanley. *The Antecedents of Self-esteem*. San Francisco: W. H. Freeman, 1967.
    Reports an extensive study of self-concept in 10 to 12-year-old boys with particular emphasis on family situations and behaviors that are related to the development of high or low self-esteem. Also reviews the literature in this area.

Elkin, Frederick. *The Child and Society, The Process of Socialization*. New York: Random House, 1960.
    A brief review of knowledge about socialization chiefly from the viewpoint of role theory and cultural conditioning. General and introductory rather than technical.

Hollingshead, August B. *Elmstown's Youth: The Impact of Social Classes on Adolescents.* New York: John Wiley and Sons, 1949.
> A classic study of the determining nature of culture on the personalities of members of a society. Shows how the culture of a social class determines the educational achievement, religious behavior, clique membership, occupation, marriage partners, and aspirations of sons and daughters whose parents are of a given class.

Moore, Bernice Milburn; and Holtzman, Wayne H. *Tomorrow's Parents: A Study of Youth and Their Families.* Austin, Texas: University of Texas Press, 1965.
> Analyzes data from a very large-scale survey of high school students. Focuses on the influences that various family variables have on the attitudes, aspirations, and behavior of adolescents. Includes data on families with one parent, a remarried parent, and with resident grandparents. Also includes a section on the married high school student.

Nye, F. Ivan. *Family Relationships and Delinquent Behavior.* New York: John Wiley and Sons, 1958.
> A study of delinquent behavior in the high school population of three small urban communities by means of a self-reporting questionnaire. Delinquent behavior related to numerous variables of family life.

Sherif, Muzafer; and Sherif, Carolyn W. eds. *Problems of Youth: Transition to Adulthood in a Changing World.* Chicago: Aldine, 1965.
> A series of papers dealing with youth subcultures in different social settings and situations. Analyzes the operation of socio-psychological factors in adolescents in varying environments. Chapters prepared especially for this book.

Woods, Sister Frances Jerome, CDP. "Family Roles and Values," *Cultural Values of American Ethnic Groups.* New York: Harper, 1956, Part III, pp. 149–338.
> Excellent analysis of the role of culture in determining values. The approach is to study family values not only of native-born white American, but of various ethnic groups, such as Chinese, Japanese, Negro, Mexican, and Jewish. Presents the implications of understanding the values of groups for professional social workers.

Chapter 9
Interaction and Socialization

> *When a baby is born into a family, he enters into a network of interactions and relationships. He lives in an emotional environment that is composed largely of the ways members express their feelings toward each other, and, especially, toward him. As he develops the capacity to enter actively into this network of interactions and relationships, he too will form ways of expressing himself to other family members. Interaction and the consequent conditioning in infancy and early childhood are very influential for setting general patterns for subsequent ways of behavior.*

INTERACTIONS WITH A YOUNG CHILD

The following account by an educated couple describes their goals for and behavior with their two-year-old son. It also gives their perceptions of his responses:

Husband: Larry now is two years old and from the beginning we engaged in ways of behavior to develop him into the kind of person we wanted him to be. Regardless of whether what we did was important in his personality development, he is turning out the way we wanted.

We wanted him to have a sense of humor. By the age of 5 months he was enjoying and laughing at incongruous ways of behavior, such as my wearing one of my wife's hats.

We wanted him to be affectionate. The model of showing affection was present, for my wife and I are quite affectionate toward each other. In addition we told him how to hold his lips in a kiss—at first he kept his mouth wide open. He has two other affectionate gestures—probably from models: an embrace, and a gentle patting of me or his mother.

We wanted him to be gentle. To some extent this was developed in him by the age of 16 weeks. We have a picture taken at that age in which

Larry is petting the dog and not pulling at him. He is also gentle with his mother and to some extent with me. This has been done by verbal instructions. If he were rougher than his mother or I enjoyed, we would say, "Be gentle with Daddy" or "Be especially gentle with Mother."

We wanted him to be a happy person with a minimum of angry behavior. Again the models are important. My wife and I are happily married and show happiness in a great many ways. We do not frustrate him any more than is absolutely necessary. Possibly this is simply respecting him as a person and not doing anything to him which we would not like if we were in his place. And we play with him on his level and somewhat surprisingly I enjoy this kind of play.

We wanted him to be interested in reading and writing. So we have given him models both in our own reading and in reading to him. We have provided, also, carefully selected books for him and a writing pad on an easel on the porch off the kitchen where he can write without objections—we are not interested in his writing on the walls of the rooms.

We wanted him to get into the habit of solving problems which he faces. So from the start we have given him problems which we think he can handle. For example, we live on a fairly steep hill and we have a rough foot path down to our fence at the bottom of the hill. If his ball goes down the hill, he is supposed to go down this path and get it. And he does, especially with a little coaching and encouragement from the top of the hill.

We wanted Larry to have muscular self-confidence. So, when he was one year old we bought him a climber; 3½ feet high with two rungs on each side. This was a little too early for him, but by the age of 15 months he began climbing it and well before two years he was climbing up the sides and swinging on the rungs.

Our techniques for conditioning him have been probably like those used by most parents—applauding him when he does something right and verbally commending him. But probably more important than these is paying attention to the models presented to him. My wife says that by the time we get him through the pre-school period my language will certainly be cleaned up. An example of deliberately giving him a model is as follows. Larry has not been too keen about having his hair shampooed. Yesterday, I decided I would give him an enjoyable model. So we both got into the bathtub and I stuck my head down into the water and then put soap on it, all the while indicating how much fun this really was. He had water and soap put on his hair without objection and did not object to having it rinsed out.

Wife: In addition to the things my husband has told you, I think of two or three goals that I have especially felt have influenced the ways I behave with Larry.

One of these goals is that I think it is important to be comfortable with words and verbal skills. So I have talked with Larry a great deal and from the very beginning. I have named things and described what I was doing or what he was doing. A real stream of chatter. And I have acted as if he could understand most of ordinary conversation. He is still too young to know whether this way of dealing with him will result in verbal skills that we hope for, but at 24 months he has a very large vocabulary for his age and uses quite complex grammar. And he is a chatterbox, accompanying his own acts with verbal descriptions of them. Yesterday when he was getting into the bath tub he was saying, "One foot in. More—other foot in."

Another goal is really something that I want to share with him—my own delight in ordinary things, especially the kind of enthusiasms that many people call childish. And I think this came from my parents' attitudes—a household where everything stopped while we all went to look at a sunset or to see a robin struggle to get a long worm out of the lawn. So I have shared my pleasures with Larry and he is developing ways of expressing his own interests. The other day he found an earthworm while he was "helping" his father in the garden and his later description of it to me included his wiggling his hand in little waves to tell me how it moved, accompanying this with a body-wiggling delighted reaction.

It has been very interesting to watch Larry learn to give appropriate responses to our behavior—to see how affectionateness brings out an affectionate response, how quiet talking results in his own quietness, and how boisterous play leads to a rough and tumble reaction. He has had a very wide range of emotional reactions for many months now—no longer the simple pleasure or displeasure of a tiny infant.

A child is born, not only into a society and its culture, but also into an environment of interpersonal relations. From birth the infant is in emotional interaction, first with its mother and then with the other members of its family. This emotional interaction and conditioning in the family environment will be discussed under these main topics: the nature of emotional interaction, emotional interaction within the family, and interrelationships between emotional and cultural conditioning.

THE NATURE OF EMOTIONAL INTERACTION

The Meaning of Emotion Social scientists have great difficulty in isolating and stating precisely what is meant by the term "emotion" or its approximate equivalent, "feeling." Emotion is an internal state of an individual and consequently may be observed introspectively. Objective observation of emotion is limited to the reports persons make about their own self-observations and to inferences from behaviors believed to be expressive of emotion.

Emotion is an internal response to the perception and appraisal of something as "good for me" or "bad for me." There is some evidence that the internal response involves changes in the physiological state of the individual, but there is little present evidence that particular physiological states are associated with particular emotional responses. The nature of this internal response is not yet understood. The person becomes aware of his internal responses and identifies them as giving pleasure or distress. He learns to distinguish between major categories of emotion, such as fear, anger, love, and elation. The arousal is broadly that of approach or avoidance. The person learns culturally acceptable ways of expressing various emotions or inhibiting the expression of certain emotions.

Apparently children are not born with complex emotional reactions but rather with a generalized emotional reactive tendency which gradually becomes differentiated into two broad patterns of reaction: a series of behaviors which indicates relaxation or pleasure and is interpreted as expressive of a state of well-being, and a series of behaviors which indicates tension and is interpreted as expressive of distress. Development from broad reaction patterns to specific emotions probably requires the acquisition of symbolic communication. Parsons expresses this view:

> The child's interaction with the mother is not only a process of mutual gratification of needs, but is on the child's part a process of learning of the symbolic significance of a complicated system of acts on the part of the mother—of what they signify about what she feels and of how they are interdependent with and thus in part consequences of his own acts. That is to say, there is developed a complex language of emotional communication between them. Only when the child has learned this language on a relatively complex level, can he be said to have learned to love his mother or to be dependent on her love for him. There is, thus, a transition from "pleasure dependence" to "love dependence." One primary aspect of learning to love and to be loved is the internalization of a common culture of expressive symbolism which makes it possible for the child to express *and communicate* his feelings and to understand the mother's feelings towards him.[1]

The Meaning of Emotional Interaction Let us consider first the general model of interaction. The acts of one person serve as a stimulus to another, who responds by some acts which in turn are a stimulus to the other. So interaction is really a series of responses between persons. In making a response to the acts of another person, one learns to take into consideration the meaning of the acts of the other. If two persons do this over a considerable period of time, some aspects of each will be incorporated into the other. In interaction the attitudes, values, preju-

---

[1] Talcott Parsons, "The Superego and the Theory of Social Systems," in *Working Papers in the Theory of Action,* Talcott Parsons, Robert F. Bales, and Edward A. Shils (eds.) (Glencoe, Illinois: The Free Press, 1953), pp. 22–23.

dices, likes, and dislikes of one person may modify to some extent those of the other person. Thus persons who are interacting in love, fear, hate, or jealousy tend to have their own emotional responses modified by the emotional behavior of the other.

Emotional interaction may be seen as ranging along a continuum of varying degrees of emotional involvement. At one end of the continuum is interaction predominantly nonemotional in content—for example, an intellectual discussion of a legal point. At the other end is interaction predominantly emotional in content, such as an embrace of affection or curses of anger. Most interaction, of course, falls between these extremes in degree of emotional involvement and has both emotional and nonemotional components.

Behavior within the family is likely to have a fairly high degree of emotional content. Almost any act has the potential of evoking an emotional response. This occurs partly because family members have a fairly high degree of emotional involvement with each other and partly because there is a general expectation that emotions may be appropriately expressed within the family.

When an infant is born into a family, he enters into an existing network of emotional relationships. Probably the most important to the child is that part of the network which consists of the emotional relationships between the mother and father. These may vary from a maximum of affection and love to a maximum of bitterness and antagonism. A child born into the first of these has a radically different emotional environment than one born into a parental relationship dominated by conflict. Within the network of his family's emotional relationship, the child learns how others feel about him and develops his own habitual emotional expressions toward other family members.

Learning Emotional Patterns In most cultures the learning of habits of emotional expression occurs first mainly in interactions with the mother. As she cares for his physical needs, the mother expresses her feelings toward the child in a variety of ways. The infant reacts and the mother encourages the responses she enjoys or approves and discourages those she considers undesirable. The child also experiences emotional relationships with other family members. His emotional development may be expected to follow the patterns established in these early interactions within the family.

Present evidence for this is chiefly in studies of child-rearing in various cultures rather than in variations between families within a given culture. From a compilation of recent anthropological field studies of child-rearing done with explicit and comparable observational techniques, we have selected two illustrations. The first describes behavior and attitudes

210   *Interaction and Socialization*

toward infants in a group of landowners called Rājpūts in a village about 90 miles from Delhi, India:

> The life of the Rājpūt baby is, aside from the daily bath, bland and free from stress, but it is also free from deliberate creative stimulation. A person in the village is viewed as a member of a group rather than as an individual. . . . Assuming that the child will live to maturity, its future life can be predicted with great accuracy. A boy will become a farmer; a girl will be a farmer's wife. . . . Throughout his or her lifetime, the person will function in a group; seldom, if ever, will he be called on to act independently of the group, let alone oppose it. Whereas a mother who conceives of her child as a unique individual emphasizes how he differs from other children, the Rājpūt mother, for whom all people are transient elements in a permanent group structure, insists that "all children are alike." . . . Babies are neither the objects of interest nor the objects of anxiety that they are in this country (the United States). A mother does not fear that her baby is sick every time it cries; she knows better. But, by the same token, she is not as delighted with its smile because she also knows that all babies smile. She therefore continues with her usual routine, attends to her infant's needs but does not hover over it or "drop everything" to rush to its side. . . . Thus the baby spends his first two years as a passive observer of the busy courtyard life. He is never alone, never the center of attention.[2]

The emotional passivity in dealing with infants apparent in this passage is echoed in adaptation to group life. "In general, the apparent lack of self-reliance in both adults and children is one of the first characteristics that strikes an American observer."[3]

The second illustration is of the early patterns of interaction with infants in Nyansongo, a community in the highlands of Kenya, Africa:

> The Nyansongo does not act very affectionately toward her infant. . . . It is rare to see a mother kissing, cuddling, hugging, or cooing at her child. Individual variability among mothers on this score is considerable, but in the main it is not done. . . . The mother nurses the child mechanically and only occasionally takes it from the nurse (an older child between six and ten years of age who is placed in charge of the infant for most of the daytime hours, carrying him and caring for him, from the time the umbilical cord drops off) when unprovoked by its crying. Most mothers saw to it that their infants did not get into trouble and were not neglected by the nurses but intervened only when they felt the nurses or the infants were doing wrong. When things were going smoothly, the mothers tended to remain aloof. The caretakers who were most affectionate were

[2] Leigh Minturn and John T. Hitchcock, "The Rājpūts of Khalapur, India," in *Six Cultures, Studies of Child Rearing*, Beatrice B. Whiting (ed.) (New York: John Wiley and Sons, 1963), pp. 316–318.
[3] *Ibid.*, p. 336.

nurses, grandmothers, and occasionally fathers' brothers' wives. When she is alone with the infant, the child nurse frequently hugs him, kisses him, tickles him, and indulges him in other kinds of affectionate play. Sometimes, however, she does this in a rough manner which tends to alarm the infant and other times she ignores her charge in favor of interacting with her peers. There is, then, little consistency in the nurse's affectionate behavior, and it may not always be communicated to the infant as nurturance.[4]

A common way of quieting older infants is to frighten them. When a one-year old on a nurse's back begins whimpering, she will say, "aso, aso, esese," which is a way of calling a dog. There may or may not be a dog nearby, but the calling of it (or, more rarely, a cat) is intended to make the child think that the animal will come and harm him if he does not stop crying. This often works to silence him. The infant is prepared to respond in this way by his mother, grandmother, and other caretakers, who often point out animals of any kind—cows, chickens, dogs, insects—and label them all *ekuku*, who "will bite you," a name (in baby talk) which is supposed to inspire terror in the child. The mother and grandmother believe that this fear is good because it will safeguard the child from actual harm incurred by animals, such as being stepped on by a cow, and also explicitly because it can be used by a parent to control the child's behavior, particularly excessive crying.[5]

The general picture of the Nyansongo child as he emerges from infancy is that of a dependent, fearful individual, capable of making demands on his mother and other caretakers for food and attention, but unaggressive, quiet, and timid in his approach to the physical environment and to strange things.[6]

Evidence of variations in emotional interaction with children and subsequent personality development is not limited to underdeveloped countries. For example, in an extended and intensive study of a small number of Japanese families the Vogels found that dependency in infants and small children was fostered by such customs as the mother almost invariably keeping the small child physically close to her, never placing him in the care of another, carrying him while he is small on her back while she worked or to put him to sleep, soothing his cries immediately, sleeping next to him until about elementary school age, and protecting him from imagined fears of the outside world.[7]

Emotional dependency in a Japanese family continues to be manifested throughout childhood and adolescence and in varying ways in adulthood,

[4] Robert A. LeVine and Barbara B. LeVine, "Nyansongo: A Gusii Community in Kenya," in Whiting, pp. 144–145.
[5] *Ibid.*, pp. 142–143.
[6] *Ibid.*, p. 147.
[7] Ezra F. Vogel and Suzanne H. Vogel, "Family Security, Personal Immaturity and Emotional Health in a Japanese Sample," *Journal of Marriage and the Family*, 23 (1961): pp. 161–166.

where, in part, even employing firms adopt a paternalistic attitude toward their employees which facilitates continuing dependency.

INTERACTION WITHIN THE FAMILY

Husband-Wife Emotional Interaction The predominant emotions between husbands and wives are of a binding rather than a disruptive nature. Forces of internal attraction within marriages or external pressures on them are strong enough to keep almost 8 in 10 American couples in their first marriage; of those in their second marriage about a third are those in which the first mate is deceased. No other human association has such an enduring character as the family.

Some of the studies on predicting adjustment in marriage collected information on its emotional components. These studies indicate that couples emphasize love, affection, happiness, enjoyment, and satisfaction as interactive factors in marriage. There are other couples in which the predominant emotions are anger, bitterness, and jealousy.

Love is considered an inner feeling of affection, rapport, and attachment. Demonstration of affection is an outward manifestation. Burgess and Wallin indicate that the type of love reported by couples in their study was of "friendship deepening into love."[8] It has its origin in the companionship of courtship and reached its full development in the marital relation. In successful marriages love tends to be stronger after than before marriage.

Burgess and Wallin suggest the hypothesis that love is a component in a companionship relation in marriage and is reinforced by satisfying sexual relationships. They give the following case of a wife who felt a strong positive relationship between love and sex in marriage:

> My idea of love goes much deeper than even companionship and understanding. I have found love to be not merely an attraction, but something live and growing that makes you forget yourself in an effort to bring complete happiness to your husband—to do things with him and for him that will make his whole being glow with the warmth of satisfaction. We have so many times said to each other that the love we had when we were first married seems so small compared to the love we have come to know now. Sex life is not merely the physical satisfaction I thought it was going to be, but is an expression of love—a much needed outlet for deep-rooted emotion.[9]

Burgess and Wallin computed love, sex, companionship, and happiness scores for the husbands and wives they studied.[10] They found moderate

---
[8] Ernest W. Burgess and Paul Wallin, *Engagement and Marriage* (Philadelphia: Lippincott, 1953), Ch. 14.
[9] *Ibid.*, p. 421.
[10] *Ibid.*, pp. 421–423.

correlations between love and companionship.[11] between love and happiness,[12] between love and satisfying sexual relations,[13] and between satisfying sexual relations and happiness.[14] The highest relationship was between love and happiness in marriage. Satisfying sexual relationships and companionship were also significantly associated with love and happiness.

In emphasizing the emotions which bind the marital partners together, we do not mean, of course, that emotions of a disruptive type are not also operating in many marriages. Fear, anger, and jealousy are of this nature. We will discuss jealousy as reported in the study of happily-married and divorced persons as an illustration of the type of emotions that tear a family apart.

Persons were asked if their mates were inclined to be jealous if they danced, talked, or otherwise associated with those of the opposite sex. Divorced persons reported much more jealousy than did the happily married. The percent reporting the mate jealous was 16 for happily-married men, 55 for divorced men, 13 for happily-married women, and 45 for divorced women.[15]

Jealousy was a primary factor in the disruption of the couple in the following case:

> *Wife:* We were very happy in the first years of our marriage. We both engaged in the same professional work. I guess I was more interested in my profession than in my home. Even in these early years, I began to be skeptical of him. He took my savings, and said that in his marriage he was going to handle the money. Then, when his brother died and we were going through his things, I found a letter in which my husband had written him about a couple of women whom they had taken on a trip. About four years after our marriage, I found he had gotten a girl pregnant, and we had to pay $500 to fix it up. But I thought that maybe he had been framed. The final thing was when I found that he was going out with another woman. After that, I would not have anything to do with him sexually. I took complete charge of the money; in fact I did not want to live with him. I wanted separation, but not divorce.
>
> *Interpretation:* This is a case of the gradual development of estrangement between the husband and wife. When the wife discovered a few "indiscretions," the reaction of the husband was a demonstration of more affection than formerly. But the wife's reaction was one of complete withdrawal. He felt that he could not live at home because of her psychological

---

[11] For husbands, .39; for wives, .40.
[12] For husbands, .65; for wives, .63.
[13] For husbands, .37; for wives, .38.
[14] For husbands, .45; for wives, .29.
[15] Harvey J. Locke, *Predicting Adjustment in Marriage: A Comparison of a Divorced and a Happily-Married Group* (New York: Henry Holt, 1951), p. 153.

withdrawal. He secured the divorce, married again, got a job in his profession in another city, and is happier than formerly. The wife is still working, is lonesome and discouraged. Tears came into her eyes when she said that he was always so cheerful and fine around the home.[16]

Spouse Interaction in Relation to Child-Rearing For mothers and fathers the rearing of their children is a matter both of great interest and great importance. Much of the interaction of parents with children living in the home may center around the children, both when they are in the company of the children or by themselves. Nevertheless, very few studies have focused on this form of interaction. The relationships between mothers and their children have, of course, been studied most extensively, both because of the significant position of the mother in child-rearing and, one suspects, because of the greater availability of mothers as research subjects. Most data reported on fathers have been obtained from information supplied by the mother. Children of school age or older have also been used as informants. An exception to this usual situation is a study of 39 families reported by Stolz.[17] Several extended interviews with each mother and father separately were tape-recorded, transcribed, and carefully coded. Almost all (92 percent of the mothers and 82 percent of the fathers) volunteered information about interaction with their spouses as an influence in the rearing of their children.[18] Of those giving data about such interaction, 69 percent of the mothers and 92 percent of the fathers cited talking over what they should do as a frequent occurrence. About two-thirds of the parents stated that their discussions typically ended in mutual agreement. When disagreement did occur, the mother's opinion tended to prevail. Husbands are more conscious of their wives' influence on their own attitudes and behaviors in child-rearing than the wives are aware of exerting influence. Similarly, wives are more conscious of their husbands' influences. Fifty-six percent of the wives reported being influenced by their husbands, while only 15 percent of the husbands indicated an awareness of having influenced their wives.

Many statements of values the parents held for parenthood and child-rearing were made in the interviews. In the order of their emphasis by the parents these values were: moral, family, egoistic, interpersonal, emotional security, educational, orderly living, biological, play, and economic.[19] Factor analysis of value codings revealed the value for a close-

---

[16] *Ibid.*, pp. 153–154.
[17] Lois Meek Stolz, *Influences on Parent Behavior* (Stanford, California: Stanford University Press, 1967).
[18] *Ibid.*, pp. 171–175.
[19] *Ibid.*, Chapters 4 and 5.

knit, unified family and this was emphasized by more than two-thirds of mothers and fathers. The desire to have their children learn independence was also a strong motivating force for these parents. For a number of other values, there was a tendency for variation with the age of the children.

Parent-Child Interaction   The Berkeley study of child and family behavior has thrown light on the importance of the birth of a child in husband-wife relationships and the significance of interpersonal relationships of the husband and wife for the personality development of the child. This study investigated 252 children and their families over a twenty-year period. Macfarlane describes the competition for affection which may develop with the coming of the child. The father may manifest feelings of jealousy and insecurity, or the mother may sense definite changes in the responses of her husband:

> Important . . . is the changed relationship which often occurs between husband and wife by the introduction of a triangular situation of affection. It is almost pathetic to find how frequently a husband has made the statement that he feels very much at loose ends and uneasy since he has been displaced in his wife's affections by his child. "I am merely supporting the two of them. If I am in the middle of a sentence she always stops to listen to his requests and interruptions." And the wife will say, "George has never felt the same toward me since I had a child. I don't know whether I am less attractive physically, or what it is." . . . Certain it is that some affectional competition is unavoidable.[20]

Macfarlane also describes how the relationship between husband and wife modifies the personality patterns of the child:

> The relationship between the parents in a home, whether it be a straining or supporting one, looms much larger in its bearing upon the children's behavior than do such things as education or the economic advantages or handicaps which the parents have had. In fact, the marital relationship appears to be more important than any other factor in the homes thus far studied. Food finickiness, overdependence, attention-demanding, negativism, temper tantrums, and urinary incontinence in the daytime are recruited more largely and consistently from homes where a straining and inharmonious parental relationship exists. To some degree one may regard this behavior (in the young child, at least) as symptomatic of uneasiness and discouragement in the parents which have interfered with wise and steady training of their children. In our study we found that if too many areas of adjustive difficulties exist between the parents, it brings them insecurity which communicates itself to the child, who then uses devices

[20] Jean Walker Macfarlane, "Inter-Personal Relationships within the Family," *Marriage and Family Living*, 3 (1941): p. 30.

we call aggression, withdrawal, or problem-behavior in his efforts to recapture equilibrium.[21]

The birth of a baby at once transforms the relationships of husband and wife to each other. The orderly adjustments which have developed between husband and wife tend to be disturbed. The demands and needs of the child take precedence over the desires and interests of the parents. Time and energy previously devoted to companionship and social affairs are absorbed in providing for the child's physical needs.

In a study of 46 middle-class couples LeMasters reports that 38 of the couples said that the birth of the first child precipitated a crisis for them, regardless of the anticipatory preparation they had made.[22] They had been relatively unprepared for the readjustments of roles required by the presence of the child and they found it necessary to reorient some values.

Changes in the family and in its members influence both the interaction and the emotional climate within the family. There are indications of both continuity and change in interaction and in the emotional climate. In an analysis of the limited research knowledge available, the Yarrows emphasize that there is only fragmentary evidence about this important issue.[23] For example, in a longitudinal study comparing data of mother-child interaction during infancy and middle childhood (9 to 14 years), consistency was indicated by fairly high correlations (.73 for boys and .61 for girls) for a dimension of parent hostility and love.[24] However, for the same group there was no significant correlation over time for the mothers' control of the children. Two earlier studies indicate changes in the mother's relationship with existing children during pregnancy and after the birth of the new child.[25] During pregnancy mothers became less directive and exhibited more understanding of their children. After the birth of the new child there was less warmth displayed toward the older children and the mothers became more restrictive and more severe in discipline. These changes were greatest after the birth of a second child. Also, there are some data, primarily clinical, which suggest that

---

[21] *Ibid.*, p. 31.

[22] E. E. LeMasters, "Parenthood as a Crisis," *Marriage and Family Living*, 19 (1957): pp. 352–355.

[23] Leon J. Yarrow and Marian Radke Yarrow, "Personality Continuity and Change in the Family Context," in *Personality Change*, Philip Worchel and Donn Byrne (eds.) (New York: John Wiley and Sons, 1964), pp. 489–523.

[24] E. S. Schaefer and Nancy Baley, "Consistency of Maternal Behavior from Infancy to Preadolescence," *Journal of Abnormal and Social Psychology*, 61 (1960): pp. 1–6.

[25] A. L. Baldwin, "Changes in Parent Behavior During Pregnancy: an Experiment in Longitudinal Analysis," *Child Development*, 18 (1947): pp. 29–39; and Joan K. Lasko, "Parent Behavior Toward First and Second Children," *Genetic Psychology Monographs*, 49 (1954): pp. 97–137.

some mothers relate more effectively to children of certain ages or of a certain sex.[26]

Sibling Interaction Sibling relationships have received little attention from sociologists.[27] In a review of the literature, Irish points out that most studies of children in families have focused on the parent-child relationship.[28] The effects of the ordinal position of siblings have also been examined, but typically without regard to interactional factors. An exception to this is clinical literature on sibling rivalry, frequently focused on the reaction of a young first-born child to the birth of a sibling. The first-born finds himself deprived of the exclusive position he has held in the affection of his parents and may manifest reactions of jealousy. A very early study suggests that age at the birth of a sibling is related to jealousy, particularly the period between 18 months and three years, and there is less jealousy as there are more children in the family.[29]

Rivalry of siblings begun in infancy may continue in a modified form into childhood. The following case provides an illustration:

> *Amy:* When I was just a kid, I wore horn-rimmed spectacles. I was sort of chubby, while Nellie was very pretty. Everybody said how pretty she was but no one said anything about me except what a good girl I was. This gave me an inferiority complex and it carried through high school. I still have a little of it. I used to tease Sister a lot. That was when I was very small. We used to argue about who would get the funny paper first. They were just children's quarrels. After we got into high school, we got on better.
>
> *Nellie:* Amy was not quite two years older. I was the baby, but I wasn't treated like a baby by other children. I was bossed and teased—like kids do. Being very sensitive, I would come home to Mama. Amy and Mother have always made my decisions for me, except in the last few years. There's always been a boy in my life. The first one was in the first grade—holding my hand and telling me he loved me. I've always looked up to Amy, although I never wanted to be her or like her. She did not have boy friends until she was in high school.

Three different types of negative reaction of the older to the younger sibling may be distinguished. He may imitate the behavior of the baby,

[26] Yarrow and Yarrow, p. 492.
[27] For example, in the excellent two-volume *Review of Child Development Research*, edited by M. L. Hoffman and L. W. Hoffman, only one entry appears in the index for siblings.
[28] Donald P. Irish, "Sibling Interaction: A Neglected Aspect in Family Life Research," *Social Forces*, 42 (1964): pp. 279–288.
[29] Mabel Sewall, "Some Causes of Jealousy in Young Children," *Smith College Studies in Social Work*, 1 (1930): pp. 15–22.

who seems to get attention and care from the mother by his helplessness. One three-year-old reverts to crawling. Another demands to be carried like the baby. A third takes up baby talk again after he has abandoned it. A second reaction is aggressive behavior. The older child may attempt physical violence, such as slapping the infant. A third kind of behavior is for the older child to ignore the baby, to refuse to look at it, or even to deny that he has a little brother or sister.

An intriguing hypothesis about sibling relationships is advanced by Toman, who suggests that basic patterns of peer relationships may be learned from the patterns of interaction with siblings.[30] He suggests that these patterns can carry over into almost all subsequent interaction. Of special importance is the possibility that individuals seek to repeat some aspects of their sibling relationships with their spouses. For instance, he suggests that an older sister who had a younger brother might well choose as a spouse a man who had been a younger brother with an older sister in his own family. Each would have learned how to relate to persons of the opposite sex through the interaction with his own siblings and there would be congruency between their basic patterns.

There is some empirical evidence that some characteristics of young children are influenced by the presence of siblings. Koch's extensive study found, among other things, that girls with older brothers tend to be more tomboyish than girls with older sisters.[31] A supplementary analysis of Koch's data found that children who have siblings of the opposite sex have more traits of the opposite sex than do children who have only siblings of the same sex.[32] These traits are more pronounced when the opposite-sex sibling is older than the child being studied.

The area of sibling interaction is particularly in need of research if interaction within the family is to be understood. When one considers the proportion of early childhood that is spent in the company of siblings, the importance of further knowledge for understanding personality development within the family becomes apparent.

CHILD-TRAINING PRACTICES

Feeding, Weaning, and Toilet Training In the mother-child interaction, certain child-training practices have been regarded as important in personality development. Psychoanalytic theory has suggested that practices used in feeding and toilet training a child may be permanently reflected

---

[30] Walter Toman, *Family Constellation: Theory and Practice of a Psychological Game* (New York: Springer, 1961).

[31] Helen L. Koch, "Sissiness and Tomboyishness in Relation to Sibling Characteristics," *Journal of Genetic Psychology*, 88 (1956): pp. 231–244.

[32] Orville G. Brim, Jr., "Family Structure and Sex Role Learning by Children: A Further Analysis of Helen Koch's Data," *Sociometry*, 21 (1958): pp. 1–6.

in certain aspects of his personality. Many research studies have attempted to discover relationships between childhood, adolescent, and adult personality traits and types of feeding practices, age at weaning, severity of weaning, age at toilet training, or severity of toilet training. Two systematic reviews of these studies have concluded that there is little support for the belief that such child-training practices as these will have lasting discernible influence on the personality of children.[33]

One criticism of most such studies has been that they depended upon mothers' retrospective reports about training practices. One analysis does not have this defect. The subsequent personality adjustment of infants who were breast or bottle fed was investigated as a part of the comprehensive longitudinal study begun in Berkeley in the 1930's by Macfarlane. A recent monograph describes follow-up studies of 47 boys and 47 girls through 18 years and shows no personality advantage or disadvantage related to breast or bottle feeding at any age period through 18.[34] Boys who had a longer duration of total nutritive sucking showed slightly more problem behavior during middle childhood; this was not true for girls.

Affection and Permissiveness The effects of child-rearing on personality may be studied by examining general dimensions of mother-child interaction, such as permissiveness and affectionateness of the mother. Sears, Maccoby, and Levin obtained detailed information about child-rearing and children's behavior in tape-recorded interviews with 379 mothers of five-year-old children.[35] The data were analyzed by ratings on nearly 200 specific items. Three aspects of the mother's interaction with her child were related to the child's personality. (1) Warmth of the mother, including the open demonstration of affection for the child, was associated with few problems developing in the child, while maternal coldness was associated with the development of feeding and toilet-training problems, high aggressiveness in the child, and slower development of conscience. (2) Permissiveness for aggression was a source of continuing aggressive behavior; however, permissiveness for dependency had no discernible effect on dependency. (3) Punishment was not effective, over

[33] Harold Orlansky, "Infant Care and Personality," *Psychological Bulletin*, 46 (1949): pp. 1–48; Irving L. Child, "Socialization," in *The Handbook of Social Psychology, Special Fields and Applications*, Gardner Lindzey (ed.) (Cambridge, Mass.: Addison-Wesley, 1954), 2, Ch. 18; and *The Handbook of Social Psychology*, Gardner Lindzey and Elliot Aronson (eds.) (Reading, Mass.: Addison-Wesley, 1969), particularly 3, pp. 505–516.

[34] M. I. Heinstein, "Behavioral Correlates of Breast-Bottle Regimes Under Varying Parent-Infant Relationships," *Monographs of Social Research in Child Development*, 28 (1963), No. 4.

[35] Robert R. Sears, Eleanor E. Maccoby, and Harry Levin, *Patterns of Child Rearing* (Evanston, Illinois: Row, Peterson, 1957).

the long term, as a technique for eliminating the behavior against which it was directed.

Factor analysis of the ratings of the interview materials found five major clusters of behavior and attitudes of the mothers: permissiveness, general family adjustment or a euphoric response to questions about the family, warmth of the mother-child relationship, responsible child-training orientation, and aggressiveness and punitiveness. These factors suggest possible dimensions of the mother-child interaction which may be related to the personality development of children.[36]

Research which attempts to delineate specific parent-child interaction patterns is beginning to be reported. For example, different parent-child patterns have been found for children who persisted in problem-solving tasks despite distractions from those of children who were extremely distractible.[37] Given a series of tasks requiring adult help in a semi-experimental situation in the families' homes, nondistractible children and their parents showed a pattern of parents giving less specific suggestions, more positive encouragement, and paying more attention to the child's contributions. The amount of parent-child interaction was the same for distractible and nondistractible children, but the quality differed.

Discipline The ways in which parental methods of discipline affect children is obviously a matter of interest and concern to many parents as well as an important issue in understanding how children are socialized within the family. A substantial body of research has focused primarily around a few main areas.[38] The use of "love-oriented" techniques such as praise and reasoning, reward or withholding of rewards, showing disappointment, isolating the child, and actual or threatened withdrawel of love has been compared with the use of "power-oriented" techniques including physical punishment and shouting. Love-oriented techniques tend to be used by accepting, affectionate parents and seem to promote the adoption of the desired behavior by the child as a matter of his own responsibility along with generally cooperative social rela-

---

[36] See also Daniel R. Miller and Guy E. Swanson, *The Changing American Parent: A Study in the Detroit Area* (New York: John Wiley and Sons, 1958) for an analysis of ways in which general family orientation toward bureaucratic or entrepreneurial organizations may influence child training.

[37] Helen L. Bee, "Parent-Child Interaction and Distractibility in 9-Year-Old Children," *Merrill-Palmer Quarterly*, 13 (1967): pp. 175–190.

[38] Wesley C. Becker, "Consequences of Different Kinds of Parental Discipline," in *Review of Child Development Research*, Martin L. Hoffman and Lois Wladis Hoffman (eds.) (New York: Russell Sage, 1964), 1, pp. 169–208. This chapter is an excellent review and integration of the research in the United States in this area for the 1950's and early 1960's.

tions and internalized reactions to transgressions. Power-oriented techniques seem to be used primarily by somewhat hostile parents (at least in the populations studied) and to promote aggression in young children, resistance, and externalized reactions to transgressions, such as fear and hostility.

Restrictiveness or permissiveness of discipline is another area in which considerable research has been done. Here it tentatively appears that restrictiveness fosters well controlled and acceptable behavior and also tends to develop dependent and submissive behavior accompanied by a reduction of intellectual striving and curiosity and an increase in hostility. Permissiveness seems to lead to less controlled behaviors, outgoing and assertive behaviors, more intellectual striving, more aggressiveness, and less persistence. Very early restrictiveness leads to dependent behavior more than later restrictiveness.

The question of consistency in discipline frequently arises. This is an area which has not been well defined and in which information is meager. Some indirect evidence on consistency is found in studies of delinquency, especially those by the Gluecks,[39] McCords,[40] and Bandura and Walters.[41] These studies repeatedly show that erratic or inconsistent discipline is associated with antisocial behavior of boys. This seems to be true whether the inconsistency is by one or both parents with great fluctuation in discipline from time to time or major differences between parents in discipline. It should be remembered that these studies deal with an extreme inconsistency and that many other factors are also involved in the development of delinquency.

CHILD-REARING IN UNUSUAL SITUATIONS

Will the socialization of children differ in unusual situations as compared with the usual? This question will be explored by a consideration of large families, the family environment of schizophrenic and normal children, and child-rearing in the Kibbutzim.

Interaction in Large Families There has been considerable interest in how the number of children in a family affects patterns and outcomes of family interaction. Bossard and Boll indicate that families with six

---

[39] Sheldon Glueck and Eleanor Glueck, *Unraveling Juvenile Delinquency* (Cambridge: Harvard University Press, 1950).
[40] William McCord, Joan McCord, and I. K. Zola, *Origins of Crime* (New York: Columbia University Press, 1959).
[41] A. Bandura and R. H. Walters, *Adolescent Aggression* (New York: Ronald Press, 1959).

or more children placed great value on organization, cooperation, and conformity within the family.[42]

In a survey of a large number of high school students, Elder and Bowerman found that children from larger families more frequently reported that their parents were autocratic or authoritarian, were more likely to use physical punishment and less likely to use rewards.[43] Children from smaller families show higher achievement motivation and academic performance.[44] There is substantial evidence that children from smaller families tend to score somewhat higher on intelligence tests even when social class is held constant. A study done in Great Britain was especially intensive. Douglas used a sample selected from the children born in one week in 1946 and obtained intelligence test and school data on them at ages eight and eleven.[45] As family size increased, intelligence scores decreased, most markedly in children of manual workers, but also among children of professionals. All of these research results suggest that more intensive and perhaps more verbal interaction occurs between parents and children in smaller families. This interaction may act as a stimulus in the development of intellectual and verbal abilities.

Attitudes of children in large families were examined in a study of a large representative sample of high school youth in Texas.[46] Young people from families of six or more children were consistently more negative and pessimistic, and more distrustful of relationships with others. Authoritarian discipline was frequently considered preferable. They felt problems with parents, siblings, and peers were more numerous and they had a pronounced resentment of family life-style. High-school-age girls in these large families were considerably more aware of family problems and tensions than were boys from similar sized families, probably reflecting the greater involvement of girls in household and childcare activities.

---

[42] James H. S. Bossard and Eleanor Boll, *The Large Family System* (Philadelphia: University of Pennsylvania Press, 1956).

[43] Glen H. Elder, Jr. and Charles E. Bowerman, "Family Structure and Childrearing Patterns: the Effects of Family Size and Sex Composition," *American Sociological Review*, 28 (1963): pp. 891–905.

[44] Glen H. Elder, Jr., "Family Structure: the Effects of Family Size, Sex Composition, and Ordinal Position on Academic Motivation and Achievement," in *Adolescent Achievement and Mobility Aspirations* (Chapel Hill, N. C.: Institute for Research in Social Science, 1962); and B. C. Rosen, "Family Structure and Achievement Motivation," *American Sociological Review*, 26 (1961): pp. 574–585.

[45] J. W. B. Douglas, *The Home and the School: A Study of Ability and Attainment in the Primary School* (London: MacGibbon and Kee, 1964).

[46] Wayne H. Holtzman and Bernice Milburn Moore, "Family Structure and Youth Attitudes," in *Problems of Youth: Transition to Adulthood in a Changing World*, Muzafer Sherif and Carolyn W. Sherif (eds.) (Chicago: Aldine, 1965), pp. 46–61. This study is more fully reported in *Tomorrow's Parents* (Austin, Texas: University of Texas, 1965) by the same authors.

Family Environments of Schizophrenic and Normal Children One way in which the influence of family interaction on personality development in children has been studied is through examination of family situations involving children with abnormal personality development. Thomes compared the family environment of schizophrenic children with that of normal children who were of the same sex, age, and race, and whose families were of the same socioeconomic and educational status.[47] The families of the normal children were in the circle of acquaintance of the families of the schizophrenic children. The schizophrenics had developed major signs of abnormal personality development before the age of three and did not have organic damage to account for the abnormality.

Three measures were used to assess the family environment. The first was adjustment in marriage. Both mothers and fathers of schizophrenic children were significantly less adjusted in their marriages than the mothers and fathers of normal children. This conclusion was based on scores on Locke's marital-adjustment test, which taps some of the emotional interactions and tensions between husbands and wives. Interview information indicated that the relatively poor marital adjustment of the parents of schizophrenic children existed some time before the illness of the child. Second, mothers of schizophrenic and normal children differed in their perception of parental role behavior. Mothers of schizophrenic children saw only themselves as the parent primarily involved in certain daily activities with their children. By contrast, the mothers of normal children saw themselves and their husbands as engaging in these activities together. Thus the two groups of mothers differed in the degree to which they felt common concern with their husbands about the child. Third, parents of schizophrenic children were rated as having significantly less freedom and warmth of communication between them than parents of normal children. This was true for both verbal and nonverbal communication. In addition, the parents of schizophrenics were rated as having significantly less affection evident in the relationship between them.

This study supports the theory that the nature of the interaction in the homes of emotionally disturbed children differs from that found in the homes of normal children. The three components of parental interaction investigated are indirect indexes of the emotional climate in the home. The emotional climate in the homes of schizophrenics, as compared with that of normal children, was significantly more tense, showed less mutuality, and warmth and affection.

[47] Mary Margaret Thomes, "Parents of Schizophrenic and Normal Children: A Comparison of Parental Attitudes, Marital Adjustment, Role Behavior, and Interaction" (Ph.D. Dissertation, University of Southern California Library, 1959).

The question arises as to why all children in such families are not schizophrenic. One suggestion derived from interview data is that emotional or other problems within the family were particularly acute within the first two years of the life of the child who developed schizophrenia.

Child-Rearing in the Kibbutzim Child-rearing in the Israeli Kibbutzim has been the focus of considerable attention in the last two decades because, with some variations, the Kibbutzim may have a unique form of the family in which the socialization and control of children is not primarily a prerogative of the nuclear family. The Kibbutz movement began about 1910, with emphasis on ideals of economic collectivism and social equality. The typical Kibbutz is a collective agricultural settlement of about 200 adults and 200 to 300 children of various ages.[48] Living arrangements place married couples in sleeping and sometimes sitting quarters, with all children housed in a series of separate "children's houses." Fundamentally, the children are reared in small peer groups under the supervision of child-care workers. Daily contacts with parents are maintained, from very frequent visits by the mother for nursing and caring for the infant in the early months of life to once-a-day visits to the parents' quarters from about the middle of the first year. In the Kibbutz the housekeeping, economic, and child-rearing functions of the family are collective. In the mid-sixties there were about 230 Kibbutzim, with a population of about 100,000. The movement has not been growing in recent years.[49]

The effects of Kibbutz methods of child-rearing have been systematically studied by Rabin using several types of psychological and social test instruments. His sample included groups of one-year-olds, ten-year-olds, 17-year-olds, and 19- to 20-year olds. Each group of Kibbutz-reared children was matched with a similar group selected from cooperative but not communal agricultural villages. The control groups of children were reared in nuclear families living in their own households.[50] Results indicate some lag in development, especially of a social type, on the part of the Kibbutz one-year-old infants as compared with the family-reared infants.[51] However, the ten-year-old Kibbutz children at least equal the family-reared children intellectually, and over-all maturity and adjustment are somewhat better in the Kibbutz children. In dimensions more directly related to family interaction, there seems to be a greater diffusion of identification processes in the Kibbutz children,

---

[48] A. I. Rabin, *Growing Up In the Kibbutz* (New York: Springer, 1965).
[49] *Ibid.*, pp. 1–9.
[50] *Ibid.*, Ch. 4.
[51] *Ibid.*, Ch. 5.

less sibling rivalry, and somewhat more positive attitudes toward the family unit.[52] Kibbutz adolescents (17-year-olds) function intellectually as well as and sometimes better than the control group; are as well adjusted personally and socially; are less involved with and have less conflict with their families; and are more opposed to early sexual expression.[53] With an army sample of 19 and 20-year-olds, the trends indicate less aggression in the Kibbutz group, somewhat more concern with sexuality and more dependence on the group.[54]

The following selected quotations from Rabin describe his conclusions on some of the questions raised about communal child-rearing in the Kibbutz:

> Our findings would certainly not support the notion of social immaturity which is alleged to be a consequence of maternal deprivation. . . . It may be stated that the predictions based on the maternal deprivation hypothesis with respect to personality characteristics do not hold for the children who grow up under the Kibbutz conditions of collective education.[55]

> From the very beginning attachments and ambivalences are less intense than in the ordinary family situation. Early emotional independence and self-reliance are characteristic of the growing Kibbutz child. . . . Adolescence itself is not so much of a *storm* and *stress* period; the child need not struggle for his independence and identity—he gained them long before. Intrapsychic conflict, at this and other periods, of the kind ultimately stemming from intrafamilial relationships is minimal.[56]

This study by Rabin is one of the more recent investigations of Kibbutz child-rearing. The research methods employed were particularly appropriate and the control group relatively similar on most cultural values except those specific to the collective family and child-rearing practices of the Kibbutz. However, even when this knowledge is added to earlier investigations with somewhat varying results, one needs to remember that the results of this alternative to family child-rearing are still understood in only a fragmentary way.

INTERRELATIONSHIPS BETWEEN EMOTIONAL AND CULTURAL CONDITIONING

The process of cultural and emotional conditioning are intertwined in a network of interpersonal interaction. For purposes of analysis they have been considered separately. But for an adequate understanding of

[52] *Ibid.*, Ch. 6.
[53] *Ibid.*, Ch. 7.
[54] *Ibid.*, Ch. 8.
[55] *Ibid.*, p. 200.
[56] *Ibid.*, p. 208.

human behavior and personality development, they must be viewed in their synthesized relationship and the aspects of each seen in its dynamic relation to the other.

Accordingly, it is now proposed to select two areas of behavior and examine them for emotional interaction and cultural conditioning, but with particular emphasis on the latter. Let us first consider personality traits and then, for further analysis, sibling jealousy.

Personality Traits Early influences in the emotional interactions of families tend to give a "set" to certain personality characteristics. Through a combination of emotional and cultural influences, for example, a child may acquire a tendency to dominate or to be submissive. An older child may take charge of younger brothers and sisters, who in turn develop dependent attitudes which may persist into adult behavior. In certain societies, as in Japan until the early twentieth century, the little girl was taught the three obediences—to obey her father, her husband, and her son. The pattern of female submission to male dominance was so universal and so powerful that it prevented overt expression of feminine aggressiveness, at least in relations with men.

A crucial test of the extent to which culture may influence the process of personality development is the comparison of differences between men and women in personality characteristics. Mead reports on differences she found in the approved personalities of men and women among three primitive peoples living near one another in New Guinea. She was interested in determining whether certain traits which in our culture are rather specifically associated with one sex are also associated with that sex in other societies. The following is a summary of her findings:

> We found the Arapesh—both men and women—displaying a personality that, out of our historically limited preoccupations, we would call maternal in its parental aspects, and feminine in its sexual aspects. We found men, as well as women, trained to be cooperative, unaggressive, responsive to the needs and demands of others. We found no idea that sex was a powerful driving force either for men or for women. In marked contrast to these attitudes, we found among the Mundugumor that both men and women developed as ruthless, aggressive, positively sexed individuals, with the maternal cherishing aspects of personality at a minimum. Both men and women approximated to a personality type that we in our culture would find only in an undisciplined and very violent male. The Arapesh ideal is the mild responsive man married to the mild responsive woman; the Mundugumor ideal is the violent aggressive man married to the violent aggressive woman. In the third tribe, the Tchambulli, we found a genuine reversal of the sex attitudes of our own culture, with the woman the dominant, impersonal, managing partner, the man the less responsible and the emotionally dependent person. These three situations suggest, then, a

Interrelationships Between Emotional and Cultural Conditioning 227

very definite conclusion. If those temperamental attitudes which we have traditionally regarded as feminine—such as passivity, responsiveness, and a willingness to cherish children—can so easily be set up as the masculine pattern in one tribe, and in another be outlawed for the majority of women as well as for the majority of men, we no longer have any basis for regarding such aspects of behavior as sex-linked. And this conclusion becomes even stronger when we consider the actual reversal in Tchambuli of the position of dominance of the two sexes, in spite of the existence of formal patrilineal institutions.

When we consider the behavior of the typical Arapesh man or woman as contrasted with the behavior of the typical Mundugumor man or woman, the evidence is overwhelmingly in favor of the strength of social conditioning. In no other way can we account for the almost complete uniformity with which Arapesh children develop into contented, passive, secure persons, while Mundugumor children develop as characteristically into violent, aggressive, insecure persons. Only to the impact of the whole of the integrated culture upon the growing child can we lay the formation of the contrasting types. There is no other explanation of race, or diet, or selection that can be adduced to explain them. We are forced to conclude that human nature is almost unbelievably malleable, responding accurately and contrastingly to contrasting cultural conditions.[57]

Sibling Jealousy It is often assumed that sibling jealousy or rivalry is always present in families with two or more children. From the material below one concludes that rivalry and competition may or may not be present in a society. Horney points out that the culture of a society determines the degree to which sibling jealousy is manifested:

> The rivalry between father and son, mother and daughter, one child with another, is not a general human phenomenon but is the response to culturally conditioned stimuli. This rivalry itself is not biologically conditioned but is a result of given cultural conditions and, furthermore, the family situation is not the only one to stir up rivalry, but the competitive stimuli are active from the cradle to the grave.[58]

In her report on Arapesh people Mead described a society with an entire absence of rivalry, or indeed any competitive activity:

> Arapesh small boys are protected from aggression and struggle as is the most tenderly reared and fragile little daughter among ourselves. As a result, Arapesh boys never develop "good sportsmanship." The slightest

---

[57] From *Sex and Temperament in Three Primitive Societies*, by Margaret Mead. Reprinted by permission of William Morrow and Company, Inc. Copyright 1935, 1950, © 1963 by Margaret Mead.
[58] Karen Horney, *The Neurotic Personality of Our Time* (New York: W. W. Norton & Company, 1937), pp. 284–285.

gibe is taken as an expression of unfriendliness, and grown men will burst into tears at an unfair accusation.[59]

At the opposite pole is Pilaga society, where many factors in the social situation make for insecurity and where the rejection of the child by its parents at the birth of a new baby leads to the manifestation of intense hostility and jealousy directed against the new arrival.[60]

Evidence from these and other studies indicates that sibling jealousy is stimulated or minimized according to the type of parental relations to the child. These, in turn, are conditioned by the cultural patterns of competition and co-operation within the society.

SUMMARY

An emotion is an internal response to the perception and appraisal of a person, a material object, an idea, or a situation as good or bad for a person. Emotional interaction is like other forms of interaction, since it consists of interresponses between two or more persons, but it is different in at least two respects. First, the content of the interaction is emotions of love, affection, and other approaching feelings, and bitterness, fear, hate, and other feelings of avoidance. Second, it is relatively spontaneous and impulsive. Early emotional interactions of a person occur almost exclusively with members of his family.

Early childhood relationships within the family *in their totality* mold the personality structure of the person in ways which predetermine much of his future behavior. This does not mean that infantile patterns of behavior persist and control the conduct of adults, but rather that personality structure takes form in early interaction within the family and tends to develop according to the trends established in childhood. It is evident that certain emotional patterns of response are more permanent than others, although it is not yet established what the limits of their modifiability or unchangeability may be. This opens a most promising field of research to the student of personality.

Certain patterns of relationships of the child with his parents and his brothers and sisters tend to be reproduced by the adult in his parent-child and his husband-wife relations. The significance of this lies in the fact that early affectional and emotional relations become patterned and consequently set the mold for the type of intimate association, in both affectionate and hostile manifestations.

[59] Mead, pp. 52–53.
[60] Jules Henry, "Some Cultural Determinants of Hostility in Pilaga Indian Children," *American Journal of Orthopsychiatry*, 10 (1940): pp. 118–119; see also J. and Z. Henry, "Symmetrical and Reciprocal Hostility in Sibling Rivalry," *ibid.*, 12 (1942): pp. 256–257.

The dynamic elements of personality structure take their form in interpersonal relationships within the family. Expression of impulses is a major process providing spontaneity in personality development. Jealousy, aggression, and hostility are rooted in particular emotional situations in interpersonal relations. This means that these phenomena should be studied, not as if they were static elements in the personality, but as factors in the dynamics of the relation between the self and others.

PROBLEMS FOR RESEARCH

Modifiability of Emotional Traits There is marked divergence of opinion concerning the modifiability of emotional characteristics. Part of the confusion is due, no doubt, to the fact that emotional traits, or at least the emotional component of a particular personality trait, have not been clearly defined and identified. Then, too, there has been a tendency to describe emotional and other personality traits as dichotomies—extroversion and introversion, egocentrism and sociocentrism, dominance and submission, security and insecurity—whereas it is evident that these are two ends of a continuum. In spite of these and other difficulties, it should be possible to make exploratory studies by tracing the development of these and other traits by means of a series of interviews and findings from personality tests made from infancy to youth. Such studies are now feasible, and data are available in child-study institutes which have for many individuals records of interviews, repeated physical and psychological examinations, and social histories over a period of years. The results already secured should be utilized in planning even more systematic studies directly focused on these problems.

Cultural Framework of Emotional Conditioning While cultural factors may not directly affect emotional conditioning, there remains the consideration of the extent to which culture indirectly influences the development of emotional traits. Studies should be made to determine the degree to which cultural values in a society, through their influence on parental responses to children, mold personality patterns. One study that might be carried on is to take the children of one group of parents who believe in the efficacy of punishment and compare them with children of parents who try to rear their children through reasoning with them. This is only one way in which definitions of behavior by parents may affect the emotional conditioning of the traits of a person.

Combination of Techniques in Personality Research In the past, studies in personality have typically been made by a single method—one person using psychological, or biological, or sociological techniques. Much human behavior, however, cannot be so neatly segmentalized and successfully studied in its separate phases. The result is that the findings of most studies of this type are not only one-sided but inconclusive. At present there have been some attempts to make studies in the area of human behavior by combining the techniques of the different disciplines. A few of the many subjects awaiting co-operative investigation are sex differences in behavior, jealousy, inferiority feelings, sense of humor, sociability, altruism, conscience, personal morale, and leadership ability.

The subject of sex differences in behavior may be taken to illustrate the desirability of studying the different aspects in relation to each other by utilizing different techniques. Obviously, there are physiological aspects of sexual differences, and biological techniques are needed to investigate these. There is also emotional conditioning of sexual manifestations, with psychiatrists emphasizing the role of repression in leading to minor and marked deviations. The cultural conditioning of sex behavior has been emphasized by the sociologist and the cultural anthropologist, who point to phenomena such as the wide variety of the definitions of what is masculine or feminine in different places and at different times. A co-operative study by a biologist, a psychologist, and a sociologist could yield findings which would differentiate much more clearly the distinctive aspects of sex behavior that are biological, emotional, and cultural and would show how these three influence one another.

QUESTIONS AND EXERCISES

1. What are some of the basic differences between biological, emotional, and cultural traits?
2. Indicate the ways in which additions to the family affect the emotional interactions of family members.
3. Define emotion and list as many emotions as you can.
4. What is the difference in speed of response between emotional and intellectual interaction? What are the particular values of each?
5. Analyze the introductory case as an example of interrelationships between emotional and cultural conditioning.
6. What are the components of jealousy? Is there evidence that jealousy is the result of feelings of insecurity? Specify.
7. What is the evidence that emotional interaction patterns vary in different societies?

BIBLIOGRAPHY

Ackerman, Nathan W. *The Psychodynamics of Family Life.* New York: Basic Books, 1958.

Analyzes the interdependence of the individual and the family from the standpoint of mutual stability; the emotional development of the child; the family as the conveyor of anxiety and conflict; and the relationship of conflict between family members and conflict within individual family members.

Arnold, Magda B. "Emotions and Personality," *The Psychology of Emotion.* New York: Columbia University Press, 1, 1960, Part III.
Shows the relationship between perceptions, objectives, and emotional behavior; the nature of motivation; and describes anger, fear, and anxiety.

Hess, Robert D.; and Handel, Gerald. *Family Worlds: A Psychosocial Approach to Family Life.* Chicago: University of Chicago Press, 1959, particularly Chs. 1 and 7.
Examines family emotional organization and the process of social interaction. Case studies of five families are used to illustrate emotional interactions and social processes. Presents framework for analysis of whole families.

Hoffman, Martin L.; and Hoffman, Lois Wladis. *Review of Child Development Research.* New York: Russell Sage, 1, 1964, and 2, 1966.
A series of extensive and well-documented reviews of knowledge on the social and psychological aspects of child development. Covers topics from early periods of socialization by adults and peers to the development of higher mental processes. See especially chapters on infant care and parental discipline. All chapters have extensive bibliography.

Miller, Daniel R.; and Swanson, Guy E. *The Changing American Parent: A Study in the Detroit Area.* New York: John Wiley and Sons, 1958.
Survey of 582 mothers asking questions about child-rearing practices such as feeding, bladder and bowel training, discipline, and the mother's reaction to the birth of the child and her expectations for the child's adult role. Analyzes data into categories of families with bureaucratic or entrepreneurial occupations of the father, as well as middle and lower socioeconomic status. Finds bureaucratic and entrepreneurial occupations significant dimensions differentiating child-rearing practices in families.

Rabin, A. I. *Growing Up In the Kibbutz.* New York: Springer, 1965.
Reports a carefully controlled study of Kibbutz-reared children ranging in age from infancy to young adulthood. Analyzes both psychological and social adjustment. Results suggest few if any deleterious effects from child-rearing in the unique Kibbutz communal and family system.

Sears, Robert R.; Maccoby, Eleanor E.; and Levin, Harry. *Patterns of Child Rearing.* Evanston, Illinois: Row, Peterson, 1957.
An intensive interview study of 379 mothers of kindergarten-age children in the Boston area. Semi-structured interviews were tape-recorded and the results of the content analysis are reported in detail. Attention given to the meaning of the findings for a general understanding of child-rearing.

Sewell, William H. "Social Class and Childhood Personality," *Sociometry*, 24, (1961): pp. 340–356.
>Reviews and analyzes studies of infant-training practices and of personality differences in children in different social classes in America. Concludes that there is a relatively low correlation between social class and some aspects of personality, and very little or no relationship between infant-training practices and childhood personality. Good bibliography.

Stolz, Lois Meek. *Influences on Parent Behavior*. Stanford, California: Stanford University Press. 1967.
>Reports an intensive interview study of parents in 39 families with varying backgrounds. Both mothers and fathers were interviewed repeatedly. Beliefs, values, situational factors, background, and contacts with various sources of information were studied. Emphasizes network of factors influencing parent behavior.

Chapter 10
Expectations and Roles

> It is in the family that the expectations of society first impinge on the infant, forming his habits, setting his standards, and defining his roles. Family expectations define the initial roles of the child in his family and prepare him for later roles in the community. These expectations he uncritically accepts until they are challenged by divergent expectations. Complications arise when there is conflict between the expectations of the family and those of other groups in the community.

ROLES AND EXPECTATIONS OF A HUSBAND AND WIFE

A man and woman enter marriage with expectations of the proper roles of the husband and wife. These expectations have developed from observations of the behavior of their parents and from observing the behavior of others. They also develop from their own ideas about marriage. In the following case, a husband and wife describe some of their expectations of ways in which the husband and wife should interact and also of how they should behave toward each other:

> *Husband:* The most important thing is that there must be a great deal of love and mutual understanding. One other thing is that the husband and wife should have some common interests in activities outside the home. They should have some future goal they are working for. We are both working now so I can go to school and become a hairdresser. This will give us security which is very important in marriage; insecurity in money matters is probably what people fight most over. A satisfactory adjustment sexually is also important. I don't believe in one person making a decision. I believe that the people involved should have some say in the decision. I would say this is true of us in most areas. My main duty is to be the breadwinner: you should make it a duty to do all you can for your

family. I've never balked at doing the dishes. Even if the husband is tired, he should help. . . . My wife is very nice. . . . She's very generous, understanding in certain areas. She's not as understanding in certain areas like finances but she's certainly not a spendthrift. . . . I believe I am very understanding and considerate. Sometimes I'm too emotional, with a tendency to drown my sorrows in a couple of beers. Being impulsive is my worst fault. . . . My wife thinks I am pretty good with the kids. Actually I'm too easy with them, we both are.

Wife: I guess we're both looking for a future together, and making each other happy. My husband enjoys family life; there was no family life in my first marriage. My first husband made good money but he was never around. . . . My husband gives me his check and I pay the bills. With the children, except when they're very naughty and he tells them to stand in the corner and sees that they stay there, whichever one of us is nearest corrects them. We decide together if we want to go to the beach or go out. We relax together mostly. . . . He's very considerate. He hasn't got many bad points; he can't hurt people even with words. When he gets a bottle of beer, he likes to talk. He's the type that anyone can get along with. He's independent, too. . . . I'm impatient and I'm independent. . . . We had some financial problems, but nothing much else. We haven't been married long so he wants lots of attention. He's the type of person who sits down and talks things out when there's a problem before it grows.[1]

The husband expected that he and his wife would love each other and that they would have understanding, common interests, security, satisfaction in sexual relations, and shared authority in decision-making. He expected to be the chief breadwinner and to help in housekeeping activities. The wife agreed with him regarding the desirability of making each other happy, having common interests, and shared authority in decision-making. She included, in her role, paying the bills and giving her husband the attention he desired.

The topics considered in this chapter are (1) the nature of expectations and roles, (2) the influence of family expectations, (3) family roles of husband and wife, (4) the learning of sex roles by children, and (5) roles of adolescents and young adults.

THE NATURE OF EXPECTATIONS AND ROLES

Men and women enter marriage with rather definite expectations of how a husband and wife are supposed to behave in the marriage situation. These expectations have developed over the years, largely patterned after the parental models. Regardless of their origin, a man and

---

[1] Lee Rainwater, *Family Design: Marital Sexuality, Family Size, and Contraception* (Chicago: Aldine, 1965), pp. 34–35.

woman entering marriage each has a set of expectations of the proper role of a husband and of a wife. This is the basis for the conception of marriage as an adjustment of roles, defined as an organization of activities and attitudes appropriate to a given position in a network of social relationships.

Differences in Expectations of Husband and Wife A man and woman entering marriage in the United States generally have some differences in their expectations of the proper roles of a husband and a wife. Each set of parents have had different experiences; possibly they are from somewhat different cultural backgrounds; and possibly each set of parents have different conceptions of the proper roles of a husband and wife. So almost inevitably a new husband and wife will have differences in their expectations of what roles the husband and wife will play.

Adjustment of Roles of Husband and Wife Some of the adjustments of roles may have occurred in the premarital period, particularly if the courtship is sufficiently long and communication is intimate and unrestricted. In courtship a man and woman may learn what each expects the role of the husband and wife to be in marriage. If these expectations are too divergent it may result in the couple terminating their association. But if the differences are surmountable each will begin to make adjustments to the other's expectations of the role of the husband and wife, at least on the verbal level.

Questions which will arise in the courtship period or in the early months of marriage include the following: Should the wife be employed in a full-time job? In making major decisions, should some be made by the husband, others by the wife, or by consensus? Should sexual activities be mutually enjoyable? Should they be engaged in whenever one or the other desires it? Should the wife, the husband, or both be responsible for the prevention of conception until planned? In housekeeping activities, is the expectation that the wife will take care of these exclusively, or that the husband will help? What is the expectation of the frequency and intensity of associations with in-laws? What is the expectation concerning the desirable number of children and the role of the father and mother in rearing them? What are the expectations of each on such personal relationships as demonstration of affection, emotional support, degree of talkativeness, and sociability?

In interaction between the husband and the wife, each will learn the expectation of the other on roles they expect to play and on roles they expect the mate to play. Some of these expectations will be completely acceptable, others will be acceptable if modified somewhat, and still others will be quite unacceptable. In the process of communication, adjustments are likely to develop on some of these while others will be given up as not too important.

A person can engage in symbolic interaction with himself and consider the kinds of roles he will engage in. For example, a husband may weigh the desirability of being the head of the house with the major voice in making decisions or sharing this role with his wife. If he has respect for her judgment, he may come to the conclusion that better decisions will be made if she has a voice in making them. This means that the person is not just a passive receiver of roles from his family and other groups, but actually has a hand in determining the roles he will play.

The Inner and Outer World of Experience To understand the behavior of a person, one must consider both forces within himself and forces impinging on him from without. Realistic analyses of conduct stress this interplay between the inner and outer factors. For example, expectations of others for the roles one plays become internalized and may be accepted as a person's own, so that he desires what society demands of him. However, changes in the situation may introduce new expectations. When this occurs, the person may be influenced either by the expectations that he accepted previously or by the new expectations. Under these conditions, conflict may ensue. Or the person may develop personal expectations which are a compromise between the old and new conflicting expectations.

This interaction between the inner world of personality and the outer world of society must always be kept in mind, even when, for purposes of examination, it is necessary to concentrate for the moment on either external or internal aspects of behavior.

Definition of Roles A role may be defined as an organization of behavior in response to group expectations. It is a pattern of behavior which a child or an adult develops on the basis of what others expect or demand of him. Role is the "part" a person plays in the family or other social group. A role is an organized set of activities and attitudes expected of a person with a given status or position in a group. Roles for certain positions may remain the same from generation to generation; or they may be different and fluid, as in periods of social change.

The conception of the person as one who has a role and a status in a social group has thrown light on the nature of personality development in the family. Every person has some awareness of his roles in all groups of which he is a member. Not only does the person have a conception of his own role in the family, but he has a sense of the roles of all the other members and ideas of what family life is or ought to be. The ideas of what behavior and attitudes are appropriate for a given role are developed in the family through the communication of the expectations of various family members. These expectations have arisen both from the individual experiences of each person and from ideas of proper behavior found in the culture.

Among the early sociologists who developed the concept of roles was W. I. Thomas. He was one of the first to emphasize the idea that it is the family and the community which define the expected behavior of the person and the way his role is to be played in various situations. From his analysis of personal documents, Thomas concluded that the "definition of the situation" by the family and society determines in large part the behavior of a person:

> Preliminary to any self-determined act of behavior there is always a state of examination and deliberation which we may call the *definition of the situation*. And actually not only concrete acts are dependent on the definition of the situation, but gradually a whole life-policy and the personality of the individual himself follow from a series of such definitions.
>
> The child is always born into a group of people among whom all the general types of situations which may arise have already been defined and corresponding rules of conduct developed, and where he has not the slightest chance of making his definitions and following his wishes without interference.
>
> The family is the smallest social unit and the primary defining agency. As soon as the child has free motion and begins to pull, tear, pry, meddle, and prowl, the parents begin to define the situation through speech and other signs and pressures: "Be quiet," "Sit up straight," "Blow your nose," "Wash your face," "Mind your mother," "Be kind to Sister," etc. This is the real significance of Wordsworth's phrase, "Shades of the prison house begin to close upon the growing child." His wishes and activities begin to be inhibited, and gradually, by definitions within the family, by playmates, in the school, in the Sunday school, in the community, through reading, by formal instruction, by informal signs of approval and disapproval, the growing member learns the code of his society.[2]

The concept of roles is one of the fundamental tools in a sociological or social psychological analysis of the family. Consequently, the use of this concept, either explicitly or implicitly, will be found in various chapters of the book. The following are some of the explicit discussions of roles and role expectations: roles of rural and urban wives, Soviet expectations for parents and children, roles of the wife in India and Japan, role expectations in courtship, the role of intermediaries in mate selection, interdependence of family roles as a component in family unity, reduction of parental roles in the middle and later years of marriage,

---

[2] W. I. Thomas, *The Unadjusted Girl* (Boston: Little, Brown, 1923), pp. 42–43.

changing patterns of family roles, and changes in the role of family members in a crisis situation.

Learning of Roles Role expectations are learned chiefly through interactions with others in a group. Sometimes the others will be acting in roles similar to the role to be learned. In this situation the role may be learned largely by copying the model or by imitation. Frequently this would be the case in a family with young children copying the behavior of older ones. Under different situations other persons may be acting in related but quite different roles, as in the case of a parent and child, or a husband and wife. The father and mother will use many ways to define the way they expect the child to behave. A child may tell the parents how he thinks parents ought to behave. In a very real sense this informal instruction or education contributes to role learning.

The ways in which husbands and wives may define proper behavior for themselves or for each other are illustrated in the following comments made in response to a projective "story." This was used as a stimulus to obtain information about companionable conversation between husband and wife in research interviews with working-class families. In the first two comments, the women thought that the wife should adjust to the husband. The third thought that the husband should make an adjustment to the wife:

> I don't know what is the matter with some women. Their husbands will come home and wish they could lie down and just forget everything, and a woman will come yakity yak about nothing at all until a guy has to go out and get a drink. I don't know what they think their husbands are made of. They work their guts out making a living, trying to get along, and then they come home and their wives want them to be some kind of fancy pants, say silly things to them.

> She should make it interesting enough around the house to get him away from the T.V. and the newspaper; invite people over or find some things like church work or hobbies that they can work at together.

> He should listen to her and talk to her. He can't expect her to sit in the house all day and do her job and not have anyone to talk to at night.[3]

Parents, brothers and sisters, and other relatives sometimes try to teach roles by giving negative definitions to children. In the following two cases, a brother and a father gave negative definitions which influenced the behavior of a sister and a playmate of a child:

> My brother was especially mean to me, but his explanation was that he would not want me to be a "sissy." He made me fight hornets and yellow

---

[3] Mirra Komarovsky, *Blue-Collar Marriage* (New York: Random House, 1967), pp. 115–116.

jackets, and if I had a sting I could not cry or he would say that "all girls are sissies." If he dared me to do anything I would do it, regardless of the consequences. Once he said, "Do you dare to burn your hair off?" I said that I did. He burned one side of my hair so short that I had to have my hair cut short as a boy's.

When I was seven years old I spent the day with some relatives whose little granddaughter was visiting them. She and I were playing with our dolls on the porch when she said, "My dolls have nothing to wear so I will let them go naked." Her father heard the remark and said that "nice little girls do not talk about being naked." I felt that we had been wicked and for years I had a guilty feeling when I heard the word.

Eventually the role expectations to which a person responds are patterns of behavior he has learned to expect of others and of himself. When these expectations have been incorporated within him, they are used as standards in evaluating his own behavior as well as the behavior of others. Expectations stamped with the approval of significant persons—parents, the extended family, or a peer group—do not impinge on group members as alien and imposed, but as socially desirable personal standards. These standards have developed in experience through communication with others and with oneself.

Learning of Roles in a Homogeneous Culture The learning of roles is facilitated by living in a homogeneous culture. An illustration of learning role expectations with ease in a homogeneous distinctive subculture in the United States is provided by a study of the Amish. Among the white middle class, urban population of the United States, it is generally accepted that the behavior of a child is decidedly different from that expected of an adult. Then as he grows older it is expected that the child will abruptly give up most of his childish attitudes and activities and behave like an adult. What happens, however, when children live in a group where there are many links and similarities between the world of the child and the world of the adult? A partial answer to this question is provided by Kuhn's study of Amish and non-Amish children in Iowa.[4] He collected information about the Amish culture and secured questionnaire data from 134 fourth- through eighth-grade children in 15 one-room schools, about equally distributed between Amish and non-Amish children.

Amish culture includes roles which are expected of the child, of youth, and of older persons. These roles, however, are not clearly differentiated for each age group. The child has part-time work roles to perform

---

[4] Manford H. Kuhn, "Factors in Personality: Socio-Cultural Determinants as Seen Through the Amish," in *Aspects of Culture and Personality*, Francis L. K. Hsu (ed.) (New York: Abelard-Schuman, 1954).

which are similar to those of adults. Boys help in the outdoor farm activities; girls help in housework. The continuity of roles for children, young people, and adults is promoted by the expectation that the associations of children and early adolescents will be confined to siblings and others within the Amish community. Kuhn describes this as follows:

> The Amish infant and child are immersed in their families, and their widest horizons are Amishdom. Even at the ages of fourteen and fifteen some of my Amish subjects in the Kalona area had never visited Iowa City, only sixteen or seventeen miles away. This is, apparently, a very deliberate practice for adult Amish people shop regularly in Iowa City. The horizon of the Amish child is thus bounded largely by his family, and as a consequence his earliest roles are much less age-graded than are those of our children. He associates mainly with his fellow siblings, who are thus not as precisely his age-peers as are the associates of our children.[5]

The two primary values of the Amish are that a child should learn to farm and should acquire and retain the values of the Amish religion. Therefore he should go to school only through the eighth grade. On leaving school the Amish child begins more definitely to prepare for adult life. Boys are expected to work, save, and engage in courtship; girls are expected to be full-fledged household help.

From the responses of Amish children to 13 questions, Kuhn concludes that Amish children have internalized certain expectations of the Amish group: adult roles, roles connected with farming and housewifely activities, and those associated with abstract values of the Amish religion. The Amish child conceives of himself as a young adult engaging in important farming activities or housewifely activities of the farm home. He accepts Amish religious practices as good and right. Relative isolation from "worldly people" or "nonbelievers" prevents internalizing competitive and conflicting roles. He is assured by his family and the Amish group that farming and the Amish way of life are absolutely good. On the whole the Amish have succeeded in defining proper behavior for their group members and in having these definitions and expectations incorporated into group members. This is true even though the expectations are very different from those of the surrounding culture. However, in recent years it has become somewhat more difficult to maintain isolation.

The child growing up in a homogeneous culture gradually and uncritically assimilates definitions of expected behavior of that culture; he does not question the goodness or rightness of roles which he is expected to play in group relationships.

[5] *Ibid.*, p. 54.

Adults Who Join New Groups For adults who join new groups, such as immigrants to a new country, converts to Catholicism, or a professor who decides to enter business, group expectations at first may appear strange, meaningless, and sometimes opposed to his own principles. This reaction of the new member to group expectations occurs to the degree that (1) the person belonged to other groups with a different body of expectations, (2) the new group lacks or has prestige for him, and (3) he has not yet fully assimilated the expectations of the group. Through initiations and other induction rituals, the group may attempt to impress on the new member its history, its objectives, and the significance of its activities.

Conformity and Nonconformity While the main result of giving definitions of expected behavior is conformity, the process inevitably involves the potentiality of nonconformity. If for any reason the person fails in his effort to meet group expectations, and if he is in contact with a group with different expectations, he may turn to this other group and fulfill their expectations. He may be thought of as a renegade, a rebel, or a genius. The divergent behavior of the person is often sanctioned by another group to which he transfers his allegiance. Thus the son who rejects the standards of the family may follow unquestioningly the expectations of his peer group.

THE INFLUENCE OF FAMILY EXPECTATIONS

The Force of Expectations The behavior of a person in a particular situation is motivated by attitudes and ideas formed in his various experiences from birth to the time of acting in that situation. For example, the tendency on the part of a husband to expect his wife to be a homemaker depends on all his prior experiences with roles of wives. Consequently, an understanding of behavior in a family involves knowing the expectations to which the persons have been exposed before as well as during marriage. From this viewpoint, the family as a unit of interacting persons signifies the fitting together of the expectations of a husband and of the wife acquired both during marriage and in the years before they became acquainted.

The expectations of intimate and informal groups, like the family, define proper behavior and usually control the conduct of group members. Parental expectations control the early habits formed by the child. What the person will eat and how he will eat it, how he will walk and talk, what he may and may not do, standards of decency, and other approved behavior, require no compulsion other than that of a consistent group definition and expectation.

The potent effect of family expectations may be seen by posing the question: To what extent are a person's life activities determined by the status of his parents and by their expectations? For the vast majority, religious affiliation, social class, and educational level of the childden are about the same as those of their parents. The effect of the educational expectations of a mother on a child is shown in the following case:

> I passed in all of my studies the first year of high school but flunked in all but one the second. I was so surprised at my failure that I hurried home to Mother, then throwing myself into her arms I sobbed out my disgrace. At first she forgot her daily attitude toward me and kissed me and loved me into calm; then suddenly she pushed me from her and demanded why I had failed. I did not dare to tell her that it was too much basketball or she would forbid me to play, so I told her that the studies were too difficult. She looked at me and said, "Well, young lady, you are going to finish high school if it takes a hundred years, so you had better get busy." Needless to say I worked hard the next year and in my fourth year I carried both junior and senior work and finished with my class.

Not only do the expectations of husbands and wives influence their conduct and that of their children, but the expectations of children as to the desirable behavior of parents affect the latter's behavior. This is particularly true in a companionship family, where children are encouraged to express themselves.

Parental expectations as regards family objectives and standards may exert a rather uniform influence on all sons and daughters in the family. However, when parental expectations are linked with preferential treatment of different children, there may be differential conformity to family expectations. How family expectations may result in approved behavior by one son and disapproved behavior by another is seen in the following case:

> Jim and Tom were brothers. Jim, the older, was an unusually attractive boy. When he was three years old Tom was born and this presented him with a problem, but he met it by conforming to parental standards and by developing winsome manners, thus maintaining first place in his parents' affections.
>
> Tom was up against a difficult situation. He first attempted to outdo Jim in obedience to parental wishes. He was painstaking, orderly, and neat. At five years of age he would spread a paper on the grass so as not to soil his suit. In spite of this strenuous effort Tom did not succeed in displacing Jim in first place in his parents' affection. In school he found himself called a "sissy," while his brother was popular. In high school Tom went to the other extreme and gained attention by being wild and tough.

In this case the younger brother gave up his attempt to be a model boy when he found that it did not win his parents' preferential affection and made him lose status with his fellows.

Expectations and the Formation of Personality Up to this point, parental expectations have been considered as a very important factor in the personality development of the child. But just what part do parental expectations play in the process by which the family biologically, emotionally, and socially shapes the personality of the child?

Biological characteristics are those that are inherited, like physiognomy, skin color, and possibly temperament. The influence of parental expectations on the genetic traits of the child at most is slight and indirect. It might seem at first glance that social expectations have no influence at all on the biological inheritance of the child, but indirectly parental expectations exert some effect. This happens because persons tend to marry others physically and mentally, as well as culturally, like themselves.[6] The assumption is that the tendency to fall in love and to marry someone physically and mentally similar to oneself is the effect of selection on the basis of social expectations. This selective process has a definite effect on the physical characteristics of children.

Emotional traits arise principally in the emotional interaction of the child and his parents and with his brothers and sisters. Cultural expectations of approved family roles and other cultural patterns may indirectly affect the conditioning of emotional traits. For example, let us assume that a dominant parent tends to induce submission in the child. Cultural approval or disapproval of parental domination may affect the behavior of the father or mother and thus modify parent-child interaction. To the extent, then, that cultural influences modify the expression of emotional traits of parents, they will influence the development of emotional traits in their children.

Social traits are formed by social expectations and patterns of behavior derived from others. This occurs in the family and then in outside groups. Habit formation, character development, social attitudes, and values are obtained in large part from roles assumed by the person in his family and in society. A low level of achievement may be of social rather than biological origin. It may reflect the absence in the person and in his family of the expectation to acquire an education or to rise in the economic scale. Then, too, the unambitious person may be conforming to the expectations of his family and friends but failing to meet the standards of the larger society. A high cultural level of parents, relatives, and friends and their expectations are potent factors in stimulating mental growth and in setting up levels of aspiration. The achieve-

---

[6] See the discussion of homogamy in Ch. 12.

ment of a person is a result of his ability and of his determination to attain a goal. His ambition is not something inborn but acquired in interaction, first within the family and later in the circle of his associates.

Thus family expectations exert a slight and only indirect influence on the biological traits of a person, a somewhat greater but still indirect effect on his emotional characteristics, and a great and direct impact on his social development.

Patterns of Husband-Wife Expectations Each family begins with newlyweds, relatives, and friends having certain expectations of what roles should be played by family members. The bridegroom has a conception of himself as a husband and of his bride as a wife. The bride has an idea of her role as a wife, and of how her husband will behave. If husband and wife are in agreement on the roles each should play, the union may be harmonious, regardless of whether the agreement is on control by the husband, by the wife, or by concensus. However, an element of discord may be introduced if the expectations of relatives or friends are in conflict with those of the couple.

A case in point is that in which the wife tends to dominate, the husband to yield, and the source of conflict is the attitudes of relatives and friends reflecting the tradition that the husband should be head of the family and have the final word in decisions. In situations of this type it may be psychologically satisfying to both husband and wife for her to take the lead in family affairs. However, discord may result because this dominating role of the wife runs counter to cultural expectations. The tradition of masculine domination has a stronger place in our society than the conception that equality "ought" to characterize relationships between the sexes.

The husband may conceive the role of a wife as the old-fashioned role of his mother, while the wife thinks of herself as a modern woman; he wants his wife to be a homebody, while she is intent on a career. He may be content to make a modest living, while his wife prods him to become a money-maker like her father. Or the husband may work overtime and study at night, imbued with the ideal of success, while the wife longs for his companionship.

Even if the mate does not live up to the expectations of the other or up to his conception of his role in marriage, the marriage may survive because of the expectations of one or both of the permanent nature of the marriage. When divorce is against the mores, the wife is disposed to tolerate behavior contrary to her conception of satisfactory conduct of a husband, such as infidelity, drunkenness, and cruelty, to a far greater degree than when the expectation is that these are justifiable grounds for the dissolution of the union. The following case reported by a daughter shows the mother choosing the lesser of two evils, a drinking husband rather than violation of the conception of permanent husband-wife relationships:

> Mother "disapproved" of Father's more recent friends without ever having met them. The realization that she was having less influence on him, especially in regard to what was as yet an occasional drink, began to undermine her sense of security. Morally, to Mother, this was a terrible wrong. *Her* husband drank, the father of *her* children drank; *her* friends were coming to *know* he drank; she feared to allow her adolescent children to have guests because he might have had a drink. She begged, she cajoled, she taunted, she threatened to leave, but tradition held her fast. Mother was a martyr to traditions. Staying or leaving of her own volition did not really exist, for *he* was her husband; *he* was the father of her children—"for better or worse."

FAMILY ROLES OF HUSBAND AND WIFE

Although the concept of roles has been widely used in the analysis of the family, a relatively limited amount of empirical study has been devoted to the examination of role behaviors and role expectations within the family. This may be, in part, because the study of roles requires close examination of interaction and tools for this are only in the process of being developed. Almost all studies have relied on reports of behavior, expressions of attitudes and expectations, paper and pencil tests of choice of behavior, or observations made in experimental sessions. Certain areas have received the most intensive study. Among these are certain aspects of husband-wife interaction, especially conjugal role relationships and division of labor.

Conjugal Role Relationships Central in delineating the marriage and family life of a husband and wife are the typical ways in which a husband and wife organize their relationships to one another—their performance of tasks, their modes of interacting, their reciprocal expectations, and their characteristic ways of communicating their values and beliefs about desired ways of interacting. One way of characterizing the role relationships of husband and wife is suggested by the theme of this book; families may be seen along a continuum from those with major focus on traditional expectations as an economic and child-rearing unit to those families with major focus on interpersonal relationships and satisfactions, especially companionship. A characterization more specifically directed at roles has been suggested by Bott.[7] Husband-wife relationships are seen as ranging from jointly organized to highly segregated.

[7] Elizabeth Bott, *Family and Social Network* (London: Tavistock, 1957).

In joint conjugal role relationships the marital life of the couple is characterized by sharing of time, interests, and activities. The usually necessary division of labor for occupational and housekeeping responsibilities is expected, but joint involvement is a dominant theme for the couple. The sharing of time, interests, and activities may involve the husband and wife carrying out an activity together or by either partner at different times. This applies to social and recreational events as well as task performance. Family affairs are considered as joint affairs with a minimum of task differentiation or separation of interest. A high value is placed on the sharing of all possible aspects of marital life, and also on interest in and sympathy toward activities which are of necessity more independently carried out.

By contrast, the segregated conjugal role relationship is characterized by a pattern of marital life in which the activities of the husband and wife are separate and distinct and a considerable number of separate interests are expected. The life of the couple is divided into the husband's or male spheres of activity and interests and the wife's or female spheres.

This division is viewed as appropriate. These descriptions of joint and segregated role relationships apply to the ends of a continuum, with intermediate degrees between.

Bott's study was carried out through intensive interviews with a small number of London families. In this group, she found that husband and wife roles were related to the kind of social environment in which they lived. Segregated role relationships were likely to occur when a couple lived in a situation which made possible close ties and frequent contacts with members of the kinship group (usually for the wife), or with a friendship group (usually for the husband). When a couple lived in an environment without close contact with kinship or personal friendship groups, joint role relationships were more likely.

The idea of joint or segregated role relationships between husband and wife was used by Rainwater in a study gathering data on 257 urban American families. He found conjugal roles differed by social class, most strikingly the prevalence of joint relationships in upper middle-class families and of segregated relationships in lower lower-class families. Table 13 presents these findings. A study of middle-aged couples by Udry and Hall came to a somewhat similar conclusion, finding that role relationships were associated with the educational level and employment role of the wife.[8] College educated, employed wives were most likely to have joint role relationships with their husbands.

[8] J. Richard Udry and Mary Hall, "Role Segregation and Social Network in Middle-class, Middle-aged Couples," *Journal of Marriage and Family*, 28 (1965): pp. 392–395.

Table 13. Social class and conjugal role relationships*

		Percent Joint	Percent Intermediate	Percent Segregated
Class and Race		ROLE RELATIONSHIPS		
Upper middle class	(32)	88	12	—
Lower middle class	(31)	42	58	—
Upper lower-class				
Whites	(26)	19	58	23
Negroes	(25)	12	52	36
Lower lower-class				
Whites	(25)	4	24	72
Negroes	(29)	—	28	72

*Adapted from Lee Rainwater, *Family Design: Marital Sexuality, Family Size, and Contraception* (Chicago: Aldine, 1965), p. 32.

Instrumental and Expressive Roles Although a great deal of laboratory research has been devoted to examining the roles of persons in small groups, very little of this work has involved families as subjects. Nevertheless, some of the ideas gained from such research have been applied to the family. For example, from research on five-man problem-solving groups, Bales and Slater concluded that certain persons in the group would devote themselves primarily to the performance of tasks and other members would be primarily engaged in the maintenance of relationships between the persons in the group.[9] Parsons suggested that this distinction applied to the family with the husband-father being a task-performance specialist, called the "instrumental" role, and the wife-mother being specialized in the maintenance of the social and emotional relationships of the family, called the "expressive" role.[10] An analysis of anthropological reports suggested that on a very general level this distinction might be seen in many cultures, but not in all.[11]

Attempts to test this idea of the husband playing an instrumental role in the family and the wife playing an expressive role do not lend support to it. For example, Levinger studied 60 middle-class couples, married on the average 13 years, and with an average of three children.[12]

[9] Robert F. Bales and Philip E. Slater, "Role Differentiation in Small Decision-Making Groups," in *Family, Socialization, and Interaction Process*, Talcott Parsons and Robert F. Bales (eds.) (New York: Free Press, 1955), pp. 259–306.
[10] Talcott Parsons, "The American Family," in Parsons and Bales, pp. 45–47.
[11] Morris Zelditch, Jr., "Role Differentiation in the Nuclear Family," in Parsons and Bales, pp. 307–352.
[12] George Levinger, "Task and Social Behavior in Marriage," *Sociometry*, 27 (1964): pp. 433–448.

He obtained data on task and social-emotional performance and on the relative importance of these areas to husbands and wives. Results showed clearly that task specialization occurred, with some tasks done exclusively by the husband and others by the wife. However, in the social-emotional area, a great deal of equality and mutuality was apparent. Other studies also support the central importance of social and emotional factors in American middle-class marriages. One might conclude that when the maintenance of close affectional relationships is a major function of the family, one person or one role in the group will not be specialized in this area. Rather, participation by all will be required.

Division of Labor The allocation of tasks within and around the home to husband or wife seems to be based to a considerable extent on who is available to do the job and on whether the task is heavy or outside work. Tasks within the home, such as the routine of meals, laundry, and home care are usually done by wives, while care of lawns and repairs are usually done by husbands.[13] There appears to be increasing specialization of task performance from early marriage through the years of childbearing and child rearing. However, when the wife is employed, especially full time, the husband is much more likely to assist with routine housekeeping tasks. Komarovsky's study of working-class families examined the degree to which the husbands participated in domestic tasks traditionally performed by the wife.[14] The percents of husbands never or hardly ever doing given activities were: cooking, 88; laundry, 83; cleaning, 75; and doing dishes, 63. However, there was much greater involvement of husbands in other types of family tasks. Over a third of husbands frequently or regularly helped with grocery shopping and with care of infants; and over half with care of older children. The question of attitudes toward division of labor was systematically explored, with results indicating that for eight out of every ten of these working-class couples, "who does what" around the house did not present any significant problems. Household tasks were in fact divided according to somewhat traditional expectations of what women are to do and what men are to do. Such divisions of tasks were a matter of convenience and habit rather than ideas about what is right.

THE LEARNING OF SEX ROLES BY CHILDREN

From many cues and definitions given to him, a child gradually learns that he is a member of a sex—a boy or girl. Being a boy or girl has many

[13] Robert O. Blood, Jr., and Donald M. Wolfe, *Husbands and Wives* (Glencoe, Illinois: Free Press, 1960), Ch. 3.
[14] Komarovsky, *Blue-Collar Marriage*, pp. 50–56.

expectations attached to it—ways in which one will dress, ways one will behave, toys one will play with, whether one is rough or gentle in play with others, whether one may show fear and cry openly or must try to hide it. Much of this process of definition of how to be a boy or a girl takes place in the nuclear family, with subsequent reinforcement by others. Most of the definitions of appropriate sex-role behavior are given somewhat incidentally in the course of family living and are absorbed by the child without special attention to them. When there is conflict about sex-role behavior, the issue is more likely to be remembered. This is the case in the following examples cited by college women:

> My brother was caught taking a doll to bed with him. He must have seen me and my sister do it. We made fun of him and the nurse told him that if he doesn't want to be taken for a little girl he'd better take the teddy bear instead.
>
> I started life as a little tomboy, but as I grew older Mother got worried about my unladylike ways. She removed my tops, marbles, football, and skates and tried to replace these with dolls, tea sets, and sewing games. To interest me in dolls, she collected dolls of different nations, dressed exquisitely in their native costumes. She bought me small pocketbooks and lovely little dresses. When, despite her efforts, she caught me one day trying to climb a tree in the park, she became thoroughly exasperated and called me a little "freak."
>
> I was ten years old when I attended the funeral of some relative. I was awed but I didn't cry. I remember thinking that I must *try* or else people would think me very unfeeling. The irony of it was that my brother was biting his lips to keep from crying. He, too, remembered the occasion and confessed years later that he tried hard not to appear a "softy" by bursting into tears.
>
> I thoroughly enjoyed my high school years, but I remember the real disappointment at not being allowed to take "shop," which was given only for boys, and of spending many dreary hours over a piece of cloth that somehow never quite became a skirt.[15]

There is evidence to support a generalization that the behavior expected of children is learned at an early age, varies with the sex of the child, and varies somewhat with the social class to which a child belongs. Rabban studied children in a middle-class suburb of New York and a working-class community of New Jersey.[16] The children were 3 to 8 years old. The problem was to see whether boys and girls would differ

---
[15] Mirra Komarovsky, *Women in the Modern World: Their Education and Dilemmas* (Boston: Little, Brown, 1953), pp. 55-56. Copyright, 1953 by Mirra Heyman.
[16] Meyer Rabban, "Sex-Role Identification in Young Children in Two Diverse Social Groups," *Genetic Psychology Monographs*, 42 (1950): pp. 81-158.

in their selection of "male" and "female" toys and if their selections would vary with age and social class.

Boys and girls differed in their choice of toys. Boys selected the following toys more frequently than did girls: gun, steam roller, dump truck, racer, fire truck, cement mixer, soldiers, and knife. Girls selected the following toys much more frequently than did boys: high chair, buggy, crib, beads, dishes, purse, doll, and bathinette. Irrespective of sex or class, there was a steady increase in appropriate choices as the children advanced in age. Middle-class girls lagged behind working-class girls in appropriate choices.

Eight case studies of the awareness of appropriate sex roles were analyzed intensively by the investigator. For example, one boy aged four and a half years selected all toys considered appropriate for boys. He had two older brothers and his parents were actively interested in training him for a boy's role. His mother expressed the following attitude: "I would actively encourage boyish play, would put away dolls." A girl aged five years and two months also had made all the appropriate choices for her sex. Her only sibling was a brother age seven, but her mother had very definite attitudes toward the proper role played by girls. She always reminded her that "girls don't climb trees. Little girls should sit down and be quiet." This little girl was always rewarded for girlish behavior and punished for boyish behavior. Another girl, four years old, who had an older sister, selected a majority of boys' toys at two experimental sessions. The mother, who did most of the disciplining and rewarding, did not seem to care whether her girl played with sex-appropriate toys or not. The girl was attached to her father and helped him in carpentry, gardening, and other work.

A study of approximately 1400 elementary school children secured information on the kinds of behavior expected of girls and of boys by their classmates. The average girl was expected to be quiet, popular, good looking, not quarrelsome, not inclined to get angry, not to show-off, and not bossy. Boys were rated higher than girls on only three traits: takes a chance, good at games, and not bashful.[17]

Other evidence suggests that both boys and girls have an understanding of sex-role differentiation and appropriate sex-role behavior by four years of age.[18] In an analysis of the processes that occur in the early years, Hartley suggests that various factors act to develop early incorporation of sex-role typing: channeling of perceptions into sex-

[17] Read D. Tuddenham, "Studies in Reputation: I, Sex and Grade Differences in School Children's Evaluations of Their Peers," *Psychological Monographs: General and Applied*, 66, No. 1 (1952): pp. 1–39.

[18] H. Abel and R. Shahin Kaya, "Emergence of Sex and Race Friendship Preferences," *Child Development*, 33 (1962): pp. 939–943; and Walter Emmerich, "Parental Identification in Young Children," *Genetic Psychology Monographs*, 60 (1959): pp. 257–302.

appropriate areas; the use of labels and symbols to identify the child's sex together with appropriate behaviors and objects for that sex; and the provision of opportunities and approval for engaging in sex-appropriate behavior.[19] It is readily observed in most groups in the American culture that there are both direct and subtle ways in which infants and young children are treated in a manner adults consider appropriate to the sex of the child. For example, little girls may be "gentled" and little boys "roughhoused," girls have their hair fluffed and curled, while boys' hair is slicked and trimmed, girl infants may be freely described as pretty, while there may be some embarrassment at describing even a six-week-old boy as beautiful. The frequent use of phrases such as "just like mommy" to girls, or "like daddy does" to boys, teaches imitative sex-typing, even when the specific behavior involved may not be very sex-typed by itself. Direction of activity occurs through the provision of toys and opportunities considered suitable for the sex of the child. Such continuing ways of defining and reinforcing behaviors are some of the interactions which develop appropriate sex-typing in children.

Family Relationships and Sex-Role Learning The emotional quality of the interaction between parent and child may also influence the degree to which a child adopts traits of the same-sex parent. A study of first-grade boys and girls found that both more masculine boys and more feminine girls perceived the parent of the same sex as warm, nurturant and affectionate.[20] Several other studies, particularly with boys, tend to confirm this finding.

Masculinity of boys seems to be related to some degree to the role which their fathers play within the family.[21] When the father is the more powerful parent, especially in decision-making and in the general setting of limits for the child, the boy is likely to be relatively high on a variety of measures of masculinity.[22]

Learning the Sex Roles of Parents Components of the family roles of men and women are apparently perceived and formulated into sex-role stereotypes by American children approximately five years of age.

[19] Ruth E. Hartley, "A Developmental View of Female Sex-Role Identification," *Merrill-Palmer Quarterly*, 10 (1964): pp. 3–16.
[20] Paul Mussen and Eldred Rutherford, "Parent-Child Relations and Parental Personality in Relation to Young Children's Sex-Role Perception," *Child Development*, 34 (1963): pp. 589–607.
[21] While there are many issues about the measurement of masculinity, the usual procedures include choice of socially sex-typed toys or activities and behaviors or traits considered to be assertive or independent.
[22] E. Mavis Hetherington, "A Developmental Study of the Dominant Parent on Sex-Role Preference, Identification, and Imitation in Children," *Journal of Personality and Social Psychology*, 2 (1965): pp. 188–194.

Fathers are perceived as more powerful, punitive, aggressive, fearless, and less nurturant than mothers.[23] There is little difference in these role conceptions between middle-class and lower-class children, or between children from the predominant white culture and those from a presumably more "matriarchal" Negro subculture. Boys who do not have fathers present in their homes differ from those with fathers only in being less likely to see the father as carrying out physical punishment. Girls with working mothers appear to have the same predominantly domestic definitions of mothers' roles as girls whose mothers do not work.[24] These data suggest that early learning of appropriate sex-role behaviors is not limited to the child's own family experience, but may be based also on his experience with other families and possibly from various media of communication.

Effect of Siblings on Learning Sex-Roles The question might be raised as to what effect interaction with siblings has on the learning of sex-role behavior by children. Brim analyzed data on two-child families and concluded that boys with a girl sibling tend to have more traits judged feminine (those dealing with social and emotional, as opposed to task-oriented behavior) than do boys with a boy sibling.[25] This tendency is much more pronounced when the boy is the younger child than when he is the older. Similarly, girls with a boy sibling exhibit more traits judged masculine than do girls with a girl sibling, and again the tendency is more pronounced when the girl is younger than the boy.

A study by Lansky suggests that parents may also be influenced by the sex composition of young children in a family. Parents of children of just one sex tend to have more definite attitudes about appropriate sex-role behavior for young children than parents of children of both sexes. Also, all parents tend to have more definite attitudes about appropriate sex-role behavior for boys and relatively neutral attitudes toward sex-roles for girls.[26]

Thus both the definition and the learning of appropriate sex-role behavior are influenced by the total interactional situation in the family. In the ordinary course of daily living the child is taught both directly and in many subtle ways how to act out his role both as a child and as

---

[23] C. Smith, "The Development of Sex-Role Concepts and Attitudes in Father-Absent Boys," (Unpublished Master's thesis, University of Chicago, 1966).

[24] Ruth E. Hartley and F. Hardesty, "Children's Perceptions of Sex-Roles in Childhood," *Journal of Genetic Psychology*, 105 (1966): pp. 43–51.

[25] Orville G. Brim, "Family Structure and Sex-Role Learning by Children: A Further Analysis of Helen Koch's Data," *Sociometry*, 21 (1958): pp. 1–16.

[26] Leonard M. Lansky, "The Family Structure Also Affects the Model: Sex-Role Attitudes in Parents of Preschool Children," *Merrill-Palmer Quarterly*, 13 (1967): pp. 139–150.

a boy or a girl. What he learns is likely to be influenced both by what a sibling is being taught by the parents and also directly by the child's own interaction with the sibling.

Father Absence The absence of the father from the home is an important issue related to the sex-role identification of children, particularly boys, and also to other aspects of children's personalities. The frequency of father-absence is indicated by Clausen who reports data from the 1960 census showing that of households with children under 18, slightly more than ten percent had only one parent present.[27] This, of course, is for a single point in time. Data from other studies are cited indicating that the proportion of all children who have experienced a broken home at some time before they reach age 18 is much larger since there is a good deal of remarriage. Clausen estimates that between 30 and 40 percent of all children live with only one parent at some time. In the vast preponderance of cases the mother is the parent who is present and the father is absent.

Studies of boys with absent fathers present somewhat confusing evidence concerning the effects of a father's absence on the son's sex-role development. There have been some investigations of young children whose fathers are absent for prolonged periods because of their occupations. This work has been done primarily with young children of European sailors, and contradictory results have been reported. Using projective doll play, researchers found the sons of Norwegian sailors to be more dependent and manifesting more conflict about masculine identification than boys whose fathers were present.[28] A study of children of Italian sailors used similar techniques but did not find important differences between children whose fathers were absent and those who were present.[29] Pedersen compared American military officers' sons who were referred for treatment of emotional or behavioral problems with a matched control group on the extent of father-absence and found no significant relationship between father absence and the boys' problems.[30]

[27] John A. Clausen, "Family Structure, Socialization, and Personality," in *Review of Child Development Research*, Lois Wladis Hoffman and Martin L. Hoffman (eds.) (New York: Russell Sage Foundation, 1966), 2, p. 27.

[28] P. O. Tiller, "Father Absence and Personality Development in Children in Sailor Families," in *Studies of the Family*, N. Anderson (ed.) (Gottingen, Norway: Vandenhoeck and Ruprecht, 1957), 2, pp. 115–137; and David Lynn and W. Sawrey, "The Effect of Father Absence on Norwegian Boys and Girls," *Journal of Abnormal and Social Psychology*, 59 (1959): pp. 258–262.

[29] L. Ancona, M. Cesa-Bianchi, and C. Bocquet, "Identification with the Father in the Absence of the Paternal Model: Research Applied to Children of Navy Officers," *Archivio di Psicologia e Psichiatria*, 24 (1964): pp. 341–361.

[30] Frank A. Pederson, "Relationships Between Father-Absence and Emotional Disturbance in Male Military Dependents," *Merrill-Palmer Quarterly*, 12 (1966): pp. 322–331.

Two studies of very young children whose fathers were temporarily absent because of military service during World War II used projective techniques and found the overt and fantasy behavior of boys in father-absent families to be somewhat effeminate and lacking in aggression.[31] Other investigations have more recently studied young men who were separated from their fathers for a few years as young children; one, using projective techniques, reported less identification with the father.[32] Another examined college entrance scores and reported lower scores in areas of typical masculine interest and proficiency.[33]

The age at which father-absence occurs may be an important influence on the effect of the absence, particularly since it appears that sex-role identification takes place in the very early years. One study which investigated this question compared father-absent with father-present boys, dividing each group into those whose fathers had left before the boys were five years old and those leaving after the boys were five.[34] The father-absent boys had less masculine scores on a sex-role preference test and also were rated as more dependent and less aggressive—but only if the father's absence had begun before the child was five years old. Two factors may be at work here. One is the lack of a male model to whom the small boy can become emotionally attached; the other is the fact that the older boys have the additional environment of school with many male peers as well as older male children who might serve as models for the male role. Also, school groups probably are important sources of continuing reinforcement for sex-role preferences.

The social class of the family may also be an important influence on the effect of father-absence on children. Social class or socioeconomic status has been shown to be related to patterns of interaction within the family.[35] Thomes studied families with low socioeconomic status, using both boys and girls between nine and eleven years of age as subjects and matching father-absent with father-present children.[36] She found very few differences between the groups on measures of the

---

[31] George R. Bach, "Father-Fantasies and Father-Typing in Father-Separated Children," *Child Development*, 17 (1946): pp. 63–79; and Pauline S. Sears, "Doll Play Aggression in Normal Young Children: Influence of Sex, Age, Sibling Status, Father's Absence," *Psychology Monographs*, 65:6 (1951): No. 323.

[32] Mary M. Leichty, "The Effect of Father-Absence During Early Childhood Upon the Oedipal Situation as Reflected in Young Adults," *Merrill-Palmer Quarterly*, 6 (1960): pp. 212–217.

[33] Lyn Carlsmith, "Effect of Early Father Absence on Scholastic Aptitude," *Harvard Educational Review*, 34 (1964): pp. 3–21.

[34] E. Mavis Hetherington, "Effects of Paternal Absence on Sex-Typed Behavior in Negro and White Preadolescent Males," *Journal of Personality and Social Psychology*, 4 (1966): pp. 87–91.

[35] See Ch. 4.

[36] Mary Margaret Thomes, "Children with Absent Fathers," *Journal of Marriage and the Family*, 30 (1968): pp. 89–96.

children's peer relationships, self-concept (including measures of masculinity and femininity), and their feelings and attitudes toward family members. The few differences were for girls rather than boys, suggesting that girls may learn certain aspects of the feminine role by playing them out in relationships with their fathers. Children whose fathers were absent differed in their concepts of parental roles, perceiving all fathers as having a very inactive role in the rearing of their children. These results show very limited influence of father-absence in lower socioeconomic status families, perhaps because the father who has a low educational and occupational level does not have a very prestigious or very active position in his family.

ROLES OF ADOLESCENTS AND YOUNG ADULTS

Adolescent Roles In our urban society the child's roles through early adolescence are very different from adult roles. Then in late adolescence suddenly several new adult roles are expected of him. He is expected to select an occupation, to get a job or begin training for a profession, to become a responsible member of social organizations, and to take the responsibility for the selection of a mate.

The adolescent, however, is not without role definitions for adult behavior. These definitions of adult roles have been incorporated by him from models, from specific instruction on how to behave in certain roles, and from his family, his peer group, and mass media. The various investigations of the relative influence of parents and the adolescent's best peer friend on future plans have not been completely consistent. However, a recent study by Kandel and Lesser, using sound methods and a large sample, found that for future life goals parents have a stronger influence than peers.[37]

What, in general, are the expectations of adolescents with reference to their roles in marriage? Dunn studied the marital expectations of 436 white high school seniors, 238 girls and 198 boys, of northern Louisiana.[38] It was found that in certain relationships both boys and girls favored an equalitarian, companionship relationship, and in others, traditional role expectations. As compared with the number who favored traditional roles, more boys and girls favored equalitarian relationships in participation in religious and civic affairs, in the care of children, and in such matters as personal freedom, making decisions, and being the "head" of the home.

[37] Denise B. Kandel and Gerald S. Lesser, "Parental and Peer Influences on Educational Plans of Adolescents," *American Sociological Review*, 34 (1970): pp. 213–223.
[38] Marie S. Dunn, "Marriage Role Expectations of Adolescents," *Marriage and Family Living*, 22 (1960): pp. 99–111.

In the past the so-called "stress and strain" of adolescence was attributed to the physiological changes taking place at puberty. Or "adolescent" behavior was ascribed to emotional traits assumed to be associated with these biological developments. The studies of Margaret Mead, reported in *Coming of Age in Samoa,* and investigations of other cultural anthropologists disclose that adolescent problem-behavior is absent from some primitive societies in which the culture provides a socially recognized and controlled transition from childhood to adult status.

Adolescents are in transition to an adult status. Some persons pass from childhood into an adult status without experiencing stress and strain in adolescence. This may result from one or more conditions: (1) residence in a community which is well organized to provide social activities for adolescents which help to mediate the transition, (2) membership in a social group which performs this same function, (3) parental or other adult guidance during this period, and (4) the early selection of an occupation or other central interest which directs the attitudes and interests of the adolescent.

Young Adults For present purposes young adults will be defined as persons 18 through 24 years of age. One of the major changes in roles for these young adults is from a single to a married status and this is relatively sudden. For those 18 to 19 years old, 98 percent of the men and 91 percent of the women are single. However, for those 20 to 24 years old, nearly half (44.2 percent of the men and a little less than two-thirds (61.7 percent) of the women are married. This is a radical change in roles.[39]

Young adults are in the process of emancipating themselves from parental control. Some, of course, continue the role of dependence on parents for economic support and are satisfied with the role of participant in the activities of the parental family. Others, particularly those who are married, are aware of the social expectation that adults will establish homes of their own. Many of these develop a dual role—independence from the control of parents and dependence on parents, especially for affection, recognition for achievements, and economic and emotional support in time of difficulty. Still others almost completely withdraw from their parents and siblings.

The following is the case of a girl who, as she grew into adulthood, resolved the conflict between family and outside definitions and expectations by psychologically and then spatially withdrawing from her family:

> My environment since leaving home has been entirely different. To some extent I am more likely to define the situation for myself. I have not the same views on many things with which I grew up, for after all they

[39] *Statistical Abstract of the United States,* 1969, p. 32.

were more or less imposed. Little by little I found that my change of views disturbed my family. More and more I closed to them one side of my make-up and then another. For example, only two years ago my sister was discussing with her husband the terrible drought and said something about the Lord not sending rain. Without thinking of the outcome, I said, "The Lord didn't have anything to do with it." The fact that I, four years younger than herself, should think such a thing, shocked my sister very much. At another time I made some remark which made my sister feel that I questioned immortality and they never did get over trying to do something about it. Change of views, new and different interests, marriage, and many other things have tended to separate me from my family.

What, in general, are the expectations of young adults with reference to roles in marriage? Dyer and Urban studied the marital-role expectations of young adults attending Brigham Young University, 150 single men, 150 single women, and 100 married couples.[40] Almost all of these were Mormons who had been exposed to the patriarchal tradition of the Mormon Church. With regard to several marital roles, most of these young adults had moved away from the patriarchal tradition of family relationships. Both single and married young adults favored an equalitarian relationship more than a traditional one in child-rearing, decision-making, and recreation. However, in family finances the traditional expectations appeared not to be clearly defined and new norms in these areas were not clearly established.[41] In household tasks there was the traditional expectation of a division of labor. Thus, while some traditional expectations of marital roles continued, particularly in certain areas, there was at the same time the expectation of an equalitarian, companionship relationship in the family.

The emphasis on the effect of parental expectations on the behavior of the child, the adolescent, and the young adult should not lead the reader to minimize the influence of others in the community who also have expectations of role behavior. There are the social pressures of the play group, with its condemnation of the roles of "teacher's pet" and "mama's boy." There are the expectations of the adolescent group of what is correct in dress, appropriate in conduct, and up-to-date in social relations. Finally, the expectations of one's occupational group and of one's class or social set influence attitudes and behavior.

SUMMARY

There appear to be three stages in the development of expectations of the person: (1) as a small child, when his own expectations are uncon-

---

[40] William G. Dyer and Dick Urban, "The Institutionalization of Equalitarian Family Norms," *Marriage and Family Living*, 20 (1958): pp. 53–58.
[41] *Ibid.*, p. 56.

sciously formed for him by those of his parents; (2) as an older child and adolescent, when he substitutes for parental expectations some of the expectations of his peer group; and (3) as a young adult, when he formulates his own set of expectations as a guide for his conduct.

The taking of roles in the family has a profound and permanent influence on the person. The boy is taking the role not only of the son but of the father and husband. The girl, as playing with dolls indicates, takes the role not only of the daughter but of the mother and wife. Life in the parental home is thus preparation for living later in one's own home.

A man or woman enters marriage with definite expectations of the proper roles of the husband and the wife. Roles are learned by copying models, in informal instruction and training, in thinking about choices of roles, and by negative definitions of some behaviors. A child growing up in a homogeneous culture gradually and uncritically assimilates definitions of expected behavior of that culture. Family expectations exert only a slight and indirect influence on the biological traits of a person, a somewhat greater influence on his emotional characteristics, and a great direct influence on his social development.

The conceptions of family roles which a man and woman brought to marriage in the traditional family of the past were essentially those of their parents. With the companionship family, the conceptions of family roles held by engaged and newly married couples may be widely different from those of their parents. In fact, a man entering marriage may react against the role patterns presented by his father and mother and strive to carry out quite different roles in his own family. Or a wife may seek information from the pediatrician and the psychologist about the proper role of a mother in rearing her children.

PROBLEMS FOR RESEARCH

Further research is needed on the way in which expectations and roles are transmitted by the family and shape personality development.

Differences by Social Class Hollingshead, in his study of adolescents and their families in a small city in the Middle West, found significant differences in family relationships by social class.[42] Although he did not deal specifically with social expectations and roles, a fairly adequate picture of differences by social class can be secured by analyzing his descriptions. It is, of course, limited to a single city of about 10,000 population in the 1940's. One wonders whether there have been changes

[42] A. B. Hollingshead, *Elmtown's Youth: The Impact of Social Classes on Adolescents* (New York: John Wiley & Sons, 1949).

in family roles in the decades since his study. Research is also needed to discover the extent to which family expectations and roles differ by social class, in communities of various sizes, including metropolitan areas, in different ethnic groups, and in rural and urban areas.

Roles of Children in the Family There is a need for studies of the roles taken by children in the family and in their play groups. This investigation should be carried on at different age levels in order to determine the relative degree of family and outside influences on the behavior of the preschool child, the preadolescent, and the adolescent. Mothers with social and psychological training might be induced to participate in a project in which they would make comparable observations on the roles taken by children at selected age levels. It would be important to include in this study such items as the sources of roles and the way in which roles taken in play function for the expression of attitudes inhibited in their direct expression because of parental or other social disapproval.

The Adolescent and Family Expectations From the standpoint of the sociologist and the cultural anthropologist, one problem of adolescent behavior is the conflict between the expectations of the family and the peer group. Systematic studies should be made of the conflicts of the adolescent which arise out of the parents' conception of him as a child and his idea of himself as an adult; conflicts which result from the heterogeneity of American culture and the presence of multiple and incompatible choices; and conflicts arising from rapid cultural change in the roles and expectations of parents and adolescents.

QUESTIONS AND EXERCISES

1. What is the relationship between roles and social expectations?
2. Enumerate some roles you perform as the result of family expectations. What are some of the expectations of your family which differ from the expectations of your peer group?
3. Show how social expectations have an indirect influence on biological and emotional traits.
4. Give examples of the point that personal roles are determined by the situations in which they are expressed.
5. Give illustrations of the conflicting social expectations in American culture of the roles which should be played by husbands and wives, and by parents and children.
6. Contrast the traditional American expectations of husband-wife and parent-child roles with the roles played by members of your family.

7. How do you account for the absence of adolescent problems in some cultures, as reported by anthropologists, and their presence in American culture?
8. How is social class related to joint and segregated roles of husbands and wives?

BIBLIOGRAPHY

Borow, Henry. "Development of Occupational Motives and Roles," in *Review of Child Development Research*, eds. Lois Wladis Hoffman and Martin L. Hoffman. New York: Russell Sage, 2, 1966.
> Reviews social and psychological factors related to occupational aspirations and choices. Related chiefly to adolescents but also contains some data on younger children and achievement orientation.

Biller, Henry B.; and Borstelmann, Lloyd J. "Masculine Development: An Integrative Review," *Merrill-Palmer Quarterly*, 13 (1967): pp. 253–294.
> An extensive review and analysis of theories and research on masculinity in boys. Considers as key variables the degree to which the father is available, masculine, nurturant, and the setter of limits, and the mother's attitude toward and encouragement of masculinity.

Brim, Orville, G. "Family Structure and Sex-Role Learning by Children," *Sociometry*, 21 (1958): pp. 1–16.
> Subjects were 384 children, five- and six-year-olds, originally studied by Helen Koch. Reports that cross-sex siblings have more traits of opposite sex than same-sex siblings; and that this is more pronounced in younger than in older children, particularly for boys.

Herbst, P. G. "Task Differentiation of Husband and Wife in Family Activities," *Human Relations*, 5 (1952): pp. 3–35.
> Used 96 sixth-grade children in Australia as informants about the role behavior of their parents. Describes relative participation of husbands and wives in six areas designated as wife's household duties, common household duties, husband's household duties, child control and care, economic activities, and social activities. Attempts to predict in which areas the husband or wife will participate from the order of areas as listed.

Kagan, Jerome; and Moss, Howard A. *Birth to Maturity*, New York: John Wiley and Sons, 1962.
> Reports a longitudinal investigation of 89 subjects from birth to 20–30 years of age. Focuses on the stability and changes in behavior from the early years of life within the family to the period of young adulthood. An important report on a major longitudinal study.

Komarovsky, Mirra. *Women in the Modern World: Their Education and Their Dilemmas*. Boston: Little, Brown, 1953.

Attempts to answer the question of what in contemporary society causes the problems of women and tensions between the sexes. Traces the college-trained middle-class woman from adolescence to middle age in order to reveal social forces which cause conflict throughout her life.

Maccoby, Eleanor E., ed. *The Development of Sex Differences.* Stanford, California: Stanford University Press, 1966.
A compilation of chapters written after three years of interdisciplinary discussions of this area. Summarizes and analyzes.

Nye, F. Ivan; and Hoffman, Lois Wladis, eds. *The Employed Mother in America.* Chicago: Rand McNally, 1963.
Compiles and analyzes research on why mothers work, what effects a mother's working may have on her children, on the husband-wife relationship, and on the adjustment of the mother. An important volume summarizing knowledge in a controversial area.

Rainwater, Lee. *Family Design.* Chicago: Aldine, 1965. "Social Class and Conjugal Role-Relationships," Ch. 2.
Describes joint and segregated conjugal role-relationships and gives case illustrations from upper-middle, lower-middle, upper-lower, and lower-lower class families. Follows Bott's conceptualization, applying it to American urban families.

Toman, Walter. *Family Constellation: Theory and Practice of a Psychological Game.* New York: Springer, 1961.
Based on a psychological study of 400 persons over a 10-year period. Data about a person's brothers and sisters, his sibling position, and the sibling position of his parents. Holds that from such data one can predict the nature of interpersonal problems and specific attitudes toward authority, politics, religion, death, and economic relationships.

Part III
Family Organization

Over a million and a half couples in the United States get married in any given year. While some of these have been married previously, over three-fourths are having this experience for the first time. The prior experiences of young people have prepared them, in part, for meeting a possible marriage partner, going through the courtship process, getting married, and establishing a family. Persons have what might be called an apprenticeship for courtship and marriage through living for some twenty years in their parental families, through dating, and through going steady without commitment to marry.

In spite of the knowledge, ideas, and feelings one has acquired about courtship, marriage, and family life, it is to be expected that one will face questions and situations which are new for him. The following are illustrations of such questions: How can one tell whether he is really in love and is loved by another? How can one meet persons who closely correspond to his conception of an ideal mate? What are desirable and permissible activities during courtship and engagement? What are the factors involved in the development of unity in a family? Can one measure and predict the chances of success in marriage? What happens to the marriage relationship as one moves from the early through the middle to the later years of marriage? The chapters in this part of the book will help in answering these and other questions. They also suggest areas for future research.

Chapter 11
Courtship

> For generations Americans have believed that courtship, including falling in love, is the natural prelude to marriage. Courtship behavior, however, has been continuously changing for more than two centuries. Courtship in colonial times was strictly supervised and controlled by parents. Since that time there has been a trend toward increased freedom of choice of a mate and increased contact between young men and women without parental supervision. In courtship a young person is trying to find someone who meets as far as possible his expectations and prescriptions for a marriage partner. In the early stages of courtship there is competition for desirable dating partners and this is greatly influenced by the sex ratio. There is progressive commitment from dating to going steady and from going steady to engagement. In the United States a feeling of love and affection is considered one of the most important features of the courtship process.

CHANGES IN COURTSHIP

Interviews with a mother and her daughter show the degree to which courtship has been modified in a generation:

Mother: Bill was 18 and I was 17 when we met in 1932. We became acquainted through our places of employment, which were adjacent. He worked as a clerk in a drug store and I was a dental assistant. Although I had frequent dates with other fellows and he with other girls, we liked one another right off and almost immediately began "going with" one another. Our courtship had a practical tone. The depression was on and we had very little money to spend either for necessities or pleasures, and the future looked grim indeed. Our conversation often dealt with the careful appropriation of money—trying to save a mite here and there so that we would one day have enough money to buy the necessary household items to begin housekeeping. I remember we generally went to a restaurant and movie one night a week, and on the other nights (after Bill got off work) we would go for a drive in his little open roadster. Bill was very proud to own this car! We didn't have a lot of time together as I worked during the day and he worked until 10 o'clock at night.

Morally, there were no parental restrictions for me. My mother had died and my father lived in another city. I do not remember Bill's parents, with whom he lived, restricting him in any way. My parental situation precluded any promiscuous behavior—there was no one to whom I could turn in a dilemma. Yet, our courtship was warm, loving, and satisfying. In 1936 my aunt willed me $100.00 and this magnificent sum permitted us to get married.

In conclusion, the pressing problem of economic survival for both of us most certainly was a dominant factor during our four-year courtship.

Daughter: I met Don three years ago at the university we both were attending. The year before I had been going with another boy and, although we were not engaged, we were pretty serious about each other. There were two difficulties: my folks disapproved of him, particularly my mother, and then his parents wanted us to get married soon and thought education for a girl was unimportant.

Don was a senior and I a junior when we began going together. We had known each other casually before we began really to look at each other. After our first few dates, we saw each other almost every day. That was in the spring. We both live in the same city and so returned there for the summer. Don went to Hawaii with some fraternity brothers, but decided he wanted to come back early and see me. We saw a lot of each other during the remainder of the summer and before I went back to the university we knew we were in love and became formally engaged.

He had to spend six months in the service and so we planned that I would speed up my final year at the university by crowding three quarters of work into two, while he was doing his stint in the army. His camp was not too far from the university and we saw each other about every other week.

We decided not to have a large church wedding, but to have a large supper-dance engagement party back home. My folks made arrangements to have it at one of the nicest hotels in the city and all my friends and all of Don's friends were invited.

The process of getting acquainted with Don's family was something I would not choose to do over again. Not that they were not nice to me or that I did not like them. Their attitudes and ways of behavior were quite different from those with which I had grown up. In a very real sense they were strangers. I suppose Don had somewhat the same problem. Then his folks are wealthy, had a large estate in a rather exclusive section of the city, had conservative political attitudes, and were conformists.

As the day of the wedding approached I found I was becoming very nervous and irritable. I would criticize my folks, was snappy to Don and, although I had to put on a good front with his parents, I felt like expressing my irritation at them.

But all that is in the distant past. We have been married over a year and I really like married life.

The courtship experiences recounted here emphasize the prudential considerations of the mother's courtship, with much attention focusing on economic problems. In the daughter's courtship adequate financial resources allowed the couple to focus on interpersonal relationships. The four-year courtship of the mother is in contrast to the one-year courtship of the daughter. Another contrast is that the mother was emotionally involved with only one man, while the daughter had seriously contemplated marriage with at least two men.

This chapter will be organized around the following major points: (1) the development of American courtship behavior, (2) romantic love, (3) the nature of courtship, (4) the courtship process, and (5) sexual behavior during courtship.

DEVELOPMENT OF AMERICAN COURTSHIP BEHAVIOR

Perspective on current courtship practices may be obtained from an examination of the history of American courtship behavior. It will be seen that there has been a long-term trend from parental control and supervision toward intimate personal interaction between the couple, with minimum supervision.

Colonial America   The customs of courtship in early colonial New England were based on the belief that parents were responsible for the marriage arrangements of their children.[1] It was also believed that the sooner a man was married the better and, consequently, laws were passed to discourage bachelorhood. In Connecticut, for example, a bachelor had to have special permission to live alone or he was subject to a fine of one pound a week. Since a father was believed to be carrying out God's will in arranging marriage for his daughter, it followed that any young man who attempted to gain the girl's affections was frustrating the intentions of God and man. One may assume that such attempts were made, since laws were passed to discourage them. For example, a Massachusetts law of 1647 was as follows:

[1] E. S. Turner, *A History of Courting* (London: Michael Joseph, 1954), p. 70.

It is common practice in divers places . . . for young men irregularly and disorderly to watch all advantages for their evil purposes, to insinuate into the affections of young maidens by going to them in places and seasons unknown to their parents for such ends, whereby much evil hath grown among us, to the dishonor of God and damage of parties.[2]

A similar law in Connecticut detailed "endeavors to inveigle," including "speech, writing messages, company keeping, unnecessary familiarity, disorderly night meetings, sinful dalliance, [and] gifts."[3] Early New England records contain many cases of persons being cited for offenses against laws like these. Nevertheless, for the most part, considerations of prudence were expected to influence the marriage choices of parents and children, with love expected to develop after marriage rather than before.

The ideas of love and happiness as basic to marriage were acknowledged, although it is difficult to obtain evidence about the prevalence of such beliefs. One study based on the analysis of magazines published between 1741 and 1794 is available.[4] Fifteen magazines were examined, a total of 546 issues. In a sample of articles from these magazines, there were 337 discussions indicating the existence of romantic love in a given situation. Such discussions appeared primarily in fiction. Happiness as a motive for marriage was mentioned 97 times. These magazines were aimed at a middle- and upper-class audience, and the appearance of discussions of love and happiness in them only indicates that such ideas were in the culture of at least these groups.

Actually, courting couples had opportunities to become fairly well acquainted. One custom which permitted this was bundling, a practice in which a man and woman would lie together in one bed during the night without undressing.[5] Bundling was practiced especially in rural New England and the Middle-Atlantic colonies, where the winters were long and cold and at a time when candlelight and fuel were not to be wasted. When a young man had done a hard day's work on his father's farm and gone a considerable distance to the home of his sweetheart, he would spend the evening with her family gathered around the fireside with little chance for intimate conversation. When the family retired to bed and the fire was allowed to die down, the parents permitted their daughter and the young man to continue their courting in the warm comfort of a bed. Frequently the bed used for bundling would be in the

[2] *Ibid.*, p. 71.
[3] *Ibid.*
[4] Herman R. Lantz, *et al.*, "Pre-industrial Patterns in the Colonial Family in America: A Content Analysis of Colonial Magazines," *American Sociological Review*, 33 (1968): pp. 413–426.
[5] William J. Fielding, *Strange Customs of Courtship* (Garden City, New York: Garden City Books, 1960), pp. 67–69.

single large room of the farmhouse in which the entire family lived and slept. Bundling was the prerogative of a couple who were engaged or who were courting with the intention of marrying.

Early Nineteenth-Century America In the early 1800's economic and social conditions permitted early marriage and encouraged freedom of choice by the young people. Calhoun cites a German-American in 1826 as saying that as soon as a young man had gathered a few dollars, he thought of marriage.[6] Land was cheap and abundant, and a wife and children were of great assistance in its development. The possibility of maintaining a family adequately lay within the grasp of any reasonably energetic young man.

Freedom of choice by the young rather than parental control seems to have been prevalent. Foreign observers traveling in America in the first half of the nineteenth century were struck by the freedom allowed young girls and by the fact that the young couples, rather than their parents, made matrimonial choices.[7] De Tocqueville described the education of girls as offsetting the risks of the freedom allowed them: "If democratic nations leave a woman free to choose her husband, they take care to give her mind sufficient knowledge, and her will sufficient strength to make so important a choice."[8] Calhoun quotes a French visitor: "The young girls and men . . . do not marry unless both are pleased, and don't postpone until too late the discovery that they have been deceived. The object of both sexes is to learn each other's character."[9] From a survey of documents of the period between 1800 and the Civil War, Calhoun concludes that "American maidens enjoyed great freedom, cherished their independence, and used it cleverly."[10]

The 1890's By the end of the nineteenth century the expectation of companionship between boys and girls before marriage was well established. Henry Seidel Canby describing events in the period of his youth writes that the associations of boys and girls were based on comradeship, good spirits, and character, but "sex, naked and unashamed," was kept in its place. He goes on to describe the result of this emphasis:

The result was a free association of boys and girls in their teens and

[6] Arthur W. Calhoun, *A Social History of the American Family* (New York: Barnes and Noble, 1945), 2, pp. 14–15.
[7] *Ibid.*, pp. 70–71. See also Frank F. Furstenberg, "Industrialization and the American Family: A Look Backward," *American Sociological Review*, 31 (1966): pp. 326–337. An analysis of accounts by 42 foreign travelers in the United States between 1800 and 1850.
[8] Calhoun, p. 74.
[9] *Ibid.*, p. 30.
[10] *Ibid.*, p. 72.

early twenties that perhaps never has existed on the same plane elsewhere in the history of the modern world. We had confidence in each other, and we were confided in. All through the Adirondack woods we climbed together in summer, sleeping in cabins, girls on one side, boys on the other, following by couples all day lonely and difficult trails, and in the winter skated far-off ponds or sat all night in the spring on moonlit Delaware hills, falling in and out of love with never a crude pang of sex, though in a continuous amorous excitement which was sublimated from the grosser elements of love. . . . It was laissez-faire again, and possible of success only because we had our code and lived by it. . . . One met one's girl not in the transitoriness of a week-end, or at the end of three hundred miles of auto road, but for long acquaintance. She would be there and you would be there next week, next year. She was one of a family, and that family part of a community which was yours. She carried with her the sanctions and refusals of society.[11]

These young men expected women of their own social class to avoid sexual experience before marriage. At the same time, there was considerable pursuit of girls of lower social classes for sexual gratification.

The 1920's The First World War introduced the pressures of impending separation and wartime dangers into the courtship of American couples, and many wartime courtships were swift and uninhibited. Courtship in the decade that followed was characterized by greater freedom and more open interest in sex and sex appeal than had been true in prewar America.[12] Courtship was no longer characteristically associated with the home. Young men and women first met each other among strangers, at work, or at school. The expressions "boy friend and girl friend" came into use, symbolic of a new easy companionship between the sexes. Dresses were shortened, hair was bobbed, silk-stocking-clad legs became a symbol of sex appeal. The telephone made possible the extension of courtship beyond the earlier barriers of time and place. A former United States president is reputed to have telephoned his future wife fifteen times on the day after he first met her.

It was in the twenties that the advertisers seriously began the business of selling products as aids to the winning and keeping of a mate, with the florists and personal-care industries in the vanguard. Some of the literature of the time has given rise to the legends of "flaming youth" and the "roaring twenties." Actually, the courtship customs of the 1920's were a continuation of a trend toward less parental control in mate selection and of greater personal freedom for young people. Conditions

[11] Henry Seidel Canby, "Sex and Marriage in the Nineties," *Harper's Magazine,* 169 (1934): pp. 428–429.
[12] Turner, Ch. 16.

following World War I may have accelerated the trend, and the mass-communication industries coming into use during this period publicized changes in behavior.

The fairly rapid changes in courtship customs which characterized the 1920's laid the basis for American courtship behavior in the last half of the twentieth century.

Contemporary American Courtship   A review of the courtship practices of American couples from colonial times to the present reveals a long-term trend toward increased freedom of choice of a mate for a young person and of increased contact between young men and women without parental supervision. In addition, the trend has been toward choice of a mate for personal reasons rather than for economic considerations. This does not mean that parents and family members do not function in the mate-selection process. Rather, their influence has become more indirect, while courtship has become an increasingly independent activity of young people. Courtship by young people today is the approved method of mate selection.

ROMANTIC LOVE

Romantic Love as a Theme in American Courtship   Through the changes that occurred in courtship in America, there developed a theme and to some extent an expectation of romantic love as a part of courtship. However, it is important to note that most of the evidence about romantic love is in the mass media rather than in systematic studies of the population or even in case studies. Consequently, we know very little about the actual incidence or course of this phenomenon. Romantic love as a part of courtship folklore developed to a greater extent in America than in most other countries. Most cultures regard romance as a most unsuitable base for marriage, viewing it as a possible threat to making a prudent match.

The concept of romantic love includes the following characteristics: (1) One person of the opposite sex is the "right" mate for an individual. (2) This person will be discovered. (3) The couple who are "right for each other" will know this unquestionably. (4) Various manifestations of emotional bliss are to be expected in this state of love.

Romantic love has been glorified by the mass-communication media, both as a dominant theme in fiction and drama and as a nearly universal appeal which will help sell anything from toothpaste to automobiles. In an analysis of a sample of short stories drawn from two mass-circulation magazines for two five-year periods, 1911–1915 and 1951–1955, England found that in the earlier period the romantic content was typically subordinated to a subplot position, while 40 years later the stories were more exclusively concerned with romantic relationships.[13] In the 1911–1915 period only 11 percent of the fictional couples met through romantic chance encounters, while later, 45 percent met in this manner. In the early stories, an acquaintance of one week or less preceded decision to marry in 11 percent, while in the 1950's this occurred in 41 percent of the stories. Horton, analyzing a sample of 1955 popular song lyrics, found that 83 percent were songs about love. Through content analysis he classified the major themes of the songs: wishing and dreaming for a romantic partner; a courtship made up of direct, sweet, and desperate approaches to the loved one; a honeymoon period with the love object; the downward course of love; and a period of hopeless love, being all alone, with a gradual transition to interest in another romantic experience.[14]

At the same time, romanticism has been decried as the cause of many incompatible marriages and much disillusionment in marriage. Two short quotations, the first by a psychologist and the second by a sociologist, illustrate the unfavorable attitude toward romantic love of some American writers:

> Romance lasting for many years is only imaginable in Utopia. . . . No person can remain in the grip of a strange fascination for a long time. . . . Romance is a nine-day wonder.[15]

> This element of capricious choice makes marriage even more of a gamble than it should be. In the romantic credo, everything depends upon the original choice, nothing on the subsequent marital interaction. . . . Any course of action based upon such dubious tenets presents difficulties for stable marriage.[16]

Romantic love is sometimes viewed as a product of unsatisfied sexual drives. Waller saw romanticism as being founded on the temporary frustration of sexual impulses,[17] while Merrill indicates that romantic love may be inversely related to permissiveness toward premarital sexual relationships.[18] There have been no systematic investigations of the

---

[13] R. W. England, Jr., "Images of Love and Courtship in Family-Magazine Fiction," *Marriage and Family Living*, 22 (1960): pp. 162–165.

[14] Donald Horton, "The Dialogue of Courtship in Popular Songs," *American Journal of Sociology*, 58 (1957): pp. 569–578.

[15] Theodor Reik, *A Psychologist Looks at Love* (New York: Holt, Rinehart and Winston, 1944), p. 295.

[16] Francis E. Merrill, *Courtship and Marriage* (New York: Holt, Rinehart and Winston, 1959), p. 35.

[17] Willard Waller and Reuben Hill, *The Family* (New York: Henry Holt, 1951), p. 123.

[18] Merrill, pp. 42–43.

relationship between romantic love and sexual drives, and, consequently, these views must be regarded as only opinions.

THE NATURE OF COURTSHIP

Courtship may be defined as all forms of behavior by which one seeks to win the consent of another for marriage. Courtship, in the modern sense, concerns the behavior of men and women who are eligible for marriage and includes activities specifically aimed at the development of affectionate heterosexual relationships. These include dating and going steady, as well as the more formalized engagement period. Clearly, casual dating and some types of steady dating are not directed toward a permanent arrangement. This is, of course, especially true for young adolescents. However, this dating serves as an important opportunity for the development of competence in heterosexual relationships and hence may be regarded as an aspect of courtship behavior.

The nature of courtship will be analyzed under the following headings: role expectations, competitiveness, progressive commitment, and love and affection.

Role Expectations An analysis of the courtship process reveals the influence of expectations and role definitions derived from interaction within the family and other groups, especially the peer group. A young person interested in dating or in finding a mate has expectations and prescriptions of how to behave in courtship and mate selection. These have been acquired from his family, his intimate peers, and from such mass-communication media as novels, movies, television, newspapers, and magazines. Both the communication media and a person's peer group may present models of courtship behavior different from the definitions given by his family.

When a man and woman enter courtship, each brings his own set of role expectations and prescriptions for appropriate courtship behavior. By the time a person is ready to engage in serious courtship, he usually has a rather precise set of expectations of appropriate behavior for himself and his partner. When he encounters a person whose behavior and expectations so mesh with his that they are mutually satisfying, the prerequisites for serious courtship are present. Dating affords interaction in which there is testing of these expectations and attitudes.

Competitiveness The early stages of courtship involve competition for desirable dating partners. Girls will give special attention to grooming and dress and will behave in ways designed to attract favorable attention from boys. Boys may test their chances of dating highly desirable girls and, if they are refused, may settle for a somewhat less desirable date. The ratings of desirability will vary from group to group and with age, but will usually include appearance, personality, and status in a peer group. In addition, there are standards of desirability held by individuals which may be somewhat at variance with the standards of the peer group.

The sex ratio in a particular area may have a significant influence on the degree of competitiveness. In rural communities, where there is a high proportion of men to women, almost all women are able to marry. By contrast, in urban areas, with more women than men, there is a higher proportion of unmarried women. The following case shows somewhat unusual attention to the sex ratio:

> Dear Sir:
> I am a young man 38 years of age with 2½ years of university training beyond the B.A. degree, which I received with honors.
> My problem is one involving contacting girls with a college education. I could have married, but I see now that I was overly idealistic in my selection of a mate.
> I plan to continue my college training, but my work will be of such a time-consuming nature that I cannot afford to spend my spare time in a social endeavor that would not be with the eventual idea of getting a mate.
> With the above statements in mind I would like to obtain data on the following:
> 1. Relative number of single males and females in the Berkeley area.
> 2. Relative number of single males and females in the Boulder and Denver, Colorado area.
> 3. Best social activities to attain the objective mentioned.
> Yours very truly,

College communities frequently have an unbalanced sex ratio. With higher enrollments of men than of women in many schools, the competition is made more difficult for men and easier for women.

Progressive Commitment Courtship involves a progressive commitment of two persons to each other. There is very little commitment with casual dating. It increases with steady dating and engagement. Courtship may be viewed as a series of events gradually leading to the development of a relatively stable interaction between a couple. From this viewpoint, dating serves as a means of testing interrelationships, with individuals exploring both their own and their partner's reactions. The relative anonymity of urban living, the frequent contacts between men and women away from their homes, and the personal mobility afforded by the automobile allow fairly extensive dating without significant commitment. In addition, the acceptance of dating by young people as a part of the general culture has resulted in many parents encouraging a wide range of dating experiences for their high school and college-age children. The expectation is that much of this dating will be without important commitment, especially at younger ages. However, family and other intimate primary groups may still exert considerable pressures toward commitment, especially on persons beyond the usual age of marriage. Among very young persons, particularly in high school, the custom of "going steady" with one dating partner gives the appearance of considerable commitment, though in fact it generally does not involve serious consideration of commitment to marriage.

Love and Affection A feeling of love and affection is possibly the most important feature of the courtship process. Love, like other sentiments, is a complex of attitudes, emotions, and desires organized around an object. Affection is an emotion involving liking, being fond of, having a firm attachment to, and desiring to be in the presence of the object of one's affections. The physical expressions of an affectional feeling, such as kissing, embracing, and caressing may be associated with either a nonpassionate or passionate sexual desire. In the case of some women there may be a great desire for demonstration of affection, and a withdrawal from the physical aspects of sex. The feeling of affection and love is characteristic of American courtship.

The emphasis on marriage as a satisfying affectional relationship goes along with the change from the traditional to the companionship family form. Willingness to do one's duty, fulfill one's obligations, and help carry out the essential functions of the family might be adequate for the traditional family. For the companionship family, love and affection between the mates is essential. Accompanying this is the feeling that the establishment of a strong affectional relationship is the only acceptable basis for marriage and that the affection will continue in marriage. Consequently, courtship activities are directed toward finding a person with whom one can establish a close mutual affectional relationship and subsequently toward the development and testing of that relationship.

The following discussion of heterosexual love involving interrelated processes is, in part, based on an analysis by Reiss.[19] Reiss identifies four processes: establishment of rapport, self-revelation, mutual dependence, and meeting personality needs. These fit in with our general theory of heterosexual love, but do not include two which we find essential: idealization of the other and the development of adequate sexual behavior. These six will be presented in the following order: rapport, self-revela-

[19] Ira L. Reiss, "Toward a Sociology of the Heterosexual Love Relationship," *Marriage and Family Living*, 22 (1960): pp. 139–145.

tion, personality needs, idealization, mutual dependence, and sexual behavior.

1. The development of a feeling of rapport occurs if the two persons feel at ease with each other, are able to communicate with each other, have common interests, and have mutually acceptable role expectations. Communication depends, of course, on a common language and some degree of articulateness. Common interests, while they may not directly evoke love, prepare a favorable situation for it and tend to sustain and maintain it. Participation in any common interest involves companionship and leads to friendship, and these are favorable to the development of love and affection. The existence or development of mutually acceptable role expectations permits a satisfying fitting together of the actions and attitudes of the couple.

2. Self-revelation operates in the development of a love relationship. In the process of revealing themselves to each other, one or both persons may like and appreciate and learn to love the traits, attitudes, values, and goals of the other.

3. One of the major gratifications obtained from an interpersonal relationship is having some of the needs of one's own personality met in the relationship. In courtship when a man and woman have established considerable rapport and have begun to know each other through self-revelation, each may find that the other provides satisfaction of his needs. For example, a woman with a well-established pattern of dominance may obtain satisfaction from a relationship with a fairly acquiescent man in part because it allows her to follow her own pattern of dominance. In general, when each person in a relationship meets the personality needs of the other, the relationship is likely to be satisfying to both.

4. Idealization is the process of constructing a mental picture of the loved one. The degree of distortion from reality in idealization depends on a number of factors, such as the intensity of attraction and the lack of knowledge of the other person.

Factors making for idealization are subject to social change. The freer association of young people before marriage in the present generation has markedly decreased the degree of distortion of the romantic images which they have of each other. It has correspondingly reduced the disillusionment in marriage. Idealization, however, is not completely eliminated from courtship and marriage, for wherever there is love, some degree of idealization will be present.

5. Intertwining of habits develops in the association and communications during courtship. Communication which is intimate, personal, and unrestricted, is particularly favorable to the development of interdependent habits. Communication during courtship is likely to be of this nature. With the growth of interdependent habits, one becomes de-

pendent for the fulfillment of some of his acts on the other. Interdependence of habits may become particularly apparent to a person if he is separated for a time from his loved one.

6. The development of socially approved sexual behavior involves the process of integrating the biological sexual drive with cultural definitions of sexual expression. The forms of sexual expression are defined by the culture and learned through social experiences. Culture defines the sex role of the man and woman, desirable sexual characteristics of each, the proper approach to an expression of a sexual interest, and the situations and conditions in which the sexual drive may be expressed.

These six processes are interdependent and tend to reinforce each other. Together they result in the development of love and affection.

THE COURTSHIP PROCESS

Dating Dating is a relatively new phenomenon in American culture. Dating involves association between young men and women which (1) is an end in itself, signifying no necessary further involvement; (2) provides an opportunity for friendly associations with many persons of the opposite sex; and (3) is based on selection of companions with little or no parental supervision and according to the standards of one's own age group.

Characteristics desired in dates by college men and women were studied by Blood, using University of Michigan students.[20] Blood found that 6 of 37 items were almost unanimously considered desirable in both casual and serious dating partners and by both men and women. These same characteristics were reported by the students to be those prominent in the campus rating of desirable dates. The characteristics were (1) is pleasant and cheerful, (2) has a sense of humor, (3) is a good sport, (4) is natural, (5) is considerate, and (6) is neat. One may conclude that these college students were placing a high value on personal qualities which would promote a companionable relationship. Items which the students considered more important for serious dating partners than for casual dates were concerned with desires for emotional maturity, intelligence, and affectionate behavior. Campus prestige items were considered slightly more important by fraternity and sorority members and by underclassmen.

A study of an unusual form of dating has been reported by Coombs and Kenkel.[21] This involved computer-selection of dates, with follow-up

---

[20] Robert O. Blood, "Uniformities and Diversities in Campus Dating Preferences," *Marriage and Family Living*, 18 (1956): pp. 37–45.

[21] Robert H. Coombs and William F. Kenkel, "Sex Differences in Dating Aspirations and Satisfaction with Computer-Selected Partners," *Journal of Marriage and the Family*, 28 (1966): pp. 62–66.

questionnaires shortly after the date and again six months later. Under these circumstances, women expressed higher aspirations for socially desirable traits in a date than did men. Also, the men were more satisfied with their computer-selected partners than were the women. One possible interpretation is that the computer-selection process allowed the women to request a date that might meet an ideal-date image, a situation quite different from the usual process of dating. Also, the characteristics that were utilized in the computer matching process did not include those personal qualities reported in the study by Blood.

The behavior of college students, rather than their attitudes, was investigated by Rogers and Havens.[22] Using students at a mid-western state university as their subjects, they found that college students date, go steady, and become engaged within their own social prestige level as this is rated on the campus.

The age at which young people begin dating varies with the expectations of their own social groups, but a general pattern seems to exist. Using a representative sample of all girls in the United States in grades six through twelve, the Survey Research Center found that 20 percent of girls under 14 years reported some dating, 70 percent of girls 14 to 16 years reported dating with some regularity, and 90 percent of girls over 16 reported dating regularly.[23] Using high school students in five rural communities of Washington, Stone found that about 3 out of 4 boys and slightly over 4 out of 5 girls reported dating.[24] In a review of literature on the time of initial dating, Burchinal concludes that on the average students begin dating in the ninth and tenth grades.[25] Bell and Chaskes compared questionnaire data on dating, going steady, and engagement collected by Bell in 1958 with data based on the same questionnaire in 1968. The samples were 250 college women in 1958 and 205 in 1968. The mean age of the first date in 1958 was 13.3 and in 1968 it was 13.2[26]

Going Steady Although dating in itself involves no further commitment, under certain circumstances it actually is the prelude to going steady. Perhaps there is always an appraisal of the other as a matrimonial

[22] Everett M. Rogers and A. Eugene Havens, "Prestige Rating and Mate Selection on a College Campus," *Marriage and Family Living*, 22 (1960): pp. 55–59.
[23] Marguerite M. Dixon, "Adolescent Girls Tell About Themselves," *Marriage and Family Living*, 20 (1958): pp. 400–401.
[24] Carol Larson Stone, *Pacific County Teen-agers' Activities and Social Relations*, Washington Agricultural Experiment Station, Circular 373 (May 1960), p. 24.
[25] Lee G. Burchinal, "The Premarital Dyad and Love Involvement," in *Handbook of Marriage and the Family*, Harold T. Christensen (ed.) (Chicago: Rand McNally, 1964), pp. 624–625.
[26] Robert R. Bell and Jay B. Chaskes, "Premarital Sexual Experience Among Coeds, 1958 and 1968," *Journal of Marriage and the Family*, 32 (1970): p. 82.

possibility. There are various factors that transform dating *many* into dating *one:* (1) mutual responsiveness and preference for each other, (2) protection of one's self-esteem against the risk of being turned down, (3) the economy of time and money, (4) group arrangements and expectations which favor pairing rather than dating, and (5) emotional involvement.

The practice of going steady has been the subject of widespread discussion in recent years. As the term is commonly used, it refers to the practice of dating exclusively with one person, but does not necessarily involve specific commitments looking toward probable marriage. The extent to which going steady is practiced or favored by teenage girls is indicated by the Survey Research Center's study of girls 11 through 18 years.[27] Only 10 percent of these girls reported that they were going steady, less than 20 percent reported that they like the idea and, of the girls 16 to 18, 60 percent felt there were more disadvantages than advantages in going steady. Stone's report on high school students in rural Washington counties indicates that less than one-fifth of the boys and about one-third of the girls were going steady.[28] The degree to which going steady is popular varies greatly from one high school to another. Where going steady is popular among high school students, it is usually a symbol of high status in the group and is also regarded as a source of personal security, eliminating the necessity of competing for dates. Going steady among college students or young men and women out of school usually implies more personal commitment to each other than is true for high school students. Some college students may differentiate between dating "steadily" or going with one person more than anyone else but without a formal arrangement and "going steady" which is an acknowledged exclusive arrangement involving very frequent contact of the couple and providing considerable companionship.[29]

On college campuses several factors may prevent involvement beyond the expression of mutual preference through going together. These include (1) the advice of parents to postpone consideration of marriage; (2) the prudential attitude of making certain of one's choice through further associations with the opposite sex; (3) resistance on the part of the man to matrimonial implications of going steady and the apprehension on the part of the girl that emotional involvement may result in sexual intimacies without matrimonial intention; (4) the sensitivity of the person to the frank and critical comments of his associates, which tends to prevent idealization; and (5) the fear that emotional involve-

---

[27] Dixon, pp. 400–401.
[28] Stone, p. 27.
[29] Jack Delora, "Social Systems of Dating on a College Campus," *Marriage and Family Living*, 25 (1963): pp. 81–84.

ment will interfere with educational progress in training for and success in a career.

The transition from dating to going steady is the result of factors making for and against emotional involvement. Keeping steady company signifies mutual preference; it may, however, represent only friendship and not love. There is often a tendency on the part of one or both members of a couple to limit the relationship and also to refrain from making further affectional commitments. But, in general, going steady is regarded by college-age couples as a period of exploration in which a couple tests their personality needs and satisfactions, temperamental compatibility, common interests, and ideals. There may be increasing commitment by one or both.

Private Understanding and Engagement If the course of love runs smoothly, the agreement to go steady passes into the stage of a private understanding or private engagement. It may be just taken for granted, but generally there is an understanding of the intention to marry. Often at this stage the young man and the young woman take each other to visit their families, if this has not occurred earlier on a casual basis.

The process of falling in love, culminating first in a private understanding and then in a public announcement, is described by one young man:

> I met my future "better half" in the autumn as we were doing dishes together one evening over at the Co-op. She was pretty as a picture but she was also "outgoing," friendly, and alert.
>
> Our first "date" was a double date. This particular night, a girl I'd been dating a bit was having a date with another fellow. Here was my chance to change women, to get to know this girl who had walked into my world.
>
> On our double date with the other couple, we saw that two was company in their case, and we felt the same way, so we took our first walk-talk out by the lake. We soon found we talked the same language and we knew we had found mutual satisfaction in this first "date."
>
> We began to meet each other at meals, in classrooms, and would take walk-talks along about 9:30 evenings in our old clothes, across the campus, weaving our lives as "good friends."
>
> Within a month we were going steady. At school affairs we paired off. We began to share our work. We proofread each other's papers.
>
> We decided to "go steady" about Thanksgiving time. As we continued to share vital interests, school affairs, and one night a week as co-leaders of a youth club, our affection increased.
>
> At Christmas time we knew we were in love and began to exchange tokens of mutual affection. She gave me a book I wanted, I gave her my picture. We parted for Christmas vacation.

It seemed that being apart, writing daily letters, brought us back together with a new rush of feeling, and our relationship emerged onto a new level. On New Year's Eve we celebrated our new "private understanding." We toasted our new relationship, wished each other "A Happier New Year," and exchanged rings.

We each had pictured a person of certain qualities, and a quality of relationship which we wanted. When we saw these fulfilled and the joy of our growing affection, we knew we wanted to share the rest of our lives. I had not definitely, in so many words, asked her to marry me; but we knew everything moved in that direction.

My big brother-in-law came to the city for a convention and naturally we entertained him. After having his enthusiastic approval of the young woman as a potential sister-in-law I asked her to marry me.

We went first to visit my family and then visited first her sister and brother-in-law and then her family. We began to marry each other's family. We've been apart this summer. We look forward eagerly to being married next June.

This relationship is characterized by personal interaction and companionship. There is a distinct difference between the private understanding and the formal engagement. The former signifies the mutual expression of love with the expectation of marriage. Engagement, however, takes into account parents, relatives, and friends and adds the social to the personal commitment. In general, as indicated by this case, the approval of parents and relatives of the relationship is a secondary, although highly desired, consideration.

The engagement period is increasingly utilized by young couples to become better acquainted with each other and to determine whether they possess the combination of characteristics favorable for a happy marriage. At this point it is sufficient to point out that the intimacy of engagement gives the young man and the young woman the opportunity to make sure of their mutual love; of their compatibility in personal traits; of their similarity in familial and cultural backgrounds; of their common interests, ideas, and ideals; and of their complementing of each other's personality needs.

Studies show that a rather long period of acquaintance, courtship, and engagement increases the probability of a successful marriage. The mere passage of time is, of course, not the significant point. It is only a symbol of the opportunity given the couple to test their relationship and to determine whether they have developed the affection and companionship adequate for a lifelong union. The engagement also affords the couple the opportunity to solve problems in their relationship before rather than after marriage. The high proportion of broken engagements shows that many couples find out before marriage that they are not well matched.

Broken Engagements In the Burgess-Wallin study of one thousand engaged couples, 24 percent of the men and 36 percent of the women had broken one or more previous engagements, and 15 percent later broke their current engagements.[30] These figures indicate that broken engagements are quite frequent in our society, and they raise the question, first, of cause, and second, of the reaction of the couple to breaking the engagement.

Our discussion of the causes of broken engagements will be largely based on the findings of an unpublished study by Charlotte A. Cooper.[31] The specific difficulties making for broken engagements may be grouped under five factors, of which the last two appear to be the most important: (1) superficial attraction, (2) separation, (3) parental influence, (4) cultural divergence, and (5) major personality problems.

In cases of superficial attraction the couple appears to have been drawn to each other romantically only to find in the engagement period an absence of one or more of the elements essential for a lasting union, such as deep affection, temperamental compatibility, or common interests. Often one member of the couple is much more emotionally involved than the other, and the other breaks the relationship. A period of separation is often a factor in broken engagements. Certain of these undoubtedly fall under the heading of superficial attraction, since the relationship has not sufficient depth to be maintained during separation. But it also seems that many engagements would have led to marriage if the separation had not occurred. Parental influence is also a common factor in breaking engagements. Sometimes its influence is direct, often it is indirect, and perhaps most frequently it is a reinforcement of an attitude shared by the son or daughter. Cultural divergences include those of marked difference in race or nationality, in religion, in economic or social class, and in family background. In addition, cultural divergences are seen in few common interests, differences in expectations with reference to having children, or to behavior toward each other during engagement. Important also as a factor in breaking engagements is the presence of a major personality problem which adversely affects personal adjustments. Such problems appear to stem from feelings of insecurity and inferiority.

The breaking of the engagement is often a major emotional crisis. There is the loss of status in being rejected and the problem of facing and perhaps explaining to one's friends. More disturbing is the feeling of not being wanted, and the examination of one's own deficiencies. In self-defense one may deprecate the personality and the character of

---

[30] Ernest W. Burgess and Paul Wallin, *Engagement and Marriage* (Philadelphia: Lippincott, 1953), p. 273.

[31] A manuscript in the files of the Department of Sociology, University of Chicago.

the former loved one, finding defects and flaws where previously there seemed to be only perfection.

The individual differences in the rate of recovery from a broken love affair are due to several factors, including temperament, the number and importance of other interests, and the beginnings of a new attachment. In retrospect, at least after another engagement which is successful, the person tends to minimize the seriousness of the experience and to be thankful that the break took place.

At one time in the United States, engagements were seldom broken. If broken, suits might be instituted for breach of promise, and damages secured. Legal actions in cases of broken engagements are passing out of legal procedure with the recognition that marriage should be based on love and that an engagement is not a legal contract but a period in which both members of the couple determine their compatibility in temperament, common interests, and ideals.

SEXUAL BEHAVIOR IN COURTSHIP

The Nature of Sexual Behavior For the purpose of the following discussion the term sexual behavior will be defined as all forms of physical contact between a man and woman which are aimed, either directly or indirectly, toward intercourse and which are an expression of a biological sex drive. Forms of sexual behavior include kissing, caressing, petting without genital manipulation, petting with genital manipulation, and sexual intercourse.

In humans, sexual behavior to some extent is always subject to cultural conditioning. All societies impose regulations and restrictions on ways in which the sex drive may be acceptably expressed. In the United States there are some proscriptions which are generally held. The taboo against incest is conspicuous among these. There is also a general attitude against the conception of a child out of wedlock. At the same time, there are many variations in sex regulations by ethnic background, social class, and religious affiliation. The sexual behavior of an individual at any given time in any given situation is determined by both the strength of his biological sex drive and the influence of cultural definitions.

The Kinsey Reports The most widely known studies in sexual behavior are those directed by Kinsey.[32] The basic design of these studies was intensive interviewing of men and women who were accessible and who could be persuaded to cooperate in such interviews. Obviously, the data

---

[32] Alfred C. Kinsey, Wardell B. Pomeroy, and Clyde E. Martin, *Sexual Behavior in the Human Male* (Philadelphia: W. B. Saunders, 1948); and Alfred C. Kinsey, Wardell B. Pomeroy, Clyde E. Martin, and Paul H. Gebhard, *Sexual Behavior in the Human Female* (Philadelphia: W. B. Saunders, 1953).

were based on recollection and on the willingness and ability of the subjects to report accurately on behavior which occurred over a period of years. Over 12,000 persons were interviewed. This large number was subdivided into relatively small samples for different parts of the analysis. Since the subjects were volunteers, the cases secured were not representative of the general population. The reports have been widely publicized and, disregarding the unrepresentativeness of the cases, some consider the Kinsey studies as reporting an accurate picture of the sexual behavior of American men and women. The unrepresentative character of his cases may be illustrated by an analysis of the female sample: 75 percent of Kinsey's sample had some college education, while in 1950 the median years of education of adults in the United States was 9.9 years, or approximately the second year of high school; 90 percent were from urban areas, although only 64 percent of the total population in 1950 was urban; and 58 percent were single, while only 20 percent of women 14 years of age and over were single in 1950. Nevertheless, with these limitations in methodology in mind, we may still gain insight about sexual behavior in America from the Kinsey studies.

Incidence of Petting Petting is defined as any physical contact between a man and a woman for the purposes of erotic arousal, but without necessarily terminating in intercourse. While investigators have used slightly different definitions of petting, they generally include kissing and hugging, body caressing, and manipulation of the genitals. On this basis Kinsey reports that 91 percent of women and 89 percent of men had engaged in premarital petting by the age of 25.[33] Using much the same definition as Kinsey, Ehrmann studied the premarital sexual behavior of 1,423 college students.[34] His data indicate that about 97 percent of both men and women engaged in some form of premarital petting. However, when he analyzed different forms of petting, he found that for 13 percent of the men and 44 percent of the women the most intensive form of petting behavior engaged in was kissing and hugging. For girls, kissing is much more acceptable than other forms of petting, and consequently they either restrict their petting to kissing or report that they do. Most of the girls of Ehrmann's sample, 86 percent, reported they were virgins.

Incidence of Premarital Intercourse In various cultures throughout the world and at different times, virginity at marriage has had different values. It has been considered as completely incidental, as undesirable

[33] *Sexual Behavior in the Human Female*, p. 267.
[34] Winston Ehrmann, *Premarital Dating Behavior* (New York: Henry Holt, 1959), p. 46.

because there was no evidence that a woman could bear children, and as an indispensable requirement for marriage. The predominant and socially supported value in the United States has been chastity before marriage. The value placed on chastity has been especially important for women and for the middle class.

In actual practice, this value represents an ideal rather than existing behavior. Terman, after analyzing and describing the incidence of premarital intercourse of older and younger men and women, predicted in 1938 that virginity at marriage would vanish within a few decades:

> If the drop should continue at the average rate shown for those born since 1890 virginity at marriage will be close to the vanishing point for males born after 1930 and for females born after 1940. It is more likely that the rate of change will become somewhat retarded as the zero point is approached and that an occasional virgin will come to the marriage bed for a few decades beyond the dates indicated by the curves. It will be of no small interest to see how long the cultural ideal of virgin marriage will survive as a moral code after its observation has passed into history.[35]

How does actual behavior fit Terman's prediction? A partial answer to this question can be secured from Ehrmann, who has reviewed the incidence of reported premarital intercourse found by various investigators since 1915. Several general trends appeared from an examination of the reports: (1) more men report premarital intercourse than women; (2) the incidence of premarital intercourse for men rises with increasing age; (3) studies made at more recent dates in general report higher incidence of premarital intercourse for men than earlier studies. No such consistent pattern for either age or recency of investigation appears for women. Almost all studies of the incidence of premarital intercourse have used subjects of college level and consequently the behavior may be limited to persons from middle- and upper-middle-class families.[36]

The findings of two of the more recent investigations illustrate the rather large difference in the incidence of premarital intercourse reported by men and women. Kinsey found for his subjects that by age 25, 83 percent of the men and 33 percent of the women reported premarital intercourse.[37] Ehrmann obtained questionnaire data from students enrolled in marriage and family courses in a single college and found that

---

[35] Lewis M. Terman, *Psychological Factors in Marital Happiness* (New York: McGraw-Hill, 1938), p. 323. Copyright 1938. McGraw-Hill Book Co. Used by permission.

[36] The lack of studies of representative samples for investigating the incidence of premarital intercourse is a serious limitation of present knowledge. Furthermore, since investigators must rely on personal reports of behavior in an area in which there may be reticence about disclosing information, one must assume some variance of the reports from actual behavior.

[37] *Sexual Behavior in the Human Female*, p. 333.

57 percent of the men, aged 18 through 21, and 13 percent of the women, aged 18 through 22, reported premarital intercourse.[38]

Some premarital intercourse occurs between persons who will subsequently marry. Of the 288 women in the Burgess-Wallin sample who reported having engaged in premarital intercourse, 75.6 percent did so only with their future spouse; of the 394 men who had engaged in premarital intercourse, 25.6 percent did so only with their future spouse.[39] In Terman's study, using his two youngest groups—those born in 1900–1909 and 1910 and later—67 percent of the 205 women who had engaged in premarital intercourse did so only with their future spouse. The corresponding percent for 203 men was 26.6.[40] From these data one may infer that a substantial amount of premarital intercourse occurs between persons with fairly intensive emotional involvement. This seems to be particularly true for women.

A British study obtained data on the incidence of various forms of petting and of premarital intercourse as well as background data from a representative sample of 934 boys and 939 girls 15 through 18 years of age.[41] This was an urban sample, selected from London and two other cities, and included subjects from various social classes. It involved careful field work and interviewing. The results indicate that 34 percent of the boys and 17 percent of the girls had experienced premarital intercourse, while 56 percent of the boys and 46 percent of the girls had experienced petting to the extent of genital stimulation. The most rapid increases in experience occurred between 15 and 17 years of age. There was little relationship between the sexual activity of the teenager and the social class of his family (except for more petting by upper-class girls), the religious affiliation and churchgoing of his family, and whether or not the home had been broken. Personal relationships within the family were related to sexual activity, somewhat more for girls than for boys. Girls who are not sexually experienced were more likely to get on well with both their fathers and their mothers and to perceive their parents as happily married. The only association in this area for boys was that those who did not get along well with their mothers were more likely to be sexually experienced. Less supervision of the teenager by the parents was associated with sexual experience, especially the opportunity for the teenager to entertain friends at home without the presence of a parent. A factor analysis of attitude scales disclosed that sexually experienced boys and girls had a teenage ethnocentrism

---

[38] Ehrmann, pp. 34–35.
[39] Burgess and Wallin, p. 331.
[40] Terman, p. 321.
[41] Michael Schofield, *The Sexual Behavior of Young People* (London: Longmans, 1965).

(that is they were favorable to their own teenage group and opposed to all other groups) and they were relatively permissive on items dealing with control and morality.

The relatively young age at first marriage for both men and women today—median age 23.2 and 20.8 respectively (1969)—as compared with earlier times tends to reduce the time for premarital intercourse. It is fairly well established that at younger ages there is less premarital intercourse. If one would be rash enough to venture a prediction at this time, it appears that there will be a leveling off of the incidence of premarital intercourse rather than an increase to the point at which virginity at marriage would be a thing of the past, as Terman predicted in 1938.

Attitudes Toward Premarital Sexual Behavior The most comprehensive study in this area has been by Reiss whose work includes data obtained from a national sample of adults and samples from several high schools and colleges.[42] The questions dealt essentially with the degree of approval of kissing, petting, and premarital intercourse. The general results indicated that 42 percent of the students felt abstinence from intercourse was proper under all circumstances, with about half of these approving petting. Another 25 percent approved a double standard. Twenty-six percent approved premarital intercourse. With the national adult group (a representative sample of 1,345) 77 percent approved only abstinence, with 27 percent in this group approving petting. Only 11 percent approved premarital intercourse. There was considerable variation of standards for different groups. In both the student and adult samples many more females than males accepted abstinence, and many more whites than Negroes accepted abstinence. The Negro-white differences were not due to social class since the differences remained when tests were made controlling social class. Other findings on the student sample included 63 percent perceiving themselves as having attitudes similar to those of their mothers, and 77 percent perceiving themselves as similar to their peers. More permissive individuals felt more similar to their friends. In the adult sample, there was no relationship between social class and permissive attitudes for whites and only a slight relationship for Negroes. It is important to note that this study deals with attitudes rather than behavior. An additional finding of particular interest to students of the family is that parents of teenage or older children were the least permissive group in the adult sample. This was not related to the age of these parents, and suggests that the role of the parents of children for whom premarital sexual activity is a real

---

[42] Ira L. Reiss, *The Social Context of Sexual Permissiveness* (New York: Holt, Rinehart and Winston, 1967).

and present issue has important effects on attitudes. There was no difference in attitudes between parents of teenage daughters and those of teenage sons.

Bell and Chaskes, in the study referred to earlier, compared premarital intercourse during the dating period, going steady, and engagement in 1958 with its incidence in 1968. The incidence of premarital intercourse during the dating relationship increased from 10 percent in 1958 to 23 percent in 1968. In the going steady relationship the increase was from 15 percent in 1958 to 28 percent in 1968. And for the engagement period the increase was not as striking—from 31 percent in 1958 to 39 percent in 1968.[43]

Control of Premarital Sexual Behavior In the past in Western cultures almost all forms of sexual behavior were controlled through supervision, limitation of privacy, and internalization of community mores in the unmarried. Today supervision and lack of privacy have been practically eliminated, and community mores have been weakened. There is very little interest in or attempt to control some forms of sexual behavior, such as kissing and caressing. However, there is concern about genital petting and premarital intercourse. The control of such behavior is almost entirely in the hands of young people. Some of the factors which influence the sexual behavior of young people are their ethical standards, their religious commitment, fear of pregnancy or forced marriage, feelings of guilt, the standards of their peer group and, for women, a fear of being devalued as potential marriage partners. Finally, many young people feel that virginity is a highly desirable status at marriage.

SUMMARY

The practices of courtship in modern American society are not only different from those of other cultures but reflect the influence of factors which are associated with the urban way of life, particularly individualism as contrasted with familism. Dating is essentially an individualistic practice and is significant in mate selection. It greatly enlarges the circle of prospective matrimonial partners and, involving no commitment to marriage, permits young people to determine their compatibility in temperament and their congeniality in interests and values before they decide to keep steady company.

Engagement in American society has changed from a contract enforceable by legal action to an intimate relationship which gives a couple the opportunity to discover the strength of their affection and their congeniality in temperament, interests, and ideals.

[43] Bell and Chaskes, pp. 81–84.

Broken engagements are losing their public stigma. There is a growing recognition that they perform an important function in preventing unhappy marriages.

PROBLEMS FOR RESEARCH

Differential Courtship Behavior Studies of courtship should be made in communities of different sizes, in various regions of the country, by educational levels, and by social class. Differences in courtship practices should be noted for each of these categories. Attention should be given to such factors as the sex ratio, mobility, and the effects of the motion picture, radio, television, and popular magazines.

A Three-Generation Study of Courtship An effective method of identifying, comparing, and measuring changes in courtship behavior is the three-generation technique. Personal documents could be secured from young people, their parents, and their grandparents in different social classes and from different nationalities. This would make possible an interpretation of courtship behavior in its relation to the systems of family relations and the social conditions of the three periods.

Broken Engagements A study of broken engagements will throw light on the relative significance of such factors in courtship as role expectations, competitiveness, degree of commitment, and the development of love and affection. In addition, the degree to which a broken engagement is a crisis for the man and for the woman should be investigated.

QUESTIONS AND EXERCISES

1. What are the major differences between courtship in colonial America and today?
2. Analyze romantic love from the standpoint of its essential characteristics and the favorable and unfavorable attitudes toward it.
3. How do role expectations, competitiveness, and progressive commitment enter into the development of love and affection?
4. What are the essential characteristics of dating? What factors encourage the transition from dating to going steady, and what factors tend to prevent it?
5. What is the most important difference between a private understanding and a formal engagement?
6. How do you account for the probable increase in the incidence of premarital intercourse?
7. Analyze the introductory case in the light of (1) changing courtship

patterns, and (2) the advantages and disadvantages of early pairing as compared with dating.

BIBLIOGRAPHY

Bell, Robert R. *Premarital Sex in a Changing Society.* Englewood Cliffs, New Jersey: Prentice-Hall, 1966.
> A small book, 182 pages, presenting a summary of empirical research in this area and written from the perspective of sociological analysis.

Ehrmann, Winston. *Premarital Dating Behavior.* New York: Henry Holt, 1959. (Also available paperbound, Bantam Books)
> Reports on data obtained from college students in marriage and family courses from 1946 to 1953 (990 questionnaires and 100 interviews). Analyzes premarital sexual behavior according to degrees of intimacy of contact; reports characteristics related to the various degrees of intimacy.

Fielding, William J. *Strange Customs of Courtship.* Garden City, New York: Garden City Books, 1960.
> Descriptive accounts of courtship and mate selection practices in various cultures and at various times. Deals with specific courtship practices. Little documentation.

Kinsey, Alfred C.; Pomeroy, Wardell B.; and Martin, Clyde E. *Sexual Behavior in the Human Male.* Philadelphia: Saunders Company, 1948; and Kinsey, Alfred C.; Pomeroy, Wardell B.; Martin, Clyde E.; and Gebhard, Paul H. *Sexual Behavior in the Human Female.* Philadelphia: Saunders Company, 1953.
> The most comprehensive study of human sexual behavior to date. In spite of the serious limitation of using volunteers, it gives an idea of such things as types of sexual outlets, age and sexual outlets, marital status and sexual outlets, sources of sexual outlets, homosexual behavior, and premarital and extramarital intercourse.

Kirkendall, Lester A. *Premarital Intercourse and Interpersonal Relationships.* New York: Julian, 1961.
> Based on interviews with 200 male students who reported a total of 668 premarital intercourse experiences. Analyzes data according to experiences with women with whom the subjects had varying degres of interpersonal involvement, ranging from prostitutes to fianceés.

Reiss, Ira L. *The Social Context of Premarital Sexual Permissiveness.* New York: Holt, Rinehart and Winston, 1967.
> Reports attitudes toward sexual behavior of a student sample from high schools and colleges and also of a representative national sample of adults. Main emphasis of analysis is on social factors related to high levels of permissiveness.

Schofield, Michael. *The Sexual Behavior of Young People.* London: Longmans, 1965.

Based on interviews with 934 single boys and 939 single girls ages 15 through 18, a representative sample of given areas in London and two other English cities. Reports incidence of various types of sexual activity and relates them to social factors.

Turner, E. S. *A History of Courting.* London: Michael Joseph, 1954.
Examines courtship behavior principally in Western Europe and America from Ovid's discourse on love in Roman society to mid-twentieth-century American customs. Relies chiefly on historical and literary sources. Detailed reports of courtship practices for various periods, generally supported by documentation.

Chapter 12
Mate Selection

If one asks married or engaged persons why they were attracted to each other their answer is likely to be "we fell in love." If one asks why they fell in love, they would probably credit it to a liking for each other, luck, or Providence. There are explanations, however, for mate selection, just as for other kinds of behavior. For one thing, an ideal of the kind of person one would like to have as a mate is formed during childhood and adolescence. In addition, such factors as common values, common backgrounds, and personality needs are determinants of the mate one finally selects.

THE PROCESS OF MATE SELECTION

Personal documents obtained from young people throw light on some of the factors that enter into the choice of a mate. In the following case the young man was highly conscious of certain influences and somewhat aware of others which determined his decision:

My idea of an "ideal mate" is a girl who loves the home, the church, the simple things of life; who likes to be quiet and doesn't just "jabber." She should not be boisterous. She must not enjoy "crude" jokes and stories, but she should enjoy good music, good books, all kinds of games—both athletic and those in which no physical exertion is required. Should be warm and friendly, not still and reserved. Yet she must have poise. She must love children. She should not be a "career" woman, nor should she be one who doesn't know how to work. She should be able to think. She should be able to have fun but should not desire an endless round of movies and dances. It would be preferable if she did not smoke.

She must be honest, fair, patient, and self-controlled. She need not be beautiful, but she must be neat and careful about the way she dresses. She should be sensitive, conscientious, kind. She should be popular, but not "cheaply" so. She should be well educated. She must have no prejudices, class, racial, religious, or political.

I have known girls who fit very well into my "ideal mate" pattern, but they did not reciprocate in their response to me. They considered me a friend, but no more. Often I would examine myself and ask why I couldn't have a girl as other fellows did. Girls would be friendly when first introduced. Then they would draw up a reserve which meant "you haven't got a chance." But there were girls who practically "worshiped at my feet," but even though they might possibly have come up to my standards for the ideal mate, they did not rate anything more than my friendship.

With the young lady I have learned to know in the last year things are different. To my affection she responds; to her affection I respond. Little formalities of social codes do not worry me when I am with her. If I make a mistake, she understands rather than condemns. Self-consciousness is at a minimum when I'm with her. I can understand what she means without her having to say a thing directly. She meets my ideal standard, but that doesn't seem to be too important in comparison with the compatibility of personalities.

It seems to me that in her personality there are traits like those of both my parents. In her, too, there is something of me. Of the two parents, she is more like my mother, in physical appearance as well as psychologically.

She gives me encouragement and understanding. Then, too, our friends give their approval. This builds up a feeling of pride which enters into the process of falling in love.

There were causes behind my inability to have dates and girls in abundance, no doubt. There was something of the monogamous ideal ingrained in me along with the romantic concept that sometime the one and only would come along and that I would not have associated intimately with any other before or after.

The influences in the process of selecting a mate recognized by the young man in this case were his picture of an ideal mate, proximity, and group approval. He appears to have been less conscious of the full effect of such factors as previous failure in securing response from girls, competition with other young men, and the fact that the girl resembled his mother. Additional factors were undoubtedly present in the situation, of which he was entirely unconscious.

Many of the factors in mate selection just mentioned do not operate in societies where parents control marriage arrangements. In such societies parents are influenced by considerations of social standing, economic status, and financial return. In the United States, where young people have secured almost complete freedom in mate selection, there are still many circumscribing factors, such as the sex ratio, circle of acquaintances, and cultural standards.

The discussion of these and other points will be taken up under the following headings: (1) patterns of arranging marriage, (2) the role of intermediaries, and (3) factors in mate selection.

PATTERNS OF ARRANGING MARRIAGE

Before the rise of courtship practices and when parents still had direct control over marriage, the patterns of arranged marriage differed widely from culture to culture. Only a few can be presented here; they have been chosen to represent mate selection in different types of family relationships.

Choice of Mates in the Apache Family   The Apache Indian, with a matrilocal residence, lived in an extended family numbering on the average from twenty to thirty members. It was composed of parents, unmarried sons, daughters, husbands and children of the married daughters, granddaughters, and unmarried grandsons. The family group in Apache society dictated the reciprocal rights, duties, and obligations of an individual to his fellows. This social unit supervised the person's early training, tested his manhood, determined whom he could not marry, and, if he was killed avenged his death. Courtship practices in the early 1930's have been described by Opler:

> In the social dancing it is the girl who takes the initiative. All men who desire to dance stand in a designated place. The girl chooses a partner by tapping one of this group on the shoulder, and the man so selected has no choice but to accept the invitation.
>
> In this way the Apache girl is able to indicate her preference for a mate, but she can do little more than hope that her obvious interest will awaken a like sentiment in her favorite.
>
> An Apache youth has somewhat more control over the choice of his wife. If he is of marriageable age and has become interested in a girl, he takes the matter up with his parents and their siblings. It is quite necessary to gain their consent, for one of them must act as intercessor for him in obtaining permission from the girl's family, and the bulk of the presents to be given to the girl's parents, when the marriage is agreed upon, must come from them. But if the members of his immediate family disapprove of the girl or are unenthusiastic about an alliance with the girl's family, there is little the young man can do save look for another and more suitable mate.
>
> Though the wishes of the young people are not entirely ignored, it cannot be overemphasized that marriage among the Apaches is not nearly so much an agreement between individuals as it is a contract between families.[1]

[1] Adapted from Morris E. Opler, "An Analysis of Mescalero and Chiricahua Apache Social Organization" (Ph.D. Dissertation, Chicago, University of Chicago Libraries, 1933), pp. 43–45.

Arranging Marriage in Japan Until recently in the Orient—China, India, Japan, Korea, and the Philippines—as in ancient society, arrangement for marriage was even more controlled by the parents than among the Apache Indians. Japan has been selected for the description and analysis of the pattern of arranging marriage. In both the upper and the lower social classes of Japan, parents emphasized practical considerations—social status and economic standing—and, on the whole, ignored sentiment and the personal preferences of the children.

How completely the individual a generation ago accepted marriage as a family affair rather than a personal matter is portrayed in *A Daughter of the Samurai*, the autobiography of a Japanese girl who was betrothed at thirteen. This is her account of the event:

> There was a meeting of the family council, the largest that had been held since Father's death. Two gray-haired uncles were there with the aunts, besides two other aunts, and a young uncle who had come all the way from Tokyo on purpose for this meeting. They had been in the room a long time, and I was busy writing at my desk when I heard a soft "Allow me to speak!" behind me, and there was Toshi at the door, looking rather excited.
>
> "Little Mistress," she said, with an unusually deep bow, "your honorable mother asks you to go to the room where the guests are." I entered the big room. Tea had been served and all had cups before them or in their hands. As I pushed back the door they looked up and gazed at me as if they had never seen me before. I made a low, ceremonious bow, Mother motioned to me, and I slipped over beside her on the mat.
>
> "Etsu-ko," Mother said very gently, "the gods have been kind to you, and your destiny as a bride has been decided. Your honorable brother and your venerable kindred have given much thought to your future. It is proper that you should express your gratitude to the Honorable All."
>
> I made a long, low bow, touching my forehead to the floor. Then I went out and returned to my desk and my writing. I had no thought of asking, "Who is it?" I did not think of my engagement as a personal matter at all. It was a family affair.[2]

In this case the personal preferences of the young people were not consulted. In the Japanese village of Suye Mura, studied by Embree and inhabited by 1,663 people, marriage was also arranged by the parents, but not until after the boy and girl had had a preliminary meeting ostensibly to take place by sheer chance and to have no significance.[3] Yoshino made a restudy of Suye Mura and reported that "in practice, marriage is still primarily a family affair promoted by parents through

---
[2] From *A Daughter of the Samurai*, by Etsu I. Sugimoto. Copyright 1928 by Doubleday and Company, New York, pp. 87–89.
[3] John F. Embree, *Suye Mura, A Japanese Village* (Chicago: University of Chicago Press, 1939), pp. 203–204 and 213–214.

the services of a go-between."[4] In the chapter on the family in Japan, China, and India, data were presented showing that in Japan in 1955 the percent of marriages arranged by parents or a matchmaker was 73 in large cities and 86 in farming areas.

Matchmaking in the Irish Rural Family A description was given in Chapter 3 of the Irish system of transferring a farm from the father to the chosen son in connection with the latter's marriage and under an arrangement whereby the girl's father turns over a "fortune" to the boy's father equivalent to the value of the land. Naturally the father takes a keen interest in the transaction. In fact, the young people may not be introduced until the financial negotiations have been practically completed. The marriage itself does not take place until the papers have been drawn up and signed. Arensberg and Kimball describe courtship practices in the Irish rural family a generation ago as follows:

> When a young man is on the lookout for a young lady it is put through his friends for to get a suitable woman for him for his wife. It all goes by friendship and friends and meeting at public houses. The young man sends a "speaker" to the young lady, and the speaker will sound a note to know what fortune she has, will she suit, and will she marry this Shrove? She and her friends will inquire what kind of a man he is, is he nice and steady. If he suits, they tell the speaker to go ahead and "draw it down." So then he goes back to the young man's house and arranges for them to meet in such a place, on such a night, and will see about it.
>
> The speaker goes with the young man and his father that night, and they meet the father of the girl and his friends or maybe his son and son-in-law. The first drink is called by the young man; the second by the young lady's father. The young lady's father asks the speaker what fortune do he want. He asks him the place of how many cows, sheep, and horses it is. . . .
>
> If it is a nice place, near the road, and the place of eight cows, they are sure to ask £350 fortune. Then the young lady's father offers £250. Then maybe the boy's father throws off £50. If the young lady's father still has £250 on it, the speaker divides the £50 between them. So now it's £275. Then the young man says he is not willing to marry without £300—but if she's a nice girl and a good housekeeper, he'll think of it. . . . After this, they appoint a place for the young people to see one another and be introduced. . . . If they suit one another they will then appoint a day to come and see the land. If they don't, no one will reflect on anybody, but they will say he or she doesn't suit. They do not say plainly what is wrong.[5]

[4] Roger Yoshino, "Selected Social Changes in a Japanese Village, 1935–1953" (Ph.D. Dissertation, University of Southern California Library, 1954), p. 149.

[5] Conrad M. Arensberg and Solon T. Kimball, *Family and Community in Ireland* (Cambridge: Harvard University Press, 1968), pp. 107–108.

The Bride Price The selection of a groom who can pay a high bride price in the form of a dowry is found in several African and other countries. Young bachelors who desire a higher education at inflated prices and at the same time desire to be married are in a dilemma. It is reported that in Kenya the bride price is equivalent to five years of the groom's expected income, payable in postmarital installments of cattle, bicycles, and money. However, they do not want to eliminate the tribal laws, for after marriage, if there is a break-up because of the wife's misdeeds, the husband gets his bride price back. At a conference in Uganda women stated their attitudes toward the bride price: "How will our husbands value us if they have not given value for us?" Another said, "How can our husbands keep us faithful unless there is a dowry they can demand back?"[6]

The following is a description of the inflated price of brides in Australian New Guinea. In this case it was suggested that the government place price controls on brides, depending on skill, earning power, and appearance:

> Not so long ago a young man would take a few pigs, walk to a neighboring village and after a pleasant day's barter come home with a wife.
>
> Now a prospective bride has become a valuable unit in the economy.
>
> For tribes in and around the larger towns and cities where a western style of economy is heavily superimposed on the old barter system, the problem is serious, because a bride can cost $3,500.
>
> She need not be good looking, but she would have been trained as a nursing aid, school teacher, or typist.
>
> Some more sophisticated tribes have asked the government for bride price controls, fixing maximum prices depending on skill, earning power, and appearance.
>
> "The prices of brides is just plain ridiculous," said the president of one native council.
>
> The record price paid recently in Port Moresby was $4,050. It obtained Mary, a pretty, 21-year-old school teacher, for Reuben, an $18-a-week government clerk.
>
> Reuben had saved $900. Members of his clan raised $1,575. Reuben will pay off the remaining $1,575 in installments. If Mary fails to produce children, the $1,575 he owes will be substantially reduced. His payments cease if Mary dies a natural death or from sorcery. If the couple turn out to be incompatible and Mary goes home to mother, Reuben gets back all he has paid plus some extra for his trouble.
>
> In primitive areas bride prices are lower than in cities and towns.
>
> In Madang District an average price for an uneducated girl, 18, as shown in a government survey, was one pig, five net bags, 10 sauce pans, 10 plates, one string of pig's teeth, one string of dog's teeth, two bows,

---

[6] "The Bride Price," *Time*, 86 (1965): pp. 25–26.

six dozen loaves of bread, 70 pounds of sugar, 112 pounds of rice, and 36 tins of canned meat, with a total value of $132.

Nobody really benefits from the inflated costs. The tribe foots most of the bill for a bride, and because each tribe has about the same number of brides to sell as its young men need to buy, the money and goods are just passed around in larger quantities.[7]

These four cases of arranging marriage have one element in common: an almost complete absence of love and courtship before marriage. There was in these and many other societies little or no thought of love as a prerequisite to marriage.

THE ROLE OF INTERMEDIARIES

Let us consider the following three questions on the role of intermediaries in mate selection in the United States: In what ways do parents still influence the selection of marriage partners for their children? What is the role of voluntary associations in mate selection? How do other intermediaries function in the courtship process?

Parental Role At present in the United States every kind of parental role in the selection of mates may be found. In a country with many heterogeneous cultural groups and in a period of transition, a wide range of behavior is to be expected. Our attention is focused not on the variations, however, but on the main trends and the emerging general pattern.

The most powerful parental influence on mate selection is largely through the development of expectations and patterns of behavior in childhood. There are family expectations related to culture, social class, and conceptions of qualities desirable in a person. And the emotional interaction in the family creates the response pattern the young adult typically seeks to perpetuate in a love relationship and in marriage.[8] The role of the family in mate selection will be treated in greater detail later in this chapter under the headings "Ideal Mate" and "Parental Image."

The influence of parents in mate selection appears to be exerted (1) by control of the social contacts of young people, (2) by attempting to break up a disapproved match, and (3) by the conscious desire of young people to select a mate who will meet the approval of the family.

In the upper-middle and upper classes parents influence to a marked

---

[7] This is by permission of the *Chicago Tribune*, published in *The Los Angeles Times*, July 2, 1965, Part I, p. 18.

[8] Ernest W. Burgess and Leonard S. Cottrell, *Predicting Success or Failure in Marriage* (New York: Prentice-Hall, 1939), pp. 172–217.

degree the social contacts of their children. This occurs in many different ways: entering their sons and daughters, even when very young, in select dancing schools; sending them to private schools; moving to a more desirable neighborhood; providing them with the social privileges of a country club, from which nonmembers and their children are excluded; sending their children to the college from which the father or mother graduated or to other situations of high social status; or exerting pressure on their daughters to join a sorority, which presumably will somewhat control their social contacts.[9] In these and other ways, parents create situations and build up expectations of marrying within one's social class or higher.

Parents seeking to disrupt a relationship employ various methods. A direct attack succeeds in some cases, but in others only strengthens the determination of the young people to marry in defiance of opposition. An indirect approach is generally more effective. When a daughter seems to be developing an attachment to a young man of a lower class or with "undesirable" characteristics, the parents may arrange a trip or a visit, or send her away to school, counting on a new environment to provide new associations and to bring about a shift in affections. In the case of a son infatuated with a pretty and charming but uncultured girl, one upper-middle-class mother handled the situation by inviting his fiancée for a visit. All the differences in social class which the young man had previously ignored, such as mistakes in table manners and English and crudities in dress and action, induced him to end the relationship without an open expression of disapproval from his mother.

The Role of Voluntary Associations With young people in cities, voluntary associations are important in facilitating courtship and accelerating engagement and marriage. Many voluntary associations composed of young unmarried people have as their principal function, though not their formal stated purpose, provision for association of the sexes. These include young people's societies in churches, organizations for civic and welfare objectives, and recreational clubs.

When groups either have an exclusive membership or are otherwise isolated from outside social contacts, they may be designated as closed groups. If these are also primary groups, they provide a situation unusually favorable for promoting friendship, courtship, engagement, and marriage.

Secondary Contacts In the city secondary contacts tend to predominate over primary associations. For decades there has been a trend away

[9] John F. Scott, "The Sorority: Its Role in Class and Ethnic Endogamy," *American Sociological Review*, 30 (1965): p. 524.

from neighborhood to city-wide recreation for youth. Young people follow the crowd for fun, adventure, and romance. Commercial recreation places become centers for contacts and associations that may lead to matrimony.

The findings of studies on the way married persons first met each other show the part now played by secondary contacts in initiating courtship. Terman found that slightly less than one-half of the couples he questioned had met as a result of such associations as neighborhood acquaintance, home of a friend, church, or social organization.[10]

In his study of marital adjustment, Locke asked happily married and divorced subjects where they had first met their mates. Their responses are summarized in Table 14. Neglecting the minor variations between the happily married and the divorced, it is apparent that the places in which these people met their mates were radically different from what they would have been a few generations ago, when most would have been living in a rural area and would have met their mates in the neighborhood. Neighborhood acquaintance ranked below school, home of a friend, a place other than those listed, and just above business.

Table 14. **Place of meeting of happily married and divorced couples, by percent***

	HAPPILY MARRIED		DIVORCED	
Place	Husbands $N=172$	Wives $N=171$	Husbands $N=163$	Wives $N=183$
Church	17.4	19.3	11.7	13.1
Home of a relative	17.4	18.1	12.9	16.9
School	15.7	15.8	16.6	12.6
Home of a friend	14.0	11.1	22.7	22.4
A place other than those listed	14.0	12.9	6.7	6.0
Neighborhood acquaintance	9.3	10.5	14.1	13.1
Business	7.0	7.6	7.3	5.5
Pickup	2.9	2.9	3.7	1.6
Dance hall	1.7	1.8	4.3	7.7
Travel	0.6	0.0	0.0	1.1
	100.0	100.0	100.0	100.0

*Data from Harvey J. Locke's study, *Predicting Adjustment in Marriage: A Comparison of a Divorced and a Happily Married Group*, New York: Henry Holt, 1951, p. 88.

The so-called "blind date" is an interesting combination of primary and secondary contacts. It could not exist in the old-time village, where

[10] Lewis M. Terman and others, *Psychological Factors in Marital Happiness* (New York: McGraw-Hill, 1938), p. 196.

everyone knew everyone else. It arises under urban conditions, where the number of people one does not know greatly exceeds the number of one's acquaintances and friends. An essential aspect of primary relations is retained, since the two persons are introduced by a mutual friend.

Lonely-Hearts Introduction Clubs A combination of factors in modern American society makes it almost impossible for some persons to find desirable and eligible mates. As we have seen, there is an unbalanced sex ratio in urban and rural areas and in various age groups. For the United States in 1968 there were 6,069,000 more single, widowed, and divorced women than men in the total civilian group of 14 years old and older.[11] In the 20-34 age group, however, there were 1,427,000 more civilian men than women who were single, widowed, or divorced. In the 35-64 age group there were 2,789,000 more women than men who were single, widowed, or divorced. Finally, urban persons are exposed to heterogeneous attitudes, ideals, and expectations of marriage, the result being that they have increased difficulty in meeting those they are willing to marry.

This need for assistance in mate selection has led to the establishment of commercial agencies throughout the country. One, Personal Acquaintance Service, Inc., was established by a sociologist, Wallace, under the name of Karl Miles, to study mate selection in introduction clubs.[12]

Introduction clubs in America operate under great difficulties. First, the resistances of prospective clients must be overcome. Second, there is an unfavorable image of such introduction clubs. Finally, there are the inherent difficulties involved in the mechanics of operating the club profitably, such as an unbalanced sex ratio, disparity in ages of the two sexes, unrealistic demands of clients, and high operating costs involved in the great amount of detail necessary for the operation of a successful club.

A reading of the form letters addressed to prospective patrons reveals five types of resistance clubs attempt to overcome. First, there is the reluctance of the potential client to substitute an impersonal approach by correspondence for the introduction in person by a mutual friend. Second, there is prejudice against patronizing a commercialized enterprise dealing in affairs of the heart. Third, there is often prejudice against the type of person who would solicit the help of an introduction service. Fourth, there is doubt as to the honesty and integrity of both club operators and their members, and suspicion of ulterior motives.

[11] *Statistical Abstract of the United States*, 1969, p. 32.
[12] See Karl Miles Wallace, with Eve Odell, *Love is More than Luck: An Experiment in Scientific Matchmaking* (New York: Wilfred Funk, 1957).

Finally, there is scepticism about the possibilities of success in such a venture.

Wallace reports that there are about twice as many men as women in introduction clubs and that this was the main problem of his and other clubs. The sex ratio of men to women varies with age. For the 18–34 age group the ratio was 3½ or 4 men to 1 woman; for the 35–44 group the ratio was about 2½ to 1; for those 45–55 the ratio was 1 to 1; and for those over 55 there were more women than men. Women who join lonely-hearts clubs are, on the average, much older than men. Wallace reports that the average age of men in his club was 38, and of women, 47.

FACTORS IN MATE SELECTION

Some people believe that of all the millions of people in the world two individuals are predestined for each other and will find supreme happiness in their union. Others believe that Providence has decreed a marriage for a purpose, perhaps inscrutable to the spouses, that fate determines the outcome, or that chance results in good or bad luck in mating.

These unscientific ideas about mate selection help us understand why many persons are averse to finding in science an explanation of why people fall in love. Yet love and marriage are behavior and, like all behavior, are subject to observation and study.

Studies of mate selection suggest a number of factors as chiefly determining "who marries whom." These are (1) propinquity, (2) homogamy, or the tendency of those who are similar in social characteristics to be attracted to each other and marry, (3) conception of the ideal mate, (4) parental image, and (5) personality needs.

Propinquity The theory of propinquity assumes that persons tend to marry those who live near them, those with whom they go to school, and those with whom they work. Stated in this way, the theory merely asserts what is obvious: that marriage may take place between those who have an opportunity to meet each other. The chief findings of research on factors in mate selection indicate that there is a positive association between residential propinquity and mate selection.[13] Propinquity, however, is only a circumscribing factor in choice of mate; it is not, or is only in rare exceptions, a specific factor determining the individual with whom one will fall in love. One of the more recent studies of propinquity is that of Catton who collected data from

---

[13] For a bibliography on propinquity, see Alvin M. Katz and Reuben Hill, "Residential Propinquity and Marital Selection: A Review of Theory, Method, and Fact," *Marriage and Family Living*, 20 (1958): pp. 34–35.

marriage-license applications of 413 couples. He found the usual pattern of grooms marrying brides who are near them in residence. He holds that within a geographical area there will be homogamy and so persons marry each other because they are alike.[14]

Social Characteristics Which tendency is stronger in mate selection: for those with similar characteristics to be drawn to each other or for those with dissimilar characteristics to attract each other? The first is known as homogamy or assortative mating, and the second heterogamy. Couples are attracted to each other both by likenesses and by differences. The question, then, is not if those with like or unlike characteristics choose one another, but which tendency is greater in given situations.

Approximately a hundred studies have been made on homogamy. Until recently these studies were concerned with married couples. They dealt with characteristics such as age, stature, health, and intelliegnce. For example, Kiser reports that homogamy is present in educational attainment for both white and nonwhite couples; Garrison, Anderson, and Reed found homogamy in intelligence as measured by IQ; and Spuhler lists a host of physical traits in which there is homogamy, such as age, weight, eye color, and stature.[15] In every case, with the exception of a few early inquiries using questionable methods, it was found that every difference over chance expectation was in the direction of homogamy rather than of heterogamy. These studies were all open to the objection that the findings on homogamy might be the result of marriage rather than the cause of it.

Data on homogamy before marriage is now available. In one study, that of Burgess and Wallin, findings on physical, psychological, and social characteristics substantiate the conclusions of the previous studies of married couples. Their findings, based on data on 1,000 couples during engagement and then restudy of the couples after marriage, are in the direction of homogamy.[16]

Research indicates that on race and religious affiliation there is a greater than chance proportion of homogamous unions. In general, research also shows a tendency for persons to marry within the same

---

[14] William R. Catton and R. J. Smircich, "A Comparison of Mathematical Models for the Effect of Residential Propinquity on Mate Selection," *American Sociological Review*, 29 (1964): p. 529. The same was the conclusion of the authors in the first edition of this book in 1945. See p. 422.

[15] Clyde V. Kiser, "Assortative Mating by Educational Attainment in Relation to Fertility," *Eugenic Quarterly*, 15-2 (1968): pp. 98–112; Robert J. Garrison, V. Elving Anderson, and Sheldon C. Reed, "Assortative Marriage," *Ibid.*, pp. 113–127; and J. N. Spuhler, "Assortative Mating with Respect to Physical Characteristics," *Ibid.*, pp. 128–140.

[16] Ernest W. Burgess and Paul Wallin, "Homogamy in Social Characteristics," *American Journal of Sociology*, 49 (1943): pp. 109–124.

social-economic class and with those having the same leisure-time interests.

Only a few studies have analyzed the actual factors determining homogamy. Those factors which have been suggested include: (1) propinquity, insofar as residential segregation may bring together persons who are like rather than unlike each other; (2) group membership, such as in church and other voluntary associations, which select persons of common culture, interests, and values; (3) social disapproval of marriage outside the in-group, such as persons of different race, religion, nationality, and social class; (4) the conception of the ideal mate tends to exclude persons who are much different from one's self, one's family, and friends; (5) the tendency to fall in love with a person whose psychological characteristics are those of one's parents. This is based on the assumption that since the child is like the parent, marrying a person like his parent will make for homogamy; and (6) consensus on values was found to be significant in a study of 194 couples who were engaged, pinned, or seriously attached.[17] In a reanalysis of their data, Kerckhoff and Bean had to modify somewhat their conclusion that agreement leads to liking.[18] Culture defines men as more likely to be oriented to power than women and more likely to have the role of providing for the economic needs of the family, while women play the expressive role more than men. Men have more power orientations and are able to tolerate a lack of consensus in some areas. Some deviation from the generalization that agreement leads to liking arises from the instrumental-expressive role division in engagement or marriage. A strongly instrumental-oriented man is unlikely to select a woman if she, also, has strongly instrumental orientations. Agreement leading to liking is found more in women than in men. If some or all of these six factors operate to determine assortative mating, it is understandable why the tendency for like to mate with like is greater than for opposites to attract each other.

Homogamy of attitudes was studied by Snyder who collected data from 561 sophomore students in 13 rural high schools.[19] An analysis of those who subsequently married a person from their class (20 couples) showed that prior to their serious involvement they did not have a high degree of homogamy of attitudes. Most data on homogamy have samples of married or engaged persons and so similarity of attitudes may have

---

[17] Alen C. Kerckhoff and Keith E. Davis, "Value Consensus and Need Complimentarity in Mate Selection," *American Sociological Review*, 27 (1962): pp. 295–313.

[18] Alen C. Kerckhoff and Frank D. Bean, "Role-Related Factors in Person Perception Among Engaged Couples," *Sociometry: A Journal of Research in Social Psychology*, 30 (1967): pp. 176–186.

[19] Eloese Snyder, "A Study of Homogamy and Marital Selectivity," *Journal of Marriage and the Family*, 26 (1964): pp. 332–336.

developed in interaction during engagement or marriage, but might not have been present at the beginning of the interaction.

There is considerable homogamy on some items associated with mate selection and not on others. There is some heterogamy with reference to age, education, marital status, and religious affiliation.

Baber asked 642 New York University students and Komarovsky asked 559 Columbia students whether or not certain specified characteristics would be important to them in choosing a mate.[20] One question was whether a person would prefer the mate to have less, more, or the same education. Over half of the women wanted the husband to have more education and none wanted the husband to have less. Equal education was preferred by 60 percent of the men in Komarovsky's sample and 78 percent in Baber's sample.

Preferred age difference between the mates has been studied by a number of persons.[21] The vast majority of women want their husbands to be older; a vast majority of men want their wives to be younger. Evidence supplied by McGinnis seems to indicate that preferred age difference is declining. For Wisconsin University students in 1939 it was 2.3 for men and 3.4 for women; in 1956 it was 1.2 for men and 2.1 for women. This is supported by the difference in age at first marriage. The long-term trend has been toward homogamy in age. In 1890 the difference in age of brides and grooms was 4.1 years, 22.0 and 26.1 years respectively.[22] In 1968 the median age of brides was 2.4 years younger than that of grooms, 20.8 and 23.2 respectively.[23]

If homogamy were always operating in mate selection, it would result in single persons marrying single persons, divorced marrying divorced and widowed marrying widowed. Actually, while homogamy is very high for single persons, it is relatively low for the other two groups.[24] About 9 out of 10 single persons marry single persons; their order of choice is single, divorced, and widowed. About half of divorced men and women marry divorced persons; their order of choice is divorced, single, and widowed. About half of widowed men and $4\frac{1}{2}$ out of 10 widowed

---

[20] Ray E. Baber, *Marriage and the Family* (New York: McGraw-Hill, 1953), pp. 118–121; and Mirra Komarovsky, "What Do Young People Want in a Marriage Partner?" *Journal of Social Hygiene*, 31 (1946): pp. 440–444.

[21] Ray E. Baber, *Marriage and the Family*; Reuben Hill, "Campus Values in Mate Selection, *Journal of Home Economics*, 37 (1945): pp. 554–558; and Robert McGinnis, "Campus Values in Mate Selection, *Social Forces*, 36 (1958): pp. 368–373.

[22] Department of Health, Education, and Welfare, *Vital Statistics of the United States*, 1 (1959): pp. 2–7.

[23] *Current Population Reports*, Population Characteristics, Series p-20, No. 198, 1970.

[24] Department of Health, Education, and Welfare, *Marriage Statistics Analysis, United States, 1963*, Washington, D.C.: National Center for Health Statistics, Series 21, No. 16, September, 1968, pp. 29–30.

women marry widowed; their order of choice is widowed, divorced, and single. Obviously, other factors than homogamy were operating, particularly for divorced and widowed.

To what extent do Protestants marry Protestants, Catholics marry Catholics, Catholics marry Protestants, and Jews marry Jews? While there are a few small studies of interfaith marriages between Protestants, Catholics, and Jews, the only nationwide statistics are for Catholics and non-Catholics.

The percent of valid interfaith marriages between Catholics and non-Catholics has been relatively high for a number of years; in 1945 it was 27.5; in 1950, 27.6; in 1955, 26.7; in 1961, 32.5, and in 1968, 33.7.[25] Obviously, the rate of marriage between Catholics and non-Catholics would be much higher if, in addition to those sanctioned and considered valid by the Catholic Church, the nonsanctioned and invalid marriages were included. The interfaith marriage rate may go up in view of the 1970 relaxation of two major rules of the Catholic Church by the Pope: (1) the non-Catholic partner no longer has to pledge not to impede the Catholic partner in raising their children as Catholics; and (2) diocesan bishops may permit mixed marriages to take place without the presence of a Catholic priest.[26]

A generalization on the rate of interfaith marriage has been formulated and supported in a study by Locke, Sabagh, and Thomes: The rate of interfaith marriage increases as the proportion of a religious group in an area decreases.[27] Data on Catholics in the United States, Catholics and Anglicans in Canada, and Catholics and Protestants in Switzerland support the generalization.

The fact that interfaith marriages increase as the proportion of a religious group in the population decreases probably indicates that religious homogamy operates rather effectively only when a sufficient number of a religious group are in an area. Otherwise, one is more likely to meet and marry a person of a different religious faith.[28]

Ideal Mate The "ideal mate" is the term used to indicate the image which the adolescent or youth constructs of the characteristics of the

---

[25] Data from the *Official Catholic Directory*, New York: P. J. Kenedy and Sons. (Issued Annually.)

[26] Reported in the *Los Angeles Times*, April 29, 1970, Part I, p. 4.

[27] Harvey J. Locke, Georges Sabagh, and Mary Margaret Thomes, "Interfaith Marriages," *Social Problems*, 4 (1957): pp. 329–333. Data for Switzerland from Kurt B. Mayer, *The Population of Switzerland*, (New York: Columbia University Press, 1952), pp. 178–187.

[28] For a detailed discussion of intermarriage among Protestants, Catholics, and Jews see J. Richard Udry, *The Social Context of Marriage*, (New York: Lippincott, 1966), pp. 215–223.

person he would like to marry. Nearly every young person from highschool days, or earlier, cherishes in his imagination a picture, sometimes very clear and definite, of the person he hopes to marry. He may visualize the physical features and appearance of the future mate and delinate mental, temperamental, moral, and social characteristics. Conceptions of desirable personal traits in an ideal mate are part of the culture of a group, are assimilated by new members of the group, and, while persistent over a time period, change somewhat under changing conditions. The characteristics of an ideal mate as valued by students at the University of Wisconsin were studied first in 1939[29] and then in 1956.[30] Students were asked to rank an identical set of 18 personal traits according to their importance in an ideal mate. McGinnis, who replicated the study in 1956, concluded that there seemed to be a high degree of consistency over time in the rank given to the 18 traits.[31] There were, however, some changes. Having similar religious backgrounds and interests increased in importance over the time period for both men and women. Not having previous experience in sexual intercourse decreased in importance for both men and women. McGinnis emphasized that companionship family values are replacing traditional values among males in the culture of the university studied.

Case studies indicate that the conception of the ideal mate operates in the initial stages of mate selection. In only a few cases does the person fall in love with and marry a person with all the traits of his ideal mate. Typically he makes a compromise. He discovers other factors are more important in the choice of a life partner, as in the following case:

> What was my ideal? Oh, somebody tall, dark, and handsome. With a little mustache and a clipped British accent, and who wore tweeds. Somebody who shared all my religious, philosophical, and political beliefs, and was very serious about the future and the destiny of the world. We were going to go out and conquer everything together. Wait till you hear about Dick, though—he's short and blond with a Southern drawl (she laughs).
>
> I thought it was going to be one of those soul-mate businesses, that there would be an immediate attraction and a deep understanding of what was hidden inside. Oh, and another thing—he had to have a social conscience. Dick doesn't fit any place as far as I can see. We've never been soul mates. When we're together all we think of is each other and we never get around to religion or philosophy or anything like that.[32]

---

[29] Hill, "Campus Values in Mate Selection."
[30] McGinnis, "Campus Values in Mate Selection."
[31] Spearman rank correlations between 1939 and 1956 were .97 for men and .91 for women.
[32] Anselm Strauss, "A Study of Three Psychological Factors Affecting Choice of Mate" (Ph.D. Dissertation, Chicago, University of Chicago Libraries, 1945), pp. 62–63.

Does a person's conception of an ideal mate change as a result of interaction with an esteemed person of the opposite sex? Udry attempted to answer this question by securing conceptions of the ideal mate from 90 engaged persons and from 58 men and 69 women who were not engaged. He concluded that there is little relationship between the conception of an ideal mate one has before engagement and the conception of the ideal mate by persons who have had interaction with a fiancée during the engagement period.[33]

Parental Image The hypothesis regarding the role of the parental image is that a person tends, typically and generally unconsciously, to fall in love with a person similar to his parent of the opposite sex. A more detailed statement of this theory is as follows: In early childhood a person normally develops a strong affectional relationship with one or more persons in the family circle. In general it is directed in the case of the boy to his mother and of the girl to her father. Sometimes the major affectional response of the boy is to his father and of the girl to her mother. Occasionally the boy or girl feels a strong affectional attachment to a sister or brother. Whatever the actual constellation of response relationships in the family, the person as an adult attempts to continue this pattern or to reproduce it in the person with whom he falls in love.

Case histories secured by interviewing couples both before and after marriage seem to substantiate this hypothesis, though not to prove it conclusively. The boy appears to fall in love with a girl who possesses the temperamental and other personality traits of his mother, or who sustains toward him the type of relation which exists between him and his mother. If his relationship with his mother as a child was not satisfying, the boy may seek a girl with characteristics quite different from his mother's and establish with her the kind of relation which he desired as a child. Or, if the relation to his father or sister nearest in age was meaningful to him in childhood, he may attempt to reinstate this type of response pattern in marriage. A study by Prince and Baggaley raises the question of whether it is the opposite sex parent which is influential or whether it is the mother. A study of 170 advanced students revealed that the ideal mate for both men and women had qualities similar to those of the mother.[34] The theory of parental image would help explain how "falling in love" is not determined by conscious and prudential influences but by motivations below the conscious level.

[33] Richard Udry, "Influence of the Ideal Mate on Mate Selection and Mate Perception," *Journal of Marriage and the Family*, 27 (1965): pp. 477–482.
[34] Alfred James Prince and Andrew R. Baggaley, "Personality Variables and the Ideal Mate," *The Family Coordinator*, 12 (1963): pp. 93–96.

Personality Needs The personality needs of the individual are another important factor to be considered in the analysis of mate selection. The hypothesis is that because of certain experiences and situations persons develop personality needs that are best satisfied by intimate association in marriage and family life. Many, but not all, of these center on the wish to be loved, to have emotional security, and to be appreciated.

A significant aspect of being in love is the realization by couples that they are interdependent. Some sociologists and psychologists feel that this interdependence is based on complementary rather than similar needs. For example, Winch has developed a theory of complementary needs to explain why a certain person falls in love with a particular other person. His central hypothesis is that "in mate selection the need-pattern of each spouse will be complementary rather than similar to the need-pattern of the other spouse."[35] This hypothesis was tested on a homogeneous sample of 25 middle-class married, undergraduate students. After analyzing his data, Winch concluded, "It is my judgment that the data support the general hypothesis."[36]

Winch feels that homogamy, or that persons attract and select as mates persons who are like themselves, operates in social characteristics, such as religion, educational level, and social status.[37] These social characteristics establish a field of eligibles within which mate selection occurs. On the level of psychological motivation, complementary needs are the determining factor in mate selection. This is called heterogamy, and means that opposites attract and select each other as mates. The theory is that a highly dominant person, for example, needs and selects a submissive person as a mate. A highly submissive person needs and selects a dominant person as a mate. Or a highly maternal person needs and selects a mother-son relationship, and a highly dependent person who needs a mother selects a maternal person.

The theory of complementary needs has been criticized on various grounds, the most serious being that the evidence of other studies does not support it. For example, Bowerman and Day studied the needs of 60 college couples who were formally engaged or considered themselves regular dating partners. They report that "the findings of our study do not support the theory of complementary needs."[38] Shellenberg and Bee studied the needs of 36 couples who were engaged or

[35] Robert F. Winch, *Mate Selection: A Study of Complementary Needs* (New York: Harper & Brothers, 1958), p. 96. See his article "Another Look at the Theory of Complementary Needs in Mate Selection," *Journal of Marriage and the Family*, 29 (1967): pp. 756–762.

[36] *Ibid.*, p. 333.

[37] *Ibid.*, p. 331.

[38] Charles E. Bowerman and Barbara R. Day, "A Test of the Theory of Complementary Needs as Applied to Couples during Courtship," *American Sociological Review*, 21 (1956), pp. 602–605.

going steady and 64 recently married couples. They conclude that "the theory of complementary needs cannot be considered as adequately grounded empirically."[39] Two other studies, Hobart[40] and Heiss,[41] found no empirical support for the theory of complementary needs.

It may be that some needs of some couples are complementary and other needs are not. This was the conclusion of Goodman who used a sample of 102 couples at a state university. He found that mates who had high self-acceptance were complementary in their need structures in that they were attracted to persons who presumably provided sources of need satisfaction.[42]

Functioning of Ideal Mate, Parental Image, and Personality Needs
These factors obviously work together in mate selection. To a great extent the conception of the ideal mate, the parental image, and the personality needs of the individual are all products of the interaction of the person with other members of his family. The conception of an ideal mate is in large part derived from the family. The parental image specifically influences the formation of the conception of one's ideal mate. And the personality needs of the person derive in large part from the satisfactions received and withheld in the family circle.

Coombs has proposed that factors in mate selection be analyzed in terms of values.[43] Propinquity brings persons of similar values together, if one assumes that given geographical areas are characterized by given values. The ideal mate is composed of valued behavior and traits of a possible mate. Parental image would function if one values the parent of the opposite sex. And personality needs are those ways of behavior and traits which a given person desires or values.

SUMMARY

Two extremely different methods of mate selection are (1) a situation where arrangements for marriage are completely in the control of parents and (2) one where they are entirely in the hands of young people.

---

[39] James A. Shellenberg and Lawrence S. Bee, "A Re-examination of the Theory of Complementary Needs in Mate Selection," *Marriage and Family Living*, 22 (1960): pp. 227–232.

[40] Charles Hobart, "The Theory of Complementary Needs: A Re-examination," *Pacific Sociological Review*, 6 (1963): pp. 73–79.

[41] J. Heiss, "Complementarity—A Test," *Journal of Marriage and the Family*, 26 (1964): pp. 337–339.

[42] Marvin Goodman, "A Pilot Study of the Relationship Between Degree of Expressed Self-Acceptance and Interpersonal Need Structure in the Mate Selection Process," *Dissertation Abstracts*, 24 (1963), pp. 867–868.

[43] Robert H. Coombs, "A Value Theory of Mate Selection," *The Family Life Coordinator*, 10 (1961): pp. 51–54.

The closest approximation to absolute control by parents in the cases considered was that of the traditional pattern of Japan, where the daughter did not even ask the name of the young man to whom she was betrothed. Theoretically, courtship in the United States exemplifies the other extreme of choice of mates by young people. Courtship in the present generation of young people has tended to replace parental standards with those of the youth group and to extend the circle of selection by the practice of dating. Increasingly, young people make their choices on the basis of a companionship formed by mutual experiences, compatibility of temperament, personality needs, and common interests and ideals.

Mate selection when arranged by parents stressed social and economic considerations and assumed that satisfactory interpersonal relationships would develop after marriage. With the transition from parental control of marriage to freedom of young people to select their mates, choices tend to be on the basis of propinquity, homogamy, ideal mate, parental image, and personality needs.

Today in our society young people may have difficulty in finding mates, especially since parental assistance is no longer available or desired. Commercial enterprises called "lonely-hearts clubs" have developed to meet this need. These services have undoubtedly resulted in some marriages.

PROBLEMS FOR RESEARCH

There have been many studies in the area of mate selection. They have been concentrated, however, largely on the factors of propinquity and homogamy. Studies are needed on the underlying factors which determine the selection of a mate.

Mate Selection as the Development of a Love Relationship Bolton criticizes past research on mate selection as concentrating on variables in the characteristics and behavior of two individuals.[44] He suggests a process approach to focus on the interaction of a couple in building up the love relationship. In an intensive study of twenty couples he identified five developmental processes in mate selection: (1) *personality meshing*, in which there is early attraction and mutual perception of personality fit; (2) *identity clarification*, in which the process of resolving identity problems builds up a strong structure of shared understandings; (3) *relation-centering*, in which there is no spontaneous meshing of personalities and the effort is directed consciously to building up

[44] Charles D. Bolton, "Mate Selection as the Development of a Relationship," *Marriage and Family Living*, 23 (1961): pp. 234–240.

shared understandings and commitments; (4) *pressure and interpersonal conflict,* in which personalities do not mesh and one of the pair uses direct pressure and the other subtle manipulations; and (5) *expediency-centering,* where there is a strongly felt pressure toward marriage by one or both of the parties.

The conceptual theory proposed by Bolton provides a promising lead for the study of the dynamics of mate selection by the process approach to the development of the love relation.

Primary Group Controls The direct and immediate control of parents and friends over mate selection has greatly diminished in the United States. Yet their indirect and subtle influence remains. There is opportunity and need for systematic research of the control still exerted by parents, as well as by the intimate social group of which the young people are members. Differences by social class should also be investigated, on the hypothesis that overt and covert influences vary with class membership.

Organizations Promoting Mate Selection There are numerous organizations providing social contacts for unmarried persons. Little is known about their role in the courtship process. These organizations include young people's church societies, young people's voluntary social groups, dancing clubs, beach clubs, and such clubs as Parents Without Partners, composed of divorced and widowed persons. Representative types could be studied to investigate their effectiveness in promoting social contacts between men and women, the types of persons who join such organizations, and whether contacts made in these organizations eventuate in marriage.

QUESTIONS AND EXERCISES

1. Show the similarities and differences in the way mates are selected among the Apache Indians and in a Japanese village.
2. Enumerate specific ways in which parents in the United States overtly influence mate selection.
3. What modern social situations encourage the development of lonely-hearts clubs?
4. Describe the theory of propinquity as an explanation of mate selection and indicate why it is inadequate.
5. How does one's conception of the ideal mate operate in mate selection?
6. Analyze the case at the beginning of the chapter, listing in order of their importance the factors of proximity, ideal mate, personality

needs, parental image, and homogamy in mate selection. What other factors are present in this case?
7. Write a personal document, either of yourself or of someone with whom you are intimately acquainted, illustrating the different factors operating in mate selection.

BIBLIOGRAPHY

Bowerman, Charles E.; and Day, Barbara R. "A Test of the Theory of Complementary Needs As Applied to Couples During Courtship," *American Sociological Review*, 21 (1956): pp. 602–605.

Tests Winch's theory of complementary needs on 60 college couples who were engaged or dating regularly. Needs assessed by means of responses of couples on Edwards Personal Preference Schedule. Score correlations give very little evidence of complementary needs being used as basis of mate selection.

Burchinal, Lee G. "The Premarital Dyad and Love Involvement," in *Handbook of Marriage and the Family*, ed. Harold T. Christensen. Chicago: Rand McNally, 1964, Ch. 16.

Extended discussion of dating and courtship and various factors with reference to mate selection: homogamy, previous marital status, physical and psychological characteristics, and complementary needs.

Carter, Hugh; and Glick, Paul C. *Marriage and Divorce: A Social and Economic Study*. Cambridge: Harvard University Press, 1970.

An excellent analysis and interpretation of both historical and contemporary national statistics on marriage and divorce. Includes a discussion of the development of statistics on marriage and divorce; comparative international trends; trends and variations in marriage rates, divorce rates, and marital status; variations in age at marriage; intermarriage among educational, ethnic, and religious groups; family composition and living arrangements; work experience and income; variations among separated and divorced persons, widows and widowers; and marital status and health.

Heiss, Jerold S. "Premarital Characteristics of the Religiously Intermarried in an Urban Area," *American Sociological Review*, 25 (1960): pp. 47–55.

Analyzes data from a representative sample of midtown Manhattan. Compares 304 religiously intermarried subjects with 863 inmarried. Examines these two groups with reference to intensity of early religious ties, early family relationships, and emancipation from parents.

Katz, Alvin M.; and Hill, Reuben. "Residential Propinquity and Marital Selection: A Review of Theory, Method, and Fact," *Marriage and Family Living*, 20 (1958): pp. 27–35.

The chief finding of the various studies is that there is a positive association between residential propinquity and mate selection.

Udry, Richard. "Influence of the Ideal Mate on Mate Selection and Mate Perception," *Journal of Marriage and the Family*, 27 (1965): pp. 477–482.
> Studied a group of men and women before engagement and a group of those who were engaged. He concluded that there was little correlation between the characteristics of the ideal mate given before engagement and those given after interacting with a person in engagment.

Wallace, Karl Miles; with Odell, Eve. *Love Is More than Luck: An Experiment in Scientific Matchmaking.* New York: Wilfred Funk, 1957.
> An account of Wallace's establishment of an introduction or lonely-hearts club for the purpose of studying the nature of such clubs, the problem of attracting clients, and type of clients. Describes the attempt to meet the needs of clients through matching characteristics punched on IBM cards.

Winch, Robert F. *Mate Selection: A Study of Complementary Needs.* New York: Harper & Brothers, 1958.
> Presents the theory that on the level of psychological motivations persons select mates with different personality patterns from their own in order to fulfill their own personality needs. Gives evidence for the theory of complementary needs from his study of 25 upper-middle class, undergraduate, homogeneous, married couples.

Chapter 13
Measuring Success in Marriage

During the last few decades a large number of studies have attempted to measure and predict success in marriage. A variety of instruments have been used ranging from a single question such as "How happy would you rate your marriage?" to an elaborate instrument with several sets of questions. What indicates the success of marriages? Is it permanence, happiness, satisfaction, sexual compatibility, adjustment, integration, agreement, companionship, or some combination of these? The instrument used to measure success in marriage should be as adequate, reliable, and valid as possible.

DIFFICULTIES IN MEASURING MARITAL SUCCESS

The following case shows some of the difficulties of trying to measure marital success. The statements by the husband and the wife reveal the disintegrating forces in the marriage:

Husband: As far back as we know, there never have been any domestic breaks in our family. Mother didn't want me to have any trouble of that sort. When Jennie and I had our break, one of the things that made me quite sure that I didn't want a divorce and really want to separate, except temporarily, was that I didn't want to be the one who would bring open domestic strife into our family. Jennie did not look on divorce with such distaste as I.

My wife did want to be a lawyer, but her ambitions changed and she wanted to try social work. Then she got so she didn't know what she wanted to do.

Her parents are not religious and she isn't at all. My parents are very religious and I had to go to church and to Sunday school every Sunday when I was a child. I continued my interest in religion until I got away from home and in college and then I dropped out gradually. We didn't have any disagreements on that.

On one occasion after our separation she was over at my parents' home with my sister and she called her father up from there. Her father wanted her to come home, bawled her out something awful, and she got to crying and hung up. It was then she realized how much my parents cared for her. They were very nice and very sympathetic. My mother called me on the phone and I asked to talk to Jennie. She said she couldn't talk because she was still crying so much. Finally I got her and she told me what the matter was. I called up her old man and for once said what I thought. I gave him hell, and he apologized profusely and then I told Jennie what he said. That raised my stock a hundred percent and then he called Jennie and apologized to her and she called me back and told me what her father had said.

After this incident with her father, she called me and asked me if she could see me. I had already told her that any move for reconciliation would have to come from her because she had decided to separate. Then she said she would like to see me. Of course, I wanted to see her, but I took on a very business-like air and told her that a couple was coming over to see me and if she wanted to she could come too. She came along and we had a good time together.

This couple had planned to stay all night. We had three bedrooms; one had a single bed, one a double bed, and the other had twin beds. When bedtime came, I said: "Well, how will we sleep?" I told her, "You can take the front room with the single bed, or you can take my room and I'll take that, and the friends can take the room with the twin beds." She said: "Well, what's the matter with sleeping with you?" So we slept together that night. That night we realized we wanted to come back together.

Her mother, I am sure, is sexually cold and I am quite sure that from the time Jennie was a child, her mother instilled in her the idea of sexual coldness, that sex relations are something that a woman has to submit to. I could sense it somehow throughout the whole time we were married and up until the time we were separated. At first she seemed to enjoy it reasonably well, but by the end of the second year I could notice she was becoming colder and colder. Since our renewal of relationships she has been very desirous of sex relations. Sometimes even more desirous than I am, although I think I am a little higher sexed than she is.

After we came back together Jennie said that she wanted a home, a Ford, a dog, and a baby and she would be satisfied and happy. She says she wants to make a career out of being a housewife.

Wife: After we were married I continued in college. I felt sort of constrained. My freedom wasn't particularly limited, but I felt as if it were. I had become acquainted before marriage with a rather unconventional couple who lived in the same building. They didn't like my husband. Our friends simply weren't mutual. Both of us were working very hard and we didn't plan anything to do together very often. Our interests were too separate.

After graduating I went home to Mother. I remember I was awfully tired. At that time I was very nervous and irritable and felt like I wanted to get away from everything. I had thought of separation and possibly divorce. I wasn't very anxious to get a divorce, but I wanted to get away and give myself time to do some thinking. I was very unhappy all my last year at school. We saw very little of one another and most of the time that we were together we were rather irritable. I finally decided to return to college in the fall, rejoin my husband, and take some graduate work. In the fall we still did not get along well and I thought of separation. I was dissatisfied with everything. The college boy I liked before I married came back to visit and I got interested in him. I was over at his friends' a lot of the time and he and his friends were over at my house. My husband didn't like it. We became rather snappy and actually rude to each other. These friends didn't seem to like the way he treated me and they seemed to blame it on him. I could take my troubles to them and they were sympathetic. Finally, I decided to leave my husband. We talked it over; we agreed to separate and give me time to think it over. He told me that he was still of the same mind and wanted to live with me, but he wanted me to make up my own mind and decide what I wanted to do. I got a job, and one of my girl friends and I took a room in a hotel. I told her that I wasn't getting very far in making up my mind whether to stay separated and get a divorce or to go back. She said: "You are always noticing your husband's faults. Have you ever thought of your own faults and how they might strike another person?"

For the first time in my life I began to think about my faults. It came to me as something of a shock. I realized that a lot of my friends were influencing me, that I didn't have much ability to make up my own mind, and that I was too much interested in another man, although I could never marry him, because our backgrounds were far too different.

You can't always be thinking of yourself if you are going to make a success of marriage and I am very anxious to make a success of mine. I very definitely made up my mind to go back and try it again.

For some time before our last separation I was disgusted with any sex relations with my husband. This was during the time that I was interested in the other man, but since our reunion, I get much more pleasure out of it and feel no disgust at all.

One time after my examinations I was all tired out and I went to my in-law's home. My father called up and told me to take the next train and come home. He wouldn't hear no. I told him I just couldn't, but he was very unreasonable. I got to crying and stopped talking to him. My husband called him up and for once stood up and said what he thought. He said I was too tired to come and wasn't coming. Daddy was real nice when my husband called his bluff.

How can one measure the marital success of the couple in this case? Could one use happiness, or satisfaction, or integration of the husband and wife as standards? Would one have to make two measurements, one in the period of "trial separation," the other after the reconciliation? It is evident that any measure of success that might be used—happiness, satisfaction, or integration—would give different results in these two periods.

CRITERIA OF MARITAL SUCCESS

In measuring marital success, the first problem is to select the criterion or criteria by which marriages may be evaluated. The criteria to be considered are those which have been used in one or more major studies: (1) permanence of the marriage, (2) happiness of the husband and wife, (3) satisfaction with the marriage, (4) sexual adjustment, (5) marital adjustment, (6) integration of the couple, (7) consensus, and (8) companionship.

Permanence Some persons judge the success or failure of a marriage by its actual or potential permanence. They say that successful marriages are those which survive and unsuccessful unions are those which are broken by separation and divorce, or in which husband and wife are seriously considering divorce. Lack of permanence or divorce was one of Locke's indexes of marital adjustment.[1]

To consider as successful those marriages in which husband and wife continue living together has two distinct advantages. First, a marriage in modern society might well be rated a success if it manages to survive despite such disintegrating influences as economic insecurity, the decline of religious and moral control, and the liberality of divorce laws. Second the status of being separated or divorced is an objective and easily applied criterion, and is useful in determining the extremely unsuccessful marriages. This criterion, however, is not sufficient by itself, for many marriages that do not end in separation or divorce are as unhappy as those that are broken.

Happiness To many persons the success or failure of a marriage is judged by the happiness of the couple. This involves the personal reaction of husband and wife and recognizes the fact that in American society happiness is assumed to be the object of marriage and the standard by which it is to be evaluated. Above all other conditions implied in the marriage contract is the obligation of husband and wife to

---

[1] Harvey J. Locke, *Predicting Adjustment in Marriage: A Comparison of a Divorced and a Happily-Married Group* (New York: Henry Holt, 1951).

make each other happy, an obligation which reflects the personal character of marriage in our society. Accordingly, studies of marriage often include an appraisal of its happiness by the husband and wife, either individually or together.

Many objections have been raised to the use of happiness as a way of judging a successful marriage. Because happiness is subjective, how can any two persons agree on rating the happiness of their own marriage or that of anyone else? A marriage may be happy for the husband but not for the wife. Too, will persons be honest in rating their marriage? Can they be honest even if they wish to be so? Indeed, can persons know whether they are really happy or not?

Actually, studies have found that these doubts about happiness as a criterion of marital success are not justified. Persons readily report the state of happiness in their marriage. Husbands and wives generally, though not always, agree in their rating of the happiness of their own marriage. A member of a couple and an outsider come close to giving the same rating. In other words, even if happiness is a subjective reaction, the person is aware of it and can report on it and those who know him well can rather accurately appraise it.

Studies having happiness as the criterion of marital success have used only a five-point or a seven-point scale of measurement, because people have difficulty in discriminating lesser degrees of happiness. By using a seven-point scale Terman thought he would minimize the effect of persons tending to rate their marriage toward the happy end of the continuum.[2] His categories were extraordinarily happy, decidedly more happy than the average, somewhat more happy than the average, about average, somewhat less happy than the average, decidedly less happy than the average, extremely unhappy. Burgess-Cottrell and Locke, in his first study, used five degrees: very happy, happy, average, unhappy, and very unhappy. After his data were collected, Locke suggested that an attempt be made to minimize the tendency of subjects to rate their marriages as very happy, happy, or average. He suggested the use of a scale line similar to that given below. Each end of the line is defined and a subject can check any one of 10 possible places on the line.[3]

> The squares on the line below represent different degrees of happiness in marriage. The range is from very happy to very unhappy. Check the square which, everything considered, *you feel* is the happiness in your marriage.
> Very ☐—☐— ☐—☐— ☐—☐— ☐—☐— ☐—☐— Very
> Happy   Unhappy

[2] Lewis M. Terman and others, *Psychological Factors in Marital Happiness* (New York: McGraw-Hill, 1938), p. 440.
[3] Ernest W. Burgess and Leonard S. Cottrell, *Predicting Success or Failure in Marriage* (New York: Prentice-Hall, 1939), p. 32; Harvey J. Locke, *Predicting Adjustment in Marriage*, pp. 48–49 and 65.

Satisfaction with the Marriage Many couples judge the success or failure of their marriage by the amount of satisfaction they receive from it. In most cases, of course, satisfaction with the marriage is associated with its harmony and happiness.

Hamilton, in his pioneer study of 100 married men and 100 married women, used this criterion to determine the success or failure of marriage.[4] He used 13 questions to measure satisfaction. Four of his questions have been used, with modifications, by subsequent investigators:

1. If by some miracle you could press a button and find that you had never been married to your husband (or wife), would you press that button?
2. Knowing what you now know, would you wish to marry if you were unmarried?
3. What is there in your marriage that is especially unsatisfactory to you?
4. What things in your married life annoy and dissatisfy you the most?

Satisfaction with a marriage is not by itself an adequate measure of success, for either husband or wife may be dissatisfied in a marriage where there is no conflict or incompatibility, or they may be highly satisfied in a union which has unsolved problems of adjustment. For example, the status of being a married woman may cause a wife to be satisfied with marriage even when there are many conflicts in the marriage and she is unhappy. Or the inhibited and shy husband may prefer remaining in an unhappy marriage to the problem of divorce.

In the following case the wife is satisfied with her husband although she is frank in giving the characteristics which she likes and dislikes in him and talks freely of their conflicts:

The things I liked about Roy were and are:
He is good natured, always making jokes, and while he is quick tempered, afterwards he lets me know that he is sorry by showing me that he cares for me. He is very loving, he always comes in and puts his arms around me; of course I like that.

During the first two years we were together Roy gave me gifts rather frequently; then for the next two or three years somewhat less frequently; during the last two years Roy has given even fewer gifts; he seems to think that I belong to him now.

The things I don't like about Roy are:
The thing that makes me maddest at Roy is that when he comes home he just gets on the bed and reads western stories. He is always buying them. Then after reading a while he may go to sleep. If I wake him up to talk to him, it makes him mad—he just roars. I will talk to him and he

---

[4] Gilbert V. Hamilton, *A Research in Marriage* (New York: Albert and Charles Boni, 1929), pp. 60–76.

won't pay any attention, and then I will say, "Hey, I want you to talk to me." He will stop in a minute and say, "What did you say?"

He may come by in the daytime and jump out of his truck, stick his head in the door and say, "Are you all right," and maybe before I have a chance to say a word, goes on back saying, "I will see you after a while."

Then he doesn't keep his promises. He promised to get me a four-room house three months ago but hasn't done it.

I am very jealous and he always teases about girls. He has only stepped out a couple of times. While I know he is only joking, it makes me so mad I could almost die. And he is just that jealous of me too. I walked into the garage last night and said to one of the men, "Hello, honey," and the man replied, "Hello there, sugar baby." Roy, as serious as could be said, "I didn't know that he was your honey." I told him I was just kidding, but it still made him mad.

Sexual Adjustment Sexual adjustment has never been used as the sole criterion of marital success. Some, however, have regarded it as a sensitive index of adjustment in other areas of behavior. Several studies have included items on sexual adjustment.[5] Burgess and Wallin, Locke, King, and Karlsson used sex items as one of their criteria of marital success. Terman and Oden employed 9 items which were associated with marital happiness for both the husband and the wife: ratio of reported to preferred frequency of intercourse; rated equal passionateness of spouse; wife has orgasm; release and satisfaction from intercourse; never or rarely desires extramarital intercourse; never, rarely, or sometimes refuses sexual intercourse; agreeable or not displeased for long on being refused intercourse; few or no sexual complaints; no premarital intercourse or intercourse with future spouse only.

Marital Adjustment Another criterion of a successful marriage used in several studies is adjustment of the husband and wife to each other. A well-adjusted marriage may be defined as a union in which the husband and wife are in agreement on the chief issues of marriage, such as handling finances and dealing with in-laws; in which they have come to an adjustment on interests, objectives, and values; in which they are in harmony on demonstrations of affection and sharing confidences; and in which they have few or no complaints about their marriage. Questions

---

[5] Ernest W. Burgess and Paul Wallin, *Engagement and Marriage* (Philadelphia: Lippincott, 1953); Georg Karlsson, *Adaptability and Communication in Marriage: A Swedish Predictive Study of Marital Satisfaction* (Uppsala Sweden: Almqvist and Wiksells, 1951); Charles E. King, "Factors Making for Success or Failure in Marital Adjustment Among 466 Negro Couples in Southern City," (Ph.D. Dissertation, University of Chicago Libraries, 1951); Locke, *Predicting Adjustment in Marriage;* Terman and others, *Psychological Factors in Marital Happiness;* Lewis M. Terman and Melita H. Oden, *The Gifted Child Grows Up: Twenty-Five Years' Follow-up of a Superior Group* (Stanford: Stanford University Press, 1947).

in these areas are included in a marital-adjustment index. With adjustment as the criterion, emphasis is on the harmonious relations of husband and wife in marriage, on consensus, on mutuality of interests, and on joint participation in activities.

A factor analysis by Locke and Williamson of a 20-item marital-adjustment index led to the following conclusions:[6] (1) The items cluster under five factors: companionship, consensus, affectional intimacy, wife accommodation, and euphoria or halo effect. (2) Some items may be general indexes of marital adjustment, inasmuch as they fall under more than one factor. One item falls under four of the factors: "If you had your life to live over would you marry the same person?" Three appear in three factors: agreement on conventional conduct, engage in outside activities together, and kiss every day. (3) Marital adjustment can be redefined as an adaptation between the husband and wife to the point where there is companionship, agreement on basic values, affectional intimacy, accommodation, and euphoria. In addition, there are probably other components of marital adjustment not being measured by the test. However, if one single criterion is to be used, adjustment is probably the most satisfactory measure of success in marriage available at the present time.

Integration Another criterion of a successful marriage is the degree of integration achieved. Marital unity has been defined as "the integration of the couple in a union in which the two personalities are not merely merged, or submerged, but interact to complement each other for mutual satisfaction and the achievement of common objectives. The emphasis is upon intercommunication, interstimulation, and participation in common activities."[7]

In their study of 1,000 engaged couples and follow-up interviews with the couples three years after marriage Burgess and Wallin employed 14 categories of integration.[8] Each of these was rated on a five-point scale: highly integrating, somewhat integrating, neither integrating nor disintegrating, somewhat disintegrating, and highly disintegrating. Burgess and Wallin gave each of these levels of integration numerical values, ranging from zero for neither integrating nor disintegrating to plus two for highly integrating and minus two for highly disintegrating. Then by adding the number of points for the 14 factors, it was possible to assign a total integration score. This method provided a marital-integration scale for the measurement of the relative degree of strength of the marital relationship of different couples.

[6] Harvey J. Locke and Robert C. Williamson, "Marital Adjustment: A Factor Analysis Study," *American Sociological Review*, 23 (1958): pp. 562–569.
[7] Burgess and Cottrell, p. 10.
[8] Burgess and Wallin, pp. 585–588.

Past studies of engaged and married couples reveal great differences in the degree of integration. Some couples are so highly integrated emotionally and in ideas that it would seem that nothing could endanger the relationship. The members of other couples may be so slightly integrated in their sentiments, attitudes, and values that it would seem their union could hardly survive even the minor problems of life. Between these two extremes fall almost all couples.

Consensus Consensus as a criterion of marital success denotes the degree of agreement or disagreement of a couple on the primary values or objectives of their marriage. Three studies—by Burgess and Wallin,[9] Farber,[10] and Locke and Thomes—used consensus as one of their specific criteria of success in marriage. Burgess and Wallin included the degree of agreement or disagreement on such matters as handling finances, recreation, religion, demonstration of affection, friends, intimate relations, conventional behavior, ways of dealing with in-laws, and philosophy of life. They also included absence of quarrels, how disagreements are settled, similarity of attitudes toward having children, and attendance at the same church. Most of these items are included in marital-adjustment tests used by Burgess and Cottrell, Terman, Locke, and Karlsson.

In the factor-analysis study made by Locke and Williamson, one of the five clusters of items in the marital-adjustment test was labeled agreement or consensus. All but one of the agreement and disagreement items listed above were found in this factor.

Farber measured consensus by the degree of similarity of husband and wife in ranking independently the importance for family success of the following 10 family values: a respected place in the community, healthy and happy children, companionship, personality development, satisfaction with the amount of affection shown, economic security, emotional security, moral and religious principles, everyday interesting activities, and home.

Locke and Thomes used three measures of consensus. (1) The subject's perception of the degree of agreement on eight items similar to those of Burgess and Wallin. (2) The degree of agreement in the way a husband and wife rated the agreement on the eight items. And (3) the agreement in the way a husband and wife ranked six values.[11]

Companionship When couples are asked what they have gained from marriage, one of the most frequent answers is "companionship." Com-

[9] *Ibid.*, pp. 489–497.
[10] Bernard Farber, "An Index of Marital Integration," *Sociometry: A Journal of Research in Social Psychology*, 20 (1957): pp. 117–134.
[11] Harvey J. Locke and Mary Margaret Thomes, "A Comparison of Negro and White Marriages," in process.

panionship has four principal components: joint participation in common interests and activities, confiding and talking things over, understanding the ideas and feelings of the other, and demonstration of affection. The following report by a wife and her husband illustrates the importance of companionship to many married couples:

> *Wife:* The biggest thing in marriage is being compatible, doing things together, and having our own home. I think you have a sense of security that you don't have before marriage.
> *Husband:* It is difficult to put into words. The idea of being continually with the person you are in love with; then, too, the idea of you two together in your home. Spending your evenings together at home instead of running around. I think it is more or less companionship.

Burgess and Wallin used 12 questions to measure the four components of companionship listed above.[12] Eeach question had several possible responses. Burgess and Wallin then scored the couples on the 12 questions, which gave them a total companionship score.

THE USE OF MULTIPLE CRITERIA

Several studies, rather than having one criterion, have used multiple criteria. Three will be used to illustrate this procedure: Locke's in Indiana;[13] Locke's and Karlsson's in Uppsala, Sweden;[14] and Burgess' and Wallin's in chicago.[15]

In the Indiana study there were three criteria: lack of permanence of marriage as indicated by divorce, happiness in marriage as judged by an outsider, and a test of marital adjustment. In the Swedish study there were five criteria: the marital-adjustment test and four more-or-less objective and independent criteria—happiness in marriage, as judged by persons in the general population; average success, based on the assumption that a sample from the general population would be average in marital adjustment; unhappiness, as judged by the happily married; and separation while waiting for a divorce.

In both studies the marital-adjustment test included several criteria. The test included questions indicative of satisfaction with the marriage, marital happiness, permanence of the marriage, common interests and

---

[12] Burgess and Wallin, pp. 500–501, and 809–810.
[13] Locke, Ch. 3.
[14] Harvey J. Locke and Georg Karlsson, "Marital Adjustment and Prediction in Sweden and the United States," *American Sociological Review*, 17 (1952): pp. 10–17.
[15] Burgess and Wallin, Ch. 15 and p. 673.

activities, consensus (or agreements and disagreements), sexual adjustment, companionship, and demonstration of love and affection. In the Indiana study the scores secured on this test by the divorced group were very much lower on the average than those secured by the happily married. In the Swedish study the average scores secured on the marital-adjustment test were significantly different for the four groups. These groups had the following order of success in marriage as measured by the test: happily married, general or rank-and-file population group, unhappily married, and separated while waiting for divorce. The marital-adjustment test has validity, since it differentiates degrees of marital success as indicated by independent criteria.

Burgess and Wallin used 9 criteria to measure success in marriage: permanence, happiness, general satisfaction, specific satisfaction, consensus, love, sex adjustment, companionship, and compatability of personality and temperament. The number of items used to measure these various criteria ranged from 5 to 26.

DIFFERENCES OF MARITAL SUCCESS OF HUSBANDS AND WIVES

Husbands and wives often differ in the degree of their marital success as measured by a composite or multiple index. This is indicated by the correlation between the scores of husbands and the scores of wives. Terman found a correlation of .59 in his first study.[16] Terman and Oden, in their study of the marital adjustment of the "genius" children that Terman had studied, found a .52 correlation between the happiness scores of husbands and wives.[17] Burgess and Wallin, in their study of 1000 couples, reported a .41 correlation between marital-adjustment scores.[18] Locke found no correlation between the marital-adjustment scores of divorced subjects and only .36 for the happily married husbands and their wives.[19] These correlations indicate that in a considerable proportion of cases a union regarded as very satisfactory by one partner is viewed in a somewhat or entirely different light by the other.

The following summary statements secured from a couple three years after their marriage illustrate how a husband and wife may have widely different reactions to their marriage:

> The husband and wife differ in their expressions of satisfaction with the marriage. The wife reports that she is very much pleased and satisfied

---

[16] Terman, p. 82.
[17] Terman and Oden, pp. 241–242.
[18] Ernest W. Burgess and Paul Wallin, "Predicting Adjustment in Marriage from Adjustment in Engagement," *American Journal of Sociology*, 49 (1944): pp. 324–330.
[19] Locke, pp. 58–59.

while the husband states that he is very much dissatisfied with their marriage.

The wife is satisfied because her love for her husband is very much stronger than before the marriage, they are very much in love with each other, the marriage is very happy, her husband and she are well mated, she kisses her husband every day, sex has considerably strengthened the union, and nothing annoys or dissatisfies her with the marriage. While she admits that her husband smokes, swears, is impatient, is always wrapped up in his business, and criticizes her, she says none of these things interferes with the happiness of the marriage.

Only matters pertaining to in-laws and choice of friends have made the marriage less happy than it should have been. While she once considered the possibility of divorce, she has never regretted the marriage.

Th husband is dissatisfied because he feels that his love for his wife is considerably weaker than before the marriage, being now only somewhat in love; he would be happier being married to some other woman; occasionally she makes him feel miserable; he thinks a man is a fool to get married; his marriage could not be very much worse than it is; and marrying his wife was his biggest mistake. The unhappiness of his marriage is due to the fact that his wife is argumentative, unaffectionate, unfaithful, narrow-minded, selfish, inconsiderate, insincere, a poor housekeeper, desirous of much visiting and entertainment, tries to improve him, and nags him.

Sex relations have considerably weakened the union. He has seriously considered divorcing his wife. The only reason for not securing a divorce is his dislike of admitting failure. What annoys and dissatisfies him most about his marriage is "the hypocrisy connected with it, the lack of freedom, and the constant bickering over what is not important."

CONSTRUCTING A MARITAL-ADJUSTMENT INDEX

An index to measure success in marriage can be constructed in two different ways. One way (1) combine the various criteria into an expanded multiple index or (2) delete as many items as possible and thereby secure a short test of marital adjustment. Burgess in his study with Wallin favored the first approach. Locke and Thomes have used the second.

An Expanded Multiple Index of Marital Success Combining the 8 criteria for appraising marital success described in this chapter gives one a profile of marital success. Permanence of the union, happiness of the husband and wife, satisfaction with the marriage, sexual adjustment, marital adjustment, integration, consensus, and companionship are evidently not mutually exclusive. In fact, as far as studies offer evidence on this point, they indicate that the various criteria are interrelated. Undoubtedly there is a common element in all these criteria. At the same time, in each one of the criteria there is a separate variable which is important in determining the success of the union. For this reason it may be desirable to combine some or all of these, and possibly others, into a single instrument. This would have the advantage of an all-round representation of the outcome of the union, rather than the selection of only one criterion which may not be significant in certain cases.

Figure 14 exhibits how the 8 criteria may be combined into profiles of marital success. These two particular profiles are rough approximations of the case given at the beginning of the chapter, before the couple's temporary separation. Each item is scored on the basis of 10 possible points, which makes 80 points the maximum score a person could secure. In these particular profiles the husband and wife differ markedly on practically all of the 8 criteria. If these profiles are a correct picture of the marriage, the degree of marital success, while not high for either the husband or the wife, is higher for the husband. The husband has a score of 60 out of 80 possible points, and the wife only 38.

A Short Marital-Adjustment Index The expanded marital-success schedule of Burgess and Wallin, including the subitems, requires answers to approximately 246 items. This may take more time than is available, for in any given study one generally wants to ask many questions in addition to those on marital adjustment. A short test form has been constructed and is about as reliable and valid as the longer and more complex adjustment indices.[20]

Table 15 gives a short marital-adjustment instrument based on the Locke-Williamson factor analysis of a 20-item marital-adjustment test.[21] It will be noted that the items are listed under five general factors. A marital-adjustment score can be secured from answers to the questions. To take the test, one circles the number opposite the answer which best describes the relationship between the husband and wife.[22] For example, if a person in answering the first question decides that when disagreements arise neither gives in, he would circle 22. This is a code number and has nothing to do with the degree of adjustment in marriage. The code or key for the test is found in the footnote on p. 333. Of course, one would not look at the key before taking the test. With minor changes, these questions can be answered also by an engaged person.

---

[20] Harvey J. Locke and Karl M. Wallace, "Short Marital-Adjustment and Prediction Tests: Their Reliability and Validity," *Marriage and Family Living*, 21, (1959): pp. 251–255.

[21] Locke and Williamson, "Marital Adjustment."

[22] The weights are those secured in Harvey J. Locke's study of predicting adjustment in marriage and thus are arbitrary for any other sample.

328   *Measuring Success in Marriage*

Figure 14. Marital-success profiles of husband and wife

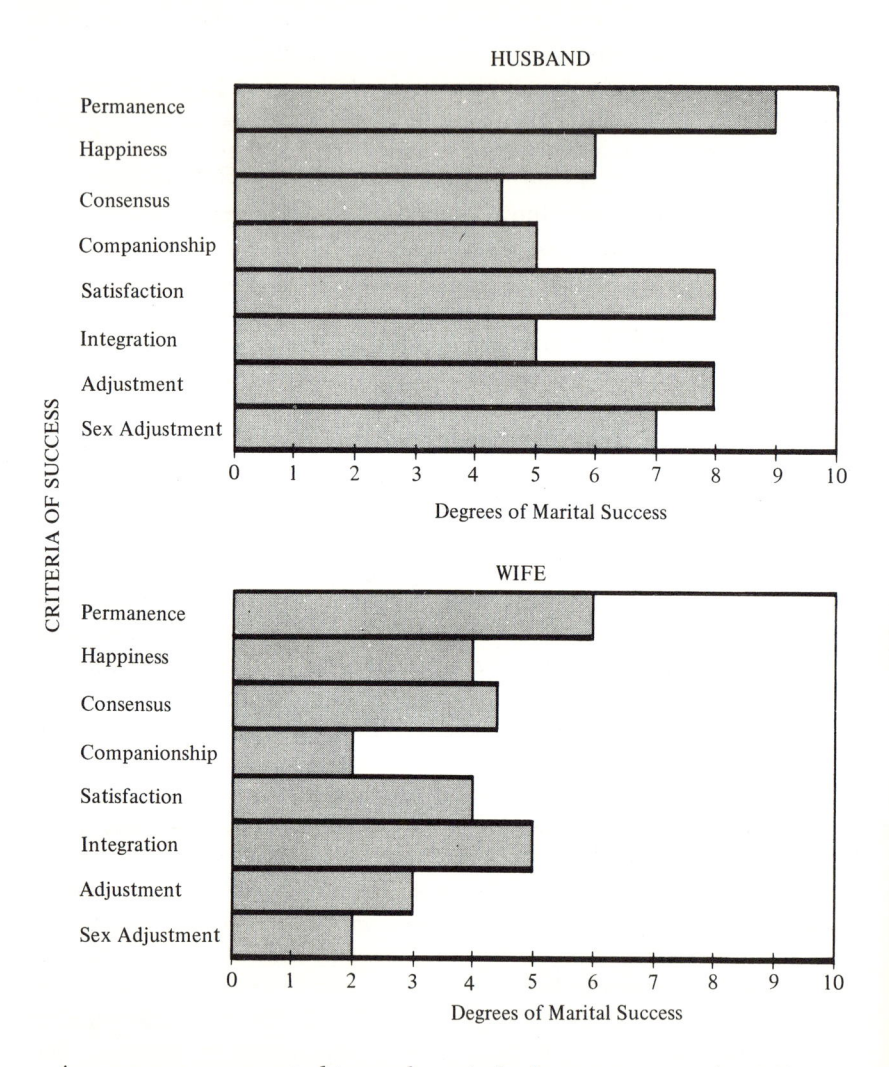

CRITERIA OF SUCCESS

HUSBAND

- Permanence
- Happiness
- Consensus
- Companionship
- Satisfaction
- Integration
- Adjustment
- Sex Adjustment

Degrees of Marital Success

WIFE

- Permanence
- Happiness
- Consensus
- Companionship
- Satisfaction
- Integration
- Adjustment
- Sex Adjustment

Degrees of Marital Success

A person can compute his total marital-adjustment score by following the instructions in the footnote on p. 333. The maximum score is 120 and the minimum is 49. Thus there is a spread of 71 points between the highest and the lowest possible score.

Anyone taking the marital-adjustment test generally wants to compare his score with some standard. A standard can be constructed by dividing the possible range of scores into approximate quarters. Scores from 103 through 120 represent the upper 25 percent of possible scores and can be considered an index of "good" marital adjustment. Scores from 85 through 102 represent the second 25 percent and indicate "fair" ad-

Table 15. An instrument to measure adjustment in marriage*

Instructions: The questions may be answered by either the husband, the wife, or both. Frank and honest replies are of the highest importance. There are no "right" or "wrong" answers. The following points are to be observed in answering the questions: (1) Be sure to answer all questions. Do not leave any blanks to signify "no" reply. (2) Do not confer with your mate in answering the questions or show your answers to him or her. (3) For each question circle the number given after the most appropriate answer.

I. *Companionship Factor*
1. When disagreements arise they generally result in:
   a. Husband giving in 50
   b. Wife giving in 31
   c. Neither giving in 22
   d. Agreement by mutual give-and-take 53
2. Do you and your mate agree on right, good and proper behavior?
   a. Always agree 61
   b. Almost always agree 51
   c. Occasionally disagree 40
   d. Frequently disagree 40
   e. Almost always disagree ..13
   f. Always disagree 22
3. Do husband and wife engage in outside activities together?
   a. All of them 34
   b. Some of them 24
   c. Few of them 13
   d. None of them 40
4. In leisure time, which do you and your mate prefer?
   a. Both husband and wife to stay at home 44
   b. Both to be on the go 51
   c. One to be on the go and the other to stay home 31

II. *Consensus or Agreement*
1. Do you and your mate agree on aims, goals, and things believed important in life?
   a. Always agree 26
   b. Almost always agree 15
   c. Occasionally disagree 40
   d. Frequently disagree 22
   e. Almost always disagree ..31
   f. Always disagree 13
2. Do you and your mate agree on friends?
   a. Always agree 25
   b. Almost always agree 70
   c. Occasionally disagree 40
   d. Frequently disagree 13
   e. Almost always disagree ..31
   f. Always disagree 40
3. Do you and your mate agree on ways of dealing with in-laws?
   a. Always agree 43
   b. Almost always agree 52
   c. Occasionally disagree 23
   d. Frequently disagree 23
   e. Almost always disagree ..32
   f. Always disagree 50
4. Do you and your mate agree on handling family finances?
   a. Always agree 25
   b. Almost always agree 16
   c. Occasionally disagree 22
   d. Frequently disagree 22
   e. Almost always disagree ..13
   f. Always disagree 40
5. Do you and your mate agree on amount of time spent together?
   a. Always agree 16
   b. Almost always agree 60

330 *Measuring Success in Marriage*

      c. Occasionally disagree 41
      d. Frequently disagree 40
      e. Almost always disagree ..31
      f. Always disagree 13

III. *Affectional Intimacy*

1. How often do you kiss your mate?
    a. Every day 25
    b. Now and then 23
    c. Almost never 50
2. How frequently do you and your mate get on each other's nerves around the house?
    a. Never 52
    b. Almost never 60
    c. Occasionally 50
    d. Frequently 23
    e. Almost always 32
    f. Always 41
3. Do you and your mate agree on demonstration of affection?**
    a. Always agree 16
    b. Almost always agree ...33
    c. Occasionally disagree 41
    d. Frequently disagree 14
    e. Almost always disagree ..23
    f. Always disagree 32

4. Check any of the following items which you think have caused serious difficulties in your marriage:
    Difficulties over money   ———
    Lack of mutual friends   ———
    Constant bickering   ———
    Interference of in-laws   ———
    Lack of mutual affection
      (no longer in love)   ———
    Unsatisfying sex relations   ———
    Selfishness and lack of
      cooperation   ———
    Adultery   ———
    Mate paid attention to
      (Became familiar with)
      another person   ———
    Drunkenness or alcoholism   ———
    Other reasons   ———
    Nothing   ———
    a. Nothing checked 44
    b. One checked 80
    c. Two checked 61
    d. Three checked 24
    e. Four or five checked 23
    f. Six or more checked 22

IV. *Satisfaction with the Marriage and the Mate*

1. Have you ever wished you had not married?
    a. Frequently 31
    b. Occasionally 22
    c. Rarely 34
    d. Never 26
2. Do you and your mate generally talk things over together?
    a. Never 31
    b. Now and then 40
    c. Almost always 33
    d. Always 16
3. How happy would you rate your marriage?
    a. Very happy 17
    b. Happy 43
    c. Average 40
    d. Unhappy 22
    e. Very unhappy 13
4. If you had your life to live again would you:
    a. Marry the same person? .27
    b. Marry a different person?.12
    c. Not marry at all? 21
5. What is the total number of times you left mate or mate left you because of conflict?**
    a. No times 54
    b. One time 13
    c. Two or more times 22

V. *Sexual Behavior*
1. What are your feelings on sex-relations with your mate?**
   a. Very enjoyable 43
   b. Enjoyable 52
   c. Tolerable 13
   d. A little enjoyable 22
   e. Not at all enjoyable 31
2. Do you and your mate agree on sex-relations?**
   a. Always agree 43
   b. Almost always agree 33
   c. Occasionally disagree 23
   d. Frequently disagree 50
   e. Almost always disagree ..41
   f. Always disagree 14
3. During sexual intercourse are your physical reactions satisfactory?**
   a. Very 34
   b. Somewhat 25
   c. A little 23
   d. Not at all 14
4. Is sexual intercourse between you and your mate an expression of love and affection?**
   a. Always 52
   b. Almost always 34
   c. Sometimes 42
   d. Almost never 22
   e. Never 13

---

*Based on Harvey J. Locke and Robert C. Williamson, "Marital Adjustment: A Factor Analysis Study," *American Sociological Review*, 23, 1958, pp. 562–569.
**Item not included in the factor analysis.

justment. Scores of 67 through 84 are in the third quarter and indicate that the adjustment is "questionable." Scores of 49 through 66 are in the lowest quarter and indicate "poor" marital adjustment.

A poor or questionable rating does not always mean that a marriage is failing. And if the score is above average or good, the marriage may still be less adjusted than indicated by the test. As will be shown more clearly in the next chapter, any individual score must be considered in an actuarial framework. In measuring marital adjustment, the term "actuarial" refers to the level of risk as determined by a large number of cases. For a group the test will give an approximate measure of marital adjustment. For any given individual, however, it may be an incorrect measure of his marital success.

SUMMARY

Eight different, though related, criteria have been used to measure success in marriage: permanence of the marriage, happiness of the husband and wife, satisfaction with the marriage, sexual compatibility, marital adjustment, integration of the couple, consensus, and companionship. Some of these are composite indexes, which actually include several of the other criteria.

Some investigators advocate combining several criteria into a measure of marital success, which would provide a profile of the husband and of the wife. This might be of particular value for the clinical analysis of a case. A short form of marital adjustment may be more economical in a research investigation.

PROBLEMS FOR RESEARCH

Criteria of Marital Success This chapter has shown that several criteria have already been developed and used in predictive studies of marital adjustment. It is desirable, of course, to revise and improve these instruments of measurement. It is also important to explore the possibilities of other facets of marital success, such as social expectations, personal expectations, and personality development. Aller, for example, found a correlation between a person's self-concept and marital adjustment.[23] A person's self-concept might be another index of marital adjustment. Veen and associates developed an 80-item Q sort composed of statements on family relationships.[24] This and other criteria to measure marital adjustments should be used to develop an efficient and reliable index of marital adjustment.

Comparison of Criteria No adequate comparison has been made of the relative value of the different criteria so far employed. To what extent are they measuring the same or different things? These different criteria may be applied to cases of married couples from whom detailed interview data has been secured to test the hypothesis that some criteria are more important for certain couples than for others.

An Empirical Measure of Marital Success The indexes of marital success which have been used by investigators were constructed on the basis of criteria used in previous studies and by common sense. By using the experiences of couples in their marriages, a more effective measure of marital success might be developed. Several methods of doing this in other areas of behavior have been devised. One is known as the critical-incident technique. This would involve going to a relatively large sample of husbands and wives and securing from them brief descriptions of an incident in marriage which they thought indicated success in marriage and a second incident which they thought indicated an unsuccessful marriage. Through content analysis the behavioral aspects of the incidents could be secured and would constitute the basis for a marital-adjustment test. A second method of using marital experiences is to

---

[23] Florence D. Aller, "The Self-Concept in Student Marital Adjustment," *Family Life Coordinator*, 11, (1962): pp. 43–45.

[24] F. van der Veen, B. Huebner, B. Jorgens, and P. Neja, "Relationships between the Parents' Concept of the Family and Family Adjustment, *American Journal of Orthopsychiatry*, 34 (1964): pp. 34, 45–55.

interview a sample of husbands and wives about things which indicate success or failure in marriage. A third method could be a modified Likert-type technique. This would involve four essential steps. (1) Formulate a large number of statements believed to be indicative of success or failure in marriage from interviews with married subjects, from common sense or from experts. (2) Submit these statements to a large sample of husbands and wives to indicate the degree of their agreement with the statements on a five-point scale: strongly agree, agree, uncertain, disagree, and strongly disagree. (3) Analyze responses item-by-item for internal consistency. Responses to each item are analyzed to determine which items discriminate most clearly between the highest (quartile) scorers and the lowest (quartile) scorers on the *total* items. (4) The most discriminating items are retained and are arranged in a marital-adjustment test. The main point in each of these methods is that the actual experience of married persons are used in the construction of a marital-adjustment test.

Criteria of Family Success In this chapter consideration has been confined to criteria of marital success. Children have been considered only to the extent to which they influence the nature of the relationship between a husband and wife. When children are added to the husband-wife unit, the interests of the family may supersede those of the husband-wife relationship, and family success may then become the more important area for study. This will necessitate devising criteria to measure family success which will include the criteria of marital success and also appropriate criteria of parent-child and sibling relations.

QUESTIONS AND EXERCISES

1. Describe the essential features of each of the 8 criteria of marital success.
2. Examine these criteria from the standpoint of the degree of difficulty which you would have in grading them, and then arrange them in order from the least to the greatest difficulty.
3. What are the objections to the use of some of these criteria? Are the

Computing Scores The first step in computing the marital-adjustment score is to add the digits of the number circled. For example, assuming a person circled 22 for the first question, his score for this question would be 2 + 2. A score for each question is obtained in this way and all are added together. Then 44 is subtracted from this score. This is because we added 2 points to the weight of each answer of the 22 questions in order to secure more combinations of digits.

For the marital-prediction test presented in the next chapter, follow the procedure as outlined above, but subtract 60 from the total score rather than 44.

objections to the use of happiness as a criterion of marital success warranted?
4. To what extent do these criteria measure the same or different aspects of marital success?
5. Analyze the introductory case according to each of the criteria. Which seem most adequate and which most inadequate for the measurement of the success of this particular family?
6. Write a description and explanation of a case of a married couple who are not well adjusted and yet are satisfied with their marriage.
7. Interview a divorced couple and a presumably happily married couple, using one or more of the criteria as a measure of the marital success of each couple.

BIBLIOGRAPHY

Burgess, Ernest W.; and Cottrell, Leonard S. *Predicting Success or Failure in Marriage.* New York: Prentice-Hall, 1939, Chs. 4 and 5.
> Sample consisted of 526 marriages. Marital adjustment was measured by a 26-item test on five areas of behavior: agreements and disagreements, common interests and activities, demonstration of affection and confiding, dissatisfaction with the marriage, and feelings of personal isolation and unhappiness.

Burgess, Ernest W.; and Wallin, Paul. *Engagement and Marriage.* Philadelphia: Lippincott. 1953.
> Based on study of 1000 engaged couples; 666 of the couples were interviewed after three years of marriage. Engagement adjustment measured by slightly modified Burgess-Cottrell marital-adjustment test. Success in marriage measured by a multiple index composed of nine criteria.

Farber, Bernard. "An Index of Marital Integration," *Sociometry: A Journal of Research in Social Psychology,* 20 (1957): pp. 117–134.
> Sample consisted of 99 couples. Success measured by similarity of husband-wife scores on 10 family values or objectives.

Hamilton, Gilbert V. A. *Research in Marriage.* New York, Albert & Charles Boni, 1929: Ch. 3, "Kinds of Degrees of Spousal Satisfaction and Dissatisfaction."
> Based on study of 100 married men and women, including 55 couples. Satisfaction measured by a marital-satisfaction test composed of 13 questions. This was the earliest attempt to construct a marital-adjustment test. Some of the test items have been used by subsequent investigators.

Kirkpatrick, Clifford. "Community of Interest and the Measurement of Marriage Adjustment," *The Family,* 18 (1937): pp. 133–137.
> Based on study of 58 well-adjusted and 47 poorly-adjusted couples: relatives

and friends of students. Success based on ratings by students as "well and "poorly" adjusted.

Locke, Harvey J. *Predicting Adjustment in Marriage: A Comparison of a Divorced and a Happily Married Group.* New York, Henry Holt, 1951: Ch. 3.
> Based on study of 201 divorced couples, plus 123 persons where only one side co-operated; 200 happily-married couples, plus 4 with only one co-operating. Success measured by a marital-adjustment test.

Locke, Harvey J.; and Williamson, Robert C. "Marital Adjustment: A Factor Analysis Study," *American Sociological Review,* 23, (1958): pp. 562–569.
> Sample consisted of 171 husbands and 178 wives. Factor analysis revealed five general factors: companionship, consensus, affectional intimacy, wife accommodation, and euphoria. Data were not collected on sex items in this study; consequently, items on sex adjustment should be added to this test.

Terman, Lewis M.; and others. *Psychological Factors in Marital Happiness.* New York: McGraw-Hill, 1938: Ch. 4.
> Sample consisted of 792 husbands and their wives. Happiness measured by scores on a marital-happiness test composed of 9 general questions, the subparts consisting of most of the Burgess-Cottrell items.

Chapter 14
Predicting Adjustment in Marriage

Studies of predicting adjustment in the marriage dyad followed closely on attempts to predict personal adjustment in other areas of human behavior. Prediction techniques had already been applied to school achievement, vocational adjustment, personnel selection, and behavior of persons on parole from prison. Predicting adjustment in marriage, involving as it does the interaction of two persons, is more difficult than predicting behavior in areas involving only one person.

The basic assumption in predicting adjustment in marriage is that the personality characteristics and past experiences and interactions of two persons conditions their future conduct. The primary feature of the prediction technique is, therefore, the investigation and analysis of past experiences of persons in a particular area and then the use of this information to predict the probable future behavior of others in that area of behavior. The conclusion of marital-adjustment studies is that the success or failure of marriage in the future may be predicted not only before but after marriage with some degree of accuracy.

A CASE STUDY IN PREDICTION

People are always engaged in making common-sense "predictions" about the behavior of their fellows. Particularly before marriage the parents and friends of the bridegroom and bride discuss their family backgrounds and characteristics and forecast their chances for marital success. Psychologists and sociologists in making predictions utilize much the same data, but organize them systematically and develop theories and hypothesis. Burgess and Wallin gathered personal case materials through interviews with some of their engaged couples. In the following case they predicted that in marriage this couple would be in the high-adjustment group:

James (during engagement): We were a very happy family. There was occasional jealousy between me and my next oldest brother. I was closer to Father than to Mother. My mother was very good to me. But I confided more in my father, even as a child. I didn't feel at all dependent upon my mother for affection and advice. I went to my father in all cases. It seems as though my father took a more personal interest in me. We used to go hunting and fishing together. My father was my pal.

My parents' marriage was happy. I think they had happiness in their children. There was a lack on my mother's part to give Father credit for the things that he had done. We might call it "nagging" at times.

I met Eleanor first about three years before I started going steady with her. It was at a party. The first time I met her, I was interested. We met off and on, mostly at parties and several times at church. Then one time two years ago I drove her home and we had a chance to talk over things. From that time on, we've been going steady. Our love became real as our friendship developed. I don't think either of us would say that it was love at first sight. Her interests were so similar to mine, and I was yearning for some companionship at the time. I am receiving the most happiness I ever could receive from anyone or anything. But I am not blindly or unreasonably in love. I'm pretty self-sufficient, but she has encouraged me, done many little things for me, and helped me to be more aggressive. I think she needs sympathy and encouragement more than I do.

We have no disagreements whatsoever. We like just about all the same things. Our friends are all practically mutual. I said kiddingly that I didn't want a church wedding, but deep down in my heart I wanted it. She wants a large wedding and I don't. We will have a church wedding, but it won't be very large.

There is not much similarity between Eleanor and Mother. Eleanor is not quick tempered, but my mother is. My mother is stubborn, Eleanor is not. My mother is inclined to agree but not mean it. Eleanor will not agree with people unless she means it.

Eleanor (during engagement): My father has always been closest to me. My mother, too, but my father a little more. Father is more easygoing. He always let me have my own way. Mother was always more strict. I have always been called "Daddy's baby." I think my mother preferred my younger brother. He and I got on just fine.

Jim and I first met at a party. We attended a number of parties, and finally Jim took me home. I took a particular liking to him from the first time I saw him. I thought he was pretty swell and fell in love with him before I started going with him.

I don't think I have an even temper. I fly off the handle, but I usually get over it quickly. I get along with everyone. If something is not done the way I think it should be, I won't come out and say it, but you can tell, by the way I act, how I feel. I think perhaps I'm more stubborn than Jim.

Jim claims he always admired me. From the first he has always been very attentive and very unselfish. About a month after we were going steady he told me he loved me. He is pretty self-sufficient. I like to a certain extent to be sympathized with, which he does. Our interests are very much the same, church work, the same sports, etc. We have a lot of the same friends.

All my family are for him. They think he is a wonderful boy. His mother would just as soon have him at home, but she has been very kind to me. Both Father and Jim have a very even temper, are very congenial, and go out of their way to help people. Jim is more self-sufficient. My mother is always self-sufficient like Jim. That is the chief way in which they are alike.

James (three years after marriage): The biggest things I've gotten out of marriage are companionship, being able to work together, sympathy, and understanding. Now that we have a child, it adds more. It is something to work for. It draws two people together. After the child came, we began to realize how much we love each other. Marriage gives one a feeling of responsibility and an incentive to succeed. I am a very happy man and have no complaints. Our love has increased tremendously.

We belong to the church, and our common interests have been built around the church. We belong to several clubs, and we play cards. We play golf occasionally. We always take our vacations together.

Eleanor (three years after marriage): My greatest gains from marriage have been happiness, a lot of pleasant experiences, and a fine little son. Just an all-around life, that is all. I feel my family is the most worth while thing in life. I know his family stands high with him.

I think that Jim takes the lead. We always talk over our decisions and make them together. We belong to several groups. We do almost everything together. The majority of our friends are from the church. We both enjoy church. Our sports are similar.

Let us enumerate some of the factors in the above case that entered into mate selection and marital success. (1) James and Eleanor had numerous social contacts before they began going together through attendance at parties. (2) They were of similar cultural backgrounds and had the same interests in church, friends, sports, and other recreation. (3) Their love was based on association and friendship and was not a sudden infatuation. (4) Their relationship reproduced the response pattern that had been the most important to each in childhood. James thought of his fiancée in her personality characteristics as the opposite of his mother. Eleanor, however, described herself as having the very traits which he disliked in his mother: getting angry, being stubborn, and not expressing feelings of disapproval. Perhaps James was attracted to her because she had the same personality traits as his mother but in a form that was agreeable rather than irritating to him. (5) These young people appear to have adjusted excellently to each other. (6) Both are of the domestic type, placing family life above all other values. The interplay of dynamic factors in the relation as inferred from the interview data seems to presage a very happy married life.

This chapter is devoted primarily to a description and analysis of predictive items associated with marital adjustment. Consideration will be given to four main topics: (1) studies predicting adjustment in marriage, (2) predicting adjustment in marriage, (3) general predictive factors of marital adjustment, and (4) predicting future marital adjustment.

STUDIES OF PREDICTING ADJUSTMENT IN MARRIAGE

Six major studies of predicting adjustment in marriage have been published,[1] in addition to many less inclusive ones dealing with individual items or specialized investigations. All the major studies included a marital-adjustment index in which several items were combined. They also included a large number of predictive items on such things as courtship experiences, educational level, influence of in-laws, sexual adjustment, and personality characteristics.

The major investigations, except the two in which Locke was involved, used samples composed of volunteers having high income and education. The studies by Locke and by Locke and Karlsson had two unique features: (1) the samples were representative of the general population, and (2) marital adjustment was measured by not only a marital-adjustment index but by independent indexes, such as divorce or happiness in marriage.

The annotated bibliography at the end of the chapter provides a more complete description of the major studies. The analysis of predictive

---

[1] Ernest W. Burgess and Leonard S. Cottrell, *Predicting Success or Failure in Marriage* (New York: Prentice-Hall, 1939); Lewis M. Terman and others, *Psychological Factors in Marital Happiness* (New York: McGraw-Hill, 1938); Lewis M. Terman and Melita H. Oden, *The Gifted Child Grows Up: Twenty-Five Years' Follow-up of a Superior Group* (Stanford: Stanford University Press, 1947), Ch. 19; Harvey J. Locke, *Predicting Adjustment in Marriage: A Comparison of a Divorced and a Happily-Married Group* (New York: Henry Holt, 1951); Georg Karlsson, *Adaptability and Communication in Marriage: A Swedish Predictive Study of Marital Satisfaction* (Uppsala, Sweden: Almqvist and Wiksells, 1951); and Ernest W. Burgess and Paul Wallin, *Engagement and Marriage* (Philadelphia: Lippincott, 1953).

factors of marital adjustment presented in this chapter is based primarily on the research findings of these studies.

PREDICTING ADJUSTMENT IN MARRIAGE

A marital-adjustment test and a marital-prediction test are designed to do different work for an investigator. The first measures the degree of adjustment which exists at a given time; the second predicts the degree of adjustment which will exist in the future. The conclusions from both are always stated in terms of probabilities.

Three Procedures of Prediction The prediction of marital adjustment involves three procedures: the search for items associated with adjustment in marriage, the combination of items into a test, and the formation of an actuarial table.

1. A physician differentiates between the symptoms of a disease and the factors involved in its origin and development. So, likewise, the investigator differentiates between the items predictive of marital adjustment and the causative factors producing it. The person not familiar with prediction procedures may be disturbed to find that some symptoms of adjustment are absent in adjusted marriages, and that some adjusted persons answer a few questions like the unadjusted. Similarly, some symptoms of unadjustment may be absent in the poorly adjusted, and some unadjusted person may answer a few questions like the adjusted. But these variations tend to disappear when a large number of items are combined in a prediction test.

2. In prediction one combines a number of items into a prediction index. No one item, or even a few items, can be used to predict the success or failaure of a marriage. The procedure is to discover a series of items which, in general, are answered differently by the adjusted and unadjusted. Scores are determined for each answer, and then these scores or points are added and the total is a person's prediction score for marital adjustment. The size of the prediction score indicates the probability of a person's adjustment in marriage.

3. The prediction index is always placed and interpreted in an actuarial framework. Investigators have used different methods to show how much marital adjustment can be expected for a given marital-prediction score. The one used by Locke in his Indiana study was as follows: His prediction test included 137 items for men and 140 for women. The test had a lowest possible score, a neutral or nondiscriminating score, and a highest possible score. For men, the respective lowest, neutral, and highest scores were 389, 548, and 693; and for women, 381, 560,

and 721.[2] Using the neutral score as a point of reference, the more one's prediction score approaches the lowest score, the less one's probable marital adjustment, and the more one's score approaches the highest score, the greater his chances of marital adjustment. Words such as likelihood, probably, expected, and chances indicate the actuarial nature of a prediction test. The prediction score indicates the expected degree of marital adjustment for a group of persons, not for a particular person. The prediction score of an individual simply indicates the expected risk level of his marital adjustment.

An Example of a Marital-Prediction Index A short marital-prediction index is given in Table 16. It is composed of 30 of the most discriminating items from the various marital-adjustment studies.[3] Scores are obtained by the same procedure as described above for the marital-adjustment test.

Table 16. An index to predict adjustment in marriage

Instructions: This set of questions is prepared for persons who are seriously considering marriage. Although designed for couples who are engaged or who have a private understanding to be married, they can also be answered by other persons who would like to know the probability of their adjustment in marriage. The value of the results of the questions depends on your frankness in answering the questions. The following points should be observed in filling out the questions: (1) Be sure to answer every question. Do not leave a blank to mean a "no" answer. (2) The word "fiance(e)" will be used to refer to either the man or the woman to whom you are engaged or are considering as a possible marriage partner. (3) Do not confer with your fiance(e) on any of the questions. (4) Circle the number opposite the most appropriate answer.

1. What do you think the length of time will be between your engagement and marriage?
   a. Less than a month 50
   b. 1 to 5 months 14
   c. 6 to 11 months 24
   d. 12 months and over 61
2. How much conflict is there between you and your fiance(e)?
   a. None 43
   b. A little 25
   c. Moderate 41
   d. A good deal 22
   e. Very great 13
3. How much affection is there between you and your fiance(e)?
   a. None 13
   b. A little 22

---

[2] Locke, p. 319.
[3] The weights are those secured in Harvey J. Locke's study of predicting adjustment in marriage and thus are arbitrary for any other sample.

    c. Moderate 31
    d. A good deal 60
    e. Very great 44
4. What is the attitude of your parents toward your fiance(e)?
    a. Approval 61
    b. Disapproval 14
    c. Indifferent 23
    d. Do not know him (her) .60
5. What is the difference in age between you and your fiance(e)?
    a. Equal or not more than 2 years 70
    b. 3 to 10 years 50
6. How happy would you rate your childhood?
    a. Very happy 52
    b. Happy 16
    c. Average 33
    d. Unhappy 23
    e. Very unhappy 41
7. What was the discipline in your parental home?
    a. Never had own way 41
    b. Usually had own way ...61
    c. Always had own way ...41
8. What was the degree of happiness of your parents' marriage?
    a. Very happy 70
    b. Happy 60
    c. Average 32
    d. Unhappy 23
    e. Very unhappy 14
9. What is the highest level of education you will have completed by the time of your marriage?
    a. Elementary (eighth grade) 23
    b. High school 32
    c. Two years of college ...60
    d. College graduate 25
    e. Graduate work 16
10. Is your fiance(e) jealous of you?
    a. Yes 22
    b. No 17
11. Do you and your fiance(e) both desire to have children during marriage?
    a. Yes 16
    b. No 14
12. What is the church affiliation of you and your fiance(e)?
    a. Only one of you is a member of a church 23
    b. Neither belongs to a church 41
    c. Both belong to same church 61
    d. Belong to different churches 33
13. What is the frequency of your monthly church attendance?
    a. No times 23
    b. Once or less 60
    c. 2 or 3 times 52
    d. 4 or more times 61
14. Do you feel that your fiance(e) is over-modest and shy in attitudes toward sex?
    a. Very much 50
    b. A good deal 14
    c. Some 70
    d. Very little 16
    e. Not at all 42
15. Do you feel that the strength of your interest in sex, as compared with that of your fiance(e), is:
    a. Very much greater 23
    b. Much greater 42
    c. About the same 16
    d. Much less intense 23
    e. Very much less intense ..41
16. Do you feel that during marriage you will refuse sexual intercourse when your mate desires it?
    a. Frequently 41
    b. Sometimes 23
    c. Rarely 16
    d. Never 15

Rate your fiance(e) on the following personality traits. Be sure to rate each trait. Put the score for each question in the right-hand column.

Trait	Very much so	Considerably	Somewhat	A little	Not at all	
17. Takes responsibility willingly	25	52	24	32	22	——
18. Dominating	41	23	33	42	70	——
19. A leader in school or other group	43	52	61	32	23	——
20. Able to make decisions readily	61	16	33	23	14	——
21. Easily influenced by others	13	32	15	61	52	——
22. "Gives in" in arguments	43	52	43	14	22	——
23. Gets angry easily	13	14	16	25	34	——
24. Gets over anger quickly	52	43	33	14	23	——
25. Affectionate	25	25	32	14	23	——
26. Demonstrative	33	24	61	32	23	——
27. Sociable—makes friends easily	52	33	42	41	23	——
28. Likes belonging to organizations	33	34	52	33	32	——
29. Cares what people say and think	33	34	61	23	14	——
30. Has a sense of humor	61	33	33	13	22	——

A person can compute his total marital-prediction score by following the instructions of the key in the footnote on page 333. The maximum score is 152 and the minimum score is 81. The neutral score, which predicts neither adjustment nor maladjustment, is 4 times the number of questions (30), or 120.

A person answering the marital-prediction questions generally will want to compare his score with some standard. One can use the neutral score as the point of reference and say that the closer one's score is to the maximum, the greater his chances of adjustment in marriage, and the closer it is to the minimum score, the less the chances of adjustment in marriage. A more specific standard can be constructed by dividing the range from the minimum to the maximum scores into approximate quarters. Scores of 135 through 152 represent the upper quarter of possible scores and can be considered an index of "good" chances of adjustment in marriage; scores of 117–134 can be considered "fair"; scores of 99–116 are termed "questionable"; and those of 81–98 are "poor."

One should use the results of this index with extreme caution. For one thing, it is but a part of the larger validated index.[4] Moreover, it simply gives an actuarial picture of the risk group into which a person's prediction score falls, and, like all actuarial tables, it is not predictive of an individual case.

Premarital- and Marital-Predictive Items To predict the marital adjustment of an engaged couple, one obviously has to use premarital items. On the other hand, to predict the future marital adjustment of a married couple, one uses both premarital and marital items. A list of premarital- and a list of marital-predictive items, found to be significantly related to marital adjustment by one or more studies, is included in Appendix A. The findings of the various investigators on each item are also included. An analysis of the significant items reported in the six major studies and the more limited studies completed before publication of this text reveals much agreement by the different investigators. This is particularly interesting, since the studies were made in different places, in different years, and with different types of subjects. There were 70 significant *premarital*-prediction items, and of these 49 were reported by two or more studies and of these 26 by four or more studies. There were 45 *marital*-prediction items, and of these 32 were found by two or more studies and of these 12 were reported by four or more studies.

The following list gives the 26 premarital and the 12 marital items reported by four or more studies, along with the characteristic of the item which is associated with marital adjustment:

Premarital-Predictive Items	*Number of Studies Reporting*
1. Acquaintance: well, or over 6 months	6
2. Adaptability: good general adjustment	4
3. Age at marriage: 20 or older for women, 22 or older for men	7
4. Age differential: man older or the same age as woman	6
5. Attachment to father: close	4
6. Attachment to mother: close	4
7. Church attendance: 2 to 4 times a month	4
8. Church membership	4
9. Conflict with father: none or very little	5
10. Conflict with mother: none or very little	5
11. Discipline: not harsh	4
12. Educational level: some college or college graduate	6

[4] *Ibid.*, pp. 319–337.

13. Engagement: 9 months or longer[5] 4
14. Friends before marriage: few or several women friends 4
15. Happiness of childhood: happy or very happy 4
16. Happiness of parents' marriage: happy or very happy 7
17. Married by: clergyman 4
18. Mental ability: equal 4
19. Occupation: professional 4
20. Organizations: member of some 4
21. Parents' attitude toward mate: approval 6
22. Savings: some 4
23. Sex instruction: adequate 4
24. Sex, source of information: parents 4
25. Sex relations, premarital: none or only with future spouse .. 8
26. Sunday-school attendance: some and beyond childhood 5

Marital-Predictive Items
1. Children: desire for[6] 4
2. Conflict, over activities: none 4
3. Economic level: home owned 6
4. Employment: regular by husband 4
5. Employment of wife: employed and husband approves 4
6. Equality of husband and wife (not superior or inferior) 5
7. Mental ability: rated equal by partner 4
8. Occupation of husband: professional 4
9. Personality traits: nonneurotic and culturally approved 7
10. Sexual intercourse: confined to marriage, little refusal of ... 4
11. Sex: equal strength of desire 5
12. Sex enjoyment: enjoyable or very enjoyable 5

GENERAL PREDICTIVE FACTORS OF MARITAL ADJUSTMENT

The above items, along with others which are correlated with marital adjustment, may be classified under the following nine basic factors: personality characteristics, cultural backgrounds, social participation, courtship experiences, age at marriage, education, adjustment to the kinship group, sexual behavior, and number of childden.

Personality Characteristics Marital adjustment is associated with the presence or absence of certain personality characteristics. Most of the evidence on the predictive value of personality characteristics is from

---

[5] The studies were not entirely consistent as to length of engagement: 1 was nine months or longer, 1 was 12 months or longer, and 2 were 24 months or longer. In addition, 1 study reported 3 months or longer for women and 6 months or longer for men.

[6] Six studies found no relationship between the presence or absence of children and marital adjustment.

ratings of the mate on 16 traits; from certain indexes of sociability, such as the number of friends; from indexes of conventionality, such as whether one is affiliated with a church; and from psychological characteristics, particularly the presence or absence of neurotic tendencies.

In the studies by Locke and Locke and Karlsson, ratings of the mate on 16 personality traits were much more predictive than ratings of self. In Locke's study, on ratings of mate, there were 14 which differentiated between adjusted and unadjusted for both men and women; in the Swedish study there were 13.[7]

The following are predictive of marital adjustment when ratings of mate are used: the ready assumption of responsibility, strictness in dealing with children, leadership in the community, quickness in making decisions, expressions of determination, resistance to the influence of relatives and friends, yielding in arguments quickly, not being dominating, slowness in getting angry, quickness in getting over anger, enjoyment in belonging to organizations, moderate concern over what people say and think, a sense of humor, affectionateness, and demonstration of affection.

Similarity of personality characteristics of the husband and wife is associated with marital adjustment.[8] The degree of agreement between the image a subject has of the mate on a particular personality trait and the mate's image of him on this trait was studied by Hurley and Silvert. They used the Personal Preference Schedule, PPS, of Edwards for the personality characteristics. They report: "PPS mate-image congruity is generally and positively associated with marital adjustment." Also mate-image correspondence appears to be more highly associated with marital adjustment than is self-report.[9]

The following excerpt from an interview with a happily married couple shows the value placed by the husband on one of these personality traits—not being dominating:

> I think that a dominating person is about the worst person to be around. But neither of us tries to dominate the other. I have a horse and sometimes after getting through work, I go out to my horse. She does not enjoy such things, but she appreciates my interest. I do the same with the

---

[7] Locke, Chs. 9–11, particularly p. 173; and Karlsson, pp. 198–203. Similar findings are reported by Eleanor Braun Luckey, "Marital Satisfaction and Personality Correlates of Spouse," *Journal of Marriage and the Family*, 26 (1964): pp. 217–220.

[8] John A. Pickford, Edro I. Signorie, and Henry Rempel, "Similar or Related Personality Traits as a Factor in Marital Happiness," *Journal of Marriage and the Family*, 28 (1966): pp. 190–192.

[9] John F. Hurley and Diane M. Silvert, "Mate-Image Congruity and Marital Adjustment," *The 1966 Convention Proceedings of the American Psychological Association*, pp. 219–220.

things which she enjoys. I think of my days as my own but the evenings I spend with her, if she has nothing else to do.

Sociability, as measured by the possession of several or many friends before marriage, during marriage, and in common with mate during marriage, is a positive symptom of marital adjustment, and the absence of sociability, as measured by the relative lack of friends, is a negative factor.

Conventionality is very predictive of marital adjustment. Four or more studies found the following to be correlated with marital adjustment and these are considered to be indexes of conventionality: being married by a minister and not by the justice of the peace, attending Sunday school beyond childhood, and being a member of a church at the time of marriage. Additional indexes of conventionality associated with marital adjustment are husband older than the wife; church attendance of the husband 2 or more times a month and of the wife 4 times a month; husband with savings at the time of marriage; and weddings in church, in a parsonage, or at home.

Lucky made a study of personality perception and marital adjustment of 80 married couples, who were married from two to twenty years. She found that the longer the couples were married the less favorable personality qualities they saw in their mates.[10]

The following list of "prescriptions for a happy marriage" was given by a happily married husband and could be duplicated by excerpts from many case histories. The list is of conventional values and illustrates the point that the research investigator must look for the meaning of a subject's responses and not just at the responses themselves:

> (1) Have a religion and live up to it. If a man and wife really live their religion and read their Bible, they will not let troubles bother them, and will get along. We do not believe in divorce, for our religion is against it. Moreover, we do not even think of it, for we get along so well. (2) The man or woman should not try to be the whole boss. They should work things out together. (3) Keep away from dance halls and beer joints; they will break up a home faster than anything else. If one goes to dance halls, the wife or husband may think that the other is dancing too much or too close to someone. If one goes to a beer joint, a person may get tight and be too fresh with another person. (4) A woman should keep the house clean and have the meals ready when the husband comes home from work. (5) A man should come in from work happy and stay home with the wife and not go running around.

---

[10] Eleanor B. Lucky, "Number of Years Married as Related to Personality Perception and Marital Satisfaction," *Journal of Marriage and the Family*, 28 (1966): pp. 44–48.

The following psychological characteristics are positively associated with marital adjustment: (1) a happy temperament, as indicated by a predisposition to be optimistic rather than pessimistic; (2) a tolerant and considerate attitude toward others; and (3) nonneurotic behavior, as measured by an inventory of neurotic behavior.

Cultural Backgrounds Similarity of cultural background is favorable, and dissimilarity, if sufficiently great, is unfavorable to adjustment in marriage. Persons from different cultural levels who marry may have difficulty in forming a unity of communicating personalities, for there will be cultural barriers to communication. Such persons may cherish different meanings, behave differently in situations, have fewer common interests, and, consequently, have less unity in their relationship.

Social Participation A group of background items, constituting what might be called the social-participation factor in marital adjustment, is significantly related to success in marriage. Among these items are objective evidence of religious activity, such as duration and frequency of attendance at Sunday school and church; the degree of participation in social organizations; and the number and sex of friends. These items, taken together, constitute an index of sociability, or social participation. Participation in church activities possibly applies only to the cultural setting of the United States. Locke and Karlsson in their Swedish study found that belonging to a church was more frequent in the unadjusted than in the adjusted group, although other indexes of sociability were more frequent in the adjusted.[11]

In a probability sample of 4,452 households in Alameda County, California, the number of close friends and relatives and the frequency of seeing close friends and relatives were both related to the degree of satisfaction with the marriage. The findings are summarized as follows:

> People with few intimate associates were more likely than others to be dissatisfied with their marriages; in other words, marital satisfaction is related to the number of "close" relatives and friends claimed by the respondent. Social isolates—those who claimed no more than two close friends and no more than two close relatives—were much more likely than others of the same race, sex, and age to be unhappily married.
>
> A more objective criterion—number of friends seen, rather than felt close to—produces the same pattern. Those who saw fewer than three close friends or relatives monthly were distinctly more likely than others to be dissatisfied with their marriages.[12]

[11] Harvey J. Locke and Georg Karlsson, "Marital Adjustment and Prediction in Sweden and the United States," *American Sociological Review*, 17 (1952): pp. 10–17; and Karlsson, *Adaptability and Communication in Marriage.*

[12] Karen S. Renne, "Correlates of Dissatisfaction in Marriage," *Journal of Marriage and the Family*, 32 (1970): pp. 65–66.

Courtship Experience A unified family is one in which the members have similar or shared attitudes and values. This unification process begins before the marriage ceremony and continues afterward. Consequently, the experiences during the period of courtship and engagement are likely to be potent forces making for or against the success of a marriage. The length of the period of acquaintance and the length of engagement are indexes of the degree to which the unifying process has developed before marriage.

Differences in the length and type of engagement of maladjusted and adjusted marriages are seen in the two following excerpts from life-history materials. In the first, a divorced woman expresses regret for marrying a man whom she had known when she was a little girl but whom she had not seen as an adult until three days before the marriage:

> I had known this fellow when I was a little girl, but hadn't seen him for a long time. He had went away, and then he came back. I was 18 about then. He was there 3 days, and on the third day I married him. There wasn't no courtship or engagement. We were really just pals. He was back from the place where he was working and he says, "Let's get married, and I won't go back, but will stay here." I liked him all right, and it seemed the thing to do. So we got married. I don't think those kind of marriages are good. You didn't know no others or have any experiences. I found out later that there wasn't really love like it should be. Even at that we would have done all right, if he hadn't met up with the old friends and took to gambling again.

The second case is that of a happily married woman who was engaged for 6 months. She describes the way her brother and mother entered into the courtship process:

> From the time I started dating my husband, I knew that I wanted to marry him. I had had a few dates with him, and my brother wanted to meet him. So I asked my brother and my mother to go to church with us. On the way back I walked with my mother, and my brother walked with "Smiles," which was the nickname of my husband. When we were at breakfast the next morning, my brother told me what a fine boy he thought "Smiles" was. He had asked him about his jobs, his family, and so on. So after that my mother didn't worry about it and began to like "Smiles." In 6 months we were married.

A relatively long period of acquaintance and engagement is associated with adjusted marriages and a relatively short period with unadjusted marriages. The specific length of acquaintance which is predictive of marital adjustment varied from one study to another, but most reported a year or more. All data point to the conclusion that, on the average, the longer the period of intimate association before the marriage, the greater the probability of marital adjustment. Such marriages are likely to be based on companionship. Moreover, the longer period of association tests whether the two persons are temperamentally and emotionally compatible and whether they have similar values and attitudes. Through a long process of cultural conditioning, a person builds up a mental picture of the kind of person he would like to marry. With this mental picture of the ideal mate, the tendency is to impute to a person characteristics he may not have. Courtship involves exploration, the purpose being to discover the kind of person the other is. If the exploration is carried on only over a few weeks, chances of happiness in marriage are reduced. A period of acquaintance of two or three years and an engagement of about a year affords an opportunity to discover the differences between what the love object is imagined to be and what the person actually is, and, if the differences are too great, of separating oneself from that person. A long period of premarital association also enables the persons to become accommodated to each other on the basis of companionship. Interdependent habits built up over time condition the couple so that they will know in advance the reactions of each other to a given situation and shape their conduct accordingly.

Age at Marriage Age is a potent factor in marital adjustment. This is shown by an analysis of the rate of marital dissolution by different ages at first marriage. Carter and Glick did this for those whose marriages had been broken by divorce or death during the period 1940–1944 to 1960 and 1945–1949 to 1960. Table 17 gives the percent of all marriages which had been dissolved during these two time periods for different ages at first marriage. For white and nonwhite men the rate of dissolution was highest for those who married at the age of 14–19; it was lowest for those marrying at age 25–29. This was true for those whose marriage dissolved during a 15 to 20 year period and a 10 to 15 year period.

Marriages of very young women had the highest dissolution rates—with early teenagers having the highest rate, followed closely by later teenagers. For white and nonwhite women the highest rate of marital dissolution for both time periods—1940–1944 to 1960 and 1945–1949 to 1960—was for those marrying at the young age of 14 to 17, with the next highest rate for those who married at the age of 18 or 19. Those marrying in the age period of 20–24 had about the same low rate of marital dissolution as those marrying in the age period 25–29.

White and nonwhite men and women had the same pattern. Those who married before 20 had much higher rates of marital dissolution than those who married at a later age.

The table also shows that the nonwhite marital dissolution rate was much higher than the white rate. This was the case for the total number of marriages, as well as for each of the different ages at first marriage.

Table 17. Percent of first marriages, married in 1940-1944 and 1945-1949, dissolved by divorce or death by 1960, by age at marriage, sex, and color*

			Age at first marriage	
Year of first marriage	Total	14–19	20–24	25–29
White men				
1945–1949	12.3	22.5	11.8	9.4
1940–1944	16.6	27.9	16.0	13.1
Nonwhite men				
1945–1949	20.4	26.4	20.1	17.2
1940–1944	27.8	35.5	27.9	23.6

			Age at first marriage		
	Total	14–17	18 and 19	20–24	25–29
White women					
1945–1949	14.8	25.8	16.0	10.8	11.2
1940–1944	21.0	32.9	22.9	16.6	16.5
Nonwhite women					
1945–1949	24.3	27.4	23.5	21.4	23.8
1940–1944	33.7	37.0	33.2	30.6	32.4

*Data from Hugh Carter and Paul C. Glick, *Marriage and Divorce: A Social and Economic Study*, Cambridge: Harvard University Press, 1970, pp. 235–237.

Education Marital-adjustment studies indicate that those with a high level of education have a higher level of marital adjustment than those with a low educational status. Locke in his Indiana study found that a larger percentage of happily married than divorced husbands had done graduate work, and a larger percent of happily married wives than divorced had more than a high school education.[13] Terman, while finding no correlation between the amount of education of husbands and wives and their own happiness scores, did find a positive correlation between the amount of education one had and his mate's happiness score.[14] Burgess and Cottrell report a consistent relationship between increased chances of success in marriage and a rising level of educational achievement for both husbands and wives.[15] Lucky, in a study of 80 married couples, found that education and marital satisfaction were correlated.[16]

[13] Locke, p. 346.
[14] Terman and others, p. 189.
[15] Burgess and Cottrell, pp. 122 and 271.
[16] Lucky, pp. 44–48.

Level of education is an index of other variables which may be associated with marital adjustment. In their study Burgess and Cottrell point out that education may be an index of higher economic status and being older at the time of marriage, and these rather than education itself may be the factors correlated with marital adjustment.[17]

Adjustment to the Kinship Group A man or woman not only marries another person but also marries into the family of the mate. Adjustment in marriage is highly correlated with parental approval of the prospective mate and some emancipation from one's own parents.

A question as to whether the parents approved the mate before marriage was included in six of the marital adjustment studies. All found that it was correlated with marital adjustment. Table 18, which gives data on four of these studies, shows that parental approval of the prospective daughter-in-law or son-in-law was reported by more than three-quarters of the adjusted men and women as compared with about half to two-thirds of the unadjusted.

Table 18. Percent of adjusted and unadjusted men and women reporting parental approval of mate before marriage, four studies*

| | MEN | | WOMEN | |
Study by	Adjusted	Unadjusted	Adjusted	Unadjusted
Burgess-Cottrell	87.3	68.2	80.8	62.2
Burgess-Wallin[a]	82.0	77.1	82.7	64.9
Locke	76.8	51.9	82.3	45.6
Karlsson	85.8	60.0	90.5	66.2

[a]Percents refer to broken and unbroken engagements.
*Burgess and Cottrell, p. 408; Burgess and Wallin, pp. 561–562; Locke, p. 119; and Karlsson, p. 183. See annotated bibliography for complete references.

Some emancipation of children from their parents and of parents from their children appears necessary for adjustment to in-laws and adjustment in marriage. The evidence for this comes from case studies[18] by Locke and Burgess and Wallin. Frequently the parental family is a sort of closed corporation, with strong interdependent attitudes and attachments. Under such conditions the son, daughter, or parents find difficulty in accepting the reduction in strength of these attachments which ordinarily goes along with the establishment of a new family. The attempt may be made to incorporate the mate into the closed

[17] Burgess and Cottrell, p. 122.
[18] Locke, pp. 114–123; Burgess and Wallin, 597–599 and 603–607.

family group; sometimes this involves moving in with the in-laws. If the mate does not fit into the set of intrafamily relationships and habitual practices, irritation and conflict may ensue and result in the departure of the son-in-law or daughter-in-law. Locke reports that the divorced men of his sample said over and over that if they had their lives to live over again they would marry the same girl but would see to it that they did not move in with the in-laws. Burgess and Wallin give several excerpts from their cases showing problems of adjustment to the in-laws. The following shows one type of adjustment:

Husband: The biggest adjustment of all was to get along with my mother-in-law. If there are any quarrels we have ever had, I think that is where they come from. I have finally got used to letting her think she runs the whole family; just not to pay any attention to her any more. All her sons-in-law and daughters-in-law have had to become adjusted to her domination to keep peace in the family. It bothered me at first but doesn't any more. She runs the family so thoroughly that no one would think of disagreeing with her. Thank God we see her only once a year.

Wife: I don't think there were many adjustments except to keep on an even keel between my family and husband. My family didn't want us to get married when we did. They thought he ought to be further ahead. There was controversy. My mother got very much upset. They get along fairly well at a distance; we see each other only a few times a year.[19]

The following excerpt from one of Locke's unpublished cases shows that the interference of the mother-in-law was decreased by "the understanding" between the husband and wife, and by having the mother-in-law spend time with other relatives:

We allowed my husband's mother to make her home with us for the entire time of our marriage, although she had extended visits with her other children. She has felt that because my husband and I have no children the major support of her should come from us. In the early years of our marriage she was a complicating factor, and what dissension and disagreement we had centered, for the most part, around her interference in running the home. She was at an active age, felt she could manage the home better than I could, and had a strong attachment for her son, for he resembled her husband and he was her only son. Her inclination was to expect the cooking, mending, and other house work done according to the way she would do it. I really think that I learned to please my husband in the culinary arts from the coaching of my mother-in-law. However, I had been independent and in a position of responsibility for several years, and, when I was so suddenly deprived of these in our home, I just didn't like it. However, when I had taken all I could, I let go and explained everything to my husband. When he saw me so upset, he

[19] *Ibid.*, p. 605.

realized that I was more important to him than his mother and told me so. We talked things over. He had an understanding with his mother and arranged for her to stay with his sister for a time. This has occurred at intervals and each absence was like a new honeymoon. Now that she is older we do not notice her presence as much because she is not as active and seems resigned to this being our home.

Thus parental approval of the mate before marriage and some emancipation from the parents are predictive factors for marital adjustment.

Sexual Behavior Adjustment in marriage is correlated with similar values and expectations of the husband and wife on sex, and marital maladjustment is associated with wide differences between the sex behavior of one of the mates and the values and expectations of the other. The various studies of marital adjustment have found significant differences between the adjusted and unadjusted in premarital, marital, and extramarital sex behavior.

Of all items associated with marital adjustment, premarital intercourse is the one which has the largest number of studies reporting a significant relationship between it and marital maladjustment. Of the eight studies which found a statistically significant relationship between marital adjustment and premarital intercourse, seven reported no premarital intercourse or only with future spouse, and the other, the Locke-Karlsson study of Swedish couples, reported intercourse with none or only one.[20]

Marital sex relations will be analyzed from the standpoint of (1) strength of sexual interest or desire, and (2) pleasure or enjoyment of intercourse with mate. Five studies report that marital adjustment is related to about the same or equal sex interest or desire and to pleasure or enjoyment of intercourse with mate. Terman computed a "sex satiety" ratio by dividing the reported frequency of intercourse with mate by the desired or preferred frequency. He indicates that when the reported frequency of intercourse was the same or about the same as the preferred frequency, the mean happiness scores of both men and women were highest. Both those with extreme sexual hunger or extreme sexual satiety had low marital-happiness scores. In addition, the happiness of a given spouse was related not only to his own degree of sexual satisfaction but to that of his mate.[21]

Locke's findings on strength of sex interest and refusal of intercourse when desired by mate, summarized in the following tabulation, show

---

[20] See Appendix A.
[21] Terman and others, pp. 279–380, and 284–285.

that "about the same sex interest" was reported by a much larger percent of happily married men and women than of divorced.[22]

	MEN		WOMEN	
Item	Happily Married	Divorced	Happily Married	Divorced
Sex interest of spouses: about the same	70.1	47.4	61.7	39.2
Refused intercourse when desired by mate: rarely and sometimes	31.8	23.7	71.2	47.9

The question on refusal of intercourse when desired by mate had four possible answers: "frequently," "sometimes," "rarely," and "never." "Rarely" and "sometimes" were reported by a significantly larger percent of happily married women than divorced. A larger percent of divorced than happily married men reported "never," and a much larger percent of divorced women than happily married gave this response. It seems that sexual adjustment involves mutual accommodation to sexual desires. If a wife or husband rarely or sometimes refuses to have intercourse, the happily married person apparently understands the moods of the other and adjusts to them. The tendency to report "never" by the divorced may mean that they may have exaggerated the degree to which they never refused intercourse because never refusing may have been considered the mark of a good mate, and it was difficult to admit that the reason for failure of the marriage was that one was not a mate.[23]

The informal interviews revealed that husbands in adjusted marriages occasionally had a stronger desire for intercourse than their wives. Other things in the marriage, such as companionship, compensated for the relatively low sex interest of such wives.

Extramarital sex relations may or may not result in marital difficulties, as may be seen in the following excerpts from life-history documents. The first reveals a happily married husband who had an "understanding" wife:

> My wife has a great understanding of me. She knows I love her and as far as sex which I have with other women during marriage, it does not worry her, for she knows that I don't care for any of these women. She also knows that I am human.

[22] Data from Harvey J. Locke, *Predicting Adjustment in Marriage*, pp. 141–142, and 144–146.
[23] *Ibid.*, pp. 46–48.

The following excerpt from an interview with a divorced woman deals with extramarital intercourse as related to marital maladjustment:

> We were having difficulties the first two years of our marriage, and then we were separated for 5 years. I decided I wanted other company. I wanted to go out too, so I sued for divorce. Oh, yes, I have two or three boy friends now, but I won't marry unless I lose my mind.
> He lived with that other woman the last two years of our marriage, and then for the 4 years we were separated. I reckon he did commit adultery. She had a baby, and she didn't get that by sitting in the water. He still lives with her, and isn't married to her.

In his studies of sexual behavior of men and women, Kinsey obtained some impressions of the relationship between marital adjustment and sexual attitudes and activities.[24] However, since he paid only incidental attention to marital adjustment and did not systematically study the marital adjustment of his cases, the following must be regarded as suggesting possible relationships rather than demonstrating them. Kinsey reports his impressions that sexual maladjustments contribute to perhaps three-quarters of the separations and divorces of upper-class marriages and to a smaller percent of broken marriages of lower-level couples. Specifically, Kinsey felt that for upper-class marriages the following are the sexual factors which cause difficulty: (1) failure of the male to show skill in approach and technique, (2) failure of the female to participate with the abandon necessary for sexual consummation; and (3) inhibitions due to conceptions of the esthetic acceptability and moral decency of some sexual practices.

Number of Children Childless and one-child families are more adjusted, are more united, and have a more satisfying marriage than those with a larger number of children. This is the reverse of the popular belief that the presence of children increases the chance of marital happiness and tends to unite the family. The results of various studies, while not completely consistent, give little support to this popular belief. They give some support to the inverse relationship between number of children and family unity.

Earlier studies of divorce seemed to refute the inverse relationship between the number of children and family unity, for childless couples were found more frequently among the divorced than among the nondivorced. More childlessness among the divorced, however, is to be

[24] Alfred C. Kinsey, Wardell B. Pomeroy, and Clyde E. Martin, *Sexual Behavior in the Human Male* (Philadelphia: W. B. Saunders, 1948), pp. 544–546 and 589–594; and Alfred C. Kinsey, Wardell B. Pomeroy, Clyde E. Martin, and Paul H. Gebhard, *Sexual Behavior in the Human Female* (Philadelphia: W. B. Saunders, 1953), p. 12.

expected unless the divorced and nondivorced are matched for the length of living together. The time of living together for the divorced is not the period between marriage and the date of the divorce, for there is a period of separation of about two years before the actual divorce. Also cases of desertion and separation without divorce should be included.

The various marital-adjustment studies, in general, show either no relationship between number of children and marital adjustment or an inverse relationship between them. Hamilton,[25] Katherine Davis,[26] Bernard,[27] Terman,[28] and Locke[29] for the United States and Karlsson[30] for Sweden found no relationship between adjustment in marriage and the presence or absence of children and/or the number of children.

Lang, in his study of 22,000 couples, reported that for those married five years and over childless families and those with one or two children were happier than those families with three or more children.[31] Burgess and Cottrell found that couples with two or more children had significantly lower marital-adjustment scores than the childless or one-child families[32] Reed collected data from 860 couples living in Indianapolis and found that the larger the size of the family the poorer the marital adjustment.[33]

One part of the study of families in Alameda County, referred to earlier, dealt with the relationship between satisfaction with the marriage and the number of children. This study found that parents, especially those currently raising children, were definitely less likely to be satisfied with their marriage than childless couples. Moreover, regardless of sex, race, age, or adjusted family income, couples raising children were more likely to be dissatisfied with their marriage.[34]

Thus on the basis of such predictive factors as personality characteristics, cultural backgrounds of the couple, social participation in community activities and friendship groups, courtship experiences, level of

[25] G. V. Hamilton, *A Research in Marriage* (New York, Lear, 1948 edition), p. 511.
[26] Katherine B. Davis, *Factors in the Sex Life of Twenty-Two Hundred Women* (New York: Harper and Brothers, 1929), p. 42.
[27] Jessie Bernard, "Factors in the Distribution of Success in Marriage," *American Journal of Sociology*, 40 (1934): p. 51.
[28] Terman and others, pp. 171–173.
[29] Locke, pp. 58–67.
[30] Karlsson, p. 184.
[31] Richard O. Lang, A Study of the Degree of Happiness or Unhappiness in Marriage as Rated by Acquaintances of the Married Couples, M.A. thesis, University of Chicago Library, 1932, pp. 49–50.
[32] Burgess and Cottrell, pp. 258–261.
[33] Robert B. Reed, "Social and Psychological Factors Affecting Fertility: The Interrelationship of Marital Adjustment, Fertility Control, and Size of Family," *The Milbank Memorial Fund Quarterly*, 25 (1947): pp. 383–425.
[34] Renne, pp. 61–62.

education, adequacy of adjustment to the kinship group, age at marriage, attitudes toward sexual behavior, and number of children, one can predict with fair probability the likelihood of marital adjustment.

PREDICTING FUTURE MARITAL ADJUSTMENT

Most marital-adjustment studies have been confined to the construction of a marital-adjustment index or securing some other criteria of marital adjustment and then discovering those items which differentiate between adjusted and unadjusted marriages. For example, the first Terman study, the Burgess-Cottrell study, Locke's Indiana study, and the Locke-Karlsson Swedish study secured criteria of marital adjustment and then assumed that those items which differentiated between adjusted and unadjusted marriages would be predictive of marital adjustment. All these were concerned with certain marriages at one given time. The important question is: Will data on items found to be associated with marital adjustment which are collected at a given time be reliable in predicting the risk group into which marriages will fall at a later time?

Four studies have attempted to forecast future marital adjustment. The first was that of Kelly, who attempted to predict future marital adjustment from engagement data.[35] The second was a comparison of broken and unbroken marriages of Terman's genius subjects on the basis of data secured 8 years earlier.[36] The third, by Adams, compared scores on predictive tests given to 100 couples before marriage with marital-adjustment scores after marriage.[37] The fourth was by Burgess and Wallin, who attempted to predict marital adjustment from questionnaire and interview data from engaged couples.[38] All four used marital-adjustment and prediction items which were the same as or similar to those discovered by prior studies.

These four studies indicate that the future marital adjustment of couples can be predicted from premarital or marital data. The most comprehensive of these was that of Burgess and Wallin, and it will be described briefly.

Burgess and Wallin secured data from 1000 engaged couples and from these data predicted how well adjusted the couples would be three or four years after marriage. One unexpected by-product of this study

---

[35] E. Lowell Kelly, "Marital Compatibility as Related to Personality Traits of Husbands and Wives, as Rated by Self and Spouse," *Journal of Social Psychology*, 13 (1941): pp. 193–198; and "Concerning the Validity of Terman Weights for Predicting Marital Happiness," *Psychological Bulletin*, 36 (1939): pp. 202–203.
[36] *The Gifted Child Grows Up*.
[37] C. R. Adams, "The Prediction of Adjustment in Marriage," *Educational and Psychological Measurement*, 6 (1946): pp. 185–193.
[38] Burgess and Wallin, pp. 584–588.

was the opportunity to predict the likelihood that an engagement would be broken. Engagement-adjustment scores were significantly lower for the 123 couples who had broken their engagements than for the 877 who did not break their engagements.[39]

Burgess and Wallin found that adjustment in marriage can be predicted from adjustment in engagement. They secured marriage data from 666 of the 784 cases available for the marriage study, approximately three years after marriage. The marriage data included a marital-adjustment index similar to that used in other studies. A moderate correlation was found between marital-adjustment scores and engagement-adjustment scores: .43 for men and .41 for women.

At the time of securing the engagement data, they secured personal documents, including interviews from 226 engaged couples. Later, 30 judges, using a 14-point scale, forecast the probable success in marriage of the husband and wife of each of the 226 couples. Then by adding the forecast scores of the raters for a given person and dividing by the number of raters, they obtained an average forecast score of marital adjustment for each person. It was then possible to correlate the forecast scores and the scores secured on the marital-adjustment index three years after marriage. The correlations were .42 for men and .39 for women. These correlations were about the same as those secured from the engagement-adjustment scores.

These studies, particularly that of Burgess and Wallin, indicate that the level of marital adjustment at a later time can be predicted with some accuracy from data secured during engagement or marriage.

SUMMARY

The materials from the studies reviewed in this chapter can be summarized as follows: (1) The six major studies of adjustment in marriage, in addition to a score of smaller studies, all found predictive items associated with some index of marital adjustment. Some dealt exclusively with premarital predictive items, some exclusively with marital items, and most with both premarital and marital items. (2) Of 70 significant premarital-predictive items, 49 were supported by two or more studies and 26 by four or more studies. Of 45 significant marital-predictive items, 32 were supported by two or more studies and 12 by four or more studies. (3) Nine basic predictive factors associated with marital adjustment were presented: personality characteristics, cultural backgrounds, social participation, courtship experiences, age at marriage,

---

[39] Burgess and Wallin, "Predicting Adjustment in Marriage from Adjustment in Engagement," *American Journal of Sociology*, 49 (1944): p. 329, and *Engagement and Marriage*, pp. 313–315.

education, adjustment to the kinship group, sexual behavior, and number of children. (4) A marital-prediction index, combining various predictive items, will work in predicting future marital adjustment.

Studies demonstrate the feasibility of predicting before marriage the probabilities of marital success. It must be remembered that the predictive score is much more discriminating at the two extremes, in picking out those that will have the best or the poorest chances of being adjusted in their marriage.

PROBLEMS FOR RESEARCH

Research in marital prediction is promising but still in a pioneer stage. Increased efficiency in prediction by both statistical and case-study methods may be expected from the progress of research in this field.

Significant Predictive Items Research may be advanced by the inclusion of more significant items indicative of happiness in marriage. Especially desirable are those that reveal the attitudes and values of engaged couples. Case studies of the interaction of persons in going steady, in engagement, and in marriage will provide hypotheses for further exploration.

Prediction of Special Groups Predictive items associated with marital adjustment under special conditions should be investigated. This would include studies of marriages (1) which followed pregnancy, (2) of very young persons, including those married during high school, (3) of persons with extremely different backgrounds of social class or cultural group, and (4) of persons who remarry, particularly when children are part of the new family.

Experiences after Marriage Those who emphasize the importance of emotional behavior in marital compatibility are inclined to hold that emotional tendencies developed in childhood are present at the time of marriage, and that, if one had sharper methods of perception, marital behavior could be predicted before marriage. This, however, may not be completely true, for persons in marriage may undergo great changes.

An example of the use of marital items in predicting happiness and satisfaction in marriage is the study by Hawkins. He found that hostility is correlated strongly and negatively with marital satisfaction and that companionship is moderately and positively correlated.[40]

Thus it may be that a greater degree of reliability in predicting happi-

[40] James L. Hawkins, "Associations Between Companionship, Hostility, and Marital Satisfaction," *Journal of Marriage and the Family*, 30 (1968): pp. 647–655.

ness or failure at a given time in marriage will be secured if marital experiences up to that time are also taken into account. It may be feasible, for example, in addition to making a prediction of marital happiness at the time of engagement, to reinterview the couple after one or more years of marriage and then to determine whether new factors have entered the relationship or whether attributes have crystallized which make possible increased accuracy in predicting the further course of marital adjustment.

QUESTIONS AND EXERCISES

1. What is the basic assumption of prediction? To what specific areas of human behavior have prediction techniques been applied?
2. What is the difference between a marital-adjustment score and a marital-prediction score?
3. What courtship items are predictive items of marital adjustment?
4. What cultural background items are associated with marital adjustment? Can you think of any marriages where a given item has not applied? How do you account for these exceptional cases?
5. What items indicate conventionality and conformity? Why is the conventional person a better risk in marriage than the unconventional?
6. Why are the affectional and sex factors significant in marital adjustment? Which of these do you consider the more important? Give reasons for your choice.
7. Compare the similarities and differences in methods and findings of the six major studies of marital adjustment.
8. What was the procedure of Burgess and Wallin in their study of predicting during engagement the likelihood of marital adjustment?

BIBLIOGRAPHY

Bowerman, Charles E. "Prediction Studies," in *Handbook of Marriage and the Family*, ed. Harold T. Christensen. Chicago: Rand McNally, 1964, Ch. 6.
> Summarizes the six major prediction studies. Deals with criticisms of prediction studies. Considers alternate methods of measuring adjustment in marriage than those used to date.

Burgess, Ernest W.; and Cottrell, Leonard S. *Predicting Success or Failure in Marriage*. New York: Prentice-Hall, 1939.
> This study, begun in 1931, was the first major investigation of adjustment in marriage. Questionnaire data were secured from 526 individuals who had been married from one to six years and lived in and around Chicago. A

marital-adjustment test composed of 26 questions was correlated with many predictive items. Findings were limited by the characteristics of the sample: predominantly urban, upper-income, highly educated, Protestant group; volunteer subjects; and information secured from only one of the marriage partners.

Burgess, Ernest W., and Wallin, Paul. *Engagement and Marriage.* Philadelphia: Lippincott, 1953. See also "Predicting Adjustment in Marriage from Adjustment in Engagement," *American Journal of Sociology,* 49 (1944); pp. 324–330.

Begun in 1936, this study had the objective of predicting marital adjustment 3 years after marriage from information secured during engagement. Of those who married, 666 were restudied about 3 years after marriage. Also compared were couples who had broken their engagements with those who went on to marriage.

Karlsson, Georg. *Adaptability and Communication in Marriage: A Swedish Predictive Study of Marital Satisfaction.* Uppsala, Sweden: Almqvist and Wiksells, 1951. See also Locke, Harvey J., and Karlsson, Georg, "Marital Adjustment and Prediction in Sweden and United States," *American Sociological Review,* 17 (1952): pp. 10–17; and Locke, Harvey J., and Snowbarger, Vernon A., "Marital Adjustment and Prediction in Sweden," *American Journal of Sociology,* 60 (1954): pp. 51–53.

In the 1950–51 academic year, as Visiting Professor at Uppsala University in Sweden, Locke collaborated with Karlsson, a Swedish sociologist, in a study of marital adjustment. Couples recommended as happily married, rank and file marriages from the general population, unhappily married, and legally separated were contacted in their homes by Swedish interviewers and given Locke's marital-adjustment test, a large number of predictive items used by Locke in his earlier study, and certain additional questions.

Locke, Harvey J. *Predicting Adjustment in Marriage: A Comparison of a Divorced and a Happily-Married Group.* New York: Henry Holt, 1951.

Begun in 1939, this study secured interview and questionnaire data from 929 persons in a central county in Indiana. Almost all were husbands and their wives. There were two unique features: (1) the data were from a representative general population sample, and (2) marital adjustment was measured not only by a marital-adjustment test but by divorce and happiness in marriage. The divorced and happily married were compared on many predictive items.

Terman, Lewis M.; and others. *Psychological Factors in Marital Happiness.* New York: McGraw-Hill, 1938.

This study, using a sample of 792 couples, was the second major study, being initiated in 1934. Similar to Burgess and Cottrell study, but the data were obtained from both the husband and wife.

Terman, Lewis M.; and Oden, Melita H. *The Gifted Child Grows Up: Twenty-Five Years' Follow-Up of a Superior Group.* Stanford: Stanford University Press, 1947, Ch. 19. Also, Terman, Lewis M. "Predictive Data: Predicting Marriage Failure From Test Scores," *Marriage and Family Living,* 12 (1951): pp. 51–54.

In 1921 and 1922 Terman and several assistants collected a mass of information on 1,528 "genius" children. Twenty years later (1940) Terman and Oden contacted 643 who had married. These and their spouses were given a marital-happiness test, a marital-aptitude test, and a sex-adjustment test. The cases were analyzed by (1) correlating predictive items and scores on the marital-adjustment test, and (2) comparing 8 years later (1948) the 52 couples who had broken their marriage by divorce and 591 who remained married.

Chapter 15
Family Unity

Family unity has two aspects: the subjective inner lives of the members and the external structural form. The first is the unity resulting from interaction and communication between family members. Interaction and communication which is friendly and congenial results in a fusion of attitudes, values, and objectives so that family members have a "we-feeling." The external form is a configuration of a man and women living together as husband and wife and, with the addition of children, living together as father, mother, and children. Families range along a continuum in the degree to which they are unified. At one end of the continuum are families which have been broken by divorce or separation. At the other end are those which are united in attitudes, goals, values, and the various activities of the family.

A COMPANIONSHIP FAMILY

In the United States the small-patriarchal and patricentric types of family organization are in the process of being superseded. The companionship family, although lacking most or all of the factors which combine to make the patriarchal family highly integrated, may manifest an equal or even greater degree of unity, as shown in the following case:

> My family, consisting of Mother, Father, and myself, has always been very closely knit. Since the time that I could talk and share things with my parents we have been very close. Since I am an only child, the "feeling of togetherness" has been great in our family life.
> The harmony results from the democratic or companionship relation-

ship. My father is the chief breadwinner of the family; however, all of his decisions are reached only after discussions with Mother. Mother shares the financial business of the family by keeping and managing the budget. In late years I have shared the discussions of major importance.

Any outsider looking in on us would think that we are a very silly group because of our demonstrations of love for each other. My father and I are always playfully boxing and chasing one another around the house. My father does not show his love for Mother by showering her with gifts or other outward signs of affection but rather by sharing all activities with her and spending his spare time with her. Mother is a very affectionate type of person and is always doing minor unnecessary things to add to our comfort and enjoyment.

A few years ago our family passed through a major crisis. My mother became seriously ill and was in the hospital for about six weeks. I was twelve at the time and barely recognized the seriousness of her illness, but I was not too young to be afraid that she might not pull through. I can remember vividly the grave talks my father had with me in an effort to allay my fears, and my visits to the hospital with him. Going through that serious emotional crisis aided in bringing the three of us more closely together than ever.

The deep warm love that Mother and Father have showered on me has made my life seem fuller and richer. No other incentive to work hard and do well is necessary beside the anticipation of their pleasure and pride. Any temptation for me to do wrong has been quickly stopped by thoughts of my parents' disappointment in me.

Father is a football and track coach, and through him we have gained our interest in sports. It seems as though there is something added through our mutual enjoyment of these activities.

We have an annual holiday custom. Our Christmas Eve is never shared with anyone—just family. After going to church in the evening we sit together until the wee hours of the morning listening to the Christmas carols.

Our family has always worked on a system of mutual aid. Mother helps Father in planning his schedule for his school teaching program. Dad helps Mother with some household activities. I assist Mother for the most part in household tasks, but I also aid Dad in caring for the flower gardens or in such tasks as washing the car.

My Father's job has been jeopardized several times by selfish, heartless people. Mother and I realized how this troubles him, and in sympathizing with him and condemning those against him our family ties have been strengthened.

Unity in this family is very little, if at all, the result of community control, tradition, authority of the head, or participation in a common economic enterprise, as in patriarchal families. The prominent characteristics in this family are demonstration of affection; having common experiences; mutual confiding; sharing in the making of decisions; companionship; reaction to the family crisis of the illness of a family member; and combining as a unit against attack on the father by outsiders.

COMPONENTS OF FAMILY UNITY

Family unity may be analyzed in terms of several interrelated components. These can be classified as communication, love and mutual affection, emotional interdependence, sympathetic understanding, common interests, consensus on values and goals, family events, celebrations, and ceremonies, interdependence of family roles, sexual behavior, and pressures by the environing society. While the maximum of family unity exists when there is a maximum of these component parts, there can be some unity if only one of them is present. For instance, a couple who marry on the basis of strong sexual attraction may have a feeling of unity, even though there is little consensus on the general values and objectives of life, no tolerance of divergent behavior, little interdependence of family roles, and slight community pressure. However, a family established on the basis of sexual attraction or one other component alone will probably break up unless other components of family unity develop.

A decline during the marriage in some of these components of family unity was found by Burgess who analyzed the Burgess-Wallin cases in the early and middle years of marriage. There was a statistically significant decline in demonstration of love and affection, in sharing of interests and activities, and in consensus.

Communication An analysis of patterns of personal relationships in any family leads directly to the conception of the family as a unity of interacting and communicating persons. The explanation of family unity as a welding together of family members who are interacting and communicating with each other has been generally adopted by students of the family. The family as a unit of communicating persons involves the fitting together of reactions and attitudes of husband and wife which have a history reaching back to the early months and years of each person's life. These persisting attitudes and values act as a selective factor in sensitizing each person to pay attention to objects, values, and situations similar to those previously experienced. The basic principle, however, is that persons undergo modification in the process of communicative interaction within the family. Thus, through communication, particularly of the intimate type found in most families, there is an interpenetration and fusion of the attitudes of husband and wife and of parents and children, for in their reciprocal responses the members continually modify one another's behavior.

The relationship between communication and family unity is revealed, in part, by an analysis of the nature of communication. Communication is a process of symbolic interaction between a sender and a receiver in which the sender is also a receiver and the receiver is also a sender. The messages sent and received may be about feelings, attitudes, values, aspirations, expectations, convictions, conceptions, factual information, and the like. Sensory reception and interpretation of messages and the transmission of messages in response leave some residues within the communicating persons. Moreover, if traces of another person's messages occur repeatedly and over a long period, ways of behavior of the other person or persons become increasingly imbedded within one. At the same time one becomes increasingly a part of the person with whom communication is taking place.

A continuing series of corrections occurs in communicating with others. One may modify the messages he transmits and receives so that they will be meaningful or acceptable to the other person or so that they will be meaningful and acceptable to himself. Consequently, when there is extended communication between members of a dyad such as a husband-wife group, the sending, receiving, and correcting of messages and the ensuing modifications of the communicating persons are likely to result in mutual modifications of behavior.

The nature of these modifications will depend, to some extent, on the nature of the communication which is taking place. If the communication is friendly and mutually accommodating it is likely to draw persons into closer association and increasing consensus, while hostile communication is likely to separate them. This separation will also result in the reduction of communication unless other influences enter the situation to enforce communication.

Several studies have investigated the relationship between communication and family unity. Goodman and Ofshe studied the communication of engaged and married couples. They found that engaged men had lower communication scores with fiancées than husbands had with their wives. However, engaged women had higher communication scores than married women. They feel that the lower communication scores of married women may be due to husbands moving into occupational roles with a reduction of expressive behavior and a reduction of communication of wives with their husbands.[1]

Four studies have investigated the relationship between primary com-

[1] Norman Goodman and Richard Ofshe, "Empathy, Communication Efficiency, and Marital Status," *Journal of Marriage and the Family*, 30 (1968): pp. 597–603.

munication and family unity. The studies used marital adjustment as an index of family unity and all employed a 25-item primary communication index constructed by Locke, Sabagh, and Thomes. Each of the studies found a consistent correlation on the .01 level of probability between primary communication and family unity.[2]

Love and Affection Love and affection between family members is a primary dimension of family unity. There are three aspects of love and affection: the intensity of the feeling, the expression of it, and emotional security indicated by the absence of doubts about the love and affection among family members.

A love relationship beginning in courtship and continuing throughout the marriage is the accepted ideal of marriage in the United States. The sentiment of love varies from an infatuation, which is almost as fleeting as it is intense, to a companionship in which two personalities are united in a lifelong union. The sentiment of love may contribute markedly to early adjustments in marriage, and it may promote family unity over an extended period.

"Friendship deepening into love" is one way of describing love. Sharing past experiences, divulging inner attitudes, and mutual confiding build up affection that provides a solid foundation for marriage. In marriage, love is maintained and strengthened by expressions and demonstrations of affection, although it may decline over the years. While a few couples say that their love for each other has not changed or may have decreased since marriage, the majority report that it has grown stronger and deeper.[3]

Love is itself a unifying factor. It creates problems in marriage only when it leads to ignoring other factors upon which unity also is based, such as temperamental compatibility, common interests and ideals.

Loveless marriages lack an element essential to family unity, although they may survive even for a lifetime because of other unifying elements and because of habit, mutual respect, and feelings of duty. Such marriages in our society are always vulnerable, since they deviate from

[2] Harvey J. Locke, Georges Sabagh, and Mary Margaret Thomes, "Correlates of Primary Communication and Empathy," *Research Studies of the State College of Washington*, 24 (1956): pp. 116–124; Charles W. Hobart and William J. Klausner, "Some Social Interactional Correlates of Marital Role Disagreement, and Marital Adjustment," *Marriage and Family Living*, 21 (1959): pp. 256–263; Stuart Brody, "Husband-Wife Communication Patterns Related to Marital Adjustment" (Ph.D. Dissertation, University of Southern California Library, 1963); and an unpublished study by Harvey J. Locke and Mary Margaret Thomes of primary communication and family unity as reported by divorced men and women and by widowed women.

[3] Ernest W. Burgess and Paul Wallin, *Engagement and Marriage* (Philadelphia: Lippincott, 1953): p. 419.

the social expectation that love will always be present in a successful marriage. One partner may find a satisfying love relationship with another person.

How couples typically express their affection for each other is well represented in the following case of John and Ethel, from statements secured before and after marriage:

Ethel (during engagement): The things that I've always considered of paramount importance seem to be of no importance in comparison with our relationship. It is completely necessary to me. To be without him would be beyond my endurance.

Ethel (three years after marriage): During the first year I didn't think he was as much in love with me as I was with him. When he criticized me I thought he could not be as much in love with me. I think I depend on him more than he does on me in daily life. I think our love has found a more solid basis than it had before marriage. If anyone before marriage had asked if I was marrying a good man I would have said "yes." Since marriage I have found out how much better he is and how fortunate I am—extremely fortunate.

John (during engagement): I'd say I'm very much in love or head over heels in love—just as extreme as you can put it. I'd say she means more to me than anything else. I don't think I'm blindly in love with her. I think I still have pretty good judgment.

John (three years after marriage): My love has not changed so much in amount as in kind. To some extent from romantic to companionship. I think probably she is more in love with me than I with her to some extent. I think she is by nature more dependent.

Emotional Interdependence Common family experiences make for emotional interdependence through the interlocking of emotional habits which develop through years of intimate communication. With the sharing of confidences, disappointments, sorrows, aspirations, and appreciations, an interchange of emotional attitudes takes place so that emotional unity is established. As emotional experiences are shared, new habits become intertwined with previous habits, and with the habits of other members of the family. Emotional interdependence is revealed in situations where husband and wife have need for sympathy and encouragement:

Husband: Jane gives me encouragement. A sufficient amount of it; it doesn't take very much; just a word or two. Sometimes I build myself up to a big letdown when a depressive spell comes. All I need then is a little impetus and then I am back at the grind again. She brings up past performances and shows that everything turned out all right, and I feel better.

Wife: A person wants sympathy and encouragement, but I am self-reliant too. He is fairly good at giving this if he wants to. If I don't feel good he is sorry and makes it easy for me. Especially now in my condition he takes care of the baby. Will is like a baby for sympathy and encouragement. I always give him encouragement. It makes a man feel better. He doesn't often get discouraged.

The strength of such interdependent emotional attachments is indicated by their persistence after the disintegration of the family. We have found not only a high degree of emotional interdependence in happily married couples, but the persistence of considerable emotional dependence on the part of many unhappily married and divorced husbands and wives, particularly when the divorce was preceded by a relatively short period of separation. Apparently such couples find it hard to liberate themselves from interlocking emotional habits. This is illustrated in statements by a divorced wife and her former husband, both of whom are remarried to divorced persons:

Wife: My former husband was so good to me in so many ways that my present husband doesn't even think about. My present husband will sit and not even notice that I am doing the hard work, but my former man would have noticed that things needed doing and would have helped me without my even mentioning it to him. I certainly got divorced and remarried in too much of a hurry.

Husband: You may be walking down the street with two men. One has traits you like better than the other, and the other may have traits you like better. Well, that is the way it is with me and my wives. I liked the former one best in some ways and the present one in other ways. But even though I like my former wife and she likes me, it is impossible to talk to each other. If we see each other downtown we just say "Hello," for if we did much more than that our present mates would be jealous and raise hell.[4]

Sympathetic Understanding Sympathetic understanding involves the capacity to enter into and share the feelings, attitudes, interests, and experiences of others to such an extent that one is able to accept without hostility behavior quite different from that which one would engage in oneself. In the family such a close relationship may have developed that the members have the ability to take each other's roles and behave harmoniously with reference to individualistic feelings, attitudes, interests, and experiences of other family members.

Sympathetic understanding is essential to the unity and even to the

[4] Case secured by Harvey J. Locke in connection with his study *Predicting Adjustment in Marriage: A Comparison of a Divorced and a Happily Married Group* (New York: Henry Holt, 1951).

survival of a marital union when husband and wife differ widely in temperament and interests and when one or both wish to retain their individuality:

> My biggest adjustment in marriage has been living with a person who is of an entirely different nature. We made a bargain when we married that each would retain as much individuality as possible. In the beginning the adjustment was almost an impossibility. We used to have extensive arguments. Now we rarely have arguments. I feel we have become adjusted to one another.
>
> I am very dependent on him. More and more I have come to rely on him. I feel everything I do and feel I have to share with him, or else I can't enjoy it. I think he understands what I want and need out of life. Not liking the same things I do—company, and going out—he can't supply these completely, but he does the best he can. He never belittles my point of view—he understands it and he tries to do the best he can to entertain me in his own way. His idea of an ideal evening is to stay at home, take care of the budget, plan the next day's work and expenditures, and go to bed early. My idea is to go out, see people, have fun and excitement.
>
> I always feel we should do what we want to do, not what we ought to do. He says that we should do what we ought to do even *like* to do what we ought to do. That's our difference wrapped up in a package.

Sympathetic understanding of the divergent behavior of one's spouse, even though one would not engage in that behavior oneself, may be a strong bond in family unity. When this sensitivity to the other's behavior rests upon affection or community of interests, it results in unity despite divergent interests. In an interview with a married couple, the husband made this comment:

> My wife and I have a good many common interests, but we also have a good many different interests. For instance, she does not play bridge nor does she gamble. After I come home from an evening of playing bridge at a half cent a point, she may say, "Did you win or lose?" And, if I have lost, she does not nag or scold me, but may say, "I hope you were a good sport in losing." Now I think it is wonderful that we can talk things like that over in our family.

One interpretation of the unity of this family would be that a certain amount of consensus and emotional attachment had developed so that it was possible for the husband and wife to communicate sympathetically about differences in behavior, which in turn increased the feeling of unity.

Common Interests and Activities Major marital-adjustment studies all suggest that common interests and activities are an important component of family unity. It is not merely engaging in an interest or activity together but the enjoyment of the same interests and activities. This does not assume that all members of a family, regardless of age and outside-the-home experiences, will enjoy and participate in all activities together. It means that several activities will be shared and enjoyed by the members. The importance for family unity of having several common interests is supported by Luckey and Bain's study of 40 satisfactorily married and 40 unsatisfactorily married couples. They found that couples unsatisfactorily married were inclined to list children as the only mutual major satisfaction of the marriage. By contrast, the couples satisfactorily married reported one or more common satisfactions in addition to children.[5]

Consensus on Values and Objectives Consensus, as applied to the family, signifies a sharing of values, objectives, and attitudes. Consensus between husband and wife involves molding together behavior patterns acquired in the years before their acquaintance. Consensus also implies adopting family attitudes and values by young children, and later, as the children pick up deviant patterns outside the home, the adjustment and assimilation of these patterns through communication between children and parents.

Consensus of husbands and wives on the objectives of the family seems to be related to certain other variables. For example, Farber found that consensus on ten values was related to the husband's favoring such values as companionship, personality development, emotional security, and satisfaction with the amount of affection shown in the couple's sex life.[6]

This welding of dissimilar into common points of view, values, and objectives occurs most easily through a certain kind of communication, which is intimate, personal, informal, and unrestricted. When family members engage in intimate, personal, and informal communication, they come to understand each other and to share common values and expectations. In such communication one imaginatively considers the attitudes, values, and objectives expressed in the behavior of other family members, and, if this takes place over a considerable time, attitudes, values, and objectives will be modified to the point where they are shared by family members.

In a mobile, changing, urban society, culture is not internally consistent, but on the contrary includes mutually exclusive and incompatible forms of behavior. A family may be psychologically isolated

---

[5] Eleanor Braum Luckey and Joyce Koya Bain, "Children: A Factor in Marital Satisfaction," *Journal of Marriage and the Family*, 32 (1970), pp. 43–44.
[6] Bernard Farber, "An Index of Marital Integration," *Sociometry: A Journal of Research in Social Psychology:* 20 (1957): pp. 117–134.

from the contradictory parts of the culture and develop attitudes which are quite consistent; its behavior then will be relatively predictable. But if members of a family are in intimate contact with conflicting patterns, their behavior may be inconsistent and relatively difficult to predict.

Obviously, communication between persons having greatly dissimilar values, objectives, and points of view will frequently result in disagreements, conflict, and disunity. But if the persons continue to engage in primary association, with the passing of the months and years, formerly alien patterns may be changed into mutually shared patterns. This may represent the victory of one or the other, or a compromise, or even an integration of conflicting values. There is also the agreement to disagree.

Family Events, Celebrations, and Ceremonies Families vary widely in their experiences. Certain families have many events, such as large family reunions, picnics, automobile trips, and vacations. Holidays like Christmas, New Year's, and Easter may be especially significant in the experiences and memories of family members. Of great significance for unification in some families is mealtime, when the members tell each other their experiences of the day. Although family prayers have departed from almost all homes, where they are held they too are unifying.

The observance of family birthdays, ceremonies, and celebrations expresses and accentuates family unity:

> About ten days or a week before Christmas Dad brings home the Christmas tree. The ornaments for the tree are older than my sister. We have three tailless birds and three silver bells from my father's generation. The egg-cups, pickle caster, and soup tureen figure in a family ceremonial. Mother is the high priestess of this rite. The dinner is served by candlelight. We eat with the family silver off the soup plates my great grandparents bought on their wedding day in 1881. We all love this.

Interdependence of Family Roles There are two general theories on the way roles of family members are related to family organization or unity. One theory is that the family is somewhat like a business or factory and that if the organization is to function smoothly the various activities have to fit together. This theory emphasizes division of labor and the differentiation of roles. One familiar classification of roles on this basis is that the husband plays the instrumental role of providing for the economic needs of the family and the wife plays the expressive role of meeting the emotional needs of family members.

The other theory is that the family is different from a business or factory because it is a small intimate group in which personal relationships are the rule. This theory recognizes that, while the husband or wife may be more expert in the performance of some family tasks, sharing of tasks indicates consideration and cooperation. Very little or no sharing of tasks indicates lack of cooperation while the sharing of all or almost all tasks indicates lack of organization and efficiency.

Interdependence of roles refers to the fitting together of the different activities of family members to achieve common objectives. This may be difficult for the modern husband and wife, for they probably have been influenced by conflicting conceptions of family life, and often have different conceptions of the parts which they have to play in their family. Inasmuch as the husband's role as traditionally defined has been superordinate, under modern conditions he probably will tend toward minor modifications of traditional roles. Since the role of the wife as traditionally defined has been subordinate, under the impress of the same social conditions she will tend toward greater modifications of traditional roles. A wife may conceive of her role as some embodiment of the new woman, and she will probably be more favorably inclined toward an equalitarian type of family organization than her husband. The process of family organization or unity consists, in part, of adjusting the conflicting conceptions of activities and roles so that the roles of the husband and wife will fit together.

In the following case the husband reports that he performs the superordinate role and the wife's is subordinate:

> I am quite sure I take the lead more often than Kate. She does not even try to stop me. When we were first married we would make decisions together and then she would wonder if she had made the right decision. That is still a source of difficulty. Then, too, about the baby; I think in the depths of her nature Kate needed the baby but I think I had the reasoning and logical persistence that led to it. I wanted it more but she needed it more. One factor was I wanted her to quit working and I knew she wouldn't unless she had the child.

A wife may resent the fact that her mate does not fulfill her expectations of the husband taking the lead in family matters. She may not mind the actual assumption of responsibility, for she may like to manage things; but if the husband lets her do it, he may fall short of her expectation of what a husband should be and do.

Current definitions of economic roles of husbands, of wives, and of children are divergent and often conflicting. There are divergent definitions on such questions as the following: During courtship should recreational expenses be paid by the man or shared? Is a woman's place in the home, or should she work outside? If both the husband and wife work, should the earnings be combined or is a wife justified in the attitude, "What you earn is ours and what I earn is mine"? Should the money be contributed to the family when earned by children? Should children be paid for work they do at home? Family unity necessitates the adjustment of divergent conceptions of economic roles or the sympathetic understanding of the conception of the roles. After an extended period of primary communication, accommodation and assimilation may develop, so that agreement may be reached concerning the expected and acceptable economic activities of the various family members. In the following case there was accommodation:

> *Wife:* I like to squeeze the pennies and have a big explosion. He likes to spend the pennies and is afraid to spend a lot of money at a time. We always kid a lot over that.
>
> *Husband:* Grace likes to save and have fine things. Her job in life is to have fine things. I am free with nickels and dimes but it is hard for me to spend a lot of money. We have had to adjust ourselves on that point. I have endeavored to be more careful with nickels and dimes and to have a larger appreciation of fine things.

Sexual Behavior Mutual satisfaction and enjoyment of sexual activities by the husband and wife are unifying factors in marriage. Terman found that marital adjustment is associated with equality or near equality in sexual drives, as measured by the ratio of the actual to the preferred number of copulations per month and by the spouses' ratings of their relative passionateness.[7] Locke found that equal interest in sex is associated with marital adjustment and unequal interest with marital maladjustment.[8]

The sexual interrelationship in marriage is much more than the physical contact of two persons. It necessarily involves the conception of the meaning of the sexual act by the husband and the wife and the role which each plays. It may be an extremely sensitive and intimate form of communication, with emotional and symbolic meaning. On the other hand, in the case of the unhappily married, there frequently is an almost complete severance of all forms of communication between them, including sexual intercourse.

What happens during marriage to the relationship between marital adjustment and sexual adjustment? This question was analyzed by Dentler and Pineo from data in a follow-up study of 400 husbands five years and fifteen years after marriage.[9] These husbands were original cases of the Burgess-Wallin sample of 1000 engaged couples. The con-

---

[7] Lewis M. Terman and others, *Psychological Factors in Marital Happiness* (New York: McGraw-Hill, 1938): particularly pp. 285–289.

[8] Locke, pp. 141–142.

[9] Robert A. Dentler and Peter Pineo, "Sexual Adjustment, Marital Adjustment, and Personal Growth of Husbands: A Panel Analysis," *Marriage and Family Living,* 22 (1960): pp. 45–48.

clusion was that there is a high association between marital adjustment and sexual adjustment five years and fifteen years after marriage and that this relationship tends to remain stable over the ten years.

Three studies give evidence on the relative importance of sex in marital adjustment. Terman found that, while a sex-adjustment test differentiated between broken and unbroken marriages for both men and women, it was slightly less discriminating than a marital-adjustment test and a marital-prediction test.[10] Another study of a middle-class American group reported that sexual adjustment had a lower association with marital happiness than other factors, such as affection, consensus, and specific satisfactions.[11] Even when the sexual adjustment left much to be desired, some couples stated that it detracted little or not at all from the happiness of their marriage. Many wives stated that if sex were taken out of the marriage the loss would be small because other factors were much more important. In another study of a general population group, sex was assigned a role in marital adjustment equal, but not superior, to such other factors as personality traits, cultural background, and sharing values and attitudes.[12]

Husbands of happily married couples occasionally have a stronger desire for intercourse than do their wives, but other things in the marriage seem to compensate for the relatively low sex interest of the wife. This is shown in the following excerpts from happily married cases from Locke's marital-adjustment study. It will be noted that the third excerpt is from the viewpoint of the wife who reported that the husband adjusted "agreeably" to less intercourse than he desired:

> The main thing I do not like about my marriage is that I like to love and have more sex play than my wife. She is an ideal wife in every other way. She cooperates and we work well together. But she does not like loving.

> My wife says that I would want to have her if I was on the border of death. I say "Yes, I would come to you if you wanted me to even though I had double-pneumonia." We are very happy, but we would be happier if she was a little more interested in sex. She doesn't like it, and simply tolerates me.

> No, I never was very much on the kissing bug, and sex just doesn't bother me at all. Now, I do think that there are some women whom it does bother; they seem as passionate as men. I don't have time for such foolishness, especially now that we are getting older. . . . He was always

---

[10] Lewis M. Terman, "Prediction Data: Predicting Marriage Failure from Test Scores," *Marriage and Family Living*, 13 (1950): p. 52.
[11] Burgess and Wallin, p. 504.
[12] Locke, p. 125.

agreeable about it though, and at night, if I was tired, I would say, "Now you turn over there and go to sleep, for I don't want to monkey with such foolishness." And he wouldn't bother me any more. I just don't have any complaints about my husband. When he's here, he always helps me with the work. He always helps clean the house, and all such stuff as that. So you see, I just don't have a kick coming.[13]

The Environing Society The family derives part of its unity from the social matrix in which it exists and interacts. Persons contemplating marriage generally do not appreciate the multitude of extrafamilial relationships and associations into which they are marrying and those which will develop around the family during marriage. When a person marries he marries into a person's circle of relatives and friends, his occupational and other economic relationships, his civic and military obligations, his educational, recreational, and religious relationships; moreover, he marries into the statuses connected with these various relationships and associations.

The pressure for family unity exerted by extrafamilial attachments is illustrated by an incident in a visit to a happily married couple. A neighbor belonging to a fundamentalist church dropped in and, on being briefly informed of the reason for the interviewer's presence, remarked:

> Brother, belief in Jesus Christ and God the Father makes for happiness in home life. Isn't that right, Sister Mary? Now, if one is saved, happiness floods the home and he just doesn't think of separating if a little sin comes into the life of the other. Now Brother Ben here used to sin a lot, used to drink quite a lot, but through Sister Mary's prayers and the prayers of our people at the church, he has been saved from his sin. Also, in our church we just don't believe in divorce. If God is in the house, people will get along all right.

The following is a part of the interpretation of the case, written after the interview:

> This happily-married couple is highly religious as contrasted with the divorced group. Three factors appear to be involved: (1) Religion is an indication of conventional and conforming behavior. (2) It is significant that the friends of this couple are religious and that their religion is opposed to divorce. Consequently the pressure and support of a circle of religious friends with their expectation that families would stay together determined in part the unity of this family. (3) In many of these families in which religion is significant, the members participate in religious activities together, which psychologically unites the husband and wife. The function of religion in these homes is to reinforce each other religiously

---

[13] *Ibid.*, p. 142.

and thereby create conforming attitudes with reference to the maintenance of the family.[14]

The family in its internal interaction develops a conception of itself, but this conception is modified and adjusted to the conception which persons outside have of it. Extrafamilial relationships give the family status and support, and to a considerable extent control its activities. Thus the family often is affected decisively by its relationship to groups and institutions in the community.

TYPES OF MARITAL RELATIONSHIPS

Cuber has made a five-fold typology of husband-wife relationships of permanent, on-going, affluent families.[15] The data came from interviews lasting from three hours to several days. Excluding those with marriages of less than 10 years and those who had considered divorce, he based his classification on the remaining 211 persons. The five types were conflict-habituated, the devitalized, the passive-congenial, the vital, and the total. These types do not indicate different degrees of marital happiness or adjustment, but rather different types of adjustment and different conceptions of marriage.

In the *conflict-habituated* type of relationship, the husband and wife conceive of their marriage as a battleground. They regularly engage in conflicts which occupy much of the interaction between them. Even though there is constant tension and much attention is given to handling the tensions and concealing them, there is no thought of divorce.

The *devitalized* husband-wife families conceive of their marriage as having lost much of that which they valued in earlier years. They are not currently deeply in love; little time is spent together; sexual relationships are not satisfying either qualitatively or quantitatively; and interests and activities are not shared in the way they once were. The continuity of the "apathetic lifeless" relationship is fostered by habit, by legal and ecclesiastical requirements and expectations, and the conception that "the divitalized mode is that appropriate mode in which a man and woman should be content to live in the middle years and later."[16]

The *passive-congenial* couple have from the beginning conceived of marriage as noninvolvement and at the same time congenial. The passive-congenial is differentiated from the devitalized by the fact that the passivity which pervades the relationship was there from the start. The

[14] *Ibid.*, pp. 220–221.
[15] John F. Cuber, *The Significant Americans: A Study of Sexual Behavior Among the Affluent* (New York: Appleton Century, 1965).
[16] *Ibid.*, p. 50.

couples of this type never expected anything different from what they are currently experiencing; existing ways of association are comfortably adequate; and there is no wish to invest their total emotional involvement and creative interests in the male-female relationship.

In the *vital* relationship the husband and wife conceive of the marriage relationship as one that intensely binds them together psychologically in important life objectives, goals, and values. There is genuine sharing and togetherness. The presence of the mate is indispensable to feelings of satisfaction in an activity. The husband and wife have "exciting mutuality of feelings and participation together in important life segments."[17] Other values are readily sacrificed to maintain the central value of their lives—living with and through each other.

The *total* relationship might have been called the totally vital, for that is what it is. The husband and wife conceive of marriage as complete mutuality of all interests and activities. The points of vital meshing are numerous. When faced with differences, such husbands and wives dispose of the differences without losing their feelings of unity and the centrality of their relationship. As far as possible, all interests and activities are shared and any activity which is not shared is flat. In the totally vital "it is as if neither spouse has, or has had, a truly private existence."[18]

Cuber is not specific on the frequency of these five types of family relationships. He indicates that the devitalized is exceedingly common. One gathers the impression that the conflict habituated, the passive congenial, and the vital are all small in number of cases. He indicates that the total or what we have called the totally vital are rare.

DEGREES OF FAMILY UNITY

Family unity, as a continuum, has disorganization and dispersion of the family members at one extreme and the highest degree of unity at the other. Actually, families fall on a continuum of integration from those that are loosely organized to those with a high degree of organization. Selected for consideration to represent different degrees of family unity are (1) the broken family, (2) the relatively unorganized family, (3) the habit-bound family, (4) the highly solidified family, and (5) the dynamically unified family.

In a loosely organized family there is little integration. The habit-bound family is integrated on the basis of habitual responses. The highly solidified family is integrated through interdependent habits, strong attachments, and the subordination of individual goals and values

[17] *Ibid.*, p. 56.
[18] *Ibid.*, p. 60.

to those of the family group. In the dynamically united family integration develops and is maintained through the voluntary participation of its members in achieving a common objective.

The Broken Family Families are broken by death, divorce, separation because of domestic discord, and separation for other reasons.[19] In the late 1960's those without mates because of death, divorce, or separation due to marital discord were about ten men for every 100 married men, and about 30 women for every 100 married women.[20] The larger figure for women was due, in large part, to the fact that there were about 9 million widowed women and only 2 million widowed men. Separations were more numerous among nonwhites than whites, and in urban than rural areas.

The above is on the extent of broken families. However, one should not forget the shattering of personal relationships which result from divorce or death of a family member. In a family that breaks up by divorce or separation, the husband, or wife, or both may feel married even though the spouse is absent. In the case of death the bereaved spouse may have difficulty in adjusting to the permanent absence of the spouse.

In cases of both divorce and widowhood, remarriage frequently occurs. When children by the first marriage are present, problems of adjustment arise, and family unity is impaired if these problems are not solved.

The Relatively Unorganized Family The members of some families may never have had or developed consensus on values and objectives, or interdependence based on sympathetic understanding, or division of labor for the attainment of common objectives. Becoming man and wife before the law may have occurred because of pregnancy, impulsive behavior, casual sex contacts, or economic advantage, with little or no prior unity. Such marriages may become a legal fiction and often end in separation and divorce.

But occasionally unorganized families, especially those of low economic and social status, survive when the integration of husband and wife, at least to an observer, seems slight. Sometimes, as in the following case, an isolated, rejected person will strive more to make adjustments than will a person whose family background was superior to the situation he finds in marriage:

> I was twenty-eight at the time of my marriage. I grew up in a home in which I had two stepmothers; my childhood was unhappy, and I thought

---

[19] See the discussion of family disruption, Ch. 21.
[20] Figures for this paragraph computed from data in *Current Population Reports, Population Characteristics*, Series P-20, No. 170, 1968, p. 9.

I would do anything to get away from my stepmother. I think I am very lucky in getting a good husband. Yes, I filed suit for divorce, but I canceled it three days later. I decided I would never forsake the man who had been so kind to me although he has done some things of which I disapprove. His biggest fault is periodic drunken sprees. You asked me what I would do if I found that my husband was going around with other women. I do not know, but I do know I would not leave him.

The Habit-Bound Family Some students of family behavior have indicated that intimate, spontaneous communication in a family decreases with the passing of the years, that the roles of family members become fixed, and that behavior toward each other tends to become routine. Waller refers to the "dead level of marriage interaction."[21] For many couples in which the thought of divorce may never be considered as a possibility, marriage seems to move along at a friendly jog-trot marked by sober accommodation of each partner to his share in the joint family activities.

While observable expression of communication may decrease with the establishment of stable, interdependent habits, the amount of intimate, personal, informal communication may not decrease, for it is not necessarily determined by the number of words spoken or the time span of the particular association. A slight gesture, a facial expression, a word, or a phrase may have acquired great meaning for the members of an independent family. As persons become well acquainted, a glance may signify something on which there is common understanding. So possibly the "dead level" of family interaction or the decrease of intimate communication with the passing of the years may be more apparent than real. Moreover, these habitual patterns of behavior allow members to anticipate each other's behavior in advance and adjust their conduct accordingly.

The Highly Solidified Family Certain families seem to live within and for themselves alone. The persons in these families may be not so much separate individuals as parts of a single entity. In these highly solidified families familism is emphasized, and there is disapproval of individuality.

The degree of unity in some families is so great that it is extremely difficult for a member to break away and form a family of his own. When there is this high degree of integration and a child marries, it may be practically impossible for the spouse, "this stranger," to become incorporated into the family unit:

---

[21] Willard Waller (Revised by Reuben Hill), *The Family: A Dynamic Interpretation* (New York: The Dryden Press, 1951), pp. 331–332.

Life in my family is extremely close-knit, and I wanted to bring Joe into my family as he brought me into his. Mother just can't get used to the fact that I'm grown up and that I'm not going to live at home. She tries to "win back," as she says, my affection. She says that I should have nicer clothes and that Joe doesn't support me in the style to which I've been accustomed (laughs). His folks have been wonderful and I'm very much attached to them. They feel that they have gained a daughter, but Mother says, "I've lost my little girl."

This case illustrates the point that in the parental family there may develop a closely knit organization based on interdependent attitudes and strong attachments. Upon marriage the young person may find difficulty in breaking off these attachments and separating himself from the family. The attempt may be made to incorporate the mate into the closed corporation. If the mate does not fit into the parental family and follow its practices, irritation and conflict ensue, and may result in his departure and finally in divorce.

Other cases show the difficulties sons or daughters may have after marriage in breaking the attachments and habits of confiding which still bind them to their parents:

My husband, particularly at first, was always running home with whatever troubles or problems we had. It annoyed me. He was always having to consult his mother. He used to go to her about every detail. I suppose it bothered me most because I am more independent.

My husband compares me unfavorably with his mother too much. I didn't cook like his mother or do this and that the way she did it. It seemed like she was always more or less in the background.

The Dynamically Unified Family The dynamically unified family has the following characteristics: (1) Its unity is based on the consensus of its members. (2) It emphasizes the individuality of its members and their personality development rather than their subordination to the family. (3) It is characterized by the adaptability of the family and its members in meeting crises.

The cooperation of the members of the dynamically unified family in common activities may actually be stimulated by the freedom given to individual expression of diverse interests and by the flexibility and informality of its organization. Certain families manifest in unusual degree the participation of their members in a collective endeavor to which each makes a vital contribution. All members of a family may be united by a common objective, such as buying a home, sending children to college, or participating in a family council in which budget and other matters are discussed and decided.

Often the participation of the whole family in a career or a project of one of its members is highly unifying. Husbands and wives who are engaged in the same profession may be unified by this common occupational interest.

Behavior in a dynamically unified family is pictured in the account by a daughter in the case at the beginning of this chapter.

SUMMARY

The unity of the extended-patriarchal family was based on tradition, the mores, community pressure, law, elaborate ritual and ceremony, authority, superordination and subordination of family members, definite roles, especially in the division of labor, and rigid discipline. Most of these factors making for family integration are absent or at a minimum in the modern urban American family. Unity in the companionship family develops and is maintained in communication, love and affection, emotional interdependence, sympathetic understanding, common interests and activities, consensus on family objectives and values, family events, celebrations, and ceremonies, interdependence of family roles, and mutual enjoyment and satisfaction of sexual activities. Social pressure of the community, particularly that of relatives, friends, and neighbors, still exerts an influence, although it is diminishing.

In a society like that of the United States, characterized by heterogeneity of cultural patterns, there is not the same uniformity in family integration as found in a homogenous society. In the United States at present, various types of marital relationships and varying degrees of family unity are found, ranging from the disrupted family through the unorganized family, the habit-bound union, the highly solidified family, to the dynamically unified family.

This latter type is one that deserves special study to discover the combination of integration and flexibility which will contribute to family unity and at the same time will foster the development of differentiated personalities. Other possibilities of research will now be indicated.

PROBLEMS FOR RESEARCH

Affectional and Prudential Marriages What is the difference in unity of families where strong emotional attachments are basic to the marriage and those where marriages are more utilitarian? It would be interesting to take a group of marriages where love is at a minimum and utility at a maximum and investigate the unifying factors and compare these factors with those in marriages where love is at a maximum and utility at a minimum. What, if any, are the differences by economic status and class?

Family Personnel There are marked differences in the personnel of such family groups as childless families, families with different numbers of children, no minor children living at home but unmarried adult children living at home, in-laws living with the family, families with boarders, remarried widowed, remarried divorced, families with stepchildren, and various other types. How is family unity affected by these and other differences in personnel?

Parents and Parents-in-Law In ancient society and Oriental civilizations, the parents and parents-in-law were unifying influences because the small-family group was subordinate to the extended family or the lineage group. Now, where the unit of husband, wife, and children is independent, the parents on one or both sides of the family may be either unifying, disruptive, or indifferent. The problem for research is to determine the conditions under which parents of young married couples act to strengthen or undermine the new union. Several hypotheses may be tested: (1) Antagonism expressed before marriage, particularly between a mother-in-law and her son-in-law or daughter-in-law, is likely to persist after the marriage. (2) Conflicts between mother-in-law and daughter-in-law are more frequent than between mother-in-law and son-in-law. (3) Conflicts between parents-in-law and children-in-law are more likely when the husband or wife is an only child.

Religion Religion as a unifying and, under certain circumstances, a disintegrating factor in family life needs further study. Research might discover whether disagreements between husbands and wives who are affiliated with very different religious groups may be greater after the birth of children. Another significant problem for study is the extent to which parents resume religious activities after the birth of a child.

QUESTIONS AND EXERCISES

1. Discuss the family as a unity of communicating persons from the standpoint of (a) internal modifications of personalities, (b) reciprocal responsiveness of the members of the family, (c) interaction on the level of the senses, and (d) interaction resulting in organization and accord.
2. Rank in the order of importance for family unity (a) primary communication; (b) love and affection; (c) emotional interdependence; (d) sympathetic understanding; (e) temperamental compatibility; (f) common interests; (g) consensus on values and objectives; (h) family events, celebrations, and ceremonies; (i) interdependence of roles; (j) sexual behavior; and (k) the environing society.

3. To what extent does conflict with outsiders intensify family unity?
4. Under which types—disorganized, unorganized, habit-bound, highly solidified, and dynamically organized—would you classify the following families: divorced; those resembling a closed corporation; the farm family; a young married couple who before marriage had a minimum of contact and who married on the spur of the moment?
5. Which of the various factors promoting family unity were most important in the case introducing this chapter?
6. Write an account in the first person of unity in your family or in one with which you are intimately acquainted.

BIBLIOGRAPHY

Bell, Norman W.; and Vogel, Ezra F. *A Modern Introduction to the Family.* New York: Free Press, 1960, Introductory Essay, pp. 1–33.
> Describes the nuclear family as related to other parts of a society—the economic, political, community, and value systems; its internal activities; and the personality development of its members.

Blood, Robert O.; and Hamblin, Robert L. "The Effects of the Wife's Employment on the Family Power Structure," *Social Forces,* 26 (1958): pp. 347–352. Also in Norman W. Bell and Ezra F. Vogel, *A Modern Introduction to the Family,* Ch. 11.
> Based on 160 interviews with wives made by upper-division students at the University of Michigan. Husband-wife power relationships of both wives who worked and those who did not were equalitarian.

Cuber, John F. *The Significant Americans: A Study of Sexual Behavior Among the Affluent.* New York: Appleton-Century, 1965.
> Based on extended interviews with 437 men and women. The families were affluent in that they had incomes from business or a profession. The emphasis is on different kinds or types of marriages.

Luckey, Eleanore Braun. "Perceptual Congruence of Self and Family Concepts as Related to Marital Interaction," *Sociometry,* 24 (1961): pp. 234–250.
> Compares 41 couples having high scores on marital adjustment with 40 couples having low scores. Analyzes differences in concepts of self, spouse, mother, father, and ideal self as indicated by responses on Interpersonal Check List. There were significant differences between high- and low-scoring couples.

Middletown, Russel; and Putney, Snell. "Dominance in Decisions in the Family: Race and Class Differences," *American Journal of Sociology,* 65 (1960): pp. 605–609.
> Compares four groups of 10 members each on husband-wife making of minor decisions: white professors, white skilled workers, Negro professors,

and Negro skilled workers. There were no significant differences in relative dominance of husband and wife. All four groups had equalitarian relationships.

Parsons, Talcott; and Bales, Robert F. *Family, Socialization, and Interaction Process*. New York: Free Press 1955.
Views the family as a network of patterns of relationship or as a social subsystem, the chief role of the man is occupational or instrumental, and the chief role of the woman is the giving of affection, or an expressive role.

Zimmerman, Carle C.; and Cervantes, Lucius F. *Successful American Families*. New York: Pageant Press, 1960.
Based on questionnaires filled out by 9,253 high school seniors about their parents' intimate friends, and found that successful families—without divorce, separation, or police records—associated with other successful families. The more intimate the relationship and the more similar the friends were in income, religion, and region of origin, the more successful the families.

Chapter 16
Family Relations in the Middle and Later Years

New intergenerational family relations are emerging in the United States. These are developing as a reaction to economic and social trends which have modified the kinship system, have taken the worker out of the home, and have changed the average man from entrepreneur to employee. The role of the patriarch has all but disappeared. The new roles of grandparents, adult children, and grandchildren are manifestations of companionship within an area of common social life. The vitality and meaning of family relations to the older person is evident when consideration is given to the desolation and loneliness of the widowed, especially of those lacking the emotional support of their children.

AN INTERGENERATION FAMILY

The following case of intergeneration family relations consists of excerpts from interviews with the parents, who are in the later years of marriage, and with their middle-aged son and daughter-in-law. The son and daughter-in-law are in the process of social mobility. The parents are lower-middle class, their son and his wife are becoming upper-middle class, and they are ambitious to prepare their children for the same or next higher class level. The excerpts reveal many of the crucial points in family relations in the middle and later years of family life.

Changes in Interests and Activities with Aging
Father: You don't enjoy the things you used to. Things change. I used to enjoy going to ball games. When I was a kid movies were good but look at them now. I did take an interest in politics, but no more. It is too

crooked. You have to be in with a clique, but singlehanded, you'd better stay in your own backyard. Now I like to see my grandchildren, visit with my children, see nature, and walk in the park.

Mother: I enjoy a nice dinner, dancing, seeing a show, visiting people, watching T.V. I still do all of them off and on, but not as much. Too much crooked stuff goes on in politics. Everyone is out for the dollar.

Son: I enjoy music, a good play, a good television show, a good book, anything concerned with outdoors. I'm not a cause-bearer but I keep daily abreast of things political.

Daughter-in-law: Now I like things on a higher level than when I was younger. I liked night clubs. I like them less every year now. Now I prefer a quiet dinner in a restaurant. I've slowed down in the last few years. My energy is a little less now. I never miss voting. I try to follow the candidates and listen to others.

Attitudes Toward Retirement

Father: In the last ten years I retired. I don't have to hustle and bustle like I used to. Now that I have retired, I just take things easy. I quit work of my own accord. Today the most important thing in my life is to see my children and grandchildren get a little headway in life. I am happy that my children and grandchildren are getting along.

Mother: Retirement used to be the rocking chair for older people. Grandmothers are not old now.

Son: I would like to retire as early in life as possible. I am looking forward to it. But it is going to be a retirement that is planned—not just doing nothing. I want to be active—but do only what I want to do when I want.

Daughter-in-law: I think retirement is wonderful but it depends on the individual. People who can enjoy life and have an interest in people can have an easier time of it.

Attitudes Toward Children Leaving Home

Father: It wasn't a bad time when the children left home. We just didn't have to spend as much money.

Mother: When children grow up and leave home husband and wife get much closer but you have lonely minutes too. It's a difficult period. You're back where you started with your husband. It was a bad time in my life—I shouldn't feel that way but that's what you bring them into the world for—to grow up and leave you.

Son: When children leave home it's bad in one respect. Unless the wife knows how to fill the void, she can run into a lot of trouble. But it can create a more harmonious and romantic situation. They can do a lot that they were postponing, that they could not do before.

Attitudes of Parents Toward Son and His Wife

Father: I get along with my son and daughter-in-law. We just see them once in a while—not too much—it bores them.

Mother: She is not as warm and friendly as I'd like a daughter-in-law to be. Maybe I'm expecting too much. She takes advantage of my son. She knows how to get around him. You can't expect anything from your son after he's married.

Attitudes Toward the Grandchildren
Father: My grandchildren are very important. They are my family. When they get sick it seems like the love is really there. It's not like your own. It's different. It's more sometimes.
Mother: I like my grandchildren very much. I'm closer to the children who were raised here.
Son: The children have been an excuse for not seeing my parents as much.

Joint and Separate Lives of Middle-Aged Husband and Wife
Daughter-in-law: With four children and more work we get more wrapped up in our separate activities than with each other. Today's father has more to do and it is harder to make a living. He has more things to do away from the house. As for me, the children become my drive. I would be more social minded if my husband were. I'd do more entertaining. I'd probably go out more.
Son: With children my wife had to devote more of her time to the raising of children and the home. The husband's position is pushed into the background. I believe a small amount of a man's time should be away from the family.

The excerpts from this case focus on crucial issues in intergenerational relations. In both the older and the younger couple, changes in interests and activities have taken place with aging. The father thinks of retirement as "taking things easy"; the son emphasizes planning for it and being active in doing what he wants to do. The father, with his life work completed, is ambitious for successful careers for his children and grandchildren. When adult children leave home for marriage, it is a crisis particularly for the mother, who loses what often is her central function in the family. The upward social mobility of the young couple may, as in this case, produce an emotional strain on the personal relations of the two generations which is keenly felt by the old couple in restrictions on visiting with children and grandchildren. Finally, there is the appreciation by both son and daughter-in-law that demands of work on the husband and the preoccupation of the wife with rearing children and housework have encroached on their life in common.

The relations of husband and wife in the middle and later years may be viewed in the light of three sets of roles: The roles they have in common, the separate roles of the husband, and the separate roles of the wife. The roles they have in common center on companionship. The separate roles of the husband are connected with his occupation. The separate roles of the wife center on her homemaking and child rearing.

THE FAMILY LIFE CYCLE

The developmental approach emphasizes the sequences in the family life cycle.[1] Before engagement the man and woman have lived separate lives. They have had different experiences in childhood and adolescence. Typically, during adolescence they begin casual associations and dating. During courtship and engagement the couple forms a network of interpersonal relationships, although individual interests tend to predominate. A woman at the present time (1970) will enter into her first marriage at about 21 years of age (20.8) to a man who is just over 23 years of age (23.2).

Between marriage and a year to a year and a half after marriage, when the first child is born (1.3 years), the husband and wife will have the opportunity to develop common interests, to enjoy companionship, to share feelings, attitudes, and values. When the children are young, they often are a source of interest and enjoyment for both husband and wife. The wife will complete her child-bearing between her 30th and 31st birthday. Subsequently, her primary activity is child-rearing.

The child-rearing period in the typical family begins shortly after the marriage and continues until the last child is married. At this time the mother is about 52 years of age. During these middle years of marriage, the general tendency is for the husband and wife to become absorbed in separate interests—the husband in his work and in sports, the wife in care of the home and the rearing of children. This generally means that common interests decline, together with a decline in companionship and intimacy.

In about 8 out of 10 couples both the husband and wife survive to see their last child married. With the marriage of the last child the mother is retired from one of her chief functions—the care and rearing of the children.

The retirement of the husband from work usually means a reduction of family income by more than one-half and the loss of friends he enjoyed on the job. But it also may be a turning point in the relationship of the husband and wife, providing an opportunity to appraise their common and separate activities and to select those they wish to continue and new ones they wish to pursue in the later years.

Couples who survive until the last child is married will have several

---

[1] Age at marriage is from *Current Population Reports, Population Characteristics*, Series P-20, No. 198, 1970; other statistical data are from Paul C. Glick and Robert Parks, "New Approaches in Studying the Life Cycle of the Family," *Demography*, 2 (1965), pp. 187–202, and Hugh Carter and Paul C. Glick, *Marriage and Divorce: A Social and Economic Study* (Cambridge: Harvard University Press, 1970), particularly pp. 147–148.

years together before one of the couple will die. It is estimated that on the average, a wife will become a widow by age 61. Widows will have an average period of about 19 years before death. If the husband survives his wife, he will live an average of 15 years.

The death of the husband or wife is a crisis for the surviving member. Widowhood means that the common life and activities of the husband and wife have been destroyed, except in memory.

FAMILY RELATIONS IN THE MIDDLE YEARS

The chief manifestations of changing relationships of husband and wife in the middle years of marriage will be discussed from the viewpoint of (1) a comparison of the early and middle years of marriage, (2) occupational frustration of the husband, and (3) the effect on parents of the children's leaving home.

Comparison of the Early and Middle Years of Marriage Burgess has made two restudies of the Burgess-Wallin cases. The first examined the early years of marriage and the second the middle years.[2] These longitudinal studies provide data on family relationships which changed significantly and those which remained essentially stable from the early to the middle years of marriage. We will first present six significant changes between the early and middle years of marriage.

1. Husbands and wives report a substantial decline in companionship in the transition period from childlessness to having children up to the age of three. This is followed by a leveling off in the degree of companionship. These were the conclusions of Rollins and Feldman from their study of a representative sample of 799 upper-middle and upper class families residing in Syracuse, New York. The items used to measure companionship were laughing together, calm discussion with each other, having a stimulating exchange of ideas, and working together on a project.[3]

The decline in companionship is revealed in the personal documents obtained from the couples in the early and middle years of marriage. There is a decline in the scope and meaning of their common life together and a growth of separate interests and activities. This begins after the first three or four years of marriage. Particularly in the middle-class family, the husband becomes increasingly absorbed in his work

[2] Ernest W. Burgess, unpublished manuscript, "The Study of Marriage in the Middle Years," based on a restudy of the Burgess-Wallin cases described in Ernest W. Burgess and Paul Wallin, *Engagement and Marriage* (Philadelphia: Lippincott, 1953).

[3] Boyd C. Rollins and Harold Feldman, "Marital Satisfaction Over the Family Life Cycle," *Journal of Marriage and the Family*, 32 (1970): pp. 20–28.

and in the prospects for advancement. His career role often makes demands on his time and limits his effective functioning in his roles of husband and father. Statements by husbands and particularly by wives illustrate how the career aspirations of the husband limit the time he has for companionship with his family:

> *Wife:* My husband's business has taken too much of his time. I feel that the strong competition in business has caused us to miss the best years of our life together. He has achieved great success in his business. His gains have been much more than we ever expected. The changes I would make in my marriage for more happiness would be that my husband spend more time with the family in leisure, in taking trips, and in just having time for us to talk with each other.

The wife for her part gets increasingly involved in her roles of child care, of homemaking, and often of community activities:

> *Wife:* A housewife's job is just as important as any job a person can hold. It requires a lot of time and thought. I think that making a nice home can be like a career. She can learn to be a good cook and a gracious hostess and be able to meet people and perhaps take a place of responsibility in the community.

> *Wife:* The biggest problems in marriage have always involved the children, particularly in the area of disciplining. I have to do all of it. I think parents should share this equally for the sake of the children.

2. There is a statistically significant decline in demonstration of love and affection between husbands and wives from the early to the middle years of marriage. The frequency of sexual intercourse decreases over the years, a finding which was also supported by Kinsey's data.[4] Frequency of intercourse tends to decline over the years; satisfaction of husbands and wives with sex decreases when the children are of school age (6 to 12 years of age), and then gradually rises to the time when all children have left the home.[5] Demonstration of affection, as indicated by the husband and wife kissing each other, also drops by the later years of marriage.

There appears to be a change in the quality of affection from romantic to a deeper feeling of love. This is illustrated by statements of a middle-aged wife and husband:

---

[4] Alfred C. Kinsey, Wardell B. Pomeroy, and Clyde E. Martin, *Sexual Behavior in the Human Male* (Philadelphia: Saunders, 1948), pp. 252–257; and Alfred C. Kinsey, Wardell B. Pomeroy, Clyde E. Martin, and Paul H. Gebhard; *Sexual Behavior in the Human Female* (Philadelphia: Saunders, 1953), pp. 350–354.

[5] Wesley R. Burr, "Satisfaction with Various Aspects of Marriage Over the Life Cycle: A Random Middle Class Sample," *Journal of Marriage and the Family*, 32 (1970), pp. 29–37.

Wife: There is a good deal of maturation, give and take much more than in the beginning—a deeper meaning of love over and above the purely romantic.

Husband: My love for my wife has mellowed as the years have past. I don't think it has decreased any. It is more of a companionable love.

3. There is a statistically significant decline in the sharing of interests and activities. One wife put it thus:

Our interests have grown apart, and our thoughts on life have changed. Each of us has concentrated on the fields with which we are most concerned. We have lost some of our togetherness.

4. A statistically significant decrease takes place in consensus, as measured by agreements as compared with disagreements on the main issues in marriage. A husband makes the following comment:

I'd like to see a change made for a better understanding between us and for a situation more of a 50-50 arrangement, with each of us giving the other the opportunity to hear the other side.

5. The growing apart of husband and wife is reflected also in the reduction of those believing in the permanence of the marital union. A rating of permanence was secured by answers to questions involving having ever considered or thought that the spouse had considered divorce or separation. There was an increase in affirmative answers in the middle as compared with the early years of marriage.

6. A decline takes place in scores on the marital-adjustment index. This is an overall measure of growing apart of husband and wife. The marital-adjustment test showed a large decline between the early and middle years af marriage.[6]

We now turn to the personal characteristics and marital relationships which remain stable over the period between the early and middle years of marriage. Like the above, this will be based on both interview and statistical data. There was little or no statistically significant change between the reports in the early and middle years of marriage on the following indexes of personal characteristics and marital relations:

1. Own marital happiness as reported by husband and wife.
2. Personal autonomy or nonneuroticism
3. Sexual adjustment
4. Favorable attitudes toward having children

---

[6] These same statistical data have been analyzed by Peter G. Pineo relative to disenchantment. See "Disenchantment in the Later Years of Marriage," *Marriage and Family Living*, 23 (1961): pp. 1–11.

5. Traditionalism in the marriage
6. Dominance in the marriage
7. Personal growth due to marriage
8. Number of felt personality needs
9. Rating of own personality traits
10. Rating of mate's personality traits
11. Idealization of mate's personality

Thus, Burgess found that by the middle years of marriage there was a drop in certain factors and no drop in others. The six things which declined were indexes of growing apart: a decline in companionship, demonstration of affection, common interests, consensus, belief in the permanence of the union, and scores on the marital-adjustment test. There was no decline in the 11 listed above. What common element, if any, exists in the 11 indexes as compared with the 6 in which there was a drop? Obviously none of the 11 are measures of the growing together or apart of husbands and wives. On the contrary, practically all of them are measures of personal *reactions,* such as own marital happiness and nonneuroticism, and personal *attitudes,* such as those in favor of having children, traditionalism, and dominance in the family.

There is a change in the types of problems persons have in the middle years as compared to the early years of marriage. Brayshaw, in an analysis of 25 thousand marriage counselors' records, found that the reasons given for dissatisfaction with marriage change in order of importance between those who had been married less than three years and those who had been married eighteen or more years. Table 19 shows the percentage of persons responding to the various reasons for marital dissatisfaction.

Table 19. Marital problems of couples married 3 years or less and those married 18 years or more, by percent*

Serious problems	LENGTH OF MARRIAGE	
	3 years or less	18 years or more
Sex	40	15
Living conditions	24	7
Parental influence	22	9
Ill health	14	29
Incompatibility	12	23
Infidelity	6	26
Income	3	6

*Data from A. Joseph Brayshaw, "Middle-Aged Marriage: Idealism, Realism, and the Search for Meaning," *Marriage and Family Living,* 24 (1962): pp. 358–364.

It is apparent that the serious problems in the early years of marriage are different from those of the middle years of marriage. Sex, living conditions, and parental influence were mentioned most frequently by those in the early years, whereas ill health, infidelity, and incompatibility were mentioned more often by those in the middle years of marriage.

Career Frustration of the Middle-Aged Husband The American dream of success in an occupational career is almost an obsession with many middle-class men. Yet the plain facts of economic life show that the odds favor the few. The majority are doomed to disappointment. Statistics for all employed men indicate declining rather than increasing income for men in their late fifties.

There is a definite income pattern by age of the head of the family. With inflation, income may go up but the pattern remains essentially the same. The pattern is that income is low in the early years of economic activity, reaches a high level in the age period 35–54, declines between 55–64, and drops drastically for those 65 and older. This is illustrated in Table 20 which gives the median family income by age of head.

Table 20. Median family income by age of head*

Age	
14–24	$5,611
25–34	7,335
35–44	8,589
45–54	8,861
55–64	7,586
65 and over	3,645

*Current Population Reports, Consumer Income, P-60, No. 53, 1967, p. 24.

By 45, or perhaps as early as 40, a man realizes that the chance of further advancement as measured by increase in occupational rank and income are increasingly doubtful. At this time many men are dissatisfied with their occupational progress, especially those who have cherished aspirations for a higher level of achievement. In the following example, a middle-aged husband expresses his dissatisfaction with his occupational status, while his wife expresses hope for his advancement:

Husband: No man is ever satisfied. I'm accepting it, but am not completely satisfied. I think my talents and capabilities are such that I could operate as president of a company the size of the one I am now in.

Wife: He might be vice-president some day. They have lots of them. He works for a large corporation.

The failure to fulfill one's self-image may find expression in restlessness, ill health, and maladjusted behavior, such as excessive drinking and gambling. Or a person may place the blame for his failure on the organization that did not recognize his merits or on some circumstance beyond his control. He may seek to maintain his self-image by substituting noneconomic for occupational success, such as achieving prominence in activities of a church, lodge, or charity organization. He may picture himself as winning fame and fortune by an ingenious invention or a best-selling book. Or he may withdraw from these associations and organizations which remind him and others of his failure, consoling himself that he has quit the "rat race."

This unhappiness of husbands with their occupational progress often affects adversely the roles of husband and father. Wives generally show less dissatisfaction with the husband's occupational progress. A wife states that she is completely satisfied with her husband's work and income. "I am only unhappy because he is unhappy."

There are husbands, however, who place the self-image of the family man ahead of the occupational-success image. The husband in the following put his wife and family first and was fully conscious that he was doing it at the expense of his success in his career:

> The thing that makes our home so happy is that I've keyed all my happiness to make her happy. It's an unusual situation where two people readjust themselves, each trying to be the best for one another. As far as my business goes, I could have been way up there, but I would have had to drink and been out three or four nights a week.

The Reduction of Parental Roles The middle years of marriage are a transitional period in the relations of parents and children. The change involves the growing independence of children and the lessening control of their behavior by parents. For children this is a time of dating, going away to college, and choosing an occupation and a mate. In asserting their independence they are responding to the pressures and codes of their peer group.

The growing interest of youth in the other sex poses a new situation for parents. Many feel that they should intervene to prevent mistakes in the choice of a mate or to promote the chances of a favorite person the parents would like as a son-in-law or daughter-in-law. Children, on the other hand, believe that the choice of a life partner is theirs to make. Burgess and Wallin report parental disapproval in two out of five broken engagements, 42.7 as compared with 21.6 percent of unbroken engagements.[7]

---

[7] Burgess and Wallin, p. 288.

Parental disapproval of the marriage often results in strained relations after marriage. These strains may be overt to the point where all communication and contact ceases. Or they may be subtle and concealed but still have an adverse effect on the relationships of parents and married children. Or the parties may agree to "let bygones be bygones."

The occasion of the last child leaving home greatly reduces and radically changes the parental role. The loss of the responsibility of rearing children is viewed by middle-aged parents with mixed feelings of regret and relief. The wife is retired from the role of motherhood and usually will need to find significant activities.

A mailed questionnaire study[8] provides data on the postparental adjustments of 199 husbands and 265 wives having a married child under 25. Comparisons were made of the responses of (1) those with no single children under 18 years remaining at home and (2) those still having one or more single children living with them.

Both groups of husbands and wives reported increased satisfaction with their marital adjustment and more activities with husband or wife now than when the child was in high school. Both fathers and mothers claimed much less financial worries since the marriage of the last child than if there were single children under 18 years remaining at home. Mothers in both groups and fathers with no single children under 18 at home stated that they now had less concern than earlier for the married child's welfare and that they participated less in community activities. Finally it is significant that the mothers and not the fathers confess to more loneliness now that no single child under 18 is at home.

Deutscher,[9] who studied postparental adjustments, asserts that when the last child leaves home most couples perceive this situation as a time of new freedom. They are now freed from the economic support of children and from much of the housework. They are free to travel and free to act exactly as they wish instead of serving as models of conduct for their children. In fact, 78 percent found the present stage of life as good or better than the preceding stages.

FAMILY RELATIONS IN THE LATER YEARS

In the later years of marriage the husband and wife typically face many situations to which adjustment is necessary. The following will be the topics discussed in this section: (1) decline in economic role of

[8] Leland J. Axelson, "Personal Adjustment in the Postparental Period," *Marriage and Family Living*, 22 (1960): pp. 66–68.

[9] Irwin Deutscher, "Socialization for Postparental Life," in *Human Behavior and Social Processes*, Arnold M. Rose, (ed.) (Boston: Houghton Mifflin, 1962), p. 523; also, "The Quality of Postparental Life: Definition of the Situation," *Journal of Marriage and the Family*, 26 (1964): pp. 52–59.

older persons, (2) marital roles in old age, (3) retirement of the husband, (4) widowhood, (5) middle-aged children and the support of their parents, (6) expectations about retirement, (7) old-age insurance and assistance programs, (8) the network of kin relationships, and (9) grandparents and grandchildren.

Decline in Economic Role of Older Persons Of primary significance for its effect on the relation of the aging father to his family is the loss of his role of economic independence and authority. A century ago older and middle-aged persons alike were largely self-employed, either on the farm or in small shops and stores in towns. The gainfully employed worker is now typically one employee among thousands of a large organization.

Not only have most older persons lost their role of independence as producers, but they are losing their role as gainfully employed. Of all men 65 and over in 1890, 68 percent were gainfully employed. In 1967 the percentage was 25.3. The Census predicts that by 1975 the percent will be 23.4 and by 1980 it will have dropped to 21.8[10]

Marital Roles in Old Age In the rural community of earlier times the husband and father was also the owner and manager of a farm. In the town he ran his small business or store, often with the help of his wife and children. He was typically an entrepreneur and an employer, with the family as an economic unit of production and sales. The father tended to organize and regiment family members in the interest of the success of his business. His wife was a junior partner, and the children were unpaid employees, with allotted work or chores to suit all ages. The husband held a more authoritarian role than the wife. As owner of his business he did not retire, though he might delegate some of his responsibilities to a son. He thus maintained his status and role to the end.

Today this situation has completely changed. The United States is a country of huge industrial, commercial, and other organizations with millions of employees. Work is now outside the home. The husband's role as entrepreneur and employer has been replaced by the role of employee. The role of the father and husband is almost exclusively that of the family man whose occupation takes him outside the home. In this new situation the authoritarian role of the husband is being replaced by a democratic and companionship role. Husband and wife are tending to be coequals in authority. The strict discipline of children is

[10] *Monthly Report on the Labor Force*, September 1961, United States Department of Labor, October 1961, Table 1; 1967, computed from data in *Statistical Abstract of the United States*, 1969, p. 212.

relaxing and the adolescent and youth have gained a degree of freedom undreamed of sixty years ago. The objective of family living is no longer economic productivity but the personal development and happiness of its members.

The Retirement of the Husband Husband and wife both face a crisis when the husband retires. Giving up his job usually means a reduction in family income by more than one-half and the loss of friends on the job. Research findings indicate that on the average the adjustment is more difficult if the husband found satisfaction in his work. In general, employees for whom work had little or no meaning other than earning a living adjust more easily. Employees who have not made plans for retirement find adjustment more difficult.

The Harris survey of 1965 on retirement had one sample of adults who were active and another who were retired.[11] A good life which was satisfactory was reported by 61 percent of the retired. The two most prevalent reasons for satisfaction in retirement were that now they were enjoying leisure and hobbies and now they can do as they please. The primary problem reported by 40 percent of those who found retirement not satisfactory was financial problems.

The age at which the subjects wanted to retire varied by age groups: under 60 was reported by 59 percent of the 21–34 age group; by 53 percent of the 35–49 age group; and by 23 percent of those over 50.

The Harris Survey also asked the pre-retired where they wanted to live upon retirement and asked the retired where they lived upon retirement. The overwhelming preference of both the retired and the pre-retired was to stay in the same place or move to another place in the same community. Only one percent indicated that they preferred to move in with their children.

In retirement the husband loses his occupational role, which represented to him and others a large part of his identity. He loses his schedule of daily activities. If he remains at home he may become a problem to his wife, who still has her household work to keep her busy. The wife has already experienced the crisis of retirement, or at least partial retirement; when the last child left home she was free to devote more time to her husband and to take up activities outside the home. Many mothers may find this at first a difficult emotional experience but later perceive it as an opportunity to use their free time in congenial associations and meaningful activities. With this experience of filling the void left by the departure of the children she may better sympathize with her husband, give him her emotional support, and help him plan his

[11] The Harris Survey, "Retirement Holds Appeal," *Los Angeles Times,* Nov. 29, 1965; and "The Concerns of Retirement," *Los Angeles Times,* Nov. 30, 1965.

activities in retirement. Often it is as difficult for the wife as for the husband to adjust to his retirement. She has been accustomed to managing the household and now the husband with free time on his hands may interfere with her housekeeping or at least the wife may feel that he is "underfoot."

One new aspect of their living together is most difficult for the retired husband. The wife retains her position in the home, but the husband has lost his occupational status and his earning power. The wife continues her management of the money, which now centers around household expenditures rather than the large purchases of the middle years. The wife may put the husband to work on repairs about the house and yard.

In the *Kansas City Study of the Middle and the Later Years*, one projective test showed a picture of an aging couple. Older as well as younger people were asked to explain what the picture meant. Older people gave interpretations of the picture that indicated the reality of the shift from less to more dominance on the part of the wife. This tendency toward reversal of roles of the aging husband and wife coincides with the downgrading of the husband through retirement from work and the augmented prestige of the wife in her increased relative influence as housekeeper and grandmother.

Shortly before or just after the husband retires, the couple have a number of crucial decisions to make. For the first time in their lives, they are at long last free to do what they want to within the limits of their income. These choices include (1) whether or not to remain in the home of their middle years or to move into a home more adapted to retirement living; (2) if they move, whether to remain in the community where they have their roots, or pull up stakes and select one more in accord with their new needs and preferences; (3) what old activities to continue and what new ones to take up; (4) what old organizations to give up and what new ones to join; and (5) which activities to select for joint and which for separate participation.

All these decisions require more knowledge than many older people possess. The need to make the best use of retirement living for personal happiness and development has led to the organization of programs of planning and preparation for retirement that are now sponsored by industry, labor unions, and community groups.

Widowhood The death of a spouse is a severe crisis in the later years of marriage. The frequency of widowhood is greater for women than for men. In 1968 there were only 1.5 widowers to 5.9 million widows 65 years af age or older.[12] This discrepancy is due partly to the fact

[12] Data from *Statistical Abstract of the United States*, 1969, p. 32.

that women on the average live longer than men. They are also usually younger than their husbands at marriage. There is also a greater probability that widowers will remarry. Of the widowers who remarry, a large percentage marry wives under 65 years of age.

In his study of an English industrial community, Townsend points out that desolation is a characteristic experience of widowhood that takes time to cure.[13] Using statements of loneliness as a measure of desolation, he found the following percentages of widowed persons stating they were "very" or "sometimes" lonely with the passage of time since the death of a spouse:

Years since death of spouse	Percent lonely
0–4	91
5–10	50
11 and over	27

The percent of all persons 65 and over stating that they were "very" or "sometimes" lonely was 27, and of all widowed individuals, 46. Thus not until 11 or more years had elapsed since the death of the spouse did widowed persons report the same proportion of loneliness as the entire population of aged persons.

Townsend reports that the loss of a marriage partner is a greater disaster for men than for women. Women "had always depended less on husbands than husbands on them, and they found it easier to console themselves with their families."[14]

Support of Parents Before the turn of the century there was a moral obligation for adult children to support and care for their aging parents. Usually only care was necessary, since many parents had property to transmit to their children. But the burden of discharging the filial role became increasingly difficult for middle-aged children. This was the result of several factors:

1. The probabilities of an adult having a parent 65 years of age and over more than doubled since 1900.

2. At the same time, the number of adult children per aging parent declined. Consequently, the volume of support and care required of adult children tremendously increased.

3. Moreover, the cost and difficulty of assuming the support and care of aging parents has mounted. The standard of living has become much

---

[13] Peter Townsend, *The Family Life of Old People* (London: Routledge and Kegan Paul, 1957), pp. 172–175.
[14] *Ibid.*, p. 174.

higher. The typical home has little or no space available to take in an additional family member.

4. Then, too, the aging parent is not of much help in the city home. In the past an able-bodied father was of real assistance to his farmer son. His modern counterpart can be at best of only limited usefulness. Even the aging mother is of far less help to her daughter than her grandmother was sixty years ago.

Consequently, the unmet expectations of many aging parents and the feelings of unfulfilled duty on the part of their adult children may result in anxiety, resentment, and broken relationships. Even adult children who recognize and discharge their duty of support and care of aging parents look forward to it with apprehension and carry it out by making real sacrifices.

Expectations About Retirement The Harris Survey of 1965 asked the pre-retired and the retired if they expected or if they were receiving financial help from their children. "Do not want help" was reported by 85 percent of the pre-retired and "do not receive help" was reported by 90 percent of the retired. Half of both groups expected to see their children and grandchildren about as frequently during retirement as before retirement. However, 28 percent of the retired were seeing more of their children and grandchildren. Harris reports that retirement increases opportunities for companionship between the retired husband and his wife.

The Harris Survey asked participants in the study how life would be different if their spouse passed away; the predominant expectation was loneliness. However, on this there are some interesting variations: 29 percent of the retired whose spouse was dead reported that they felt lonesome; 34 percent of the pre-retired reported that they expected to be lonesome; but 61 percent of the retired with both living expected to be lonesome if the spouse should die. The fear of loneliness or the experience of it is one of the most disturbing aspects of retirement.

Often the most economical way for children to help a needy aging parent is to take him into their home. This is a frequent practice in the United States and in other countries of Western culture. At present, however, the preferred arrangement is for both generations to live separately but near enough for frequent communication.

A study of 1130 employees 60–64 years old in six companies in Chicago and Toledo showed marked differences in attitudes by occupational level. The percent of those agreeing with the statement "When a mother is widowed she should be invited into the home of a child" varied from 38 percent at the managerial level, to 48 percent at the supervisory grade, to 55 percent of the skilled, semiskilled, and unskilled employees.[15] In short, those who are financially best able to care for a widowed mother are most disinclined to offer her a home.

Many factors enter into this difference in decisions by economic levels of occupation. Certainly those with higher incomes are better able to make provision for an aged mother outside their own homes. But this is probably not the strongest motivation. Social and personal factors are probably more important. These include the gap in cultural values between the generations, growing differentiation of personality of the adult children, participation of aging parents and their adult children in divergent spheres of social life, and the emancipation of the adult children from the duty to care for their parents in their own home.

Burgess studied 1000 upper-middle-class engaged couples and then restudied these couples three to five years after marriage and again fifteen to twenty years after marriage. He states that in the period of three to five years after marriage 16 percent of couples in his study made cash contributions to parents.[16] After fifteen to twenty years of marriage, this percent rose to 21.

In the *Cornell Study of Occupational Retirement* 2300 retired production workers were asked, "Who do you think should provide for the older person who has stopped working if he needs help in taking care of his problems?" Their answers were as follows:[17]

	Percent
The federal government	53
The company he worked for	45
Each state government	34
His family	33
His union	17
The local government	15
Community agency	11

Only one-third of the men mentioned the family, although most of them checked one or more of the other sources of help. It seems evident that the family has declined as a source of assistance. The reliance of aging persons for help is now on the large powerful organizations in society: government, companies, and labor unions.

[15] Ernest W. Burgess and R. T. Thornbury, "Attitudes Toward Retirement Living of Older Employees," unpublished paper.
[16] "The Study of Marriage in the Middle Years."
[17] Gordon F. Streib and Wayne E. Thompson, "The Older Person in a Family Context," *Handbook of Social Gerontology*, Clark Tibbits (ed.) (Chicago: University of Chicago Press, 1960), p. 480.

Old-Age Insurance and Assistance Programs The Depression of the thirties shocked the public into a recognition that the nation could no longer rely on rugged individualism for the support of older persons. The Social Security legislation of 1935 was the outstanding step in the assumption of government responsibility for the economic welfare of the aging. The long-range program of Old-Age and Survivors Insurance was a plan under government control whereby employers and employees would make equal contributions to a fund from which benefits would be payable under conditions of eligibility to retired workers, their wives, and their survivors.

Old-age assistance, also provided by this legislation, may be regarded as a short-range program designed for older persons not covered by Social Security. It is a joint program supported both by the federal and state governments. Eligibility for old-age assistance payments is determined by need, and the amount of financial help varies widely from state to state.

Revisions of Social Security legislation have greatly broadened the coverage of workers under Old-Age and Survivors Insurance to include all but a small number. Other measures have been taken by the government for the economic benefit of older persons. Social Security benefits and payments are not subject to the federal income tax. All men and women 65 years and over have double federal income tax exemptions.

Social Security insurance payments, pensions, and related programs are changing the economic conditions of older persons. These persons are regaining their economic independence. In March, 1969, there were 19,956,000 retired persons 65 years old or older who were receiving benefits from the Social Security insurance and related programs. Also there were 6,649,000 survivors receiving benefits from Social Security. Of those 65 years old or older, about 7 in 10 receive benefits from social insurance and related programs.[18]

All studies confirm that the present level of income of a high proportion of older persons is inadequate. But the level of income is rising, for the average Old Age Insurance benefit awarded is steadily increasing. Medicare provides insurance at low cost to persons 65 years of age and over for hospital costs and medical expenses. Those on Medicare—either hospital or supplementary medical insurance, or both—totalled 19,290,000 in 1967.[19] Even a moderate but assured monthly amount of money provides a degree of economic independence not previously avail-

[18] *Social Security Bulletin*, 32, No. 7, July, 1969; also *Social Security Bulletin*, 31, No. 3, March, 1968.

[19] *Health Insurance Statistics*, U.S. Department of Health, Education, and Welfare, Social Security Administration, Office of Research and Statistics, HI-3, February 1968.

able to older persons. This new economic independence provides the aged with the basis for a reorganization of relationships with their adult children.

The Network of Kin Relationships There is a substantial amount of evidence that the kinship group is prevalent in the urban environment.[20] The viability of the kinship relationships is seen in the help patterns between parents and children such as the exchange of gifts and financial aid. This has been studied in the middle class and working class; no information is available on the upper class or the lowest class. The exchange of aid flows from parents to children in the early years of the children's marriage and from children to parents in the later years. There is some evidence that a strong network of kinship relationships is more in what "ought to be" rather than in actual behavior.[21] The principal function of the kin-family system is visitation and participation in recreation and in ceremonies.

Approximately four out of five married couples who are 65 years of age and over live in their own households.[22] A mother is more likely to live with children than an aged father.

The evidence from case studies and limited statistical inquiries indicates that the prevailing feeling on both sides is that it is generally better to live apart. Whether the members live together or separately, a new code of family relations is evolving.

Under the old system of family relationships, the aging parents looked on themselves and were regarded by their adult children as authorities, advisors, and helpers. The adult children took a subordinate role of seekers of advice and of assistance. The aging parents were the repository of experience and the dispensers of wisdom. With the advance of science and technology, the son no longer turns to his father for advice but to the expert. The daughter tends to feel that the way her mother reared her is not the way to bring up a baby. So she goes to a pediatrician, a psychologist, or a psychiatrist. Older people are realizing the loss of this role of advisor. A sample of 284 employees of a company in the Chicago area reported the following percent of agreement by different occupational levels to the statement that a married daughter "should follow her mother's advice on how to bring up children": managerial

---

[20] Marvin B. Sussman, "Relationships of Adult Children with Their Parents in the United States," in *Social Structure and the Family: Generational Relations*, Ethel Shanas and Gordon F. Streib (eds.) (Englewood Cliffs, New Jersey: Prentice-Hall, 1965), pp. 62–92.

[21] Allen C. Kerckhoff, "Nuclear and Extended Family Relationships: A Normative and Behavioral Analysis," in *Social Structure and the Family*, pp. 93–112.

[22] From *Current Population Reports, Population Characteristics*, P-20, No. 173, 1968, p. 27.

level, 17 percent; supervisory group, 28 percent; skilled, semiskilled and unskilled, 40 percent.[23]

Studies indicate that the emotional support given the older person by children is even more important to him than financial support. Frequency of contact is one way of estimating the closeness of parents and children. The *Cornell Study of Industrial Retirement* analyzed the replies of nearly 2300 active participants, nearly 70 years old, on their family relationships. Close relationship within the three-generation family is indicated by 75 percent who see their children often and by 70 percent who see their grandchildren often. But contacts with the siblings of the older men is much less frequent, as revealed by reports of seeing sisters often by 36 percent and brothers often by 30 percent. Family ties with children are stated to be "very close" by 73 percent of respondents. It is significant, however, that 48 percent of respondents without children report "very close" family ties with their siblings, as compared with only 31 percent by families with children.[24]

Shanas studied older persons and persons to whom they said they would turn in the case of need.[25] She asked both groups—the aged and the responsible persons to whom they would turn in case of need—whether they would agree to the proposed action in 7 hypothetical situations. The percent of the aged agreeing is shown in the first column on p. 407 and the percent of the persons to whom they would turn is shown in the second column.

It is interesting to note the high correspondence of replies of the older people and the responsible individuals on the duty of a son or daughter to his aging parent. It is significant also that a much higher percent of responsible individuals (40.1) report that children or relatives should take care of retired older people than do the latter themselves (26.2).

Shanas concludes:

> Older people want to be financially independent. A majority of them feel that if an older person has been unable to save enough to make such independence possible in later life, the government should assume responsibility for his support through various income maintenance programs. A substantial group of sons and daughters (about two of every five) feel that the support of older people is their duty. What older people seem to want most from their children is love and affection. Apparently many older people feel that to ask their sons or daughters for financial support would threaten the affectional relationship between the generations.[26]

---

[23] Burgess and Thornbury.
[24] Streib and Thompson, p. 476.
[25] Ethel Shanas, *Family Relationships of Older People* (New York: Health Information Foundation, 1961).
[26] *Ibid.*, p. 38.

Proposed Action in a Hypothetical Situation	Percent of Older Persons Agreeing	Percent of All Persons to whom the Aged Would Turn Agreeing
1. Married daughter should move ailing widowed mother in with her	43.7	46.7
2. Son should repair parents' roof rather than go to practice of his bowling team for tournament	68.4	68.3
3. Son should take mother to doctor on Saturdays instead of shopping with wife	54.5	56.5
4. Son should visit parents on Easter instead of staying home to entertain wife's relatives	50.3	49.5
5. Government through Social Security should take care of retired older people	41.3	34.3
6. Retired older people should provide for themselves	23.7	17.9
7. Children or relatives should take care of retired older people	26.2	40.1

All human beings need emotional support. This emotional support, day by day and in the crises of life, is derived mainly in the family and from close friends. Older persons need this emotional support today even more than in the past. They need it to meet the crises of children leaving home, of retirement from employment, and of widowhood.

Grandparents and Grandchildren The birth of the first baby of a young couple is generally an occasion of family rejoicing. It is a time for reconciliation of the grandparents and their married children if a break in their relation occurred because of parental disapproval of the marriage or for any other reason.

The first grandchild establishes a bond of common interest between the grandparents and the young married couple. It is an auspicious time for the development of a new relationship of mutual interdependence which takes account of the independence of both the older and younger couple. If the roles of aging parents and their adult children are satisfactorily resolved, the roles of grandparents and grandchildren will present few if any problems.

The role of babysitter is one that the parents of young children are happy to confer upon grandparents. They are surprised and displeased if grandparents fail to respond with enthusiasm or even reject it altogether. Many grandparents state that they want to enjoy association with their grandchildren, but that they do not want to be exploited in the process. They resent the assumption that they are at beck and call for this service and that they are expected at a moment's notice to give up their own plans for the evening. In reply to the statement "A grandmother should babysit whenever her son or daughter asks her," affirmative replies were given by only 28 percent of employees at the managerial level, 29 percent of the supervisory level, and 42 percent of skilled, semiskilled and unskilled employees.[27] This rejection of the babysitter role by grandparents leads to the question, What should be their relation to grandchildren?

Grandparents are abandoning the role of ultimate authority and taking up the role of companionship. There are, of course, grandparents who still cling to the role of authority and rigid discipline. But they are more than counterbalanced by grandparents who assume the role of overindulgence and generous giving and who are often exploited by their grandchildren. The role of companionship is one in which the association is mutually enjoyable to grandparents and their grandchildren.

SUMMARY

Interpersonal relations of husband and wife and of older parents and their married children have been discussed in this chapter from the viewpoint of the family cycle. This method has permitted a description of changes in marital roles from marriage in the early years through the middle and later years. This analysis has revealed the critical situations faced by middle-aged couples.

In the middle years of marriage as compared with the early years there is a decline in communication, demonstration of affection, sharing of common interests, consensus, and belief in the permanence of marriage. However, there is no decline in personal reactions, such as marital happiness, sexual adjustment, and rating of mate's personality. There is a considerable difference in the serious problems during the early years of marriage as compared with the middle years of marriage. The middle-aged husband faces the likelihood that, unless he has gone up the occupational ladder by this age, he probably will not be able to do so at a later age.

In the later years of marriage there is a decline in the economic role of the husband and the child-care role of the wife. When the husband retires, he loses his occupational role and when the last child leaves home the wife loses one of her primary roles. Almost all older parents

[27] Ernest W. Burgess, data from an unpublished study.

want to live in separate quarters apart from their children. And Old Age Insurance and Assistance programs have lightened the financial burden of older persons.

In the later years of marriage many husbands feel frustrated by failure to achieve aspirations of occupational success. The complete loss of the work role at retirement lowers his status and self-esteem as a husband, father, and grandfather. There is an imperative need for vital leisure-time activity, not as a time-consuming pastime but as a status-conferring function. This problem and its solution should be a central objective of research.

PROBLEMS FOR RESEARCH

Longitudinal Research Until recently, studies of the middle and later years of marriage lagged behind research in courtship, engagement, and the early years of marriage. Research is in progress on family relations in the different stages of the family cycle. It is now opportune to consider the feasibility of longitudinal studies, beginning with engaged couples. Three sets of data are available for such research. Terman and Oden have a wealth of personality and marital findings from their study of gifted children. E. Lowell Kelly has material gathered from couples in engagement and later in marriage. Burgess and Wallin have repeated their interviews with engaged couples in both the early and middle years of marriage.

Marital Roles in the Middle and Later Years Preliminary evidence is now available on the reduction in companionship due to preoccupation of the husband with his career role and of the wife with her role of rearing children. Further research is needed to test these findings and to investigate the hypotheses that the postparental period and the retirement of the husband from work will increase the companionship and joint activities of the couple.

Effect of Career Frustration on the Husband The husband faces two occupational crises. The first occurs in middle age, when he realizes that he is blocked in achievement of his level of occupational aspiration. The second is when he is retired from his job. Research should be directed to a study of the success or failure of the husband in finding compensations in meaningful activities in the family, in neighborhood associations, or in participation in the organizations of the community.

Stability versus Mobility of Residence Older people at present have the greatest stability of residence of any age group in the United States.

Certain factors seem likely to increase their mobility, such as rising retirement income, their growing independence, and the availability of rapid transportation. A comparative study of matched pairs of couples and individuals who move and who stay put would provide valuable findings on differentiating factors between the two groups and on the relative advantages and disadvantages of stability versus mobility of residence.

New Living Arrangements for Older People In the past, older people had only a limited selection of residential arrangements. Besides remaining in their own home, they might be invited to reside with children or other relatives, or be forced to live in a poorhouse. Today there are old-peoples' homes, nursing homes, hotels specially designed for retired people, mobile-home parks, and retirement villages under the auspices of churches, various lodges, and private business. These widely different living arrangements provide an opportunity for comparative study by type of resident attracted, by type of activity, by kind of organization and management, by standards of operation, and by personal adjustment and happiness of residents.

QUESTIONS

1. What is the effect on a father and mother of the departure of the youngest child? What are the values of compensating activities?
2. Compare the probable strains on family relations (a) when the married couple is living in the home of the parents, and (b) when the older couple is living in the home of a married child.
3. What is known about intergenerational relations of parents, their married children, and grandchildren?
4. Describe the successful or unsuccessful experience of a retired couple who moved to a new area. Analyze the reasons for success or failure in the new location.
5. Which has the greater difficulty in making an adjustment, a widow, a widower, a divorced husband, or a divorced wife?
6. What are the primary characteristics of family relations in the middle years of marriage?
7. What are the primary characteristics of family relations in the later years of marriage?

BIBLIOGRAPHY

Brayshaw, A. Joseph. "Middle-Aged Marriage: Idealism, Realism, and the Search for Meaning," *Marriage and Family Living*, 24 (1962): pp. 358–364.

Sampled 25,000 marriage counselor case records from England and Wales. He compares the reasons for marital disharmony of couples married less than three years and those married for eighteen or more years.

Burgess, Ernest W. (ed.). *Aging in Western Societies*. Chicago: University of Chicago Press, 1960.

Surveys information about and policies toward the aged in Western culture. Chapters prepared by experts in areas such as population trends, employment, income, and housing. Each chapter contains information about six countries selected as representative of Western culture: France, Italy, the Netherlands, Sweden, the United Kingdom, and West Germany. See particularly Chapters 1, "Aging in Western Culture," and 8, "Family Structure and Relationships."

Deutscher, Irwin. "The Quality of Postparental Life: Definition of the Situation," *Journal of Marriage and the Family*, 26 (1964): pp. 52–59.

Conducted in Kansas City in 1954. Two socioeconomic classes were sampled—upper-middle and lower-middle. Deals with the period of the family-life cycle after children leave home. Interviews with 49 individual spouses found that 37 of these thought the present stage was as good or better than preceding stages.

Glasser, Paul H.; and Glasser, Lois N. "Role Reversal and Conflict Between Aged Parents and Their Children," *Marriage and Family Living*, 24 (1962): pp. 46–51.

Based on study of 120 families in which one spouse was at least 60 years of age, and in which there was at least one child. Demographic characteristics, personal ties with children, and problems of housing analyzed.

Kosa, John; Rachiele, Leo D.; and Schommer, Cyril O. "Sharing the Home with Relatives," *Marriage and Family Living*, 22 (1960): pp. 129–131.

Fairly comprehensive review of other related studies, and data from 507 white students about their families. Religious attitudes are related to willingness to share the home with relatives. Desire for occupational success is related to preference not to share the home with relatives.

Loether, Herman J. *Problems of Aging: Sociological and Social Psychological Perspectives*. Belmont, Calif.: Dickenson Publishing Company, 1967.

Deals with the aging process, interpersonal relations, health, housing, employment, retirement, exploitation of the aged, and death.

Neugarten, Bernice L.; and Weinstein, Karl K. "The Changing American Grandparent," *Journal of Marriage and the Family*, 26 (1964): pp. 199–204.

This study is based on a sample of 70 pairs of middle-class grandparents who were interviewed at length. The objective was to measure the degree of comfort in the grandparent role, the significance of the role, and the style with which role is enacted.

Shanas, Ethel; and Streib, Gordon F. *Social Structure and the Family: Generational Relations.* Englewood Cliffs, New Jersey: Prentice-Hall, 1965.
> This is an interdisciplinary discussion of intergenerational family relationships. The emphasis is on the aged as related to their married children. It is an excellent reference book in this area.

Tibbitts, Clark (ed.). *Handbook of Social Gerontology.* Chicago: University of Chicago Press, 1960.
> Chapters prepared by experts about the theory of societal aging, the impact of aging on individual activities and social roles, and aging and the reorganization of society. See particularly Chapter 13, "The Older Person in a Family Context."

Townsend, Peter. *The Family Life of Old People.* London: Routledge and Kegan Paul, 1957.
> Based on intensive interviews with 203 older people, men over 65 years of age and women over 60. Random sample chosen from Bethnal Green, a predominantly working-class area of London. Describes and analyzes the relationships between the aged and their family groups.

Wallin, Paul; and Clark, Alexander L. "Religiosity, Sexual Gratification, and Marital Satisfaction in the Middle Years of Marriage," *Social Forces*, 42 (1964): pp. 303–309.
> Study conducted from 1956 to 1958. The sample consisted of 384 women and 386 men volunteers. Most of the people in the sample were urban dwellers. All were white and native born. Questionnaires were answered by husbands and wives separately. Religiosity was determined by the frequency of church attendance. Sexual gratification was determined by the answer to "How much do you enjoy sexual relations with your husband/wife?"

Part IV
Changing Patterns of Family Behavior

A hundred years ago in the United States a stable network of familial expectations, roles, and values controlled and circumscribed the behavior of individual families. These folkways and mores, while allowing incompatibility and conflict within certain limits, gave definitions of expected behavior and determined the extent to which conflict could be expressed. The family today, however, is radically different from this. It is so different that Rip Van Winkle, if again resurrected, would hardly recognize many present-day families, judged by his standards, as real families. Today familial patterns are characterized by innovation, multiplicity, and inconsistency. Traditional folkways and mores are found side by side with familial practices of recent origin. The control of the mores over the individual family and its members has been greatly weakened.

Our central thesis is that family disorganization is present in the confusion and disorder of familial patterns; some of the old patterns have been perpetuated and are inconsistent with new ways of acting, and also, the new patterns are not consistent within themselves. These changes also indicate family reorganization, for new modes of behavior, sets of attitudes, and social values are being accepted and practiced as the right way of life.

The following chapters will examine the outstanding conditions and manifestations of family disorganization, such as the role of mobility, family conflicts and tensions, and family crises, including deviations from expectations, disgrace, divorce, depressions, death, and war. Finally, considerations will be given to forces and movements which are reshaping the family.

Our central thesis has been that the older traditional type of family, as found in the colonial period and also in the great majority of immigrant families, has been and is being changed into the companionship family. At times this has proceeded rapidly, and at other times gradually. It is a change from a group with a large number of children and often a grandparent and even other relatives, with central authority exercised by the father and husband over the wife and children in the various activities of the family. It is a change to a small unit of husband and wife, with no child or one, two, or three children, with a reduction of the traditional economic, protective, educational, recreational, and religious functions, and with equality of husband and wife in a companionship type of family. The traditional family was characterized by permanence of marriage, unplanned parenthood, and a sense of duty as the highest obligation of family members. The companionship family accepts divorce as a means of rectifying a mistake in mate selection, engages in planned parenthood, and sees happiness as a goal and raison d'être for marriage and family living. This new type of family appears to be coming into being on the American scene.

Chapter 17
The Changing American Family

> The family has been changing from the time of its beginning, and particularly during the last three centuries. During the last three centuries the patriarchal family form has been modified so that today democratic relationships are more prevalent than formerly. In this century—with the movement of families from rural to urban areas, with industrialization, and with an increased emphasis on education—certain family values have undergone change. Some of these changes include a shift from accepting as many children as the childbearing period provides to parenthood-by-choice; from a large to a small family; from having babies born at home with possibly a midwife or physician to having babies born in hospitals with a physician in attendance; from a feeling that a woman's place is in the home to working outside the home if a woman so desires; from placing a high value on virginity to greater freedom in sex relations; and from the feeling that marriage for all should be permanent and monogamous to the possibility of separation and divorce if the husband and wife are incompatible.

FAMILY LIFE TODAY AND YESTERDAY

One way in which changes in the family may be seen concretely and vividly is to make comparisons of family life by generations:

> My great-grandparents, so I have been told, lived in a small, white, green-shuttered house surrounded by trees, cornfields, and flowers, in a community of 150 people. My great-grandmother was the youngest of six children; my great-grandfather was the youngest of five. Grandmother was born at home and her mother was by herself at the time.

My home is also a small white house, but the design is modern and the trees are transplanted. I live in a city of 400,000 population. On the boulevard in front of my home, buses, trucks, automobiles, bicycles, and motorcycles whiz noisily by, unnoticed by the occupants of the house. I am an only child and I was born in a hospital.

My great-grandfather, a doctor, was kept busy attending to the ills of the community, traveling from house to house with his horse and a buggy built by the village blacksmith, and often being paid for his services with apples, potatoes, and sorghum. The road on which he traveled was rough. In the winter it was often impassable, and he was forced to ride horseback. An occasional buggy passed by the house, causing excitement and speculation as to where the driver was traveling. Within the household the day was long and strenuous. A fire must be made in the fireplace, and the wood chopped for the day. The lamp chimneys must be cleaned so that there would be light in the evening. Canning, cooking, cleaning, and baking kept the women busy the entire day.

My father is a traveling man and has to be away for the greater part of the week; consequently, we are a whole family only two days each week. A large grocery and meat market, and a drugstore are conveniently located nearby. Gas heat and a thermostat give us any desired temperature. A vacuum cleans the rug in a few minutes, while the bakery and grocery do away with the tasks of canning and baking.

Twice a year my great-grandfather traveled to a city some two hundred miles away, where he studied the new advances in medicine. He brought back the materials for clothing the family, and also shoes; no one ever tried on shoes before they were bought. All the sewing was painstakingly done by hand, and the socks were hand-knitted.

Today we go to the department stores of the city to buy our clothes. If dresses are made at home, the material is easily bought and the sewing quickly done with a sewing machine.

On Sundays, my great-grandfather and great-grandmother would gather up their brood of children and cross the street to the one church of the village. There they would reverently sit in prayer the entire morning. After services the villagers stayed to gossip and, perhaps, to hear news of the outside world. Every morning of the week the family was gathered for prayers before the beginning of the day. No meal was begun without first saying grace. Breakfast demanded that the entire family be together. Outside of the weekly newspaper, the Bible was the chief reading material of the family.

In my home usually Saturday and Sunday dinners are the only meals which the entire family eat together. Sunday is a day of rest and relaxation following a hard week of work and play. After breakfast the Sunday paper is divided and read thoroughly from funnies to want ads. Thanksgiving, Christmas, and Easter are the only times that the family turns briefly to religion, and yet we would instantly condemn anyone who called us an irreligious family.

There was no high school until great-grandmother, the youngest child, was growing up; when she left home for college, the town was in an uproar. By the time she received her M.A., the villagers decided she would never be through school, "she was just too dumb."

I went to a large public school about three blocks from my home. Each half grade was taught separately by a well-trained teacher. I came home each day for lunch, and by 2:30 I was home for the rest of the day. My high school was a large building with about 4000 students.

This contrasting picture of the family of three generations ago with that of today shows radical changes in birth folkways, economic activities, education, and religious behavior. Each change served to separate family members from each other and to make each less dependent on the other. Some people are inclined to evaluate these changes as bad, feeling that "the American home, the cornerstone of civilization and religion, is threatened." Others appraise them as good, holding that "changes in the family form and organization are inevitable and to be desired." Those who are disturbed by modifications in the family are inclined to advocate a return to the golden age of the past, while those who see change in the family as inevitable and good are disposed to feel that many traditions should be discarded.

The function of the sociologist is not to evaluate changes as either good or bad but to secure concrete facts on actual changes in progress and to describe and analyze them. This chapter is concerned with a description and analysis of some of these changes.

This chapter is also designed to provide a perspective on present trends in the American family. Considered from the standpoint of the past, the trends have introduced radical alterations in the network of relationships in the family. Our working assumption is that at present the American family is in the process of transition from the control of the mores of an earlier, predominantly rural society, with the imprint of Puritan values, to an urban, industrial culture, with its emerging way of life. This assumption is that the family is changing to the companionship form.

Not all the changes can be treated here. Selected for discussion are the modifications which have or are taking place in authority patterns in the family, patriarchal to democratic; in the physical structure of the home, single or multiple dwelling; in birth folkways, the declining birth rate and size of the family; changing family functions, reduction of some and retention of others; and changing patterns of sex, marriage, and family roles.

FROM THE PATRIARCHAL TO THE DEMOCRATIC FAMILY

On the basis of the member exercising authority in decision-making, one may classify families as patriarchal, matriarchal, and democratic. The patriarchal family is one in which the father has authority, with the wife and children being subordinate to him. The matriarchal family is that in which the mother has authority, with the husband and children being subordinate to her. The democratic family has equal authority of the husband and wife in decision-making, with children having an increasing voice as they advance in age.

The Patriarchal Family It is difficult for us to imagine a society in which the father has almost complete authority to make the major and minor decisions of a family. Yet even a century ago the patriarchal family was considered divinely sanctioned and was the expected form in European countries and the United States. An excellent description of the patriarchal family prevalent in the past was given in 1855 by John Harris, President of New College, London:

> The family is based on the principle of subordination. . . . The man, as husband and father, holds all under God, and represents Him. The woman, as wife and mother, holds all under her husband, and represents him. By standing in a line with his authority, she presents to the eyes of the children the image of his power invested with the light of her own love. The children, again, hold all from their parents, to whom, for a time, they look up to as the only objects of reverent affection they know. Obedience—the affectionate subordination of the filial will to the parental—is as essential to the harmony and development of the child's own internal being as to the harmony and well-being of the family; and, for a time, it is the only image which can be given of obedience to God. The children themselves stand in a line of subordination. It is this which makes the family a school of self-discipline. Here, the first sacrifice of restraint is first imposed and accepted as guidance.[1]

The recognition of the father's almost complete authority in family relations went unchallenged for centuries. Then in the decades before the American revolution the divine right of kings and the divine authority of the father over the family began to be challenged. Probably people do not come to the defense of the institution unless it is under attack, for otherwise they take it for granted. At any rate as early as 1680 books were being published in defense of the divine right of the father to be the ruler of the family and the divine right of the king to be the absolute ruler of the state.[2] At about the same time, 1690, John Locke published a scathing attack on the patriarchal form of government and incidentally on the patriarchal family. He advocated a democratic society and a democratic family and attempted to undermine the

---

[1] John Harris, *Patriarchy: or The Family, Its Constitution and Probation* (Boston: Gould and Lincoln, 1855), pp. 323–324.
[2] See Sir Robert Filmer, *Patriarchy: or The Natural Power of Kings* (London: Printed for R. Chiswell, etc., 1680). (Filmer died in 1653.)

idea that the patriarchal form of government and of the family were ordained by God.[3]

The Democratic Family John Locke was probably the first to outline the modern democratic family. Reading the following on the equality of the husband and wife and the emerging equality of the children as they advance in age, one would hardly think that it was published nearly three centuries ago. It is safe to assume that at that time almost everyone accepted the patriarchal family as ordained by God:

> Parental power . . . seems to place the power of the parents wholly in the father, as if the mother had no share in it; whereas if we consult reason or revelation, we shall find she has an equal title. . . . For whatever obligation Nature and the right of generation lays on children, it must certainly bind them equal to both the concurrent causes of it. And accordingly we see the positive law of God everywhere joins them together without distinction, when it commands the obedience of children: "Honour thy father and thy mother" (Exod. xx 12); "Whosoever curseth his father or his mother" (Lev. xx 9). . . .
>
> Children, I confess, are not born in this full state of equality, though they are born to it. Their parents have a sort of rule and jurisdiction over them when they come into the world, and for some time after, but it is but a temporary one. The bonds of this subjection are like the swaddling clothes they are wrapt up in and supported by in the weakness of their infancy. Age and reason as they grow up loosen them, till at length they drop quite off, and leave a man at his own free disposal.[4]

This is almost identical with the modern definition of the democratic family. The democratic family is based on equality of the husband and wife, with consensus in making decisions and with increasing participation by children as they grow older.

The democratic family can be present without the companionship family. However, the companionship family is democratic as indicated by the first two of the four components or characteristics of the companionship family: (1) Authority is shared among family members and is based on the equality of husband and wife, with the expectations that children will express their desires and views and will have an increasing part in making family decisions as they grow older. (2) Decisions are made on the basis of consensus or agreement among the members. (3) There is intimate and congenial association and communication among the members. And (4) the emphasis is on the freedom of

---
[3] John Locke, *Of Civil Government: Two Treaties* (New York: Dutton, 1924, first printing 1690), Book 1, Ch. 2 and Book 2, Ch. 6.
[4] John Locke, pp. 141-143.

the individual member to the extent that it does not jeopardize the family unit.

The democratic family is highly favored in at least two countries with a Western-European cultural background—the United States and Sweden. Evidence supporting this is provided by Locke's Indiana study of marital adjustment,[5] and Karlsson's study of adjustment of Swedish marriages.[6] In both studies an attempt was made to discover the degree to which democratic family behavior was being practiced. Several activities were listed in the questionnaire and each husband and wife was asked to indicate whether the wife, the husband, or both about equally took the lead in given activities. Democratic behavior was the principal response of both groups for both husbands and wives. About 6 or 7 in 10 of both groups felt that the husband and wife equally made family decisions, disciplined the children, and took the lead in religious activities and in recreational activities. The proportion was lower in equality in the handling of family money, but it still was the favored response of husbands and wives of both groups.

At the same time there were variations away from the pattern of democratic behavior. When some response other than equality was made, both Locke and Karlsson report that husbands more than wives took the lead in making family decisions, in handling family money, and in recreation. Both also report that wives more than husbands took the lead in disciplining the children and in religious behavior. If the traditional expectation is that the husband should make the decisions and handle the money and the wife should handle the children and be more religious, it appears that, when not giving equalitarian responses, the behavior of the subjects was in the direction of traditional roles.

TYPE OF HOME DWELLING

The pattern of living in a single-family dwelling is the prevalent home of American families. Necessarily it has declined under urban conditions, where industrialization has resulted in individuals and families crowding into limited areas, with the consequent premium on land space.

Many city families have become accommodated to renting space in a multiple dwelling, prefer residence in an apartment, and look with disfavor on living in a single-family house and being tied down to a

---

[5] Harvey J. Locke, *Predicting Adjustment in Marriage: A Comparison of a Divorced and a Happily-Married Group* (New York: Henry Holt, 1951).

[6] Georg Karlsson, *Adaptability and Communication in Marriage: A Swedish Predictive Study of Marital Satisfaction* (Uppsala, Sweden: Almqvist and Wiksells, 1951).

Type of Home Dwelling   421

location through home ownership, and have no interest in caring for a lawn or garden. On the arrival of children, however, many parents feel that multifamily dwellings are inadequate and move to single-family units, generally in the suburbs. Some parents decide to remain in apartment-house areas, appreciating the services of supervised playgrounds and other recreational facilities and opportunities of the community.

Figure 15 shows the percent distribution of new one-family, two-family, and multifamily units constructed in the combined urban and rural-nonfarm areas for the years 1920–1968. It shows that during the building boom of the 1920 decade the percent of new multifamily dwelling units rose to a high of 31.7 in 1928, and then declined to 6.7 at the depth of the depression in 1932. In recent years the percent of new multifamily dwelling units has been increasing.

Figure 15. Percent distribution of new permanent dwelling units constructed in nonfarm areas (urban plus rural-nonfarm), by type of dwelling, 1920-1968*

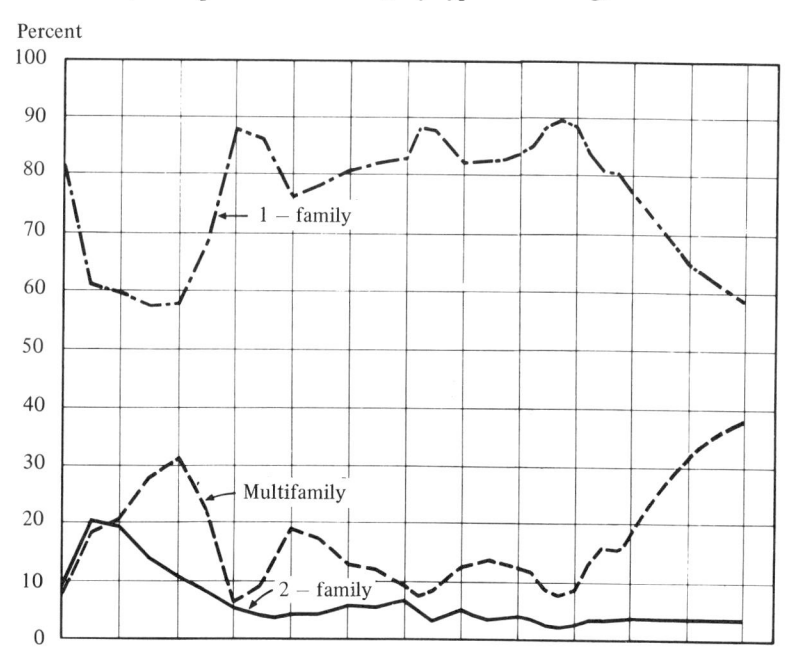

*Data from *Statistical Abstract of the United States*, 1951, p. 709; 1958, p. 758; 1961, p. 760; and 1969, p. 697.

The number of one-family dwellings fluctuated considerably in the period 1920–1932; then up to 1955 it maintained a rather steady high proportion of all dwellings constructed, varying from a low of 75.2 to a high of 89.4 percent. From 1955 to 1968 there was a steady and sharp decline in single-family units and a sharp rise in multifamily units.

BIRTH FOLKWAYS

The changes in birth folkways are in response to values which have emerged in the United States in recent decades. Students of fertility control emphasize the values which family planning attempts to achieve.[7] These values include (1) the preference to marry young, (2) a desire to limit the number of children to between two and four, and (3) the wish to have children at a controlled rate—"not as fast as biologically possible, but fast enough to compress most of the childbearing into the first half of the reproductive period."[8]

The age of women at the time of the first marriage is young as compared to an earlier time—in 1969, 20.8 for brides and 23.2 for grooms.[9] One-fourth of women enter their first marriage by the age of 19; three-fourths do so by the age of 23. Thus early marriage is a part of our values and our folkways. This, of course, lengthens the time in marriage when it is biologically possible to have children. But this runs counter to another value which American families have—to limit the number of children to between two and four. Another value of American women is to have these two, three, or four children spaced at desired intervals in the first ten years of marriage. These values cannot be attained without limiting the birth of children.

In response to these desired values, folkways and mores surrounding the birth of children have undergone radical modifications. Contrast the former attitude toward the conception of children as an act of God to be accepted with the recent tendency to control conception. There is a tremendous change from the former almost universal expectation that women should fulfill their sacred duty by having as many children as they are given and the emerging pattern of parenthood by choice.

---

[7] See Charles F. Westoff, Robert G. Potter, and Philip C. Sagi, *The Third Child: A Study in the Prediction of Fertility* (Princeton, New Jersey: Princeton University Press, 1963), particularly Ch. 2; Charles F. Westoff and Raymond H. Potvin, *College Women and Fertility Values* (Princeton, New Jersey: Princeton University Press, 1967); P. K. Whelpton and C. V. Kiser (eds.), *Social and Psychological Factors Affecting Fertility* (New York: Milbank Memorial Fund, 5 vols., 1946–1958); Ronald Freedman, P. K. Whelpton and Arthur Campbell, *Family Planning, Sterility, and Population Growth* (New York: McGraw-Hill, 1959); and R. Freedman, D. Goldberg, and H. Sharp, "'Ideals' About Family Size in the Detroit Metropolitan Area: 1954," *Milbank Memorial Fund Quarterly*, 33 (October 1959).

[8] Westoff, Potter, and Sagi, p. 11.

[9] *Current Population Reports, Population Characteristics*, Series P-20, No. 198, 1970.

The trend toward birth control is revealed by conflict over birth control, by the growing number of its proponents, by the falling birth rate, and by the decreasing size of families. Conflict over birth control is seen in early attempts to prohibit it through legislation, in a divided public opinion regarding it, and in other ways. In 1873, federal legislation banned any contraceptive device or information from interstate commerce and from the mails. Twenty-seven states followed the lead of the federal government. Court interpretations, however, have liberalized the federal and state laws by ruling that any device for the prevention of disease can be sent through the mails and in interstate commerce. It is now legal for a physician to give pregnancy-spacing advice to his patient when her health requires it.

The values leading to the use of contraceptives vary by religion and, for Protestants, by social class. These conclusions are supported by interviews with 1165 wives in seven large metropolitan areas. All of the families had two children. Religious differences were marked. The percent initiating the use of birth control practices before the birth of the first child was over 85 for Jews, 71 for white-collar Protestants, 51 for blue-collar Protestants, and slightly over 35 for Catholics.[10] In the successful use of birth-control practices, Jews were found to have the highest percentage, 81; blue-collar Catholics were next, with 68 percent; Protestants were third, with 58 percent; and white-collar Catholics were least successful, with 51 percent.[11]

The values associated with the birth of children vary within a given religious group. For example, graduates from nonsectarian high schools who selected a Catholic college prefer 4.9 children; Catholics who went to a nonsectarian college, prefer 4.2 children; and Catholics who attended parochial elementary schools, Catholic high schools, and were freshmen in a Catholic college prefer 5.7 children.[12]

To understand the use of birth-control practices among Catholics one must understand the position of the Catholic Church and the beliefs and practices of the laity. Historically the Church has maintained strong opposition to the use of artificial methods of birth control. Today Catholics are divided on the issue of birth control. Some favor the use of pills and other birth-control techniques while others insist that only abstinence or possibly the rhythm method can be used. When in August of 1968 the Pope banned all forms of birth control except abstinence and rhythm, there was an immediate and strong condemnation of this

---

[10] Charles F. Westoff, Robert G. Potter, Philip C. Sagi, and Elliot G. Mishler, *Family Growth in Metropolitan America* (Princeton, New Jersey: Princeton University Press, 1961), p. 72.
[11] *Ibid.*, p. 92.
[12] Westoff and Potvin, pp. 42–43.

by segments of the Catholic clergy and by lay groups. In late August a Gallup poll was taken on Pope Paul's encyclical[13] and found that 93 percent of Catholics and 86 percent of Protestants had read or heard about the Pope's banning of artificial methods of birth control. Gallup reports that these "awareness scores" are among the highest in the 33-year annals of the Gallup poll. American Catholics were strongly opposed to the position of Pope Paul: 54 percent said they opposed the Pope's position, 28 percent approved, and 18 percent expressed no opinion. Among devout Catholics who attended mass at least once a week, "criticism is nearly as strong." Among young Catholic couples, 8 in 10 disagreed with the Pope's position. Those opposed to the encyclical did so because they felt Catholics should be allowed to follow their consciences in family planning; the world was becoming overpopulated; and families should have only those children they can properly care for. The minority in favor of the Pope's position did so because they felt it was the duty of a Catholic to abide by any papal decision; Catholics should trust in the Pope as the head of the Church; and it is against the laws of nature to prevent births. The opposition of the laity was also indicated by the fact that 65 percent of Catholics believed it is possible to practice artificial methods of birth control and still be a good Catholic.

The American hierarchy supports the encyclical of Pope Paul and holds that birth control only by abstinence or rhythm is the official position of the Church. Many Catholics are in a dilemma: they favor and may practice birth control through pills and other techniques and in doing so they are violating the official position of their Church.[14]

Negro wives do not want more children than white wives: 2.9 and 3.3, respectively. But in spite of their reported desires, they have had and expect to have more children than white wives have had or expect to have. Negro couples living on farms in the South average 4.5 births as compared with 2.1 for white wives living on farms in the South. Negroes moving from Southern farms to towns and cities greatly reduce the number of children born (2.6) or that they expect to have (3.5). There is a gradual adoption by Negroes of values and practices favoring small families as they move from farms to cities and as their educational achievement increases.[15] Negro wives in the age group 35-44 whose

---

[13] Reported in the *Los Angeles Times*, Sept. 1, 1968, Section A, pp. 1 and 10.

[14] It should be noted that the average number of children ever born per 1000 ever-married women, 15 to 44 years old, according to a national survey, was only slightly higher for Catholics than for Protestants. Reported in Pascal K. Whelpton, Arthur A. Campbell, and John E. Patterson, *Fertility and Family Planning in the United States* (Princeton, New Jersey: Princeton University Press, 1966), pp. 77-78.

[15] The material above is based on Arthur A. Campbell, "White-Nonwhite Differences in Family Planning in the United States," *Health, Education and Welfare*

families were in the lower half of socioeconomic scores have more children than white wives and those in the upper half of socioeconomic scores have fewer children than white wives.[16]

One of the conclusions of Rainwater, in an interview study of 409 individuals from 257 families, was that in the lower class neither religion nor race seems to make a difference in desired family size. However at higher status levels, Protestants desire fewer children than Catholics. He also found that middle-class Protestants do not desire four or more children as often as lower-class Protestants.[17] Lower-class Catholic wives use the rhythm method and find that it is ineffective as a birth-control technique. This is due, in part, to the hit-and-miss method used in determining the safe period.[18]

The folkway on contraception was a part of the transition from the values of a rural society to those of an urban industrial civilization. On the farm a child can be an economic asset; in the city he is an economic liability. Also education is valued more now than formerly. With the high cost of education, families prefer to give more education to two, three, or four children than less education to a larger number of children. Then, too, the sanction of the mores on the duty to have large families was weakened by the decline in religious controls, the emancipation of women, and the growth of individualization and secularization of human values.

Declining Birth Rate Figure 16, which shows the number of births per 1,000 population from 1870 through 1969, indicates that the birth rate declined sharply and steadily up to 1930, and that it remained at this low level during the depression and postdepression decade, 1930–1940. It then rose sharply during World War II and remained at this high level in the 1950–1960 decade. In 1960 it resumed its long-term decline, so that by 1969 the birth rate was the lowest on record—17.4.

What has happened to the birth rate in other countries? An attempt to shed light on this question was made by an analysis of the birth rate of 64 countries over a 20-year period.[19] As a general rule industrial countries have had low birth rates and even these rates have declined over the period. In underdeveloped and nonindustrial countries the

---

Indicators, Feb. 1966. This article is based on a national probability sample of 270 nonwhite wives (256 of these were Negroes) and 2414 white wives. More details are given in "White and Nonwhite Differences in Fertility," in Pascal K. Whelpton, Arthur A. Campbell, and John E. Patterson, Ch. 9.

[16] *Current Population Reports: Technical Studies*, Series P-23, No. 12, 1964, p. 2.
[17] Lee Rainwater, *Family Design: Marital Sexuality, Family Size and Contraception* (Chicago: Aldine, 1965), p. 122.
[18] *Ibid.*, p. 222.
[19] Metropolitan Life Insurance, *Statistical Bulletin*, April, 1968, pp. 10–11.

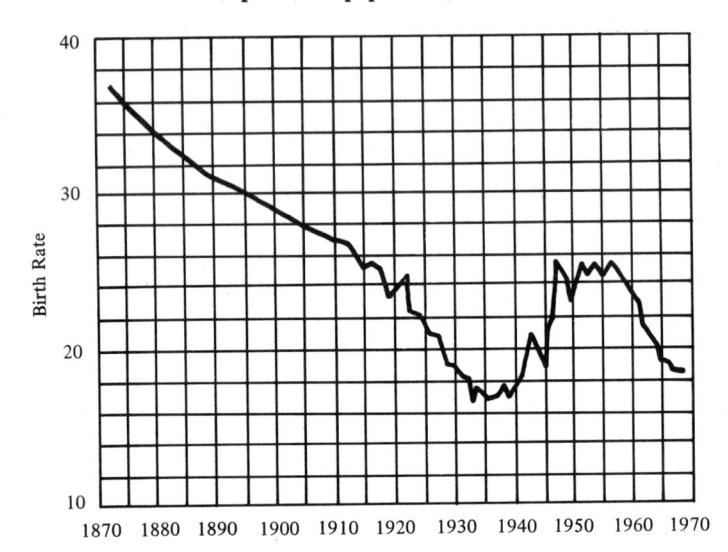

Figure 16. Number of births per 1,000 population, 1870-1969*

*Alfred J. Lotka, "Modern Trends in the Birth Rate," *The Annals of the American Academy of Political and Social Science*, 188 (1936), pp. 2–3; *Statistical Abstract of the United States*, 1969, p. 47.

birth rates were high in the beginning and they remained high in 1967.[20] In 24 of the 26 European countries studied, the birth rate in 1967 was under 20; the other two were just above 20—21.0 and 22.4. Of the 15 countries of South America, Central America, and Mexico, 7 had birth rates above 40; 6 had rates between 30 and 40; and 2 had rates under 30—22.4 and 25.7. Of 9 countries classified as Asian, 4 had rates above 40; 3 had rates from 30 to 40; and 2 had rates under 30—Japan and Taiwan. Of 7 countries of Africa, 5 had rates above 40, and the other 2 were 29.9 and 30.4. In general the rates above 40 were in underdeveloped countries and those below 30 were for more industrialized countries.

Declining Size of the Family Table 21 shows that between 1790 and 1850 the median size of the family in the United States remained almost unchanged at about 5.6. During the hundred-year period, 1850–1950, there was a steady and constant decline in the size of the American family. Then from 1950 to 1968 the median size of the household remained almost unchanged.

One secures somewhat different figures if husband-wife rather than households are used. The advantage of using household rather than husband-wife families is that long-term data are available only for

[20] The latest year for which birth rates were available for 18 countries was 1966 and for 5 countries it was 1965.

households. However, the figures that are available indicate that the size of the husband-wife family declined between 1850 and 1950 but increased slightly between 1950 and 1968; the median size for 1940, 1950, and 1968 was respectively 3.76, 3.54, and 3.70. The tentative conclusion is that the size of the husband-wife family is becoming stabilized at about 3.70.[21]

Table 21. Average number of persons per family household, 1790-1968*

Year	Persons per Household	Year	Persons per Household	Year	Persons per Household
1790	5.7	1890	4.9	1940	3.7
1850	5.6	1900	4.8	1950	3.5
1860	5.3	1910	4.5	1960	3.7
1870	5.1	1920	4.3	1968	3.7
1880	5.0	1930	4.1		

*Various census publications.

The declining size of the family is indicated also by a comparison of the percent which are childless at different times. Between 1900 and 1930 the number of unbroken families which were childless or had no related child living at home increased from 28 to 31 percent. In 1968, 44.2 percent of husband-wife families were childless or had no related child under 18 living at home.[22] These percents include both couples who never had a child and those in which the children have departed. Thus, more than 4 out of 10 families have no children in the home at the present time.

Table 22 gives the percent of families having different numbers of family members related to each other by blood, marriage, or adoption in 1790, 1900, 1930, and 1968. The great decline in the size of the family is indicated by the percent of families having 6 or more members, dropping from 50.8 in 1790 to 13.9 in 1968. By contrast, the percent of small families of two or three members was 20.2 in 1790, 34.3 in 1900, and 54.5 in 1968.

[21] Various census publications, including issues of *Statistical Abstract of the United States; Current Population Reports, Population Characteristics*, Series P-20, particularly No. 114, 1962, and 166, 1967; and Metropolitan Life Insurance, *Statistical Bulletin*, June 1969, p. 9.
[22] 1900 and 1930 percents from President's Research Committee on Social Trends, *Recent Social Trends in the United States* (New York: McGraw-Hill, 1933), pp. 683 and 687; 1968 percent from *Statistical Abstract of the United States*, 1969, p. 39.

428   The Changing American Family

Table 22. Percent of private families[a] having specified number of persons, 1790, 1900, 1930, and 1968*

Number of Persons	1790	1900	1930	1968
2	8.1	15.8	25.4	33.9
3	12.1	18.5	22.6	20.6
4	14.3	17.8	19.0	19.0
5	14.4	15.0	13.0	12.5
6 and over	50.8	32.8	20.1	13.9

[a]Figures are for the "natural" family, defined as "a group of persons related either by blood or by marriage or adoption, who live together as one household, usually sharing the same table." The figures for 1790 and 1900 are not exactly comparable, since they are for the "private" family, which inclues lodgers, servants, and other unrelated persons.
*Data for 1790 and 1900: Bureau of the Census, *A Century of Population Growth from the First Census of the United States to the Twelfth, 1790–1900*, 1909, p. 98; data for 1930 from *Sixteenth Census of the United States, 1940, Population, Families, Size of Families, and Age of Head, Region and Cities of 1,000,000 or More*, 1944, p. 3; data for 1968 from *Statistical Abstract of the United States*, 1969, p. 38.

The decided decline in the size of the family is shown also by comparing the size of the household by states in 1940 and 1960, as shown in Figure 17. In 1940 there were 11 states with an average of 4 or more persons per household, while in 1960 no state had that high an average. In 1940 there were only 4 states with under 3.4 persons per household, while in 1960 there were 32 states with this small size of family.

The modern family of husband, wife, and three, two, one, or no children, living in an apartment on the tenth floor of a skyscraper apartment building in the city of New York, is a family in a somewhat different sense from the large rural family of the past. The mere size of the family has an effect on the interactions between the members, the roles they play, the kind of housing needed, and various other aspects of marriage and family relationships.

Does family size vary in different countries of the world? Burch has answered this question by tabulating family size in 64 countries based on data in the United Nations *Demographic Yearbook* for different years.[23] Using these data, we find that 22 countries had an average family size of 3.7 or less; 20 countries had families of 3.8 to 4.9; 19 had families of 5.0 to 5.7; and only three had families of 5.8 to 6.5 Thus the average family size of one-third of the countries was about that of the United States or less; one-third had on the average of one member more than the United States; and almost all others had but two members more

[23] Thomas K. Burch, "The Size and Structure of Families: A Comparative Analysis of Census Data," *American Sociological Review*, 32 (1967): pp. 347–363.

Birth Folkways 429

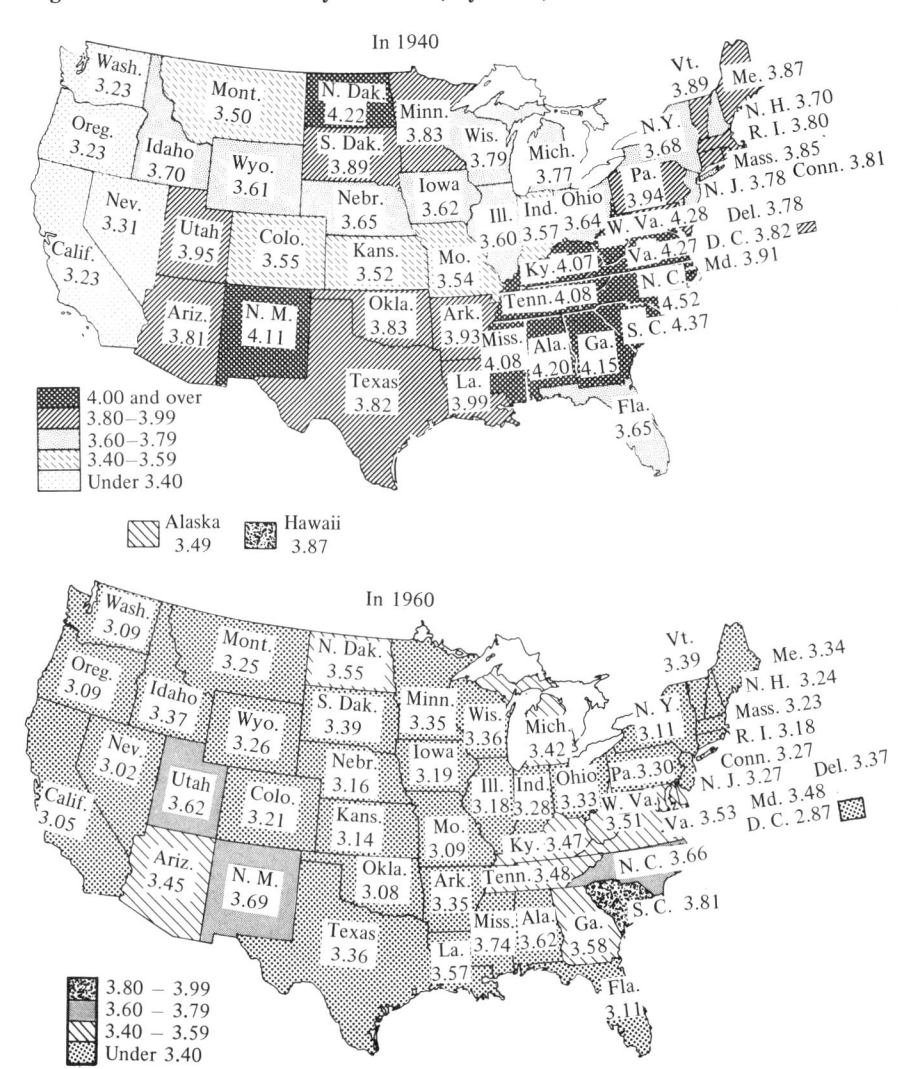

Figure 17. Size of the family household, by states, 1940 and 1960*

In 1940

Wash. 3.23; Oreg. 3.23; Calif. 3.23; Nev. 3.31; Idaho 3.70; Mont. 3.50; Utah 3.95; Ariz. 3.81; Wyo. 3.61; Colo. 3.55; N. M. 4.11; N. Dak. 4.22; S. Dak. 3.89; Nebr. 3.65; Kans. 3.52; Okla. 3.83; Texas 3.82; Minn. 3.83; Iowa 3.62; Mo. 3.54; Ark. 3.93; La. 3.99; Wis. 3.79; Ill. 3.60; Miss. 4.08; Mich. 3.77; Ind. 3.57; Ky. 4.07; Tenn. 4.08; Ala. 4.20; Ga. 4.15; Ohio 3.64; W. Va. 4.28; Va. 4.27; N. C. 4.52; S. C. 4.37; Fla. 3.65; Pa. 3.94; N. Y. 3.68; Vt. 3.89; Me. 3.87; N. H. 3.70; R. I. 3.80; Mass. 3.85; Conn. 3.81; N. J. 3.78; Del. 3.78; D. C. 3.82; Md. 3.91

- 4.00 and over
- 3.80–3.99
- 3.60–3.79
- 3.40–3.59
- Under 3.40

Alaska 3.49   Hawaii 3.87

In 1960

Wash. 3.09; Oreg. 3.09; Calif. 3.05; Nev. 3.02; Idaho 3.37; Mont. 3.25; Utah 3.62; Ariz. 3.45; Wyo. 3.26; Colo. 3.21; N. M. 3.69; N. Dak. 3.55; S. Dak. 3.39; Nebr. 3.16; Kans. 3.14; Okla. 3.08; Texas 3.36; Minn. 3.35; Iowa 3.19; Mo. 3.09; Ark. 3.35; La. 3.57; Wis. 3.36; Ill. 3.18; Miss. 3.74; Mich. 3.42; Ind. 3.28; Ky. 3.47; Tenn. 3.48; Ala. 3.62; Ga. 3.58; Ohio 3.33; W. Va. 3.51; Va. 3.53; N. C. 3.66; S. C. 3.81; Fla. 3.11; Pa. 3.30; N. Y. 3.11; Vt. 3.39; Me. 3.34; N. H. 3.24; Mass. 3.23; R. I. 3.18; Conn. 3.27; N. J. 3.27; Del. 3.37; D. C. 2.87; Md. 3.48

- 3.80 – 3.99
- 3.60 – 3.79
- 3.40 – 3.59
- Under 3.40

*Sixteenth Census of the United States, 1940, Population, 2, Housing, General Characteristics, Part 1, p. 60; and Statistical Abstract of the United States, 1961, p. 40. Data show population per occupied dwelling unit.

than that of the United States. This shows rather conclusively that the small family, rather than the large or extended family is the existing family size in most of the countries of the world.

Family size is related to certain psychological characteristics. Two of the four indexes which frequently have been used to measure alienation—meaninglessness, normlessness, powerlessness, and social isolation—are related to family size. Groat and Neal secured data from 754 women who had given birth to a child during the calendar year of 1962 in the Standard Metropolitan Area of Toledo, Ohio.[24] They found women who had high scores on meaninglessness had significantly more children than those who had low meaninglessness scores: 4.38 and 3.73. They also found that those with high normlessness scores had more children than those with low scores: 4.12 and 3.64. An analysis of their data indicates that the other two components of alienation—powerlessness and social isolation—were not consistently related to fertility.

Groat and Neal had the hypothesis that successful family planning results in small families and should be correlated with rational decision-making, a sense of mastery over social events, and the perception of social relations as integrative and supportive. They also thought that large families would be related to the operation of drift and failure to make long-range rational planning. One would raise the point, however, whether alienation is related to lower-class families and lower-class families have larger families than higher social classes.

Hospital-Born Babies Changing birth folkways also include the practice of having babies born in hospitals, which is in sharp contrast with the former almost universal practice of having babies born at home with the assistance of a midwife or doctor.

Figure 18 shows the great increase in the proportion of babies born in hospitals. In 1935 less than 40 percent of babies were born in hospi-

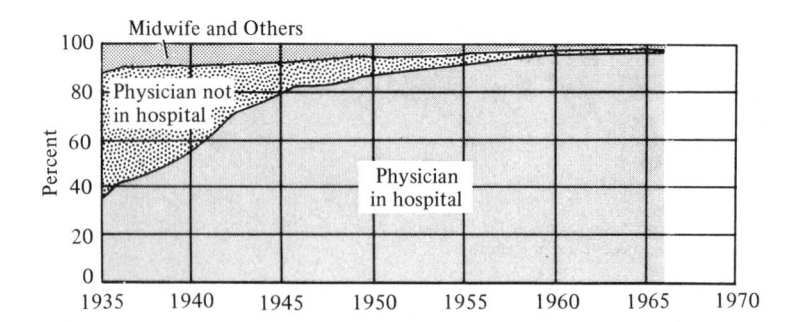

Figure 18. Percent of babies born in hospitals and not in hospitals, 1935-1967*

*From "Births by Person in Attendance, United States, Each Division and State, 1949," Vital Statistics, Special Reports, National Summaries, 36, No. 5, 1951, pp. 63 and 66; Vital Statistics of the United States, 1966, 1, Nativity, pp. 1-21; and Statistical Abstract of the United States, 1969, p. 48.

[24] H. Theodore Groat and Arthur G. Neal, "Social Psychological Correlates of Urban Fertility," *American Sociological Review*, 32 (1967): pp. 945–959.

tals, compared with 98 percent in 1967. The practice of having babies born in hospitals is about the same for rural and urban whites and for urban Negroes. The percent of nonwhites having babies born by help of a midwife, or at least not born in a hospital, and not with the help of a physician outside a hospital dropped from 49.2 percent in 1940 to only 7.1 percent in 1966.[25]

CHANGING FAMILY FUNCTIONS

Historically the family has discharged several characteristic functions which have been of service to its members and to the community. These include bearing and rearing children, giving and receiving affection, and economic, protective, recreational, educational, and religious activities. The following discussion of changing family activities will be based partly on the assumption that increases in certain outside-the-home activities are indexes of decreases in certain traditional functions of the family.[26]

Economic Activities The economic function of the family has been modified greatly during recent decades, and the change is still proceeding at a rapid rate. In the past the manufacture of articles and the production and consumption of food were largely within the family. It is well known that factories have taken over most of the production of goods, but not everyone is aware of the changed function of the family in food consumption and the degree to which labor-saving devices have been introduced within the home.

The use of household appliances and conveniences has greatly increased. This can be seen, in part, from the percent of homes owning appliances. Table 23 gives a list of some of these appliances and the percent of homes owning them in 1953, 1960, 1967, 1968, and 1969.

These great changes are vividly illustrated by a case which compares household activities today with those in homes around 1900:

> My great-grandmother churned her own butter; raised her own broom corn for her brooms; canned all her own vegetables and fruits; carried in all her own firewood, which she had previously chopped herself, or had her children do it; raised practically all the foodstuffs that the family consumed; did her ironing on a board laid across two chair backs, with an old heavy flatiron; washed the clothes by hand, and carried the water from a well in the woods a half mile away. The children each had to do his share of the work.

[25] *Vital Statistics of the United States, 1966*, 1, *Nativity*, p. 1–21.
[26] Unless otherwise documented, the basic data are from publications of the United States Bureau of the Census.

432 The Changing American Family

Table 23. Percent of homes with given appliances, 1953, 1960, 1967, 1968, and 1969*

	1953	1960	1967	1968	1969
Air conditioners (room)	1.3	12.8	29.9	36.7	42.5
Dishwashers	3.0	6.3	15.9	18.1	20.8
Freezers	11.5	22.1	25.7	27.2	28.5
Refrigerators	89.2	98.0	99.6	99.7	99.8
Television					
Black and white	46.7	89.9	97.8	98.1	98.5
Color	—	—	15.0	26.2	35.7
Vacuum Cleaners	59.4	72.5	90.6	92.0	93.1

*Statistical Abstract of the United States, 1969, p. 704.

Our family life is different. We can sleep later in the morning because much of the drudgery of housework has been taken off our hands by labor-saving devices. We get our milk in a bottle on the doorstep, our breakfast food out of cardboard boxes, light the gas for the coffee, plug in the toaster, and breakfast is over. We go over the house with the vacuum cleaner, toss something in the electric refrigerator for dessert for dinner, open a can of vegetables, and that takes care of lunch. The rest of the day is typified by the same sort of labor-saving methods and, in the meantime, Mother has read a book, attended her favorite club, or gone to the city twenty miles away to do some shopping.

Table 24. Gainfully employed married women, their number, and the percent they are of all married women, 1890-1968*

Year	Number of married working women	Percent of all married women
1890	515,260	4.6
1900	769,477	5.6
1910	1,890,661	10.7
1920	1,920,281	9.0
1930	3,071,302	11.7
1940	5,040,000	16.7
1950	9,273,000	24.8
1960	13,485,000	31.7
1967	17,486,000	37.9
1968	18,233,000	39.1

*Data from publications of the Bureau of the Census; 1967 and 1968 from Statistical Abstract of the United States, 1968, p. 224, and 1969, p. 220.

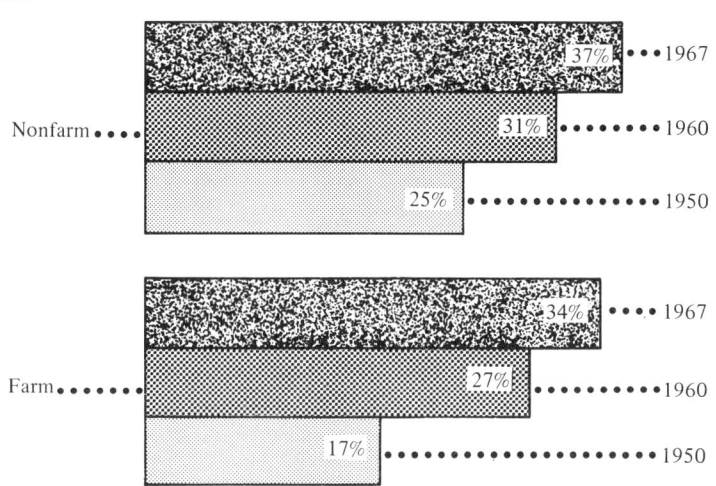

Figure 19. Percent of nonfarm and farm wives in the labor force, 1950, 1960, and 1967*

Nonfarm
- 37% ···1967
- 31% ········1960
- 25% ···············1950

Farm
- 34% ····1967
- 27% ···········1960
- 17% ·················1950

*Adapted from U. S. Department of Agriculture, *Handbook of Agricultural Charts*, 1968, p. 59.

A growing proportion of married women are working outside the home. Table 24 gives the number and percent of married women who worked outside the home for the period 1890 to 1968. It shows that only 1 in 20 worked in 1890, compared with almost 4 in 10 today. The table shows that since 1920 there has been a steady and sharp increase in the proportion of married women gainfully employed.

Figure 19 shows a dramatic increase since 1950 of both nonfarm and farm wives in the labor force. It will be noted that this was particularly true for farm wives—the percent working doubling between 1950 and 1967.

Of all women 14 years of age or older, single women are most likely to be employed (51.4 percent in 1968); married women are next with slightly less than 4 in 10 employed (39.1 percent); widowed and divorced are lowest with a little over a third employed (35.8 percent). However, of all women in the labor force in 1967, 63.5 percent were married; 21.5 percent were single; and only 15.0 percent were widowed or divorced. Of the total labor force in 1969 (men and women combined) 37.5 percent were women.[27]

A detailed analysis indicates that only a third of married women in the labor force work full time, and that those who work receive decidedly

[27] *Statistical Abstract of the United States*, 1969, p. 224.

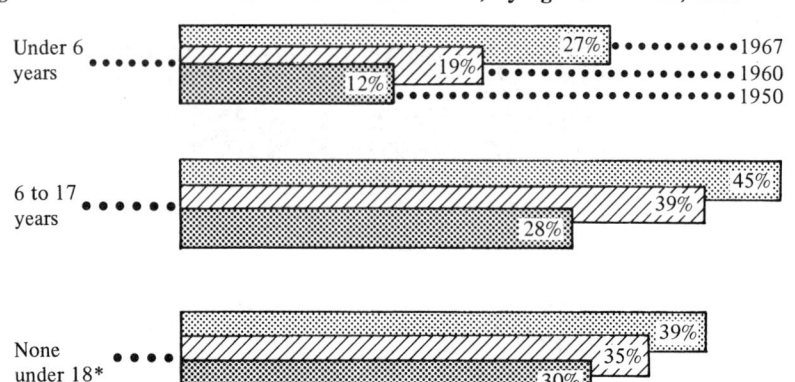

Figure 20. Percent of mothers in the labor force, by age of children, 1967*

Under 6 years: 27% (1967), 19% (1960), 12% (1950)

6 to 17 years: 45% (1967), 39% (1960), 28% (1950)

None under 18*: 39% (1967), 35% (1960), 30% (1950)

*Department of Agriculture, *Handbook of Agricultural Charts*, 1968, p. 59. (Includes wives who worked without pay 15 hours or more on family farm or business; includes wives with no children.)

lower income than men.[28] The contribution to the family budget by married women who work is only about one-fourth that of their husbands. Despite their relatively small incomes, the wife's earnings are an important factor in the family's standard of living. In 1960 the wife worked in over half of all families with incomes of $7,000 to $15,000. By contrast, in families with incomes from $3,000 to $5,000, only about 40 percent worked. Full-time work by the wife was about twice as prevalent in higher-income families as in lower.

The age of children has a decided influence on whether a wife works. Figure 20 shows that mothers with children under six years are least likely to work and those with children 6 to 17 years are most likely. However, an increasing percent of those with young children are working: between 1950 and 1967 the percent of mothers with children under 6 years who worked more than doubled.

Women have attained the first objective of the social movement for the emancipation of women—entry into the world of activities formerly monopolized by men. World War II, like World War I, accentuated the trend toward equality of vocational opportunities and equality of pay. The mores which are being undermined by this economic emancipation of women are those associated with the subservice of women to the "head of the house." Readjustment of familial patterns in the direction of companionship and mutual affection is promoted by women's actual or potential economic independence and by their educational and social equality.

[28] Jacob Shiffman, "Marital and Family Characteristics of Workers, March, 1961," *Monthly Labor Review*, 85 (1962): pp. 9–16.

The effect of the mother's employment on marital success was studied by Nye.[29] He collected data from 1,993 mothers residing in three small cities in Washington. He found that employed mothers, compared with nonemployed, reported more conflicts in their families and less permanence of the marriage. However, the two groups were equally happy and satisfied. When a marital-success score was used, a significant but small difference was found between the employed and nonemployed, favoring the nonemployed mothers. When married-only-once mothers were compared, the difference between marital success scores increased.

Protective Activities In the pioneer community the man of the family kept firearms in his home to protect his family. Today it is policemen and firemen who protect the lives and property of families; and municipal, county, state, and federal health departments help give protection from disease. Insurance companies, agencies of the individual states, and the social security program of the federal government help protect a family from the economic consequences of death of a member, accident, illness, unemployment, and old age.

One index of the transfer of protective activities from the family to outside agencies is the fact that between 1900 and 1968 total life insurance owned increased from $7.6 billion to $1,245 billion. In 1900 only 13 percent of the total population owned life insurance. A survey made in 1967 found that 71 percent of all Americans owned life insurance. Some form of life insurance was owned by 88 percent of men (91 percent of husbands); 70 percent of all women (71 percent of wives); and 58 percent of children under 18. The average amount of insurance owned per family was approximately $20,000.[30]

Government intervention to deal with these problems was well under way before the 1930's. A great impetus was given to governmental participation by the financial depression of that decade. Finally, in 1935, the various projects and proposals were merged into a federal system of social security. The families of workingmen are now safeguarded by compensation, insurance, and pension against the contingencies of accident, unemployment, and old age. Most significant, perhaps, for the family unit is the provision of assistance and insurance benefits for the aged, which permits them to live in independence and relieves their children of responsibility for their support.

The scope of the security given to families and to individuals by federal and state governments is shown by such facts as the following:

[29] F. Ivan Nye and Lois W. Hoffman, *The Employed Mother in America* (Chicago: Rand McNally, 1963), Ch. 19.
[30] Institute of Life Insurance, *Life Insurance Fact Book*, 1961, p. 5 ff and 1969, p. 9 ff.

in 1968, 24.6 million aged persons received assistance from old-age, survivors, and disability insurance, and 2.0 million from public assistance; financial aid was given to 81,000 blind persons and 4.6 million dependent children.[31]

The adoption of the program of social security was a revolutionary change. In the past the family recognized provision for its members as a sacred obligation. The popular support of the social security program is an index of the profound change in public attitudes. There is no longer the expectation that younger family members should provide economically for aged members. Rather, there is the expectation that the financial needs of the aged will be met through pensions, the old-age social insurance program, and other governmental programs.

Educational Activities The family today does not assume as much direct responsibility for the education of the children as formerly. In colonial times a child went to school three months of the year, as compared with the nine or ten months today. The following excerpt contrasts the extent and quality of formal education around 1900 with the quality of education in the city in which this middle-aged person now resides:

> My grandparents attended a one-room schoolhouse, where they were taught from the primer to the fifth grade. The schoolmaster or marm was paid forty dollars a month and usually boarded with the family closest to the school. It lasted six months, but not many attended full time, as spring was a busy time on the farm. High school or college was for only the very rich or for one with enough nerve to run away from home to the big city.
>
> In the city in which I live, one can go from the kindergarten through college with the best teachers available, patronize public libraries in every community with trained assistants to aid in supplying your books, and attend night courses held in our high schools. We have art schools, commercial schools, extension schools, laboratory schools, and almost any other kind of school.

Great increases in educational attainment are revealed by data assembled by the census. Between 1940 and 1968 the median grade attained rose from 8.4 to 12.0. In 1968 the median grade attained by whites was 12.6 and by Negroes 12.2.[32] A comparison of educational achievement in 1967 with 1947 is provided in Figure 21. Education limited to elementary levels was drastically reduced in this period, from 47 percent

---

[31] Data from *Statistical Abstract of the United States*, 1969, pp. 281 and 296.
[32] *Current Population Reports, Population Characteristics*, Series P-20, No. 169, 1968; and No. 182, 1969.

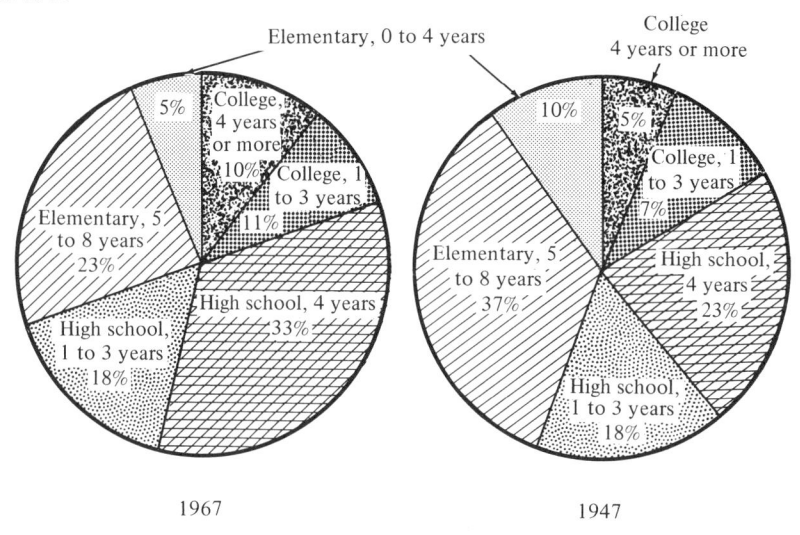

Figure 21. Years of school completed by persons 20 years of age and older, 1947 and 1968*

[Two pie charts. 1967: Elementary 0 to 4 years 5%; Elementary 5 to 8 years 23%; High school 1 to 3 years 18%; High school 4 years 33%; College 1 to 3 years 11%; College 4 years or more 10%. 1947: Elementary 0 to 4 years 10%; Elementary 5 to 8 years 37%; High school 1 to 3 years 18%; High school 4 years 23%; College 1 to 3 years 7%; College 4 years or more 5%.]

Current Population Reports, Population Characteristics, Series P-20, 169, 1968, p. 2; and *Statistical Abstract of the United States,* 1969, p. 106.

in 1947 to 28 in 1967; high school graduates increased from 23 in 1947 to 33 percent in 1967; and one or more years of college increased from 12 percent in 1947 to 21 percent in 1967.

Between 1940 and 1968 the number of children enrolled in public elementary and secondary schools rose from 25,484,000 to 44,769,000. Between 1900 and 1960 the average number of days school were in session rose from 144.3 to 178.0. The average number of days attended annually increased from 99.0 to 160.2.[33] The number of high-school graduates increased from 95,000 to 2,759,000 with the number of college graduates increasing from 27,000 to 685,000.

Recent years have witnessed the expansion of education into the preschool level. Nursery schools are taking children from two to five years of age out of the home. Kindergartens have become almost an expected part of the school program. There were about four times as many children in kindergarten in 1970 as in 1940: This extension of the school program is a reversal of the former attitude that one of the home's primary "intrinsic" functions is the training of the preschool child during the formative years of his life.

---

[33] Days in session and the number of days attended annually from *Advance Data, from Statistics of State School Systems,* 1959–60 (Formerly *Biennial Survey of Education of the United States*), Ch. 2.

Recreational Activities In the past, recreation was largely centered in the home. Today it is increasingly outside. In the rural family of yesterday the social expectation was that persons would work hard all day and part of the evening and that little or no time would be spent in recreation. Today, with most families in the city, the social expectation is that people will work much shorter hours and that the individual will engage in recreation and exercise in his leisure time. Many facilities and activities have developed to meet leisure-time demands, such as bowling, swimming, skating, golf, tennis, baseball, picnicking, and the like.

Not only has there been a change in the type of activity, but recreation today less often involves the family as a whole. Children play with the neighborhood children, or, if they are older, go off with groups of young people; Father may go to his lodge or play golf; and Mother attends club meetings, card parties, and other organizations. And while television has resulted in family members staying at home more, it may also have led to a decrease of interpersonal communication within the family.

Religious Behavior Major changes have occurred in familial religious behavior. The change in religious attitudes and behavior is described in the following excerpt from a case which contrasts the loyalty and devotion to the church around 1900 with the liberal and secular attitude of the interviewee's family:

> Because of their firm Presbyterian beliefs, my great-grandparents were rigorous advocates of the philosophy of self-denial. In all things they were temperate and self-controlled. They never enjoyed pleasure for the sheer love of living—they would have thought that foolish and self-indulgent. They could not understand enjoyment of recreations such as movies, dancing, and card parties. They had a tenacious loyalty to the Church; it was infallible and they would tolerate no criticism of it. Their attitude toward the Bible was no less firm; it was unquestionably and absolutely true.
>
> Our family is much more liberal. We hold proper reverence for God, but realize, through our more advanced knowledge, that many unusual events, supernatural to our great-grandparents, are not directly attributable to Him. This understanding of the world and nature removes many of the fears that oppressed their time. Our philosophy of living in the family group is not restriction and self-denial but rather pleasure and self-expression. We never have prayer before meals because we are always in too big a hurry. No one is home in the evenings for family prayers. There are too many places to go on Sundays, or we were out too late Saturday evening; so consequently we do not always go to church.

Retention of Affectional and Child-Rearing Functions While various forces are decreasing some of the functions of the family, it maintains its affectional and child-rearing activities. More and more the American family is becoming a union of husband and wife, parents and children, based on love, common interests, and companionship. Child rearing is one of the primary functions of the family, particularly for the mother, and this has been retained. Child rearing is affected by varied and important home activities. Perhaps the most significant is the socialization of the child through transmitting to him attitudes, behavior, values, and goals. The emphasis on the child-rearing function of the family was emphasized in the chapters, "Culture and Socialization" and "Family Relations in the Middle and Later Years."

CHANGING PATTERNS IN SEX, MARRIAGE, AND FAMILY ROLES

Sex In 1900 the Puritan taboo regarding sex still held sway. Evidences of this are numerous: long dresses and high collars for women; covering of the feminine figure, even in swimming; prudery in speech and writing; the ban of churches on dancing, card playing, and theater going; and Victorian novels with the beautiful and virtuous maiden ever triumphant over the villain.

The lifting of the Puritan taboo was the result of a combination of factors: the freedom of city life; the emancipation of youth from parents greatly accelerated by the automobile; the dissemination of Freudian theory; the growth of the movement for sex education; and the movement for women's rights, aiming among other things for a single standard of morals.

Terman and Locke compared the sex experiences of those born before 1890 with the experiences of those born in 1910 or later. Terman compared the premarital sex experiences of 760 men and 777 women. Table 25, which summarizes his findings, indicates that more younger

Table 25. Percent of Terman's subjects born before 1890 and in 1910 or later reporting premarital intercourse*

Reported intercourse	HUSBANDS Born before 1890	HUSBANDS Born 1910 and later	WIVES Born before 1890	WIVES Born 1910 and later
None	50.6	13.6	86.5	31.7
Only with future spouse	4.6	31.9	8.7	45.0
Only with others than future spouse	35.6	13.6	1.9	3.3
Future spouse plus others	9.2	40.9	2.9	20.0

*Data from Lewis M. Terman and others, *Psychological Factors in Marital Happiness* (New York: McGraw-Hill, 1938), p. 321.

440   The Changing American Family

husbands and wives had premarital intercourse than older husbands and wives.

Terman's percentages of husbands born in 1910 and later reporting premarital intercourse are higher than those found by Kinsey[34] for his younger generation of married college males. They are also higher than those found by Burgess and Wallin, whose findings correspond closely with Kinsey's data.[35]

Locke, in his study of representative samples of happily married and divorced persons, found that reported premarital, and also extramarital, intercourse was more prevalent among younger than older persons. Table 26 gives the data for both happily married and divorced and for both men and women.

Table 26. Percent of Locke's subjects born before 1890 and in 1910 or later reporting premarital and extramarital intercourse*

	HUSBANDS		WIVES	
Reported intercourse	Married	Divorced	Married	Divorced
Premarital with future mate				
Born before 1890	5.7	38.1	4.5	20.0
Born 1910 or later	42.0	57.4	38.9	33.3
Premarital with one or more persons				
Born before 1890	52.9	76.2	4.5	20.0
Born 1910 or later	71.4	89.9	22.7	34.3
Extramarital				
Born before 1890	5.9	29.3	0.0	0.0
Born 1910 or later	21.2	38.8	1.4	8.0

*Data secured in connection with Harvey J. Locke's study of marital adjustment. See also, "Sexual Behavior" in his *Predicting Adjustment in Marriage: A Comparison of a Divorced and a Happily Married Group* (New York: Henry Holt, 1951), Ch. 7.

Permanent Marriages   Mores pertaining to the permanence of marriage have undergone a radical change. In earlier times separation or divorce did not enter into the thought of people as a solution for family difficulties. Thus the increasing divorce rates do not necessarily indicate a greater amount of discord within individual families than in the past. They do show, however, that the mores on marriage as an indissoluble union have been and are breaking down. The progressive decline in the

[34] Alfred C. Kinsey, Wardell Pomeroy, and Clyde Martin, *Sexual Behavior in the Human Male* (Philadelphia: W. B. Saunders, 1948), p. 552.
[35] Ernest W. Burgess and Paul Wallin, *Engagement and Marriage* (Philadelphia: Lippincott, 1953), p. 331.

cultural pattern of permanent monogamous marriage, as measured by divorce, is shown in Figure 21 in Chapter 21. The number of divorces per 1,000 population is about 9 times larger than in 1870 and 3 times larger than in 1900. It should be kept in mind, however, that 92.8 percent of all wives in the United States in 1968 were living with their husbands in their own homes; that 1.4 percent were living with their husbands in the home of a relative; and that only 3.5 percent were separated from their husbands because of marital discord. The remaining 2.3 percent had other living arrangements.[36]

Increasing Length of Marriage One significant change in family relationships is the increased length of married life a couple will have together. Since 1900 about 9 years have been added to the married life of a couple. For those born since 1900 about 79 percent of all couples survive to see their last child married, as compared to 52 percent of those born before 1900. This is partly due to the decrease in the number of children and the concentration of births before the wife reaches the age of 30.

The increase in the length of time that a husband and wife will probably live together can be determined by dividing all married couples into the oldest and youngest groups. For the oldest couples there will be 35.4 years between the median age at first marriage and the death of one spouse. For the youngest couples there will be 44.5 years.[37]

Age at Marriage The median age at first marriage declined during the period 1890–1968; for men from 26.1 to 23.2 years, and for females from 22.0 to 20.8. It remained about the same from 1950 to 1964. Since 1964 there has been about a half-year increase in the median age at marriage. However, one-fourth of all women marry under the age of 19 and one-fourth of all men under the age of 20.[38] While both brides and grooms are younger, the difference in their ages has declined. One explanation for the decline in the difference of age of men and women at marriage is the trend toward the companionship character of modern marriage.

Familial Roles Present family roles reflect changed social situations, which have made many time-honored roles obsolete. The roles of family members have been changed by the mother working outside the home

---

[36] Metropolitan Life Insurance, *Statistical Bulletin*, 41, January 1970, p. 6.
[37] Hugh Carter and Paul C. Glick, *Marriage and Divorce: A Social and Economic Study*, (Cambridge: Harvard University Press, 1970), p. 147.
[38] *Current Population Reports, Population Characteristics*, Series P-20, No. 198, 1970.

for wages, by adolescent members of a family sometimes earning as much as the father, by the father traveling some distance to his job, or by a member of the family going away from home for higher education. The roles of family members in cities differ from the roles of their forefathers in the country. And changing functions of the family have altered the positional arrangement and relationships of the various members of the family. When economic production and a rapidly increasing proportion of consumption are outside the home, when commercialized entertainment takes the place of home amusements, when the state assumes protection over life, security, and property, and when the religious and educational functions of the home are delegated to the church and school, radical adjustments of roles necessarily take place.

In 1924 Sumner analyzed the relationship between changing social conditions and the changing status of women. His analysis of the competition between marriage and family life and other interests and enjoyment reflects a situation not very different from that today:

> The modern tendencies of society . . . have opened to women careers and ambitions which have dislodged marriage from its supreme place in their interest and life plan. Within a hundred years, and more especially within fifty years, there have been opened for women both numerous and attractive chances for independent existence. These offer alternatives to marriage. Women have such a deeply rooted love of children that alluring opportunities for marriage easily win them away from other careers, but the importance of the fact that for great numbers of them it is no longer the sum of life to find husbands can be easily appreciated. Moreover, modern life, especially in cities, offers a great number of interests and enjoyments which make domesticity less attractive for either sex.[39]

There has been a great decline in the authority of husband over wife and of parents over children. The decline of the family as an economic unit in production tended to free women from economic dependence on the husband, and the possibility of economic independence emancipated them from living under undesirable family relationships. Instead of the husband's having the legal right to discipline his spouse, the wife may sue for divorce if she experiences cruel and inhuman treatment, or for irreconcilable differences as in California in 1970. The subserviency of women in a "gladsome, womanly way to the head of the house" is to be contrasted with her emancipated position with reference to actual or potential economic independence, voting power, spending most of the family income, and frequently managing the whole household, either through overt dominance or through subtle methods of control. The position of children has changed from that of being

---

[39] William G. Sumner, "Modern Marriage," *The Yale Review*, 13 (1924): pp. 274–275.

under the complete authority of the father to that of enjoying the protection of the state in case of cruel or inhuman treatment by parents. Compulsory school attendance, factory and child labor legislation, and juvenile-court procedures illustrate the new position of children in modern social relationships. The following case describes this transition from autocratic control by the husband over his wife and children to democratic control through discussion and guidance by the father and mother on the basis of their greater experience:

> In my grandfather's family, the husband was king, his wife was a very obedient little servant who served him in every way and subordinated all her desires to his. He treated her kindly in a paternal fashion, but he never shared with her any of his business confidences, nor ever gave anyone the impression that her judgment was of any value except in household matters—yet she was devoted to him and never minded his little slights. His children were subservient, too, with perhaps a little more freedom and independence. In all things, however, his will was law, and this relationship continued until his children had homes of their own.
> Our family relationships are more democratic. Even the smallest child enjoys an important position in the family group. Father's judgment is final ultimately, but in any problem, we ourselves have an opportunity of and take pleasure in making our own decisions and acting upon them providing they are wise. Mother and Father cooperate in the discipline, as in all other matters of interest and importance; their relation is one of mutual co-ordination. We share their pleasures, and they take delight in ours. Our parents love us and demonstrate their affection in their excellent guidance, not rule, of us.

These variations from traditionally defined familial activities and roles are symptoms in the present, as in similar times in the past, that society is undergoing change. The family becomes reorganized according to new definitions of expected activities and roles, only to be modified later by new social changes.

SUMMARY

The emphasis in this chapter has been on values families attach to certain changes in folkways and activities. Evidence indicates that the degree of change in values varies by socioeconomic status, by education, and by affiliation with a particular religious group. In general, however, families today value the following among other things: democratic behavior; marrying young, having two, three, or four children, and completing childbearing within ten years after marriage; family planning through an effective birth-control technique; babies born in a hospital with a physician in attendance; employment of a woman outside the home if she so desires; adequate insurance or other provision against accident, illness, unemployment, and old age; extended educational training and facilities; enjoyment of sexual behavior; separation or divorce if a marriage is intolerable; and flexibility in family roles.

More specifically, the radical modifications that have occurred in family behavior are shown in the decreasing birth rate, declining size of the family; diminution of historic family functions—economic, protective, educational, recreational, and religious; the lifting of the Puritan taboo on sex; increases in various forms of sexual freedom; the rise of the divorce rate as an index of the growing impermanence of marriage; and changing roles of family members, with the weakening of the authority of the husband over his wife and children.

PROBLEMS FOR RESEARCH

Many questions arise about the American family in transition. A few have been selected for special consideration as research projects.

Comparisons by Generations In this chapter comparisons by generations have been employed to show the nature and meaning of changes taking place in the family. This method might be used more systematically to investigate the changing functions of the family. The meaning of changes for family living might be profitably investigated. These include the transition of the family from a large to a small unit, the shift from parental control to the emancipation of young people, the modification of attitudes toward sexual activity, and the declining value placed on chastity before marriage.

Survival of the Patriarchal Family Many different forms of the patriarchal family, or of cultural patterns once associated with it, survive in the United States. These should be studied at a time when they still may be examined and recorded before they disappear. There are cultural islands where patriarchal patterns of family living still prevail, as in the Acadian villages of Louisiana, in the Amish communities of Pennsylvania, and in the Ozark Mountain region. Survivals of the patriarchal patterns even in so-called companionship families should also be studied: the husband's control of the purse strings, opinions on rigid discipline and severe punishment of children, intervention by parents in mate selection of young people, and so on.

Single and Multiple Dwellings Factors and conditions in housing that demand study include (1) the family cycle from youth to old age as affecting type of housing, (2) the degree to which multiple dwelling is by necessity or by preference, (3) the differences in requirements by social and economic class, and (4) the possibility of new construction and new materials favoring single houses.

Birth Control and the Mores The aspects of birth control which most appropriately fall within the scope of sociological research are those related to the mores. Comparative studies might be made of the practice of birth control in spite of religious sanctions of varying degrees of strength. Particularly significant would be a study of the behavior of Catholics, where personal documents already secured reveal a severe conflict between feelings of religious duty and the heavy economic cost of additional children.

A limited number of investigations have been made on motivations for having children. Additional studies should attempt to find out individual differences in couples in desire to have children, the strength of economic motives, and the relative influence of other factors, such as group opinion and status.

QUESTIONS AND EXERCISES

1. Enumerate some of the changes which have occurred in birth folkways. What are the social forces operating for and against the continuance of these trends?
2. What forces or factors are related to the retention of traditional values or the adoption of new values?
3. In the last ten years, what has been the trend in the birth rate and in family size?
4. For each of the traditional functions of the family give what you consider the most important indexes of change.
5. Which traditional functions of the family have been retained most and which least? Have any new functions been added?
6. What is the evidence of changes in cultural patterns relating to sex, permanent marriage, and roles of family members?
7. What are your personal values on democratic family authority; age at first marriage; the most desirable number of children; child spacing through birth-control techniques; women's working outside the home; freedom in sex relations; permanent monogamous marriage; and the husband helping with some of the housework.

BIBLIOGRAPHY

Bureau of the Census. *200 Million Americans*. Washington, D. C.: U. S. Government Printing Office, 1967.

A description of the standard of living, the birth rate, illegitimacy rate, marriage rate, the sex ratio, housing, city and suburban problems, decline of farms, recreation, education, and economic relationships.

Freedman, Ronald; Whelpton, Pascal K.; and Campbell, Arthur A. *Family Planning, Sterility, and Population Growth*. New York: McGraw-Hill, 1959.

Based on a nationwide area-probability sample of 2,713 white married women 18–39 years old. Presents findings on the number of children in families by social and economic classes, and on expected fertility. Income and education seem to be related to actual fertility but not to anticipated fertility.

Ogburn, W. F.; and Nimkoff, M. F. *Technology and the Changing Family*. New York: Houghton Mifflin, 1955.

Presents changes in the trend toward romance, age at marriage, decreasing family size, decreasing functions of the family, working wives, equality in authority, emphasis on personality development of the child, and family disruption.

Rainwater, Lee. *Family Design: Marital Sexuality, Family Size, and Contraception*. Chicago: Aldine, 1965.

Interview study of marital and family relationships of 409 persons representing 257 families. Deals with social class, sexual relations, preferences on family size, family limitation.

Westoff, Charles F.; Potter, R. G.; Sagi, P. C.; and Mishler, E. G. *Family Growth in Metropolitan America*. Princeton, New Jersey: Princeton University Press, 1961.

A report of the first interviews with 1,165 wives having two children, living in seven large metropolitan areas. Interest focused on fertility-planning behavior and its relationship to such variables as adherence to traditional values, religious affiliation, amount of education, and social and psychological factors.

Westoff, Charles F.; Potter, Robert G.; and Sagi, Philip C. *The Third Child: A Study in Prediction of Fertility*. Princeton, New Jersey: Princeton University Press, 1963.

A report of interviews with 905 couples of the original sample of 1,165 three years after the first interviews. Emphasizes fertility behavior, the relationship between actual fertility and previously expressed attitudes and preferences. Deals not only with fertility and fertility control, but with the social and psychological factors related to fertility. An excellent feature is a summary of major findings, Chapter 16.

Westoff, Charles F.; and Potvin, Raymond H. *College Women and Fertility Values*. Princeton, New Jersey: Princeton University Press, 1967.

The authors used a probability sample of 45 American colleges from which they secured data from about 15,000 freshman and senior women students. Primary interest in the effects of education and religion on preferences for family size, on family-planning intention. Analyzed the influence of social factors and beliefs on family-size preferences and on family-planning intentions.

Whelpton, Pascal K.; Campbell, Arthur A.; and Patterson, John E. *Fertility and Family Planning in the United States*. Princeton, New Jersey: Princeton University Press, 1966.
Studied 3,322 white and nowhite wives on number of pregnancies and births; number of children wanted by wives and husbands; physical defects that make future births unlikely or impossible; and the use of birth control techniques and their effectiveness. Also includes social factors related to fertility.

Chapter 18
Mobility and the Family

Mobility is a primary characteristic of American society. Almost all persons change their residence at least once in their lifetime and most do so several times. Vertical mobility means movement up or down the social status ladder and is generally a shift in occupational level from that of one's father. In the United States the majority of persons have a different occupation from that of their fathers or grandfathers. Ideational mobility, the acceptance and practice of different ideas and values, can hardly be avoided in the United States for we are constantly bombarded by new ideas from books, newspapers, movies, and radio and television. Mobility of residence, movement up or down in occupational status, and the experiencing of new ideas profoundly affect the family in both its structure and in its activities. Some of these effects are disorganizing while others are organizing.

A TRANSPLANTED FAMILY

The movement of a rural family to the city exemplifies many of the effects of mobility on the internal structure of the family and the personality development of its members. The following case describes the changes in family organization and in the roles of husband and wife and of parents and children resulting from such transplanting:

> When Bob, my oldest brother, got a good job in the city, we older children began raising the question of moving there. John went next and also got a steady job paying high wages. Their success induced Father to go.
> At first it was very pleasant for Father to be in the city and to get such high wages. But within a year he became discontented. The children were

now carrying their share of the burdens of the family, and some were making more than he, but that rather increased the problem for Father, for now they were becoming the dominant part of the family and were usurping his functions. When Mother and the older children decided to buy a home, they made the choice largely without Father's advice.

Father is very generous, sociable, and sympathetic, but is crude in manners and dress. On many occasions he insisted upon visiting and approaching people in the rural manner, much to the chagrin of the more sophisticated members of the family.

On the farm Father always took his place at the head of the table and said grace at meals. All the family ate together; but no longer. Some of the members now have to leave for work very early, others later. At no time during the day or week are all the members together in a family circle.

The children have varied in their reaction to the city environment. Helen, as soon as she reached the city, took a job at the place where she is still employed. She rose steadily and is satisfied. Meanwhile, she has entered into various groups where her social, vocational, and educational interests are satisfied. She and Bob have made the most satisfactory adjustment of all.

The adjustment or maladjustment of Ted has come during the last six years, the period of his adolescence. He was taken from the rural area, where he had never become adjusted, and before he had found himself he was thrust into a turbulent urban community. Here he has been forced to work out his own destiny unguided by the experience of others. Recently he has been sharing more intimately in family interests and goals.

My mother has projected upon her children all the ambitions and childhood dreams she had for her own life. She was disappointed in her marriage, and when she saw her desires running athwart of the man she was learning to care less for, she revolted and set up standards for the family; and to the task of maintaining them she dedicated her life. Thus she became the dominant figure.

There would be much less family spirit if Mother were not exercising the control she does. Mother has been able to curb the individualism of family members to a great degree, such as unwillingness to share possessions, and has brought about a surprising amount of unity.

I have never felt that there was any maladjustment in connection with my shift from the small town to the city. For me the move to the city was gradual, for I was left behind to complete a term of school. When I followed the rest to the city I went into a place already formed for me.

When I look back upon the environment out of which we moved and see the miles of social distance that lie between it and the one we live in now, I am amazed that there has not been more strain upon the family organization.

This family may be considered a specimen of hundreds of thousands of families who have migrated from rural communities in America and

Europe to large industrial cities. It exhibits both the disorganizing and organizing effects of the adjustment of the family and its members to the urban way of life, and the variation in adaptation of family members to the new environment.

In the following discussion the emphasis will be on the significance of mobility, whether physical or social, on personality development, and on family organization. The topics to be considered are (1) types of mobility, (2) mobility and family disorganization, and (3) mobility and family organization.

TYPES OF MOBILITY

Continuity denotes that a social group remains fixed in space with the transmission through generations of an unchanging culture. Mobility denotes change both in residence and in culture. Movement in space thus becomes a symbol and a measurement of cultural change, since leaving one location means a break in continuity and entrance into a new place signifies the necessity for making adjustments and adopting new patterns of behavior.

Mobility should be differentiated from routine movement which is regular and repeated. Mobility, objectively, is change from place to place; subjectively, it means the stimulation that comes from new contacts and new experiences. The central idea of mobility is the effect of movement on attitudes and behavior. Through mobility the family and its members are introduced to new patterns of behavior, often differing markedly from those which have been customary. The different types of mobility—residential, personal, vertical, and ideational—all tend to free the members of the family from familial control and thus to individualize them.

Residential Mobility By residential mobility is meant change in the location of the home. The American family is not strongly attached to a given place of residence. This is manifested in different ways. (1) Living in the ancestral home is of little importance to American people. (2) There is much movement from community to community and within the same community.

1. The family living in an ancestral home is surrounded by visible, physical symbols of family continuity and solidarity. The family history is intertwined with its locaton, with the growth of its physical structure through additions and improvements, and with its furnishings accumulated through the years.

The growth of cities served to undermine the importance of the ancestral home. Young people began leaving the farm for the shorter hours and higher wages of the factory and the bright lights of the city. Then, gradually at first but in increasing numbers later, farm owners on retirement moved to small cities and villages to enjoy the conveniences and sociability of living in the neighboring town or small city. The fact that only 1.5 percent of persons 18 years of age and older have lived in the same house through their lives indicates the low value attached to living in the ancestral home.[1]

2. Both in the city and in the country there is increasing movement from community to community and change of residence within the community. Early studies gave evidence of relatively great mobility within communities. The evidence from early studies is as follows: the Lynds (1929)—"the working-class group today appear to exhibit more mobility than the families of their mothers" and move oftener than the business-class group;[2] Zorbaugh (1929)—in a roominghouse district of Chicago the "whole population turns over every four months";[3] Mowrer (1932) —people in a random sample of 1,000 telephone subscribers in Chicago moved on the average of every 2.8 years, and 35 percent moved within a year;[4] Lundberg (1934)—70 percent of suburban families moved at least once in ten years;[5] Cowgill (1935)—in St. Louis 32 percent of the population moved on the average of once during a given year.[6]

During recent years the census has collected data on both intercommunity and intracommunity movement, where people live in comparison with a year earlier. Figure 22 shows that about 1 in 5 persons one year of age or older moves annually; about two-thirds of this migration is within the same county.

Additional data on migration are provided by the census: (1) men are slightly more mobile than women; (2) young adults, aged 20–24, are more mobile than other age groups, (3) Negroes are slightly more mobile than whites; (4) rural-nonfarm people move most, urban next, and rural-farm least; (5) those with incomes less than $5,000 move more than those with incomes of $5,000 or more; and (6) those with one or more years of college move more than those with less education.[7]

[1] *Current Population Reports, Population Characteristics*, Series P-20, No. 104, 1960.
[2] Robert S. Lynd and Helen M. Lynd, *Middletown* (New York: Harcourt Brace, 1929), p. 109.
[3] Harvey W. Zorbaugh, *The Gold Coast and the Slum* (Chicago: University of Chicago Press, 1929), p. 72.
[4] Ernest R. Mowrer, *The Family* (Chicago: University of Chicago Press, 1932), p. 196.
[5] George A. Lundberg and others, *Leisure: A Suburban Study* (New York: Columbia University Press, 1934), p. 175.
[6] Donald O. Cowgill, *Residential Mobility of an Urban Population* (St. Louis: Washington University Library, 1935).
[7] *Current Population Reports, Population Characteristics*, Series P-20, No. 188, 1969.

Figure 22. Percent of population one year old or older moving to a given area in a one-year period, 1947-1969*

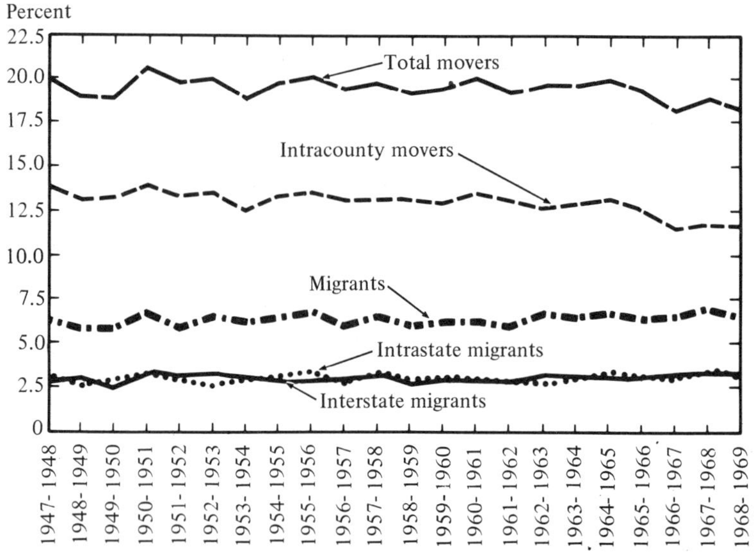

*Current Population Reports, Population Characteristics, Series P-20, No. 193, 1969.

A family which has a conception of itself as belonging to a community will be inclined to live up to community expectations more than a transient family, which is emancipated from gossip and other forms of social control.

A selection process operates in spatial migration in that the better educated are disproportionately high in the migrant group. The correlation between migration and education becomes more pronounced as distance of the move increases. Nonwhites moving out of the South are better educated but they are lower in education than those in the area to which they go.[8]

The effect of spatial migration on the migrant and on his parental family was studied by Schwarzweller.[9] He took a survey of male children enrolled in the 8th grade in 1949-1950 in 11 counties in Eastern Kentucky. He then followed up these subjects as young men 10 years

---

[8] See Elizabeth M. Suval and C. Horace Hamilton, "Some New Evidence on Educational Selectivity in Migration to and from the South," *Social Forces*, 43 (1965): pp. 536–547; and Henry S. Shryock and Charles B. Nam, "Educational Selectivity of Interregional Migration," *Social Forces*, 43 (1965): pp. 299–310.

[9] Harry K. Schwarzweller, "Parental Family Ties and Social Integration of Rural to Urban Migrants," *Journal of Marriage and the Family*, 26 (1964): pp. 410–416.

later. His sample shrank from 757 to 307. Those who remained in Eastern Kentucky were termed nonmigrants and all who moved outside the 11 counties were termed migrants. The following were his primary findings:

1. Migration results in a sharp reduction of face-to-face interaction with the family of origin.
2. Nevertheless more than half of those living over 100 miles from parents visit home or are visited by parents at least once a month.
3. There is some evidence that spatial separation is associated with intergenerational support—parents to children and children to parents.
4. The greater the interaction of migrant with the parental family the greater his dissatisfaction with the urban environment in which he resides.

Personal Mobility The invention of the steam engine, the airplane, and the automobile were prerequisites to today's high rate of personal mobility. First, let us look at airplane travel. In a 1961 Gallup poll, 48 percent of a representative sample of adult men and women reported that they had flown in airplanes.[10] The following shows the great increase in this type of personal mobility. It shows the number of airline passengers per year in millions for the years 1964–1967.[11]

Number of passengers in millions

1964................ 81.8
1965................ 94.7
1966................109.4
1967................132.1

Between 1954 and 1964 there was an increase of 130.7 percent in passengers per year and between 1965 and 1967 the percent increase was 39.6. Flying has become a common form of personal mobility.

In 1900 there were only 8,000 automobiles in the United States, as compared with 83.3 million in 1968. The number of registrations and the number per 1,000 population for the 1900–1968 period are given below.[12] In 1968, 79 percent of all families had a car and 26 percent had two or more.[13]

[10] *Los Angeles Times*, Nov. 17, 1961.
[11] *1968 Air Transport Facts and Figures*.
[12] Automobile Manufacturers Association, 1969, *Automobile Facts and Figures*; and *Statistical Abstract of the United States*, 1969, p. 550.
[13] *Statistical Abstract of the United States*, 1969, p. 553.

Year	Number	Number Per 1,000 Population
1900	8,000	1.1
1910	458,377	5.0
1920	8,131,522	76.4
1930	22,972,745	186.7
1940	27,372,397	207.9
1950	40,185,146	264.2
1961	61,683,865	296.2
1968	83,281,000	411.3

Sixty years ago the radius of movement of the family and its members was limited to that of the horse and buggy. While the horse and buggy would seldom carry one far outside the neighborhood, so that neighborhood control was always operating, the automobile can quickly transport the individual into a different community, far away from the family and the gossip of neighbors.

Furthermore, the automobile has extended the radius of mate selection. Today young people may meet at a considerable distance from home and court in the privacy of the car or in the anonymity provided by the place the car takes them. In freeing the individual from the control of the family and the neighborhood, the automobile has increased the opportunity for casual contacts. It has facilitated nonmarital sex relationships. Not only does it provide a place for premarital and extramarital relations, but it makes possible the use of the hotel and the motel for the same purpose.

Vertical Mobility The movement of a person or a family from one social class to another is termed vertical mobility. A comprehensive survey by Lipset and Bendix of studies of social mobility in various countries, including the United States, led to the following specific conclusions:[14] (1) There is a high correlation between occupational mobility and educational attainment. (2) Children from low-status families drop out of school earlier than those from high-status families. (3) When educational attainment is held constant, sons of manual workers usually enter the labor market in manual jobs, while sons of nonmanual workers usually enter in nonmanual jobs. (4) Occupational and social status tend to be self-perpetuating: if a son comes from a working-class family, he typically will receive little educational or vocational advice, and his job plans for the future will be vague. The job opportunities for some-

[14] Seymour M. Lipset and Reinhard Bendix, *Social Mobility in Industrial Society* (Berkeley: University of California Press, 1960), particularly pp. 197–199.

one from a working-class family are handed down from generation to generation. Sons of well-to-do families have the advantages of the social status of their parents, the education which such families can afford, and traditional opportunities for higher-status jobs.

Occupational groups vary in degree of vertical mobility. A survey by the Michigan Survey Research Center revealed the following order of occupational mobility, measured by the percent of sons being in the same broad occupational group as their fathers.[15] Clerical and sales had the greatest mobility, with only 19 percent of sons reporting the same occupation as their fathers. Professional and semiprofessional had the next highest mobility, with 25 percent of sons in the same occupation as their fathers. Proprietors, managers, and officials had about the same mobility as professional, 26 percent reporting the same occupation as their fathers. The fourth group was farm owners, with 30 percent in the occupation of their fathers. Sons of unskilled and farm labor ranked fifth, with 32 percent in their father's occupation. And sons of fathers in skilled and semiskilled work had the least mobility, with 54 percent in the same kind of work.

The greatest shift of sons from the occupation of their fathers for all occupational groups, except clerical and sales, was into skilled and semi-skilled jobs. The percent reporting this shift for professional and semiprofessional was 32; for proprietors, managers and officials, 25; for clerical and sales, 22; for unskilled and farm labor, 38; and for farm owners, 30. This great shift of sons into skilled and semiskilled occupations possibly is a reflection of technological developments in American society.

Occupational mobility and affectional attachment to parents were studied by Adams.[16] He secured interviews with 799 white- and blue-collar workers who had been married not more than 20 years. The question was if love, affection, and admiration for the father, mother, and siblings would be related to whether the son or daughter had experienced upward mobility, downward mobility, or stability. An analysis of the data Adams collected and published warrant the following conclusions:

1. Occupationally stable white-collar men and women (same class as father) have more love and affection for the father than do white-collar mobile men and women.

---

[15] *Ibid.*, p. 100. The fact that the various occupations were not proportionately represented is a deficiency of this study.
[16] Bert N. Adams, "Occupational Position, Mobility, and Kin Orientation," *American Sociological Review*, 32 (1967): pp. 364–377. See also Glen H. Elder, "Appearance and Education in Marriage Mobility," *American Sociological Review*, 34 (1969): pp. 519–533.

2. Occupationally stable white-collar men have more affection for their fathers than blue-collar men who are occupationally stable.

3. Downwardly mobile blue-collar men have more affectional attachment to their fathers than do stable blue-collar men.

4. Occupationally stable white-collar women have more affection for their fathers than the occupationally stable blue-collar women.

5. Mutually downwardly mobile siblings are affectionally close, but distant from the parents, particularly the mother.

The above indicates that occupational mobility or stability has an effect on the kind of affectional attachment a person has to parents and siblings. Vertical mobility and stability are associated with affectional attachments to kin in specific situations.

A person acquires the social status of his family and may tend to continue to be identified with this status even though he has attained a new status. In the following case the father had started out as a fruit peddler but now owns a large wholesale fruit business and the son is a senior in college and aspires to a higher status:

> In my home town I have no social status of my own—I have my father's—he has a social level. My last visit home last year verified I have not improved socially or even managed to start climbing the ladder of social status. While home I met a woman I had not seen in some fifteen years. While talking to her her husband happened upon us. When introduced as John, he showed no sign of recognition. Finally she said, "He's Peter Cervanti's son—you know the fruit peddler's son." Recognition was immediate through my father's early social level and position—not through my own efforts and rise upward which they knew. Further they ignored the fact that my father built his peddler's business to one of the largest wholesale fruit businesses in New York. It seems my father's social level is still that of a fruit peddler. As for me, I'll always be Peter Cervanti's son—you know the fruit peddler's son.

A sample of 917 lower-class and middle-class high school boys was divided into those who expected to follow the occupation of their fathers and the socially mobile—those who expected to follow a different occupation than their fathers. It was found that the socially mobile had the support of parental influences and friends in the class to which they aspired significantly more than those who expected to follow the occupation of their fathers.[17]

The United States has been called the land of "open classes." Warner and Lunt, in their pioneer study of social classes in Yankee City, recognized the possibility of rising from a lower to a higher class, but emphasized that barriers are present. In the following case Paul Stanley, the

[17] Richard L. Simpson, "Parental Influence, Anticipatory Socialization, and Social Mobility," *American Sociological Review*, 27 (1962): pp. 517–522.

son of a Polish immigrant who had raised himself from the lower-lower class to the upper-lower class, made the hurdle to the lower-middle class and found that further advance for himself and his wife was difficult, if not impossible. When his father objected to Paul's marrying a girl whose family was in the lower-lower class but who had moved upward herself, Paul married the girl anyway. Warner and Lunt described Paul's vertical mobility as follows:

> Within the year Paul was a member in good standing of the Antlers (a club ranging from upper-upper class to lower-middle class, but predominantly lower-middle), and he played bridge there several nights a week. He still belonged to the Caribou (a club from lower-lower class to lower-middle class), but some of the members of the latter organization were beginning to complain that he didn't come around any more.
>
> The Stanleys were now in a clique with Mr. and Mrs. Tim Pinkham (lower-middle), Mr. and Mrs. Dick Jones (lower-middle), and Mr. and Mrs. Jerry Thomas (lower-middle), but people like the Camps, the Frenches, and the Flahertys (all upper-middle), whom Paul knew at the Antlers, never invited them to dinner, nor did any of the "nice ladies from Hill Street" (a residential section of upper-class families) ever call on Annie. It is possible that this occasionally worried them, but there is more evidence that their past success was still a pleasant reward and that the present filled them with hope for the future.
>
> "And anyway," they said, "we're going to see to it that our children have every advantage."
>
> Paul's wife had made new friends in her neighborhood and had attended one or two meetings of the Art Club. She was not yet a member of this organization, but she was pleased, she told her husband, to be "introduced to several of the nicest ladies in Yankee City."[18]

In their rise in social status, the Stanleys broke social relations with their parents on both sides. They themselves had not yet given up hope of a still higher social status in the future, but were already beginning to project this ambition onto their children, just as Paul's father had done for him.

The upwardly mobile attempt to adopt the attitudes, values and standards of the higher class to which they aspire. This is not completely realized, for the adoption of values and norms of the higher class is segmental and discrepancies tend to appear. Ellis and Lane question whether upwardly mobile people ever fully develop the outlook of the class to which they aspire.[19]

Hollingshead, in his study *Elmtown's Youth*, found five stratified

---

[18] W. Lloyd Warner and Paul S. Lunt, *The Social Life of a Modern Community* (New Haven: Yale University Press, 1941), p. 193.
[19] Robert A. Ellis and W. Clayton Lane, "Social Mobility and Career Orientation," *Sociology and Social Research*, 50 (1966): pp. 280–296.

social classes and relatively little mobility across class lines. He concluded that those who date, marry, associate in religious activities, and engage in recreational and leisure-time activities are from the same social class or one immediately adjacent to it. Also, for the most part, the occupation one "chooses" is similar to the occupations of the social class to which one belongs.[20]

Ideational Mobility By ideational mobility is meant the degree to which a person or family is in contact with different ideas and values. Physical movement is only one way of acquiring new ideas. Modern means of communication, such as books, magazines, newspapers, motion pictures, the radio, and television, are essential for keeping abreast of the world of events and thought. The increasing development of these media is an index of their increasing role in American society.

The circulation of daily and Sunday newspapers has increased greatly over the decades but so has the number of families. In 1945 there was 1.28 daily and 1.06 Sunday newspapers per family;[21] in 1968 there was 1.05 daily and .84 Sunday newspapers per family.[22] Thus there has been some decline in the proportion of newspapers per family. This probably reflects the use of radio and television for news by some persons rather than a newspaper or two newspapers.

Millions of persons have been influenced by the motion picture, the radio, and television. While there has been a decided decline in attendance at motion picture theatres, probably as the result of television, still over 40 million persons attend weekly.[23]

The radio has come to be an almost standard possession of families in the United States. In 1969, 99.7 percent of all dwellings in the United States had at least one radio. The increase in radios is seen by the percent of all occupied dwellings and urban and rural dwellings having radios in 1930, 1940, 1950, and 1960.[24]

Year	All	Urban	Rural
1930	40.3	50.0	26.9
1940	82.8	91.9	69.6
1950	95.7	97.2	92.7
1960	91.5	92.4	89.1

[20] A. B. Hollingshead, *Elmtown's Youth: The Impact of Social Classes on Adolescents* (New York: John Wiley and Sons, 1949).
[21] *Statistical Abstract of the United States*, 1968, p. 505.
[22] N. W. Ayer & Sons, *Directory of Newspapers and Periodicals*, 1968, p. xix.
[23] *Film Daily Yearbook of Motion Pictures, Film Daily*, 1961, p. 105, gives this estimate. Attendance for 1947–1948 was 90.0 million.
[24] Data from various censuses. 1969 figure from *Statistical Abstract of the United States*, 1969, p. 704.

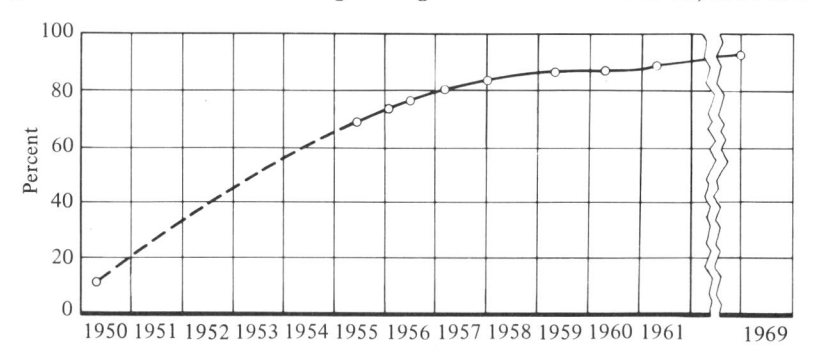

Figure 23. Percent of all dwellings having at least one television set, 1950-1969*

*Bureau of the Census, "Households with Television Sets in the United States, May, 1960," *Current Housing Reports, Housing Characteristics*, Series H-121, No. 7, 1967 percent from *Statistical Abstract of the United States*, 1969, p. 500.

Television has become a major avenue of ideational mobility. In spite of its short history—there were only about 10,000 sets in the United States in 1945[25]—it has swept the country. As is shown in Figure 23, in 1950, 12 percent of all occupied dwelling units had at least one set; by 1955 the figure had increased to 67 percent, and by 1969 to 95 percent. By 1960 11 percent had two or more sets and by 1969, 29 percent had two or more sets. Television sets are fairly evenly distributed for urban, rural-nonfarm, and rural-farm areas.

A study of the use of television by children in San Francisco and in five Rocky Mountain communities showed that by the first grade nine out of ten children watched television, and that the average time spent watching television was two hours in the early grades, went up to three or four hours by the sixth and seventh grade, and then declined through high school.

The influence of television viewing on the behavior of children is of increasing concern to parents, teachers and others. This is especially true since estimates are that the average American child from three to sixteen years of age spends about one-sixth of his waking hours watching television.[26] By the first grade 40 percent of children's viewing is spent on programs not intended primarily for children, and by the sixth grade 80 percent. A major question which concerns most persons is the influence on children, adolescents, and young adults of the portrayal of violence.

---

[25] M. F. Nimkoff, "What Do Modern Inventions Do to Family Life?" *The Annals of the American Academy of Political and Social Science*, 272 (1950): p. 55.

[26] Wilbur Schram, Jack Lyle, and Edwin B. Parker, *Television in the Lives of Our Children* (Stanford: Stanford University Press, 1961), Ch. 9.

The amount of violence in television programs was the subject of a survey of network television programs from 7 to 11 PM on weekdays and from 8:30 to noon on Saturday—a total of 85½ hours for three networks—for a single week in the summer of 1968. The report stated that there was a total of 81 murders and killings, and 372 incidents of violence or threatened violence, 162 of which appeared on Saturday morning.[27]

The influence of television on the behavior of children was studied by Maccoby.[28] She concluded the following from a review of studies in the United States, Britain, and Japan:

1. Television has relatively little effect on school performance. Some apparent relationships between high degrees of viewing and poor school performance disappear when IQ is controlled. Children with higher IQ levels both watch television less and have better school grades.

2. From experimental studies it appears that with normal children, the effect of viewing aggression on film or television is to arouse aggressive impulses which may be acted upon if subsequent real-life situations present appropriate opportunities.

3. There is a limited amount of evidence suggesting that television may influence moods (pessimism about the future among adolescent girls who see many daytime serials) or transmit pervasive attitudes (diminishing of sensitivity among viewers of crime dramas).

4. There is essentially no evidence that television has substantially increased children's knowledge or range of interests in any lasting way. This may be partly because most studies have concentrated on areas considered to be possible problems but not all studies have been of this type.

Before the development of television and its widespread presence, parents, teachers, and the public were concerned about the influence of movies on children and adolescents. Three or four decades ago the effects of movies were studied by several persons, including Blumer who described the function of motion pictures in giving definitions of behavior in conflict with those of the family and other institutions:

> In a genuine sense, motion pictures define his [the adolescent's] role, elicit and direct his impulses, and provide substance for his emotions and ideas. Their modes of life are likely to carry an authority and sanction which make them formative of codes of living. Despite their gay and entertaining character, motion pictures seem to enter seriously into the lives of young men and women, particularly of high-school age.

[27] Survey conducted by the staff of the *Christian Science Monitor* and reported in the *Los Angeles Times*, August 12, 1968, Part 2, p. 4.

[28] Eleanor E. Maccoby, "Effects of the Mass Media," in *Review of Child Development Research*, Martin L. Hoffman and Lois Wladis Hoffman, (eds.) (New York: Russell Sage Foundation, 1964), 1, pp. 323–348.

Because motion pictures are educational in this sense, they may conflict with other educational institutions. They may challenge what other institutions take for granted. The schemes of conduct which they present may not only fill the gaps left by the school, by the home, and by the church, but they may also cut athwart the standards and values which these latter institutions seek to inculcate. What is presented as entertainment, with perhaps no thought of challenging established values, may be accepted as sanctioned conduct, and so enter into conflict with certain of these values.

Where, as in disorganized city areas, the school, the home, or the community are most ineffective in providing adolescents with knowledge adequate for the new world into which they are entering, the reliance on motion pictures seems to become distinctly greater.[29]

The figures on the increasing ideational mobility of the American people indicate how far the outside world has invaded the home and the degree to which man is living and moving in an increasingly wider and changing world. The effects of contact with new ideas through the motion picture, radio, television, books, and pamphlets, daily and Sunday newspapers, and periodicals are not confined to the city or to any one class, but reach out and touch the remotest hamlet and in varying degrees impinge on every social class.

Agencies of communication introduce persons to ways of behavior divergent from those sanctioned by the family, the school, and the church. Through these agencies of communication persons contact different norms and this may result in a decrease in the influence of family and community standards. The total effect of mobility in its various forms—residential, personal, vertical, and ideational—is the relaxation of control by the family and the emancipation of its members. The major changes are individualization of interests and secularization of ideas and values. In short, there is a marked decline in familism and an increase in individualism. Under certain conditions the outcome may be family disorganization.

MOBILITY AND FAMILY DISORGANIZATION

Family organization arises out of intercommunication between its members, with resulting consensus and collective action. Disorganization develops when communication ceases or is disrupted, when individual aims take precedence over common objectives, and when family members, instead of working together, act at cross-purposes.

The disorganizing effects of mobility have been suggested in the discussion of the individualizing effect of mobility on family members. Let

[29] Herbert Blumer, *Movies and Conduct*. By permission of The Macmillan Company, publishers, New York, 1933, p. 197.

us now illustrate concretely the influence of mobility on family disorganization. First, we will discuss the case of immigrant families transplanted from Mexico and Puerto Rico to a new urban environment. Second, we will consider internal migration. Third, we will see that a family may move out of the social matrix of one community to another community in the same society and experience disorganization caused by the breaking of old social relationships and the difficulty of forming new ones. Fourth, we will see that spatial separation of family members may weaken their attachments and relationships.

The Immigrant Family Mexicans and Puerto Ricans are among the current or recent migrants into the United States. At first the immigrant families reside in areas with people speaking their own language and are quite isolated from the general culture of the new country. At first families typically are highly organized, but they become disorganized as their members progressively participate in the economic, educational, and recreational activities of the American community and differentially assimilate the attitudes and values of the new culture.

Differential assimilation of the culture patterns of the new community results in differential allegiance to the old values and ways of behavior. The children attend public schools and, through formal training and informal association at school, frequently are introduced to a radically different set of patterns from those of their parents. Various family members participate in the economic life of the community and gradually the allegiance to the traditional values and behavior patterns which unified the family breaks down.

The loss of allegiance to traditional values and the development of individualism in more recent migrants are seen in the following account by a Puerto Rican mother of three children living in a slum area of New York City:

> The children are more respectful to old people in Puerto Rico than here . . . I know. I never used to argue with my mother in Puerto Rico. If she had a reason or no, I keep quiet. And with my father, too. The word that he said was the only word to me. If he said not to go to a movie, I didn't discute (argue) that with him. I didn't go. No here. The children are more free here. Tommy, when I say, do that, and he don't want to and he explains me why, I don't mind that. I think it is better for him. You know, we didn't do that but it was not good inside.[30]

Internal Migration Internal migration, like immigration, may also have disorganizing effects, since cultures are plural within many countries

[30] Elena Padilla, *Up from Puerto Rico* (New York: Columbia University Press, 1958), p. 307.

today. The United States has wide cultural differences in folkways among regions, rural and urban areas, various nationality groups, and social classes. Anthropologists call these cultural areas of a country "subcultures." Migration between subcultures brings into contact people who differ from each other in religious, political, economic, and familial attitudes and values.

If individuals are in intimate contact with divergent patterns of behavior over a sufficiently long period, formerly alien standards tend to become their standards. Consequently, if members of a family, because of necessity or desire, move in different social worlds, hold different types of jobs, or are in regular and intimate contact with different patterns of behavior, they tend to become individualized. This is the situation in modern societies, where ease and speed of transportation and communication tend to bring the individual members of families into differential association with cultural values. Whenever there is a high degree of mobility, in the sense indicated above, there will be a high degree of actual or potential disorganization of the individual family. Under such conditions the inner unity and even the structure of the family may be disrupted.

Moving Out of a Social Matrix A family moving to a strange community is torn from its social matrix and detached from the extrafamilial social attachments which gave it support in the former location. If the members of a family had few social relationships before or if in the new location the time and energy of the various members are sufficiently absorbed in satisfying pursuits, the breaking of extrafamilial associations will probably not be very disorganizing. But, if a member of a family has built up satisfying attachments or has had positions of importance in the former location and finds no satisfying outlets for his talents in the new location, he may feel lost, homesick, and depressed. When a family moves into a strange community, it generally takes considerable time to form satisfying attachments or to secure positions of prestige. This is especially true of wives and older children as contrasted with husbands and young children. A wife may patiently wait for social acceptance later, or turn for consolation to the members of the family and be more firmly united with them than formerly. However, she may also become discontented, irritable, and nervous. Situations which formerly would have caused no difficulty now create tension and strain, and the inner unity of the family may be imperiled.

Moving out of a social matrix seems to be particularly disrupting to working-class wives who move to suburbs. Tallman found this to be true in his study of 45 suburban and 51 central-city working-class families. Both were new residents in the respective communities. Tallman presents the following sequence of events which characterize working-class wives who move to suburbs:

> The sequence begins with migration away from the neighborhood and family of orientation leading to both increased isolation and greater demand for changes in conjugal and extra-familial roles. This, in turn, results in increased marital conflict, a state which, given the condition of separation from friends and relatives, results in an increased sense of general disaffection. This situation is exacerbated if the family move is seen as indicating upward mobility, since such mobility may imply status changes which emphasize the social distance of wives from their families of orientation. In addition, perceived upward mobility provides a visible locus for the distress suburban working-class women may experience and, in this sense, may contribute to increased marital conflict.[31]

Spatial Separation of Family Members Family members separated in space may grow apart even though they are living in similar cultural situations. Continued and intimate communication seems essential for the perpetuation of interpersonal attachments. An extended absence of any member means that the roles which he had been playing in the family will either go unperformed or be assumed by other persons, and in either case the former unity will be disturbed.

The movement of persons to a new location removes them from the social restraints and social controls of primary relationships, makes them free to neglect or violate traditional folkways and mores, allows them to express overtly behavior which previously had been inhibited because of social pressures, and thus makes it possible for the divergent patterns to become more firmly entrenched in individuals. When these individuals go back to their original groups, they may constitute a real threat to traditional family behavior. This is particularly true if the number of such deviant persons is large. The new ways of behavior may be practiced unwittingly or conscious attempts may be made to undermine established customs and traditions and thus increase family conflict.

MOBILITY AND FAMILY ORGANIZATION

Under certain conditions, mobility may have an organizing rather than a disorganizing effect on family relations. Among these are vacations and trips taken together or separately; temporary and prolonged separations; family movement as among gypsies, trailer families, hotel families, and other families continuously on the move; and the change of resi-

---

[31] Irving Tallman, "Working-Class Wives in Suburbia: Fulfillment or Crisis?" *Journal of Marriage and the Family*, 31 (1969): p. 72.

dence of the family not adjusted in one community seeking to improve its social relationships by moving to a new community.

Vacations and Other Travels Vacations in which all the members of the family enjoy together the interesting experiences of camping out or making an automobile trip typically heighten family unity. When the family participates in joint activities in which each member has a vital role in an atmosphere of play rather than work, its unity resembles that of the old-time rural family, but without its drudgery and rigid discipline.

A vacation freed from the responsibility and care of the children may be especially unifying for the husband and wife. A younger child when away from one or both parents may become homesick and is the more appreciative of parents on his return. With the adolescent, separation in camp, school, or otherwise from the family aids both in the emancipation from parents and in enabling him to take a more adult role in the family. Thus conflicts occasioned by his desire for independence and the reluctance of parents to grant him autonomy are mitigated.

The social institution of the honeymoon recognizes the unifying effect on husband and wife of going away together immediately after the wedding, thus separating themselves from relatives, friends, and all other distracting influences during the initial period of marital adjustment.

Extended travel later in marriage, when both members of a couple have similar interests, is highly unifying. When husband and wife have divergent interests, they may plan an itinerary which satisfies both. Or if they have sympathetic understanding of one another's individual interests and desire for freedom in travel, they may arrange separate trips and be more unified because of the appreciation of this mutual accommodation.

Temporary and Prolonged Separations Short separations seem to have little or no disturbing effect on family relations and often appear to heighten family solidarity because of the concentration of interest on the trip made by one of its members and his return as a great event in family life. In many cases, homesickness of the absentee is at its height in the first days and weeks of separation, when he is most keenly aware of his isolation in the new situation and least adjusted to it. In this period his letters are frequent, long, affectionate, and intimate. As he becomes accustomed to his new surroundings and forms friendships, his letters become occasional, shorter, and less intimate and affectionate. While this is the general rule, there are, of course, wide individual differences. In the case of a wife and husband separated over a long period, letters may continue frequent and intimate on the part of both, or neither, or of only one. A long absence may "make the heart grow fonder" if communication is maintained, particularly if neither has made new and satisfying attachments while apart or developed divergent interests. A prolonged separation may be unifying or at least involve a minimum of disorganization when both husband and wife realize that the separation is necessary, and particularly if it is the expression of a family objective, such as the husband completing his education, or of a national purpose, such as his service in the armed forces.

Occupational Separations Certain occupations, like that of traveling salesman, require absence from the home during the week or for longer periods. The general effect of these sparations is disorganizing, as indicated by the high rates of divorce and marital unhappiness in occupations of high mobility. Nevertheless, in these occupational groups the enforced and necessary absence of the husband leads in many marriages to a closer relationship between husband and wife and father and children because of the enhanced pleasure of association on his periodic returns to the home.

In certain couples, temperamentally incompatible or having widely divergent interests, the separation of the husband from the family because of his occupation has actually prevented conflicts which would have led to the breakup of the marriage. The husband and wife are able to adjust satisfactorily in the holiday atmosphere of the weekend, when before his traveling there were many irritations and annoyances in day-in and day-out existence together.

Mobile Families Families that are constantly on the move, such as those that live in trailers and hotels, remain unified apparently because of mobility.[32] Why is mobility a unifying factor with these families when it is disorganizing in certain other families? One reason for the immunity of these families to the disorganizing effects of mobility seems to be that, although there is movement, there is at the same time a high degree of isolation. Since these families are constantly on the move, they do not remain in any one place long enough to make vital and sustained contacts with divergent patterns of behavior. The trailer family and the hotel family participate very little in the community life in which they are physically located. And when they do take part in social activities, it is likely to be on a formal and superficial level, like that of the tourist in a foreign country.

[32] Other mobile families in American society are those employed in the circus, construction-camp work, and migratory farm work, such as fruit picking and sugar-beet harvesting.

Another reason for the unifying effect of movement on this type of family is the participation of all the members in the frequent changes of residence, especially in the stages of planning, anticipation, the journey, and the first experiences in the new location.

The trailer family is the outstanding example of the mobile family in our society. It differs from other mobile families not only in the long distances it may cover in a short time but because it usually travels as an independent unit. The trailerite takes his residence, which he almost always owns, with him. In fact, the trailer family typically looks forward to the day when it can own a "bigger and better" trailer.

Many families live in trailers only during their vacations, but an increasing number are permanent trailer dwellers. Trailer life is an escape from many of the complexities and problems of urban life. For this reason the extreme mobility of the trailer family does not result in as high a degree of family disorganization as might be expected. This is due, in fact, to the fact that so much of the existence of all members of the family is organized around the trailer.

Hotel life involves social isolation in which the family is thrown more upon its own resources than in a well-integrated neighborhood environment. For children in most apartment hotels, a play group is almost entirely lacking. The child is thus with its parents the greater part of the day not taken up by school. Mobility also involves frequent changes in schools. Indeed the only unchanging feature of the child's environment is his parents. The family group is the only primary group with which the child has any sustained contact.

Adjustment Through Relocation Although movement to a new location is in general disorganizing, we must not overlook the fact that it may contribute to the adjustment of families who for one reason or another have been maladjusted in the old community. Such maladjustments are reflected in inferior or uncertain status in the old community, conflict with its standards, delinquency of a member of the family, difficulties with in-laws, or some other dissatisfaction of one or more members of the family with the community. When the move to a new community is for the fulfillment of a family objective, as for superior educational opportunities for the children, the change of residence is also unifying.

SUMMARY

Mobility has been examined in this chapter as an important factor in the explanation of family disorganization. In this analysis of the ways in which mobility is disorganizing, seven types have been described: (1) moving from one culture into an entirely different culture, as in immigration; (2) moving to a different subculture, as in internal migration; (3) moving within a culture or subculture but to a new community, thereby breaking old associations and being faced with the necessity of forming new personal relationships; (4) remaining in the community but moving up or down in the social scale; (5) temporary or prolonged but not permanent separations from primary associations, particularly the family; (6) personal mobility with the increase in rapid means of transportation; and (7) coming in contact with new stimulations and patterns of behavior through communication, particularly through the newspaper, the motion picture, radio, and television.

The chief disorganizing effect of mobility is that it individualizes the person by detaching him from his family and other personal associations. This takes place (1) by the interruption of communication with family and friends, (2) by bringing the person into communication with those engaging in divergent practices, (3) by freeing him from primary social controls over his conduct, (4) by weakening personal attachments and loyalties to his family and friends, and (5) by increasing the opportunity of choice between various patterns of behavior.

Mobility has organizing effects which counteract, at least to a certain extent, its disorganizing tendencies. Examples of these are situations in which the family participates in travel as a unit; when mobility makes for nostalgia and, therefore, greater appreciation of home and family; and when the family improves its social adjustment and status by a move to a new community.

PROBLEMS FOR RESEARCH

This résumé of the relation of mobility to family disorganization and reorganization provides the background for further research on mobility.

Vertical Mobility and Family Relationships When sons and daughters have more education than their parents, they may have higher social status by young adulthood. It is frequently assumed that the relationships between the two generations will be disrupted by differences in social class. Research is needed on the following questions: (1) Is this assumption valid, and if so, what are the conditions most and least likely to contribute to breaking of intergeneration ties? (2) In what specific kinds of family relationships is the disruption greatest and which least? (3) Is movement out of a very low social class less disruptive than upward mobility in other social classes? (4) What differences are there when the movement is to an adjacent social class as compared with greater changes in status? (5) Are there changes in the degree of disruption at different periods of the family life cycle?

Change of Social Matrix In moving from one community to another within the same culture and subculture, the family meets the problem of change in its matrix of personal and social relationships. The simplest situation for study is that in which a family moves to a new community. Four types of residential change might be studied: (1) movement into a new community similar to the old one, (2) movement from village to city or the reverse, (3) movement from smaller to larger cities or the reverse, and (4) movement from a lower to a higher residntial status or the reverse. Many factors are involved in the differences of adjustments of family members to the new community, such as the degree of spatial or social distance, frequency of previous changes of residence, and personality differences, such as sociability, aggressiveness, and emotional independence.

Mobility and Family Attachments A study could be made of the comparative effect on family attachments and personality of separation of members with infrequent visits home and with frequent or occasional visits home. The emancipation from parental attachments of students coming from a considerable distance to a university could be compared with that of students living within a seventy-five-mile radius of the university. How does nostalgia—the yearning for the accustomed and familiar—vary by persons, cultures, ages, or distances from the old and familiar? Is nostalgia or homesickness a factor contributing to family solidarity? What are the factors in parents' emotional reaction, lonesomeness, or resentment on separation from children at marriage? To what extent is this accentuated if the married couple is in a higher social class, lives in a different community, and has developed different interests?

QUESTIONS AND EXERCISES

1. Indicate specific ways in which the family has been changed as a result of the increased rapidity of transportation by railroad, automobile, and airplane, and as a result of the increase in communication with the outside world through radio, television, books, newspapers and periodicals.
2. Give what you consider the most important data on each of the following showing the transiency of the American family: absence of an ancestral home, increased residential mobility, and life in a trailer.

3. Make an outline of the manifestations of family disorganization occasioned by movement out of a social matrix, vertical mobility, and spatial separation of family members.
4. What are some ways, other than those presented in the text, in which families may be more united as the result of mobility?
5. What is the meaning of individualization? What are the specific ways in which mobility results in individualization?
6. What is the relationship between upward and downward vertical mobility and affectional attachments to parents?
7. In what ways could moving out of a social matrix be organizing or disorganizing?

BIBLIOGRAPHY

Adams, Bert N. "Occupational Position, Mobility, and Kin Orientation," *American Sociological Review*, 32 (1967): pp. 364–377.
> Deals with occupational mobility as related to affection and admiration of father, mother, and siblings. Sample consisted of 799 white-collar and blue-collar men and women. Found significant correlations on several comparisons.

Goldstein, Sidney. *Patterns of Mobility, 1910–1950: The Norristown Study.* Philadelphia: University of Pennsylvania Press, 1958.
> Studies residential and occupational mobility through the use of data in successive city directories. Shows that high in- and out-migration is largely attributable to repeat migrants, rather than to the displacement of established residents by immigrants.

Leslie, Gerald R.; and Richardson, Arthur H. "Life-Cycle, Career Pattern, and the Decision to Move," *American Sociological Review*, 26 (1961): pp. 894–902.
> Analyzes earlier studies of residential mobility and reports a survey of mobility of families in a relatively new subdivision in a small city. Suggests that upward occupational mobility potential and stage of the family life cycle may be the most significant variables influencing decisions of families to move. Factors such as dissatisfaction with present housing are of much less importance.

Lipset, Seymour Martin; and Bendix, Reinhard. *Social Mobility in Industrial Society.* Berkeley: University of California Press, 1960.
> Reviews studies in vertical mobility in Europe and the United States, drawing pertinent conclusions from them. Also includes an analysis of the authors' 1949 Oakland mobility study. Chiefly concerned with the sources of social mobility in industrial societies.

Litwak, Eugene. "Occupational Mobility and Extended Family Cohesion," *American Sociological Review*, 25 (1960): pp. 9–21; and "Geo-

graphic Mobility and Extended Family Cohesion," *ibid.;* pp. 385–394.
Both articles present the thesis that a modified form of the extended family exists in urban United States, with personal relationships being maintained even though the extended family as an economic and occupational unit has disappeared. Include limited data from a survey of middle-class housewives. Indicates that neither geographic nor occupational mobility significantly interferes with the maintenance of personal relationship ties with relatives.

Maccoby, Eleanor E. "Effects of the Mass Media," in *Review of Child Development Research*, eds. Martin L. Hoffman and Lois Wladis Hoffman. New York: Russell Sage Foundation, 1964.
This is an excellent review of the influence of television on children and adolescents as indicated in studies in the United States, Britain, and Japan.

Rossi, Peter H. *Why Families Move: A Study in the Social Psychology of Urban Residential Mobility.* New York: Free Press, 1955.
An excellent description and analysis of mobility and why people move. Mobility considered as a process. Concern with the determinants of mobility inclinations, role of complaints in the decision to move, and on specifications persons have in mind when selecting a new residence. Study of area of high and low mobility in Philadelphia.

Schramm, Wilbur; Lyle, Jack; and Parker, Edwin B. *Television in the Lives of Our Children.* Stanford University Press, 1961.
Reports on 11 studies of children's use of television and the influence of television on children. Data chiefly from San Francisco and five Rocky Mountain and two Canadian communities. Analyzes some relationships between children's use of television and family relationships.

Chapter 19
Family Conflicts and Accommodations

There are increased chances that persons will meet and marry persons quite different in backgrounds if they have experienced residential, personal, vertical, and ideational mobility. It is to be expected that a bride and groom will bring to their marriage different personal characteristics and divergent behavior patterns. Children, as they grow older, acquire attitudes, values, and standards somewhat divergent from those of their parents. It is to be expected that under these conditions there will be both potential and actual conflict in families. Accommodations of family members to each other can lessen the conflict and enhance the possibility of family unity.

A CASE OF MARITAL CONFLICT

In the transition from the traditional to the companionship family, as in any other major social change, forces arise which make conflicts almost inevitable. Certain of these stand out clearly in the following case of marital conflict. The critical factor here is the disparity in conceptions of the husband and wife of their respective responsibility toward the home when the wife is working. This case was written with no audience in mind; the author simply talked her problem over with herself:

> I am sitting at home alone. My husband has gone out to the home of a friend for a poker game. Our little boy of eight is sleeping soundly here by my side. My question is this: Which should come first with a man, the comforts and necessities of life for his family, or his entertain-

ment. Note this—if a woman allows her thoughts to creep out a bit and he senses her disapproval, he thinks, "Oh, well, you can't please her anyway," goes out, slams the door, and is gone.

Now, that's what happened tonight, and that is what stirred me to the point of spending the evening in this manner. And here is another thing that is hard to take. Tonight a big show is being staged. Last week a woman sold him two tickets for it. They are paid for, there is to be every kind of entertainment, and yet after all plans were made to use the tickets and get an evening's entertainment from them, some friend calls and instantly he changed his mind. He asked me to lend him five dollars, and for the first time I refused, because the little five dollars I made myself and I wasn't going to take a chance on letting it slip so easily through my fingers.

Of course, you may think, "Oh goodness, that's nothing to have all this hullabaloo over." But this is not the whole thing, this is just the straw that broke the camel's back and sent me to this desk with this pen.

And I tell you I've got to decide something. This thing is no nearer a solution now than ten years ago, except that I'm stirred up, while ten years ago I would have done anything for peace in the family. Of course, I realize that my husband is not to blame for his utter lack of responsibility, for it was not taught him in his youth, but I do believe that he should grow up by the time he's thirty-five. He has never supported me since we've been married. I've made my own living even up until two months before my baby was born, and beginning again when he was less than three months old. Am I wrong in thinking that I'm not sure I did right when I married for love? Isn't a man supposed to support his family, or is the modern way living together and each supporting himself?

I am certainly standing at the crossroads, and before next January 1st I am going to decide what I shall do. I can't go on this way any longer.

I'll either have to wake him up, or carry this hurt through life, or leave. Now, which is best? I've tried everything but leaving, and I hate the shock it would be to us and our friends. Then we have the dearest little boy and it's hard to know what is best for him.

I am trying to make all allowances for the differences in home environments of our youthful days. The two homes were as different as two homes could be. I was the oldest of a large family of poor but respectable people; and, oh, such an ambitious mother, who felt that nothing was too good for her brood of eight. She taught us to hitch our aims high. She struggled hard for us so that we might all have an education. When I was grown, I taught and worked my way through a special school in expression and dramatic art. It's been the means of my livelihood before and after my marriage. My home life was not a happy one, and after twenty-five years my father and mother separated. When I was twenty-four I fell so madly in love that everything in life faded out but that. I knew this man worshiped me, and words can never express my overflowing joy at loving and being loved.

Now, his early home life was so different. He was an only child until sixteen; then a little sister came. His parents were the most quiet, peace-loving, and agreeable people in the world. I have been a daughter-in-law now nine years and never once have known any one of them criticizing another, not even uncles or cousins. We were married without any money, but I felt so sure that time and patience would solve the problem. I even opened a studio to help out until he could find himself and get started, and each year it was promising for the next, but let me say that his salary has been about the same for ten years and I'm still helping out till next year. He changed firms four times.

Now, about three times in the last year, I've simply exploded and we have had it round and round. He says he wants me to be happy and that, if I'd be happier without him, he'd leave. But he says he is this way about money and regrets that the financial arrangement is so unsatisfactory, but he does not believe that he will ever change. But I know he could help it is he wanted to badly enough.

There is one thing, though, I'll always remember with pleasure. He courts me every day. I can't have the part in my hair changed or put on a new collar that he doesn't compliment me. If I change the furniture or put a different colored pillow on the davenport, he always tells me how nice it looks. He thinks I am just grand about everything. When he is irritable and hurts my feelings, he always apologizes, then takes me out to a dinner, and borrows the money from me to pay for it.

What about our love for each other during all this time, did it hold out? Well, yes and no! My husband is the dearest lover in the world, and I still care for him. I can truthfully say that most of the time in our marriage relationship we loved as passionately as in the first years, although in the last year or two as my hope died and as I lost hope of everything financially, I do not desire our love feasts as often. Of course, I'll never let him know that; I'll never even let myself admit it.

Well, it is midnight and again I ask myself, what must I do? I really have tried to see this thing from every angle. I've tried to be fair and considerate. I'll not mention this to any living soul. It has helped to write it all down, and I must say I feel better for doing it.

The difference in expectations of the economic roles of husband and wife is, of course, not a complete explanation of the conflict in this marriage. However, for the wife it was the critical area of conflict. The case illustrates the fact that major conflicts may exist between a husband and wife even while their marriage may be a significant source of satisfaction in certain areas. Different conceptions of husband and wife about their respective economic roles may be found in a society where a woman pursues a career after marriage. If the woman does not subscribe to the tradition that the husband bears the responsibility for the support of the family, she may accommodate herself to an attitude of irresponsibility on the part of the husband.

This case raises certain of the chief questions to be dealt with in this chapter: the difference between conflict and tension, the types of tensions that may arise in marriage and their interrelations, the effect of tensions between parents on the personality development of children, and the accommodations that limit and control conflict. The following questions will be considered: (1) the nature of family conflict and tension, (2) types of family tensions, (3) parent-child conflicts, and (4) accommodation to conflicts.

THE NATURE OF CONFLICT AND TENSION

In the past the mores dictated that families adjust their difficulties. The arrangement of marriage by the parents eliminated problems of adjustment before marriage. Even after marriage, adjustment was mediated partly by the parents and partly by custom, so that a disintegration of the marriage seldom occurred. The mores also controlled the behavior of the small-patriarchal family. They allowed for incompatibility and conflict within certain limits but circumscribed the extent of its expression.

Today the traditional aspects of the family have been reduced by the modification of its historic functions and by the growing freedom of the individual. Patterns of family and personal behavior are numerous and inconsistent. The control of the kinship group over the individual family has declined drastically.

Inevitability and Normality of Conflict Some conflict is inevitable and normal in the family, as it is in every area of human life. Conflict has its origin both in the personal characteristics of individuals and in cultural patterns of behavior. In the modern urban community, family conflict is the result primarily of cultural factors. Conflicts arise when the husband and wife have different cultural backgrounds, or when they develop different patterns of behavior after marriage. The speeding up of the social processes of mobility, industrialization, urbanization, and secularization has led to confused and inconsistent cultural standards. This confusion is reflected in the divergent and often conflicting behavior of husband and wife, parents and children, and brothers and sisters.

Functional Value of Conflict There is a popular conception that conflict is detrimental and harmful. According to this view, any expression of conflict in the family is cause for alarm. But conflict often has a definite functional value. Strong differences in beliefs, values, and attitudes of husband and wife may be present without hostility or clash of wills. The husband and wife may talk their differences over to the point of consensus, or they may value the individuality of each other and develop tolerance and sympathetic understanding. The dynamic, progressive family in an urban area is continually facing, discussing, and handling differences which arise from individual experiences; consequently, conflict in this sense may be considered normal and functional. Indeed, in some families conflicts are an expected, if not a welcomed, break in the family routine. In other families serious conflicts are matters of grave concern, not so much in themselves, but because they are conceived to be disruptive of the basic unity of family life.

The Difference Between Solved Conflicts and Tensions In analyzing the difficulties in marital and familial relationships it is desirable to differentiate between conflicts which are solved and those which persist. Tension may be defined as an unsolved conflict in which certain basic frustrations are not resolved. When impulses, habits, wishes, and expectations are blocked, the person is restless and attempts in one way or another to find self-expression. If no solution is reached, there is an accumulation of resentments and irritations which finds various expressions. Of particular importance for our present discussion is the fact that frustrations create tensions which disturb the normal functioning of family life.

Symbolic Nature of Much Marital Conflict Studies of marital conflict demonstrate that much overt conflict is symbolic of some underlying tension in an area of behavior other than the one in which the overt conflict is manifested. This symbolic character of marital conflict may be illustrated by economic conflict which may be symbolic of sex conflict. In such situations the husband may withhold money from the family budget after repeated refusals of sexual relations on the part of the wife. A conflict may also arise from the attempt of a husband to regulate and dominate the activities of the wife and children, but it may develop and be expressed in the refusal of the wife to participate in sexual relations.

The Cumulative Nature of Tensions The process of alienation rests upon a series of tensions, after each of which there occurs a redefinition of the marital and familial relationships on a level of greater social distance and instability. The trend toward permanent separation is periodically interrupted by attempts of the wife or husband or both to adjust to living together. Mates experiencing intense marital conflict generally experience two desires: to live together and maintain the marriage, and to free themselves from the marriage relationship and live separately. The process of alienation seems to follow the pattern:

after very serious tension, there is reconciliation; after every period of reconciliation, more serious tensions and hostilities. The cumulative nature of marital and familial tensions means that a slight incident toward the end of the alienation process may produce a disproportionate effect.

That tensions result in the development of social distance between the marriage partners is illustrated by incidents reported in "The Diary of Miriam Donaven."[1] These tensions, pictured by use of a diagram in Figure 24, accumulated until they resulted in divorce and then in the suicide of the wife. An analysis of this case reveals tensions over money matters, the failure of the wife to adjust her conduct to the expectations of the husband's mother, the failure of the husband to give indirect sexual responses in the form of caresses, and direct sexual incompatibility. These tensions seem to have their roots in differences in the cultural background of the couple. While temporary periods of social nearness occurred, there was, nevertheless, an increasing distance between the husband and wife.

Extension of Conflict Unsolved conflicts between family members, when accompanied by anger, bitterness, or hostility, are not only extended in time but tend to be extended to include other persons. Such conflicts may spread out and draw in individuals and relatives not originally associated with the conflict situation. Members inside the family circle and in-laws tend to line up on one side or the other, and, as alienation increases, outsiders may interfere with the solution of conflicts and stir up tensions, or they may mitigate the conflicts. Our studies have shown that, from the viewpoint of the husband, marital difficulties are with the wife's parents, whereas from the viewpoint of the wife, they are with the husband's parents. It appears that difficulties are caused more by mothers-in-law than by fathers-in-law.

TYPES OF FAMILY TENSION

One way in which family tensions have been studied has been to inquire about complaints and serious difficulties in a marriage. A number of studies have found that a high incidence of complaints is an index of poor adjustment in the marriage.

The complaints given are evidently only concrete manifestations of deeper conflicts and tensions. It is therefore desirable to determine how conflicts may be grouped into significant categories.

Locke employed an empirical method of determining the relative inci-

[1] See Ernest R. Mowrer, *Family Disorganization*, (Chicago: University of Chicago Press, 1927), pp. 231–250.

478   Family Conflicts and Accommodations

Figure 24. Development of social distance between a husband and wife

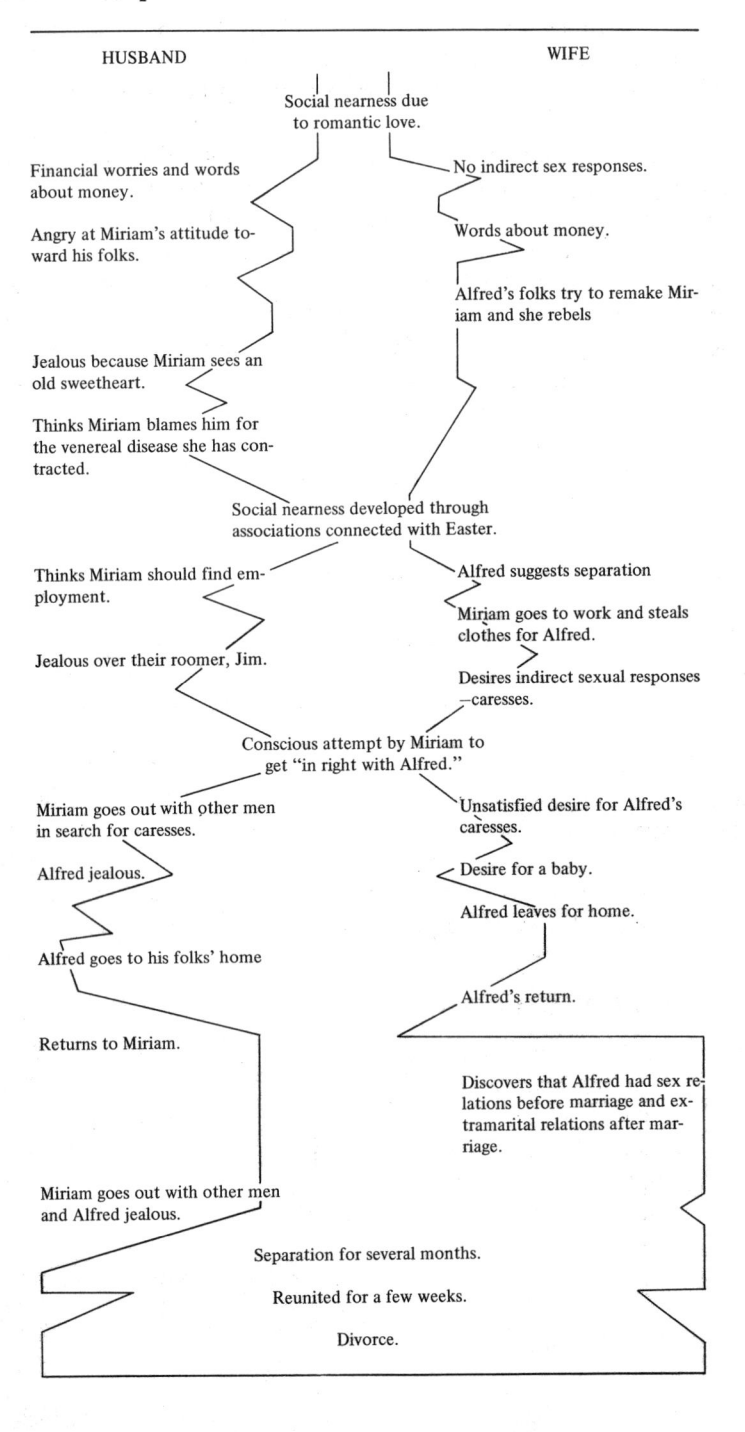

HUSBAND	WIFE

Social nearness due to romantic love.

Financial worries and words about money.

No indirect sex responses.

Angry at Miriam's attitude toward his folks.

Words about money.

Alfred's folks try to remake Miriam and she rebels

Jealous because Miriam sees an old sweetheart.

Thinks Miriam blames him for the venereal disease she has contracted.

Social nearness developed through associations connected with Easter.

Thinks Miriam should find employment.

Alfred suggests separation

Miriam goes to work and steals clothes for Alfred.

Jealous over their roomer, Jim.

Desires indirect sexual responses —caresses.

Conscious attempt by Miriam to get "in right with Alfred."

Miriam goes out with other men in search for caresses.

Unsatisfied desire for Alfred's caresses.

Alfred jealous.

Desire for a baby.

Alfred leaves for home.

Alfred goes to his folks' home

Alfred's return.

Returns to Miriam.

Discovers that Alfred had sex relations before marriage and extramarital relations after marriage.

Miriam goes out with other men and Alfred jealous.

Separation for several months.

Reunited for a few weeks.

Divorce.

dence and seriousness of marital difficulties for the stability of the union. He asked the happily married and the divorced persons in his study to check the presence of marital difficulties from a list in the schedule. Their responses are given in Table 27.

Table 27. Percent of happily married and divorced persons checking items as serious marital difficulties*

	MEN		WOMEN	
Item	Married $N=111$	Divorced $N=123$	Married $N=125$	Divorced $N=147$
A. Affectional and Sex Relationships				
1. Mate paid attention to (became familiar with) another person	2.7	65.9	5.6	73.5
2. Lack of mutual affection (no longer in love)	4.5	60.2	1.6	61.2
3. Adultery	0.9	43.9	1.6	55.1
4. Unsatisfying sex relations	8.1	46.3	5.6	32.7
5. Venereal disease	0.0	1.6	0.8	12.2
6. Unsatisfied desire to have children	2.7	8.1	8.8	3.4
7. Sterility of husband or wife	0.9	3.3	4.8	0.7
B. Economic Difficulties				
1. Mate's attempt to control my spending money	9.0	26.8	7.2	21.1
2. Other difficulties over money	14.4	34.1	19.2	38.1
3. Nonsupport	0.0	7.3	0.0	49.0
4. Desertion	0.0	20.3	0.0	27.2
C. Socially Disapproved Behavior				
1. Drunkenness	2.7	26.0	1.6	56.5
2. Gambling	2.7	6.5	3.2	26.5
3. Mate sent to jail	0.0	4.9	0.0	16.3
D. Individualistic Behavior				
1. Do not have mutual friends	10.8	38.2	6.4	25.2
2. Selfishness and lack of cooperation	6.3	22.0	12.0	29.9

E. Miscellaneous Items
   1. Interference of
      in-laws 17.1   52.8   20.0   29.9
   2. Ill health 3.6   13.8   15.2   10.2
   3. Constant bickering 5.4   48.0   8.8   34.7
F. Undifferentiating
   Items
   1. Different amusement
      interests 28.8   34.1   20.0   28.6
   2. Religious differences 6.3   8.1   4.8   7.5
   3. Other reasons 6.3   12.2   15.2   19.0
G. No difficulties at all 38.7   0.0   27.2   0.0

*From Harvey J. Locke, *Predicting Adjustment in Marriage: A Comparison of Divorced and a Happily-Married Group*, (New York: Henry Holt, 1951), pp. 75-76.

There were great differences between the number of difficulties checked by the two groups. Only one item was checked by over 20 percent of the happily married men, while 13 items were checked by more than 20 percent of the divorced men. Two marital difficulties were admitted by 20 percent or more of the happily married wives, as compared with 15 by this proportion of divorced women.

The marital difficulties which placed the greatest strain on the relationship, as measured by the difference in incidence between the married and divorced, have the following rank order for the men: (1) mate paid attention to another person, (2) lack of mutual affection, (3) adultery, (4) constant bickering, and (5) unsatisfying sex relations. For women the order was the same for the first three, but (4) was forms of socially disapproved behavior, and (5) was nonsupport.[2]

Marital difficulties which were reported much more frequently by divorced men than by divorced women were unsatisfying sex relations, interference of in-laws, constant bickering, and lack of mutual friends. Those more often checked by divorced women were venereal disease, nonsupport, drunkenness, gambling, and husband sent to jail.

Types of family tensions will be considered under the following headings: (1) temperamental incompatibility, (2) differences in cultural patterns, (3) social roles, (4) economic tensions, and (5) affectional and sexual tensions.

Temperamental Incompatibility Temperamental incompatibility may develop whether husband and wife are of the same temperament or of different temperaments. Conflicts may arise in which both the husband

[2] Those given are statistically significant at the five percent level.

and wife are of an excitable disposition, or in which one is of this type and the other is calm and slow in his reactions. The following is a case in which temperamental differences made for both harmony and disharmony in husband-wife relations:

Husband: I think I am even-tempered—perhaps a little too even-tempered. My wife fluctuates more in moods than I. She is more easily excited or angered about something. I am probably not aggressive enough; too inclined to procrastinate. Because of this there are some clashes. Usually we adjust quite well. I like my wife's vivaciousness. I feel her criticisms of me for something I do or fail to do are awfully good. Usually she is right.

Wife: The thing that is the hardest is the fact that he is so easygoing and runs along on such even keel that he is not affected like me. I am very much either way up in the clouds or down in the depths. It seems I can't find and keep a happy medium. He is much more the steady type than I am. I am very flighty and terribly sincere and I mean to do right, but little things can get me so irritated and under these circumstances I say things I don't mean. For the most part he is generous enough to overlook it. I can't imagine any person not getting disturbed at times. At those times we will have a fight. Up until last month George would just be silent; just submissive. Once or twice he has talked back. I have loved it when he does.

The wife in this case adjusted to her husband as a life partner because, with her vivacious and excitable disposition, she felt soothed and comforted by his calm and easygoing reactions. He in turn was stimulated by her impulsive and emotional behavior. Certain expressions of his temperament irritated his wife, and he in turn was sometimes annoyed and made miserable by her "belligerent" criticism. In other cases of mutual attraction and repulsion of divergent temperaments, the wife may criticize severely the husband's lack of ambition and tendency to be satisfied with things as they are, which often is associated with an easygoing disposition. At first, the unambitious husband may appreciate his wife for her efforts to "push" him ahead, but later he may react negatively to her persistent nagging. Finally, the wife may give up the vain attempt to infuse energy and ambition into her husband and turn her attention to instilling into her children, especially her sons, the determination to get ahead in life.

Differences in Cultural Patterns Differences between the husband and wife, resulting from cultural conditioning, may be present at the time of marriage or may arise from differential experiences after marriage. At marriage, husbands and wives may vary considerably in their habits, attitudes, manners, memories, sentiments, and basic values, which they in large part acquired in the early years of life, and these differences may cause conflicts. Even greater conflicts may develop after marriage from the adoption of different folkways and mores. This may occur in cases of long separation of husbands and wives, through migration of one or the other to another area, and immigration of whole families when differential assimiliation may take place. Too, cultural differentiation may occur when an individual or a family goes up or down in the scale of occupations or of social classes. The essential point is that the chances of marital and familial conflicts are greatly increased whenever an individual member of a family enters a new social environment and other members remain in the old cultural area, or whenever a family moves to a different place and its members vary in the degree to which they assimilate the new culture.

Certain cultural tensions, especially those having to do with life values, need to be placed in the perspective of changes in man's thinking about nature, society, and himself, resulting from the scientific discoveries and mechanical inventions of the past century. Man's ability to control his physical environment has shaken his reliance on the supernatural. All fields of activity are experiencing a transition from a sacred to a natural or secular interpretation of reality. In the past the stability of the family was to a considerable extent derived from the belief that marriage was a divine institution. With secularization of thought has come the view that marriage is a man-made institution. Conflicts within a family are probable if the members differ greatly in the degree to which they are sacred-minded or secular-minded. If a predominantly sacred-minded person marries a predominantly secular-minded person, the great divergencies in their attitudes and values increase the possibility of conflict.

Over fifty years ago Thomas and Znaniecki in their analysis of family disorganization formulated three principles which show the relationship between cultural differentiation, individualization, and conflict.[3] These may be summarized as follows: (1) The cause of manifestations of family disorganization is found in cultural differentiation in which new individualistic "I" attitudes develop, in contrast with the former collective "we" attitudes. (2) These individualistic attitudes may be suppressed by a strong social opinion favoring family solidarity and condemning individualistic tendencies; or the individualistic atttudes may be expressed if the community has become disorganized, if the individual is isolated from it, or if his contact with the outside world makes him

---

[3] W. I. Thomas and F. Znaniecki, *The Polish Peasant in Europe and America* (New York: Knopf, 1927), 2, pp. 1167–1176. (A reprint of original edition, 1918–1920.)

relatively independent of the opinion of his immediate milieu. (3) If the individualistic behavior of a person is not opposed by his family, there will be a loss of family interests but not conflict; if there is opposition but the individual feels free from his family and community, conflict may be minimized by the individual's withdrawing; if, however, the individual meets strong opposition and is not sufficiently free from his family and community to ignore them, hostility will arise. These principles seem to hold true today.

Social Roles Tensions may arise when members of a family change roles and status. Within the family tensions centering around status tend to appear with any change in roles, as, for example, when a husband loses his job and the wife or one of the children becomes the chief breadwinner. Another example is the adolescent boy who feels frustrated in his attempt to play the adult role when his father treats him as a boy and his mother still thinks of him as her baby. Anything which affects the positional relationships of the family members may create conflict.

The following case shows how conflict develops in relation to changing roles of family members and their struggles for position, and the way in which affection mediates compromises and adjustment:

> The father of the family frowned upon early romance, particularly for his daughters. This brought about a conflict, waged largely by the eldest daughter of the family. There was insistence, determination, wrath on the part of the daughter—cajolery, bribery, disappointment, and defeat on the part of the father. There was conflict between the father and the youngest son, who persistently violated the mores of the family group. In both cases, the father was the one who made the concessions. The most successful part of his career as head of the family was knowing when to relax his authority. He was most devoted to this older daughter and very proud of the youngest son, who was in many ways a replica of the father. The mother had a special sympathy for her youngest son. Consequently, the three "middle" children formed a close, compact organization. This combination soon obtained control.

Conflict may also take place because of the differential relations of parents and children to the class structure of a community:

> At the marriage of my two sisters, a conflict arose in the family. We children said that invitations should be sent to those individual families in the town who were on a par with us and that the others should be left out, but Father and Moher insisted that this would never do. His work as a minister would be harmed by such a procedure. We finally gave in. We saw the necessity for it, but were rebellious. Just before each marriage Father gave a public invitation.

Economic Tensions Economic conflicts, when they arise in families, seem to be related to differences in attitudes of family members toward economic goals and differences in the members' conceptions of their economic roles. A husband may not recognize the fact that social attitudes in American society virtually compel women to spend money in ways in which husbands have little or no interest. Women are expected to follow fashions and spend more money on clothes and personal beautification than are men. These obligations imposed by social expectations on women, if not understood by husbands, may cause conflicts and tensions.

Tensions may arise if there is dissimilarity of attitudes on spending money for a good time, putting it in the bank for a rainy day, or putting it into a home. If the husband and wife are both spendthrifts, they may have a glorious time without any conflicts between them, even if they continually experience periods of financial embarrassment. If both are equally thrifty, they will be harmonious on economic matters. But if one is a prodigal and the other a pennysaver, they will probably find themselves in conflict.

Differences of attitudes of family members on their individual economic roles are indicated in the case at the beginning of the chapter. If the statement of the wife is true, her complaint was not that there was inadequate income, but that her husband did not assume the responsibility of supporting his family. In some other cases there are clashes between husbands and wives in which the husband thinks it his responsibility to earn the living and resents the fact that the wife wants to work rather than fulfill her role of being a housewife.

Affectional and Sexual Tension Conflicts between men and women in the expression of affectionate behavior and in sexual intercourse are particularly prone to develop into tensions. Various studies have found that failure to secure satisfying expressions of affection and to achieve satisfying sexual adjustments within the family have resulted in conflicts and tensions. From an intensive analysis of 49 case histories, Burgess and Cottrell concluded that (1) there are wide variations in sex behavior from couple to couple and from time to time in the same couple; (2) sex conflicts are generally either emotional or cultural in origin; and (3) variations in the sexual act do not constitute a problem of adjustment unless they operate to produce chronic frustration of sexual satisfaction or chronic reactions against sex activity.[4] Terman found that (1) sex factors contribute decidedly to marital happiness or unhappiness; (2) all the sex factors combined are far from being the

[4] Ernest W. Burgess and Leonard S. Cottrell, *Predicting Success or Failure in Marriage* (New York: Prentice-Hall, 1939), Ch. 12.

major determinant of success in marriage; and (3) the two sexual factors of primary importance are the orgasm adequacy of the wife and the relative strength of the sex drive in the two mates.[5]

Locke found that happily married and divorced persons differed in most of their answers to the sex questions included in his study.[6] The happily married reported fewer extramarital sex relations, a more equal interest in sex, more enjoyment in sex behavior, less frequent refusal when mate desired it, and little or no jealousy.

Burgess and Wallin report that (1) the sex-adjustment scores of husbands and wives have a lower correlation with marital-happiness scores than do their scores on love for spouse, conception of the spouse's general satisfaction, and consensus; (2) the relationship between sex-adjustment scores and marital-success scores is about the same for husbands and wives; (3) the odds are strongly in favor of the person with good sex adjustment having a high marital-success score; (4) a substantial proportion of husbands and wives with low sex-adjustment scores have high marital-success scores; and (5) although good sexual adjustment increases the chances of high marital success, poor sexual adjustment by no means precludes it.[7]

The conclusion is that marital compatibility is correlated with agreement of husbands and wives in their attitudes toward sex.

PARENT-CHILD CONFLICTS

Certain parent-child conflicts have already been considered in the preceding discussion of family tensions. The treatment of conflicts in parent-child relations will be limited to those involving (1) emotional adjustment, (2) differences in cultural patterns, and (3) roles.

Emotional Conflicts Emotional conflicts often arise out of incompatibility of members of the family in temperament and a clash of certain personality traits. Emotional conflicts are illustrated in the following case:

> When I was in my fifteenth year my father and mother had a quarrel. Father left the house, his supper uneaten, and slammed the door. My mother burst into tears, and gathered my two sisters and myself close to her. She cried bitterly. And as she cried, my sisters cried, too. But I,

[5] Lewis M. Terman and others, *Psychological Factors in Marital Happiness* (New York: McGraw-Hill, 1938), pp. 373–376.
[6] Harvey J. Locke, *Predicting Adjustment in Marriage: A Comparison of a Divorced and a Happily-Married Group* (New York: Henry Holt, 1951), Ch. 7, pp. 125–157, particularly pp. 156–157.
[7] Ernest W. Burgess and Paul Wallin, *Engagement and Marriage* (Philadelphia: Lippincott, 1953), pp. 504 and 692.

after a few sobs, began to consider the advisability of giving my father a sound thrashing upon his return. I felt myself physically and morally capable.

My father for some years had shown great favoritism toward my older sister. Actions which coming from her gained chuckles brought me harsh rebukes. Not that he ever struck me—except once, when I had lied about going to the store—but I found the scornful rebukes wounded me more deeply than blows would ever have done. And so, large as I was, I often cried on my mother's breast, or prayed, as I lay sobbing in bed, that death might make my father sorry through his loss of me.

The prospect of striking my father gave me a kind of primitive exultation. If he had returned at that moment I believe I should have leaped upon him, yelling like a savage.

We were all in bed and asleep when Father came home. The next day he was very cheerful, and we felt that everything must have been settled, even though Mother was a bit reticent and subdued.

Not long afterward I said to her, "Mother, why does Father hate me so?"

And I thought she was going to cry as she said, "He doesn't hate you, child. Doesn't he get you everything you need and want?"

"Of course he does," I answered, "but he gets the girls everything they want, too. And besides that, he never sends them to bed to cry themselves to sleep and wish they were dead."

Then Mother did cry. I tried to comfort her, and wanted again to strike my father. I knew that Father was somehow to blame for this unhappy mystery. "Mother," I said, "let's you and me run away from Father. Let him stay here with his darned girls if he likes them so well."

She said, "I can't leave Father. Even if I did, I should have to take the girls with me, too."

"Do you love the girls as much as me?" I asked. She nodded.

My mother loved my sisters and me, but my father loved only my sisters. That night I cried myself to sleep.

I think the happiest moment of my youth was when I heard my father say to a neighbor, "I'm proud of that kid of mine. He doesn't have to sit back for any of them. The only trouble with him is he lacks nerve. He has hardly enough spunk to keep him alive."

The next day I asked him for two dollars to buy a book. He looked surprised, but I got the money.

Curiously enough, my standing with my father improved as that of my sisters lost ground. They were now of an age when, in father's terminology, they "began to run about with the fellows," which annoyed him. He disliked the boys who came about at night blowing automobile horns, and whistling prearranged signals.

One day I expressed my intent of going to college. Father was delighted. He said, "I didn't think you had the nerve."

Emotional conflict in this case is exhibited in the husband's leaving the house and slamming the door with the resulting crying by the mother; the son's anger directed toward the father coupled with his strong love for his mother; and the son's resentment that the father seemed to love his sisters more than him.

Differences in Cultural Patterns Serious conflicts between parents and children arise when the standards of the family differ markedly from those which the child meets outside the home. As children increase their contacts, they often encounter patterns of behavior decidedly different from those approved by the parents. Then, too, the child frequently surpasses his parents in formal education. If the parents were born and reared in a foreign country and the children have been brought up in America, there is a world of difference between the folkways and mores of the two generations. Similarly, rural-reared parents may differ from their urban-reared children in attitudes toward religious and recreational activities, the duties and obligations of childen and of parents, and their attitudes toward life. These differences in attitudes and values act as barriers to communication or, if there is communication about these differences, the likelihood is that conflict will ensue.

The following is from an autobiography written by a college senior for one of the authors. This girl gives an intimate account of behavior and conflicts in her Italian family. The father attempted to make the children conform to Italian customs of a generation ago and the children wanted to behave according to patterns current among their American friends. The first to rebel openly was Tony, a brother a year younger than this student, and then toward the end of her senior year she herself openly rebelled:

> Before anything can be said about my life, I must state some things about the family before I became a part of it. My father was left fatherless at the age of eleven and assumed the role of father to his four younger brothers. I presume my father's and mother's marriage was arranged according to the Italian custom. My mother was given a dowry and a house for a wedding present. My mother had her widowed mother-in-law live with her from her wedding day forward. I was born in 1937 and my brother in 1938 in San Tomago di Quino, Italy. When I was two years old, my maternal grandfather decided that he, grandmother, mother, Tony and I would go to the United States, with the expectation that my father would follow. But the war started, he was drafted into the Italian army, and he was a prisoner of war for seven years. After the war ended in 1945 my father joined us in Cleveland, where we were then living.
>
> Upon his arrival he took immediate command of the family. It was arranged that he would buy my grandfather's shoe repair business and my Mother and later Tony and I also worked in the shop. He expected us to help out, particularly in cleaning the store. He chose to do this on Sunday and, being conditioned to go to church on Sunday or it was a

mortal sin, I objected strenuously; my brother did also, but it got us nowhere.

My father wanted a doctor or a lawyer in the family, for he desired to let everyone know that his family had risen to a high status. My brother was to be a doctor and since the age of 13 I have been planning on being a lawyer.

All through high school and college I have never been allowed to have a date, or stay at a friend's house. Tony was also very restricted. One evening it seemed that the daily arguments about little things blew up into one large one. My brother told me later that it was about ocean cables. My father didn't believe it possible and an argument ensued. My brother was almost 19 and my father hit him. The next day my brother joined the army for 3 years. My family and the relatives were shocked when this became known. But Tony had been thinking about leaving for a long time. As soon as my father found out where he was, he went to see Tony. He didn't argue or yell at him. Tony told me later that father put his arms around him and cried.

The next big conflict was when Tony and Becky, the girl he had been going with for two years, told my parents they were married. My brother was on a furlough. My father exploded—but it did no good, for my brother and his wife just walked out.

Up to last year I obeyed my father's commands with minor open rebellion. Down through the years he has insisted that he take me to and from school, or if I came home by bus I must call him at the store and tell him I was home. I didn't like this, but I did comply. But things have changed this last year. I have begun to question so many things. I have begun to think for myself. I did not desire to remain a narrow-minded moralistic child. I could no longer live my parent's way of life. I must live my own. I became more and more rebellious and this antagonized my father. He threatened that he would not finance my law school expenses.

The big rebellion, resulting in my moving out of the house, came over dating. It seemed to me that whenever I showed interest in any male other than my father, he became very upset. About the middle of my senior year a boy in one of my classes asked me to go on a date with him. When I talked to my father he absolutely forbade it. Here I was a grown woman and never allowed to date.

I told him it didn't make any difference what he said, for I was going to have this date. He said for me to come down to the store and I had an idea what that meant. He had given me lickings there in the past. I went to the store and in his rage he struck me. I walked out of the store and went home and packed my suitcase. He followed me home and tried to detain me forceably. I had called a girl friend who had a car and she had come over to help me move. I left my suitcase, went out to my girl friend's car, and we drove away. I had a little money saved and was working, so I could probably pay my way.

This extreme strain in our relations continued for a few weeks and then Mother called asking me to come home for a visit on Mother's Day.

My father seems to have accepted my independence. He has asked me to please let him help financially with my law school. Moreover, he has arranged to buy me a new car for a graduation present.

This case is significant in showing how parent-child conflict occurs when the behavior expected by the parents is too different from that expected by their child's peer group. It also shows that when the alienation of the child has progressed to an extreme point, concessions may be made to preserve some family unity.

Conflict of Roles Parents often have conceptions of the roles their children should play in the community which are widely different from those approved by the adolescent group. When parents intervene, frustration and rebellious behavior may result.

The problems of adolescents have received widespread attention but little sympathetic observation and treatment.[8] The following statements by John, a tall high school boy of seventeen, show the readiness of young people to unburden themselves when assured of a sympathetic listener. John's main interests are movies, parties, being with girls, dances, and automobile riding. He is frequently punished, the usual method being deprivation of some one of his main interests. John "hits back" by revolting against his home, the school, religion, and various social standards:

> My mother is always picking on me or nagging at me. I'm sure getting sick and tired of it all, but I realize that if I left home I would never be able to live, dress, and eat as I do now. Besides, if I did go away, it would break my mother's heart, so I guess I will stick it out as long as possible. They never let me do what I want to do, so I do it anyway and tell them afterwards. Then it's too late to deprive me of my fun and I can stand my punishment easily enough.
>
> Often I ditch school and go with several other fellows downtown to a show. Sometimes a gang of fellows and girls go for a ride either in my car or some other fellow's car. When I get home I cook up a good excuse to get out of it, and it usually works fine. My report card always shows low grades, especially in language. Everybody expects so much more from a boy as big as me than they do of the ordinary fellows my age. My folks though treat me like a regular baby. One is just as bad as the other.
>
> Ever since I can remember I have been made to go to church, Sunday school, and young people's societies. My folks insist that I believe everything about religion. Well, I can't that's all! I do believe in the rudiments of Christianity, and that's enough for anybody, isn't it?
>
> I like movies, shows, dances, and parties where girls are. You can do

---

[8] See "Teen-Age Culture" in *The Annals of the American Academy of Political and Social Science*, 538 (1961).

almost anything with most girls nowadays, but a few of them are decent in every way. I like the decent girls most, but a fellow can't be in style these days and be decent, it seems.

This case shows how readily the adolescent accepts the roles presented by his own age group, even though they are in conflict with the standards of the home, the school, and the church.

Development of autonomy at adolescence may be seen, in part, as a change in the patterns of role relationships within the family. The dependency of childhood is changed into a pattern of self-regulation and responsibility preparatory to the assumption of a full adult role. The adolescent becomes much more mobile than the child and spends less time with his family and more in the company of his peers. In both his emotions and his behavior, he is disengaging himself from the patterns which have supplied the focus of his life to that time. Both popular and psychiatric literature have frequently emphasized the difficulties and struggles of adolescence. However, a review of studies of normal populations does not support this emphasis. In an extensive review of the literature on modal patterns in adolescents in the United States, Douvan and Gold conclude:

> In the large-scale studies of normal populations, we do not find adolescents clamoring for freedom or for release from unjust constraint. We do not find rebellious resistance to authority as a dominant theme. For the most part, the evidence bespeaks a modal pattern considerably more peaceful than much theory and most social comment would lead us to expect. "Rebellious youth" and "the conflict between generations" are phrases that ring; but, so far as we can tell, it is not the ring of truth they carry so much as the beguiling but misleading tone of drama.[9]

Emphasis on the problems of independence and role changes in adolescents may have arisen, at least in part, from studies of deviant subgroups, especially delinquents and clients in child-guidance and counseling centers. It appears that most adolescents achieve autonomy and independence gradually, and that most parents accede, with varying degrees of ease, to gradual changes in the family role structure. A national survey by Douvan and Adelson indicates that girls achieve a considerable degree of behavioral autonomy by age 18, with 94 percent dating or going steady; 60 percent having some kind of job outside the home; and only 44 percent still spending most of their free time with their families.[10] Sixty-four percent play a part together with their

---

[9] Elizabeth Douvan and Martin Gold, "Modal Patterns in American Adolescence," in *Review of Child Development Research*, Lois Wladis Hoffman and Martin L. Hoffman (eds.) (New York: Russell Sage Foundation, 1966) 2, p. 485.

[10] Elizabeth Douvan and J. Adelson, *The Adolescent Experience* (New York: John Wiley and Sons, 1966), pp. 386–389.

parents in establishing family rules; 71 percent feel that friendship can be as close as a family relationship; and just slightly more than one-third, 36 percent, choose a parent as confident.[11] Some data indicate that boys are somewhat less independent than girls of the same age.

ACCOMMODATION TO CONFLICT

The family is in a process of constant accommodation to environing and to internal forces. Perhaps more than any other social group, it is an experiment in the integration of diverse elements, heterogenous in age, sex, and often in social experience, economic activities, and cultural background.

In view of the heterogeneity of marriage partners in modern societies and the potentialities of conflicts and tensions between husbands and wives and parents and children arising out of their different experiences, certain powerful influences must be present to maintain the unity of the family, set limitations on conflict, and bring about accommodations.

The factors which make for the unity of the family have been analyzed as love and affection; emotional interdependence; sympathetic understanding; common interests; consensus on values and objectives; primary communication; family events, celebrations and ceremonies; interdependence of family roles; sexual behavior; and pressures by the environing society.[12] The present discussion will focus on the factors which make for the accommodation of family members to conflict. Outstanding among these are (1) the determination to make a success of marriage and family life; (2) romantic attitudes, especially during the first year or two of marriage; (3) personal adaptability of family members; (4) social pressures, particularly those of primary group association; (5) fear of losing cherished values; (6) avoidance of divisive issues; and (7) crises.

The Will to Make a Marriage a Success When both husband and wife enter marriage with a strong determination to make it succeed, both are disposed to make major concessions. When the will to make the marriage a success is much stronger in either the husband or the wife, the burden of accommodating to conflict falls upon that person. Family counselors report that many families, faced by adversity and internal conflicts, would disintegrate if it were not for the will of one of its members to hold the family together.

[11] *Ibid.*, p. 390.
[12] See Ch. 15.

Romantic Attitudes Romantic attitudes, holding over from the engagement period, aid in the early adjustments of husband and wife. Often they still see each other through rose-tinted glasses and respond to the image which each has constructed of the other. The courtship tendency of each to "put one's best foot forward" continues. In some marriages romantic attitudes and the idealization of the other persist long after marriage. Romantic love functions to facilitate the day-by-day adjustments necessary for the success of marriage.

Personal Adaptability Adaptability is defined as the ability of a person to modify his roles, attitudes, and behavior in order to adjust to those of other persons and to new situations. Angell, in his study of the reaction of the family to the Depression, found that he needed to take into account not only the integration of the members of the family but their adaptability or flexibility.[13] This is also evident in marital-adjustment studies. In some cases in which an unfavorable prediction of the success of the marriage was made, the union turned out well. The explanation is often adaptability.

Other research confirms the importance of adaptability as a factor in marital success. Hill reports that family adaptability was associated with the adjustment of a group of Iowa couples to separation because of wartime service of the husband and also to reunion upon the husband's discharge.[14] Locke measured adaptability, as associated with marital adjustment, by responses to "giving in" in arguments, not being dominating, slowness in getting angry, and quickness in getting over anger. He found that, on the basis of these indexes, adaptability was more prevalent in the happily married than in the divorced group.[15]

Locke and Karlsson, in their study of marital adjustment in Sweden, found that the "most adjusted" husbands and wives were more adaptable, as measured by Locke's indexes, than were the "less adjusted."[16] In addition, Karlsson constructed an adaptability index, composed of Locke's items and four others: gets easily into conversation with new acquaintances, understands mate's wishes, understands mate's feelings, and does not expect others to accept his opinions.[17] He found that the correlation of this index with marital adjustment showed a moderate

---

[13] Robert C. Angell, *The Family Encounters the Depression* (New York: Charles Scribner's Sons, 1936), pp. 285–292.

[14] Reuben Hill, *Families Under Stress* (New York: Harper & Brothers, 1949), p. 306.

[15] Locke, pp. 192–205.

[16] Harvey J. Locke and Georg Karlsson, "Marital Adjustment and Prediction in Sweden and the United States," *American Sociological Review*, 17 (1952): pp. 10–17.

[17] Georg Karlsson, *Adaptability and Communication in Marriage: A Swedish Predictive Study of Marital Satisfaction* (Uppsala, Sweden: Almqvist and Wiksells, 1951), pp. 118–133.

relationship between rating the mate as adaptable and marital adjustment.

Burgess and Wallin, in analyzing interviews with married couples, differentiated four components of adaptability in marriage.[18] These were degree of motivation to adapt; flexibility of personality; empathy, or the capacity to view a conflict situation from the standpoint of the other person; and knowledge of appropriate marital roles and techniques. They found that the chances of a successful marriage are greatest if both spouses are highly adaptable.

Additional evidence of the association between adaptability and marital success is supplied by one of the findings of Terman and Oden's study of the marriages of gifted children.[19] Husbands rated by the field workers as satisfactory in general adjustment had a mean marital-happiness score significantly higher than those judged to be somewhat or seriously maladjusted.

On the basis of the conclusions of the above studies, it appears that success in marriage is related, in part, to the general personality pattern of adaptability.

Social Pressures Outside pressures frequently prevent marital tensions from disrupting a marriage. These include fear of the disapproval of relatives and friends; the active assistance of a mother or mother-in-law in the adjustment of difficulties; concern about the loss of status in the church, the religious definition that conflict beyond a certain point is wrong; the risk of being condemned by one's occupational associates; and the possibility of scandal and newspaper notoriety. There are, of course, wide variations in the degree to which outside pressures impinge on families.

Fear of Losing Cherished Values Accommodation to conflict may occur if the conflict jeopardizes more important values. For instance, there may be accommodation to conflict over extramarital sex behavior if the conflict is tending toward divorce and is jeopardizing one's economic and social security or the welfare of the children. A wife who places a high value on the affectionate behavior of her husband may adjust to sex relations if conflict seems to be resulting in less caressing and other manifestations of affection by the husband.

Avoidance of Divisive Issues Some conflicts in marital and familial relations are avoided by the agreement of family members not to discuss

---

[18] Burgess and Wallin, Ch. 19, particularly pp. 635–636 and 650–653.
[19] Lewis M. Terman and Melita H. Oden, *The Gifted Child Grows Up: Twenty-five Years' Follow-up of a Superior Group* (Stanford: Stanford University Press, 1947), p. 246.

certain issues. In some cases husbands or wives report that they know the mate is likely to be particularly disturbed by certain behavior, and, consequently, they either do not confide in the other about this, or they refrain from engaging in it. A father reports that he overlooks certain misconduct of his children, for by so doing he avoids conflict with them over minor issues and thinks he will have greater control over them on more important matters.

Crises The chapters which follow, "Family Crises," "Family Disruption," and "War and the Family," show how family members adjust to each other under conditions of crisis. While deviations from expected behavior, disgrace, a depression, departure of family members, divorce, death, and war may disrupt a family, various studies have shown that any one of these may bring about greater family unity. A death almost invariably brings about a temporary rallying of family members together, and sometimes it eventuates in greater permanent unity. In times of crisis, disagreements and conflicts may be forgotten or minimized. Members may be so busy trying to meet the crisis that they have little or no time to give to divisive issues.

A Case Study in Accommodation Several of the factors which may result in accommodation to marital and family conflict are involved in the following case of a marriage which remained for some time in an uncertain balance between forces of harmony and disharmony:

> Alice, the daughter of a well-to-do businessman, had had a careful upbringing and a good education. She had a willful and headstrong temper, a great deal of nervous energy, an abundance of enthusiasm, and a charming manner. Before the end of her freshman year at the university, when she was just eighteen, she fell in love with Tom, a good-looking senior about to graduate, and they were married that June. Tom was quite a wonderful chap, and Alice's friends thought her very lucky. Tom and Alice seemed very happy. They lived in a small, attractive apartment. Alice went right on seeing her friends and having a good time.
> Their friends were former friends of Alice's. Tom did not come of a very good family. His folks were poor and had made a big sacrifice even to send him to college. He also had been carefully brought up, but in an atmosphere quite different than Alice. His family were strict Methodists, and he had always thought a great many things ought not to be done on Sundays, and had quite set and conventional ideas of how a wife ought to act. Luckily, he was intelligent enough to realize that his way of life was not the only one.
> Alice had to have excitement and an outlet for her energy. She adored Tom, but what he gave her did not satisfy her, and so she began drifting into an affair, harmless enough at first, with another man. She liked the

excitement of playing with fire, but she did not really think it would come between Tom and her. The other man had a great deal of money and was a man of the world, had traveled, seen, and read much. Alice had not as yet been actually unfaithful to her husband, but that was the direction in which she was moving. Tom found out and at first he was horror-stricken. According to the ideas in which he had been brought up, she had practically dishonored as well as deceived him. But being quite an intelligent man, and still much in love with his very young wife, he took time to think it over. He had been quite conscious of the fact that she was not really old enough or prepared enough for marriage. He knew her very well and so he looked around to find a solution to the problem. It came a little later in the shape of an offer of manager of a branch bank in a neighboring state. The question was, how to persuade Alice. He painted in glowing colors pictures of what a cute little house they could have, how much more money to spend by reason of lower prices, and how she would be the leader of society, instead of just one of the littlest pebbles of the great city. Alice grew excited over the prospect. It was characteristic of her that with this new excitement and with her energy and interest turned in a new direction, she ceased to care about the other man. And so the Jays moved to the small city.

Things went very smoothly for another year or so. Alice was accepted in the little town as a sort of leader, and therefore had a lot of fun at first. But it didn't stand the test of time. She wanted the bright lights of the big city again. She made no effort to curb her restlessness, and Tom grew worried again. Again she grew dissaisfied with him. He did not satisfy her mentally nor even physically now, for as she approached greater maturity, her sex desires, which had been less active when she had been married so young, grew more passionate. With Tom it was the other way around, and also he was overworked, so that he was always tired at night. The tension between them grew stronger, and it was really more serious than the other time, since now it was more or less on both sides. Alice was more dissatisfied because the harder Tom worked, the less he was able to satisfy her sexually. So it went in a vicious circle. Alice had reached the point where she was about to pack up her things and run back to the city. But Tom, too, had reached the breaking point. He had been working too hard and he had a nervous breakdown. From the day when he was brought home from his office, Alice stopped thinking of going back to the city. If ever she needed something to use up her surplus nervous energy, to stimulate her to work, she got it now. Just as the idea of coming to a new place and being a leader there had diverted her attention in the first crisis, so this crisis diverted her attention from going back to the city. All her love for Tom returned in those days when he was so helpless and when he was getting better.

All through Tom's illness, Alice had known that they were to have a child, and now she awaited its coming with a good deal of fear and uneasiness. But after the baby was born, she changed considerably. For one thing, she grew much older, much more mature. She gained more control over herself and her desires. Also, she had plenty to do now to use up her surplus energy. Tom found that his child-wife had at last grown up.

When differences in temperament, cultural background, and philosophy of life are as wide as in this case, solution of conflicts which arise is especially difficult. Adjustments and integration are likely to be secured, if at all, when mutuality of interests and common objectives develop, which afford a substantial basis for cooperation and partnership.

SUMMARY

Conflicts, inevitable in marital and family relationships, tend to grow in time if not solved, and tend to draw in relatives and friends. Cultural patterns which were quite adequate in the rural community of a few decades ago are obsolete in an urban industrial civilization. Much of the current conflict and tension in marital and in parent-child relations must, therefore, be regarded as incidental to these social changes and to the transition from the small-patriarchal to the companionship form of the family.

Conflicts in the family can often be understood as resulting from differences in the conceptions which its members have of their roles within and outside the home. These divergent attitudes are generally evaluated by husbands and wives or parents and children in moral terms. Actually they often represent only the clash of traditional *versus* emerging values.

It is important, for purposes of analysis, to distinguish between conflicts that arise (1) from temperamental incompatibility, (2) from divergent cultural patterns, and (3) from differences in expectations and roles. In any actual family conflict they all may be present, but the adequacy of the interpretation consists in disentangling these different elements and in perceiving their various interrelationships in the total configuration of behavior.

So far as family conflict finds expression today, where formerly it was inhibited, the result is probably a lessening of the tensions which arise from suppressed and unsolved conflicts. Family conflicts are accordingly not to be regarded as generally symptomatic of the pathological. If expressed, discussed, and solved in the spirit of sympathetic understanding, they strengthen rather than weaken family unity.

In a period of social change, families often find it difficult to resolve the conflicts between members. Especially in the city, a husband or a wife is not as disposed to turn to a relative as in the past. In addition, under the mobile conditions of today, their parents may be so far away that it is more difficult to run home than before, and this in itself is a curb on the extent to which a conflict may go.

PROBLEMS FOR RESEARCH

Our present knowledge does not make possible a complete and adequate analysis of family conflict and tension, and accommodations. An understanding of certain questions of marital and familial conflicts and tensions will have to wait until more complete information is available.

Economic Conflict It appears that income, as such, is not significant for adjustment in marriage. However, as yet no adequate studies have been made of the effect on the home of the economic independence of women. What are the conditions under which women may follow an occupational career other than housekeeping with a minimum of family conflict and tension? Other questions concern types of financial conflict in families and modes of dealing with them, comparison of successful and unsuccessful arrangements between parents and children in regard to spending money, division of labor between husband and wife in domestic responsibilities and duties, and a comparison of financial procedures such as budgeting, joint bank accounts, and paying bills.

Sex Conflicts and Adjustment Some students of family behavior hold that sex conflicts are invariably the source of all or almost all marital and family difficulties. Studies have shown that, while many family conflicts and tensions are associated with sex behavior, sex conflicts may be symbolic of tensions in other areas of behavior. There are cases in which the couples continue to have satisfying sex behavior but have conflicts over other matters.

Questions pertinent for research might include the following: What factors, emotional and cultural, predispose to frigidity in a married woman and to impotence in men? What are the determining factors in the social situation and in personality which make some married persons wish for variety in sexual relations and others completely content with monogamy? What is the influence of pregnancy or menopause on the sexual adjustment of husband and wife?

Conflicts Between Parents and Children It would be desirable to make studies of family attitudes and values in relation to conflict between parents and their children in the following social situations: (1) when the family attitudes and values and the community standards are practically the same, (2) when the family attitudes and values and community standards are widely different, (3) when the attitudes and values of the family are well defined but the community is disorganized, and (4) when the family is without well-defined attitudes and values but is in a community with well-developed standards. The hypothesis is that homogeneity of family and community standards makes for family integration, while disparity between the culture of the family and that of the community tends to result in the disruption of family control, personal disorganization, and marital and family conflicts and tensions.

The Stepchild and the Adopted Child Two special types of parent-child conflict merit more study than they have yet received: those of the stepchild and of the adopted child. With reference to stepchildren, case studies are needed to reveal the effect of various factors, such as attitudes of relatives and close friends, on the reaction of children to the step-parent; whether the mother, the father, or both bring children to the new marriage; and whether or not children are born to this union. Under what conditions does the stepparent feel as much affection for the stepchild as for his own child?

With adopted children society intervenes in controlling the adoption process. In an increasing number of states, prospective foster parents must submit to a thorough investigation by trained social workers, who consider not only the economic and social status of the applicants but also their moral fitness and their personality qualifications for parenthood. This investigation before the placement of the child may be followed by periodic visits during a probationary period. Consequently, a growing body of records is available for research on factors making for harmonious or inharmonious relations between parents and their adopted children.

It is important to study the personality development of the adopted child in the foster family. Among the questions requiring research are best age of child and parents at adoption, how and at what age to tell a child he is adopted, effect on the child of definition of the adopted child by play group and community, degree of self-consciousness of foster parent and child about the adoption, and the influence of the presence of other adopted or natural children in the family. An interesting project would be to compare adopted children with children reared by mothers widowed shortly after the birth of a child, with children brought up by mothers who are divorced, and with children brought up by their unmarried mothers.

QUESTIONS AND EXERCISES

1. Differentiate between conflict and tension. Which of these is likely to result in family disorganization?

2. What is meant by the symbolic nature of some marital and family conflicts?
3. Give an example of an overt family conflict which is symbolic of underlying tension.
4. How do you explain the fact that economic factors as a whole are not important in family conflict, but individual economic activities may be of paramount importance?
5. Give the major findings of research which demonstrate that conflict arises out of failure to secure satisfying affectional expressions and sexual adjustment in marriage.
6. How would you rank in order of their importance the factors which make for accommodation of family members to conflict?
7. What is the current view of the degree of conflict between adolescents and their parents?

BIBLIOGRAPHY

Burgess, Ernest W.; and Wallin, Paul. "Disagreements and Stresses in Engagement," *Engagement and Marriage*. Philadelphia: Lippincott, 1953, Ch. 8.
> Deals with agreements and disagreements with reference to money, recreation, religion, demonstration of affection, friends, conventionality, philosophy of life, in-laws, and interpersonal relationships. Stresses during engagement included subjects about which the person was sensitive and insecure in the present relationship.

Kephart, William M. *The Family, Society, and the Individual*. Boston: Houghton Mifflin, 1966, Chs. 20, 21, and particularly 22.
> These three chapters are "The Divorce Process," "Socio-Demographic Aspects of Divorce," and "Family Breakdown: Causes and Effects." Deals with both factual information about divorce, such as legal grounds, and conflicts leading up to divorce.

Locke, Harvey J. "Marital Disagreements and Conflicts," *Predicting Adjustment in Marriage: A Comparison of a Divorced and a Happily-Married Group*. New York: Henry Holt, 1951, Ch. 4.
> Two aspects of agreement and disagreement were discussed: on basic interests and activities, and who gives in when disagreements arise. Marital conflicts discussed include things mate does that the spouse doesn't like, number and kinds of marital difficulties, feelings about marital difficulties, times either spouse left home because of conflict, and talking to a third party about marital difficulties.

Pincus, Lily (ed.). *Marriage: Studies in Emotional Conflict and Growth*. London: Methuen, 1960.

Presents a psychoanalytic framework for the understanding of conflict in marriage, and detailed presentations of five cases seen for extended marital counseling by persons using this framework. Useful especially for its detailed case histories.

Spiegel, John P. "The Resolution of Role Conflict within the Family," in *A Modern Introduction to the Family*, eds. Norman W. Bell and Ezra F. Vogel. New York: Free Press 1968, pp. 391–411.

Presents a detailed conceptual scheme outlining possible techniques for reducing role conflict. Suggests two major ways in which conflict may be resolved: inducing the other to appropriately fulfill his role and modification of the role structure of the group. Several techniques are outlined for each

Chapter 20
Family Crises

> *A crisis is any decisive change which creates a situation for which the habitual behavior patterns of a person or a group are inadequate. Extreme deviations by children from the expectations of parents may be a crisis for parents; extreme deviation by parents from the expectations of children may be a crisis for children. Disgrace may be experienced by a family if a member is an alcoholic, is an unwed mother, engages in crime, has a mental illness, or commits suicide. A severe economic depression reduces the marriage and divorce rates, disrupts the security of the family, and disintegrates the loosely organized and unadaptable family.*

THE "TRIANGLE" AS A FAMILY CRISIS

The discovery by a husband or wife that the other has become involved in a new affectional relationship often results in a crisis which is most difficult to resolve. This may shatter the conception of faithfulness to each other, which in our society is symbolic of the unity of a couple. The shock of this type of experience may lead a person, as in the following case, to contemplate suicide:

> Mother wrote me at college that Father, the night before, had broken down and made a rather complete confession, telling her of his infidelity and his great remorse. He spared himself nothing, admitted that he had been immoral with a Mrs. W., and took all the blame upon himself. He explained that the occasion was the year before, when my mother and I had taken an extended trip. He had been very lonesome and had accidentally met Mrs. W., an attractive young widow.
>
> Mother was overwhelmed by this revelation and had, as she said in her letter, "gone to pieces." Soon, however, she "got a grip on herself," forgave him, providing he broke off immediately with Mrs. W.

That same day my parents telephoned me, asking if they could come in and see me. The three of us talked it over and it was settled that Father and Mrs. W. would have nothing more to do with each other.

The following Monday Father went to see Mrs. W. and told her that they would have to stop seeing each other. She threatened to blacken his name, to kill him, and to commit suicide if he would not leave Mother and marry her. Just how far would Mrs. W. go? We all feared that she was likely to do something rash which would create a big scandal.

Father and I went for a walk and he told me some details that he had not told Mother. He said that while he knew Mother and I loved him, he always felt "sort of out of things." When he had first married Mother, he realized he had made a mistake, for Mother had a bad disposition and sought to get her own way by any means she could. She would even feign illness if other methods failed. He had never been really happy with her.

Everything went well for about two weeks and then Mother phoned me, saying that she had walked into Father's office the day before and discovered him talking over the telephone in a kind voice to Mrs. W. She discovered that Mrs. W. was doing some work for Father at her home. I went home and it was agreed that Father would quit giving her work and paying her. I noticed that Father's attitude had changed. I tried to talk to him, but there seemed to be a shell through which I could not penetrate. At last he confided that Mother talked about the affair a great deal, especially at night, and that he didn't get the opportunity to forget the thing.

Mother frequently made the statement that if it were not for the disgrace it would bring to her son, she would commit suicide. Indeed, she "attempted" suicide on one or two occasions, but didn't go through with it. Neither Father nor I took her threats or attempts very seriously.

It was discovered that Father was continuing to see Mrs. W.; in fact, he had an apartment for her. One day Mother chanced to meet Mrs. W. on the street, and on the spur of the moment, stopped to talk to her. She talked as kindly as possible and evidently gained her confidence, for this talk was followed by several others and according to Mother, they became "good friends." Father was quite disturbed and felt that he was being "double-crossed."

It was decided that Mrs. W. would leave town. A few days later I met Mother, Mrs. W., and her younger daughter at the station, had dinner with them, and we saw her off. But within a week Mrs. W. was back in response to a telegram from Father. At present little is being said about the affair, but it is continuing.

This case reveals not only the crisis occasioned by the shattering of the wife's image of her husband as faithful and loyal but, after the initial shock, her strategic use of various techniques to restore the former status of faithfulness. There was family pressure by the mediation of the son, who was already aligned with her; the threat of suicide; and even winning the friendship, confidence, and cooperation of the other woman.

The husband in explanation of his behavior refers to the disillusionment he experienced after marriage in discovering a personality quite different from his idealized conception. The husband faced conflict between duty to his wife and family and romantic attraction to a more congenial companion. For him this turned out to be a double crisis, involving the emotional explosions of the two women, both of whom threatened suicide.

The modern family is more likely to experience crises than the family of the past because of the characteristics of a complex, changing society. Mobility and improved means of communication have resulted in the diffusion of divergent patterns of behavior. As a consequence, a person may deviate from the behavior expected of him by his family, and this may lead to a crisis. If the disapproved behavior is against the mores and if it is discovered by outsiders, it brings disgrace to the family.

This and the following chapters will analyze six crises. Three of these—deviations from expected behavior, disgrace, and economic reverses—will be treated in this chapter; crises which involve the disruption of the family—departure of family members, divorce, and death—will be discussed in the following chapter. The critical effect of war on families will be considered in Chapter 22.

DEVIATIONS FROM EXPECTATIONS

Husbands and wives enter marriage with certain expectations. They have conceptions of what each expects of the other and of community attitudes and values. Parents also have preconceptions of how children ought to behave, and sons and daughters as they come in contact with other children tend to develop their own notions of filial and parental roles.[1]

Husband-Wife Crises Crises between husbands and wives may have two origins: (1) the shattering of the conceptions which each holds of the other, and (2) divergent conceptions which are present at the time of marriage or develop afterward.

Certain idealistic conceptions derived in the romance of courtship and engagement are likely to break down in the routine of everyday married life. A crisis develops if one remains incurably romantic and the other becomes stolidly matter-of-fact. In addition, there may be the shock of discovering that the personality of the mate is very different from expectations, or that the other has concealed or misrepresented such information as age, the existence and status of certain relatives, the amount of income, physical defects, or a previous marriage.

[1] See Ch. 10.

When husbands and wives have widely divergent conceptions of expected behavior, crises are almost certain to arise. Many of these concern questions which are not settled or even discussed in the engagement period. These include differences in ideas of rearing and disciplining children, religious training of children when the parents are of different faiths, the wife working after marriage, and social relations after marriage with persons of the opposite sex.

Different experiences after marriage also may result in the development of divergent conceptions. Examples are marked religious differences, as when the wife of a physician becomes a Christian Scientist; decided educational differences, such as the husband's completing his professional training after marriage and becoming ashamed of his wife, who is out of place in his new circle of associates; or different values, as when either the husband or wife joins a social set whose ideas and values are radically different from those of the prior group to which the other still adheres.

Parent-Child Crises Crises in parent-child relations concern (1) problem behavior of children, (2) major emotional disturbances, and (3) adolescence.

In parent-child relations there are those deviations from parental expectations which may be included under the broad term of "problem behavior." These include not only such common difficulties as thumbsucking and enuresis, but any conduct defined as "bad" by the family or community. The latter include such deviations from expectations as playing with "bad" children, failing to fulfill obligations and responsibilities assumed by the child or initiated by the parent, disobedience, deception, delinquency, and any kind of play condemned by the parents. A crisis sometimes is precipitated when the child, under conditions of fatigue, overstimulation, or exceptional provocation, loses the self-control expected of him by his parents.

There are the crises which result from major emotional disturbances. Acute emotional disturbance is occasioned by the shock of the shattering of a cherished conception which a child has of himself or of another member of the family. Illustrations are the discovery that a parent in whom he has implicit confidence has deceived him or has been dishonest in a business matter; the discovery of any marital irregularity of parents, such as the unfaithfulness of father or mother, their common-law marriage, forced marriage, an unknown previous marriage or divorce; or the discovery that one is an adopted child.

A third type of crisis arises in the transition from the role of a child to that of an adult. The parent may continue to think of and treat the son or daughter as a child, while the adolescent thinks of himself as an adult and finds himself often so defined by his associates at school and in the community.

The essence of this type of crisis is the inability of the parents to shift from either a benevolent or an autocratic role to that of the democratic relationship to which the child may aspire. This is illustrated in the following case:

> I started to regulate my own conduct in all affairs and to arrange hours for study and social life to suit my own convenience. This did not appeal to my father at all. He informed me that I was still a boy and that he had no idea of giving me free range to do as I pleased. Quite often when I would start out in the evening he would ask: "Where are you going?" If I managed to get out without his seeing me, he would never fail to ask the next day: "Where did you go?"

A serious crisis may arise when the occupational choice of an adolescent differs from that desired by the parents. It may be particularly severe if the status of the vocation is definitely lower than that expected by the family and especially so if, as in the following, it is considered in the community as a blind-alley job and somewhat disreputable:

> My folks didn't like the idea of my working as a bellhop in a hotel. My mother and aunt came and tried to coax me home. I told them that I would not go back to work for my father. My brother and sisters said that I was disgracing the family. They did all kinds of things to get me away, but it was no use. I never stayed at home a night all the time I worked at the hotel. Sometimes I ate at home, but never with the family.

Occasionally the child finds himself in the critical situation of crossfire between the father and mother in their insistence on different vocational careers. There is also the situation in which a youth averse to taking adult responsibilities comes in conflict with the expectations of a parent who, if poor, may demand that the son or daughter go to work and contribute toward the support of the family or, if well-to-do, may bring pressure on a grown-up offspring to select a career and settle down.

The crises arising from deviations from expectations place a severe strain on the interpersonal relations of husbands and wives and of parents and children. These are not necessarily known to outsiders. When an unfavorable reaction of the community is foreseen or experienced, a new type of crisis develops—the threat of disgrace.

DISGRACE

A disgraced family is one in which all or some of the members feel dishonored, humiliated, ashamed, discredited, or degraded in the public eye. The stigma of disgrace is experienced when outsiders discover the socially disapproved or deviant behavior of a family or of one or more of its members.

A strongly united family with standards in harmony with community standards reduces the likelihood of family members engaging in unconventional behavior. The well-organized family exerts itself strenuously to discipline a deviant member before his behavior becomes known to outsiders, or at least before it becomes flagrant.

In our society the following behavior generally brings disgrace to a person and to his family: drug addiction, abortion, failure to pay one's debts, embezzlement, and occupational failure. Disgrace is also generally associated with the following which are discussed below: alcoholism, known loss of virginity, illegitimacy, crime, mental illness, and suicide.

Alcoholism Today drinking is socially accepted in many circles, but in nearly all groups it is disgraceful to become an alcoholic. There have been several studies of the reactions of the family to the alcoholism of one of its members.[2] It is generally agreed that most frequent reactions are anxiety and uncertainty as to how to handle the problem. Some investigators analyze the behavior of family members in the crisis of alcoholism in steps or stages: (1) The failure of the alcoholic to fulfill his role expectations in the family—father and husband or mother and wife. (2) Other members take over his duties and responsibilities. (3) If alcoholism is arrested, reorganization of the family, drawing the reformed person back into the family circle. (4) If it is felt that there is no likelihood that the alcoholic will reform, possibly there may be withdrawal from him through separation or divorce.[3]

The following is a daughter's description of the crisis in her family resulting from excessive drinking by her father:

> The real trouble was my father's periodic drinking sprees. When he was sober, he was kind and companionable and used to romp with us in the evening just before going to bed. When he was on one of his sprees, the whole family energy was bent toward concealing our terrible secret from the neighbors. How they could help knowing, I don't know; but they never said anything and we were all too proud to tell any one. The effect on my mother can be realized when one knows that she was brought up in a community where drunkenness was practically unknown and was consid-

---

[2] See Barbara R. Day, "Alcoholism and the Family," *Marriage and Family Living*, 23 (1961): pp. 253–258, for reviews of several of these studies.

[3] Joan Jackson, "The Adjustment of the Family to Alcoholism," *Marriage and Family Living*, 18 (1956): pp. 361–369.

ered the depth of degradation. This weakness of my father caused her to withdraw within herself and avoid people.

My father's trouble had drawn my sister and me closer to Mother. We talked over and decided family matters. As the frequency of my father's drinking sprees increased, Mother and my sister sometimes talked of leaving him, but I always championed him because I knew what would happen if he had no home. If it hadn't been for Father's intemperance, we would have been ideally happy.

In the above case the folowing reactions to crisis are evident: (1) The mother withdrew and avoided people. (2) The mother and children became more united as a consequence of their common endeavor to conceal the family secret from neighbors. (3) Pressure was placed on the father to conform to family standards by the threat of abandoning him. (4) Conflict developed between the "erring one" and the others.

Loss of Virginity The high incidence of premarital intercourse might lead one to conclude that it is no longer thought to be disgraceful. There is a tendency, however, to be secretive about it, and this indicates that there continues to be some disgrace associated with it. This is particularly true for girls, for those who are not engaged, and for some cultural groups. The following from Padilla's study of Puerto Ricans in a slum in New York City indicates that in this cultural group a girl's family feels disgraced if she simply goes out with a boy unchaperoned, for it is felt that this will lead to loss of virginity:

> If a girl goes out on unchaperoned dates with a boy friend to whom she is not engaged or with different boy friends or pals, she is *cabra* (goat), and it is expected that she will lose her virginity and thus her chances of getting married legally. Should a girl be deflowered, she is expected to feel ashamed of herself. Knowledge of the event will be kept within the family as long as possible because it involves shame for all of them. . . .
>
> The family of a girl who has lost her virginity and "cannot be honored" by the man who deflowered her is likely to go through a time of great emotional stress. So, of course, will the girl herself. They may discontinue many of their current associations with other people in the neighborhood, and many even leave it to live elsewhere.[4]

Illegitimacy Having a child outside of wedlock is not always a crisis. A study of illegitimacy over three generations found that illegitimacy runs in some families. If one knows that either the paternal or maternal grandmother or one's mother had some illegitimate children, it can be

---

[4] Elena Padilla, *Up from Puerto Rico* (New York: Columbia University Press, 1958), pp. 190–191, and 192.

assumed that one would be more able to handle the problem than if one had no knowledge of illegitimacy in one's nuclear or extended family.[5]

Facing the stigma of bearing an illegitimate child is extremely difficult for most unmarried mothers. They may attempt an abortion or, if a child is born, great efforts may be made by the mother and her family to keep others from knowing that the child was born out of wedlock.

Some people believe that having a child out of wedlock is symptomatic of a particular kind of personality disorder and a set of unconscious needs; others hold that unwed mothers have character and neurotic disorders. Berstein stresses the fact that unwed mothers, interviewed at the time of the crisis, may exhibit reactions which are not a part of customary reactions:

> We know that in a crisis situation current functioning may be disrupted, past vulnerabilities exposed, and hitherto manageable conflicts stirred up. Earlier feelings of guilt, deprivation, and the like may be reactivated. The unmarried pregnant woman, seen at a point of crisis, may exhibit a whole range of disturbed reactions . . . crisis can produce distortions of one's customary patterns and we cannot assume that her reactions in a crisis situation represent her characteristic mode of adaptation to a reality anymore than we can say that an acute pneumonia is characteristic of a person's physiological endowment, even though he may have some pulmonary susceptibility.[6]

Being an unwed mother may be much less a crisis when the father is unmarried than when he is married. If the father is unmarried, the child and the union may be legitimized by marriage which may soon be followed by a divorce. If the man and woman are emotionally attached, the forced marriage may become permanent. In some cases the girl may be willing to bear the child in secret and place it through an adoption agency. Or, if her parents are agreeable, the girl may continue to reside with them and retain the child.

When the father is a married man, two additional adjustments occasionally are found: (1) If the man is threatened with paternity action in court and the consequent scandal, he may avoid this by divorcing his wife and marrying the girl. (2) If the man can pass as single, he may marry the girl without divorcing his wife, with the hope of extricating himself from the forced marriage without jeopardizing his other marriage. In the following case the man was unsuccessful in keeping

---

[5] Clark E. Vincent, C. Allen Haney, and Carl M. Cochrane, "Familial and Generational Patterns of Illegitimacy," *Journal of Marriage and the Family*, 31 (1969): pp. 659–667.

[6] Rose Berstein, "Are We Still Stereotyping the Unmarried Mother?" in *The Unwed Mother*, Robert W. Roberts (ed.) (New York: Harper & Row, 1966), pp. 109–110.

his bigamy secret, but those involved in this critical situation were interested in avoiding scandal:

> Well, I faced the relatives on Sunday. But to my great surprise they had not gossiped. I have seen John twice since he left me. We heard that he has been with his folks with Grace, "the other wife." My father and I were going into Cleveland, so I stopped off at his folks and Dad was going to stop for me on his way home.
>
> John's mother told me first thing that it was Grace, John's "wife," who had let me in. John had told them that he hadn't married me. "Well," I said, "I'm staying right here till John comes home." When my father came, I sent him home for my marriage certificate.
>
> I had just gone into the kitchen when John came up the back stairs. "Hello, John," I said, "Hello," says John, eyes big. "Hello, Daddy," said Grace, flinging her arms around his neck. My dad moved into view and thundered, "You better come clean." John pushed Grace away, blustered up, and words flew between him and my father.
>
> After a three-hour session, with both licenses shown, with John saying, "I don't know," to most questions, he agreed to try and straighten things out. Grace offered to get out right then. I said that after the baby came, I'd be willing to give him a divorce, and let him return to Grace.
>
> John tried to take his two wives into the other room where his mother was to own up. He had one on each side, but when his mother saw us she burst into hysterical weeping.
>
> It was decided that my father and I and John and Grace would meet the next day. We met and it was agreed that John and Grace would get that marriage annulled. But rather than do that, they must have skipped the country, for I haven't heard from them. I guess the only thing left for me to do is to get a divorce from him.

An illegitimate child bears a stigma, especially when it is reared by its unmarried mother. It will be remembered that in the two cases of extreme social isolation discussed in the chapter on culture and socialization, Anna and Isabelle were illegitimate children who had been hidden for nearly five years. In both cases the mother's father felt so disgraced at his daughter's having an illegitimate child that he was averse even to seeing it, and insisted that it be isolated so that the neighbors would not know about it.

Crime The degree of family disgrace experienced because of the criminal behavior of a family member varies with the nature of the crime and with the type of family relations. Four different situations will be considered: (1) In homes familiar with delinquent behavior, little or no disgrace may be felt because of the delinquent behavior of the children. (2) In a home lacking family unity, a criminal act by one of its members may not be greatly disturbing. (3) In homes with strong affectional ties, the disgrace experienced may be relatively great. (4) In well-organized homes where a member is a white-collar criminal, great disgrace will be felt by the family.

1. In many cases delinquent acts which bring children in contact with the police and the courts are not very critical to a family, for the family has had prior experiences with law-enforcing agencies. Sutherland and Cressey conclude that "the homes in which delinquents are reared are in an extraordinary degree situations in which patterns of delinquency are present."[7]

2. Families with one or more criminal members very often lack emotional interdependence and unity. Investigators frequently report that delinquents lack affection for their families, that they often express hatred for one or both parents, and that the parents express little attachment to their children.

This lack of unity and control in homes from which many delinquents and criminals come is documented in a classic study by Shaw, McKay, and McDonald of the criminal careers of five brothers.[8] The activities of the children were largely unknown and inaccessible to the parents. The father spent his earnings on drinking sprees. The parents and children were separated a great deal, not only because the boys were sent periodically to correctional schools, but because both parents worked, the mother leaving very early and returning very late. This continued for eight years. There was continual conflict between parents and children about religious values, attendance at school, and certain kinds of stealing. "The parents received the bread, milk, and coal which children brought home," because "various forms of stealing were generally acceptable in the neighborhood"; but "in later years, when the brothers brought home jewelry and other merchandise which obviously had been stolen, the parents refused to accept it and in many instances turned it over to the police."[9] Such a home does not immunize its members from engaging in criminal behavior, and the parents do not feel greatly disgraced by the delinquent acts of the children.

3. Families with a high degree of unity are likely to feel disgraced by delinquent or criminal behavior of a member. Such families often make restitution, both to avoid disgrace and to save a family member from prison. In the following case the family was so united that its members cooperated in repaying the amount embezzled by the narrator's brother:

[7] Edwin H. Sutherland and Donald R. Cressey, *Principles of Criminology* (Philadelphia: Lippincott, 1960), p. 175. See Ch. 10, "The Home and Family in Relation to Crime."

[8] Clifford R. Shaw, Henry D. McKay, and James F. McDonald, *Brothers in Crime* (Chicago: University of Chicago Press, 1938), Ch. 7.

[9] *Ibid.*, footnote on pp. 149–150.

One of my younger brothers in many ways is considered the "black sheep" of the family. He is unmanageable in school and was taken out. Then he wanted to "see the country" and ran away. On one of these trips he secured a position as traveling salesman for a novelty company and then appropriated about $500 from his sales and disappeared. A representative of the firm visited the family and brought the first intimation of what had happened. The money was paid back by several family members in order to keep the matter out of the courts.

4. If a member of a white-collar family commits a crime, such as embezzlement and fraud, generally it creates a greater crisis than in lower-class families when a member engages in crime. The person engaging in "white-collar" crime is likely to have had a respectable and honored status in the community. Persons in positions of financial responsibility must have an unimpeachable personal record and an unstained occupational record to meet the standards of fidelity companies. If an embezzler is discovered, he will be unable to secure another position of financial responsibility. It is especially disgraceful when a member of a white-collar family commits a crime, for almost all such criminals come from families in which no other member has a criminal record.

Mental Illness A person who is mentally ill tends to be stigmatized. Stigma is an extreme degree of disgrace in which a person has the status of an outcast. It involves fear, rejection, and abandonment of the stigmatized person.

A longitudinal study of 17 wife-mother persons who were admitted to a state hospital and diagnosed as schizophrenic was made by Sampson, Messinger, and Towne.[10] They conducted about 50 interviews with each patient and her spouse, and with professional persons involved with the case. They concluded that some pattern of accommodation develops between the patient and other members of the family. They described two types of accommodation before hospitalization: withdrawal of the husband and moving in of a mother or mother-in-law. In 11 of the cases the accommodation was with withdrawal of the husband and wife into separate worlds:

> The marital relationship was characterized by mutual withdrawal and the construction of separate worlds of compensatory involvement. At some point during the marriage, usually quite early, one or both of the partners had experienced extreme dissatisfaction with the marriage. This was ordinarily accompanied by a period of violent, open discord, although in

[10] Harold Sampson, Sheldon L. Messinger, and Robert D. Towne, "Family Process and Becoming a Mental Patient," *American Journal of Sociology,* 68 (1962): pp. 88–96.

other cases, the dissatisfaction was expressed only indirectly, through reduced communication with the marital partner. Whatever the means of managing the dissatisfaction when it occurred in each of these families the partners withdrew and each gradually instituted a separate world. . . . The partners would rarely go out together, rarely participate together in dealing with personal or family problems, and seldom communicate to each other about their more pressing interests, wishes, and concerns. The marriage would continue in this way for some time without divorce, without separation, and without movement toward greater closeness. The partners had achieved a type of marital accommodation. . . . This pattern of mutual withdrawal eventually became intolerable to one or the other partner, pressure for a change was brought to bear, and the family suffered an acute crisis.[11]

The second type of accommodation was the overinvolved mother who moved into the new family almost from its beginning. In four of the cases the mothers took over the wifes' domestic duties and child-rearing functions. These mothers were possessive and tried to perpetuate their daughters' dependency. Symptoms of mental disturbance were of great concern to the mothers. The wives came to view the mothers as nondesirable additions to the family and rebelled. However, cycles of reliance on the mother followed by repudiation of her recurred over the years. Under these conditions the husbands withdrew to the periphery of the family. It was a disturbance in the accommodation which led to seeing a physician or a psychiatrist and eventually being admitted to the state hospital.

The slow process of accepting the fact that a family member has a mental illness is revealed in the following. This is a condensed version of what a wife told an interviewer a few weeks after her husband, Robert F., a cab driver, was admitted to a hospital for treatment of schizophrenia. The interpretative statements, italicized in parentheses, are by Clausen and Yarrow:

> Mrs. F. related certain events, swift and dramatic, which led directly to the hospitalization. The day before admission, Mr. F. went shopping with his wife, which he never had done before, and expressed worry lest he lose her. This was in her words, "rather strange." (*His behavior is not in keeping with her expectations for him.*) Later that day, Mr. F. thought a TV program was about him and that the set was "after him." "Then I was getting worried." (*She recognizes the bizarre nature of his reactions. She becomes concerned.*)
>
> That night, Mr. F. kept talking. He reproached himself for not working enough to give his wife surprises. Suddenly he exclaimed he did have a surprise for her—he was going to kill her. "I was petrified and said to him, 'What do you mean?' Then he began to cry and told me not to let

---
[11] *Ibid.*, pp. 90–91.

him hurt me and to do for him what I would want him to do for me. I asked him what was wrong. He said he had cancer. . . . He began talking about his grandfather's mustache and said there was a worm growing out of it." She remembered his watching little worms in the fish bowl and thought his idea came from that. Mr. F. said he had killed his grandfather. He asked Mrs. F. to forgive him and wondered if she were his mother or God. She denied this. He vowed he was being punished for killing people during the war. "I thought maybe . . . worrying about the war so much . . . had gotten the best of him." *(She tried to understand his behavior. She stretches the range of normality to include it.)* "I thought he should see a psychiatrist . . . I don't know how to explain it. He was shaking. I knew it was beyond what I could do . . . I was afraid of him . . . I thought he was losing his normal mental attitude and mentality, but I wouldn't say that he was insane or crazy, because he had always bossed me around before . . ." *(She shifts back and forth in thinking his problem is psychiatric and in feeling it is normal behavior that could be accounted for in terms of their own experience.)* Mr. F. talked on through the night. Sometime in the morning, he "seemed to straighten out" and drove his wife to work. *(This behavior tends to balance out the preceding disturbed activities. She quickly returns to a normal referent.)*

At noon, Mr. F. walked into the store where his wife worked as a clerk. "I couldn't make any sense of what he was saying. He kept getting angry because I wouldn't talk to him. . . . Finally, the boss' wife told me to go home." En route Mr. F. said his male organs were blown up and little seeds covered him. Mrs. F. denied seeing them and announced she planned to call his mother. "He began crying and I had to promise not to. I said, . . . 'Don't you think you should go to a psychiatrist?' and he said 'No, there is nothing wrong with me.' . . . Then we came home, and I went to pay a bill. . . ." *(Again she considers, but is not fully committed to, the idea that psychiatric help is needed.)*

Back at their apartment, Mr. F. talked of repairing his cab while Mrs. F. thought of returning to work and getting someone to call a doctor. Suddenly, he started chasing her around the apartment and growling like a lion. Mrs. F. screamed, Mr. F. ran out of the apartment, and Mrs. F. slammed and locked the door. "When he started roaring and growling, then I thought he was crazy. That wasn't a human sound. You couldn't say a thing to him . . ." Later, Mrs. F. learned that her husband went to a nearby church, created a scene, and was taken to the hospital by the police. *(Thoroughly threatened, she defines problem as psychiatric.)*[12]

This case shows the impact of mental illness on the family. The mentally ill are unable to carry out their normal patterns of relationships with other family members. Moreover, the fact that the illness finds expression in extremely deviant behavior makes both the patient

[12] John A. Clausen, Marian Radke Yarrow, and others, "The Impact of Mental Illness on the Family," *The Journal of Social Issues*, 11, No. 4, (1955): pp. 12-13.

and his immediate family feel anxious and confused, for they have had no prior experience with such behavior.

The removal of the mentally ill to a hospital changes the structure and functions of the family. The removal of the father or mother in a family with children means that the structure of the family is changed to a one-parent home. The functions of the remaining members are changed to include the duties and activities previously performed by the absent member.

Generally relatives, neighbors, and others have observed some of the deviant behavior and know about the absence from the home after hospitalization. Now the members face the problem of deciding who should be told about the illness and what they should be told. They feel that people know little about mental illness and tend to fear and reject the mentally ill. Public-opinion polls reveal this to be a fact.[13] Concealment is often the immediate plan of action, but it is rarely successful.

The first to be informed are adolescent and adult sons and daughters. The parents of the one who is mentally ill are the next to be informed. A limited number of friends are more likely to be told than are neighbors. The meaning of this desire for concealment is interpreted as follows by Clausen and Yarrow:

> Almost without exception, and regardless of the extent to which they have informed others, signs of discomfort, uncertainty, and unwillingness to reveal the situation to others occurred along with expressions of need and eagerness to talk about the illness.[14]

Suicide Suicide in American society is both a disgraceful act and a way of adjusting to disgrace. If a person commits suicide, relatives, friends, and acquaintances gossip about it and raise the question "why?" The death of a person from an accident or an illness results in a change in the structure and functions of the family and a sense of bereavement. The death of a person through suicide leads to these and in addition may lead to a sense of guilt and a feeling of being disgraced.

The following are some of the things from which people flee through suicide: unemployment, disgrace, unrequited love, jealousy, tangled personal relationships, and feelings associated with acute mental illness. Frequently the person who attempts suicide tries to control the behavior of others. For example, Shneidman and Farberow report as follows:

> The suicidal person is an individual who, when he is really faced with the prospect of seriously considering leaving this world, departs with a

---

[13] Findings of the Survey Research Center, and the National Opinion Research Center. (Reporting by Clausen and Yarrow, *ibid.*, footnote on p. 33.)
[14] *Ibid.*, p. 35.

blast of hate and self-blame and an attempt to leave definite instructions and restrictions on those he has purposely left behind.[15]

In their study of 44 persons who attempted suicide but were unsuccessful, Rubenstein, Moses, and Lidz indicated that attempted suicide is an attempt to improve one's life. They judged that 34 out of the 44 actually did succeed in improving their lives.[16]

ECONOMIC REVERSES

Financial reverses in families may be due to many causes: the death of the breadwinner, failure in business, unwise investments, speculation, loss of employment, bank failure, and insufficient or no savings. In addition, severe financial depressions resulting from major fluctuations of the business cycle bring acute economic distress to many families. Recent major economic crises in this country occurred in 1907–1908, 1913–1914, 1920–1921, and the severe Depression of the early 1930's.

Significant sociological research on the effect of a depression on families is available for only the last of these. The studies of Angell, Bakke, Cavan and Ranck, Komarovsky, and Stouffer, Lazarsfeld, and Jaffee[17] will be used, in addition to available statistical data, to indicate (1) the extent of the Depression of the 1930's; (2) the decrease in marriages and divorces which accompanies or follows depressions: (3) the insecurity of the family and its members; (4) adjustment of economic standards to the crisis; (5) changes in roles of family members; (6) a comparison of the adjustment of organized and disorganized families; and (7) patterns of reaction to a depression.

Extent of Depression Figures on unemployment and relief indicate the extent of a depression. As contrasted with the 1,813,000 unemployed in the prosperity year of 1929, in 1933, the depth of the Depression, there were 13,176,000 unemployed.[18] Figure 25 shows the total number

[15] Edwin S. Shneidman and Norman L. Farberow, "Some Comparisons between Genuine and Simulated Suicide Notes in Terms of Mowrer's Concepts of Discomfort and Relief," *Journal of General Psychology*, 56 (1957): pp. 251–256.

[16] Robert Rubenstein, Rafael Moses, and Theodore Lidz, "On Attempted Suicide," *American Medical Association Archives, Neurological Psychiatry*, 79 (1958): pp. 103–112.

[17] Robert C. Angell, *The Family Encounters the Depression* (New York: Charles Scribner's Sons, 1936); E. W. Bakke, *Citizens Without Work* (New Haven: Yale University Press, 1940); Ruth S. Cavan and Katherine H. Ranck, *The Family and the Depression* (Chicago: University of Chicago Press, 1938); Mirra Komarovsky, *The Unemployed Man and His Family* (New York: The Dryden Press, 1940); S. A. Stouffer, Paul F. Lazarsfeld, and A. J. Jaffee, *Research Memorandum on the Family in the Depression* (New York: Social Science Research Council, 1937).

[18] Dorothy C. Kahn, *Unemployment and Its Treatment in the United States* (New York: American Association of Social Workers, 1937), p. 27.

of recipients of public assistance and persons employed on federal works programs in the United States from 1933 through 1939. In January, 1934, 8,019,000 households and 28,228,000 persons, or approximately 1 in 4.5 of the population, were receiving relief.[19]

Figure 25. Total persons receiving relief through public assistance and federal works programs in the United States, 1933-1939

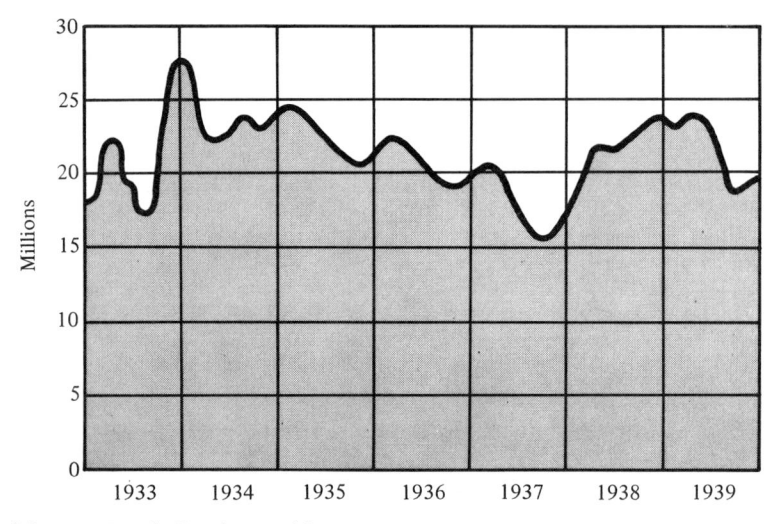

*Social Security Board, *Trends in Public Assistance*, 1933-1939, Bureau Report No. 8, 1940, p. 8.

Decrease in Marriages and Divorces Thomas has demonstrated a close relationship (correlation of .67) between business cycles and marriage rates for the 1854–1913 period in England.[20] This means that marriages increase in prosperity and decrease in depressions. Stouffer and Spencer estimated that during the early years of the 1930's between 607,000 and 806,000 marriages that were expected to occur did not take place.[21] All studies support the conclusion that a depression results in thousands of persons not getting married who otherwise would.

Figure 26, giving the distribution of marriages and divorces in the United States for 1925 through 1941, shows that both decreased during the depth of the Depression. The decrease in the divorce rate may be

[19] *Social Security Bulletin* (Washington, D.C.: Social Security Board, 3, 1940), pp. 54–55.
[20] Dorothy S. Thomas, *Social Aspects of the Business Cycle* (New York: Knopf, 1927), Ch. 3.
[21] Samuel Stouffer and L. M. Spencer, "Marriage and Divorce in Recent Years," *The Annals of the American Academy of Political and Social Science*, 188 (1936): pp. 456–465.

due, in part, to the fact that in hard times a person cannot afford to pay for a divorce.

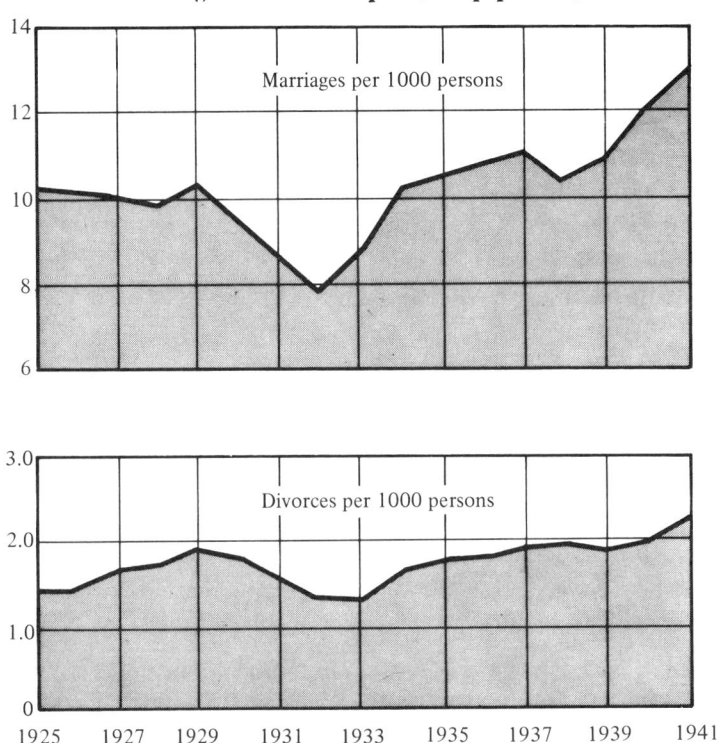

Figure 26. Annual marriages and divorces per 1,000 population, 1925-1941*

*Philip M. Hauser, "Population and Vital Phenomena," *American Journal of Sociology*, 48, 1942, p. 311.

Insecurity of the Family and Its Members The crisis of a depression disrupts the security of the family and disintegrates the loosely organized and unadaptable family. The effect of economic reverses on individual families in periods of relative prosperity however, should not be minimized. In fact, severe economic upsets of an individual and his family may be more disastrous to morale in good times than when millions are out of work during a general financial slump.

Even during times of relative prosperity, millions of families lack security. For example, the average monthly unemployment in 1970 was 4,290,000, or 5.5 percent, of those in the labor force.[22] The number unemployed has been markedly increased by the disappearance of the

[22] Released by the U.S. Department of Labor.

frontier and free land, by the growth of cities, and by advances in industrial technology. When a depression or recession descends on a nation, those living on the thin margin of security are the first to suffer, and the activities and relationships of those above this poverty group may be radically disturbed.

Cavan, a sociologist, and Ranck, a psychiatric social worker, studied the experiences before and after the Depression of the 1930's of one hundred families known before 1929 to the Illinois Institute for Juvenile Research. Of the 100 families, 18 had had experience with relief, 2 had been dependent on relatives, and 10 were classified as marginal or near the border of relief.[23] Those in the lower economic class had little to lose through unemployment and, moreover, it was no new experience to them.

Economic reverses are particularly disturbing to persons in the middle class, for, in general, they use time payments to meet payments on purchases, and a loss of income brings them quickly to the crisis of losing the objectives toward which they have been working.

Adjustments of Economic Standards   Families faced with economic reverses tend to maintain for a time their previous economic standards. The speed with which they change their habits of living to meet the crisis varies from those who make an almost immediate adjustment to those who persist in attempting to maintain the old social status. The following illustrates the latter:

> The Hursts, who had wealthy relatives, had at one time been prosperous. The whole pattern of family life seems to be an attempt to live up to standards set by the mother's ambitions and perhaps controlled by standards of wealthy relatives. The external or public phases of life (the type of living quarters, the private physician for Marcia, the mother's ambitions for her daughter, and so forth) indicate wealth. This "front" is maintained chiefly at the expense of other people: the hotel is induced to cut the rent in half, physicians are induced to give free or almost free treatments, credit is run at stores until further credit is refused, aid is accepted from relatives until the relatives refuse further aid. There is a naive hope that some day the debts may be paid—at the same time that further debts are contracted.[24]

Changes in Roles of Family Members   A depression in our society changes the role of the father more than that of any other member of the family, for his status and position rest more on his occupational level and income than that of other family members. Angell concludes

[23] Cavan and Ranck, p. 44.
[24] *Ibid.*, pp. 100–101.

that when a depression results in extreme psychological effects, it is without exception the father and chief breadwinner who is affected. This occurs because either the father reacts to the loss of responsibility for the security of his family or because the wife's preoccupation with household tasks serves to distract her to some degree from family troubles.[25]

Cavan and Ranck differentiate between families in which there was normal worry associated with planning and those in which there was excessive worry. In the former, members tended to maintain their old roles relative to each other or, if a shift in roles occurred, to consider the change as temporary. Families characterized by excessive worry had greater changes in family roles.[26]

In cases like the following, where a daughter supported the family during the depression of the 1930's, there tended to be a change in status of the members coinciding with the roles which they played. For the most part these shifts were made without much emotional disturbance:

> I am now 20 years old and my responsibility in recent months has increased because of the fact that my father and several brothers have joined the great army of unemployed. Since there is practically no other source of income I have systematized my budget, including bills which had never been included under my budget plan, such as the notes on the home, groceries, gas, light, clothes, insurance, automobile notes, automobile repair bills, telephone, telegraph, some entertainment, dentist, and doctor. On my vacation trip I included my mother and two brothers, and my brothers have termed me their "lifesaver" because of monetary gifts and loans.

In American society a husband may still consider his wife's working as an index of his failure to maintain his role as the financial supporter of the family. The following case describes crises resulting from (1) the failure in business of the husband, (2) the economic success of the wife, and (3) the insistence of the husband that the wife close her business and return to the home:

> Before marriage Mrs. Jones was a milliner, and financially independent. Mr. Jones was in the clothing business, and was wealthy, and they had everything that money could buy. During the first years of marriage, Mrs. Jones did not work outside the home, but devoted herself to her child. When Dorothy was nine years old, Mr. Jones lost his money and they had to sell their home.
> To help out, Mrs. Jones opened a millinery store and was very successful. Mr. Jones approved, inasmuch as it was necessary. He went into the

---
[25] Angell, p. 254.
[26] Cavan and Ranck, pp. 55–64, 83, and 94–95.

real-estate business, and before long had sufficient income to give his family a modest living, but very inferior to their previous mode of life. With the added income from the wife's store, their standard of living was higher than would have been possible otherwise. With his wife's rising success, however, Mr. Jones became jealous. Her contribution to the family income threatened to pass his; he frankly told her that she would have to stop working, because it didn't "look right," when he was making enough for them to get along on. She opposed him, but when he would not give in, she decided that she would, for the sake of their daughter.

Mrs. Jones is unhappy and feels imposed upon, since by keeping her millinery store she could have hired menial work done. The home atmosphere is anything but agreeable. Dorothy is perfectly conscious of the lack of harmony between the parents. Mrs. Jones says now that as soon as Dorothy is old enough to go away to school, she will start her business again, whether he approves or not, even if it necessitates separation.

The Adjustment of Organized and Disorganized Families Cavan and Ranck studied the patterns of reaction of their group of 100 cases to the impact of the Depression. Few definitive conclusions were reached. Nevertheless, several major points seem to stand out. Of these, three will be mentioned: (1) well-organized families met the Depression with fewer catastrophic consequences than families that were already disorganized; (2) families and their members tended to react to the Depression in much the same way they had to previously encountered crises; and (3) the period of disorganization characterized by emotional strain which typically was manifest in the early stages of the Depression generally was succeeded by a period of adjustment or maladjustment. Seemingly significant is the finding that the types of adjustment (including maladjustment) to the Depression attempted by the families were much the same for both the well-organized and disorganized families, but that the final outcome in organization or disorganization of family life was different. Well-organized families, even when greatly affected by the Depression, remained organized; disorganized families became further disorganized.

Adjustment seems to have been as much or more an attribute of family organization as of the degree of external pressure exerted by the Depression. In short, the adjustment of the family to the Depression turned out apparently to be a function of the adjustment of the members of the family to each other. Angell in his penetrating study of 50 families, *The Family Encounters the Depression*, found that the vulnerability of the family to the Depression appeared to vary inversely with its integration and adaptability. In general, the more integrated and adaptable families were better able to meet the crisis of the Depression than were those less integrated and adaptable. In a restudy of these cases, the Committee on Appraisal of the Social Science Research Council arrived at the conclusion that adaptability of the family was more important than its integration for its adjustment to the Depression.

Patterns of Reaction to the Depression Ten general types of reaction to the crisis of the 1930 Depression may be summarized.[27] Five of these represent practical adjustments made with little or no emotional disturbance. The sixth indicates greater family unity. The remaining four reactions represent maladjustments, three of them serious enough to imperil family unity and integrity.

1. The first reaction was to think of the Depression as temporary and to attempt to tide over this period by tapping such available financial resources as savings, by accumulating debts, and by borrowing on life insurance or on assets, such as furniture, or from relatives, or occasionally from friends.

2. Another early reaction was the willingness to curtail the family's expenses, plans, and objectives. This involved securing cheaper rent, giving up recreation and material goods, and postponing sending a child to college.

3. Cheaper rent generally meant smaller and more crowded living quarters. Less money for recreation led to more staying at home and fewer contacts with people outside the community.

4. Many families doubled up. Previously independent families moved in with the in-laws; a newly formed family lived with the in-laws, generally with the wife's parents. Both situations were potential sources of conflict.

5. Some families, faced with poverty, accepted relief gratefully, with little disorganization.

6. The reaction of a considerable number of families was for the members to rally together under the impact of the Depression crisis. Cavan and Ranck found that in 27 of the 100 families studied there was evidence that new group responsibility was developing, and this in turn increased the unity of the family.

7. Many families expressed worry and discouragement which, in view of the seriousness of the crisis were not especially excessive.

8. In a few families one or more members were so worried and depressed that they had a nervous breakdown and/or thought of, attempted, or committed suicide.

9. A small number of people became demoralized and violated standards of conduct previously accepted by the person or by his family.

---

[27] See books listed in footnote 17, p. 515, particularly Cavan and Ranck, Chs. 4 and 5.

10. A few families became disintegrated; the members drifted apart and the husband and wife separated or secured a divorce.

The last three reactions were not always the result of the Depression alone. In some families other crises, such as illness, bereavement, or family tensions, were associated with it, and the reaction of the family was to the total situation, rather than only to the Depression.

Losing One's Skilled Job to a Machine An economic reverse of a different nature is having one's skilled job taken over by a machine. This is a crisis for many persons, particularly those who are older. Rapid technological developments in recent years have meant that thousands of persons proficient in given jobs have had their jobs taken over by machines. These persons have had to start over again. The United States Department of Labor has made an extensive study of the relative performance of older and younger workers in industrial retraining courses. Courses were given to train replaced workers in three companies: a telephone company, an oil refinery, and an aircraft industry company. In all three companies older workers were lower in performance than younger workers.[28] Having one's skilled job taken away by a machine takes away a part of one's identity and is a crisis for the worker and for his family.

SUMMARY

A crisis has been defined as any decisive change that creates a situation for which the habitual behavior patterns of a person or a group are inadequate. Crises are created by major deviations from expected roles of parents or of children. Such deviations interfere with interpersonal relationships of husbands and wives and of parents and children.

Disgrace is experienced when one or all members of a family feel ashamed of deviant behavior of a family member. This feeling may come when a member becomes an alcoholic, is discovered to be engaging in premarital sexual relations, has a child out of wedlock, engages in crime, becomes mentally ill, or takes his own life.

Decisive economic reverses are critical events in the life of families. Families experiencing economic upsets often have a shift of roles and must reformulate goals and objectives.

[28] Arnold Tannenbaum and Gary Greenholm, "Adaptability of Older Workers to Technological Change," *B. Int. Association, Applied Psychology,* 11 (1962): No. 2, (July–Dec.) pp. 73–83.

PROBLEMS FOR RESEARCH

The above are tentative generalizations derived from studies now available. Among the many topics significant for further research on family crises, a few have been selected for special consideration.

Deviations from Expectations and Disgrace Subjects desirable for study include (1) changes in expectations of husbands and wives and of parents and children caused by vertical mobility; (2) relative seriousness of different forms of deviation for men and for women, with reference to expectations of the family and the community; (3) attitudes and behavior of persons under social stigma, such as the drunkard, the drug addict, the illegitimate child, the juvenile delinquent, and the adult criminal; and (4) a comparative study of the effect on relations of husband and wife of the concealment or revelation of premarital deviations.

Adjustment of Illegitimate Children Do illegitimate children differ in their personal adjustment from children who are legitimate? Jenkins studied two groups of Negro children, illegitimate and legitimate. The groups were matched on a number of variables, including low economic status. He concludes that "illegitimate birth status may have an adverse effect on the adjustment of Negro children."[29] Further research is needed in this area.

Sudden Changes in Economic and Social Status A rapid shift in economic circumstances creates a new situation for the family and its members. Studies so far made indicate that marked reduction in income is not as disintegrating in its effects on the integrated and flexible family as on the unintegrated and unadaptable family. Similar studies should be made of the effect of sudden prosperity in relation to family integration and flexibility. An interesting research project would be a comparison of the stability of marriage in cases where the advance of a husband in his career was rapid or gradual.

Disaster Disaster, a type of crisis with devastating effects on families, should be studied more thoroughly than it has been. Disasters considered as a mass rather than an individual phenomenon are of many different kinds: floods, earthquakes, cave-in of mines, fires, railroad

[29] Wesley W. Jenkins, "An Experimental Study of the Relationship of Legitimate and Illegitimate Birth Status to School and Personal and Social Adjustment of Negro Children," *American Journal of Sociology*, 64 (1958): pp. 169–173.

accidents and so on. Each kind of disaster has its particular aspects, but they all have the elements of the unexpected and the sudden. Are reactions and adjustments of families to disasters similar to those associated with other kinds of crises? Do families whose property and personal belongings are destroyed by a disaster behave the same as or differently than those who lose their possessions in a depression? Are there significant differences when a disaster falls on only one family rather than many families?

QUESTIONS AND EXERCISES

1. What are the underlying causes of parent-child crises associated with the maturing of a child and with his choice of occupation?
2. Analyze husband-wife crises involving the shattering of conceptions of each other and divergent conceptions of each other from the standpoint of the definition of crisis as a decisive change which creates a situation in which the habitual behavior patterns of a person or group are inadequate.
3. Analyze the situations resulting in disgrace—alcoholism, premarital sexual relations, illegitimacy, crime, mental illness, and suicide—from the viewpoint (1) of self-judgment and (2) of the social definitions of these types of behavior.
4. How does the family feeling of being disgraced interfere with the curtailment of the disgraceful behavior? Apply your reasoning to crime and mental illness.
5. What are the situations in which a family feels little or great disgrace when a member commits a crime?
6. Under what conditions do changes of roles of family members in a depression constitute a crisis for those involved?
7. Enumerate the various adjustments to depressions.

BIBLIOGRAPHY

Angell, Robert Cooley. *The Family Encounters the Depression*. New York: Charles Scribner's Sons, 1936.
   One of the classic studies of the family during the depression of the 1930's. Based on 50 student reports on the effect of the Depression on their families. Families classified by degree of integration and adaptability.

Cavan, Ruth Shonle; and Ranck, Katherine Howland. *The Family and the Depression: A Study of One Hundred Chicago Families*. Chicago: University of Chicago Press, 1938.
   Combined study by a sociologist and a psychiatric social worker. Investi-

gated 100 families before the Depression, the impact of the Depression on them, and differential reactions to the Depression.

Farber, Bernard. "Effects of a Severly Mentally Retarded Child on Family Integration," in *Monographs of the Society for Research in Child Development*, 24, No. 2, Serial No. 71, 1959.
> Reports a study of 240 Chicago families with one mentally retarded child. Degree of agreement by the husband and wife on the rank-ordering of 10 domestic values used as an index of marital integration. Integration related to characteristics of the retarded child. Also related adjustment of siblings to characteristics of the retarded child.

Myers, Jerome K.; and Roberts, Bertram H. *Family and Class Dynamics in Mental Illness*. New York: John Wiley & Sons, 1959.
> Reports an intensive interview study of the families of 50 schizophrenic and neurotic patients in hospitals and clinics serving the New Haven area. Analyzes environmental and family conditions in middle- and lower-class groups. Limited by fact that comparative analysis is based on four subgroups of 13 subjects each.

Padilla, Elena. *Up From Puerto Rico*. New York: Columbia University Press, 1958.
> An anthropological report on the life of Puerto Ricans living in a section of New York City. Based on three years of field work in the area. Examines the problems of the migrants from Puerto Rico, their adjustments to urban life in a large metropolis, and their family and community relationships.

Sauber, Mignon; and Rubinstein, Elaine. *Experiences of the Unwed Mother as a Parent: A Longitudinal Study of Unmarried Mothers Who Keep Their First-Born*. New York: Community Council of Greater New York, 1965.
> This is a longitudinal study of 321 unwed mothers who decided to keep their babies. They were interviewed shortly after birth of their babies, again 12 months and 18 months later. The book reports the demographic characteristics of the girls, their living arrangement, their socioeconomic situation, and arrangements for caring for the baby.

Vincent, Clark E. *Unmarried Mothers*. New York: Free Press, 1961.
> Reports a variety of information about unmarried mothers in Alameda County, California, in the early 1950's. Information was obtained from private physicians, maternity homes, and a county hospital. In addition, questionnaire data were obtained from a limited group of unmarried mothers.

Wimperis, Virginia. *The Unmarried Mother and Her Child*. London: George Allen and Unwin, 1960.
> Reports characteristics of unmarried mothers from a 1949 survey of Midboro, England, and a follow-up study of their children. These are essentially studies from official records, supplemented by some social agency reports.

Chapter 21
Family Disruption

Family disruption is a break in not only the network of interdependent activities but also in the family structure. Situations involving the disruption of the family structure include the departure of children from the home, separation or divorce, and death. The extent to which these are crises depends on the degree of emotional involvement and the strength of the network of interdependent activities. When these are great, the departure of children from the home, divorce, and death will be major crises for family members.

A CASE OF BEREAVEMENT

The following case by an 18-year-old girl describes the crises of an accident in a foreign country, resulting in the hospitalization of four members of a family and the subsequent death of the father. It shows how the youngest member of the family and a sister had to assume adult roles and manage the affairs of the family for a number of months. It shows also how this youngest member—now eighteen—looks back on the tragedy:

Awakening to a beautiful day as only Southern France can fashion proved to be a day that changed my life.

Gathering for a leisurely breakfast my family planned our anticipated drive to Avignon. We were seven in number—my mother, father, two sisters (fifteen and seventeen), my thirteen-year-old brother, and a French Governess. I was eleven and life was wonderful.

To facilitate our study of French we had just made the rule that all food must be asked for in French. I realize now the fun my father must have been having as we passed the butter back and forth before him and he asked for it in English, Italian, and German. We tossed bits of rolls out the window to fat geese in the flower garden, and packed our pockets with sweet rolls and fruit for an anticipated mid-morning snack.

We hurriedly explored the pension sitting rooms bulging with a strange array of souvenirs. The fireplace mantle heavy with vases, portraits of family soldiers, a peacock feather, greeting cards and trinkets. The yawning open mouth of the fireplace grinned with fillings of copper kettles and an iron grate.

Porters ran back and forth with our luggage which was being tied on the roof of our station wagon. The innkeeper anticipated our every need and his buxom wife chattered incessantly. Noisy townsmen bossed the placement of the luggage.

On our way at last we were a happy contented family inside the warm automobile. The world was awakening and passing before us like a movie-reel. Smoke poured from farm-house chimneys, and vineyards bulged with their harvests.

We had opened our notebooks to start our French lesson. The assignment was twenty-five words of our own choosing. I was busy selecting words from a French menu. My sisters chose phrases to simplify French greetings. My brother chuckled as he selected phrases like "drop dead," "who said so," "try and make me," and "you stink," to say in French with a smile to upper classmen who shouted orders to him upon his return to military school in California. Never was there a happier, busier family, more intent with their own problems.

And then—in a split second we lay unconscious on the road side. We were victims of an accident caused by a double-van skidding sideways across the highway and forcing us into a tree—and then afraid to stop and help us.

Since then I have sometimes awakened to moans, muffled screams, pains, and the sight of blood. It is still impossible to separate nightmares from reality. Screaming sirens of ambulances taking us to four different buildings in the Lyon hospital.

My fifteen-year-old sister and I showed the least injury so we watched members of our family carried on carts—covered with sheets. Because of our inadequate French we could not hear who was alive or dead.

In Lyon, France, the American Consul took us to his home and the rest of the family were in the hospital. I slept for two days ill with a basal-skull fracture that everyone thought was fatigue.

During the following months, my sister and I lived in a hotel while my family remained in the hospital. We rode public conveyances, struggled with a foreign language and currency, supervised the needs of a family too ill to make decisions. We ran errands, carried messages between hospital buildings and tended to all their individual requests. Finally we were forced to break the news of my father's death to my mother and a sister who was in traction with twenty-four fractures in her legs, and then see that the news was kept from my brother who was too ill for the shock. We arranged for my father's funeral and offered our prayers for the life of our mother. We knew the governess was already planning an $85,000 suit against our estate and tried to gather accident information from the police. Finally, we arranged to take the family to Paris in an ambulance and passage by ship to New York and plane to Los Angeles.

The most difficult adjustment was being forced to face reality and join our carefree friends at our old exclusive girls' school. We cried easily, we could not seem to study, we found no interest in sports or social events. One can never know what it means to be an eleven-year old at a father-daughter baseball game without a father. We had no car—no one was well enough to drive. Our estate was tied up by probate and the suit of our governess for five and a half years. My sister was in a wheel chair, and my brother very ill. I felt ill adjusted and very unhappy.

I am convinced today that I grew from childhood to adulthood in the one split second of timing that caused our accident. One can only ask "why" and accept it. I am also convinced that I would never have again adjusted to normal life without the rich reserve of love accumulated by eleven happy years of love and companionship. Our family association had been very close and adequate to help me surpass any obstacle.

Facing reality was the only way to force me to accept the inevitable, although I must admit I hid many times from well-meaning but thoughtless friends who seemed far more interested in the gruesome details of our tragedy than in my reluctance in relating the events.

At eleven I ceased being the baby of the family and learned the meaning of pain, tragedy, despair, and acceptance of the inevitable.

The crisis of family disruption described above was particularly severe, for (1) its suddenness made preliminary adjustments impossible, (2) it happened in a foreign land in which people spoke a different language, and (3) the fact that adult members of the family were incapacitated resulted in an abrupt change of roles for the eleven-year-old girl —from a child role to an adult role.

Other crises, such as separation, divorce, or a severe illness which eventually results in death, generally are preceded by a period in which two things are occurring: interpersonal relationships are being disrupted and preliminary adjustments are being made to the possible absence of a family member.

The crises discussed in the preceding chapter—deviations from expectations, disgrace, and economic reverses—may lead to the disintegration of the family and to its disruption if satisfactory adjustments or solutions are not worked out. Whatever the causes of family disruption, they take one of three forms, which will now be considered: (1) departure of family members; (2) separation and divorce; and (3) death. Two additional points will be discussed: contrasting attitudes toward the bereaved and the divorced, and characteristics common to crises.

DEPARTURE OF CHILDREN

The expectation in the United States is that when a child becomes an adult he will leave the parental home and establish a home of his own. In some other societies, however, children, though married, continue to live with their own parents or with the parents of the mate. In the matriarchal form of the family among preliterate peoples, the grown-up children never leave the household of the mother. A man upon marriage still lives with his mother and visits his wife in her mother's home. In the extended-patriarchal family the son upon marriage remains with his parents but brings his wife into their home. His sister, when she marries, leaves her parents' home and resides with her husband and his parents. In Western societies both the son and the daughter generally leave the parental home and set up a new household.

Marriage of Children Today the likelihood is that a marriage is less a crisis for the young people than for their parents. The parents, typically the mother, may be very attached to a daughter or son. This is true particularly in the following types of situations: (1) when the parent is overly protective and possessive; (2) when the parent, lacking other interests, centers hopes, ambitions, and attentions on the child; (3) when the mate selected by the child diverges in personality characteristics, status, or values from parental expectations; and (4) when the child is the partial or sole support of a parent, especially when the parent expects that support to continue. Often in such cases the child refrains from marriage rather than risk the crisis of strained relationships with the parent.

Leaving Home for Reasons Other than Marriage Family members leave home for reasons other than marriage. When the children go to college or to trade school, or leave the farm for the city, or move to another community for vocational advancement or a change of scene, the family is partially disrupted. These departures from the home generally do not take the form of acute crises, such as are experienced in connection with divorce or bereavement, but the experience of a son or daughter going away may be extremely painful:

> After John left for college I thought I could not stand it. I felt his absence especially when we sat down at the table without him, or when I went into his empty room. John is in a nearby college and therefore can come home every few weeks, but even at that I feel sometimes as though I would almost die from longing for him.

It is not surprising that the departure of children is a crisis for the parents, and sometimes for the children. Over the years a network of interrelations has developed. Some of these interconnections depend for their fulfillment on the presence both of the parents and of the children. The departure of a child severs completely or at least to some extent these interrelations and may be a crisis for those concerned.

DIVORCE[1]

In considering divorce and separation one should keep in mind the degree of permanent marriage in the general population. The figure of one divorce in three or four marriages is misleading in that this is based on the divorce applications and marriage applications in a given year and not on the total married couples in the population. Actually only one in every 109 married couples obtained a divorce in 1960. Of the 1,523,000 marriages in the United States in 1960, seventy-eight percent were first marriages and twenty-two percent involved either a divorced or widowed person—sixteen percent involved a divorced bride or groom and six percent a widowed bride or groom. Moreover the divorce rate has remained fairly stable since 1950: the rate per 1,000 population ranged from 2.1 to 2.7 and the rate per 1,000 married females ranged from 9.2 to 10.3[2] Marriages in the United States are much more stable than many people think.

Separation of the husband and wife generally precedes divorce and actually constitutes the disruption of the marriage. It is the divorce, however, or the legal dissolution of the marriage, which gives public announcement that the husband and wife have been unable to compose their marital difficulties. Many couples are so reluctant to face the unfavorable publicity attendant on divorce that they postpone this action until either the husband or the wife desires to marry again.

We shall discuss divorce under the following headings: (1) divorce an index of family disruption; (2) increase in divorce; (3) varying divorce practices; (4) situations in which divorce is not a crisis; (5) situations in which divorce is a crisis; (6) situations in which divorce is a greater crisis for one spouse than the other; (7) reconciliation; (8) differentials in adjustment; and (9) types of adjustment to divorce.

Divorce an Index of Family Disruption When a family is in the process of becoming disrupted, its members no longer act together as a

[1] A large part of the material in this section was collected by Harvey J. Locks for *Predicting Adjustment in Marriage: A Comparison of a Divorced and a Happily-Married Group* (New York: Henry Holt, 1951).

[2] Hugh Carter and Alexander Plateris, "Trends in Divorce and Family Disruption," *Health, Education, and Welfare Indicators*, August 1963.

unit. Typically a high degree of family disruption is signified by permanent separation of husband and wife and of parents and children. Disintegration of the network of family relationships may take place, of course, even though the husband and wife are still living in the same house, and even though they have not maintained conjugal relations or engaged in common activities for a long time.

Nevertheless, for research purposes divorce is the most practical index of family disruption. It is not a perfect index, because it does not include desertions and other separations that do not end in divorce, but there are no reliable and complete statistics on separations. The figures for divorce are relatively satisfactory, primarily because divorce requires legal action and many countries keep records which permit comparison of rates over a period of years.

Table 28 compares divorce rates for selected countries in 1966 with those for the 1910–1914 period. The rapid rise of the divorce rate in every country except Japan and Portugal is the outstanding fact emerging

Table 28. Divorce rate in 1910-1914 and 1966 per 1,000 population for specified countries, with ratios of 1966 to 1910-1914*

Countries	Rate 1966	Rate 1910–1914	Ratio of 1966 to 1910–1914
Australia	.9	.1	9.0
Belgium	.6[a]	.2	3.0
Canada	.5	.05[c]	10.0
Denmark	1.4	.3	4.7
England and Wales	.8[a]	.05[c]	16.0
France	.7	.4	1.8
Japan	.8	1.1	1.4
Mexico	.7	.05[c]	14.0
Netherlands	.6	.2	3.0
New Zealand	.8	.2	4.0
Norway	.7	.2	3.5
Portugal	.1	.1[b]	1.0
Scotland	.7	.1	7.0
Sweden	1.3	.1	13.0
Switzerland	.8[a]	.4	2.0
United States	2.5	1.0	2.5

[a] 1965
[b] 1915–1919
[c] Rate less than .05
*Data for 1910–1914 from Metropolitan Life Insurance Company, *Statistical Bulletin*, 33, June 1952, p. 7; for 1966 from *Demographic Yearbook*, 1967, New York: United Nations, 1967, pp. 757–760.

from this table, particularly the column giving the ratio of the 1966 divorce rates to those of 1910–1914. Evidently in European countries and the United States there is a trend toward either marital instability or to a greater willingness to sever marital relationships which have already been disrupted. Undoubtedly there are factors in modern life, more or less common to all these countries, which disturb relationships in the family.

Factors Associated with Variations in Divorce Rates A comparison of the countries in Table 28 and other data suggest several explanations for the wide differences in rates of divorce. These may be briefly stated as follows:

1. Differences in legislation markedly affect the divorce rate. The liberal grounds for divorce in most states in the United States greatly facilitate divorce. England and Wales, with language and customs similar to those of the United States, liberalized their statutes as late as 1937. Previously only the adultery of the wife and adultery in conjunction with physical cruelty on the part of the husband constituted grounds for divorce. Some European countries, such as Portugal, with relatively low divorce rates have strict divorce laws as compared with countries with higher rates, like France.

2. However, to explain differences in divorce rates between countries by variations in legislation is an oversimplification. The law itself is an expression of public opinion, which is a result of more basic factors in national life. Attitudes toward marriage and divorce are in the mores; therefore, differences in the mores not only affect legislation but determine the attitudes of people toward divorce. The mores of Portugal are much more against divorce than those of France, which in turn are less favorable to divorce than those of the United States, especially in Western states.

3. Another influence is the attitude of religious groups toward divorce. Catholic countries, in general, have low divorce rates, and Protestant countries higher rates.

4. Countries that are rural typically have lower divorce rates than those that are predominantly urban. This is illustrated by a comparison of the more urban Sweden and the more rural Norway, where other factors are relatively constant.

Census data indicate that divorced persons are more likely to live in urban areas than in rural areas.[3] Although in 1960 only 69.9 percent of the population of the United States resided in urban areas, 75.1 percent of all divorced men and 85.1 percent of all divorced women were in

[3] Census data on the residence of divorced persons in urban, rural-nonfarm, and rural-farm are available for decennial censuses.

urban areas. Farm areas have decidedly fewer divorced persons than urban areas or rural-nonfarm areas; in 1960, 7.5 percent of the population lived in rural-farm areas, while only 5.4 percent of divorced men and 2.0 percent of divorced women resided on farms.

5. Divorce varies by length of marriage and separation. Divorces are preceded by a period of one and a half to two years of separation. The first year of marriage has the highest percentage of couples who had separated. The percent divorced does not reach its maximum until the second and third year of marriage.[4]

6. Cultural homogeneity of the population appears to be correlated with a low divorce rate, while heterogeneity seems to be associated with a high rate. The high rate of the United States in comparison with the lower rate in England is due partially to this factor.

7. Another factor, mobility, must be added to help explain the rapid increase of the divorce rates in the different countries since the 1910–1914 period and the much higher rate in the United States. Since the turn of the century there has been a rapid expansion, particularly in the United States, of new means of transportation and communication, such as the automobile, the airplane, motion picture, radio, and television, which have greatly increased personal and mental mobility.

Carter and Glick give an excellent analysis of the factors associated with the rise of the divorce rate, although it is somewhat different from that presented above. In the following they give urbanization, the changed status of women, higher education of women, and the decrease in the social disapproval of divorce as the primary factors:

> Many factors are involved in the rise of the divorce rate since 1890. During these years the United States has become increasingly an urban society. The position of women has changed drastically; the proportion who are farmers' wives and unpaid family workers has declined, while the proportion employed in business and industry has risen sharply. The education of women has advanced dramatically. Women who contemplated divorce in 1890 were unlikely to obtain a comfortable livelihood. If they sought employment, their limited education and training made the outlook, other than for unskilled or semiskilled work, anything but bright; if they returned with their children to their parents, they might be placing a heavy responsibility on persons who were approaching retirement age. Remarriage following divorce was made difficult by the widespread disapproval of divorced persons. Thus the unhappy wives of 1890 were often constrained to tolerate conditions that wives of the 1960's would find intolerable. So, also the unhappy husbands of 1890 were reluctant to seek divorce because of strong community disapproval of such action. And if the husband was a farmer, as so many were, the wife was an indispensable

[4] Thomas P. Monohan, "When Married Couples Part: Statistical Trends and Relationships in Divorce," *American Sociological Review*, 27 (1962): pp. 625–633.

534   Family Disruption

member of the production team. This fact was a strong economic motivation for avoiding a legal ending of the marriage.[5]

Figure 27 shows the divorce rate of the United States for the years 1870–1968. Three facts are observable in the figure: (1) There has been a general tendency for divorce to increase over the period. (2) There have been marked fluctuations, as in downward movement during depressions and upward swings in prosperity. (3) The divorce rate rises after a war, as in 1920 and 1946.

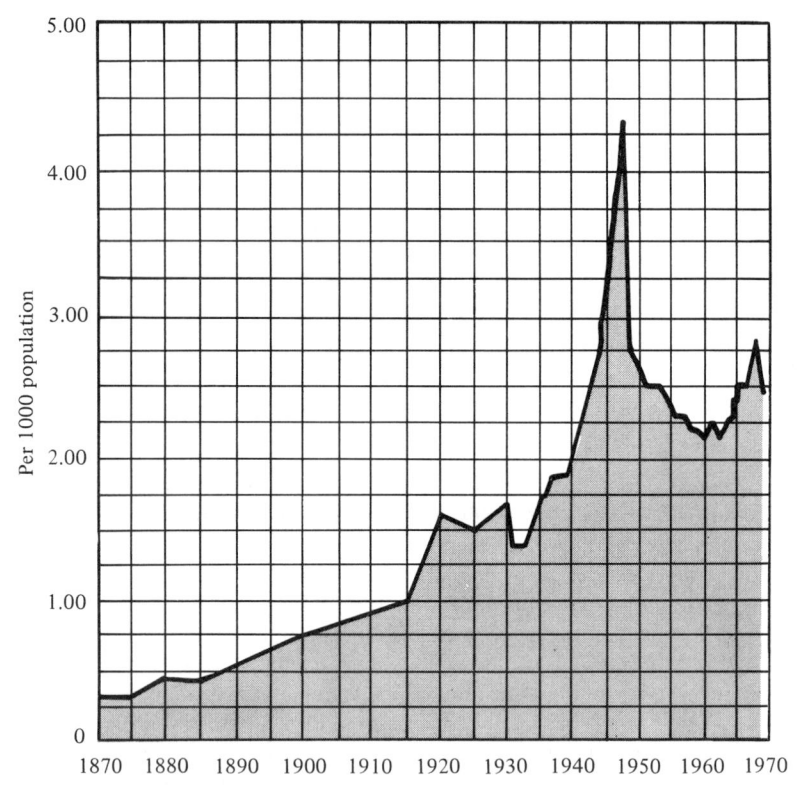

Figure 27.   Divorces per 1,000 population, 1870-1969*

*Data from Statistical Abstract of the United States, 1949, p. 80; 1962, p. 70; and 1969, p. 47.

Differences in Divorce Practices and Divorce Rates   Divorce practices and rates vary from nation to nation, from state to state, from country

[5] Hugh Carter and Paul C. Glick, *Marriage and Divorce: A Social and Economic Study* (Cambridge: Harvard University Press, 1970), p. 55.

to city, from area to area within a city, according to religious and nationality groups, educational position, by length of time married, and for different age groups.

Within the fifty-three jurisdictions[6] of the United States there are two primary differences in the divorce laws: (1) whether or not provision is made for "separation from bed and board" and (2) variations in the grounds for divorce. In absolute divorce there is full and complete legal dissolution of the marriage contract, leaving the parties with the status of single persons, while partial divorce is merely separation and does not restore either party to the status of a single person. All jurisdictions grant absolute divorce; over half provide for limited divorce. The principal grounds for divorce and the number of the fifty-three jurisdictions of the United States granting divorce for each ground are as follows: adultery, 52, conviction of a felony, 48; cruelty, 47; desertion, 45; habitual drunkenness, 44; insanity, 38; impotence, 34; and nonsupport, 32.[7]

The trend may be toward making the legal grounds coincide more closely with the real reasons for divorce. In California on January 1, 1970, the ground of insanity was retained and "irreconcilable differences" was substituted for all other grounds for divorce: adultery, cruelty, desertion, willful neglect, habitual intemperance, and conviction of a felony. If, in an uncontested case, a person testifies that irreconcilable differences have caused an irremediable breakdown of his marriage, a dissolution of the marriage is granted.

Variations in divorce rates from state to state and the increase in divorce in two and a half decades, 1940–1966 are shown in Figure 28. The variations between states was about the same in 1940 and 1966, with the highest rates in Mountain states (Wyoming, Arizona, Nevada), and Idaho, Alaska, Florida, Oklahoma, and Texas. All of these states had rates of 4.0 or more in 1966. Very low rates are found in states north and east of Kansas and a few in the southeast. In general, the divorce rate increases from east to west.

Changes and stability in divorce rates are revealed by a comparison of high divorce rates of states in 1940, 1950, 1960, and 1966. Table 29 gives the divorce rates for these years for nine states. It will be noted that divorce rates in 1950 were higher for all states, except Wyoming and Arizona, than in 1940, 1960, and 1966. The decided decrease in the divorce rate in Nevada may be due to the increase in population in that state.

[6] The 50 states, Washington, D.C., Puerto Rico, and the Virgin Islands.
[7] J. T. Collman, *The Law of Separation and Divorce* (Dobbs Ferry, New York: Oceana Publications, 1967).

536 Family Disruption

Figure 28. Divorces per 1,000 population by states, 1940 and 1966*

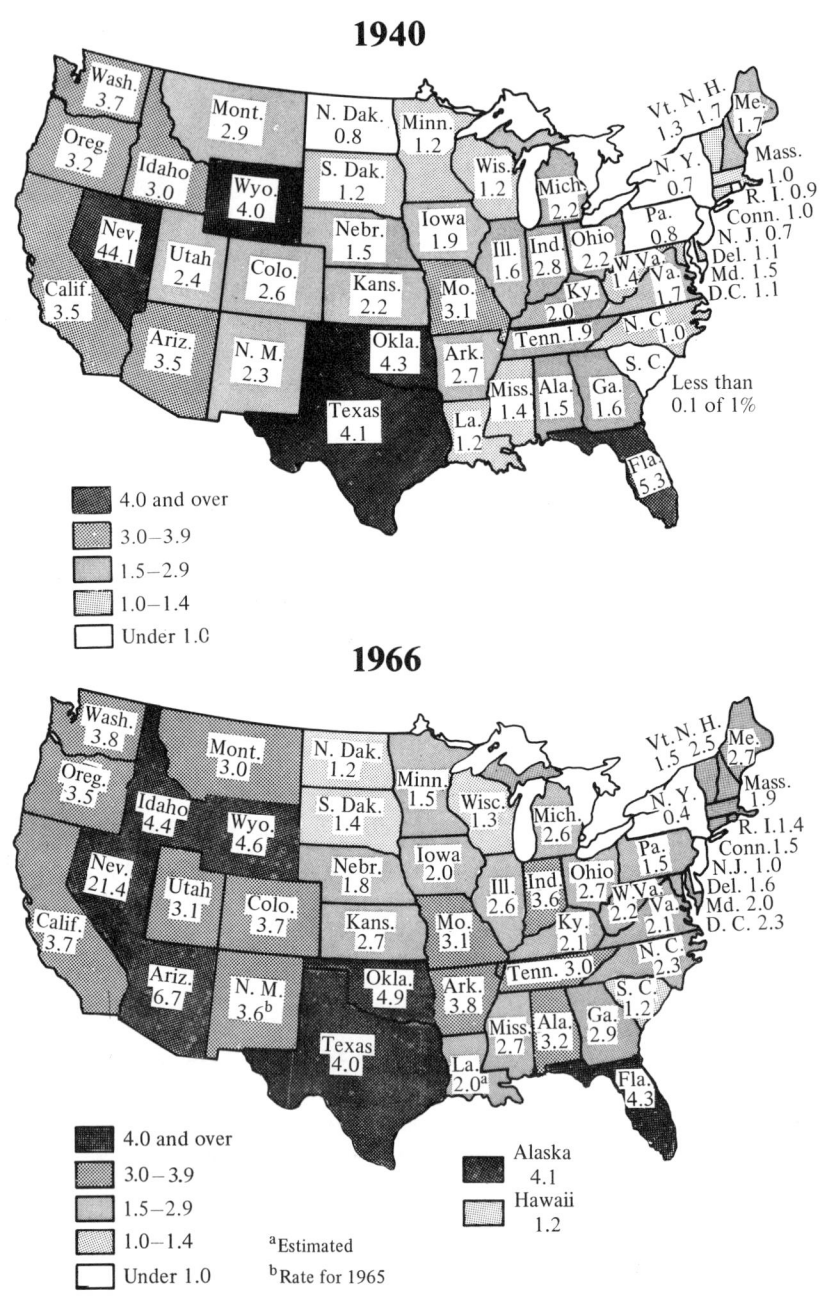

1940

Wash. 3.7; Oreg. 3.2; Mont. 2.9; Idaho 3.0; Wyo. 4.0; N. Dak. 0.8; S. Dak. 1.2; Minn. 1.2; Wis. 1.2; Mich. 2.2; Vt. 1.3; N.H. 1.7; Me. 1.7; N.Y. 0.7; Mass. 1.0; R.I. 0.9; Conn. 1.0; Nev. 44.1; Utah 2.4; Colo. 2.6; Nebr. 1.5; Iowa 1.9; Ill. 1.6; Ind. 2.8; Ohio 2.2; Pa. 0.8; N.J. 0.7; Del. 1.1; Md. 1.5; Calif. 3.5; Ariz. 3.5; N.M. 2.3; Kans. 2.2; Mo. 3.1; Ky. 2.0; W.Va. 1.4; Va. 1.7; D.C. 1.1; Okla. 4.3; Ark. 2.7; Tenn. 1.9; N.C. 1.0; S.C. Less than 0.1 of 1%; Texas 4.1; La. 1.2; Miss. 1.4; Ala. 1.5; Ga. 1.6; Fla. 5.3

- ■ 4.0 and over
- 3.0–3.9
- 1.5–2.9
- 1.0–1.4
- □ Under 1.0

1966

Wash. 3.8; Oreg. 3.5; Mont. 3.0; Idaho 4.4; Wyo. 4.6; N. Dak. 1.2; S. Dak. 1.4; Minn. 1.5; Wisc. 1.3; Mich. 2.6; Vt. 1.5; N.H. 2.5; Me. 2.7; N.Y. 0.4; Mass. 1.9; R.I. 1.4; Conn. 1.5; Nev. 21.4; Utah 3.1; Colo. 3.7; Nebr. 1.8; Iowa 2.0; Ill. 2.6; Ind. 3.6; Ohio 2.7; Pa. 1.5; N.J. 1.0; Del. 1.6; Md. 2.0; Calif. 3.7; Ariz. 6.7; N.M. 3.6[b]; Kans. 2.7; Mo. 3.1; Ky. 2.1; W.Va. 2.2; Va. 2.1; D.C. 2.3; Okla. 4.9; Ark. 3.8; Tenn. 3.0; N.C. 2.3; S.C. 1.2; Texas 4.0; La. 2.0[a]; Miss. 2.7; Ala. 3.2; Ga. 2.9; Fla. 4.3

- ■ 4.0 and over
- 3.0–3.9
- 1.5–2.9
- 1.0–1.4
- □ Under 1.0

Alaska 4.1
Hawaii 1.2

[a] Estimated
[b] Rate for 1965

*Data for 1940 from *Statistical Abstract of the United States*, 1943, p. 93; for 1966, ibid., 1969, p. 61.

Table 29. High divorce rates in nine states, 1940, 1950, 1960, and 1966*

	1940	1950	1960	1966
Nevada	44.1	55.7	29.6	21.4
Florida	5.3	6.5	3.9	4.3
Oklahoma	4.3	6.2	4.6	4.9
Arizona	3.5	5.4	3.7	6.7
Texas	4.1	4.9	3.6	4.0
Washington	3.7	4.7	3.3	3.8
Arkansas	2.7	4.6	3.2[a]	3.8
Idaho	3.0	4.6	3.9	4.4
Wyoming	4.0	4.0	4.0	4.6

[a] rate for 1959
*Various issues of Statistical Abstract of the United States.

Divorce Not Always a Crisis Divorce is not a crisis if the bonds of emotional involvement never existed or have been weakened. Emotional involvement is relatively weak in the following situations: (1) those in which husband, wife, and children are spatially separated over a long period or are living together but are psychologically separated; (2) forced marriages; and (3) second marriages of persons who still have a high degree of emotional involvement with a deceased mate. Persons in these families may move from marriage to divorce without experiencing a crisis.

The disruption of a family through divorce does not create much disturbance in the lives of persons who have drifted apart. Periodic or prolonged separation or different work schedules may result in a relative cessation of communication, with consequent loss of consensus, common interests, interdependence of activities, and emotional involvement, as in the following case analyzed by the wife:

> The real difficulty in our marriage was that we both worked and had different schedules so that we were home together very little. At the beginning of our marriage we had a great deal in common. We thought of ourselves as well mated and were very happy. But little by little we lost each other. While I missed Tom some when we were first separated, I wasn't troubled so much. As far as I was concerned it was more that I was losing my home and was somewhat uneasy about the future rather than the fact that I was being separated from my husband. For these reasons I did not want the divorce, even though he had been paying attention to other women. I felt that if we stayed together we might get back to the intimacy which had been present in the early months of our marriage.

Locke collected data on forty-one forced marriages which ended in divorce. He found that when such a marriage occurs, after brief acquaintance and casual contact, divorce generally is not a crisis. The crisis occurs in being forced to marry, and divorce is a release from an unexpected and undesirable predicament. The following is from one of these cases:

> I hate to think of my first wife. She was just a streetwalker. I had known her just about two weeks. We were out on a drinking party. The first thing I knew she said she was pregnant. I married her but never lived with her. I was going with the girl I am now married to. I went downtown a free man; the next time I went I was a married man. I did not get a divorce for four years. The same day I divorced this woman, I married my present wife.[8]

Christensen compared the marriages which ended in divorce by the length of time between the date of marriage and the birth of the first born. From his data we are taking two samples—one a county in Indiana and the other from Copenhagen, Denmark. The samples are divided into four groups by length of time married—0-181 days, 182-272 days, 273-363 days, and 2 years. One can assume that a large part of groups one and two were forced marriages. One can also assume that persons in group one resisted getting married to a greater extent than those in group two. For the Indiana sample, the percent of those in groups one, two, three, and four who were divorced was respectively 17, 13, 9, and 7; for Denmark, 31, 25, 23, and 19.[9] This indicates that those who are forced to marry get a divorce much more frequently than those who are not married due to pregnancy.

Divorce is not a great crisis in casual second marriages when the first marriage ended in bereavement. If the first marriage was happy, adjustment to divorce in the second marriage may take the form of heightened idealization of the first mate. A widow who had lived forty-three years with her first husband married a man who had been married six times (the first two wives died, and the other marriages ended in divorce). She divorced him because he did not live up to her idealized picture of her first husband.

> One day I was in the courthouse, where a lot of old people visit, and Jim came up to me and said: "Howdy-do." I said: "Howdy." He said: "I don't believe I know you." I told him my name. He said: "Are you a widow woman?" I said: "I am." He asked: "Is your man dead?" I said: "He is." I saw him at the store and he made a date with me. He told me tall tales about his fine house and furniture. I went with Jim about six months and then we were married. He came and lived in my house and paid the rent only two months.

[8] Locke, p. 92.
[9] H. T. Christensen, "Timing of First Pregnancy as a Factor in Divorce—Cross-Cultural Analysis," *Eugenic Quarterly*, 10 (1963), pp. 119–130.

> I would be awful happy if I could just go home to my first husband. Hugh was always so good to me and Jim was always so mean. After Jim and me were separated, he told some stories about me sleeping with another man. But as God is my judge I am innocent. Since my divorce from Jim, an old man has been coming to see me once a week. I don't want him around much. I don't want any man around much. They get on my nerves.[10]

When she talked about her husband, she invariably had in mind her first husband. Jim was just a man. All her marital attitudes were associated with the husband with whom she had lived for so many years. The disruption of the marriage in this case was a crisis for neither the wife nor the husband.

Another illustration of divorce without a crisis is that of a man who had lived with his first wife fifty-four years, and after her death married his landlady, found his freedom restricted in marriage and secured a divorce. For this old man the disruption of the marriage would have been a crisis only if it involved pushing him out of his rooming accommodations and if it deprived him of companionship. He was able to salvage these desired things by continuing to live in the home of his divorced wife as a "boarder":

> I went to board at the home of the woman whom I later married. I lived there a couple of years and then the children began raising questions about my living with this woman without being married to her. So, we got married. But it didn't work out. After I was married to her, she tried to keep me from going uptown, tried to get more money from me, and in other ways bossed me. So I got a divorce.
>
> I continue to stay there. I like being a boarder much better than being her husband.

Divorce Generally a Crisis In the vast majority of cases, however, divorce is a crisis for the husband, the wife, or both. Most couples go through an extended period of indecision and conflict before getting a divorce. This is shown by Goode in his study of 425 divorced urban mothers, between the ages of 20 and 38 years:

> The evidence is clear, however, that divorcees do not characteristically dash off for the nearest divorce lawyer when the first spat occurs. Divorces are preceded by a long period of conflict, and the final action is the result of a decision and action process that lasts on the average about two years.[11]

In an analysis of the time elapsing between divorce and remarriage, Locke found that, of the 281 divorced men and women who reported

[10] Locke, p. 93.
[11] William J. Goode, *After Divorce* (Glencoe, Illinois: Free Press, 1956), p. 137.

that they had remarried, 30.6 percent had done so by the end of a year. The average length of time between divorce and remarriage was 2.0 years.

The conflicts in this period are generally critical experiences for a couple. Apparently time is necessary for most couples before they are able or willing to accept divorce as a solution to marital difficulties.

When Divorce Is a Crisis Divorce as an extreme crisis for family members is associated with a situation in which there is strong community opinion against divorce and in which there is emotional involvement and interdependence of activities. In the past, divorce was regarded as so great a disgrace that husbands and wives would endure almost unbearable situations rather than resort to the divorce court. Even though there has been a great decline in the stigma attached to divorce, negative values are still associated with being a divorcée. If one's friends and associates recognize that divorce is a solution for a problematic marriage, the feeling that divorce is a stigma tends to decrease or disappear entirely. But even in such situations the person may have a sense of failure, particularly the one who feels forsaken.

The second condition is approximated in the divorce of couples whose lives have been fused by participation in common activities over many years and who are held together by common memories and continued emotional attachments. Such persons can be separated only with great difficulty and with great emotional disturbances. While occasionally one or the other of such a couple decides to secure a divorce and gets it as quickly as possible, in the majority of cases there is a considerable period between the decision that a divorce may be desirable and actually securing it.

The inner conflict experienced by spouses who are emotionally attached to each other is revealed in the typical process associated with the disruption of the family by divorce. The sequence includes some and often all of the following: talking it over and debating the issues with oneself, mentioning it as a possibility to the mate, intermittent attempts to solve the marital difficulties, sleeping in different beds or different rooms, spatial separation, reconciliation, making application for a divorce, getting the application dismissed, reapplying for divorce, securing the divorce, remarrying one's former mate, and securing a second divorce. Any stage in the above sequence may be omitted, and the process may be interrupted or permanently terminated at any stage.

Reconciliation Application for a divorce does not always result in disruption of a family. Studies have revealed that between a quarter and a third of all applications are dismissed. It is estimated that about half of these people reapply later for divorce.

Children are important in the reconciliation of some divorced couples. The following, written by an 18-year-old girl, shows that the divorce of her parents was a critical experience for her; it describes the continued attachments of children and parents during the period of divorce; and it gives a picture of the gradual reconciliation of the parents and the reuniting of the family:

> I was about seven when I realized the tension between Mother and Father. One night I saw on the front page of the newspaper of our small town a large caption, "Harriet Gay sues Lawrence Gay for divorce."
>
> This was a great shock. The next day at school was the most unhappy day of my life. The children had heard their parents talk about the divorce, and so thoughtlessly said cruel little things to me. Some said that my father wanted to remarry; others that my mother had plans for a second marriage or that she was enough to drive any man crazy.
>
> The families of both my parents took sides. My father's relatives remained true to him, while my mother's were divided. My maternal grandmother thought the trouble was mostly due to my mother's temper.
>
> Father came to see us a lot after the divorce was final. They were both very good to us but in no way tried to win us over to their sides. Neither of them ever said anything about the other in a mean way.
>
> Our parents remained separated for two years. They knew how unhappy we were. Father's visits became more frequent, but still he pretended that he came only to see Brother and me, but he always managed to come when Mother would be home.
>
> Soon he began to come for dinner and we would have such a wonderful time. Once in a while Mother and Father would catch themselves reminiscing, and Brother and I would assume the roles of matchmakers, trying to make everything come out right. One day Mother told us that we were going to move to a new place and Father was coming with us.

The following case of a couple married twenty-five years shows how difficult a reunion becomes after a prolonged period of conflict:

> We were as happy as could be for the first twenty years of marriage. Then two things happened which led to unhappiness. I had had a good business, but it went in the red. My wife is a rather dominant woman who thinks she is a good business manager, and she tried to take a hand in the business. When I would come home at night, she would fuss and argue and make me more worried and nervous. I got to staying downtown and eating out.
>
> The second thing was that she was going through the change in life. We had been very active sexually in our earlier life. Now she became cold and wouldn't have anything to do with me. I moved into another bed and then into another room. I told her I would give her four or five years to adjust to her change. At the end of that time, things were no better and she continued to fuss. So I packed up and left.
>
> I have been back occasionally. She pays no attention to me. She talks

and laughs with the others but not with me. A few weeks ago she suggested that I come back; she would live as man and wife with me. I went back and talked with her but found the old trouble was still there.

Both the husband and the wife in this case desired reconciliation, but when they attempted it they resumed hostilities.

The process of reconciliation may be stated as follows: The persistence of old habits pulls one toward reconciliation, while the difficulties which disrupted the marriage, also based on habits, drive one away from the prior mate. If there has been great emotional involvement and interdependence of activities with the former mate and children, frustration may be experienced before and after the divorce. Some habits cannot continue if one or more members of the family are removed from everyday association. Yet these tendencies to act in habitual ways toward the former mate and children persist. The result is inner conflict and frustration, with a husband or wife being inclined to be both friendly and hostile toward each other. If the affectional attitudes and habits predominate in both, reconciliation may take place.

Differences in Adjustment   There are several variations between spouses in their adjustment to divorce, depending on who gets the children, whether one is more emotionally involved than the other, and whether or not the divorce is contested. There are variations, also, between (1) men and women, (2) young and old persons, and (3) marriages of short and those of longer duration.

In cases where children are present, the parent who retains the children experiences less crisis than the one who is cut off from both the former mate and the children. A professional man whose wife would not move with him to a town in which vocational opportunities were more adequate reports the following:

> If I had to do over again, I would not get a divorce. I would put a rope around my wife and make her go with me. I have a boy ten and it is tough to be separated from him. He comes over to see me, but even at that I think it is a mistake to be divorced where there are children. I am interested in my boy and I think about my prior marriage. My present wife does not object in the least to my seeing my boy, but my second marriage is a psychological handicap.

Frequently one member of a divorced couple may be more emotionally involved and more dependent and suffer more emotional disturbance than the other, and this tends to prolong the crisis more for one than for the other. This is particularly true when the other remarries and is successful in transferring his affections to the new mate. The transference of affection may occur before the divorce or soon thereafter.

In the following case the husband was less emotionally involved than the wife:

> We were perfectly happy, except for his interest in roller skating. I couldn't skate, but he would go in the evenings alone and we quarreled some about that. We both wanted children, but I couldn't have them. At the rink he met a girl who told him that, if he would get a divorce and marry her, she would have a child for him.
>
> He didn't get home until five in the morning. He told me about it right away. He wanted me to get a divorce. I think he would have backed out later, but we were both stubborn. I left and he got the divorce.
>
> He married this girl. Thirteen days later he called me and then came to see me often. He got a divorce from this girl and talked about coming back to me. But just before getting his divorce he got acquainted with a married woman who was having trouble with her husband and who was to have a baby in a couple of months. He married her. They now have the baby from her first husband and a baby of their own. [The husband when interviewed was found to be very fond of both children.]
>
> It was a terrible shock at first. I still loved him and could hardly stand it. It was a long time before I could get over it, but I am feeling better now.

The interviewer gathered the impression that in the flare-up following the husband's return at five in the morning both took stands from which they did not retreat because of pride, stubbornness, and anger. Underneath it all they did not want the divorce, and if both had been willing to retreat, they might have patched things up.

In cases of first marriage, adjustment to divorce is easier for the young than for the old. Not only is contracting a second marriage more difficult for older persons, particularly older women, but the old are likely to be bound more firmly to their mates.

Types of Adjustment There are several types of adjustment to divorce: (1) talking to others about one's divorce, (2) continued association of the husband and wife after the divorce, (3) involvement in a second marriage, (4) attempts to control the life of the ex-mate, (5) idealization of early relationships with the ex-mate, and (6) moving to a new location.

Some divorced persons secure catharsis through relating their experiences to friends and strangers. Locke discovered that most divorced persons like answering questions and talking about their problems.

Another adjustment to divorce is continued association after the divorce. The ex-husband may continue to live in the home with his ex-mate; or the two may live separately but see each other on the basis of friendship and affection; or they may associate, with consequent quarreling and conflict. This continued association gives the persons concerned time to adjust to the disruption of their marriage.

The continuance of association, not only after the divorce but right up to the time of the divorce, occasionally occurs, as in the following case:

> *Wife:* We never separated before the divorce. He kept staying here. But we were sleeping in different rooms. I think he thought I would not go through with it. I kept hoping he would quit drinking. When he found I had got the divorce, he got outside and cursed so that the neighbors could hear him. He then took his things and moved out.
>
> I still think a lot of him. I would do anything for him. But I don't think I would live with him again, for I would be afraid that he would keep on drinking.
>
> *Husband:* My wife is a fine woman. In fact today she helped me paper two rooms of my shack. She washes my clothes even though we are divorced.

Continued or intermittent association after the divorce allows gradual psychological withdrawal from the former mate and may be coupled with the transference of affection to another. Marrying another person is, generally, the most satisfactory adjustment to divorce. Many divorced persons report that they are very happy with their second mates and that they hardly ever think of their first marriages. Emancipation from her former husband and happiness in the present marriage are expressed in the following excerpt of a letter received from a woman in reply to a request for an interview:

> The fact that I made the mistake of marrying Frank and living with him for a year and a half has been erased from my memory during more than six years of being happily married to a fine, intelligent, and successful man. I hold no grudges, only gratitude that, after making a mistake, I have been given the greatest happiness which can come to any woman—marriage to a man whom I love, admire, and respect, plus motherhood. Being a wife and mother of three healthy children certainly gives one no time to dwell on the past.

The following from Carter and Glick reports the likelihood of marriage for divorced, widowed, and single people. The divorced are much more likely to marry than the widowed and never-married:

> The individuals most likely to marry were the younger divorcees, especially the women. Of all the divorced persons 14 to 24 years of age, more than one-half of the women and one-third of the men remarried within one year. In general, the marriage rate for divorced persons remarrying was substantially higher than for never-married persons of comparable ages. Likewise widowed persons 25 years old and over, except for widows 24 to 44 years old, married at substantially higher rathes than single persons of the same age.[12]

[12] Carter and Glick, p. 47.

Another adjustment to divorce is to distinguish between the mate with whom one lived during the first part of the marriage and the mate from whom one is divorced. This allows one to build up an idealized picture of the mate during the first years of the marriage and to continue to love the mate that used to be.

Spatial separation is another means of adjusting to divorce. There is a tendency to separate from each other and from former friends, by one or both moving to a new location. Moving serves much the same function as in bereavement when the bereaved separates himself from objects and relationships which remind him of the deceased.

If a divorced person is vindictive, he is not completely emancipated from the former mate. If a man remarries and has to support two families, he generally comes to resent the legal obligation to give money to his ex-wife, even though it is to be used for the support of his children. This is particularly true if the wife has remarried and if hostility characterized the disruption of the first marriage. The man may try to get the amount of support reduced or make payments intermittently and then cease entirely. The wife feels that she has a right to these payments. Conflicting attitudes toward support may perpetuate memories of other conflicts and interfere with the emancipation of the couple from each other.

Epithets applied to the divorced mate may tend to free one from one's former spouse, but they also indicate that one is not yet completely emancipated:

> My woman now is as good as the other one was bad. You ask what I think of my ex-wife now. I think of her just like a snake out there in the grass. Don't even think of her except when someone mentions her. Never speak to her. I figure I'm married, and have a good wife, and she's no part of me any more.

Persons not reconciled to a divorce frequently attempt to continue control over their former mates. They may threaten to bring about a scandal through suicide or to do physical injury to the mate or children. They sometimes spread stories about the behavior of their prior mate. Some wives resort to court proceedings, including having their ex-husbands jailed, in an attempt to force financial support and in other ways attempt to control their behavior.

DEATH AND BEREAVEMENT

The death of a member is in itself a disruption of the family and under certain conditions may lead to complete family disruption. The focus in the following discussion, however, will be on bereavement, which is the personal reaction of members of the family to the death of a husband, wife, son, or daughter. The topics to be treated are (1) variations in mourning patterns by different cultural groups, (2) common reactions to the death of a family member, (3) individual differences in bereavement, (4) influence of the "dead hand" over the family, (5) idealization of the deceased member, (6) adjustment of persons to a death of a member, and (7) adjustment of families to bereavement.

Widows and Widowers In 1968 there were 9.3 million widows and 2.1 million widowers in the United States. This refers to current marital status and not to those who have ever been widowed. The larger number of widows than widowers is due to two factors: (1) Women have a longer life expectancy than men; in 1968, white men and women at age 20 could expect to live to age 70.2 and 76.9 respectively; Negro men and women, 64.8 and 71.3, respectively.[13] And (2) a greater percent of widowers remarry. Widowed men are more inclined or find it easier to remarry than do widowed women. Part of the difference is the result of the greater incidence of remarried younger widowers.

Variations in Mourning Patterns The folkways and mores of bereavement differ by culture, region, class, and religion. Padilla describes behavior among Puerto Ricans in times of crisis such as death:

> Women especially may express their grief with an "attack" (ataque). The pattern involves loud screaming, falling to the floor while keeping the arms rigidly extended and the hands clenched, and occasionally shaking. . . . Men are expected to show their sorrow without tears. Their grief is "inside." Yet a man is not criticized for crying or having an attack. . . . Family members who do not conform to these expectations about grief and who continue to go about their daily routine without overtly showing their discomfort over the situation are said to "lack sentiments." Resentment over this behavior . . . may lead to extending disapproval to other areas of their lives. It is considered an essential quality of a good and worthwhile person that he "have sentiment."[14]

The Irish wake, a gathering of relatives, friends, and acquaintances prior to burial, may become an occasion for congenial visiting. In some rural communities intimate friends and relatives come to the home of the deceased in the evening of the day on which the death occurred to offer condolences but incidentally to visit with one another. The practice

---

[13] *Current Population Reports, Population Characteristics*, Series P-20, No. 187, 1969; and *Statistical Abstract of the United States*, 1969, p. 54.
[14] Elena Padilla, *Up From Puerto Rico* (New York: Columbia University Press, 1958), pp. 115–116.

of survivors of the deceased providing a meal after the funeral persists in many communities.

The family plot in the community cemetery is part of the rural culture. When one mate dies, a joint tombstone may be bought, symbolizing the affection and unity of the couple and the expectation of being side by side in death as they were in life. In the process of urbanization, bereavement customs have become more formal and secular. The following shows the secular attitude of a wife being buried beside her husband:

> To make matters worse my mother and stepfather quarreled about religion. He told her she would have to join his church if she expected to be buried beside him when she died, for that is the rule of the burying grounds of his church. She flatly refused and did not seem to be worried over the prospect of being buried elsewhere.

Changes in bereavement customs under the impact of urban life are also revealed in the use of funeral parlors and chapels, mausoleums, and crematories; in the signing of one's name in a book at a funeral parlor, rather than going to the home of the deceased to offer condolences; and in newspaper notices to announce a death and the place and time of funeral services and to thank friends for sympathy.

The shock of bereavement is so universal that in every society there has grown up a set of folkways defining the expected behavior of those who are bereaved and the ways in which the group participates. Group participation in ceremonies assists in carrying the survivors through the crisis. Incidentally, it gives the bereaved something to do. In our society, particularly in villages and rural areas, relatives, neighbors, and friends come to the immediate aid of the bereaved and join in a formal ritual. The social function of this ritual is to give community support during the initial part of the bereavement crisis. In some societies the convention is to leave the members of the bereaved family alone.

The function of mourning is to provide the surviving family members with socially sanctioned patterns of behavior which enable them to adjust to the idea of the death of the loved one and to reorganize habitual responses interrupted by his passing. The prolongation of mourning in certain contemporary societies and in our own three or four generations ago was designed to maintain the memory of the deceased and to prevent the person from resuming normal social intercourse. At present there is a tendency in our society to shorten the duration of mourning and its outword manifestations, and to encourage the emancipation of the bereaved from the departed through the early resumption of their usual community activities and relationships.

Psychologically the prolonging of mourning appears to be present in the following situations: (1) when there has been a deep emotional attachment to the deceased, (2) when the survivor has feelings of guilt because of attitudes and behavior toward the deceased in his lifetime, and (3) when one's interests and activities have been restricted almost completely to the departed.

Reactions to Bereavement Upon the death of a member, the survivors of an emotionally interdependent and united family feel frustrated and experience acute sorrow.

Frustration results from the interruption of acts which are dependent for their fulfillment on acts of the deceased. When a family is united, there is consensus, sympathetic understanding, common values, and division of labor among the members. The removal of one of those involved in the network of interdependent activities imposes a devastating frustration on the habitual behavior of the survivors. When an act is blocked, it tends to complete itself in imagination. But in bereavement the person, while conscious of his imaginary behavior, constantly realizes that the act can never be completed, for the loved one is gone forever. When ingrained habits are blocked, a person experiences acute suffering. The phenomenon of grief is an extreme form of loneliness intensified by the absoluteness of personal loss. In addition, a person may experience remorse and extreme distress associated with a sense of guilt. He may wish that he had done more for the deceased and may blame himself for not providing better care during the period of sickness.

Blocked habits may get expression in hallucinatory experiences, such as the bereaved sensing the presence of the deceased; in fantasy in which old experiences involving the deceased are relived in imagination; or in bereavement dreams. In sleep, the reality of death is less definite and absolute, and ingrained habits involving the deceased find expression. The bereavement dream reveals the dynamics of the conflict over the crisis of death.

The emotional trauma experienced by the death of a spouse can cause death of the surviving mate soon thereafter. A team of research scientists made a five-year study of 4,486 widowers, aged 55 or older. They found that the death rate of widowers was excessive during the first six months after the wife's death. This might be due to such things as the widower could have been infected with the same disease which resulted in the death of the wife; a joint unfavorable environment; and widowers may become malnourished when they no longer have wives to look after them. Their conclusion, however, is that "a more potent influence is the desolation effect immediately after bereavement."[15]

[15] Reported by Patricia McCormack, "Heartbreak: Is It One of the Killers?", *Los Angeles Times*, Dec. 12, 1963, Part 4, p. 24. Reported in *Lancet*, a British medical journal.

Increased physical and psychological stress after bereavement is also indicated by increases in the consultation of physicians by bereaved persons. A study in England found recent widows consulted their physicians for physical illness one and one-half times more frequently than they had during a control period.[16] In addition to physical illness, widows under 65 pears old also experienced psychiatric symptoms during the first six months of bereavement at a rate three times that of a control period and were given prescriptions for sedatives at a rate seven times greater.

A person experiencing bereavement may engage in violent reactions, cursing the doctor and the nurses for inadequate care or shouting against God for taking the loved one away. He may try to drown his sufferings through drink. Still another reaction may be a feeling of relief that the loved one is removed from his suffering or that death has liberated the survivor from the restraining influence of the deceased. Marriage is a combination of harmony and disharmony and involves a certain amount of confinement. Death frees the bereaved to act in ways which may have been taboo for him when he was expected to play certain roles.

The above reactions to bereavement are documented, in part, in a study by Marris, who interviewed 72 relatively young widows (average age 42) in East London and found a number of different reactions to bereavement.[17] He limited his analysis to reactions spontaneously described by the widows. The following five reactions were experienced by different proportions of these widows: (1) prolonged difficulty in sleeping, 79 percent; (2) withdrawal from people and loss of interest in life, 75 percent; (3) loss of contact with reality, especially a sense of the dead husband's presence and acting as if the husband were still present, 65 percent; (4) lasting deterioration in health, 42 percent; and (5) hostility toward a physician or pronounced resentment toward fate, 35 percent. These widows found much support and companionship in their extended families but these relationships did not increase to compensate for the loss of the husband.

Individual Differences in Bereavement Personal differences in reactions to bereavement vary with sex and age; degree of relationship; the nature, occasion, and suddenness of death; the extent to which the survivor engaged in outside-the-home activities; and the extent of emancipation from the deceased. Death does not mean much to the child of

[16] C. Murray Parkes, "Effect of Bereavement on Physical and Mental Health," *British Medical Journal*, 2-5404 (1964): pp. 274–279.
[17] Peter Marris, *Widows and Their Families* (London: Routledge and Kegan Paul, 1958), pp. 21–22, 68–85, and 145.

three or four. The following excerpt shows that very young children have not been given social definitions of how to behave in bereavement:

> I was probably three years old when my grandfather died. My first thought seems to have been that I might possess his razor and hone, which I had viewed enviously and had been denied the handling of. I have been told that while others were moaning over his bed I tried to confiscate the shaving tools but was caught.

Sudden bereavement increases the difficulty of adjustment, whereas a death which is foreseen is felt with less intensity. The following shows how an eleven-year-old boy reacted, first to the death of his father who had been sick a long time, and a year later to the sudden death of an older sister:

> At Father's death, I was eleven years old. I was called to his bedside as he was breathing his last, and it was an extremely peaceful passing. He had been sick for so long that I couldn't possibly realize the significance of the removal of the head of the house.
> That night I was sent over to my chum's house and he took me to the Boy Scout meeting as his guest. I rather questioned whether or not it was the thing to do; but nobody said it wasn't and I did want to go.
> The funeral was held two days later and many of Father's relatives came to pay their last respects. I was terribly shocked at the matter-of-factness of some of these relatives; but at the same time, I was more conscious of my actions than I had been before. I watched the other members of the family and tried to pattern my feelings after their actions. The grief manifested, the silence, the simple funeral service touched me deeply. It wasn't so much the thought that my father had died, but the emotional effect of the whole affair that made me feel badly and weep with the others.
> A year later my sister Fern was very sick and nurses were almost impossible to get. One evening Mother went out to a movie to relax and I offered to stay with Fern. She was partly delirious. These two hours will never leave my memory. I loved Fern dearly and I prayed fervently and passionately for her recovery the better part of those two hours.
> She was taken to a hospital and died two days later. It was no feigned grief this time, but an experience—a poignant, hurting sensation.

A father contrasts his feelings almost of relief at the death of his crippled son with his terrible shock at the sudden death of his wife:

> We were delighted with the thought that our first [child] would not have to grow up alone, but would have a playmate almost her own age. But we were doomed to disappointment. The second baby was undernourished and partly paralyzed. . . . When at last he passed on, it gave almost a sense of relief, and yet there was a terrible longing for the lad that he might have been.
> After we had been married about six years, my wife was found to have

a tumor. . . . She went to the hospital, confidently expecting to be back home in a couple of weeks. . . . [After the operation] peritonitis set in and within ten days she was gone. The shock was something I cannot possibly describe. I could hardly eat; I had a constant feeling of nausea. Mentally I was full of self-accusation for not having taken the whole case more seriously and provided more adequately.[18]

Men behave differently in bereavement than women, in part because of differences in cultural expectations, and in part because they have occupational activities demanding their attention and are more likely to spend more time away from the objects which remind them of the deceased.

It is evident that the reactions to a death, at least in outward expression, will differ by its nature and occasion. Family members will react differently if the deceased died through suicide, from an infectious disease, from injuries received in rescuing another, or in battle. Eliot points out that wives of men in the Navy are used to long separations and are prepared to face the risk of having husbands who undergo the hazards of wartime.[19]

The "Dead Hand" The influence of a father, a mother, a husband, or a wife continues after death. In some cases it is a controlling factor, as with the young woman who reports the following:

I am forever being inclined to stop and think to myself, "Would Father want me to?" He was the one to whom I told everything and who taught me right from wrong.

Occasionally a parent consciously attempts to prolong his control by calling the family together for his last words and pledging them to certain actions. A person may also seek to maintain his control over family members after death through legal means. A husband may create a trust fund for his widow, with the stipulation that the income from it will cease if she marries again. A father may provide in his will that a daughter will forfeit her part of the estate if she marries before a certain age, or that a son will not receive his share until he marries.

Idealization of the Dead The hold of the dead over the living is markedly increased by the process of idealization. The dead have an advantage over the living in the sense that in memory their faults tend to be forgotten and their good qualities exaggerated. The highly selec-

[18] Thomas D. Eliot, "The Bereaved Family," *The Annals of the American Academy of Political and Social Science*, 160 (1932): p. 189.
[19] Thomas D. Eliot, "—of the Shadow of Death," *The Annals of the American Academy of Political and Social Science*, 229 (1943): p. 88.

tive memories of the deceased gradually become integrated into an idealized person. This tendency to dismiss the faults of the deceased and to stress his fine qualities is illustrated by Dickinson and Beam, who studied 40 widows and reported that the group between 40 and 60 years of age tended to idealize relationships with their husband, particularly those relating to sex:

> The marriages now appear sexually golden. . . . Wifehood was happy. Sex life with the husband was interesting and desirable. The wife, smoothed and tranquilized by time, had assimilated the experience of marriage and viewed it with the sympathy accorded to one's own life.[20]

Adjustments of Persons to Bereavement The suffering connected with bereavement is so severe that normally a person tries to get relief from it. A remorseful person, however, may tend to seek self-punishment through prolongation of the sorrow. Some people adjust to an unpleasant experience by attempting to drive out all thought of it from the mind. Many bereaved spouses marry again as a means of relieving their suffering and loneliness. In a society in which so many social activities are by pairs, the death of a mate necessitates either considerable social isolation or remarriage. If the survivor is left with small children, the selection of a new mate may be viewed as a desirable method of taking care of the children. In some cases a surviving mate has idealized the deceased to such an extent that no living man or woman could possibly measure up to the mental picture of the former mate. Remarriage in such cases brings disappointment and disillusionment. This difficulty shows up in divorced persons whose previous marriage ended in widowhood, the typical reaction being to think of the deceased mate as "my husband" or "my wife." The new mate may also be at a disadvantage as a stepparent. A daughter's idealized conception of her father in the following case made it difficult for her to develop affection for the new father:

> My stepfather is, I am ashamed to admit, nothing but an outsider as far as our family life is concerned. He serves as a means of protection and of aiding the finances of the family. Both my sister and I call him "Dad" but there is no affection in the term; it is merely a convenience.

Adjustments of Families to Bereavement Death usually results in family members drawing together in the bereavement period. If one member is inconsolable, the other members assume the burden of comforting him, even though grief-stricken themselves. The loss of a child may bring

---

[20] Robert L. Dickinson and Lura Beam, *A Thousand Marriages* (Baltimore: Williams and Wilkins, 1931), p. 276.

husband and wife together; the loss of a mother or father may cement the others more firmly. Moreover, the idealized picture of the deceased may become the sentimental rallying point for a family.

Death of a member alters the configuration of the family. When the performer of a certain role passes from the scene, another member of the family usually succeeds to it. Acting a new part in family relationships may result in profound alterations in the habits of a person. For example, the death of his father tends to force a son to assume responsibility for duties and obligations previously performed by the father.

Very little is known about the adjustments of children to death. Some studies have been made in communities where disaster has occurred and children have experienced death of persons intimately involved in their lives. One such study examined the reactions of 29 children in 14 families in two small northern Mississippi Negro communities.[21] The conclusion was that the child's way of responding to a community disaster which killed members of his family and his friends was influenced "not only by the parent's own disaster reaction, but also by structural aspects of the family and community systems." The investigators presented two circumstances which they felt facilitated the children's adjustment to disaster and bereavement: (1) The nuclear families were sufficiently integrated into their extended families so that there were persons with affectional ties available to take care of the children when the parents could not. And (2) both before and after bereavement, the children had responsible roles involving work for the family welfare. These roles were usually enlarged by the death of a family member and acted as a stabilizing force for the child. Moreover, the children were allowed to discuss the disaster and deaths openly, perhaps partly because of the enormity of the impact of the disaster on the two small communities.

Contrasting Attitudes Toward the Bereaved and the Divorced In our society divorced persons are presented with no socially sanctioned means of adjustment such as those available to the bereaved. In bereavement there is a tendency to concentrate on the best traits of the departed and to give assistance to the survivors; in divorce there is a tendency to condemn the defects of one or both spouses. In bereavement the individual secures comfort and group support by the rallying around of his friends and relatives; the divorced may be confronted with gossip, unfriendliness, and the taking of sides by relatives. In bereavement it is expected that the normal person will show some signs of emotional

[21] Helen S. Perry and Stewart E. Perry, *The School-House Disasters: Family and Community as Determinants of the Child's Response to Disaster* (Washington, D.C.: National Academy of Sciences, 1959).

disturbance; a divorced person who shows signs of emotional disturbance is given little consideration—in fact, he may be thought of as emotionally unbalanced. In bereavement the person may receive consolation from his religion; the divorced may be confronted with negative evaluations from religious groups. In bereavement catharsis is secured through participation in religious ceremonies; the divorced may experience an increase in emotional disturbance through the necessity of resorting to legal advice and court procedures.

Thus the divorce situation is one the individual has to handle more or less on his own. Cut off from emotional attachments and interdependent activities with his spouse and possibly his children, the divorced person is inclined to feel frustrated, alone, and forsaken. Prior habits have not prepared him for this new situation.

UNIFORMITIES OF CRISES

The following are uniformities manifested in the crises discussed in the previous chapter—deviation from expectations, disgrace, and economic reverses—and those presented in this chapter—departure of family members, divorce, and death.

Situations resulting in family crises, other than that of death, are for the most part the outgrowth of major social changes of the last hundred years. Deviations from expectations are more common today because increased mobility and ease of communication have created situations in which there are heterogeneous folkways and mores. Periodic depressions have accompanied the development of industrialization. Because of the relatively recent origin of these social changes, there has been insufficient time for the development of controls, rituals, ceremonies, and definitions of expected behavior for these crises. Consequently, a person experiencing the crises of deviation from expectations, disgrace, depression, or divorce has his routine activities interrupted or blocked; he may not know how to act in the new situation; he gets little or no help from group support; and he has no blueprints on how to behave.

Reactions and adjustments of families to crises vary from culture to culture, region to region, class to class, by age and sex groups, with the suddenness of the crisis, with one's prior experiences with similar crises, with the emotional interdependence of family members, and with the personality characteristics of those involved.

Reactions to a crisis may include one or more of the following: a feeling of shock and numbness; sensations of physical illness; reactions of frustration and futility; self-punishment; thinking about or committing suicide; psychological isolation from others by continuance in imagination of the pre-crisis situation and relationships; withdrawing within oneself; engaging in aggressive behavior toward others, including physical violence; conflict between family members; demoralization; talking over the crisis with friends, relatives, or a professional consultant; adoption of a new role in the family; exclusion of the critical situation from one's mind; moving to a new location; forgetting the crisis by throwing oneself into activities which capture the attention, such as reading detective stories, or overexertion in one's occupation; and development of a new activity or interest.

The period of maladjustment and emotional stress is manifested in the early stages of the crisis and typically is followed either by adjustment or chronic maladjustment.

Well-organized families meet a crisis with less catastrophic consequences than families already disintegrating or disorganized. Extreme emotional reactions are least in families in which the members have developed self-sufficiency and greatest in those in which there is great emotional dependency. When emotional dependence has characterized family relationships, crises result in extremely difficult problems of adjustment.

A crisis releases emotions and breaks down inhibitions which have served as barriers to communication. The removal of these barriers may result in sympathetic expressions or hostile behavior. Under these conditions a person may get surprising insight into the thoughts and character of other family members. If the crisis is resolved, a person may have a better understanding of his obligations to other family members. A crisis puts family relationships to the test of emotional strain, revealing their strong points and their weaknesses.

The adaptability of family members determines the ease of adjustment to a crisis. A flexible person is not bound to routine activities and convention and is willing to change his behavior in response to changed situations.

Crises in one field of behavior, such as deviations from expectations or disgrace, may result in crises in other fields of behavior, such as economic adversity or divorce.

SUMMARY

A family is a network of interdependent activities of two or more persons who are joined together by common attitudes, values, and objectives, and by emotional attachments. The departure of children, divorce, or bereavement disrupts this network of relationships and makes it difficult or impossible to continue sharing attitudes, values, objectives, and emotional attachments. This means that some activities are eliminated, and others have to be modified.

The disruption generally results in frustration, emotional tensions, and a feeling of not knowing how to handle the new situation.

The degree to which family disruption results in a crisis depends, in part, on the degree of emotional involvement, the strength of the network of interdependent activities, and the suddenness of the disruption.

Some family crises, such as bereavement, are mediated through social expectations of how to behave in the crisis situation, by ritual, and by the support of relatives and friends. These are almost completely lacking in other crises, such as divorce. For example, death is still generally regarded as an act of God, while divorce is only too evidently human behavior. In addition, divorce carries with it, in the attitudes of the public and of the couple, the implication of failure.

PROBLEMS FOR RESEARCH

Projects significant for research on family disruption should be undertaken on departure of family members, separation and divorce, and death.

Departure of Family Members A comparative study might be made of the reactions of parents to a child's leaving home to be married, to go to college, or to take a position in another city. Among the hypotheses to be tested would be that the extent and intensity of the crisis for the parents depends on (1) the degree of attachment of the parent to the child, (2) the presence and vitality of interests outside the home, and (3) the extent of the maintenance of the affectional relation between the parents and the child by visits and letters.

Separation and Divorce Separation and divorce have been studied mainly as the culmination and termination of tension between husband and wife. Research from this standpoint needs to be continued with special emphasis on (1) the basic factors in alienation, and (2) personal and community reactions to the experience of divorce. Studies should also be made on the effect of divorce on children at various ages. A significant study could be made of the impact of the parents' divorce on the personality development and behavior of the child, as compared with an inharmonious home environment when parents remain married for the sake of the children. Especially valuable would be a comparative study of the factors in successful and unsuccessful relationships of divorced parents to their children.

Death Many problems of the reaction of family members to the crisis of death await study. Among these are (1) the role of mourning among different peoples as a form of familial and social control; (2) the function of mourning in personal adjustment to the death of a loved one; (3) individual differences in the intensity and duration of bereavement; and (4) the persistence of control by the deceased spouse or parent, or the emancipation of the survivor.

QUESTIONS AND EXERCISES

1. Explain the variations in divorce from nation to nation, from state to state, and between country and city.
2. In what situations does divorce represent little or no crisis to those involved? How do you explain the absence of crisis in certain cases?
3. How do you account for the fact that divorce is frequently a greater crisis for one mate than for the other?
4. What are the different types of adjustment to crises?
5. What are the likenesses and differences between the crisis of divorce and the crisis of bereavement?
6. Differentiate between mourning and remorse. What is the function of mourning in the adjustment to bereavement?
7. Analyze individual differences in reaction to bereavement from the viewpoint of (a) emotional involvement, (b) the meaning of death, and (c) social expectations.

BIBLIOGRAPHY

Blake, Nelson Manfred. *The Road to Reno.* New York: Macmillan, 1962.
    An examination of the legal history of divorce in America from colonial times to the present. Gives particular attention to political issues associated with divorce laws in the various states.

Goode, William J. *After Divorce.* New York: Free Press, 1956.
    Interview study of 425 divorced mothers in Detroit. Data collected in 1948. Considers social background of subjects, characteristics of prior marriages, and adjustment activities of the divorced mothers.

Gorer, Geoffrey. *Death, Grief, and Mourning in Contemporary Britain.* London: The Cresset Press, 1965.
    Certain information was secured from a sample of 903. Of these subjects, 80 were interviewed by Gorer. Discusses religion and the bereaved, the funeral, grief and mourning, styles of mourning, and types of bereavement.

Jacobson, Paul H.; and Jacobson, Pauline F. *American Marriage and Divorce.* New York: Rinehart, 1959.
    Gives statistics on chances of marriage and of remarriage, the duration of

marriage and of widowhood, frequency of racial intermarriage, the probabilities of divorce and widowhood, and many other topics.

Marris, Peter. *Widows and Their Families.* London: Routledge and Kegan Paul, 1958.

One of three volumes reporting the Institute of Community Studies research investigation of a community in East London. Presents the findings of an interview study of 72 widows whose husbands died in youth or middle age. Chapters 1 through 6 discuss the responses of these widows to bereavement and the adjustments made in their living situations. Chapters 7 and 8 deal with the economic conditions of these widows under the British social-insurance system.

Perry, Helen Swick; and Perry, Stewart E. *The Schoolhouse Disasters: Family and Community as Determinants of the Child's Response to Disaster.* Washington: National Academy of Sciences, 1959.

A brief report on bereavement in families in two Negro communities in Mississippi. Examines factors related to the response of children to death in their families caused by a natural disaster. Suggests family structure and role relationships may be related to children's response to bereavement.

Chapter 22
War and the Family

> *War is one of the major crises which the family has periodically experienced. Total war, as exemplified by World War II, drastically affects the family by mobilizing not only men but women for service in the armed forces, home defense, war industries, and other essential activities. No family of any belligerent nation is immune, though the effect of the war on families varies widely by the nature and degree of the participation of their members in the war effort. Even the threat or possibility of war has an impact on a large number of families.*

WAR AND INTERPERSONAL RELATIONSHIPS IN THE FAMILY

The following document shows how World War II affected an American family. It illustrates how the induction of a son, a fiance, or another family member affects family relationships:

> I am an only child of a fairly typical urban middle-class family. I was born in New York City and spent most of my life in that part of the city known as Greenwich Village. My father has worked in the same factory since shortly after he was married. It has been a secure and steady job, bringing in an adequate income even during the depths of the depression.
>
> Four years ago I was in my third year in high school. There had never been any doubt that I would go to college. I had always wanted to go to what I called a go-away college, one that was out of New York City. Mother would have liked to be able to send me to one of the better schools, but family finances were already running a bit tight as the cost of living began to rise. So I made my plans to go to one of the free city colleges for the first two years.
>
> Pearl Harbor came at the end of that year and things began to happen. My father's job turned into defense work, as the factory where he worked was converted to war production. Rationing came. The war had almost no

effect on our lives. Dad went to work every morning and came home every night as he had always done.

The most momentous change came in the summer of 1942. I graduated from high school in June and left the following day for camp, where I had a job as an arts and crafts counselor. July 14 I met David, who is now my husband. I still clung to the idea that I was to finish college and work for a year or two before marriage. The war hysteria was not hitting my friends in the same way that it seemed to hit other people. There was no mad rush to marry. David was still a civilian, a counselor at a neighboring camp. At the end of the summer he enlisted in an eight-months army training program and I decided I wanted to get married. But to no avail. He knew that he would be in uniform in eight months and then it would be overseas action in a short time. He did not think it fair to ask a girl to marry a man who might be crippled for life. All my arguments (they were good ones) did not sway him, so we compromised and were engaged.

My parents did not object, for they did not take it seriously. I was just starting college and they were sure that I would not remain with David any longer than I had with the other boys I had gone steady with.

My fiance left for a nearby camp; I continued at school. Then in the summer of 1943 I went to work during the day and to school at night. I did not want to leave the city with David stationed so near. By now Mother and Dad were beginning to like him and were taking our engagement more seriously. Luck would have it that David was chosen for the Army Specialized Training Program and was sent to the College of the City of New York for his tests and assignment. When that happened, I'm afraid that his will gave way to his desires. Nine months longer in the states were likely if he passed the tests. How or when he decided we would get married, I do not know. I only remember that we had agreed to do so if he passed. He phoned to tell me that he had passed and that I should take my blood test; he was applying for a three-day pass to get married. I blithely announced this news to my mother, and we were married. It was contrary to all my previous plans and expectations and the plans of both my parents. I was only nineteen and a sophomore in college. In normal times I would not have taken such steps at such a dizzy pace; I would have stopped to think a little longer first, but I have no doubt that the end results would have been the same. I would have married David before I finished college.

This case discloses that for Americans the chief effects of a war have been not those caused by restrictions or a change from civilian to wartime employment, but rather the crises which it occasions in family relationships. Other cases indicate the emotional disturbances involved in the speeding up of the processes of acquaintance, courtship, engagement, and marriage; the dispersion of family members; family disruption with the departure of its members; anxiety for the safety of a loved one at the front, the agony of suspense if he is reported missing, and the mourning if he is killed; and concern with the many difficult problems of postwar adjustment.

The problems arising from the impact of war or the possibility of war on the family will be treated under the following headings: (1) significance of the dispersion of family members, (2) marriage in wartime, (3) family disorganization, and (4) postwar problems of the family.

DISPERSION OF FAMILY MEMBERS

Modern war or preparation for war disturbs the settled habits of millions of persons, greatly extends their social contacts and, by separating family members, interferes with the communication by which family unity is maintained and promoted.

Significance of Dispersion of Family Members Changes in group folkways, personal habits, and interpersonal family relationships are inevitable when millions of persons move into new situations. Shocks and strains are bound to occur when individual members of families and families as groups are uprooted from their customary surroundings and dispersed to the four corners of the nation and the world. They have little or no sense of belonging to community groups, for they will be on their way again soon, and consequently do not exert themselves to get established in the new community.

Moving to an army camp or defense community may be likened to a rural person's moving into a large city. Such persons come in contact with behaviors which are different from the patterns of the home community. Married men in the service have to adjust their family habits and sex life to the habits, values, and mores of a predominantly male society. Eating and sleeping habits, religious beliefs and practices, recreational interests, and philosophy of life may be modified as dispersed persons rub elbows with strangers. Alien behavior, previously repulsive, may through continued association be tolerated or practiced.

The father who is separated from his wife and children attempts to keep contact and influence his children through letters, but it is difficult for him to continue his contribution to their personality development. Hundreds of thousands of the soldiers in World War II and thousands of Korean and Vietnam men had children born after their departure. In many families the absence of the father meant that the chief disciplinarian had been removed. This came at a time when the mother and other adult members of the family were disturbed and preoccupied by new problems. Moreover, a returning serviceman may find it difficult to adjust to his child, whom he has never seen, or to children who have grown into strangers during his absence.

Stolz studied the father-child relationships of first-born children born while their fathers were at war.[1] She used only 19 families, and consequently the findings should be viewed with caution. Some comparisons were made with a control group of families never separated. The children were young when the fathers returned, the average age being 18 months. The general conclusions were: (1) A typical pattern of early response to the father's return was a shy withdrawal by the child, followed somewhat later by stern disciplinary action by the father. (2) The war-separated fathers, as compared with those never separated, were more concerned about and more annoyed by their children's behavior in eating, sleeping, and elimination. (3) The war-separated children had more serious problems in eating, sleeping, and elimination, and more fears and expression of tension. (4) The war-separated children established less satisfactory relationships with other children and had more distant relationships with their fathers.

If husbands and wives have a prolonged separation, communication may become irregular and more formal; time and attention are consumed by immediate, pressing problems, with the resulting psychological withdrawal of the members from one another. The tendency toward disruption is especially likely when previous communication has been insufficient to provide the sharing of experiences and common feelings, attitudes, and ideals essential to a durable relationship.

MARRIAGE AND BIRTHS IN WARTIME

Marriage is immediately and profoundly affected by war or preparation for war. This is evident in many ways: (1) the changes in the marriage and birth rates; (2) the characteristic shifts in the attitudes and behavior of young people who are forced to adjust their plans to wartime conditions; and (3) the different types of war marriage, the reasons for marrying in wartime, and the prognosis for the success or failure of war marriages.

Marriage Rates The effect of World Wars I and II on marriage rates is shown in Table 30, which gives the annual marriages per 1,000 population for the years 1911–1924 and 1935–1950 for the United States, England and Wales, France, Germany, Italy, and Switzerland. The lowest rates for each period are in boldface, and the highest rates are in italics.

[1] Lois Meek Stolz, et al., *Father Relations of War-Born Children* (Stanford: Stanford University Press, 1954).

Table 30. Marriages per 1,000 population in certain countries, 1911-1924, and 1935-1950*

Year	United States	England and Wales	France	Germany (Berlin after 1935)	Italy	Switzerland
1911–1913	10.4	7.8	7.7	7.8	7.5	7.2
1914	10.5	7.9	5.1	6.8	7.0	5.7
1915	10.1	9.7	2.3	4.1	5.1	5.0
1916	10.7	7.5	3.3	4.1	2.9	5.7
1917	11.2	6.9	4.8	4.7	2.7	6.0
1918	9.7	7.7	5.5	5.4	3.0	6.7
1919	11.0	9.9	14.0	13.4	9.2	7.9
1920	12.0	10.1	16.0	14.5	14.0	9.0
1921	10.8	8.5	11.6	11.9	11.5	8.4
1922	10.3	7.9	9.8	11.1	9.6	7.7
1923	11.0	7.6	8.9	9.5	8.7	7.6
1924	10.5	7.7	8.8	7.1	7.9	7.3
1935–1938	10.7	8.7	6.8	11.0	7.6	7.3
1939–1942	12.2	10.0	5.9	11.3	6.7	8.1
1943	11.5	7.0	5.7	9.6	4.9	8.3
1944	10.5	7.1	5.4	8.7	5.0	8.0
1945	11.5	9.3	10.1	6.9	6.8	8.1
1946	16.2	9.0	12.8	6.7	9.2	8.7
1947	13.8	9.3	10.5	8.2	9.4	8.7
1948	12.4	9.1	9.1	9.3	8.3	8.5
1949	10.6	8.5	8.2	8.9	7.6	8.0
1950	11.0	8.3	8.1	—	7.5	8.0

*1911–1924 data from "The Marriage Rate in Wartime," Metropolitan Life Insurance Company, *Statistical Bulletin*, November 1939, p. 6; 1939–1950 data from "Recent International Marriage Trends," *ibid.*, 32, June 1952, p. 2.

First, let us consider World War I for the United States, England and Wales, neutral Switzerland, France, Germany, and Italy. In all these countries the marriage rate rose during the early period of entrance of men into the armed services, declined during the years of war, increased during the first two postwar years, and then returned to normal in the third postwar year.

In the 1939–1950 period the rise and fall of the marriage rate in the United States was strongly affected by the imminence of World War II, the war itself, the aftermath of the war, and the Korean conflict. First there was the introduction and passage of the Selective Service Act. The monthly marriage rate[2] jumped from the May, 1940, rate of 9.6 to

[2] Figured on an annual basis.

14.1 in June, the month in which the Selective Service Act was introduced in Congress; it receded to 12.0 in July, and then, with the passage of the Selective Service Act in September, reached the peak of 14.7.[3] Marriages during August, September, and October, 1940, were 25 percent more numerous than in the corresponding months of 1939.

The movement of millions of American men overseas was accompanied by a decline in the marriage rate from the middle of 1942 through the early months of 1945. The close of hostilities in Europe in May, 1945, and in the Pacific in August, 1945 resulted in an immediate and marked upswing in the marriage rate. In 1946 the marriage rate was 16.2, which was the highest recorded rate. Thereafter the rate declined. With the attack on South Korea in June of 1950 and the military action of the United Nations, there was an immediate boom in marriages, and this increased rate continued until March of 1951.[4]

Birth Rate In the United States the birth rate rose for the two years before entrance into World War II and continued to increase until 1943. The prewar year of 1940 with a higher birth rate (17.9) than any year since 1931, was surpassed by 1941 (18.9), by 1942 (20.9), and by 1943 (21.5). The higher rates for 1941, 1942, and 1943 followed the sharp rise in the marriage rate. Also contributing to the high rates of the 1941–1943 period was the decision of an indeterminate number of previously childless couples to have a child as a possible ground for deferment of the husband from selective service; others, with a husband in the service and a wife at home, desired a child as a link between them. Hauser, after plotting the crude birth rate by months for the 1939–1941 period, showed that birth-rate peaks occurred about nine months after the passage of compulsory conscription.[5]

Birth-rate trends from prewar, through war, and to the postwar period are indicated in Table 31, which shows the birth rate of various countries between 1937 and 1949. The figures in boldface are for the years with the highest rate. For belligerents, with the exception of Italy, Austria, and Western Germany, it was in the postwar years of 1945, 1946, or 1947. The higher rates in the years immediately following World War II were not generally preceded by unusually low rates, as in World War I. The table shows that most countries had higher birth rates during the war than in the 1937–1939 period. The table also

---

[3] Bureau of the Census; also Philip M. Hauser, "Population and Vital Phenomena," *American Journal of Sociology*, 48 (1942): p. 313.

[4] See Metropolitan Life Insurance Company, *Statistical Bulletin*, 32, December 1951, pp. 3–5.

[5] Philip M. Hauser, p. 312.

shows the percent changes in the birth rate from 1947 to 1949. In all countries except West Germany the birth rate had a small decline.

Table 31. Birth rates for selected countries, 1937-1949*

Country	\multicolumn{7}{c	}{BIRTHS PER 1,000 POPULATION}	\multicolumn{2}{c	}{PERCENT CHANGE}
	1949	1948	1947	1946	1945	1940-1944	1937-1939	1947 to 1949	1937-1939 to 1949
United States	23.9	24.2	25.8	23.3	19.6	19.9	17.3	−7	+38
England and Wales	16.7	17.8	20.5	19.2	15.9	15.5	14.9	−19	+12
France	21.0	21.2	21.3	20.9	16.5	14.9	14.9	−1	+41
Western Germany	16.6	16.5	16.5	15.0	—	—	—	+1	−15
Italy	20.0	21.6	21.9	22.7	18.5	20.9	23.4	−9	−15
Austria	15.8	17.7	18.6	15.9	14.9	19.1	15.8	−15	0
Japan	33.2	33.4	34.3	25.3	23.2	30.1	28.2	−3	+18
Belgium	17.2	17.6	17.8	18.3	15.7	13.9	15.6	−3	+10
Norway	19.6	20.5	21.4	22.6	20.2	17.7	15.7	−8	+25
Sweden	17.4	18.4	18.9	19.7	20.4	17.7	14.9	−8	+17
Switzerland	18.4	19.0	19.3	20.0	20.1	17.9	15.1	−5	+22

*Metropolitan Life Insurance Company, *Statistical Bulletin*, 32, March 1951, p. 7.

Modifications in the Sex Ratio War also disturbs the sex ratio (the number of men per 100 women). After World War I the surplus of women in the 20–39 age group for various countries was as follows: Germany, 2,021,000; France, 1,042,000; and England and Wales, 972,000.[6]

After World War II there was an excess of women in most of the major combatant countries. In 1950 the sex ratio for the 20–44 age group for various countries was as follows: Western Germany, 80.5; Japan, 90.0; Italy, 96.1; the United States, 96.9; and England and Wales, 98.7.[7] An unbalanced sex ratio affects mate selection.

The sex-ratio figures do not, however, give the entire picture of the

[6] Willard Waller, (ed.), *War in the Twentieth Century* (New York: The Dryden Press, 1940), pp. 418–419.
[7] Data from United Nations, *Demographic Yearbook, 1951* (New York: Statistical Office of the United Nations, Department of Economic Affairs, 1951), pp. 128–145.

lack of balance between the sexes. The postwar populations of various countries included large numbers of partially or totally disabled men unequal to the task of fulfilling the social expectations of the role of husband in providing a livelihood for a family.

The data on the increase in marriage rates at the onset of a war demonstrate that at the beginning of a war the factors making for marriage overbalance those preventing marriage. Insight into the nature of these influences and the reasons why so many young people marry in wartime is derived largely from a study of individual cases. Such a study indicates that a war brings about three types of marriages: postponed, hurried-up, and hasty.

Postponement of Marriage The involuntarily postponed marriage is one in which the young people are forced by circumstances to remain unmarried until after the war. Most men not engaged before entering the service remain single for the duration of a war. The voluntarily postponed union is one in which the young people are moved more by prudential considerations of the insecurity of war than by romantic reasons and, consequently, decide to wait until the war is over to marry.[8] Some of these weddings will never take place, either because one or the other will change his mind or because the young man will die or be incapacitated for marriage. Even for the couples that have decided to postpone marriage, there are various pressures which reopen the question of whether or not to marry in wartime, as in the following case:

> At present we are waiting to see what Roy's status will be in the army and whether he can afford to support a wife. I feel that if possible it is much better to be able to set up a home when getting married. If it were going to be only a year or a year and a half, we might wait; but we wouldn't want to wait for five or six years. Two friends have married during the past year. One is following her husband from camp to camp. The other has a baby and is living with her parents. That is pretty unsatisfactory. My ideal of setting up a home of our own and of being self-supporting is pretty strong, but we are terribly in love. While our present tendency is to postpone marriage, we may get married before Roy is inducted, even though the situation is very uncertain.

Hurried-Up Marriages Probably most marriages in wartime are hurried-up unions in which the marriage date is set ahead.[9] A common expres-

---

[8] On the other hand, a couple who have been postponing marriage in peacetime may be pushed into it by the war.

[9] Of course, not all war marriages are hasty or hurried-up unions. Many farm boys and boys in vital defense jobs get married and continue their regular work very much as they would in peacetime.

sion in World War II was "The war may make a difference in the time of marriage and affect us after we get married, but we would have gotten married anyway." In many cases, like the following, war shortens the period of courtship and engagement of couples who have known each other for several months, and who have similar ideas, ideals, and interests:

> The basic reasons for my decision to marry have nothing to do with the war. I've known John two years; his ideals, his religion, and his interests coincide with mine. I don't want to wait for the end of the war, which may be one year or ten years away. But there was another reason for my decision. I want to give him some reality to cling to. Really knowing that he has someone besides his parents praying for his return, he is apt to be less reckless in his undertakings. So we set the date ahead a little and got married.

However, the speeding up of courtship, engagement, and marriage does not permit the degree of selectivity which normally takes place. Probably a certain proportion of hurried-up war marriages would not have occurred in peacetime.

Hasty Marriages Hasty marriages may be defined as "meet and marry" unions. In World Wars I and II there were three types: First, there were marriages on short acquaintance to avoid the draft. Second, there were war-camp marriages, typically of the home-sick soldier or sailor and a girl attracted by the glamor of the uniform. The movement of soldiers from camp to camp made for casual contacts, and marriages often occurred after only a short period of acquaintance. A third type of hasty marriage was that of men in the overseas forces who fell in love with and married foreign girls. In World War II such marriages became so numerous that six months after its beginning the United States War Department prohibited military personnel on duty in any foreign country or possession of the United States from marrying without the consent of the commanding officer.[10] In September, 1942, when the Navy discovered that there were 167 marriages between Navy men and Australians in one single area, it put higher matrimonial hurdles before its men; in addition to the previous requirement of securing the consent of the commanding officer, the new regulation required the permission of Navy headquarters.[11]

Reasons for Marrying in Wartime The reasons given by persons for their acts are not necessarily the real reasons for their behavior. Social

---

[10] *New York Times*, June 21, 1942, Sec. I, p. 19.
[11] *Ibid.*, September 29, 1942, p. 4.

psychologists hold that, even though a person honestly attempts rationally to explain his behavior, he is often unable to uncover the hidden motivations and subtle influences which have determined it. The real reasons for marrying in wartime, therefore, should be distinguished from a person's rationalizations.

The reasons for marrying in wartime probably vary somewhat by country and in different wars. The following analysis, while applying particularly to World War II, is generally applicable:

1. Whenever there is a decline in the restraining influence of parents on young people, there will be a higher proportion of "hasty" and "hurried-up" wartime marriages. Freed from the prudential restraint of their elders, the romantic impulses of youth lead to many marriages based on short acquaintance, slight knowledge of each other, and insufficient provision for the economic and emotional security of the wife. One is more likely to marry in wartime if he is spatially separated from parents and emotionally and economically independent of them.

2. The person who is emancipated from the traditional conceptions of the approved method of getting acquainted, courting, and becoming engaged is more likely to marry in wartime than one who is not.

3. Some couples marry to obtain personal security in a world of uncertainty and chaos. A soldier may have a feeling of stability if he has a wife who belongs to him and awaits his return. Marriage is more binding than engagement, and a man may feel more secure if in the period of separation there is a decreased possibility of competition with others. The insecure girl, who feels less able to compete for the available men is likely to want the security of marriage rather than face the possibility of spinsterhood.

4. Wartime prosperity increases the marriage rate. In World War II high wages for young men in defense industries opened the door of marriage to many.

5. The romantic person is more likely than the realistic one to marry in wartime. The girl who feels that her lover may never return and wants to get as much happiness as possible now is more likely to marry than the girl who questions the wisdom of lovers marrying if they face the prospect of a prolonged separation.

Evaluating Wartime Marriages The general assumption is that the prognosis for success of hasty and hurried-up wartime marriages is unfavorable because of the short time the couple have known each other. What is important, however, is not the mere passage of time from the first meeting to marriage but the nature and stability of the relationship which has developed. Do the two persons know each other well enough to have a sound basis on which to build their future?

Have they vital, binding interests? Have they a similarity of ideas and ideals that will help carry them through the family problems of wartime? These are the important questions, and time is significant only as it permits the couple to answer them.

Marriage just before a long separation, however, means that family life for the couple is more fictitious than real. Although a marriage ceremony has taken place, the family is not organized into a unity of interacting persons. There is no more meshing of habits than had developed on the level of courtship. Such families will lack the consensus, division of labor, and sympathetic understanding which grow up in the process of establishing a home and living together.

FAMILY DISORGANIZATION AND REORGANIZATION

The acceleration of social changes during wartime or preparation for war is accompanied by many manifestations of family disorganization. These are apparent in the liberalization of the sexual code of young people; the relaxation of social controls over conduct; the decline in the establishment of the traditional home immediately following marriage; disruptions of the family through death and disability; and, in addition, the changes in the institutions with which the family is interrelated, such as the state, school, recreational agencies, and the church.

Attitudes Toward Sex and Marriage The increase of premarital intercourse after World War I[12] appears to have been further augmented by various conditions which accompanied World War II. For one thing, there was a decline in the value placed on virginity. Moreover, the fear of pregnancy was diminished by the use of contraceptives, and the danger of venereal infection lessened by preventives and prophylactics, with the possibilities of cure greatly increased.

In the code of the modern young urban person, the lessening value placed on chastity does not carry with it approval of promiscuity. For many such persons sexual intercourse is regarded as a privilege of engagement, permissible when two persons are in love, and to be condoned under certain other circumstances. But promiscuity on the part of a young woman and, to a lesser degree, of a young man draws group disapproval.

Relaxation of Social Controls In wartime, customs, conventions, laws, and the primary associations of home and neighborhood lose their effec-

---

[12] See Lewis M. Terman and others, *Psychological Factors in Marital Happiness* (New York: McGraw-Hill, 1938), pp. 319–324.

tiveness as a means of controlling personal and family behavior. This relaxation of social restraints on the serviceman, with the consequent tendency to engage in unconventional behavior, is partly the result of entering into new in-groups.

Divorce and Separation The divorce rate, too, is influenced by war.[13] Many men temporarily solve their marital difficulties by enlisting. Marriages on the brink of disaster are saved "for the duration" by the husband's entering the armed forces. Wives who otherwise might sue for separate maintenance or divorce postpone such action until after the war, a prudential course in view of compulsory allowances to dependents of men in the service. Then, too, divorce may be more difficult to obtain when the husband is in active service.

In World War II, in contrast with the experience of World War I, there occurred an upswing in the divorce rate. The rates per 1,000 population for the years 1939–1946 inclusive were 1.9, 2.0, 2.2, 2.4, 2.6, 2.9, 3.5, and 4.3. This increase seemed to be due primarily to two factors. The first was the wartime economic boom, in conformity with the well-known positive correlation between divorce rates and economic prosperity. The second was that a considerable proportion of wartime marriages culminated in early divorce, facilitated in large part by the fact that basic training of inducted men took place in this country. Moreover, courts of domestic relations and marriage-counseling centers reported cases of wives of servicemen accepting other male companionship, becoming emotionally involved, and behaving as if they were single. Such behavior would result in the waning of affection for the absent husband and the forming of a new attachment. The end result might be divorce.

It is difficult to distinguish the influence of war itself on divorce rates from prosperity associated with war. The divorce rate is known to have a high correlation with the business cycle, more divorces being granted in prosperity than in depression. Prosperity at the beginning of war would tend to increase divorces, continued prosperity during war might tend to offset the depressing effect of war on divorce, and postwar prosperity would tend to increase divorce.

Death, Disability, and Family Disorganization During war many families feel the shock of bereavement due to the loss in line of duty of a son, husband, or father. There may also be the painful readjustment of

---

[13] The war year 1918 showed a sharp decline in divorce rates, according to data reported from all New England states except Maine. See "Trend of Divorce in 50 Years," (Metropolitan Life Insurance Company) *Statistical Bulletin*, 20, February, 1939, pp. 1–2.

the wife and other relatives to the serviceman returning with a physical or mental handicap. In peacetime all families, including those that are highly organized, eventually break up with the departure of children from home and with the death of members. In wartime this type of family dissolution is accentuated.

Obviously, many of those who die or are incapacitated have little or no family attachment, but in most cases family attachments exist. The death or disablement of a son or a father disturbs the inner familial relationships and in many cases results in the complete breakup of the family.

Institutional Interrelationships War disrupts the normal equilibrium of institutional relationships and establishes new equilibriums. The various parts of a culture are interrelated, with some parts being more intimately connected than others. Modifications which develop in any one of the closely related parts, such as the state, school, recreation, church, and industry, will be reflected in modifications of folkways in other related institutions, such as the family.

1. War increases the authority and arbitrariness of the state, which means that in wartime millions of families are affected by conscription, by the expansion of governmental administration, by rationing, by limitations of medical and other services, by voluntary or forced migration, and possibly by imprisonment or internment in a concentration camp.

2. War disturbs the educational institutions of a nation, and this has repercussions in family life. As women increasingly engage in outside activities, they depend more and more on schools and other institutions to take care of their children. But in wartime, schools are faced with a shortage of personnel and with a high turnover in both teachers and pupils. Schools are less able to take care of the children than in peacetime. Fluctuations in the birth rate during and after a war put increased demands on the schools when war and postwar babies are ready for school.

3. Family adjustments are necessitated by economic disturbances of preparation for war or war itself. These disturbances include unemployment when civilian industries are being converted to war production, the speeding up of production, the replacement of men by women, and large fluctuations in income. Millions of families on stationary incomes feel the pinch of advancing prices and taxes, and fear even greater inflation; others employed in war industries experience increases in income. Both sudden depression and quick prosperity confront the family and its members with changes in habits, attitudes, and roles.

To the degree that war weakens institutions buttressing and supporting the family, it disturbs family relationships and is an indirect factor in family disorganization.

Family Reorganization Family instability in American society is essentially a phenomenon of the transition from the traditional to the companionship type of family. The effect of a crisis like war is both to accelerate the transition and to introduce temporary disrupting conditions.

Certain factors favorable to family unity emerge in wartime. First, the actual danger to family members in war may draw them more closely together. When a member of a family enters the army, with the actual or potential dangers involved, petty difficulties may be submerged and the family may become more united than before. Second, some men in the services, feeling that they are mere cogs in a huge machine, desire the intimate and personal appreciation of a sweetheart, a wife, or parents, and may be drawn more closely to their families than formerly. Third, to most men a war is a disagreeable job, to be finished as soon as possible in order that they may return to civilian life, settle down, and enjoy home life, made all the more attractive by contrast with the army camp.

POSTWAR PROBLEMS OF THE FAMILY

The effects of war on the family do not stop with the end of hostilities. The impact of war on the family, not fully apparent until the postwar period, will be considered under the following topics: (1) economic readjustment, (2) housing, (3) family disruption, (4) marital conflicts and adjustments, and (5) status of women.

Economic Readjustment One of the major problems confronting the family after World War II was economic readjustment. World War II brought unparalleled prosperity to America and at the same time great economic problems to millions of Americans: the transition from wartime to peacetime employment; returning demobilized soldiers looking for re-employment; the migration of families and industries from wartime centers back to their home communities or to new locations; the menace of inflation, probably greater after than during a war; the possibility of unemployment; and high taxes to provide for national defense, governmental running expenses, and the huge interest on a staggering war debt.

Housing A second problem confronting the family after a war is housing. The stoppage during war years of new construction for normal civilian use means a real deterioration of the nation's housing. Temporary wartime building of substandard dwelling units further increases the problems of housing.

Family Disruption A third problem reaching a peak after a war is that of family disruption and disintegration. The most obvious manifestation of it, and the one easiest to measure, is the enormous increase in the divorce rate. Many factors combined to give the United States its highest divorce rate in history after World War II.

As we have seen, a considerable number of hasty unions in wartime end in separation before the end of hostilities. A higher percentage of hurried-up, wartime unions will result in unhappy marriages, separations, and divorces than in peacetime, since they do not have the test of the normal duration of courtship and engagement to insure the existence of temperamental compatibility and similar interests, values, and ideals important for success in marriage. Separation, while it may bind some couples closer together, will in other cases lead to their growing apart, developing conflicting attitudes and ideals, with consequent disruption of the marriage relation.

Obviously, when there is a great excess of women, as after a war, their "bargaining power" is decreased, and some accept mates whose personal qualities, achievements, and physical abilities, are considerably removed from the concept of the ideal mate that had been built up in the mind of the girl. With the recognition after marriage of the disparity between the ideal and real mate, the wife may prefer to end the union.

Marital Conflicts and Adjustments The returning soldier has a triple problem of adjustment: to his family, to his job, and to civilian life. Many men, of course, will find the resumption of normal relations with their wives and children and relatives extremely easy. The nostalgia of servicemen, especially those stationed in foreign lands, predisposes them to set a high value on familiar places and resuming their civilian roles, especially those in the home.

A minority, but still a considerable proportion, of returning servicemen find adjustment to home, to industry, and to community life difficult. The thrill and excitement of fighting, the alternating discipline and freedom of military life, have left an impress on their habits and attitudes. Settling down to the routine of family activities is difficult for some and relatively easy for others. This is shown in the following two cases, one of maladjustment and the other of adjustment, of men whose ages, marital and familial statuses, length of service, and reasons for discharge are almost identical:

You will be surprised, no doubt, to be getting such a blue letter from me. Really I should be kicked good and damned hard where it hurts the most. But, I've got to be honest with myself and I ought to be honest with you. Fact is that I am making a helluvan adjustment. I can't seem to get going at all. Nothing seems right. It's been several months now—almost three. I have had five jobs in that time. I'm acting like a real psychopath; stay home from work, drink more than I ought, chase what are discreetly called "loose women"; and last night I got into a fight outside an exclusive downtown bar. If I hadn't been known by the cops as an ex-serviceman I would have spent the night in jail where I belonged—and I was sober as a judge when I did it. I try to blame my conduct on everyone—on my wife, on the army, on the boss, on the kids, on my injuries, but I know damn well that I am rationalizing something which I do not really understand and may not want to. My wife has been both considerate and intelligent about the whole thing. She has not nagged me either in the presence of the children or in private; she knows what I am doing and she knows that I know that she does not condone such conduct, but she makes no scenes. Everything she had done to facilitate my readjustment has been unselfish and objectively wise. I neither appreciate nor resent her efforts; I just accept them, like I do the good weather and the other gifts of the gods. Several of the other guys I know are having the same experiences. Bob's wife threw him out, and he came to me saying that he did not blame her.

But the other man wrote:

Most of the fellows thought that it would seem strange coming back. They told me that no employer was looking for a first-class paratrooper—that I'd be selling apples in the street, that my wife would seem like a stranger and the youngsters would not know me. I began almost to fear the homecoming—the sudden precipitation of a whole social scheme which I had once known and to which I was now, I thought, a stranger. I thought that if I could take them on one at a time, I could win, but all at once I couldn't. I didn't want to go back, but I knew that I must. My wife met me *en route* home and she suggested that we have a second honeymoon in a nearby city, which we did for seven days. We were among strangers, had no one, and wanted no one but each other. We fell in love all over again and probably acted like the kids we felt ourselves to be. She never once mentioned the kids until I began wondering if they were getting along all right with her mother, who was taking care of them. By the time I saw them, I was as eager to see them as any man could be. And so it went for all of the other people and groups with whom I had lost touch during those two and a half years. I feared being rushed in, but when I was permitted to take my time it was a pleasant experience. She made it so easy for me through her skillful planning. I made the transition gradually, not forced to take one step more than I wanted to, never losing the necessary feeling of security. Now one month later I am as completely in the accustomed groove as if I had not been away and as if I had not been injured.[14]

A returning husband may find his adjustment easier to the wife than to the child he has never seen and in whose rearing he has had no part.

Wives also may have experiences during wartime that make for difficulties in adjustment afterward. The wife who has been working may be able to retain her job at a higher rate of pay than that received by her husband, especially if he was not working before the war. She has also been on her own and has had to make many decisions, including those which normally would have been made by the husband or at least those in which he would have had a major voice.

Hill studied the factors involved in the adjustment of families to the crisis of separation and the crisis of reunion.[15] His sample was 135 Iowa families from the general population, which were confronted by these two crises: separation when the husband was inducted and reunion upon discharge. All were unbroken and had at least one child over four years of age, and all defined both separation and reunion as crises.

The following generalizations were supported by Hill's findings and the evidence from other types of crises, such as depression, bereavement, and divorce:

1. The degree of adjustment of a family to a crisis depends on the degree of (a) adaptability and integration of the family, (b) affection among family members, (c) marital adjustment, (d) companionship in family relations, and (e) the success in handling prior crises.

2. There are families, particularly those which are impoverished and otherwise inadequate, which are crisis-prone—that is, they tend to define troubles as crises.

3. The length of time a crisis disorganizes a family is inversely related to the degree of organization of the family.

4. Foreknowledge and preparation for a critical event mitigates the difficulties of the crisis and improves the chances of recovery from the effects of the crisis.

Status of Women Another problem after a war is the place of women in the home and in society. World War I gave women certain outward symbols of equality with men—suffrage and social freedom. It also

---

[14] Supplied by John F. Cuber from his personal files.
[15] Reuben Hill, *Families Under Stress: Adjustment to the Crises of War Separation and Reunion* (New York: Harper & Brothers, 1949). See pp. 324–328; for a bibliography of studies on crises, see pp. 365–367.

576 *War and the Family*

offered them the opportunity of economic independence through jobs in war-production and other industrial plants.

World War II gave women more of the substance of equality than the previous conflict, in part because of its longer duration. In World War II there was a marked jump in the employment of women, with only a small decline in the postwar period. This is shown in Table 32, which gives for the 1940–1952 period the total number of gainfully employed workers and the percent of women in this total. The table shows that, although the percent of women working in the postwar period was somewhat below the peak of war years, it was well above the percent gainfully employed in prewar years.

Table 32. **Total employed workers and percent women were of total employed, 1940-1952***

Year	Total employed workers (in thousands)	Percent women of total employed workers
1940	46,400	24.4
1941	48,760	25.0
1942	52,030	26.3
1943	52,630	32.1
1944	51,960	33.6
1945	51,300	35.0
1946	54,850	29.6
1947	58,330	28.4
1948	58,661	28.3
1949	58,694	29.3
1950	59,731	29.4
1951	61,193	30.5
1952	62,778	30.1

*Data for 1940–1945, from Bureau of the Census, Department of Commerce, *The Labor Force*, Special Surveys, MRLF—No. 36; for 1946–1952, *Current Population Reports, Labor Force*, Series P-57, Nos. 60, 83, 107, 119.

This increase in economic independence was reflected in a more secure position of equality of women in the home. The absence of husbands and fathers in the army or in a distant defense industry gave many wives a larger role of management in the home and at the same time decreased the family responsibility of the men.

Many women who had experienced a higher status, leadership, and independence were not disposed after the war to return to their old roles or to the former division of labor. But some women gladly relinquished their industrial jobs and returned to domestic activities.

SUMMARY

The immediate effect of war is an increase in the number of marriages, first to avoid service, then to enjoy married life before induction, and later to enter into a union as security against separation and the dangers of war. Economic prosperity, an indirect result of war, also increases the number of marriages, particularly of those persons previously unemployed or poorly paid. As more and more men go overseas, the marriage rate drops.

Both war and its attendant economic prosperity accelerate the processes of courtship, engagement, and marriage, with a consequent increase in hasty and hurried-up unions. After a war both marriages and divorces increase.

The basic effect of World War II, however, was the impetus it gave to further modification of the American conception of marriage, which has been in process of accelerated change. For several generations these changes, taking place at first slowly and gradually, were reflected in the rising status of the wife and mother in the family, the increase in education for women, their economic emancipation, and their gaining economic equality with men. These changes were speeded up as the result of the crises of World War I and of the depression. They were further acclerated by the impact of World War II.

The surface and immediate effect of war on the family seems disruptive; the deeper and long-time effect is probably to increase the trend toward its companionship form. This result follows from the increased freedom and higher status acquired by women and youth because of their vital participation in the total war effort. Young men seventeen to thirty bore the brunt of fighting in World War II, and women demonstrated their capacity to perform nearly every type of occupational activity with a productivity comparable to that of men.

Particularly important as a postwar problem is the readjustment of the returning veteran. The crux of the matter seems to be in the great difference between military and domestic life. The army and the modern family approximate two extremes. This may be represented by the following contrasts: The army is authoritarian, with stress on the giving and taking of orders; the modern family is tending to be democratic, with decisions made by consensus. The army subordinates the personalities of its members, eliminates privacy, and represses individual differences; the family stimulates the development of personality, provides privacy, and is considerate of the individuality of its members. The army is a one-sex, equal-age group, is mobile and tends to promiscuity in response relationships; the family is a stable group composed of both sexes and different ages and places a high value on fidelity of response.

PROBLEMS FOR RESEARCH

The impact of World War II, the postwar period, the Korean conflict, and the war in Vietnam affords a real opportunity to study marriage and the family in a time of crisis.

Wartime Marriages Young people marrying or postponing marriage in wartime give reasons for their action which are often rationalizations rather than the actual causes. Those who decide to marry may offer explanations that justify their behavior to their parents, to others, and to themselves. Four hypotheses may be tested: (1) they are more romantic, (2) they are more emancipated from parental and other forms of social control, (3) they are less influenced by traditional ideas of marriage, and (4) they are emotionally unsettled in wartime. Other factors, such as age, education, social maturity, and feelings of inferiority in competition for a mate, should be related to these hypotheses.

Army Adjustment and Family Adjustment Conflicting statements have been made about the relation between family adjustment and army adjustment. Some hold that those who adjust well in the family adjust well in the army. Others maintain that the reverse is true. Studies should be made (1) of the relation of adjustment in the family to adjustment in the army and (2) of the relation between adjustment in the army and readjustment to the family. Special groups of men should be studied separately—for example, youth overly dependent on mothers, nongregarious persons, and cultural "isolates," or members of certain sectarian or nationality groups thrown as individuals into association with members of the dominant cultural group.

Adjustment to Removal of the Father What are the specific adjustments of wives and children when the father is removed from the family for military or industrial reasons? Does the adjustment made by wives vary by type of family, such as predominantly patriarchal, matriarchal, or equalitarian? What techniques are used for the promotion of family solidarity under these conditions of separation?

Fall-out Shelters Families today are faced with the possibility of nuclear bombings. Some persons favor public fall-out shelters; others have built home fall-out shelters; and still others, on various grounds, are against any type of fall-out shelter. A study could be made of differences between families and individuals favoring these three proposals in such things as personality characteristics, values, and philosophy of life.

Family Crises in Wartime Angell's case studies of the effect of the depression on the family and Hill's study of the adjustment of family members to the crisis of separation and reunion emphasize the importance of family integration, personal adaptability, and other factors in the adjustment to a crisis. Studies should be made of adjustments of a family to the various crises associated with a war, such as loss of a family member or rising prices and declining purchasing power of family income. The hypothesis would be that integration, adaptability, and perhaps certain other factors are favorable to adjustment to the crisis.

QUESTIONS AND EXERCISES

1. In the chapter on mobility and the family, certain disorganizing effects on the family of the spatial separation of its members were noted. Does spatial separation in wartime disrupt families in the same way? What counteracting forces tend to mitigate the disorganizing influence of wartime mobility?
2. What data indicate that the status of women is higher in wartime and that it declines in the postwar period from its wartime level?
3. What are the hazards faced by wartime marriages?
4. What factors account for the instability of wartime and postwar marriages?
5. What long-term social trends affecting the family are stimulated by wartime conditions?
6. Analyze the introductory case from the point of view of mobility, wartime marriages, and parent-child relationships.

BIBLIOGRAPHY

Gabower, Genevieve. *Behavior Problems of Children in Navy Officers' Families: As Related to Social Conditions of Navy Family Life.* Washington: Catholic University of America Press, 1959.
    Based on interviews with 15 children who had come to the attention of the psychiatric service and 15 who were not known to the psychiatric service. Interviews also conducted with the mothers and fathers of the children. All fathers of the children were regular Navy officers. Discusses how problem behavior develops; whether moving, separation, and related factors are associated with problem behavior; and how problem behavior is associated with efforts of parents to deal with the problems.

Hill, Reuben. *Families under Stress: Adjustment to the Crisis of Separation and Reunion.* New York: Harper & Brothers, 1949.
   Studied adjustments of 135 families to war separations and reunions. Reviewed other studies of families in crisis situations. Emphasized that a given crisis has radically different influences in different families.

Stolz, Lois Meek, et al. *Father Relations of War-Born Children.* Stanford: Stanford University Press, 1954.
   Reports an intensive study of 19 families who had been separated by the husband's being in the armed services during World War II when their first child was born. Used interviews with the fathers and mothers, observations of the children in group situations, and projective-play observations of the children. Control groups of children used for some of the observations. Analyzed both the responses of the fathers and the children to reunion of the family and also examined the characteristics of the children.

Chapter 23
The Family in Process of Change

> The family in process of change may be considered from two interrelated viewpoints: (1) changes in the network of relationship within given families, and (2) changes in the structure of the family as a social system. When the network of interrelationships within a given family is considered undesirable by the members or by outsiders, attempts may be made to modify the interrelationships. When the structural form of the family is judged to be inadequate to meet the needs of people in a changing social order, suggestions may be made on ways of modifying the family. Often both those attempting to change individual families and those recommending changes in the structure of the family fail to realize that, to be effective, any change has to fit in with general trends within the total situation.

Most conflicts within a family are solved without obtaining outside advice. Certain critical situations, however, may arise with which the husband and wife or parents and children are unable to cope without assistance. The transition from a rural to an urban way of life has resulted in the rise of such agencies as marriage-counseling centers and child-guidance clinics to help the family solve its problems. The following case shows how a marriage-counseling center gave consultation and treatment to a couple faced with a problem of marital adjustment:

First interview: Mr. Y and Mrs. Y came into the Marriage Counsel office and, at their request, were seen together. Mr. Y is six years older than his wife, and they have similar educational and religious backgrounds. Since Mr. Y's father died, seven years ago, he has been the sole support of his mother, his brother, and his sister. Mrs. Y and her mother-in-law have had a most difficult time adjusting to each other.

Mr. Y's mother is a very dominating woman and speaks of her children as "babies." She controls them in every way possible and has kept them from mature development. Mr. Y had found it most difficult to contemplate marriage in view of his intense tie with his mother.

Mr. Y explained, "We seem to be hitting a snag in relation to my mother. We get along beautifully in every other way. Mother has been most uncooperative and has made it very difficult for my wife."

Interviewed separately, Mrs. Y stated that, from the time she first knew her husband, he never really wanted to get married. It was always difficult for him to talk about taking her to meet his mother and to tell his mother about her. "His mother's thoughts are always his thoughts."

Second interview with Mrs. Y: Mrs. Y is exceedingly concerned about her whole married future. She is beginning to feel that the problem is really with *her* and that she is about to have a nervous breakdown.

Third interview with Mrs. Y (two months later): Mrs. Y seems much happier. She couldn't say enough about the improvement, both in herself and her husband. She knows that he is cooperating. Her husband has reduced his contribution to his family by $25 a month and is now about to take off another $25. "I am going to have to push him a bit on this, but I don't want to tackle it now, as it is our anniversary month. I have not been visiting his family; he goes about every ten days and tells me what he thinks I would like to know."

Last fall when their marriage came so close to going on the rocks, Mr. Y did a great deal to hold it together and change their relationship. Mrs. Y recognized his ability in working out the various situations and their complications.

Fourth interview with Mrs. Y: Mrs. Y described a painful and humiliating visit to Mr. Y, who was ill in the hospital. Both she and her mother-in-law had unintentionally arrived at the hospital at the same time. The mother-in-law shrieked and loudly accused her of many things. Mr. Y ignored this outburst, but Mrs. Y was "burnt up."

Fifth interview with Mrs. Y: Mrs. Y expressed more dissatisfaction with Mr. Y's family and his attitude toward them, saying, "He can see things from only one angle." The counselor discussed with Mrs. Y the question of whether she was not trying too hard to make her husband's family into something she could like. The counselor brought out that, as hard as it was to accept the fact, Mr. Y's mother would never like her and that Mrs. Y would never like the mother-in-law. Mrs. Y said that her husband had mentioned his desire to come to the Marriage Counsel.

Second interview with Mr. Y (several weeks after his wife's fifth interview): The counselor was amazed at the change in Mr. Y. He seems so much more certain of himself, so much more sure of his marriage, and faces the future with much confidence and courage. "I don't know that we will ever really iron out all our problems, but we are beginning to get started in working together and much of the bickering and upset has gone."

He feels that his wife has gotten much out of her interviews. It has meant much to her that she could pour out her feelings to a neutral person.

Sixth interview with Mrs. Y (immediately following above interview with Mr. Y and including him): Mrs. Y and her husband kissed each other fondly as they met in the interview room. The counselor restated the conclusion that as hard as we might want to help Mrs. Y to accept her mother-in-law and become fond of her, and her mother-in-law to become fond of Mrs. Y, it was almost a hopeless effort. Both Mr. Y and Mrs. Y agreed that in accepting this fact they were going a long way to remove the need to change it. The counselor repeated what each one had told her of their feelings about the hospital episode. Mr. Y and Mrs. Y were able to discuss their feelings about the whole episode with warmth, understanding, and appreciation of each other's point of view.

Summary. This case illustrates the conflict which ensues when a man old enough and intellectually able to woo a wife and to establish a home is still tied emotionally to an overly possessive and jealous mother.

The counselor recognized that both Mr. Y and Mrs. Y were lonely and anxious. She made them feel that she was interested and that she cared what happened to them. She allowed them, individually, an opportunity to express freely their resentment, anger, and aggression without fear of condemnation or manipulation.

Once relieved of much of these negative feelings, Mr. Y and Mrs. Y were able to develop new and constructive attitudes. By being able to discuss their problems together with the counselor, Mr. Y and Mrs. Y gained confidence in their own and in each other's true strength and ability. They now felt an assurance of their potentialities for making a success of their marriage, even though the conditions that had previously existed remained essentially the same.[1]

In this case two networks of family interrelationships were in conflict: husband-wife and mother-son. The resolution of the conflict involved changes in attitudes and redefinitions of roles in the husband-wife relationship and in the relationships of a mother and her married son.

In America, as in other modern societies, modifications of attitudes, expectations, and roles are continuously taking place. Families and their members are interacting in situations that undermine traditional behavior and introduce modes of action adaptive to the new situation.

---

[1] This case was prepared especially for this book by Mrs. Emily Hartshorne Mudd, Director of the Marriage Counsel of Philadelphia, to illustrate the philosophy and the procedures of marriage counseling.

The resulting general trend in family relationships is from the traditional to the companionship pattern.

A consideration of the family in process of change raises certain questions: What is the relation of disorganization to reorganization? To what extent does the reshaping of the family take place without social intervention? Is governmental provision desirable and feasible to ensure the economic security of the family? Should conscious efforts be made to ensure family welfare through education, religion, counseling, and research? These subjects will be treated under the headings (1) family reorganization as a process, with disorganization viewed as mediating the companionship family; (2) family security; (3) agencies interested in the family; (4) the family as a creative group; (5) marriage and family counseling; and (6) family research.

FAMILY REORGANIZATION AS A PROCESS

Disorganization is usually considered the disruption of organization, but seldom in its equally significant function of mediating reorganization. Organization, disorganization, and reorganization may be analyzed as a social process.

A process is defined as changes taking place over a period of time through the operation of forces and conditions which, for the most part, are already operating within the situation. Our analysis of the family process in the preceding chapters has been mainly from the point of view of a traditional family system in transition from the social situation of a rural to that of an urban culture. It is now desirable to make this analysis more precise and detailed by defining the forces operating in relation to the changing situation. The forces in the situation are to be understood only as they are defined by a given society and as they become internalized in the attitudes and values of the members of the family.

The concept of family process is important because certain authorities have considered only its disorganizing aspects as exhibited in increasing divorce rates, examples of parental irresponsibility, and widespread juvenile delinquency, and have proposed made-to-order reforms of family structure. An examination of these programs shows that they were formulated without taking into account the natural forces and sequences of events which are reshaping the family.

The Companionship Family The form of the family that appears to be emerging in modern society may be called the companionship family because of its emphasis on intimate interpersonal association as its primary function. Other characteristics of the companionship family are the giving and receiving of affection; the assumption of equality of husband and wife; democracy in family decisions, with a voice by the children; the personality development of its members as a family objective; freedom of self-expression which is consistent with family unity; and the expectation that the greatest happiness is to be found in the family.

This conception of the companionship family is becoming so much a part of our culture that it is difficult to consider it objectively and critically. In fact, many of the leaders in family welfare who are concerned with problems of marriage and child development are propagandists for the companionship family. Students of the family, however, find it necessary to view this new type of family in the same detached and impartial way that they examine the Apache or the ancient Chinese family.

The basic elements in the companionship family were derived from rough beginnings in the pioneer and frontier situations. It would be possible, of course, to go back to even earlier origins, especially in the ideological formulation of these elements.

The features of the pioneer situation making for the decline of the small-patriarchal family and the rise of modifications tending toward the companionship form may be briefly summarized. First of all, the pioneer situation resulted in a breakdown of status as determined by conventional and arbitrary standards, and the evaluation of individual members within the family on the basis of the initiative, originality, independence, and particularly the contribution each could make to the family. With free land available, not only were early marriages the rule, but the young couples established independent households spatially removed from the parental family.

In the second place, pioneer isolation operated to bring about a relaxation of the rigid patterns of control of the traditional family. An outstanding example is the decline in the influence of parents over the marriages of their children and the selection of mates by the young people themselves.

A third influence of the pioneer situation and, in the long run, perhaps the most important, was the emergence of political democracy. The patterns of political democracy, of course, were already present in the colonies. They had been derived from English sources. But pioneer society stimulated the spread of democracy downward until it reached nearly all the people.

The beginnings of democracy were evident in the family in the growing freedom of children and in tendencies toward equality in the relations of the sexes. Political democracy, although at first confined to adult males, later permeated all society with its ideology, and thereby was a powerful but indirect factor in raising the status of women.

The entrance of women into industry gave them actual or potential economic independence and thereby also raised their status. It made it unnecessary for a woman to marry just to secure economic support, and made it possible, if her marriage was unsatisfactory, for her to earn her own living.

This analysis of the emergence of the companionship form of the family as a result of a social process gives perspective for differentiating between familial disorganization that disrupts the family and that which mediates its reorganization. The concept of the family process suggests also that the family itself is a dynamic agent and not a passive, inert object. The term "process" also implies that the family structure is being modified by forces within it reacting to those impinging upon it.

The companionship family is, in many respects, less stable than the previous forms of the family. This is true not merely because its unity is based on affection and comradeship instead of duty and social pressure, as in the traditional family, but because in the transition from a rural to an industrial society it has lost some aspects of its security. Therefore, provision for the economic well-being of the family becomes a central problem.

FAMILY SECURITY

By scientific discovery and invention, man has achieved an unparalleled mastery over natural forces. He has all the technical knowledge necessary for an economy of abundance. Yet in the United States, with all its wealth of natural resources, millions of families are living in insecurity. Here we will discuss the following economic needs of the family: (1) a minimum economic base, (2) adequate housing, (3) acceptable nutrition, and (4) adequate medical care.

The Economic Base of the Family Essential to family well-being is a minimum of economic security. The total annual money income of a large proportion of families, in spite of the advances in recent years, is too small to give them economic security. Table 33 shows the increase in family income between 1947 and 1967 in 1967 dollars. It also shows that in 1967 about 1 in 8 families received less than $3,000; 4 in 10 received less than $7,000; and about 1 in 3 received $10,000 or more. However, this is a very much higher family income than in 1947.

In 1967 dollars, one in four families in 1947 received less than $3,000; more than eight in ten less than $5,000; and 9 in 10 less than $10,000.

In spite of the increase in family income, additional safeguards are necessary to guarantee a minimum of economic security.

Table 33. **Percent distribution of families receiving given money income, 1967 and 1947, in 1967 dollars***

Family Income	1967 Percent	1967 Cumulative percent	1947 Percent	1947 Cumulative percent
Under $3,000	12.5	12.5	27.4	27.4
$3,000–4,999	12.8	25.3	29.7	57.1
$5,000–6,999	16.1	41.4	20.6	77.7
$7,000–9,999	24.3	65.7	13.5	91.2
$10,000–14,999	22.4	88.1	8.9	100.1
$15,000 and over	12.0	100.1		

*Statistical Abstract of the United States, 1969, p. 323.

The Social Security Program, initiated in 1935, is designed to give economic assistance to families. The principal parts of this program are (1) public assistance to elderly people, dependent children, and the blind; (2) old-age and survivors insurance; (3) medicare, insuring those 65 and over for hospital or medical expenses, or both; and (4) unemployment insurance. All parts of the Social Security Program have greatly expanded since their initiation.

Studies have shown that the economic problems of families multiply with increase in the number of children. Several proposals have been made to lessen the financial handicap of parents with children, particularly those with more than two or three. One is to grant larger exemptions from taxation to the head of the family for child dependents than those now provided on a limited scale in the federal income tax.

The most comprehensive proposal for assisting in the care of children is the system of family allowances. A better name might be children's allowances, because the plan provides for the payment of a certain amount of money to parents for each dependent child, or for each child in addition to the first one, two, or three, as might be stipulated in the law. Allowances of this type in some form have been provided in 30 countries,[2] including Australia, Brazil, Canada, Chile, Eire, France, Italy, New Zealand, the Soviet Union, Spain, Switzerland, and Uruguay.

[2] James C. Vadakin, *Family Allowances* (Miami: University of Miami Press, 1959).

Housing A prerequisite of a national housing policy is the recognition that the neighborhood area, and not the individual lot, is the unit of planning. A tract adequate for a group of families has to be large enough to support neighborhood institutions and facilities, such as the school, the church, the playground, the nursery school, and a community center. Careful community planning locates the facilities according to the needs of the people and increases their safe use by blocking off through streets. Federal housing and urban renewal concentrates attention not on the individual house but on the construction of housing for a neighborhood.

Nutrition Not only housing but also nutrition is important for family health and well-being. In so-called normal times a large percent of American families have incomes insufficient to provide for a minimum standard of health and physical efficiency. Requirements of a balanced and varied diet are often sacrificed for other family expenditures. There is room for vast improvement in the nutrition of the American people even after the economic base of the family is assured.

Education in schools, in clubs, and through magazines and newspapers provides a way to spread knowledge of the nutritional values of food. Recognition should also be given to the wide variations in diets in the subcultures and social classes in the United States and in different countries throughout the world.

Health There is need for a national health policy directed toward assuring family health. At present wealthy, well-to-do, and very poor families can obtain complete medical service. The latter are eligible for the free services offered by hospitals and clinics. The middle class and the upper-lower class often have inadequate medical service.

Economic security for the family would go a long way toward meeting the cost of adequate medical care, but not far enough. If insurance is provided in the event of illness, families will be disposed to make full utilization of the services of physicians and hospitals.

Students of the problem of adequate health protection for all families believe the solution is in some method of payment by groups of families. Some form of health insurance is prevalent in the United States. In 1968 practically all of those 65 years of age and over were covered by Medicare. For those under 65, 78.2 percent of the civilian population had hospital insurance and 76.6 percent had surgical insurance.[3]

Experiments in group organization of physicians, hospitals, and clinical facilities, combined with the group plan of payment to make a com-

---

[3] U.S. Department of Health, Education, and Welfare, *Monthly Vital Statistics Report: Health Interview Survey*, 18, No. 11, 1970.

plete medical service available to a large part of the population, have been met with strong opposition by organized medical societies. Yet some plan of either private or governmental insurance of families and individuals seems a practicable method of providing preventive and curative medicine to those most in need of this service.

AGENCIES INTERESTED IN THE FAMILY

Providing the American home with economic security in income, housing, nutrition, and medical care is only a minimum base for family living. Many interested in family welfare would stop at this point. They would contend that the family is now on its own to pursue its cultural ends.

Others, however, take issue with this position. They assert that the modern family and its members are intertwined with the community in their activities and interests. They call attention to agencies and institutions whose programs of service are, in part, oriented to reorganizing the family so that it will be better adapted to conditions of modern living. Outstanding among these institutions are (1) the church, (2) the school, and (3) the new agencies of the family-life movement.

The Church There has been an intimate association between religion and the family in most preliterate and modern societies. With the orthodox Jew, religion permeates the home. In Western civilization, Christianity, the dominant religion, not only has its chief concepts stated in family terms, such as the fatherhood of God and the brotherhood of man, but has important ideals for marriage and family relationships.

In recent years there has been a decided shift in the training program of most of the major religious groups. Sociologists and psychologists have been appointed to the staffs of seminaries. The aim has been to orient the program of local churches toward family-life education and family counseling.

Education The educational system in the United States was originally designed for a rural civilization, to teach children in the grades the "three R's," thus giving them the skills necessary for reading, writing, and figuring. Farming and homemaking were learned by example, by precept, and by imitation of parents. High school and college education was originally designed to equip those planning to enter professional training for teaching, for law, for medicine, and for the ministry.

Today our conception of education has changed. High school training is the privilege of every adolescent, and junior college education is becoming a reality for increasing numbers.

If courses on education for marriage and family life are given early in high school, they would reach the vast majority of future husbands and wives. In recent years an insistent demand for courses in preparation for marriage and family living has come from college students. College courses, however, reach only a small percentage of the population. Proponents of family-life education point out that an adequate program should begin in the grades and continue in high school and college, with selection at each level of the topics most pertinent to the age group. It is not even necessary that special courses be offered on the subject. Appropriate units on education for family living may be introduced within courses already in the curriculum.

Family-Life Movement In an urban community the relationships of persons in a family are radically different from those in a rural society. Various organizations have emerged to meet the needs and problems of families in this new setting. The work of organizations devoted to assisting in the solution of the problems of children, marriage, and the family is known as the family-life movement.

The Child Study Association of America[4] carries on an extensive program on various aspects of marriage and the family. The National Congress of Parents and Teachers[5] concentrates on securing the most helpful association between the two institutions exerting the greatest influence on the child, the home and the school, and has many local committees of parents and teachers working on various activities, including the home, family life, and parent education.

Certain organizations have been formed to bring together persons and agencies working directly with the family. The oldest of these is the Family Service Association of America,[6] composed of family-welfare agencies. Since the mid-thirties, with relief giving largely assumed by the government, the activities of family-welfare agencies have become chiefly those of skilled personal service to the family and its members in various kinds of difficulties. The shift in type of service makes it possible for a family-welfare agency to offer its assistance in solving the problems of families above the poverty level who would be able and willing to pay a small charge for the service.

The National Council on Family Relations[7] is one of the largest organizations in the family-life movement. It brings together into one organization teachers of marriage and family courses from departments of biology, home economics, law, psychology, social work, and sociol-

---

[4] Organized in 1888.
[5] Organized in 1897 under the name of the National Congress of Mothers.
[6] Organized in 1911.
[7] Organized in 1938.

ogy; persons engaged in professional service to the family, including family-life educators, lawyers, marriage counselors, nurses, physicians, psychiatrists; and specialists in research from every field dealing with marriage and the family.

THE FAMILY AS A CREATIVE GROUP

The modern family does not function primarily for the transmission of the culture from the past or the present to the future generation. Nor does it operate as a passive receiver of ideas and practices with which it is indoctrinated by the church, the school, or the family-life movement. The family has a dynamic function in being critical and selective and in making its own choices. In short, each family, as a cultural unit, develops according to its own aspirations and objectives.

Some see in the family the agency for creating a culture adapted to a scientific age, stimulating and not destructive to the personality development of its members, and preparing them for participation in the outside world. The family as a creative and active cultural agent selects from the programs offered by the church, the school, and other organizations certain activities and values which it adapts to its needs.

But difficulties may occur, as in the case at the beginning of the chapter, where diagnosis and individualized treatment are necessary to prevent family disruption or to mediate reorganization. This need has led to the rise of marriage and family counseling.

MARRIAGE AND FAMILY COUNSELING

Family reorganization so far has been treated in general from the standpoint of an on-going process affected by the totality of events in a society. Family reorganization also takes place in helping particular couples plan and conduct their life together. The outstanding example of individualized guidance is the movement for the counseling of engaged and married couples.

The emerging profession of marriage and family counseling has as its primary purpose assisting husbands and wives, parents and children, and young people contemplating marriage in the solution of their problems. Originally marriage counseling was a part of the work of the minister, the lawyer, and the teacher. Later it developed in specialized aspects of family social work, child-guidance centers, and mental-hygiene clinics. While marriage counseling continues to be an activity of these professions and agencies, specialists in marriage counseling have recently appeared.

Naturally, differences in basic philosophy and in techniques have arisen. The main divergence concerns the roles of the counselor and the client or patient. The two extreme conceptions have been called directive and nondirective counseling.

In directive counseling there is the assumption that "the counselor knows best." He has the training, the knowledge, and a wider experience. His function, almost like that of the physician whose patient has a physical ailment, is to diagnose the difficulty and to suggest a solution.

The point of view of nondirective counseling is the support of a person to arrive at his own decisions. Its philosophy and procedure have been worked out systematically by Rogers, who states:

> It aims directly toward the greater independence and integration of the individual rather than hoping that such results will accrue if the counselor assists in solving the problem. The individual and not the problem is the focus. The aim is not to solve one particular problem but to assist the individual to *grow*, so that he can cope with the present problem and with later problems in a better-integrated fashion. If he can gain enough integration to handle one problem in more independent, more responsible, less confused, better-organized ways, then he will also handle new problems in that manner.[8]

Most counselors take intermediate positions between these two extremes, presenting knowledge, advice, and suggestion, but also stating that the responsibility rests with the client to make his own decision.

The Professions and Counseling The members of several professions find that they are expected by the public to give counsel on problems of marriage and the family. Counseling has always been part of the pastoral work of the minister. It is naturally his concern to assist his parishioners in striving to attain the ideal Christian family life. He has the sometimes difficult role of maintaining high ethical standards, while understanding and making allowances for the mistakes and frailties of human beings.

An increasing number of ministers recognize the positive contribution they can make by counseling before marriage. The fact that the great majority of couples seek a minister rather than a justice of the peace to perform the wedding is evidence of a desire for a religious sanction of the union. In his religious role, the clergyman can ascertain if the couple have discussed and settled problems of their relationship in the light of religious principles and of scientific knowledge.

Almost all states require couples to take a blood test for syphilis before securing a marriage license, with the result that many couples

---

[8] Carl R. Rogers, *Counseling and Psychotherapy* (Boston: Houghton Mifflin, 1942), pp. 28–29.

visit a physician before marriage. A young man and his fiancée (separately or together) may voluntarily call upon the family doctor for a physical examination and for information on sexual matters including birth control. Certain physicians have prepared themselves, through special interest or courses, to deal with the emotional as well as the physical aspects of problems of marital adjustment.

Many problems that students bring to teachers are family problems, such as those of emancipation from parental control, conflict with family ideals, and adjustment to family crises. Often the chief function of the teacher is to be a sympathetic listener. His responsibility is not to solve the personal problems of the student but to assist him in reorientation and in making his own decisions. The teacher, like other part-time counselors, needs training not only to give help on minor problems but to decide when the difficulty is a major disturbance which should be referred to a specialist.

In addition to the part-time professional workers, a new profession in marriage and family counseling is emerging. This new profession is made up, in part, of those social workers who specialize in family case work, particularly those with training in social psychiatry. It also includes a smaller number of persons who have had their basic training not in social work but in education, psychology, and sociology and have had experience in counseling.

Professional Education Those interested in marriage counseling have raised the question of the professional training of workers in their field. It is generally agreed that while training the present personnel who are now in service is desirable and should be encouraged, it is desirable to introduce adequate courses in professional schools. The leadership in the professionalization of marriage counseling has been taken by the American Association of Marriage Counselors.[9] It has concentrated on defining professional standards, developing counseling methods, exchanging clinical experiences, and considering the certification of professional services and personnel.

A highly critical person is inclined to raise the question of whether social change has become so rapid that all the programs of agencies interested in marriage, the family, and child welfare might better be scrapped, since they may be obsolescent before they can be introduced. This question should not be dismissed lightly. Too many programs in this and other social fields suffer from cultural lag. Certain questions should always be raised about a program, particularly one that appeals to our sentiments. Does it look forward or seek to return to the "good

[9] Organized in 1943.

old days?" Does it run with or against social trends? Does it accord with or go counter to the findings of research? The studies already completed, particularly in the area of predicting success and failure in marriage, show the value and the promise of research findings. Knowledge obtained from research will help provide the material adequate for the training of workers in the field of family-life education and marriage counseling.

FAMILY RESEARCH

Constructive application of psychology and sociology to the problems of the family must await the securing of facts. Only when an adequate body of tested findings from scientific studies is at hand will it be possible to make advances in the solution of the problems of the family comparable to those in the field of health which followed the scientific discoveries in medical science.

One of the chief purposes of this book has been to arouse the interest of the student in research in marriage and the family, to suggest significant projects for study, and to present a conceptual framework in which questions might be raised and hypotheses formulated. Current research on the family is fragmentary and scattered. The following illustrate the opportunities and possibilities for the study of the family:

1. The family affords an unusually promising field for research in personality. Sociologists have long appreciated the significance of the family as an environment for personality development. Yet studies of the social factors influencing the behavior of the infant and the preschool child have been left almost entirely to psychologists. The sociologist tends to criticize the psychologist for making his studies under laboratory conditions rather than in the home, without himself utilizing this opportunity. Sporadic studies have investigated family behavior in parent-child relations; in adolescence; in dating, courtship, and engagement; in marriage adjustment; in bereavement; and in old age.

2. There is an increasing body of statistical data on the family being made available by the United States Census Bureau. These data should be analyzed to test current hypotheses and formulate new hypotheses.

3. A study of research projects undertaken in the past few years and those now in progress by home economists, psychiatrists, psychologists, and sociologists would reveal increase or decrease in research in marriage and the family and the trend of research interest in this field. This survey might be introductory to the preparation of a research-planning report on the field of marriage and the family. A survey would show (1) the present body of research findings, (2) gaps in our knowledge, (3) the methods of research now in use, and (4) the subjects for future research

which would be most significant for increasing our scientific knowledge and for practical application to problems of marriage and the family.

CONCLUSION

Ten suggestions are presented in relation to the probable future of the family in the light of our survey of the American family and the current findings of research:

1. Students should be cautious about drawing conclusions from contrasting the traditional and companionship forms of the family. The general transition has been from the former to the latter. But no pure form of either has existed or is likely to exist. Any historical form of the patriarchal family had at least a minimum of companionship among its members; and the companionship family as it exists today has definite traditional characteristics.

2. It seems safe to predict that the family will survive, because of its long history of adaptability to changing conditions, its function of giving and receiving affection, its function in child-rearing, and its contribution to personality development.

3. Increase in family disruption as evidenced by divorce seems to have reached a plateau. It is probable that there will be no radical increase in divorce in the near future.

4. A number of factors are now apparent which, within twenty to thirty years, should aid in stabilizing the family. These include the virtual end of immigration, the transition of our economy from a risk to a security basis, and the development and expansion of the services of family-life education and marriage counseling.

5. There is and there will continue to be a closing of the gap between Negro and white families in education, economic status, income, and family stability.

6. It will be interesting to observe whether current long-time trends will continue. Among such trends are the declining birth rate, the consequent smaller size of the family, the increase in the proportion of people married to those of marriageable age, the increase in the proportion of all women and of married woman gainfully employed, and the decline in the historic functions of the family—economic, educational, recreational, religious, and protective.

7. We can expect certain changes in the family as a result of new inventions. It is difficult, however, to see how any or all of these—the family airplane, prefabricated houses, air-conditioning—can have nearly as much effect as the continued influence of the automobile, the motion picture, radio, and television.

8. Services to the family will continue to expand, including those

under governmental auspices to undergird its security and those under private sponsorship to conserve its cultural values.

9. The individual family, through communication of its members and in interaction with other families in the community, will make the choices that ultimately, in a democratic society, will decide its course and its future.

10. Increased research will continue to be necessary to provide the knowledge of human behavior essential to family welfare and happiness.

QUESTIONS AND EXERCISES

1. Apply the concept of social process to family organization, disorganization, and reorganization as a whole, and to each separately.
2. What factors and forces were in the situation out of which the companionship family developed?
3. What is the relationship between family reorganization and family security resulting from a minimum economic base, decent housing, good nutrition, and adequate medical care?
4. How would you evaluate the work done by schools and churches in reorganizing the culture of the family?
5. To what extent is marriage and family counseling in your home community done by ministers, physicians, lawyers, teachers, social workers, and persons trained specifically for this work? Which of these are inclined to use the directive and which the nondirective counseling technique?
6. Do you think marriage counseling would be more effective if done by an existing agency or by an independent organization? Give reasons for your answers.
7. Analyze the introductory case from the standpoint of the process of family disorganization and reorganization, economic and other aspects of security, the counseling agencies which might have been available to this family, and forces working for its reorganization.

BIBLIOGRAPHY

Abrams, Charles; and Dean, John P. "Housing and the Family," in *The Family: Its Function and Destiny*. rev. ed. ed. Ruth Nanda Anshen. New York: Harper & Brothers, 1959, pp. 463–487.

> Describes the housing problems of American families: indecent, unsafe, and unsanitary housing; home ownership; housing for families of different marital status, different sizes, and different occupations; housing the normal family; and housing shortage.

Foote, Nelson N.; and Cottrell, Leonard S. *Identity and Interpersonal Competence*. Chicago: University of Chicago Press, 1955.
   Interpersonal competence is defined as the ability to achieve health, intelligence, empathy, autonomy, judgment, and creativity. Presents hypotheses about the relationships of each of these to family behavior. Includes a relatively complete bibliography on the family for the years 1945–1954.

Mudd, Emily H.; et al. *Marriage Counseling: A Casebook*. New York: Association Press, 1958.
   Presents 41 cases having premarital and marital problems as reported by a wide variety of counselors: sociologists, social workers, physicians, lawyers, and ministers.

Pincus, Lily (ed.). *Marriage: Studies in Emotional Conflict and Growth*. London: Methuen and Company, 1960.
   Detailed reports and analysis of marriage counseling with both husband and wife of five couples seen at Tavistock Institute of Human Relations (Great Britain). Predominantly psychoanalytic theoretical framework.

APPENDIX A

Premarital and Marital Items Associated with Marital Adjustment

Table 34. Premarital items associated with adjustment in marriage (M, man; W, woman; if M and W not given then it is for both)*

Premarital Items	Studies by Benson, Bernard, Davis, Hamilton, Hart and Shields, King, Kirkpatrick, Luckey, Schnepp and Johnson, Schroeder, Shope and Broderick, and Williamson	Studies by Terman and others and by Terman and Oden[†]	Studies by Burgess and Cottrell and by Burgess and Wallin[†]	Studies by Locke and by Locke and Karlsson[†]
Acquaintance		Extremely well acquainted (Terman) M, a year or more; W, 6 months or more (Terman and Oden)	2 or more years	W, over 2 years (Locke) M, 3 years and over; W, 6 years and over (Locke and Karlsson)

[†] In columns 3, 4, and 5 the items cited are associated with marital adjustment in both studies unless one or both studies are entered in parentheses. Then the association applies to the designated studies.

Adaptability		Rated by outsider as satisfactory in general adjustment (Terman and Oden)	Adaptable (Burgess and Wallin)	Adaptable personality
Affection toward mate before marriage			Satisfied with demonstration of affection (Burgess and Wallin)	Very great (Locke)
Age at marriage	M, 24 and over; W, 20 and over (Hart and Shields) M, 25 and over (Davis) M, 21 and over; W, 20 and over (King)	W, 20 and over (Terman) M, 23 and over; W, 23-28 (Terman and Oden)	M, 22-30; W, 19 and over (Burgess and Cottrell)	M, 24-29; W, 21-29 (Locke)
Age difference	M, 0-10 years older; W, 0-5 years younger (Bernard) Same age, and M 4-7 years older (King)	All age differences except when M is 1 to 3 years younger than mate (Terman and Oden)	M, 1-3 years older, or same age as W; self older (Burgess and Cottrell)	About the same age

Attachment to father		Good deal or very close (Terman) Very strong or none (Terman and Oden)	M, close (Both studies) M, very strong (Burgess and Cottrell)	No relationship
Attachement to mother		Good deal or very close (Terman) Very strong or none (Terman and Oden)	Very close	No relationship (Locke)
Attachment, prefer one parent to the other	W, absence of greater intimacy with one parent (Kirkpatrick)	W, absence of markedly greater attachment (Terman)		
Attachment to siblings		M, to all but younger sibling; W, no relationship (Terman and Oden)	M, none or to older brother; W, none or to younger brother (Burgess and Cottrell)	

Attractiveness of opposite-sex parent		M, average or above (Terman) Average or more (Terman and Oden)	
Babies, learned the origin of at age		W, 12-16 years (Terman)	
Brothers or sisters	W, has brothers (Hamilton)	No relationship (Terman and Oden)	
Children, desire for		Both desire (Terman and Oden)	Both desire very much (Burgess and Wallin)
Church attendance	3 or more times a month (King, Schroeder)	M, 4 or more a month; W, 2 or more (Terman and Oden)	M, 2 or more times a month; W, 4 times a month (Burgess and Cottrell)

Church membership	Church member (Schroeder) 2 or more years' membership in church organizations (Schnepp and Johnson)	M, church member (Terman and Oden)		Both belong to same church (Locke)
Confide in mate			Confide about everything. (Burgess and Wallin)	
Conflict with father	None (King)	None or very little (Terman)	None or a little (Burgess and Cottrell)	A little (Locke)
Conflict with mother	None (King)	M, none; W, none or very little (Terman) None (Terman and Oden)	M, little or none (Burgess and Cottrell)	M, moderate; W, a little (Locke)

Conflict with mate before marriage			None or very little (Locke)
Conventional behavior		High degree of conservative attitude (Burgess and Wallin)	High degree of conventional behavior (Locke)
Courtship, length of	9-23 months (King)	3 or more years	
Dates with other sex		W, objects to M having dates (Burgess and Wallin)	

Discipline in parental home	Firm but not harsh; no, rare, or occasional punishment		Usually has own way (Locke) M, treated very fairly; W, treated fairly or very fairly (Locke and Karlsson)
Drinking and smoking		M or W does not drink or smoke (Burgess and Wallin)	
Educational level	Beyond high school (King and Schroeder) College (Hamilton)	Beyond high school (Terman)	M, college graduate or professional; W, college, postgraduate, or professional (Burgess and Cottrell)	M, graduate work; W, beyond high school (Locke)
Education, differences in	Equal (Davis)	M, if not more than W's; W, if not much more than M's (Terman and Oden)		

Education of father		College (Burgess and Wallin)	No relationship (Locke)
Emotional stability		Good (Terman and Oden)	Stable (Burgess and Wallin)
Employment, length of			M, average of 15 months
Employment, regularity of			Regular (Burgess and Cottrell)
Engagement, length of	24 months (King)	M, 6 months or longer; W, 3 months or longer (Terman) No relationship (Terman and Oden)	9 months or longer (Burgess and Cottrell)	A year or longer (Locke) 24 months or more (Locke and Karlsson)

Family background, level			Superior (Burgess and Cottrell)	
Family background, similarity			Similar (Burgess and Cottrell)	
Friends, men before marriage		W, many (Terman and Oden)	M, several or many; W, a few, several, or many (Burgess and Cottrell)	M, W had several or many;; W, self had several (Locke) No relationship (Locke and Karlsson)
Friends, women before marriage	M, no excess or deficiency of woman friends (Kirkpatrick)	M, few or several (Terman and Oden)	M, several or many; W, many (Burgess and Cottrell)	M, W had several or many; W, self had several or many, M had several but not many (Locke) No relationship (Locke and Karlsson)

Appendix A 607

Future father-in-law			Like very much (Burgess and Wallin)
Future mother-in-law			Like very much (Burgess and Wallin)
Happiness of childhood		Above average (Terman) M, extremely happy; W, about average (Terman and Oden)	Above average (Locke) Very happy (Locke and Karlsson)
Happiness of parents' marriage, rated by subject	M, happy (King, Schroeder)	Happy and very happy	M, very happy (Burgess and Cottrell) M, very happy (Locke) Happy and very happy (Locke and Karlsson)

Health	W, healthy (Davis)	Self, good; other perfect or superior (Terman and Oden)	M, healthy (Burgess and Cottrell)	No relationship (Locke)
Height		M, if not 12 or more inches taller than W; W, if shorter than M (Terman and Oden)		
Identification with parents	M, self with own father; W, M with W's father (Luckey)			
Income before marriage	M, $1,200 W, none (King)	M, any except none; W, $200 or more a month (Terman and Oden)	Moderate (Burgess and Cottrell)	
Income of father				$5,000 and over (Burgess and Wallin)

Leisure-time activities			M and W prefer to stay at home; engage in most activities together (Burgess and Wallin)
Marital status of parents	Not divorced or separated (Schroeder)	Not divorced or separated or, if so, not before child was 8 years old (Terman and Oden)	No relationship (Locke)
Marriage, place of			Church or Parsonage (Burgess and Cottrell) Home (Locke)
Married by	Minister or priest (Schroeder)	M, clergyman (Terman and Oden)	Minister, priest, or rabbi (Burgess and Cottrell) Minister or priest (Locke)

Meeting place, first	Other than "pickup" or private or public recreation (Terman)		Other than home of a friend or dance hall (Locke)
Mental ability	M, does not feel much superior; W, M not inferior (Terman) M, equal or inferior to W; W, not "very superior" to M; no relationship to childhood IQ (Terman and Oden)		M and W feel equal
Occupation	White-collar, professional and executive (Williamson) M, professional business, or personal service; W, professional (King)	No relationship	M, certain occupations; W, teaching or same or similar to what she wants (Burgess and Cottrell)	W, if employed, in service, professional, or semi-professional (Locke)

Order of birth		W, not only child (Terman) No relationship (Terman and Oden)	M, not only child; if only, not married to only or youngest (Burgess and Cottrell)	No relationship (Locke)
Organizations, membership in	One to three (King)	M, luncheon club and one or more; W, none (Terman and Oden)	3 or more (Burgess and Cottrell) W, either self or mate, 3 or more (Burgess and Wallin)	No relationship (Locke and Karlsson)
Parents' approval of marriage	Approved by both (King, Schnepp and Johnson)	Approved by both (Terman and Oden)	Approved by both	Approved by both (Locke)
Petting	W, none (Davis)	W, never (Terman) No relationship (Terman and Oden)		

Physical type of W	M, resembles M's mother (Hamilton)	M, has no resemblance or of same type as M's mother	
Rearing, rural or urban	Country or small town (Schroeder)	No relationship (Terman and Oden)	Country (Burgess and Cottrell)	No relationship
Religious home training	Reception of sacrament established age; first religious instruction in home; no parental quarrels over religious matters; religious periodicals in the home (Schnepp and Johnson)	M, considerable; W, not very strict (Terman) No relationship (Terman and Oden)		
Savings	Some (King)	M, had savings; W, M's savings $500 or more (Terman and Oden)	M, some (Burgess and Cottrell)	Some (Locke)

Sex, desire to be of opposite sex		W, never (Terman)	Never (Terman and Oden)
Sex instruction	W, some (Davis)	M, adequate (Terman)	Adequate (Terman and Oden)
Sex, premarital attitude toward	Interest and pleasant anticipation (King)	M, indifference or interest and pleasant anticipation (Terman)	Indifference or interest and pleasant anticipation (Terman and Oden)
			Wholesome (Burgess and Wallin)

Appendix A 615

Sex, premarital intercourse	W, none (Davis, Hamilton) M, with 2 women; W, none (King) None (Shope and Broderick) No premarital sex liberties (Schnepp and Johnson)	M, none or only with future spouse; W, none (Terman)	None (Burgess and Wallin)	M, none, does not know, believe, or suspect W had, W does not know, believe, or suspect M had; W, does not know, believe, or suspect M had (Locke) M, not many; W, not more than one, M does not know, believe or suspect W had (Locke and Karlsson)
Sex, response of parents to child's early curiosity		Frank and encouraging (Terman) Frank (Terman and Oden)		

616   Appendix A

Sex, sources of information	Parents and books (Schroeder) W, parents and teachers (Davis)	Parents and teachers
Sex shock		W, none during years 10-15 (Terman) No relationship (Terman and Oden) M, not low in (Terman and Oden)
Sociability		M, not low in (Terman and Oden)
Sunday-school attendance	Beyond 18 years (Schroeder)	Some (Terman and Oden)	Beyond 18 years (Burgess and Cottrell) W, beyond 18 years (Burgess and Wallin)	M, beyond 10 years; W, beyond 14 years (Locke)

| Values | W, interest in home, children; M, interest in romantic love and interest in religion (Benson) |

*Burnell Benson, "Familism and Marital Success," *Social Forces*, 33 (1955): pp. 277–280; Jessie Bernard, "Factors in the Distribution of Success in Marriage," *American Journal of Sociology*, 40 (1934); p. 58; and "The Distribution of Success in Marriage," *ibid.*, 39 (1933): pp. 194–203; Ernest W. Burgess and Leonard S. Cottrell, *Predicting Success or Failure in Marriage* (New York: Prentice-Hall, 1939); Ernest W. Burgess and Paul Wallin, *Engagement and Marriage* (Philadelphia: Lippincott, 1953); Katherine B. Davis, *Factors in the Sex Life of Twenty-Two Hundred Women* (New York: Harper & Brothers, 1929); Gilbert V. Hamilton, *A Research in Marriage* (New York: Albert and Charles Boni, 1929); Hornell Hart and Wilmer Shields, "Happiness in Relation to Age at Marriage," *Journal of Social Hygiene*, 12 (1926): pp. 403–407; Georg Karlsson, *Adaptability and Communication in Marriage: A Swedish Predictive Study of Marital Satisfaction* (Uppsala, Sweden: Almqvist and Wiksells, 1951); Charles E. King, "Factors Making for Success or Failure in Marital Adjustment Among 466 Negro Couples in Southern City," Ph.D. Dissertation, University of Chicago Libraries, 1951; Clifford Kirkpatrick, "Factors in Marital Adjustment," *American Journal of Sociology*, 43 (1937): pp. 270–283; Harvey J. Locke, *Predicting Adjustment in Marriage: A Comparison of a Divorced and a Happily-Married Group* (New York: Henry Holt, 1951); Harvey J. Locke and Georg Karlsson, "Marital Adjustment and Prediction in Sweden and the United States," *American Sociological Review*, 17 (1952): pp. 10–17; Eleanor B. Luckey, "An Investigation of the Concepts of the Self, Male, Parents, and ideal in Relation to Degree of Marital Satisfaction," Ph.D. Dissertation, University of Minnesota Library, 1959; Gerald J. Schnepp and Mary M. Johnson, "Do Religious Background Factors Have Predictive Value?" *Marriage and Family Living*, 14 (1952): pp. 301–304; Clarence W. Schroeder, *Divorce in a City of 100,000 Population* (Peoria, Illinois: Bradley Polytechnic Institute Library, 1939); David F. Shope and Alfred B. Broderick, "Level of Sexual Experience and Predicted Adjustment in Marriege," *Journal of Marriage and the Family*, 29 (1967): pp. 424–433. Lewis M. Terman, and others, *Psychological Factors in Marital Happiness* (New York: McGraw-Hill, 1938); Lewis M. Terman and Melita H. Oden, *The Gifted Child Grows Up: Twenty-five Years' Follow-up of a Superior Group* (Stanford: Stanford University Press, 1947): Ch. 19; Lewis M Terman, "Prediction Data: Predicting Marriage Failure from Test Scores," *Marriage and Family Living*, 12 (1950): pp. 51–54; and Robert Williamson,"Economic Factors in Marital Adjustment," Ph.D. Dissertation, University of Southern California Library, 1951.

Table 35. Marital items associated with adjustment in marriage (M, man; W, woman; if M and W not given then it is for both)*

Marital items	Studies by Benson, Bernard, Christensen and Philbrick, Davis, Hamilton, Keeley, Kelly, Kirkpatrick, Landis and Landis, Locke, Sabagh, and Thomes, Lu, Luckey, Peterson, Quade, Schroeder, Williamson, and Winch	Studies by Terman and Terman and Oden†	Study by Burgess and Cottrell	Studies by Locke and Locke and Karlsson†
Adaptability		Rated by outsider as satisfactory in general adjustment (Terman and Oden)		Adaptable personality

†In columns 3 and 5 the findings of two research studies are reported. The item cited is associated with marital adjustment in both studies unless one study is entered in parentheses. Then the association applies only to the designated study.

Birth control	No relationship to use of (Davis) W, children were planned (Christensen and Philbrick)	Trust in contraceptives, no relation to methods of contraception (Terman)	W, used (Locke)
Children, desire for	Desire 4 children (Christensen and Philbrick)	No relationship (Terman and Oden)	No children but desired by both; one or more children, and desired by both	No children, but mate desires; one or more children and desired by both (Locke) W, desire for (Locke and Karlsson)
Children, presence of	No relationship (Bernard, Hamilton Landis and Landis) W, none (Christensen and Philbrick)	No relationship (Terman) One or none (Terman and Oden)	None or one	No relationship

Appendix A 619

Church attendance		M, 2 or more times a month; W, 4 or more times a month (Locke) No relationship (Locke and Karlsson)
Church, membership in	Not in an "authoritarian" church, in a "liberal" church (Peterson)	Both belong to same church (Locke) Not member (Locke and Karlsson)
Communication	Intimate, informal and unrestricted (Locke, Sabagh, and Thomes)	
Community lived in after marriage, size of	Country (Terman and Oden)	Country, small town, or suburb; 200,000 or less

Conflict over certain activities		Nothing which annoys about the mate or the marriage	No conflict over activities
	No complaints about behavior of spouse or about the marriage (Terman)		
Economic efforts of man			W, very satisfactory
Economic level	Home owned (Schroeder, Williamson) No debts or less than $300; W, protected by more than $5,000 insurance (Williamson)	Home owned or planning to buy	Home owned; have life insurance; own home utilities or necessities, have established credit
	No relationship to ownership of home (Terman and Oden)		
Employment, length of			W, reports M had a job for over two years

Employment, regularity of husband		M, unemployed less than 20 percent of time W, M not unemployed (Terman and Oden)	Not unemployed, or under one month	W, reports M was regularly employed (Locke) M, less than 3 jobs (Locke and Karlsson)
Employment of wife	W, employed (Davis)	No relationship (Terman and Oden)	W, works and wants to work; occupation same as or similar to what she wants	No relationship to employment; M, approves wife working (Locke) M, no or one job; no relationship to M's approval of wife working (Locke and Karlsson)
Equality of man and woman	Thinks mate superior (Kelly) M, nonpatriarchal attitude of man; M and W about equally favorable to "feminism" (Kirkpatrick) Equality (Lu)			M, inferior to mate; W, inferior to mate or equal; both take lead about equally (Locke) M, feeling of equality; both take lead about equally (Locke and Karlsson)

Fear of pregnancy	No relationship	Does not make sex less enjoyable (Locke)
Feelings during periods of difficulty		Not at all or a little lonely, miserable, irritated, angry, insecure, worried, hurt, inferior, critical of mate.
Friends, men		Several or many (Locke) M, says W has many; W, says she has several or many (Locke and Karlsson)
Friends, women		M, a few or more; says W has several or many; W, several or many (Locke) M, many; W, several; W says M has several (Locke and Karlsson)

Appendix A   623

Friends in common			Several or many (Locke) M, many; W, several or many (Locke and Karlsson)
Health		Perfect, superior, good (Terman and Oden)	No relationship (Locke)
Home management			Very satisfactory
Income	No relationship (Bernard)	No relationship to amount (Terman) M, $100-500 a month; W, $200 or more (Terman and Oden)	Reported as adequate for needs of family

Income management	Income met economic needs, had checking account, did not borrow or less than three times in 5 years (Williamson)	
In-laws, attitude toward living with		M, enjoys; W, does not mind (Locke)
In-laws, lived with during marriage	No relationship	Did not live with W's; W, did not live with M's (Locke) No relationship (Locke) and Karlsson)
Jealousy		Other does not show it

Appendix A 625

Married, number of years	W, 0-4 years (Hamilton)	0-2 years (Terman) No relationship (Terman and Oden)	0-1 year
Mental ability		M, not rated markedly superior; W, husband not rated inferior	Mates feel equal
Occupation	W, white collar or higher (Williamson)	W, if husband belongs to professional class; W's occupation no relationship (Terman and Oden)	W, professional and semiprofessional; not domestic service
Personality "traits"	Not having an overreactive touchiness or sense of inferiority (Winch) Low on Bale's categories of dominance and control (Quade)	Bernreuter items: M 69; W, 67; Strong items: M, 48; W, 50; Opinion items: M, 23; W, 15 (Terman) 36 Bernreuter items; 10 Strong items; 15 opinion items and 13 self-ratings (Terman and Oden)	Thurstone neurotic items, low score	Mate and self had specified traits

Appendix A   627

Residence, type of		Single dwelling
Residence, years lived in		2 years or more
Residential area	High social area (Williamson)	
Savings	Combined, $600 or more (Williamson)	Some (Locke)
Self concept	Spouse like own concept of ideal self; M similar to W's concept of him (Luckey)	
Sex, frequency of intercourse	Less than once a day at beginning of marriage (Davis)	Ratio of actual to preferred close to unity

Sexual intercourse	Report never committed adultery; desire no extramarital intercourse (Hamilton)	Infrequent refusal; infrequent desire for extramarital intercourse (Terman)	Rarely refuses mate; never desires with another; never has with another, does not know, believe, or suspect mate; mate does not know, believe, or suspect me (Locke) None with another; does not believe mate had (Locke and Karlsson)
Sex, orgasm of wife	In at least 20 percent of copulations (Hamilton)	Adequate capacity for orgasm	
Sex, prudishness modesty		M does not think W overmodest or prudish (Terman)	Very little or some modesty and shyness in matters of sex (Locke)

Appendix A   629

Sex, strength of interest or desire	W, not married to man with low sex desire (Hamilton) W, about the same intensity (Davis)	Equality or near equality (Terman)	Equality or near equality
Sex, pleasure and satisfaction	Pleasure at beginning and throughout marriage (Davis) No complaints about adequacy of mate (Hamilton)	W, pleasure at first intercourse; M, indifference, or interest and pleasant anticipation; high degree of satisfaction in; no complaints (Terman)	M, very enjoyable with W; W, enjoyable or very enjoyable with M
Sleeping arrangements		Not in different rooms (Terman)	

Sociability	Rated by outsider as sociable (Terman and Oden)	Sociable person
Values	Similar (Keeley) W, home and children; M, romantic love (Benson)	

*In addition to references cited for Table 34: Harold T. Christensen and R. E. Philbrick, "Family Size as a Factor in the Marital Adjustment of College Students," *American Sociological Review*, 17 (1952): pp. 306–312; Benjamin J. Keeley, "Value Convergence and Marital Relations," *Marriage and Family Living*, 17 (1955): pp. 342–345; E. Lowell Kelly, "Marital Compatibility as Related to Personality Traits of Husbands and Wives as Rated by Self and Spouse," *Journal of Social Psychology*, 13 (1941): pp. 193–198; Judson T. Landis and Mary S. Landis, *Building a Successful Marriage* (New York: Prentice-Hall, 1948), pp. 238–264; Harvey J. Locke, Georges Sabagh, and Mary Margaret Thomes, "Correlates of Primary Communication and Empathy," *Research Studies of the State College of Washington*, 24, (1956): pp. 116–124; Yi-Chuang Lu, "Marital Roles and Marriage Adjustment," *Sociology and Social Research*, 36 (1952): pp. 364–368; James Peterson, "The Relation of Objective and Subjective Factors to Adjustment and Maladjustment in Marriage," Ph.D. Dissertation, University of Southern California Library, 1951; Albert E. Quade, "The Relationship Between Marital Adjustment and Certain Interactional Patterns in Problem-Solving Situations," Ph.D. Dissertation, Ohio State University Library, 1955; Robert Williamson, "Economic Factors in Marital Adjustment," Ph.D. Dissertation, University of Southern California Library, 1951; and Robert F. Winch, "Personality Characteristics of Engaged and Married Couples," *American Journal of Sociology*, 46 (1941): pp. 686–697.

APPENDIX B
Acknowledgments

We want to thank particularly John Wiley and Sons for permission to quote extensively from *Six Cultures: Studies in Child Rearing*, by Beatrice B. Whiting, (ed.); and also from *Birth to Maturity*, by Jerome Kagan and Howard A. Moss. In addition, we want to thank the following for kindly giving us permission to quote: Aldine, *Family Design: Marital Sexuality, Family Size, and Contraception*, by Lee Rainwater; Columbia University Press, *Up From Puerto Rico*, by Elena Padilla; Granada Publishing Limited, *Leisure and Pleasure of Soviet Children*, by Deana Levin; Harper and Row, Publishers, Incorporated, *Patterns of Child Rearing*, by Robert R. Sears, Eleanor E. Maccoby, and Harry Levin; Harvard University Press, *Family and Community in Ireland*, by Conrad M. Arensberg and Solon T. Kimball; also *Marriage and Divorce: A Social and Economic Study*, by Hugh Carter and Paul C. Glick; Houghton Mifflin, "The Tibetan Family System," by Prince Peter of Greece and Denmark, in *Comparative Family Systems*, M. F. Nimkoff, (ed.); Lippincott, *The New You and Heredity*, by Amram Scheinfeld; Little Brown and Co., Inc., *The Drifters: Children of Disorganized Lower-Class Families*, by Eleanor Pavenstedt, (ed.); also, *Women of the Modern World: Their Education and Dilemmas*, by Mirra Komarovsky; Oceana Publications, Inc., *Workingman's Wife: Her Personality, World, and Life Style*, by Lee Rainwater, Richard P. Coleman, and Gerald Handel, © 1959 by Social Research, Inc. Reprinted by permission of Oceana Publications, Inc.; Prentice-Hall, Inc. *Marriage and Family Among Negroes*, by Jessie Bernard, © 1966; Springer Publishing Co., Inc., *Growing Up in the Kibbutz*, by A. I. Rabin; also, "Minority Group and Class Status as Related to Social and Personality Factors in Scholastic Achievement," by Martin Deutsch, in *Mental Health and Segregation*, M. M. Grossack, (ed.); UNESCO, "The Changing Social Position of Women in Japan, 1961," by Takashi Koyama, Reproduced with the permission of UNESCO; University of California Press, *Japan's New Middle Class: The Salary Man and His Family in a Tokyo Suburb*, by Ezra F. Vogel, Reprinted by Permission of The Regents of the University of California; Williams and Wilkins, *Deviant Children Grown Up*, by Lee N. Robins, © 1966.

The *American Academy of Political and Social Scince*, (160, 1932, p. 189), "The Bereaved Family," by Thomas D. Eliot; *American Journal of Orthopsychiatry*, (35, 1965, pp. 94–95), "A Comparison of the Child-Rearing Environment of Upper-Lower and Very Low-Lower Class Families," by Eleanor Pavenstedt, copyright, the American Orthopsychiatric Association, Inc. Reproduced by permission; *Journal of Marriage and the Family*, (31, 1969, p. 72), "Working-Class Wives in Suburbia: Fulfillment or Crisis, by Irving Tallman; also, (32, 1970, pp. 65–66), "Correlates of Dissatisfaction in Marriage," by Karen S. Renne; *Journal of Social Issues* (11, 1955, pp. 12–13), "The Impact of Mental Illness on the Family," by John A. Clausen, Marian Radke-Yarrow, and others; *Los Angeles Times* (Sept. 8, 1968), "What is it Really Like to be Poor?", by Linda Mathews, copyright 1968, Los Angeles Times. Reprinted by permission; *Pediatrics*, (32, 1963, p. 307), "Child-rearing Practices in a Low Socioeconomic Group," by H. Wortis and others; The University of Chicago Press, *American Journal of Sociology* (60, 1956, p. 12), "Some Aspects of Urbanization in the Belgian Congo," by Jean L. Comhaire; also (68, 1962, pp. 90–91), "Family Process and Becoming a Mental Patient," by Harold Sampson, Shelden L. Messinger, and Robert D. Towne.

Index

Abel, H., 250
Abrams, C., 596
Accommodation, 491–496
Ackerman, N. W., 230–231
Adams, B. N., 96, 455, 470
Adams, C. R., 358
Adams, J. B., 33
Adelson, J., 490, 491
Adjustment, to bereavement, 552–553; as a criterion of marital success, 321–322; to depressions, 520–521; to divorce, 543–545; predicting in marriage, 336–363; see also Marital adjustment
Adolescent roles, 255–256
Affection, 275–277, 368–369, 438–439, 484–485
Age, differences between mates, at marriage, 287, 305; at marriage in various countries, 23–24
Aiken, M. T., 64
Alcoholism, 506–507
Aldous, J., 67
Aller, F. D., 332
Allowances, family, 137–138, 587
Alt, E., 153–154
Alt, H., 153–154
Ancona, L., 253
Anderson, N., 75, 253
Anderson, V. E., 303
Angell, R. C., 492, 515, 519, 524
Anshen, R. N., 174, 596
Arensberg, C. M., 38, 296, 631
Aronson, E., 219
Arnold, M. B., 231
Automobile, in personal mobility, 453–454
Axelrod, M., 63, 96
Axelson, L. J., 397

Baber, R. E., 305

Bach, G. R., 254
Baggaley, A. R., 308
Bain, J. K., 372
Bakke, E. W., 515
Bales, R. F., 247, 386
Baldwin, A. L., 216
Baldwin, G. C., 183
Baley, N., 216
Bandura, A., 221
Barker, R. G., 199
Bascom, W., 66
Bauer, R. A., 146, 154
Baykov, A., 148
Beam, L., 552
Bean, F. D. 304
Becker, W. C., 220
Bee, H. L., 220
Bee, L. S., 309–310
Beegle, J. A., 48
Bell, N. W., 385, 500
Bell, R. R., 81, 278, 288, 290
Bell, W., 96
Bender, L. D., 47, 57
Bendix, R., 454, 455, 470
Benson, B., 599, 617, 618, 630
Berardo, F. M., 10
Bereavement, 545–553; adjustments to, 552–553; attitudes toward bereaved and divorced persons, 553–554; idealization of the dead, 551–552; individual differences in, 549–551; reactions to, 548–549; variations in mourning patterns, 546–548; widows and widowers, 546
Berger, B. M., 96
Berman, N., 145, 147
Bernard, J., 115, 127, 357, 599, 600, 617, 618, 624, 631
Bernstein, B., 182
Bernstein, R., 508
Besner, A., 79, 80–81, 96

633

Bharadwaj, L. K., 41, 58
Biller, H. B., 260
Biological traits, 243
Birth folkways, 422–430
Birth rate, declining, 425–426; in Russia, 137–138; in wartime, 564–565
Blake, N. M., 557
Blood, R. O., 40–41, 57, 74, 169, 173–174, 248, 277, 385
Blumer, H., 461
Boll, E., 222
Bolton, C. D., 311
Boquet, C., 253
Borow, H., 260
Borstelmann, L. J., 260
Bossard, J. H. S., 222
Bott, E., 245–246, 261
Bowerman, C. E., 222, 248, 309, 313, 361
Boynton, P. H., 193
Brayshaw, A. J., 394, 410–411
Brim, O. G., 218, 252, 260
Britton, J. H., 58
Broderick, A. B., 599, 615, 617
Brody, S. A., 368
Broken families, see Family disruption
Bruce, P. A., 113
Burch, T. K., 428
Burchinal, L., 53, 63, 278, 313
Burgess, E. W., 3–4, 10, 141–142, 212–213, 282, 286, 298, 303, 319, 321, 322, 323, 324, 325, 326, 327, 334, 337, 339, 351, 352, 353, 357, 358, 359, 361, 362, 368, 375, 376, 391, 396, 403, 406, 408, 411, 440, 454, 485, 493, 499, 517, 599–630
Burke, V. J., 139, 144
Burr, W. R., 392
Byrne, D., 216

Calhoun, A. W., 32, 264
California Test of Personality, 43
Campbell, A., 422, 424, 425, 446, 447
Canby, H. S., 269–270
Carlsmith, L., 254
Carroll, E. E., 90
Carter, H., 313, 350–351, 390–391, 441, 530, 534, 544, 631
Catton, W. R., 302–303
Cavan, R. S., 515, 518, 519, 521, 524–525
Cervantes, L. F., 386
Cesa-Bianchi, M., 253
Changing American Family, 415–447; age at marriage, 441; babies born in hospitals, 430; birth folkways, 422–430; birth rate, declining, 425–426; changes in type of home dwelling, 420–422; democratic characteristics, 419–420; economic activities, 431–435; educational activities, 436–438; family functions, changing, 430–439; family roles, 441–443; length of marriage increasing, 441; patriarchal characteristics, 418–419; from patriarchal to democratic, 417–420; permanent marriage, 440–441; protective activities, 435–436; recreational activities, 438; religious activities, 438; retention of affectional and child-rearing activities, 438–439; sex, changing patterns, 439–440; size of the family, declining, 426–430

Chaskes, J. B., 278, 288
Child, I. L., 219
Children, adjustment of farm, 42–44; adjustment of urban, 42–44; child-rearing in unusual situations, 221–225; child-training in disorganized slum families, 83–85; education of Negro, 111–114; child-training practices, 218–221; in father-absent homes, 253–255; function of communication in development of, 183–187; learning of roles, 239–241; learning of sex roles, 248–255; of lower-class mothers, 81–85, status of farm, 45
Child-training practices, 218–221
China, see Japan, China, and India
Christensen, H. T., 10, 278, 313, 361, 538, 618, 619, 630
Clark, A. L., 412
Clausen, J. A., 203, 253, 513–514, 631
Cloward, R. A., 203
Cochrane, C. M., 508
Coleman, R. P., 59–60, 97, 631
Collman, J. T., 535
Comhaire, J. L., 66, 67, 632
Communication, and family unity, 366–368; increasing for farmers, 50–53; function of personality development, 183–187; primary, in courtship, 276–277; sexual behavior as a form of, 375
Companionship, as a criterion of marital success, 323–324
Companionship family, a case history of, 364–366; decline in the middle years, 391–392; definition of, 9, 584–586; desire for by young people, 257; trend toward, 7–9, 28–29
Competitiveness in courtship, 273–274
Conceptual framework, 2–5; social groups and structures, 2; role behavior, 3; social processes, 3; culture,

3; demography, 3; symbolic interaction, 3-4
Conflict, see Family conflicts and accommodations
Consensus, as a criterion of marital success, 323
Conveniences, modern, 431-432; in rural and urban dwellings, 55
Cooley, C. H., 4, 10
Coombs, R. H., 277-278, 310
Cooper, C. A., 282
Coopersmith, S., 201, 203
Coser, R. L., 32
Cottrell, L. S., 298, 319, 322, 334, 339, 351, 352, 357, 358, 361-362, 484, 597, 599-630
Courtship, in Colonial America, 267-269; and competitiveness, 273-274; control of premarital sexual behavior, 288; dating in, 277-278; defined, 273-277; development of in America, 267-271; in early nineteenth-century America, 269; and engagement, 280-283; and engagement, broken, 282-283; and going steady, 278-280; incidence of petting in, 284; incidence of premarital intercourse in, 284-287; love and affection in, 275-277; and marital adjustment, 281; progressive commitment in, 274-275; and role expectations, 273; and romantic love, 271-273; and the sex ratio, 274; sexual behavior in, 283-288; in the 1890's, 269-270; in the 1920's, 270-271
Couvade, 183
Cowgill, D. O., 451
Cowhig, J. D., 53
Cressey, D. R., 198, 510
Crime, see Delinquency
Crises, see Family crises
Criteria of marital success, 315-335; companionship, 323-324; consensus, 323; happiness, 318-319; integration, 322-323; marital adjustment, 321-322; permanence, 318; satisfaction, 320-321; sexual adjustment, 321
Cuber, J. F., 378-379, 385, 575
Cultural conditioning and emotional interaction, 225-228
Culture and socialization, 179-204; acquisition of the family culture, 192-194; biological traits, definition of, 198-200; cultural conditioning within the family, 187-192; cultural continuity, 193-194; definition of cultural conditioning, 181-182; examples of cultural conditioning, 182-183; the family as a conditioning agent, 191-192; the function of communication, 183-184; language, the importance of, 186-187; learning deviant behavior, 192; methods of conditioning behavior, 187-191; the nature of cultural conditioning, 181-187; outside-the-home conditioning, 195-198; projection of parental goals, 194-195; relative absence of communication, 184-187; self-concept, development of, 198-201; self-esteem, development of, 200-201

Dating, 277-278
Davis, A., 129
Davis, J. P., 128
Davis, K., 184-186
Davis, K. B., 599, 600, 605, 609, 612, 614, 615, 616, 617, 618, 619, 622, 627, 629
Davis, K. E., 304
Day, B. R., 309, 313, 506
Dean, J. P., 596
Death, see Bereavement
Delinquency and crime, as a family crisis, 509-511; learned in the family, 192; in Russia, 144-145
Delora, J., 279
Dentler, R. A., 375
Depression, adjustment to, 520-522; changes of roles in, 518-520; decrease of marriages and divorces in, 516-517; insecurity in, 517-518
Deutsch, M., 113, 182, 631
Deutscher, I., 397, 411
Dickinson, R. L., 552
Disaster, 523-524
Disgrace, 505-515; and alcoholism, 506-507; and crime, 509-511; and illegitimacy, 507-509; and loss of virginity, 507; and mental illness, 511-514; and suicide, 514-515
Divorce, 530-545; crisis generally, 539-540; crisis, not always, 537-539; when it is a crisis, 540; differences in adjustment to, 542-543; differences in divorce practices and divorce rates, 534-537; an index of family disruption, 530-532; laws, 532, 535; and reconciliation, 540-542; types of adjustment to, 543-545; variations in divorce rates, 532-534; in wartime, 570, 573
Dixon, M. M., 278, 279
Dobriner, W. M., 74, 96

Dollard, J., 129
Douglas, J. W. B., 222
Douvan, E., 490, 491
Dunn, M. S., 255
Dyer, W. G., 257

Edmonson, M. S., 129
Education, changes in educational activities, 436–437; of farm and nonfarm persons, 52–53; and mate selection, 305; of Negroes and whites, 109–114; as a factor in predicting adjustment in marriage, 351–352; in Russia, 144; in South Africa, 196; in suburbs and central cities, 70, 71; variations among blue-collar workers by, 88–90
Edwards, G. F., 128
Eggan, D., 20
Ehrmann, W., 284, 286, 290
Elder, G. H., 222, 455
Eliot, T. D., 550, 551, 631
Elkin, F., 203
Elkins, S. M., 104, 128
Ellis, R. A., 457
Embree, J. F., 174, 295
Emmerich, W., 250
Emotional interaction, see Interaction and socialization
Engagement, 280–283
England, R. W., 271–272
Erlick, V. St., 32
Expectations, see Roles and expectations
Extended family in Japan, China, and India, 158–162; among the Apache, 294; See also Family, extended
Exogamy, 13–14

Familism, 39–42
Family, age and years married, 29; agencies, interested in, 589–591; authority, 28–29; companionship, 7–9, 28–29, 257, 323–324, 364–366, 391–392, 584–586; composition of, 29; conflicts and accommodations, 472–500; conjugal, 7; the courtship process, 265–291; as a creative group, 591; crises of, 501–558; cultural background, 29; cultural continuity, 193–194; definition of, 6–7; and delinquency, 144–145, 192, 509–511; democratic, 22; disruption of, 526–558; division of labor, in various countries, 27–28; emotional interaction in, 207–221; expectations and roles, 233–261; extended, 7, 20, 21, 22, 158–162, 163–171; forms in various countries, 27; housing, 588; in Japan, China, and India, 156–175; in Ireland, 38–39; in the later years of, 387–412; mate selection, 292–314; measuring success in marriage, 315–335; in the middle years of marriage, 387–412; mobility, 448–471; Negro, 99–129; nuclear, 7; nutrition, 588; of orientation, 7; personality and cultural conditioning, 179–204; predicting adjustment in marriage, 336–363; in process of change, 581–597; of procreation, 7; retention of affectional and cultural functions, 438–439; reorganization, 584–586; rural, 34–58; Russian, 130–155; size of, 426–430; in social change, 415–447; urban, 59–98; variations in, 13–33; as a valued object, 1–2; war, 559–580; widowhood, 400–401, 546
Family conflicts and accommodations, 472–500; accommodation, 491–496; and adaptability, 492–493; affectional, 484–485; and avoidance of devisive issues, 493–494; and crises, 494; cumulative nature of tensions, 476–477; economic tensions, 484; differences in cultural patterns, 481–483, 487–489; emotional tensions, 485–487; fear of losing cherished values, 493; functional value of, 475–476; inevitability and normality of, 475; nature of, 475–477; parent-child tensions, 485–491; and roles, 483, 489–491; sexual, 484–485; and social pressures, 493; symbolic nature of, 476; temperamental incompatibility, 480–481; types of family tensions, 477–485; will to make the marriage a success, 491
Family counseling, marriage and family, 591–594; professional training for, 593–594; in the professions, 592–593
Family crises, 501–558; adjustments of economic standards in depressions, 518; adjustment of organized and disorganized families to depressions, 520–521; alcoholism, 506–507; changes in roles of family members in depressions, 518–520; crime, 509–511; in depressions, 515–522; deviations from expectations, 503–505; disgrace, 505–515; economic reverses, 515–522; illegitimacy, 507–509; insecurity of the family in depressions, 517–518; marriages and divorces in depressions, 516–517; mental illness, 511–514; reactions to depressions, 521–522; skilled job, losing to a machine, 522; suicide, 514–515; uniformities of, 554–555; virginity, loss of, 507

Index 637

Family disruption, 526–558; death and bereavement, 545–554; departure of children, 529–530; divorce, 530–545; see Divorce, and Bereavement
Family, extended, 158–163; characteristics of, 159; disintegration of in Japan, China, and India, 167–171; traditional roles in, 163–167
Family of Japan, China, and India, 156–175; extended family, 158–162; industrialization and mobility, 168–169; the lineage group, 162–163; marriage laws, 169; new culture contacts, 168; reasons for changes in the traditional form, 167–171; roles of family head, 163–164; roles of mother, 164–165; roles of son, 165; roles of daughter, 165; roles of daughter-in-law, 166–167
Family-life cycle, 390–391
Family in the middle and later years, 387–412; and career frustration of middle-aged husbands, 395–396; comparison of early and middle years of marriage, 391–395; decline of companionship family in middle years of marriage, 391–392; decline in economic role of older persons, 399; grandparents and grandchildren, 407–408; in the later years of marriage, 397–408; marital roles in old age, 398–399; old age insurance and assistance programs, 404–405; network of kin relationships, 405–407; reduction of parental roles in the middle years, 396–397; retirement of husband, 399–401, 402–403; support of parents, 401–402; widowhood, 400–401
Family unity, 364–386; common interests and activities, 371–372; communication, 366–368; consensus on values and objectives, 372–373; degrees of, 379–383; dynamically unified, 382–383; emotional interdependence, 369–370; environing society, 377–378; factors in, 366–378; family events, celebrations and ceremonies, 373; habit-bound, 381; highly solidified, 381–382; interdependence of roles, 373–375; and love and affection, 368–369; nature of, 366; relatively unorganized, 380–381; sexual behavior, 375–377; sympathetic understanding, 370–381; types of marital relationships, 378–379
Farber, B., 323, 334, 372, 525

Farber, S. M., 159, 174
Farberow, N. L., 515
Feldman, H., 391
Fielding, W. J., 268, 290
Filmore, R., 418
Firth, R., 32
Foote, N. N., 597
Frampton, M. E., 37–38
Frazier, E. F., 118, 128
Freedman, R., 422, 446
Fried, M., 174
Fuggitt, G. V., 58
Functions of the Family, 430–439
Furstenberg, F. F., 269

Gabower, G., 579
Gallup, G., 194
Gans, H. H., 78
Garrison, R. J., 303
Gebhard, P. H., 283, 284, 285, 290, 356, 392, 440
Geiger, H. K., 147, 154
Gilevskaya, S., 154–155
Gillin, J., 129
Ginzberg, E., 58, 128
Glasser, L. N., 411
Glasser, P. H., 411
Glick, P. C., 313, 350–351, 390–391, 441, 534, 544, 631
Gluck, E., 221
Gluck, S., 221
Going steady, 278–280
Gold, M., 490
Goldberg, D., 422
Golden, J. F., 47, 57
Goldstein, B., 97
Goldstein, S., 470
Goode, W. J., 158, 174, 539, 557
Goodman, M., 310
Goodman, N., 367
Gorer, G., 557
Grandparents, 407–408
Greenfield, S. M., 97
Greenhohm, G., 522
Groat, H. T., 430
Grossack, M. M., 113, 631
Guerney, B. C., 78

Habenstein, R. W., 19, 33
Hall, E. T., 79
Hall, M., 246
Halle, F. W., 132, 135
Hamblin, R. L., 385
Hamilton, C. H., 452
Hamilton, G. V., 320, 334, 357, 599, 602, 605, 613, 615, 617, 618, 626, 628, 629
Handel, G., 59–60, 97, 129, 231, 631

Hansen, D. A., 4-5, 10
Happiness, as a criterion of marital success, 318-319
Hardesty, F., 252
Harris, C., 66
Harris, J., 418
Hart, H., 599, 600, 617
Hartley, R. E., 251, 252
Hathaway, S. R., 43-44
Hauser, P. M., 517, 564
Havens, A. E., 278
Hawkins, J. L., 360
Haywood, A. C., 108
Heinstein, M. I., 219
Heiss, J. G., 310, 313
Henkel, R. E., 58
Heney, C. A., 508
Henry, J., 228
Henry, Z., 228
Herbst, P. G., 260
Hess, R. D., 193, 231
Heterogamy, 303-306, 309-310
Hetherington, E. M., 251, 254
Hill, R., 4-5, 10, 272, 302, 305, 307, 313, 381, 492, 575, 580
Hindus, M., 147
Hitchcock, J. T., 210
Ho, P., 159, 162, 165, 174
Hobart, C. W., 310, 368
Hobbs, D., 47
Hoffman, L. W., 217, 220, 231, 253, 260, 261, 435, 490
Hoffman, M. L., 217, 220, 231, 253, 260, 490
Hollingshead, A. B., 30, 78, 204, 258, 458
Holtzman, W. H., 204, 222
Homogany, 303-306, 309-310
Horney, K., 227
Horton, D., 272
Hsu, F. L. K., 239
Hubbard, L. E., 143
Huebner, B., 332
Hurley, J. F., 346
Husband-wife interaction, emotional, 212-214; expectations and roles in, 244-248; see also Family conflicts and accommodations, Marital adjustment, Family unity

Ideational mobility, 458-461
Illegitimacy, 107-108, 507-509
Individualism, 39-42
Inkeles, A., 146, 149, 150, 154
Integration, as a criterion of marital success, 322-323
Interaction and socialization, 205-232; affection and permissiveness, 219-221; child-rearing in the Kibbutz, 224-225; child-rearing in large families, 221-222; child-training practices, 218-221; emotional and cultural, interrelationships between, 225-228; emotion, nature of, 207-212; family environment of schizophrenic and normal children, 223-224; husband-wife, 212-214; learning emotional patterns, 209-212; parental, and child-rearing, 214-217; and personality traits, 226-227; sibling, 217-218; and sibling jealousy, 227-228; within the family, 212-218
Intermarriage, interfaith, 306; racial, 303-304
Irish, D. P., 17

Jackson, J., 506
Jacobson, P. F., 557-558
Jacobson, P. H., 557-558
Jafee, A. J., 515
James, H., 4, 10
Japan, China, and India, See Family of Japan, China, and India
Jealousy, 227-228
Jenkins, W. W., 523
Johnson, M. M., 599, 603, 612, 613, 615, 617
Jones, L. W., 128-129
Jorgens, B., 332

Kagen, J., 196, 197, 198, 260, 631
Kahn, D. C., 515
Kandel, D. B., 255
Kapadia, K. M., 159, 174
Karlsson, G., 321, 324, 339, 346, 348, 352, 357, 362, 420, 492, 599-630
Kaya, R. S., 250
Katz, A. M., 302, 313
Keller, H., 186-187
Keeley, B. J., 618, 630
Kelly, E. L., 358, 618, 622, 630
Kenkel, W. F., 277-278
Kephart, W. M., 32, 499
Kerckhoff, A. C., 304, 405
Key, W. H., 63
Keyano, S., 174
Kharchev, A. G., 139, 143, 146, 154
Kiang, K., 166
Kimball, S. T., 38, 296, 631
King, C. E., 321, 599, 600, 602, 603, 604, 605, 606, 608, 609, 611, 612, 613, 614, 615, 617
Kinsey, A. C., 283-284, 285, 290, 392, 440
Kinship group, 63-68

Kirkendall, L. A., 290
Kirkpatrick, C., 334–335, 599, 601, 607, 617, 618, 622
Kiser, C. V., 303, 422
Klausner, W. J., 368
Kluckhohn, F. R., 20–21
Koch, H. L., 218, 252, 260
Kohn, M. L., 90–91
Kolb, J. H., 58
Kollmergen, W. M., 39–40
Komarovsky, M., 64, 88–90, 97, 238, 248, 249, 260–261, 305, 515, 631
Korshunova, E., 143, 144, 155
Kosa, J., 411
Kounin, J. S., 199
Koyama, T., 164, 166, 167, 168, 169, 170, 174–175, 631
Kozera, E. S., 135, 136, 138, 142, 149, 154
Kravchinskii, S. M., 130–132, 133
Kuhn, M. H., 239–240

Lambert, W., 23
Landis, J. T., 618, 619, 630
Landis, M. S., 618, 619, 630
Lane, W. C., 457
Lang, R. O., 358
Lansing, A. K., 57
Lansky, L. M., 252
Lantz, H. R., 268
Lasko, J. K., 216
Laws, divorce, 169, 535
Lazarsfeld, P. F., 515
Leichty, M. M., 254
Le Masters, E. E., 216
Le Play, F., 37–38
Leslie, G. R., 470
Lesser, G. S., 255
Levin, D., 146, 154, 631
Levin, H., 200, 219, 231, 631
LeVine, B. B., 13–16, 210–211
LeVine, R. A., 13–16, 210–211
Levinger, G., 247–248
Levirate, 14
Lewis, H., 78, 118, 129
Lidz, T., 515
Lindzey, G., 219
Lipset, S. M., 454, 455, 470
Litwak, E., 63, 68, 470–471
Locke, H. J., 10, 64–65, 75, 91–93, 213–214, 223, 300, 306, 318, 321, 322, 323, 324, 325, 326, 327, 331, 335, 339, 340, 341, 344, 346, 348, 351, 352, 353, 354, 355, 357, 362, 368, 370, 375, 376, 377, 378, 420, 439, 440, 477–480, 485, 492, 499, 530, 537–538, 539, 599–630
Locke, J., 419
Lonely-hearts clubs, 301–302

Loether, C. C., 411
Lotka, A. J., 426
Love and affection, 275–277, romantic, 271–273
Lu, Y., 618, 622, 630
Luckey, E. B., 346, 347, 351, 352, 372, 385, 599, 609, 617, 618, 627
Lundberg, G. A., 451
Lunt, P. A., 457
Lynd, H. M., 451
Lynd, R. S., 451
Lyle, J., 459, 471
Lynn, D., 253

Maccoby, E. E., 200, 219, 231, 261, 471, 631
McCord, J., 221
McCord, W., 221
McCormack, P., 548
McDonald, J. F., 510
McGinnis, R., 305, 307
Mace, D., 163
Mace, V., 163
Macfarlane, J. W., 199, 215–216
Mack, R. W., 172
McKay, H. D., 510
Mangus, A. R., 42–43
Marital adjustment, 315–363; and age at marriage, 350–351; constructing a marital-adjustment index, 326–331; and courtship experiences, 349–350; criteria of marital success (see Criteria of marital success), and cultural backgrounds, 348; differences of husbands and wives in, 325–326; and education, 351–352; general predictive factors of, 345–358; and the kinship group, 352–354, measuring adjustment in marriage, 315–335; and number of children, 356–358; and personality characteristics, 345–348; predicting future adjustment, 358–359; procedures of predicting, 340–341; and sexual behavior, 354–356; and social participation, 348; studies of, 339–340; test to measure adjustment, 328–331; test to predict marital adjustment, 341–343
Marriage, age at marriage, 23–24, 390, 422, 441; decrease in depressions, 516–517; definition of, 5–6; forms, of, 16–19, 27; hurried up and hasty marriages in wartime, 566–567; postponement of in wartime, 566; predicting adjustment in (see Marital adjustment); proportion married in rural and urban, 50; rate in wartime, 562–564

Marris, P., 66, 549, 558
Martin, C. E., 283, 284, 285, 290, 356, 392, 440
Martin, W. T., 74, 96
Mason, M. K., 185
Mate selection, 292–314; age differences between mates, 305; among the Apaches, 294; the bride price, 297–298; and education, 305; factors in, 302–310; homogamy, 303–306; ideal mate, 306–308; in Japan, 295–296; lonely-hearts introduction clubs, 301–302; parental image, 308; parental role in, 298–299; and personality needs, 309–310; propinquity, 302–303; role of intermediaries, 298–302; role of voluntary associations, 299; in rural Ireland, 296; secondary contacts in, 299–301; social characteristics in, 303–306; in various countries, 24–25
Mather, W. G., 58
Mathews, L., 75–76, 81–83, 632
Matriarchal family, 19, 20–21
Matricentric family, 73–74
Matrilineal family, 19
Matrilocal family, 19
Matsumoto, Y. S., 175
Mathews, L., 75–76, 81–83
Mayer, K. B., 306
Mead, G. H., 3, 4, 10, 188
Mead, M., 202, 226–228
Measuring success in marriage, see Marital adjustment, and Criteria of marital success
Meisel, J. H., 135, 136, 138, 142, 149, 154
Merrill, F. E., 272
Messinger, S. L., 511, 512, 632
Middletown, R., 385–386
Miller, D. R., 220, 231
Miner, H., 66
Minturn, L., 23, 210
Minuchin, S., 78, 97
Mishler, E. G., 423, 446
Mobility and the family, 448–471; adjustment through relocation, 467; to cities, 45–47; and family disorganization, 461–464; and family organization, 464–467; ideational, 458–462; and the immigrant family, 462; internal migration, 462–463; mobile families, 466–467; moving out of a social matrix, 463–464; Negro, 116–119; occupational, 454–457; personal, 453–454; residential, 450–453; in rural areas, 451; spatial separation of family members, 464; in urban areas, 451; and vacations and other travels, 465–466; vertical, 193, 454–458; in wartime, 561–562
Mollendorff, P. G., 166
Monachesi, E. D., 43–44
Monogamy, 17
Monohan, T. P., 533
Moore, B. M., 204, 222
Montalvo, B., 78
Mormons, 17–18
Morrison, D. E., 41
Moses, R., 515
Moss, H. A., 188, 196, 197, 198, 260, 631
Mourning practices, 546–548
Mowrer, E. R., 74, 96, 451, 477
Mudd, E. H., 583, 597
Munson, B. E., 43
Mussen, P., 251
Mustachi, P., 159, 174
Myers, J. K., 525
Myrdal, G., 118

Nam, C. B., 452
Neal, A. G., 430
Negro family, 99–129; case of, 99–103; changing Negro family, 105–114; decreasing differences between Negro and white, 108–114; differences among, 114–115; differential experiences during slavery, 105; disorganization, 119–123; education, years completed, 109–111; education, quality of, 111–112; elimination of the African heritage, 104–105; equalitarian, 124; female heads, 107; field hands, 105; forms of organization, 123–124; free Negroes, 105; house servants, 105; illegitimacy, 107–108; matricentric, 123; mobility, 116–119; small patriarchal, 123–124; urbanization, 119
Neugarter, B. L., 411
Neja, P., 332
Nimkoff, M. F., 19, 446, 459, 631
Nonfamily areas, 75–76
Nye, F. I., 10, 43, 204, 261, 435

Occupations and vertical mobility, 155–156
Odell, E., 301–302, 314
Oden, M. H., 321, 325, 339, 358, 363, 493, 599–630
Ofshe, R., 367
Ogburm, W. F., 33, 446
Ohlin, L. E., 203
Old age, among the Amish, 39; insurance and assistance, 404–405, 435–436; in the later years of marriage, 397–408

Opler, M. E., 294
Orlansky, H., 219

Padilla, E., 462, 507, 525, 546, 631
Parent-child relations, conflicts, 485–491; interactions, 205–207, 208–212, 215–217; of farm families, 42–44; among the poor, 81–85; in Russia, 145–147
Park, R. E., 105
Parker, E. B., 459, 471
Parkes, C. M., 549
Parks, R., 390–391
Parmar, Y. S., 37
Parsons, T., 10, 208, 247, 386
Pastore, J., 67
Patriarchal family, 19, 21–22
Patrilineal family, 19
Patrilocal family, 14, 19
Patterson, J. E., 424, 425, 447
Pavenstedt, E., 79, 83–85, 631
Pedersen, F. A., 253
Permanence as a criterion of martial success, 318
Perry, H. S., 553, 558
Perry, S. E., 553, 558
Personality, and culture, 182–183; definitions of biological traits and self-conception, 198–200; of farm children, 42–44; importance of communication for its development, 183–187; self-esteem, development of, 200–201; traits, 226–227; in varying cultures, 226–228
Peter, P., 18–19, 631
Peterson, J., 618, 620, 630
Petrova, L., 154–155
Philbrick, R. E., 618, 619, 630
Pickford, J. A., 346
Pincus, L., 499–500, 597
Pineo, P. G., 375, 393
Pinto, J. B., 67
Plateris, A., 530
Polyandry, 18–19, 37
Polygyny, 17–18
Pomeroy, W. B., 283–284, 285, 290, 356, 392, 440
Population, decreasing rural, 45–47; mobility of, 450–464; movement to cities, 62; suburbs and central cities, 68–73
Potter, R. G., 422, 423, 446
Potvin, R. H., 422, 423, 446–447
Prediction of marital success, see Marital adjustment
Prince, A. J., 308
Propinquity, 302–303
Putney, S., 385–386

Quade, A. E., 618, 626, 630
Queens, S. A., 19, 33

Rabban, M., 249–250
Rabin, A. I., 224–225, 231, 631
Rachiele, L. D., 411
Rainwater, L., 59–60, 79–80, 86, 87, 88, 97, 129, 183, 234, 246–247, 261, 425, 446, 631
Ranck, K. H., 515, 518, 519, 521, 524–525
Reconciliation, in family disruption, 540–542
Redfield, R., 202
Reed, R. B., 357
Reed, S. C., 303
Reik, T., 272
Reiss, A. J., 58
Reiss, I. L., 275, 287–288, 290
Rempel, H., 346
Renne, K. S., 120, 348, 357, 631
Reston, R., 137, 148
Richardson, A. H., 470
Roberts, B. H., 525
Robins, L. N., 192, 631
Rodman, H., 10
Rogers, C. R., 592
Rogers, E. M., 278
Rohrer, J. H., 129
Roles and expectations, 233–261; adjustment of roles, 235–236; of adolescents, 255–256; adult roles in new groups, 241; conjugal role relationships, 245–247; definition of roles, 236–238; division of labor, 248; family roles of husbands and wives, 245–248; in father-absent homes, 253–255; and the formation of personality, 243–244; husbands and wives, 235–236; husband-wife expectations, 244–245; influence of family expectations, 241–245; instrumental and expressive roles, 247–248; learning of roles, 238–240; learning of sex roles, 248–255; nature of expectations and roles, 234–241; siblings, effect of in the learning of roles, 252–253; and social class, 247; of young adults, 256–257
Rollins, B. C., 391
Romantic love, 271–273
Rose, A. M., 397
Rosen, B. C., 222
Rosenberg, M., 200
Rosman, B. L., 78
Rosser, C., 66
Rossi, P. H., 471
Rubenstein, E., 525
Rubenstein, R., 515

Rural Family, 34–59; adjustment of children, 42–44; changes in three generations, 34–37; changing, 45–53; communication increase, 50–53; and modern conveniences, 54–55; decline in family size, 47–48; decline of population in rural areas, 45–47; economic status of, 53–55; education of, 52–53; excess of men, 48–49; familism, 39–42; Irish, 38–39; personality characteristics of, 42–44; proportion married, 50; security of, 45; social characteristics of, 47; status of, 44–45; stem, 37–38; and systems of land tenure, 37–39
Russian family, see Soviet family
Rutherford, E., 251

Sabagh, G., 306, 368, 618, 620, 630
Sagi, P. C., 422, 423, 446
Sampson, H., 511, 512, 632
Santos, A. E., 21–22
Satisfaction, as a criterion of marital success, 320–321
Sauber, M., 525
Sawrey, W., 253
Schaefer, E. S., 216
Scheinfeld, A., 179–180, 631
Schizophrenic children, 223–224
Schnepp, G. J., 599, 602, 603, 612, 613, 615, 617
Schnore, L. F., 72
Schofield, M., 286, 290–291
Schommer, C. O., 411
Schramm, W., 459, 471
Schroeder, C. W., 599, 602, 603, 605, 608, 610, 613, 616, 617, 618, 621
Schworzweller, H. K., 47, 452
Scott, J. F., 299
Sears, P. S., 254
Sears, R. R., 200, 219, 231, 631
Separation, 72–73
Sewall, M., 217
Sewell, W. H., 232
Sex ratio, in mate selection, 48, 274; rural and urban, 48–49; in wartime, 565–566
Sexual behavior, during courtship, 283–288; definition of, 283; as a factor in marital adjustment, 321; a form of communication, 275–277; incidence of during courtship, 284–287; the Kinsey reports, 283–284; in Nyansongo, 14; premarital, 284–288; in various cultures, 25–27
Sexual satisfaction, as a criterion of marital success, 321

Shanas, E., 63, 97, 405, 406–407, 412
Sharp, H., 63, 422
Shaw, C. R., 510
Shellenberg, J. A., 309–310
Sherif, C. W., 128, 204, 222
Sherif, M., 128, 204, 222
Sheilds, W., 599, 600, 617
Shiffman, J., 434
Shils, E. A., 208
Shneidman, E. S., 515
Shope, D. F., 599, 615, 617
Shyrock, H. S., 452
Signorie, E. I., 346
Silvert, D. M., 346
Simpson, R. L., 456
Size of the family, 426–430
Slater, P. E., 247
Smircich, R. J., 302–303
Smith, C., 252
Smith, J., 17
Smith, R. T., 31
Snowbarger, V. A., 362
Snyder, E., 304
Social class, Negro class position, increasing, 108–109; and desired family size, 425; families differ by, 30; urban working-class and middle-class families, 85–93; the urban poor, 76–85; in the Soviet Union, 148–150; variations among farm families, 53–54
Soviet family 130–155; changes in divorce laws, 138–140; and communal living, 140–142; and delinquency, 144–145; early attitudes toward marriage, 135–136; early policy toward divorce, 138; education, 144; emancipation of women, 142–144; equal rights of women, 143–144; extended family, 131–132; health, 144; ideal of separate children's quarters, 140–141; ideals for parents and children, 146; marriage and divorce, 134–140; motherhood, 137–138; parental responsibility, 146–147; prerequisites to marriage, 136–137; prerevolutionary family, 132–134; reasons for changing attitudes toward the family, 147; rural communistic experiments, 141–142; size of, 137; and social class structure, 148–150; survivals of early practices, 147–148
Spencer, H., 7–8
Spencer, L. M., 516
Spiegel, J. P., 500
Spuhler, J. N., 303
Starkey, O. P., 97
Status, 54, 91–93

Stein, M. R., 83–84
Stolz, L. M., 214, 232, 562, 580
Stone, C. L., 278, 279
Stouffer, S. A., 515, 516
Straus, M. A., 58
Strauss, A. L., 307
Streib, G. F., 63, 97, 403, 405, 406–407, 412
Strodtbeck, F. L., 20–21
Strumilin, S., 137, 141, 144
Stryker, S., 10
Suburbs, 69–74
Sugimoto, E. I., 295
Suicide, 514–515
Sumner, W. G., 442
Sussman, M. B., 63, 97, 405
Sutherland, E. H., 75, 198, 510
Suval, E. M., 452
Sverdlov, G., 136, 140, 146, 148, 155
Svetlov, V., 138, 147
Swanson, G. E., 220, 231
Szelenyi, I., 63

Tallman, I., 464, 631
Tannenbaum, A., 522
Tatarinova, N., 143, 144, 155
Telephones, 51
Television, 51–52
Tension, see Family conflicts and accommodations
Terman, L. M., 285, 300, 319, 321, 325, 335, 339, 351, 354, 357, 358, 362, 363, 375, 376, 439 485, 493, 569, 599–630
Theodorson, G. A., 175
Thomas, A., 183
Thomas, D. S., 516
Thomas, W. I., 10, 237, 482
Thomes, M. M., 64–65, 91–93, 223–224, 254–255, 306, 323, 326, 368, 618, 620, 630
Thompson, L. M., 196
Thompson, W. E., 403, 406
Thornbury, H. T., 403, 406
Tibbits, C., 403, 412
Tiller, P. C. 253
Toman, W., 218, 261
Torney, J. V., 193–194
Towne, R. D., 511, 512, 632
Townsend, P., 401, 412
Tuddenham, R. D., 250
Turner, E. S., 267, 268, 270, 290

Udry, J. R., 246, 306, 308, 314
Urban, D., 257
Urban family, 59–98; broken families, 72–73; case of middle-class, 60; case of working-class, 59–60; communication, 61; growth of urban areas, 62; industrialization and the growth of cities, 62; kinship group in urban areas; 63–68, 87–88; matricentric families in suburbs, 73–74; middle-class families, 85–93; mobility, vertical, 61; Negro couples in, 64–65, 91–93; non-family men's areas, 75–76; patriarchal authority in suburbs, 73–74; poverty families, 76–85; roles of working-class and middle-class families, 86–87; self-conception, 87; socionomic status and family behavior, 90–93; suburban, 68–74; transplanting rural families to cities, 62; urban-rural contrasts, 60–61; working-class families, 85–93

Vadakin, J. C., 587
Values, 1–2, 80, 90, 113, 422–423, 443–444, 493
Varley, D. W., 72
Veen, F., 332
Vertical mobility, 61, 454–457
Vincent, C. E., 508, 525
Virginity, loss of, 507
Vogel, E. F., 156–158, 162, 163, 164, 165, 167, 169, 175, 211, 385, 500, 631
Vogel, S. H., 211

Wallace K. M., 301–302, 314, 327
Waller, W., 272, 381, 565
Wallin, P., 212–213, 282, 286, 303, 321, 322, 323, 324, 325, 326, 327, 337, 339, 352, 353, 358, 359, 362, 368, 375, 376, 391, 396, 412, 440, 485, 493, 499, 599–630
Wallis, R. S., 202
Wallis, W. D., 202
Walters, R. H., 221
War, and the family, 559–580; birth rate during, 564–566; death and disability in, 570–571; dispersion of family members, 561–562; divorce and separation, 570; and family disorganization, 569–572; and family disruption, 570–571; and family reorganization, 569–572; hasty marriages, 567; hurried-up marriages, 566–567; marriage rates, 562–564; modification of the sex ratio, 565–566; postponement of marriage, 566; postwar problems of the family, 572–576; reasons for marrying in, 567–568; relaxation of social controls in, 569–570; and status of women, 575–576

Warner, W. L., 457
Weinstein, K. K., 411
Westoff, C. F., 422, 423, 446–447
Whelpton, P. K., 422, 424, 425, 446, 447
Whiting, B. B., 5–6, 16, 23, 24, 25, 26, 27, 28, 33, 210, 211, 631
Whyte, W. F., 98
Widowhood, 400–401
Wilkening, E. A., 41, 58, 67
Williams, A. R., 135, 147
Williamson, R. C., 322, 327, 331, 335, 599, 611, 617, 618, 621, 626, 627
Willmott, P., 66, 95
Wilson, R. H. L., 159, 174
Wimperis, V., 525
Winch, R. F., 309, 313, 314, 618, 626, 630
Wolfe, D. M., 40–41, 74, 248
Women, legal emancipation of, in Russia, 142–145; equality of, in Japan, China, and India, 169; gainfully employed, 432–435; status in wartime, 575–576
Woods, F. J., 204
Worchel, P., 216
Wortis, H., 181, 182, 632
Wright, H. F., 199

Yang, C. K., 175
Yarrow, L. J., 216, 217
Yarrow, M. R., 216, 217, 513–514, 632
Yoshino, R., 296
Young, B., 17–18
Young, K., 17–18, 30–31, 33, 172
Young, L. A., 43–44
Young, M., 66, 95

Zelditch, M., 247
Zimmerman, C. C., 37–38, 386
Znaniecki, F., 482
Zorbaugh, H. M., 451
Zola, I. K., 221